P9-CLB-532

READER'S CHOICE

Third
Canadian
Edition

Kim Flachmann
California State University, Bakersfield

Michael Flachmann
California State University, Bakersfield

Alexandra MacLennan
Institute for Learning, Bank of Montreal

PROPERTY OF
SENECA COLLEGE
LEARNING COMMONS
SENECA@YORK

Prentice Hall Allyn and Bacon Canada
Toronto, Ontario

WITHDRAWN

Canadian Cataloguing in Publication Data

Flachmann, Kim
Reader's Choice

3rd Canadian ed.
First-2nd ed. written by Kim Flachmann et al.
Includes index

ISBN 0-13-020931-7

1. English language—Rhetoric. I. Flachmann, Michael. II. MacLennan, Alexandra, 1964– . III. Title.

PE1417.R42 2000   808'.0427   C99-930598-0

© 2000, 1997, 1994 Prentice-Hall Canada, Toronto, Ontario
Pearson Education

ALL RIGHTS RESERVED

No part of this book may be reproduced in any form without permission in writing from the publisher.

Prentice-Hall, Inc., Upper Saddle River, New Jersey
Prentice-Hall International (UK) Limited, London
Prentice-Hall of Australia, Pty. Limited, Sydney
Prentice-Hall Hispanoamericana, S.A., Mexico City
Prentice-Hall of India Private Limited, New Delhi
Prentice-Hall of Japan, Inc., Tokyo
Simon & Schuster Asia Private Limited, Singapore
Editora Prentice-Hall do Brasil, Ltda., Rio de Janeiro

ISBN 0-13-020931-7

Vice President, Editorial Director: Laura Pearson
Acquisitions Editor: David Stover
Developmental Editor: Susan Ratkaj
Production Editor: Cathy Zerbst
Copy Editor: Diana Thistle-Tremblay
Production Coordinator: Wendy Moran
Art Director: Mary Opper
Cover Design: Lisa LaPointe
Cover Image: Whale/Tony Stone Images
Page Layout: Michael Kelley, Christine Velakis

3   4   5   04   03   02   01   00

Printed and bound in Canada

RHETORICAL CONTENTS

   Using vivid sensory details, Richards takes the reader back to his home
   town in a loving yet starkly realistic series of vignettes drawn from his
   childhood.

   Could you imagine life in prison? Sally Armstrong shows us life inside a
   Canadian penal institution for women. The writer reveals the grim stories
   and horrific environment of P4W in a clear-eyed and unflinchingly
   perceptive essay.

. . . rtY OF
SENECA COLLEGE
LEARNING COMMONS
SENECA@YORK

CHAPTER 2

NARRATION: *Telling a Story*   83

CHAPTER 3

EXAMPLE: *Illustrating Ideas* 131

CHAPTER 6

COMPARISON/CONTRAST: *Discovering Similarities and Differences* 281

CHAPTER 7

DEFINITION: *Limiting the Frame of Reference*   337

CHAPTER 10

DOCUMENTED ESSAYS: *Reading and Writing From*
Sources   485

Defining Documented Essays   485

BARBARA EHRENREICH *The Ecstasy of War*   503
Do men and women possess a natural "warrior instinct" that enables them to kill their enemies during battle? Not so, claims Barbara Ehrenreich, though many social and cultural rituals help transform ordinary people into effective soldiers.

JILL LESLIE ROSENBAUM and MEDA CHESNEY-LIND *Appearance and Delinquency: A Research Note*   512
Criminologists Rosenbaum and Chesney-Lind offer some fascinating evidence about the relationship between the attractiveness of female offenders and the severity of their punishment.

MARILYN DAHL *The Role of the Media in Promoting Images of Disability*   526
In this documented essay Marilyn Dahl explores the ways that the media shapes our images of people with disabilities.

CHAPTER 11
ESSAYS ON THINKING, READING, AND WRITING   535

EUDORA WELTY *Listening*   536

DAVID SMITH *Burying the Hatchet in Language*   540

ROBERT FULFORD *The Fading Power of the Written Word*   545

NATALIE GOLDBERG *The Rules of Writing Practice*   548

Credits   553

Index of Authors and Titles   555

PREFACE TO THE INSTRUCTOR

Reader's Choice is based on the assumption that lucid writing follows lucid thinking, whereas poor writing is almost inevitably the product of foggy, irrational thought processes. As a result, our primary purpose in this book, as in the first edition, is to help students *think* more clearly and logically—both in their minds and on paper.

Reading and writing are companion activities that involve students in the creation of thought and meaning—either as readers interpreting a text or as writers constructing one. Clear thinking, then, is the pivotal point that joins together these two efforts. Although studying the rhetorical strategies presented in *Reader's Choice* is certainly not the only way to approach writing, it is a productive means of helping students improve their abilities to think, read, and write on progressively more sophisticated levels.

The symbiosis we envision among thinking, reading, and writing is represented in this text by the following hierarchy of cognitive levels:

1. *Literal, characterized by a basic understanding of words and their meanings;*

2. *Interpretive, consisting of a knowledge of linear connections between ideas and an ability to make valid inferences based on those ideas; and*

3. *Critical, the highest level, distinguished by the systematic investigation of complex ideas and by the analysis of their relationship to the world around us.*

WHAT IS NEW

We have made some changes in the third edition of *Reader's Choice* that represent the responses of reviewers from many different types of colleges and universities all over Canada and the United States:

• *The third edition of Reader's Choice contains 19 new essays.*

We have updated some of the selections, added new authors, and introduced new topics, such as regional traditions, and national identity, infomercials, the monument at Vimy Ridge, ethics in journalism, welfare reform, and war.

• *A new set of questions called "Making Connections" has been added to each essay.*

The "Making Connections" questions make links between the various readings throughout the book, reinforcing rhetorical strategies that are used and providing further opportunities for writing and discussion on the topics the writers address.

• *This edition includes new user-friendly checklists at the end of each chapter introduction.*

These checklists summarize the information in the chapter introduction and serve as references for the students as they complete their own writing tasks.

• *We have completely renovated Chapter 10 on Documented Essays.*

It now includes two new essays that deal with important current issues. In addition, the essays illustrate two different documentation styles: Modern Language Association (MLA) and American Psychological Association (APA).

• *A Web site—www.prenticehall.ca/readerschoice—features a glossary of useful terms for students to use in conjunction with this book.*

ACKNOWLEDGMENTS

I would like to acknowledge a number of people who helped in the preparation of this edition of *Reader's Choice*. At Prentice-Hall Canada, for their guidance, patience, and support, I would like to thank David Stover, Acquisitions Editor; Susan RatkaJ, Developmental Editor; Cathy Zerbst, Production Editor; and Diana Thistle-Tremblay, Copy Editor.

At Seneca College, I am grateful to my colleagues, especially Sarah Reid, Enid Gossin, Judith Carson, and Andrea Medovarski, as well as my students in College English, for their ongoing feedback and advice about *Reader's Choice*.

Alexandra MacLennan

PREFACE TO THE STUDENT

Accurate thinking is the beginning and fountain of writing.

—Horace

THE PURPOSE OF THIS TEXT

Have you ever had trouble expressing your thoughts? If so, you're not alone. Many people have this difficulty—especially when they are asked to write their thoughts down.

The good news is that this "ailment" can be cured. We've learned over the years that the more clearly students think about the world around them, the more easily they can express their ideas through written and spoken language. As a result, this textbook intends to improve your writing by helping you think clearly, logically, and critically about important ideas and issues that exist in our world today. You will learn to reason, read, and write about your environment in increasingly complex ways, moving steadily from a simple, literal understanding of topics to interpretation and analysis. Inspired by well-crafted prose models and guided by carefully worded questions, you can actually raise the level of your thinking skills while improving your reading and writing abilities.

Reader's Choice is organized on the assumption that as a college student you should be able to think, read, and write on three increasingly difficult levels:

1. *Literal*, which involves a basic understanding of a selection and the ability to repeat or restate the material;

2. *Interpretive*, which requires you to make associations and draw inferences from information in your reading; and

3. *Analytical or critical*, which invites you to systematically separate, explain, evaluate, and reassemble various important ideas discovered in your reading.

For example, students with a *literal* grasp of an essay would be able to understand the words on the page, cite details from the selection, and paraphrase certain sections of the essay. Students equipped with *interpretive* skills will see implicit relationships within a selection (such as comparison/contrast or cause/effect), make inferences from information that is supplied, and comprehend the intricacies of figurative language. Finally, students functioning *analytically* will be able to summarize and explain difficult concepts and generate plausible hypotheses from a series of related ideas. In short, this book leads you systematically toward higher levels of thinking and writing.

In order to stimulate your thinking on all levels, this text encourages you to participate in the making of meaning—as both a reader and a writer. As a reader, you have a responsibility to work with the author of each essay to help create sense out of the words on the page; as a writer, you must be conscious enough of your audience so that they perceive your intended purpose clearly and precisely through the ideas, opinions, and details that you provide. Because of this unique relationship, we envision reading and writing as companion acts in which writer and reader are partners in the development of meaning.

To demonstrate this vital interrelationship between reader and writer, our text provides you with prose models that are intended to inspire your own thinking and writing. In the introduction to each chapter, we include a student paragraph and a student essay that feature the particular rhetorical strategy under discussion. The essay is highlighted by annotations and by underlining to illustrate how to write that type of essay and to help bridge the gap between student writing and the professional selections in the text. After each essay, the student writer has drafted a personal note with some useful advice about generating that particular type of essay. The essays that follow each chapter introduction, selected from a wide variety of contemporary authors, are intended to encourage you to improve your writing through a partnership with some of the best examples of professional prose available today. Just as musicians and athletes richly benefit from studying the techniques of the foremost people in their fields, you will, we hope, grow in spirit and language use from your collaborative work with the writers in this collection.

HOW TO USE THIS TEXT

Reader's Choice contains essays representing the four main purposes of writing:

Description

Narration

Exposition

Persuasion

Our primary focus within this framework is on exposition (which means "explanation"), because you will need to master this type of verbal expression to succeed in both the academic and the professional worlds. Although the essays in this text can be read in any order, we begin with

description

because it is a basic technique that often appears in other forms of discourse. We then move to

narration, or storytelling,

and next to the six traditional expository strategies:

example   *comparison/contrast*

process analysis   *definition*

division/classification   *cause/effect*

The text continues with an expanded chapter on

argument and persuasion,

including two sets of opposing viewpoint essays. Chapter 10 discusses and presents

documented research papers,

and the anthology concludes with selections about thinking, reading, and writing.

"Pure" rhetorical types rarely exist, of course, and when they do, the result often seems artificial. Therefore, although each essay in this collection focuses on a single rhetorical mode as its primary strategy, other strategies are always at work in it. These selections concentrate on one primary technique at a time in much the same way a well-arranged photograph highlights a certain visual detail, though many other elements function in the background to make the picture an organic whole.

Each chapter begins with an explanation of a single rhetorical technique. These explanations are divided into six sections that move from the effect of this technique on our daily lives to its integral role in the writing process. The first section catalogs the use of each rhetorical mode in our lives. The second section, "Defining _____" (e.g., "Defining Description"), offers a working definition of the technique and a sample/student paragraph so that we all have the same fundamental understanding of the term. A third section, entitled "Thinking Critically by Using _____," introduces each rhetorical mode as a pattern of thought that helps us organize and more fully understand our experiences. A fourth section, called "Reading and Writing _____ Essays" (e.g., "Reading and Writing Descriptive Essays"), explains the processes of reading and writing an essay in each rhetorical mode, and a fifth section presents an annotated student essay showing this particular rhetorical method "at work," followed by comments from the student writer. The last part offers some final comments on each rhetorical strategy including a summary review checklist.

Before each reading selection, we have designed some material to focus your attention on a particular writer and topic. This "prereading" segment begins with biographical information about the author and ends with a number of questions to whet your appetite for the essay that follows. The prereading questions forecast not only the material in the essay, but also the questions and writing assignments that follow.

The questions following each reading selection are designed as guides for thinking about the essay. These questions are at the heart of the relationship represented in this book among thinking, reading, and writing. They are divided into four interrelated sections that move you smoothly from a literal understanding of what you have just read, to interpretation, and finally to analysis. The first set of questions, "Understanding Details," focuses on the basic facts and opinions in the selection. The second set of questions, "Analyzing Meaning," asks you to explain certain facts and to evaluate various assumptions of the essay in an effort to understand the entire selection on an analytical level. The third set of questions, "Discovering Rhetorical Strategies," guides your thinking on how the author achieved certain effects through word choice, sentence structure, organization of ideas, and selection of details. This third series of questions often requires you to apply to your reading of an essay material you learned about a particular mode of writing in the chapter introduction. And "Making Connections," the fourth group of questions, asks you to identify and process relationships and connections that you may not have noticed between the essay and others in the book.

The last section of questions consists of three "Ideas for Discussion/Writing." These topics are preceded by "prewriting" questions to help you generate new ideas. Most of the Discussion/Writing topics specify a purpose (a definite reason for writing the essay) and an audience (an identifiable person or group of people you should address in your essay) so that you can focus your work as precisely as possible. These assignments outline realistic scenes and roles for you to play in those scenes so that, as you write, your relationship to your subject and audience will be clear and precise.

Finally, the Web sites listed at the end of each selection will lead you to sites on the World Wide Web that will give you more information about reading. This might be information about the author, the original source of the piece of writing, or the topic of the essay you have read. Visit the *Reader's Choice* Web page—**www. prenticehall.ca/readerschoice**—to find a glossary of useful terms.

The word *essay* (which comes from the Old French *essai*, meaning a "try" or an "attempt") is an appropriate label for these writing assignments, because they all ask you to grapple with an idea or problem and then try to give shape to your conclusions in some effective manner. Such "exercises" can be equated with the development of athletic ability in sports: The essay itself demonstrates that you can put together all the various skills you have learned; it proves that you can actually play the sport. After you have studied the different techniques at work in a reading selection, a specific essay assignment lets you practise them all in unison and allows you to discover for yourself even more secrets about the intricate details of effective communication.

INTRODUCTION

■ ■ ■

Thinking, Reading, and Writing

Reading and writing are companion activities that involve students in the creation of thought and meaning—either as readers interpreting a text or as writers constructing one. Clear thinking, then, is the pivotal point that joins these two efforts. Although studying the rhetorical strategies presented in *Reader's Choice* is not the only way to approach writing, it provides a productive means of helping students improve their abilities to think, read, and write on progressively sophisticated levels.

We can improve the way we think, read, and write by exercising our brains on three sequential levels:

1. *The literal level* entails knowing the meanings of words—individually and in relation to one another. In order to comprehend the sentence "You must exercise your brain to reach your full mental potential" on the literal level, for example, someone would have to know the definitions of all the words in the sentence and understand the way those words work together to make meaning.

2. *Interpretation* requires the ability to make associations between details, draw inferences from pieces of information, and reach conclusions about the material. An interpretive understanding of the sample sentence in level 1 might be translated into the following thoughts: "Exercising the brain sounds a bit like exercising the body. I wonder if there's any correlation between the two. If the brain must be exercised, it is probably made up of muscles, much as the body is." None of these particular "thoughts" is made explicit in the sentence, but each is suggested in one way or another.

3. *Thinking, reading, and writing critically*, the most sophisticated form of rational abilities, involves a type of mental activity that is crucial for successful academic work. A critical analysis of our sample sentence might proceed in the following way: "This sentence is talking to me. It actually addresses me with the word *you*. I wonder what *my* mental potential is. Will I be able to reach it? Will I know when I attain it? I certainly want to reach this potential; it will undoubtedly help me succeed scholastically and professionally. The brain is obviously an important tool for helping me achieve my goals in life, so I want to take every opportunity I have to develop and maintain this part of my body." Students who can take an issue or idea apart in this fashion and understand its various components more thoroughly after reassembling them are rewarded intrinsically with a clearer knowledge of life's complexities and the ability to generate creative, useful ideas. They are also rewarded extrinsically with good grades and are more likely to earn responsible jobs with higher pay, because they can apply their understanding of the world effectively to their professional and personal lives.

In this textbook, you will learn to think critically by reading essays written by intelligent, interesting authors and by writing your own essays on a variety of topics.

Thinking Critically

Recent psychological studies have shown that "thinking" and "feeling" are complementary operations. All of us have feelings that are automatic and instinctive. To feel pride after winning first place at a track meet, for example, or to feel anger at a spiteful friend is not behaviour we have to study and master; such emotions come naturally to human beings. Thinking, on the other hand, is much less spontaneous than feeling; research suggests that study and practice are required for sustained mental development.

Thinking critically involves grappling with the ideas, issues, and problems that surround you in your immediate environment and in the world at large. It does not necessarily entail finding fault, which you might naturally associate with the word *critical*, but rather suggests continually questioning and analyzing the world around you. Thinking critically is the highest form of mental activity that human beings engage in. Fortunately, all of us can learn how to think more critically.

Critical thinking means taking apart an issue, idea, or problem; examining its various parts; and reassembling the topic with a fuller understanding of its intricacies. Implied in this explanation is the ability to see the topic from one or more new perspectives. Using your mind in this way will help you find solutions to difficult problems, design creative plans of action, and ultimately live a life consistent with your opinions on important issues that we all must confront on a daily basis.

Our initial goal, then, is to help you think critically when you are required to do so in school, on the job, or in any other area of your life.

Working with the rhetorical modes is an effective way to achieve this goal. With some guidance, each rhetorical pattern can provide you with mental practice to prepare you for writing and critical thinking. Through these various guided thinking exercises, you can systematically strengthen your ability to think analytically.

As you move through the following chapters, we will ask you to isolate each rhetorical mode so that you can concentrate on these thinking patterns one at a time. Each rhetorical pattern we study will suggest slightly different ways of seeing the world, processing information, and solving problems. Looking closely at rhetorical modes or specific patterns of thought helps us discover how our minds work. In the same fashion, becoming more intricately aware of our thought patterns lets us improve our basic thinking skills as well as our reading and writing abilities. Thinking critically helps us discover fresh insights into old ideas, generate new thoughts, and see connections between related issues.

Each chapter introduction provides three exercises specifically designed to help you focus in isolation on a particular pattern of thought. While you are attempting to learn what each pattern feels like in your head, use your imagination to play with these exercises on as many different levels as possible.

When you practise each of the rhetorical patterns of thought, you should be aware of building on your previous thinking skills. As the book progresses, the rhetorical modes become more complex and require a higher degree of concentration and effort. Throughout the book, therefore, you should keep in mind that ultimately you want to let these skills accumulate into a well-developed ability to process the world around you—including reading, writing, seeing, and feeling—on the most advanced analytical level you can master.

Reading Critically

Reading critically begins with developing a natural curiosity about an essay and nurturing that curiosity throughout the reading process. To learn as much as you can from an essay, you should first study any preliminary material you can find, then read the essay to get a general overview of its main ideas, and finally read the selection again to achieve a deeper understanding of its intent. The three phases of the reading process explained below—preparing to read, reading, and rereading—will help you develop this "natural curiosity" so you can approach any reading assignment with an active, inquiring mind.

Preparing to Read

Focusing your attention is an important first stage in both the reading and the writing processes. In fact, learning as much as you can about an essay and its "context" (the circumstances surrounding its development) before you begin reading can help you reach some degree of analysis before writing on the assigned topics. In particular, knowing where an essay was first published, studying the writer's background, and doing some preliminary thinking on the subject of a reading selection will help you understand the writer's ideas and form some valid opinions of your own.

As you approach any essay, you should concentrate on four specific areas that will begin to give you an overview of the material you are about to read. We use an essay by Lewis Thomas to demonstrate these techniques.

1. *Title.* A close look at the title will usually provide important clues about the author's attitude toward the topic, the author's stand on an issue, or the mood of an essay. It can also furnish you with a sense of audience and purpose.

To Err Is Human

From this title, for example, we might infer that the author will discuss errors, human nature, and the extent to which mistakes influence human behaviour. The title is half of a well-known proverbial quotation (Alexander Pope's "To err is human, to forgive, divine"), so we might speculate further that the author has written an essay intended for a well-read audience interested in the relationship between errors and humanity. After reading only four words of the essay—its title—you already have a good deal of information about the subject, its audience, and the author's attitude toward both.

2. *Synopsis.* The Rhetorical Table of Contents in this text contains a synopsis of each essay, very much like the following, so that you can find out more specific details about its contents before you begin reading.

Physician Lewis Thomas explains how we can profit from our mistakes—especially if we trust human nature. Perhaps someday, he says, we can apply this same principle to the computer and magnify the advantages of these errors.

From this synopsis, we learn that Thomas's essay will be an analysis of human errors and of the way we can benefit from those errors. The synopsis also tells us the computer has the potential to magnify the value of our errors.

3. *Biography.* Learning as much as you can about the author of an essay will generally stimulate your interest in the material and help you achieve a deeper understanding of the issues to be discussed. From the biographies in this book, you can learn, for example, whether a writer is young or old, conservative or liberal, open- or close-minded. You might also discover if the essay was written at the beginning, middle, or end of the author's career or how well versed the writer is on the topic. Such information will invariably provide a deeper, more thorough understanding of a selection's ideas, audience, and logical structure.

LEWIS THOMAS
1913–1998

Lewis Thomas was a physician who, until his death in 1998, was president emeritus of the Sloan-Kettering Cancer Center and scholar-in-residence at the Cornell University Medical Center in New York City. A graduate of Princeton University and Harvard Medical School, he was formerly head of pathology and dean of the New York University-Bellevue Medical Center and dean of the Yale Medical School. In addition to having written over 200 scientific papers on virology and immunology, he authored many popular scientific essays, some of which have been collected in *Lives of a Cell* (1974), *The Medusa and the Snail* (1979), *Late Night Thoughts on Listening to Mahler's Ninth Symphony* (1983), *Etcetera, Etcetera* (1990), and *The Fragile Species* (1992). The memoirs of his distinguished career have been published in *The Youngest Science: Notes of a Medicine Watcher* (1983). Thomas liked to refer to his essays as "experiments in thought": "Although I usually think I know what I'm going to be writing about, what I'm going to say, most of the time it doesn't happen that way at all. At some point I get misled down a garden path. I get surprised by an idea that I hadn't anticipated getting, which is a little bit like being in a laboratory."

As this information indicates, Thomas was a prominent physician who published widely on scientific topics. We know that he considered his essays "experiments in thought," which makes us expect a relaxed, spontaneous treatment of his subjects. From this biography, we can also infer that he was a leader in the medical world and that, because of the positions he held, he was well respected in his professional life. Last, we can speculate that he had a clear sense of his audience because he was able to present difficult concepts in clear, everyday language.

4. *Preparing to read.* The "Preparing to Read" sections following the biographies are intended to focus your attention and stimulate your curiosity before you begin the essay. They will also get you ready to form your own opinions on the essay and its topic as you read. Keeping a journal to respond to the questions in this section is an excellent idea, because you will then have a record of your thoughts on various topics related to the reading selection that follows.

Discovering where, why, and how an essay was first written will provide you with a context for the material you are about to read: Why did the author write this selection? Where was it first published? Who was the author's original audience? This type of information enables you to understand the circumstances surrounding the development of the selection and to identify any topical or historical references the author makes. All the selections in this textbook were published elsewhere first—in another book, a journal, or a magazine. Some are excerpts from longer works. The author's original audience, therefore, consisted of the readers of that particular publication.

Preparing to Read

The following essay, which originally appeared in the *New England Journal of Medicine* (January 1976), illustrates the clarity and ease with which Thomas explains complex scientific topics. As you prepare to read this essay, take a few moments to think about the role mistakes play in our lives: What are some memorable mistakes you have made in your life? Did you learn anything important from any of these errors? Do you make more or fewer mistakes than other people you know? Do you see any advantages to making mistakes? Any disadvantages?

From the sample "Preparing to Read" material, we learn that Thomas's essay "To Err Is Human" was originally published in the *New England Journal of Medicine*, a prestigious periodical read principally by members of the scientific community. Written early in 1976, the article plays upon its audience's growing fascination with computers and with the limits of artificial intelligence—subjects just as timely today as they were in the mid-1970s.

The questions here prompt you to consider your own ideas, opinions, or experiences in order to help you generate thoughts on the topic of errors in our lives.

Reading

People read essays in books, newspapers, magazines, and journals for a great variety of reasons. One reader may want to be stimulated intellectually, whereas another seeks relaxation; one person reads to keep up with the latest developments in his or her profession, whereas the next wants to learn why a certain event happened or how something can be done; some people read in order to be challenged by new ideas, whereas others find comfort principally in printed material that supports their own moral, social, or political opinions. The essays in this textbook variously fulfill all these expectations. They have been chosen, however, not only for these reasons, but for an additional, broader purpose: Reading them can help make you a better writer.

Every time you read an essay in this book, you will also be preparing to write your own essay concentrating on the same rhetorical pattern. For this reason, as you read each essay you should pay careful attention to both their content (subject matter) and their form (language, sentence structure, organization, and development of ideas). You will also see how effectively experienced writers use particular rhetorical modes (or patterns of thought) to organize and communicate their ideas. Each essay in this collection features one dominant pattern that is generally supported by several others.

The questions before and after each essay teach you a way of reading that can help you discover the relationship of a writer's ideas to one another as well as to your own ideas. These questions can also help clarify for you the connection between the writer's topic, his or her style or manner of expression, and your own composing process. The questions are designed to help you understand and generate ideas, discover various choices the writers make in composing their essays, and realize the freedom you have to make related choices in your own writing. Such an approach to the process of reading takes reading and writing out of the realm of mystical creation and places them in the realistic world of the possible; it takes some of the mystery out of reading and writing and makes them manageable tasks at which anyone can become proficient.

The following three general guidelines will help you develop your own system for reading and responding to what you have read:

1. *Read the essay to get an overall sense of it.*

2. *Summarize the essay.*

3. *Read the questions and assignments that follow the essay.*

Guideline 1. *First, read the essay to get an overall sense of it in relation to its title, purpose, audience, author, and publication information.* Write (in the margins, on a separate piece of paper, or in a journal) your initial reactions, comments, and personal associations.

To illustrate, on the following pages is the Thomas essay with a student's comments in the margins, showing how the student reacted to the essay upon reading it for the first time.

Lewis Thomas
(1913–1998)

■ ■ ■

To Err Is Human

Boy is this true!

Everyone must have had at least one personal experience with a computer error by this time. Bank balances are suddenly reported to have jumped from $379 into the millions, appeals for charitable contributions are mailed over and over to people with crazy sounding names at your address, <u>department stores send the wrong bills,</u> utility companies write that they're turning everything off, that sort of thing. If you manage to get in touch with someone and complain, you then get instantaneously typed, guilty letters from the same computer, saying, "Our computer was in error, and an adjustment is being made in your account."   1

Last spring this happened to me.

exactly

These are supposed to be the sheerest, blindest accidents. Mistakes are not believed to be part of the normal behavior of a good machine. If things go wrong, it must be a personal, human error, the result of fingering, tampering, a button getting stuck, someone hitting the wrong key. The computer, at its normal best, is infallible.   2

How can it be?

I wonder whether this can be true. After all, the whole point of computers is that they represent an extension of the human brain, vastly improved upon but nonetheless human, <u>superhuman</u> maybe. A good computer can think clearly and quickly enough to beat you at chess, and some of them have even been programmed to write obscure verse. They can do anything we can do, and more besides.   3

In what way?

Can this be proven?

It is not yet known whether a computer has its own consciousness, and it would be hard to find out about this. When you walk into one of those great halls now built for the huge machines, and stand listening, it is easy to imagine that the faint, distant noises are the sound of thinking, and the turning of the spools gives them the look of wild creatures rolling their eyes in the effort to concentrate, choking with information. <u>But real thinking, and dreaming, are other matters.</u>   4

I expected this essay to be so much more stuffy than it is. I can even understand it.

In what way?

On the other hand, the evidences of something like an unconscious, equivalent to ours, are all around, in every mail. As extensions of the human brain, they have been constructed with the same property of error, spontaneous, uncontrolled, and rich in possibilities.   5

good, clear comparison for the general reader

so true

great image!

<u>Mistakes are at the very base of human thought</u>, embedded there, feeding the structure like <u>root nodules</u>. If we were not provided with the knack of being wrong, we could never get anything useful done. We think our way along by choosing between right   6

I don't understand this

I agree!
This is how
we learn
{ and wrong alternatives, and the wrong choices have to be made as frequently as the right ones. We get along in life this way. We are built to make mistakes, coded for error.

We learn, as we say, by "trial and error." Why do we always   7
say that? Why not "trial and rightness" or "trial and triumph"? The old phrase puts it that way because that is, in real life, the way it is done.

Another
effective
comparison
for the
general
reader

A good laboratory, like a good bank or a corporation or gov-   8
ernment, has to run like a computer. Almost everything is done flawlessly, by the book, and all the numbers add up to the pre- dicted sums. The days go by. And then, if it is a lucky day, and a   *Isn't this a*
lucky laboratory, somebody makes a mistake: the wrong buffer,   *contradic-*
something in one of the blanks, a decimal misplaced in reading   *tion?*
counts, the warm room off by a degree and a half, a mouse out of his box, or just a misreading of the day's protocol. Whatever, when the results come in, something is obviously screwed up, and then the   *What?*
action can begin.

The misreading is not the important error; it opens the way.   9
The next step is the crucial one. If the investigator can bring himself   *aha!*
to say, "But even so, look at that!" then the new finding, whatever it is, is ready for snatching. What is needed, for progress to be made, is the move based on error.

Whenever new kinds of thinking are about to be accomplished,   10
or new varieties of music, there has to be an argument beforehand. With two sides debating in the same mind, haranguing, there is an   *I believe*
amiable understanding that one is right and the other wrong. Sooner   *Thomas here*

Interesting
idea
or later the thing is settled, but there can be no action at all if there   *because of*
are not the two sides, and the argument. The hope is in the faculty   *his back-*
of wrongness, the tendency toward error. The capacity to leap across   *ground.*

Could this be
related to
the human
ability to
think
critically?
mountains of information to land lightly on the wrong side repre- sents the highest of human endowments.

{ It may be that this is a uniquely human gift, perhaps even stip-   11
ulated in our genetic instructions. Other creatures do not seem to have DNA sequences for making mistakes as a routine part of daily living, certainly not for programmed error as a guide for action.

We are at our human finest, dancing with our minds, when   12
there are more choices than two. Sometimes there are ten, even   *Nice mental*
twenty different ways to go, all but one bound to be wrong, and   *image*

Yes, but this
is so
frustrating
the richness of selection in such situations can lift us onto totally new ground. This process is called exploration and is based on human fallibility. If we had only a single center in our brains, capa-   *This is a*
ble of responding only when a correct decision was to be made,   *great*
instead of the jumble of different, credulous, easily conned clus-   *sentence —It*
ters of neurones that provide for being flung off into blind alleys, up   *has a lot of*
trees, down dead ends, out into blue sky, along wrong turnings,   *feeling*

I love the
phrase
"splendid
freedom"
around bends, we could only stay the way we are today, stuck fast.

The lower animals do not have this splendid freedom. They   13
are limited, most of them, to absolute infallibility. Cats, for all their   *See ¶ 11*
good side, never make mistakes. I have never seen a maladroit,   *Look up*
clumsy, or blundering cat. Dogs are sometimes fallible, occasionally   *"maladroit"*

I never thought of mistakes this way

able to make charming minor mistakes, but they get this way by trying to mimic their masters. <u>Fish are flawless in everything they do</u>. Individual cells in a tissue are mindless machines, perfect in their performance, as absolutely inhuman as bees.

I like this idea

We should have this in mind as we become dependent on more complex computers for the arrangement of our affairs. Give the computers their heads, I say; let them go their way. If we can learn

14

Thomas makes our technology sound really exciting

to do this, turning our heads to one side and wincing while the work proceeds, the possibilities for the future of mankind, and computerkind, are limitless. <u>Your average good computer can make calculations in an instant which would take a lifetime of slide rules for any of us</u>. Think of what we could gain from the near infinity of

so true

We need to program computers to make deliberate mistakes so they can help our natural human tendency to learn thru error

precise, <u>machine-made miscomputation</u> which is now so easily within our grasp. We would begin the solving of some of our hardest problems. How, for instance, should we go about organizing ourselves for social living on a planetary scale, now that we have become, as a plain fact of life, a single community? We can assume, as a working hypothesis, that all the right ways of doing this are unworkable. What we need, then, for moving ahead, is a set of wrong alternatives much longer and more interesting than the short list of mistaken courses that any of us can think up right now. We need, in fact, an infinite list, and when it is printed out we need the

yes

Not a contradiction after all.

computer to turn on itself and select, at random, the next way to go. If it is a big enough mistake, we could find ourselves on a new level, stunned, out in the clear, ready to move again.

So mistakes have value!

■───────────────────────────────■

Guideline 2. *After you have read the essay for the first time, summarize its main ideas in some fashion.* The form of this task might be anything, from a drawing of the main ideas as they relate to one another, to a succinct summary. You could draw a graph or map of the topics in the essay; outline the ideas to get an overview of the piece; or summarize the ideas to check your understanding of the main points of the selection. Any of these tasks can be completed from your original notes and underlining.

Guideline 3. *Next, read the questions and assignments following the essay to help focus your thinking for the second reading.* Don't answer the questions at this time; just read them to make sure you are picking up the main ideas from the selection and thinking about relevant connections among those ideas.

Rereading

Following your initial reading, read the essay again, concentrating this time on how the author achieved his or her purpose. The temptation to skip this stage of the reading process is often powerful, but this second reading is crucial to your development as a critical reader in all of your courses as it allows a much deeper understanding of the work under consideration and prepares you to analyze the writer's ideas.

You should also be prepared to look closely at the assumptions the essay is based on: For example, how does the writer move from idea to idea in the essay? What hidden assertions lie behind these ideas? Do you agree or disagree with these assertions? Your assessment of these unspoken assumptions will often play a major role in your critical response to an essay. In the case of Thomas's essay, do you accept the unspoken connection he makes between the workings of the human brain and the computer? What parts of the essay hinge upon your acceptance of this connection? What other assumptions are fundamental to Thomas's reasoning? If you accept his thinking along the way, you are more likely to agree with the general flow of Thomas's essay. If you discover a flaw in his premises or assumptions, your acceptance of his argument will start to break down.

Next, answer the questions that follow the essay. The "Understanding Details" questions will help you understand and remember what you have read on both the literal and the interpretive levels. Some of the questions ask you to restate various important points the author makes (literal); others help you see relationships between the different ideas presented (interpretive).

Understanding Details

Literal   1. According to Thomas, in what ways are computers and humans similar? In what ways are they different?

Lit/Interp   2. In what ways do we learn by "trial and error"? Why is this a useful way to learn?

Interpretive	3. What does Thomas mean by the statement, "If we were not provided with the knack of being wrong, we could never get anything useful done" (paragraph 6)?
Interpretive	4. According to Thomas, in what important way do humans and "lower" animals differ? What does this comparison have to do with Thomas's main line of reasoning?

The "Analyzing Meaning" questions require you to analyze and evaluate some of the writer's ideas in order to form valid opinions of your own. These questions demand a higher level of thought than the previous set and help you prepare more specifically for the discussion/writing assignments that follow the questions.

Analyzing Meaning

Analytical	1. What is Thomas's main point in this essay? How do the references to computers help him make this point?
Analytical	2. Why does Thomas perceive human error as such a positive quality? What does "exploration" have to do with this quality (paragraph 12)?
Analytical	3. What could we gain from "the near infinity of precise, machine-made miscomputation" (paragraph 14)? In what ways would our civilization advance?

The "Discovering Rhetorical Strategies" questions ask you to look closely at what strategies the writer uses to develop his or her thesis, and how those strategies work. The questions address features of the writer's composing process, such as word choice, use of detail, transitions, statement of purpose, organization of ideas, sentence structure, and paragraph development. The intent of these questions is to raise various elements of the composing process to the conscious level so you can use them in creating your own essays.

Discovering Rhetorical Strategies

1. Thomas begins his essay with a list of experiences most of us have had at one time or another. Do you find this an effective beginning? Why or why not?

2. Which main points in his essay does Thomas develop in most detail? Why do you think he chooses to develop these points so thoroughly?

3. Explain the simile Thomas uses in paragraph 6: "Mistakes are at the very base of human thought, embedded there, feeding the structure like root nodules." Is this comparison between "mistakes" and "root nodules" useful in this context? Why or why not? Find another simile or metaphor in this essay, and explain how it works.

A final set of questions, "Making Connections," asks you to consider the essay you have just read in reference to other essays in the book. Your instructor will assign these questions according to the essays you have read. The questions may have you compare the writers' treatment of an idea, the authors' style of writing, the difference in their opinions, or the similarities between their views of the world. Such questions will help you see connections in your own life—not only in your reading and your immediate environment, but also in the larger world around you. These questions, in particular, encourage you to move from specific references in the selections to a broader range of issues and circumstances that affect your daily life. (See box, opposite.)

Because checklists can provide a helpful method of reviewing important information, we offer here a series of questions that represent the three stages of reading just discussed. All these guidelines can be generalized into a checklist for reading any academic assignment in any discipline. (See "Reading Inventory.")

Making Connections

1. Sally Armstrong ("P4W") and Cecil Foster ("Why Blacks Get Mad") refer both directly and indirectly to learning from mistakes. Would Lewis Thomas agree with their approach to this topic? In what ways do these authors think alike about the benefits of making errors? In what ways do they differ on the topic? Explain your answer.

2. Lewis Thomas and Tony Leighton ("The New Nature") both discuss the usefulness of computers. In what ways do their ideas complement each other? In what ways do they differ?

3. According to Thomas, humans are complex organisms with a great deal of untapped potential. William Golding ("Thinking as a Hobby") also comments on the uniqueness of human beings. In what ways do these two writers agree or disagree with each other on the intelligence and resourcefulness of human beings? To what extent would each author argue that humans use their mental capacities wisely and completely? Explain your answer.

Reading Inventory

Preparing to Read

Title

1. What can I infer from the title of the essay about the author's attitude toward the subject or the general tone of the essay?
2. Who do I think is the author's audience? What is the principal purpose of the essay?

Synopsis

1. What is the general subject of the essay?
2. What is the author's approach to the subject?

Biography

1. What do I know about the author's age, political stance, and general beliefs?

2. How qualified is the author to write on this subject?

3. When did the author write the essay? Under what conditions? In what context?

4. Where was the essay first published?

Content

1. What would I like to learn about this topic?

2. What are some of my opinions on this subject?

Reading

1. What are my initial reactions, comments, and personal associations in reference to the ideas in this essay?

2. What are the essay's main ideas?

3. Did I read the questions and assignments following the essay?

Rereading

1. How does the author achieve his or her purpose in this essay?

2. What assumptions underlie the author's reasoning?

3. Do I have a clear literal understanding of this essay? What words do I need to look up in a dictionary?

4. Do I have a solid interpretive understanding of this essay? Do I understand the relationship among ideas? What conclusions can I draw from this essay?

5. Do I have an accurate analytical understanding of this essay? Which ideas can I take apart, examine, and put back together again? What is my evaluation of this material?

6. Do I understand the rhetorical strategies the writer uses and the way they work? Can I explain the effects of these strategies?

Writing Critically

The last stage of responding to the reading selections in this text offers you various "Ideas for Discussion/Writing" that will allow you to demonstrate the different skills you have learned in each chapter. You will be most successful if you envision each writing experience as an organic process that follows a natural cycle of prewriting, writing, and rewriting.

Preparing to Write

The prewriting phase involves exploring a subject, generating ideas, selecting and narrowing a topic, analyzing an audience, and developing a purpose. Preceding the writing assignments are "Preparing to Write" questions you should respond to before trying to structure your thoughts into a coherent essay. These questions will assist you in generating new thoughts on the topics and may even stimulate new approaches to old ideas. Keeping a journal to respond to these questions is an excellent technique, because you will then have a record of your opinions on various topics related to the writing assignments that follow.

Preparing to Write

Write freely about an important mistake you have made: How did the mistake make you feel? What (if anything) did you learn from this mistake? What did you fail to learn that you should have learned? Did this mistake have any positive impact on your life? What were its negative consequences? How crucial are mistakes in our lives?

Responses to these questions can be prompted by a number of different "invention" techniques and carried out by you individually, with another student, in small groups, or as a class project. Invention strategies can help you generate responses to these questions and discover related ideas through the various stages of writing your papers. Because you will undoubtedly vary your approach to different assignments, you should be familiar with the following choices available to you:

Brainstorming. The basis of brainstorming is free association. Ideally, you should get a group of students together and bounce ideas, words, and thoughts off one another until they begin to cluster around related topics. If you don't have a group of students handy, brainstorm by yourself or with a friend. In a group of students or with a friend, the exchange of thoughts usually starts orally, but should transfer to paper when your ideas begin to fall into related categories. When you brainstorm by yourself, however, you should write down everything that comes to mind. The act of recording your ideas in this case becomes a catalyst for other thoughts. Then, keep writing down words and phrases that occur to you until they begin to fall into logical subdivisions, or until you stop generating new ideas.

Freewriting. Freewriting means writing to discover what you want to say. Set a time limit of about ten minutes, and just write by free association. Write about what you are seeing, feeling, touching, thinking; write about having nothing to say; recopy the sentence you just wrote—anything. Just keep writing on paper, on a typewriter, or on a computer. After you have generated some material, locate an idea that is central to your writing assignment, put it at the top of another page, and start freewriting again, letting your thoughts take shape around this central idea. This second type of preparation is called *focused freewriting*, and is especially valuable when you already have a specific topic.

Journal Entries. Journal entries are much like freewriting, except you have some sense of an audience—probably either your instructor or yourself. In a journal, anything goes. You can respond to the "Preparing to Write" questions, jot down thoughts, paste up articles that spark your interest, write sections of dialogue, draft letters (the kind you never send), record dreams, or make lists.

Direct Questions. This technique involves asking a series of questions useful in any writing situation to generate ideas, arrange thoughts, or revise prose. One example of this strategy is to use the inquiries journalists rely on to check the coverage in their articles:

Who:	*Who played the game?*
	Who won the game?
What:	*What kind of game was it?*
	What happened in the game?
Why:	*Why was the game played?*
Where:	*Where was the game played?*
When:	*When was the game played?*
How:	*How was the game played?*

If you ask yourself extended questions of this sort on a specific topic, you will begin to produce thoughts and details that will undoubtedly be useful to you in the writing assignments that follow.

Clustering. Clustering is a method of drawing or mapping your ideas as fast as they come into your mind. Put a word, phrase, or sentence in a circle in the center of a blank page. Then, put every new idea that comes to you in another circle and show its relationship to a previous thought by drawing a line to the circle containing the previous idea. You will probably reach a natural stopping point for this exercise in two to three minutes.

Although you can generate ideas in a number of different ways, the main principle behind the "Preparing to Write" questions in this text is to encourage you to do what is called *expressive writing* before you tackle any writing assignment. This is writing based on your feelings, thoughts, experiences, observations, and opinions. From this reservoir, you can then choose the ideas you want to develop into an essay and begin writing about them one at a time.

As you use various prewriting techniques to generate responses to the "Preparing to Write" questions, you should know that these responses can be expressed using lists, outlines, random notes, sentences and paragraphs, charts, graphs, or pictures— whatever keeps the thoughts flowing smoothly and productively. One of our students used a combination of brainstorming and clustering to generate the following thoughts in response to the prewriting exercise following the Thomas essay:

Brainstorming

Mistakes:

- happen when I'm in a hurry
- make me feel stupid
- love
- Bob
- learned a lot about people
- people aren't what they seem
- getting back on track
- parents
- corrections

- relationships
- trip back East
- pride
- going in circles
- learning from mistakes
- I am a better person
- my values are clear
- mistakes help us change
- painful
- helpful
- valuable

Clustering

From the free-flowing thoughts you generate, you next need to decide what to write about and how to limit your subject to a manageable length. Our student writer chose topic 2 from the "Choosing a Topic" list after the essay (see page 23). Her initial responses to the prewriting questions helped her decide to write on "A Time I Got Lost." She then generated more focused ideas and opinions in the form of a journal entry. It is printed here just as she wrote it, errors and all.

Journal Entry

The craziest mistake I think I ever made was on a trip I took recently——I was heading to the east coast from British Columbia and reached Fredericton. I was so excited because I was going to get to see the Atlantic Ocean for the first time in my life and Fredericton was one of my last towns before I reached the sea. In Fredericton I was going to have to change from a northeast direction to due east.

When I got there the highway was under construction. I took the detour, but got all skrewed up till I realized that I had gone the wrong direction. By this time I was lost somewhere in downtown Fredericton and didn't know which way was east. I stoped and asked a guy at a gas station and he explained how to get back on the east-bound highway. The way was through the middle of town. By the time I got to where I was supposed to turn right I could only turn left. So I started left and then realized I couldn't turn back the other way! I made a couple of other stops after that, and one jerk told me I "just couldn't get there from here." Eventually I found a truck driver heading toward the same eastbound highway, and he told me to follow him. An hour and forty minutes after reaching Fredericton's city limits I finally managed to leave going east. I felt as if I had spent an entire month there!

The thing I learned from this was just how egocentric I am. I would not have made this error if I had not been so damn cocky about my sense of direction. My mistake was made worse because I got flustered and didn't listen to the directions clearly. I find that the reason I most often make a mistake is because I don't listen carefully to instructions. This has been a problem all my life.

After I got over feeling really dum I decided this kind of thing was not going to happen again. It was too much a waste of time and gas, so I was going to be more careful of road signs and directions.

This all turned out to be a positive experience though. I learned that there are lots of friendly, helpful people. It was kind of reassuring to know that other folks would help you if you just asked.

I feel this and other mistakes are crucial not only to my life but to personal growth in general. It is the making of mistakes that helps people learn where they are *misdirecting their energies. I think mistakes can help all of us learn to be more careful about some part of our lives. This is why mistakes are crucial. Otherwise, we would continue in the same old rut and never improve.*

This entry served as the foundation upon which the student built her essay. Her next step was to consider *audience* and *purpose* (which are usually specified in the writing assignments in this text). The first of these features identifies the person or group of people you will address in your essay. The second is a declaration of your principal reason for writing the essay, which usually takes the form of a thesis statement (the statement of purpose or the controlling idea of an essay). Together these pieces of information consciously or subconsciously help you make most of the decisions you are faced with as you write: what words to choose, what sentence structures to use, what order to present ideas in, which topics to develop, and which to summarize. The more you know about your audience (age, educational background, likes, dislikes, biases, political persuasion, and social status) and your purpose (to inform, persuade, and/or entertain), the easier the writing task will be. In the rough draft and final draft of the essay in the section that follows, the student knew she was writing to a senior English class at her old high school in order to convince them that mistakes can be positive factors in their lives. This clear sense of audience and purpose helped her realize she should use fairly advanced vocabulary, call upon a variety of sentence structures, and organize her ideas chronologically to make her point most effectively to her intended audience.

At this stage of the writing process, some people benefit from assembling their ideas in the form of an outline. Others use an outline as a check on their logic and organization after the first draft has been written. Whether your outlines are informal (a simple list) or highly structured, they can help you visualize the logical relationship of your ideas to each other. We recommend using your outline throughout the prewriting and writing stages to ensure that your work will be carefully and tightly organized. Your outline, however, should be adjusted to your draft as it develops.

Writing

The writing stage asks you to draft an essay based upon the prewriting material you have assembled. Because you have already made the important preliminary decisions regarding your topic, your audience, and your purpose, the task of actually writing the essay should follow naturally. (Notice we did not say this task should necessarily be easy—just natural.) At this stage, you should look upon your essay as a way of solving a problem or answering a question: The problem/question is posed in your writing assignment, and the solution/answer is your essay. The three "Choosing a Topic" assignments that follow the prewriting questions in the text require you to consider issues related to the essay you just read. Although they typically ask you to focus on one rhetorical pattern, they draw on many rhetorical strategies (as do all writing assignments in the text) and require you to support your statements with concrete examples. These assignments refer to the Lewis Thomas essay and emphasize the use of example, his dominant rhetorical strategy.

Choosing a Topic

1. You have decided to write an editorial for your local news-paper concerning the impact of computers on our lives. Cite specific experiences you have had with computers to help make your main point.

2. You have been invited back to your high school to make a speech to a senior English class about how people can learn from their mistakes. Write your speech in the form of an essay explaining what you learned from a crucial mistake you have made. Use examples to show these students that mistakes can be positive factors in their lives.

3. In an essay for your writing class, explain one specific human quality. Use Thomas's essay as a model. Cite examples to support your explanation.

The following essay is our student's first-draft response to topic 2. After writing her journal entry, the student drafted a tentative thesis statement: "I know there are positive attitudes that can come from making a mistake because I recently had an opportunity to learn some valuable lessons in this way." This statement helped the student further develop and organize her ideas as she focused finally on one well-chosen example to illustrate her thesis. At this point, the thesis is simply the controlling idea around which the other topics take shape; it is often revised several times before the final draft.

First Draft: A Time I Got Lost

Parents and teachers frequently pressure us to avoid committing errors. Meanwhile, our friends laugh at us when we make mistakes. With all these different messages, it is hard for us to think of mistakes as positive events. But if any of you take the time to think about what you have learned from mistakes, I bet you will realize all the good things that have come from these events. I know there are positive attitudes that can come from making a mistake because I recently had an opportunity to learn some valuable lessons in this way.

While travelling back east this last summer, I made the mistake of turning west on an interprovincial detour in order to reach the Atlantic Ocean. The adventure took me into the heart of Fredericton, where I got totally lost. I had to get directions several times until two hours later I was going in the right direction. As I was driving out of town, I realized that although I had made a dumb mistake, I had learned a great deal. Overall, the detour was actually a positive experience.

The first thing I remember thinking after I had gotten my wits together was that I had definitely learned something from making the mistake. I had the opportunity to see a new city, filled with new people—3,000 kilometres from my own hometown, but very much like it. I also became aware that the beach is not always toward the west, as it is in British Columbia. The entire experience was like getting a geography lesson firsthand.

As this pleasant feeling began to grow, I came to another realization. I was aware of how important other people can be in making a mistake into a positive experience. My first reaction was "Oh no, someone is going to know I made a mistake!" But the amazing part about this mistake was how supportive everyone was. The townspeople had been entirely willing to help someone they did not know. This mistake helped me to learn that people tend to be nicer than I had imagined.

The final lesson I learned from getting lost in Fredericton was how to be more cautious about my actions so as not to repeat the same mistake. It was this internalization of all the information I gleaned from making the mistake that I see as the most positive part of the experience. I realized that in order to avoid such situations in the future I would have to be less egocentric in my decisions and more willing to listen to directions from other people. I needed to learn that my set way of doing things was not always the best way. If I had not made the mistake, I would not have been aware of my other options.

By making this mistake I learned that there is a more comprehensive manner of looking at the world. In the future, if we could all stop after making a mistake and ask ourselves, "What can I learn from this?" we would be less critical of ourselves and have a great many more positive experiences. If I were not able to make mistakes, I would probably not be able to expand my knowledge of my environment, my understanding of people, and my choice of various actions.

Rewriting

The rewriting stage includes revising, editing, and proofreading. The first of these activities, *revising*, actually takes place during the entire writing process as you change words, recast sentences, and move whole paragraphs from one place to another. Making these linguistic and organizational choices means you will also be constantly adjusting your content to your purpose (what you want to accomplish) and your audience (the readers) in much the same way you alter your speech to communicate more effectively in response to the gestures, eye movements, or facial expressions of your listener. Revising is literally the act of "reseeing" your essay, looking at it through your readers' eyes to determine whether or not it achieves its purpose. As you revise, you should consider matters of both content and form. *In content*, do you have an interesting, thought-provoking title for your essay? Do you think your thesis statement will be clear to your audience? Does your introduction capture the readers' attention? Is your treatment of your topic consistent throughout the essay? Do you support your assertions with specific examples? Does your conclusion sum up your main points? *In form*, is your essay organized effectively? Do you use a variety of rhetorical strategies? Are your sentence structure and vocabulary varied and interesting?

Editing entails correcting mistakes in your writing so that your final draft conforms to the conventions of standard written English. Correct punctuation, spelling, and mechanics will help you make your points and will encourage your readers to move smoothly through your essay from topic to topic. At this stage, you should be concerned about such matters as whether your sentences are complete, whether your punctuation is correct and effective, whether you have followed conventional rules for using mechanics, and whether the words in your essay are spelled correctly.

Proofreading involves reading over your entire essay, slowly and carefully, to make certain you have not allowed any errors to slip into your draft. (Most writing instructors don't look upon errors as kindly as Thomas does.) In general, good writers try to let some time elapse between writing the final draft and proofreading it (at least a few hours, perhaps a day or so). Otherwise, they find themselves proofreading their thoughts rather than their words. Some writers even profit from proofreading their papers backward—a technique that allows them to focus on individual words and phrases rather than on entire sentences.

Because many writers work well with checklists, we present here a set of guidelines that will help you review the entire writing process.

Writing Inventory

Preparing to Write

1. Have I explored the prewriting questions through brainstorming, freewriting, journal entries, direct questions, or clustering?

2. Do I understand my topic or assignment?

3. Have I narrowed my topic adequately?

4. Do I have a specific audience for my essay? Do I know their likes and dislikes? Their educational level? Their knowledge about the topic?

5. Do I have a clear and precise purpose for my essay?

Writing

1. Can I express my topic as a problem or question?

2. Is my essay a solution or an answer to that problem or question?

Rewriting

Revising the Content

1. Does my essay have a clear, interesting title?
2. Will my statement of purpose (or thesis) be clear to my audience?
3. Will the introduction make my audience want to read the rest of my essay?
4. Do I pursue my topic consistently throughout the essay?
5. Have I included enough details to prove my main points?
6. Does my conclusion sum up my central points?
7. Will I accomplish my purpose with this audience?

Revising the Form

1. Have I organized my ideas as effectively as possible for this audience?
2. Do I use appropriate rhetorical strategies to support my main point?
3. Is my sentence structure varied and interesting?
4. Is my vocabulary appropriate for my topic, my purpose, and my audience?
5. Do I present my essay as effectively as possible, including useful graphic design techniques on the computer, where appropriate?

Editing and Proofreading

1. Have I written complete sentences throughout my essay?
2. Have I used punctuation correctly and effectively (check especially the use of commas, colons, and semicolons)?
3. Have I followed conventional rules for mechanics (capitalization, underlining or italics, abbreviations, and numbers)?
4. Are all the words in my essay spelled correctly? (Use a dictionary when in doubt.)

Following is the student's revised draft of her essay on making mistakes in life. The final draft of this typical student's essay represents the entire writing process at work. We have made notes in the margin to highlight various effective elements in her essay, and we have underlined substantial changes in words and phrases from earlier drafts.

Mistakes and Maturity

Catchy title; good change from first draft

Rapport with audience and point of view established

Clear, stimulating introduction for high school seniors

Parents and teachers frequently <u>harp</u> on us to <u>correct</u> our errors. Meanwhile, our friends laugh at us when we make mistakes. With all these <u>negative</u> messages, most of us have a hard time believing that problems can be positive experiences. But if we take the time to think about what we have learned from various <u>blunders</u>, we will realize all the good that has come from these events. <u>I know making mistakes can have positive results because I recently learned several valuable lessons from one unforgettable experience</u>.

Good brief summary of complex experience (see notes from Preparing to Write)

While <u>I was</u> travelling to the east coast last summer, I made the mistake of turning west on an interprovincial detour <u>in an attempt</u> to reach the Atlantic Ocean. This adventure took me into the <u>center</u> of Fredericton, where I <u>became</u> totally lost, bewildered, and angry at myself. I had to <u>ask for</u> directions several times until two hours later, when I <u>finally found the correct highway toward the ocean</u>. As I was driving out of town, I realized that although I had made a "dumb" mistake, I had actually learned a great deal. Overall, <u>my adventure had been quite positive</u>.

Background information

Good details

First topic (Topics are in chronological order)

Adequate number of examples

The first <u>insight</u> I remember having after my wits returned was that I had definitely learned more about Canadian geography from making this mistake. <u>I had become intimately acquainted with a town 4827 kilometers from home that greatly resembled my own city, and I had become aware that the beach is not always toward the west, as it is in British Columbia. I had also met some pleasant strangers. Looking at my confusion as a learning experience encouraged me to have positive feelings about the mistake</u>.

Nice close to this paragraph

Second topic

As <u>I relaxed and let</u> this happy feeling grow, I came to another realization. I <u>became</u> aware of how important other people can be in <u>turning</u> a mistake into a positive event. Although my first reaction had been "Oh, no! Someone is going to know <u>I'm lost</u>," I was amazed by how supportive other people were <u>during my panic and embarrassment. From an old man swinging on his front porch to an elementary school boy crossing the street with his bright blue backpack, I found</u> that the townspeople of Fredericton were entirely willing to help someone they did not <u>even</u> know. <u>I realized that people in general</u> are nicer than <u>I had previously thought</u>.

Clear explanation with details

Good summary statement

The final lesson I learned from <u>making this mistake</u> was how to be more cautious about <u>my future decisions</u>. <u>This insight was, in fact,</u> the most positive part of the entire experience. <u>What</u> I realized I must do to <u>prevent</u> similar <u>errors</u> in the future was to relax, <u>not be so bullheaded</u> in my decisions, and be more willing to listen to directions from other people. <u>I might never have had these positive realizations if I had not made this mistake.</u>

Third topic

Specific details

Thus, by <u>driving in circles for two hours, I developed</u> a more comprehensive way of looking at the world. If I were unable to make mistakes, I probably would not have had this chance to <u>learn</u> about my environment, <u>improve my impressions of strangers</u>, and <u>reconsider the egocentric way in which I act in certain situations.</u> Perhaps there's <u>a lesson here for all of us. Instead of criticizing ourselves unduly</u>, if each one of us could <u>pause</u> after we make an error and ask, "<u>How</u> can I <u>profit</u> from this?" <u>we would realize that mistakes can often be turned into positive events that will help us become more confident and mature.</u>

Clear transition statement

Concluding statement applicable to all readers

Good summary of three topics without being repetitive

Nicely focused concluding remark

As these various drafts of the student paper indicate, the essay assignments in this book encourage you to transfer to your own writing your understanding of how form and content work together. If you use the short-answer questions after each reading selection as a guide, the writing assignments will help you learn how to give shape to your own ideas and to gain control of your readers' thoughts and feelings. In essence, they help you recognize the power you have through language over your life and your environment.

Conclusion

As you approach the essays in this text, remember that both reading and writing function most efficiently as processes of discovery. Through them, you educate and expand your own mind and the minds of your readers. They can provide a powerful means of discovering new information or clarifying what you already know. Reading and writing lead to understanding. And just as you can discover how to read through writing, so too can you become more aware of the details of the writing process through reading. We hope your time spent with this book is both pleasant and profitable as you refine your ability to discover and express effectively the good ideas within yourself.

CHAPTER 1

DESCRIPTION

■ ■ ■

Exploring Through the Senses

All of us use description in our daily lives. We might, for example, try to convey the horrors of a recent history exam to our parents, or help a friend visualize someone we met on vacation, or describe an automobile accident for a police report. Whatever our specific purpose, description is fundamental to the act of communication: We give and receive descriptions constantly, and our lives are continually affected by this simple yet important rhetorical technique.

Defining Description

Description may be defined as the act of capturing people, places, events, objects, and feelings in words so that a reader (or listener) can visualize and respond to them. Unlike narration, which traditionally presents events in a clear time sequence, description essentially suspends its objects in time, making them exempt from such limits of chronology. Narration tells a story, while pure description contains no action or time. Description is one of our primary forms of self-expression; it paints a verbal picture that helps the reader understand or share a sensory experience through the process of "showing" rather than "telling." *Telling* your friends, for example, that "the campgrounds were filled with friendly, happy activities" is not as engaging as *showing* them by saying, "The campgrounds were alive with the smell of spicy baked beans, the sound of high-pitched laughter, and the sight of happy families sharing the warmth of a fire." Showing your readers helps them understand your experience through as many senses as possible.

Descriptions range between extremes: (1) totally objective reports (with no trace of opinions or feelings), such as we might find in a dictionary or an encyclopedia, and (2) very subjective accounts, which focus almost exclusively on personal impressions. The same horse, for instance, might be described by one writer as "a large, solid-hoofed herbivorous mammal having a long mane and a tail" (objective) and by another as "a magnificent and spirited beast flaring its nostrils in search of adventure" (subjective). Most descriptive writing, however, falls somewhere between these two extremes: "a large, four-legged beast in search of adventure."

Objective description is principally characterized by its impartial, precise, and emotionless tone. Found most prominently in technical and scientific writing, such accounts might include a description of equipment to be used in a chemistry experiment, the results of a market survey for a particular consumer product, or a medical appraisal of a heart patient's physical symptoms. In situations like these, accurate, unbiased, and easily understandable accounts are of the utmost importance.

Subjective description, in contrast, is intentionally created to produce a particular response in the reader or listener. Focusing on feelings rather than on raw data, it tries to activate as many senses as possible, thereby leading the audience to a specific conclusion or state of mind. Examples of subjective descriptions are a parent's disapproving comments about one of your friends, a professor's glowing analysis of your most recent "A" paper, or a basketball coach's critique of the team's losing effort in last night's big game.

In most situations, the degree of subjectivity or objectivity in a descriptive passage depends to a large extent upon the writer's purpose and intended audience. In the case of the heart patient mentioned above, the person's physician might present the case in a formal, scientific way to a group of medical colleagues; in a personal, sympathetic way to the invalid's spouse; and in financial terms to a number of potential contributors in order to solicit funds for heart disease research.

The following paragraph describes one student's fond memories of visiting "the farm." As you read it, notice the writer's use of subjective description to communicate to her readers the multitude of contradictory feelings she connects with this rural retreat.

The shrill scream of the alarm shatters a dream. This is the last day of my visit to the place I call "the farm," an old ramshackle house in the country owned by one of my aunts. I want to go out once more in the peace of the early morning, walk in the crisp and chilly hour, and breathe the sweet air. My body feels jarred as my feet hit the hard-packed clay dirt. I tune out my stiff muscles and cold arms and legs and instead focus on two herons playing hopscotch on the canal bank: Every few yards I walk toward them, they fly one over the other an almost equal distance away from me. A killdeer with its piercing crystalline cry dips its body as it flies low over the water, the tip of its wing leaving a ring to reverberate outward. The damp earth has a strong, rich, musky scent. To the east, dust rises, and for the first time I hear the clanking and straining of a tractor as it harrows smooth the soil before planting. A crop duster rises close by just as it cuts off its release of spray, the acrid taste of chemical filtering down through the air. As the birds chatter and peck at the fields, I reluctantly return to my life in the city.

Thinking Critically by Using Description

Each rhetorical mode in this book gives us new insight into the process of thinking by providing different options for arranging our thoughts and our experiences. The more we know about these options, the more conscious we become of how our minds operate and the better chance we have to improve and refine our thinking skills. (For a more thorough definition of the term "rhetorical mode," see the Web site **www.prenticehall.ca/ readerschoice**.)

As you examine description as a way of thinking, consider it in isolation for a moment—away from the other rhetorical modes. Think of it as a muscle you can isolate and strengthen on its own in a weight-training program before you ask it to perform together with other muscles. By isolating description, you will learn more readily what it entails and how it functions as a critical thinking tool. In the process, you will also strengthen your knowledge of how to recognize and use description more effectively in your reading, in your writing, and in your daily life.

Just as you exercise to strengthen muscles, so too will you benefit from doing exercises to improve your skill in using descriptive techniques. As you have learned, description depends to a great extent on the keenness of your senses. So as you prepare to read and write descriptive essays, do the following tasks so that you can first learn what the process of description feels like in your own head. Really use your imagination to play with these exercises on as many different levels as possible. Also write when you are asked to do so. The combination of thinking and writing is often especially useful when we practice our thinking skills.

1. Make a list of five descriptive words you would use to trigger each of the following senses: taste, sight, hearing, touch, and smell.

2. Find a picture of a person, an animal, a bouquet of flowers, a sunset, or some other still-life portrait. List words you would use to describe this picture to a classmate. Then, list a few similes and metaphors that actually describe this still life. How would your description differ if you were seeing the subject in real life rather than in a picture?

3. Choose an unusual object and brainstorm about its physical characteristics. Then, brainstorm about the emotions this object evokes. Why is this object so unusual or special? Compare your two brainstorming results and draw some conclusions about their differences.

Reading and Writing Descriptive Essays

All good descriptions share four fundamental qualities: (1) an accurate sense of audience (who the readers are) and purpose (why the essay was written), (2) a clear vision of the object being described, (3) a careful selection of details that help communicate the author's vision, and (4) a consistent point of view or perspective from which a writer composes. The dominant impression or main effect the writer wishes to leave with a specific audience dictates virtually all of the verbal choices in a descriptive essay. Although description is featured in this chapter, you should also pay close attention to how other rhetorical strategies (such as example, division/classification, and cause/effect) can best support the dominant impression.

How to Read a Descriptive Essay

Preparing to Read. As you approach the reading selections in this chapter, you should focus first on the author's title and try to make some initial assumptions about the essay that follows: Does Ray Guy reveal his attitude toward his subject in the title "When Jannies Visited"? Can you guess what the general mood of "What a Certain Visionary Once Said" will be? Then, scan the essay to discover its audience and purpose: What do you think David Adams Richards' purpose is in "My Old Newcastle"? Who is Sally Armstrong addressing in "P4W"? You should also read the synopsis of each essay in the Rhetorical Table of Contents (on pages iii–xi); these brief summaries will provide you with helpful information at this point in the reading process.

Next, learn as much as you can about the author and the conditions under which the essay was composed, information that is provided in the biographical statement before each essay. For a descriptive essay, the conditions under which the author wrote the essay, coupled with his or her purpose, can be very revealing: Can you determine when Ray Guy's piece was written? Does it describe the narrator's life now or in the past? What do Lesley Choyce's interests tell you about his motivations for writing "Thin Edge of the Wedge"? What concerns might have led Sally Armstrong to have written "P4W"? What does Tomson Highway's background suggest about his perspective in "What a Certain Visionary Once Said"? Learning where the essay was first published will also give you valuable information about its audience.

Last, before you begin to read, try to do some brainstorming on the essay's title. In this chapter, respond to the Preparing to Read questions before each essay, which ask you to begin thinking and writing about the topic under consideration. Then, pose your own questions: What image do you have of "the north" (Highway)? Do you know what jannies are (Guy)? What have your preconceptions been about correctional institutions (Armstrong)? What might you want to learn about the life of an island (Choyce)?

Reading. As you read each essay for the first time, jot down your initial reactions to it, and try to make connections and see relationships among the author's biography; the essay's title, purpose, and audience; and the synopsis. In this way, you will create a context or framework for your reading. See if you can figure out, for example, what Highway might be saying about people's attitudes toward the land in his essay, "What a Certain Visionary Once Said," or why David Adams Richards wrote an essay about his home town in "My Old Newcastle." Try to discover what the relationship is between purpose, audience, and publication information in Lesley Choyce's essay.

Also determine at this point if the author's treatment of his or her subject is predominantly objective (generally free of emotion) or subjective (heavily charged with emotion). Or perhaps the essay falls somewhere between these two extremes.

In addition, make sure you have a general sense of the dominant impression each author is trying to convey. Such an initial approach to reading these descriptive selections will give you a foundation upon which to analyze the material during your second, more in-depth reading.

Finally, at the end of your first reading, take a look at the questions after each essay to make certain you can answer them. This material will guide your rereading.

Rereading. As you reread these descriptive essays, you should be discovering exactly what each essay's dominant impression is and how the author created it. Notice each author's careful selection of details and the way in which these details come together to leave you with this impression. Also try to determine how certain details add to and detract from that dominant impression and how the writer's point of view affects it: How does Tomson Highway create a sense of respect for the environment in "What a Certain Visionary Once Said"? How does Sally Armstrong help us to feel the genuine agony and sense of helplessness experienced by inmates in a women's prison?

Try to find during this reading other rhetorical modes that support the description. Although the essays in this chapter describe various persons, places, or objects, all of the authors call upon other rhetorical strategies (especially example and comparison/contrast) to communicate their descriptions. How do these various rhetorical strategies work together in each essay to create a coherent whole?

Finally, answering the questions after each essay will check your understanding of the author's main points and help you think critically about the essay in preparing for the discussion/writing assignments that follow.

For an inventory of the reading process, you may want to review the checklists on pages 15–16 of the Introduction.

How to Write a Descriptive Essay

Preparing to Write. Before you choose a writing assignment, use the prewriting questions that follow each essay to help you discover your own ideas and opinions about the general topic of the essay. Next, choose an assignment or read the one assigned to you. Then, just as you do when you read an essay, you should determine the audience and purpose for your description (if these are not specified for you in the assignment). To whom are you writing? And why? Will an impartial, objective report be appropriate, or should you present a more emotional, subjective account to accomplish your task? In assessing your audience, you need to determine what they do and do not know about your topic. This information will help you make decisions about what you are going to say and how you will say it. Your purpose will be defined by what you intend your audience to know, think, or believe after they have read your descriptive essay. Do you want them to make up their own minds about hometown memories or prison conditions, for example, based on an objective presentation of data, or do you hope to sway their opinions through a more subjective display of information? Or perhaps you will decide to blend the two techniques, combining facts and opinions, in order to achieve the impression of personal certainty based on objective evidence. What dominant impression do you want to leave with your audience? As you might suspect, decisions regarding audience and purpose are as important to writing descriptions as they are to reading descriptions, and will shape your descriptive essay from start to finish.

The second quality of good description concerns the object of your analysis and the clarity with which you present it to the reader. Whenever possible, you should thoroughly investigate the person, place, moment, or feeling you wish to describe, paying particular attention to its effect upon each of your five senses. What can you see, smell, hear, taste, and touch as you examine it? If you want to describe your house, for example, begin by asking yourself a series of pertinent questions: How big is the house? What colour is it? How many exterior doors does the house have? How many interior doors? Are any of the rooms wallpapered? If so, what are the colour and texture of that wallpaper? How many different shades of paint cover the walls? Which rooms have constant noises (from clocks and other mechanical devices)? Are the kitchen appliances hot or cold to the touch? What is the quietest room in the house? The noisiest? What smells do you notice in the laundry? In the kitchen? In the basement? Most important, do any of these sensory questions trigger particular childhood memories? Although you will probably not use all of these details in your descriptive essay, the process of generating and answering such detailed questions will help reacquaint you with the object of your description as it also assists you in designing and focusing your paper. To help you generate some of these ideas, you may want to review the prewriting techniques introduced on pages 17–19.

Writing. As you write, you must select the details of your description with great care and precision so that you leave your reader with a specific impression. If, for instance, you want your audience to feel the warmth and comfort of your home, you might concentrate on describing the plush carpets, the big up-holstered chairs, the inviting scent of hot apple cider, and the crackling fire. If, on the other hand, you want to gain your audience's sympathy, you might prefer to focus on the sparse austerity of your home environment: the bare walls, the quietness, the lack of colour and decoration, the dim lighting, and the frigid temperature. You also want to make sure you omit unrelated ideas, like a conversation between your parents you accidentally overheard. Your careful choice of details will help control your audience's reaction.

To make your impression even more vivid, you might use figurative language to fill out your descriptions. Using words "figuratively" means using them imaginatively rather than literally. The two most popular forms of figurative language are *simile* and *metaphor*. A *simile* is a comparison between two dissimilar objects or ideas introduced by *like* or *as*: Choyce describes "two dents in the ground as if some giant had punched down into a massive surface of dough." A *metaphor* is an implied comparison between two dissimilar objects or ideas that is not introduced by *like* or *as*: At age eight, Ray Guy's life is a collection of "pieces of the great jigsaw ..." Besides enlivening your writing, figurative language helps your readers understand objects, feelings, and ideas that are complex or obscure by comparing them with things that are more familiar.

The last important quality of an effective descriptive essay is point of view, your physical perspective on your subject. Because the organization of your essay depends on your point of view, you need to choose a specific angle from which to approach your description. If you verbally jump around your home, referring first to a picture on the wall in your bedroom, next to the microwave in the kitchen, and then to the quilt on your bed, no reasonable audience will be able to follow your description. Nor will they want to. If, however, you move from room to room in some logical, sequential way, always focusing on the details you want your readers to know, you will be helping your audience form a clear, memorable impression of your home. Your vision will become their vision. In other words, your point of view plays a part in determining the organization of your description. Working spatially, you could move from side to side (from one wall to another in the rooms we have discussed), from top to bottom (from ceiling to floor), or from far to near (from the farthest to the closest point in a room), or you might progress from large to small objects, from uninteresting to interesting, or from funny to serious. Whatever plan you choose should help you accomplish your purpose with your particular audience.

Rewriting. As you reread each of your descriptive essays, play the role of your audience and try to determine what dominant impression you receive by the end of your reading.

1. Do you communicate the dominant impression you want to convey?
2. Do you have a clear point of view on your subject?
3. How does the essay make you feel?
4. What does it make you think about?
5. Which senses does it stimulate?
6. Do you use similes or metaphors when appropriate?
7. Could you, for example, add more detailed information, reorganize some of the essay, or omit irrelevant material?

For additional suggestions on the writing process, you may want to consult the checklists on pages 26–27 of the Introduction.

Student Essay: Description at Work

In the following essay, a student relives some of her childhood memories through a subjective description of her grandmother's house. As you read it, pay particular attention to the different types of sensual details the student writer chooses in order to communicate to readers her dominant impression of her grandmother's home. Notice also her use of carefully chosen details to "show" rather than "tell" us about her childhood reminiscences, especially her comparisons, which make the memory as vivid for the reader as it is for the writer.

Grandma's House

Writer's point of view or perspective — My most vivid childhood memories are set in my Grandma Goodlink's house, a curious blend of familiar and mysterious treasures. Grandma lived at the end of a dead-end street, in the same house she had lived in since the first day of her marriage. That was half a century and thirteen children ago. A set of crumbly steps made of concrete mixed with gravel led up to her front door. I remember a big gap between the house and the steps, as if someone had not pushed them up close enough to the house. Anyone who looked into the gap could see old toys and books that had fallen into the crack behind the steps and had remained there, forever irretrievable. — *Dominant impression (right margin), Comparison (simile), Sight*

Only a hook-type lock on the front door protected Grandma's many beautiful antiques. Her living room was set up like a church or schoolroom, with an old purple velvet couch against the far wall and two chairs immediately in front of the couch facing the same direction. One-half of the couch was always buried in old clothes, magazines, and newspapers, and a lone shoe sat atop the pile, a finishing touch to some bizarre modern sculpture. To one side was an aged and tuneless upright piano with yellowed keys. The ivory overlay was missing so that the wood underneath showed through, and many of the keys made only a muffled and frustrating thump, no matter how hard I pressed them. On the wall facing the piano was the room's only window, draped with yellowed lace curtains. Grandma always left that window open. I remember sitting near it, smelling the rain while the curtains tickled my face. — *Comparison (simile), Sight, Comparison (metaphor), Sound, Sight, Smell, Touch*

For no apparent reason, an old curtain hung in the door between the kitchen and the living room. In the kitchen, a large Formica-topped table always held at least a half-dozen varieties of homemade jelly, as well as a loaf of bread, gooseberry pies, or cherry pies with the pits left in, boxes of cereal, and anything else not requiring refrigeration, as if the table served as a small, portable pantry. Grandma's kitchen always smelled of toast, and I often wondered—and still do—if she lived entirely on toast. A hole had eaten through the kitchen floor, not just the warped yellow linoleum, but all the way through the floor itself. My sisters and I never wanted to take a bath at Grandma's house, because we discovered that anyone who lay on the floor on his stomach and put one eye to the hole could see the bathtub, which was kept in the musty basement because the upstairs bathroom was too small. — *Sight, Taste, Comparison (simile), Smell, Sight, Sight, Smell*

The back bedroom was near the kitchen and adjacent to the basement stairs. I once heard one of my aunts call that room a firetrap, and indeed it was. The room was <u>wallpapered with the old</u> <u>newspapers</u> Grandma liked to collect, and the bed was stacked high with <u>my mother's and aunts' old clothes</u>. There was no space between the furniture in that room, only a narrow path against one wall leading to the bed. A sideboard was shoved against the opposite wall; a sewing table was pushed up against the sideboard; a short chest of drawers lay against the sewing table; and so on. But no one could identify these pieces of forgotten furniture without digging through the sewing patterns, half-made dresses, dishes, and books. Any outsider would just think this was a part of the room where the floor had been raised to about waist-level, so thoroughly was the mass of furniture hidden.

Sight   *Sight*   *Sight*

Stepping off Grandma's sloping back porch was <u>like stepping</u> <u>into an enchanted forest</u>. The grass and weeds were hip-level, with a tiny dirt path leading to nowhere, <u>as if it had lost its way in</u> <u>the jungle</u>. A <u>fancy white fence</u>, courtesy of the neighbors, bordered the yard in back and vainly attempted to hold in the <u>gooseberries,</u> <u>raspberries, and blackberries</u> that grew wildly along the side of Grandma's yard. <u>Huge crabapple, cherry, and walnut trees</u> shaded the house and hid the sky. I used to stand under them and look up, pretending to be deep in a magic forest. The ground was <u>cool and</u> <u>damp</u> under my bare feet, even in the middle of the day, and my head would fill with the <u>sweet fragrance of mixed spring flowers</u> <u>and the throaty cooing of doves</u> I could never find but could always hear. But, before long, the wind would shift, and the <u>musty</u> <u>aroma of petroleum</u> from a nearby refinery would jerk me back to reality.

Comparison (simile)   *Comparison (simile)*   *Sight*   *Sight*   *Sight*   *Touch*   *Smell*   *Sound*   *Smell*

Grandma's house is indeed a place for memories. Just as her decaying concrete steps store the treasures of many lost childhoods, <u>her house still stands, guarding the memories of generations</u> <u>of children and grandchildren.</u>

Dominant impression rephrased

Student Writer's Comments

Writing this descriptive essay was easy and enjoyable for me——once I got started. I decided to write about my grandmother's house because I knew it so well, but I had trouble coming up with the impression I wanted to convey to my readers. I have so many recollections of this place I didn't know which set of memories would be most interesting to others. So I began by brainstorming, forcing myself to think of images from all five senses.

After I had accumulated plenty of images, which triggered other memories I had completely forgotten, I began to write. I organized my essay spatially as if I were walking through Grandma's house room by room. But I let my senses lead the way. Before I started writing, I had no idea how many paragraphs I would have, but as I meandered through the house recording my memories of sights, smells, sounds, tastes, and textures, I ended up writing one paragraph on each room, plus one for the yard. For this assignment, I wrote the three paragraphs about the inside of the house first; then, the introduction started to take shape in my head, so I got it down; and last, I wrote the paragraph on the backyard and my conclusion. Finally, my "dominant impression" came to me: This is a house that guards the memories of many generations. My grandmother has always lived in this house, and my mother has her own set of memories associated with this place too.

This focus for my paper made the revising process fairly easy, as I worked on the entire essay with a specific purpose in mind. Previously, my biggest problem had been that I had too many scattered memories and realized I had to be more selective. Once I had my dominant impression, I knew which images to keep and which to drop from my draft. Also, as I reworked my essay, I looked for ways to make my description more exciting and vivid for the reader——as if he or she was right there with me. To accomplish this, I explained some special features of my grandma's house by comparing them with items the reader would most likely be familiar with. I also worked, at this point, on making one paragraph flow into another by adding transitions that move the reader smoothly from one group of ideas to the next. "Only a hook-type lock on the front door" got my readers into the living room. The old curtain between the kitchen and the living room moved my essay out of the living room and into the kitchen. I started my third paragraph about the indoors by saying "The back bedroom was near the kitchen and adjacent to the basement stairs" so my readers could get their bearings in relation to other parts of the house they had already been introduced to. Finally, I was content that my essay was a clear, accurate description of my view of my grandma's house. My brother might have a completely different set of memories, but this was my version of a single generation of impressions organized, finally, into one coherent essay.

Some Final Thoughts on Description

Because description is one of the most basic forms of verbal communication, you will find descriptive passages in most of the reading selections throughout this textbook. Description provides us with the means to capture our audience's attention and clarify certain points in all of our writing. The examples chosen for the following section, however, are predominantly descriptive—the main purpose in each being to involve the readers' senses as vividly as possible. As you read through each of these essays, try to determine its intended audience and purpose, the object of the description, the extent to which details are included or excluded, and the author's point of view. Equipped with these four areas of reference, you can become an increasingly sophisticated reader and writer of descriptive prose.

Description in Review

Reading Descriptive Essays

Preparing to Read

1. What assumptions can you make from the essay's title?

2. Can you guess what the general mood of the essay is?

3. What is the essay's purpose and audience?

4. What does the synopsis in the Table of Contents tell you about the essay?

5. What can you learn from the author's biography?

6. Can you guess what the author's point of view toward the subject is?

7. What are your responses to the Preparing to Read questions?

Reading

1. Is the essay predominantly objective or subjective?

2. What dominant impression is the author trying to convey?

3. Did you preview the questions that follow the essay?

Rereading

1. How does the author create the essay's dominant impression?

2. What other rhetorical modes does the author use to support the essay's purpose?

3. What are your responses to the questions after the essay?

Writing Descriptive Essays

Preparing to Write

1. What are your responses to the Preparing to Write questions?

2. What is your purpose? Will you be primarily objective or subjective?

3. Who is your audience?

4. What is the dominant impression you want to convey?

5. Do you know the object of your description well?

Writing

1. Do the details you are choosing support your dominant impression?

2. Do you use words literally and figuratively?

3. What is your point of view toward your subject?

4. Do you *show* rather than *tell* your dominant impression?

Rewriting

1. Do you communicate the dominant impression you want to convey?
2. Do you have a clear point of view on your subject?
3. How does the essay make you feel?
4. What does it make you think about?
5. Which senses does it stimulate?
6. Do you use similes or metaphors when appropriate?
7. Are you *showing* rather than *telling* your description?

David Adams Richards
1950–

■ ■ ■

My Old Newcastle

Newcastle, New Brunswick, in the Miramichi valley, is often the subject and setting of choice, and formerly the home of novelist and poet David Adams Richards. After leaving St. Thomas University in Fredericton to try a career as a writer, he published a book of poems, *Small Heroics* (1972), at the age of 22. Much of the author's writing, including these early poems, shows his ability to transmute the sombre, even grim, quality of his perceptions of place into a source of beauty and interest. While he sets most of his fiction in his native area, Richards has stated that the great Russian novelists were his strongest literary influences. Indeed, the USSR bought the publishing rights to his first novel, *The Coming of Winter* (1974), in 1980. His subsequent novels include *Lives of Short Duration* (1981); *Road to the Stilt House* (1985); *Hope in the Desperate Hour* (1996); and *The Bay of Love and Sorrows* (1998) as well as the Miramichi trilogy: *Nights Below Station House* (1987), *Evening Snow Will Bring Such Peace* (1991), and *For Those Who Hunt the Wounded Down* (1993). Richards' novels show his compassion for, and continuing concern with, social and economic suffering, as well as deep feeling for his home environment. His love of the outdoors and keen eye for fine detail and local speech patterns make him a distinctly Canadian writer of the realist school. Richards' work has become familiar to a much wider audience in the last few years through the adaptation of several of his works for television.

Richards' recent works include *Hockey Dreams: Memories of a Man Who Couldn't Play* (1996) and *Lines on the Water: A Fisherman's Life on the Miramichi* (1998) in which he has captured his fly-fishing adventures on the Miramichi. In recognition of the quality of his writing, Richards has won the Governor General's Award twice (for fiction in 1988 and nonfiction a decade later in 1998) as well as the Canadian Authors Association Award (1991), The Canada–Australia Prize (1993), a Gemini Award in 1996 for his screenplay for *Small Gifts*, and the Norma Epstein Award. Richards has held the position of writer-in-residence at six post-secondary institutions in Canada and the U.S. and currently lives in Toronto, Ontario.

Preparing to Read

In "My Old Newcastle," David Adams Richards gives us a portrait of a year in the life of his childhood locale, drawn from the standpoint of the author in 1992. He focuses his memory backward to the sights, sounds, smells, and seasons of his youth. Although an industrial town in New Brunswick may not strike the reader as the setting of much that is beautiful, Richards shows us otherwise. Indoor and outdoor life, business and the progression of natural life, all had a rhythm and a sense of their own place for the author growing up beside the Miramichi River.

Where did you grow up? In one place or several? In a small town, in a rural setting, or in a city? What do you remember best about the people and places of your childhood? Your adolescence? Have you gone back to places where you grew up? What changes did you find?

■ _____ ■

In Newcastle, N.B., which I call home, we all played on the ice 1 floes in the spring, spearing tommy-cod with stolen forks tied to sticks. More than one of us almost met our end slipping off the ice.

All night the trains rumbled or shunted their loads off to 2 Halifax or Montreal, and men moved and worked. To this day I find the sound of trains more comforting than lonesome. It was somehow thrilling to know of people up and about in those hours, and wondrous events taking place. Always somehow with the faint, worn smell of gas and steel.

The Miramichi is a great working river. 3

There was always the presence of working men and women, 4 from the mines or mills or woods; the more than constant sound of machinery; and the ore covered in tarps at the side of the wharf.

But as children, sitting in our snowsuits and hats and heavy 5 boots on Saturday afternoons, we all saw movies that had almost nothing to do with us. That never mentioned us as a country or a place. That never seemed to know what our fathers and mothers did—that we went to wars or had a flag or even a great passion for life.

As far as the movies were concerned, we were in a lost, dark 6 country, it seemed. And perhaps this is one reason I write. Leaving the theatre on a January afternoon, the smell of worn seats and heat and chip bags gave way to a muted cold and scent of snow no movie ever showed us. And night came against the tin roofs of the sheds behind our white houses, as the long spires of our churches rose over the town.

Our river was frozen so blue then that trucks could travel 7 from one town to the other across the ice, and bonfires were lit by kids skating; sparks rose upon the shore under the stars as mothers called children home at 9 o'clock.

All winter long the sky was tinted blue on the horizon, the 8 schools we sat in too warm; privileged boys and girls sat beside those who lived in hunger and constant worry. One went on to be a Rhodes scholar, another was a derelict at 17 and dead at 20. To this day I could not tell you which held more promise.

Spring came with the smell of mud and grass burning in the   9 fields above us. Road hockey gave way to cricket and then baseball. The sun warmed, the ice shifted and the river was free. Salmon and sea trout moved up a dozen of our tributaries to spawn.

In the summer the ships came in, from all ports to ours, to   10 carry ore and paper away. Sailors smoked black tobacco cigarettes, staring down at us from their decks; blackflies spoiled in the fields beyond town, and the sky was large all evening. Cars filled with children too excited to sleep passed along our great avenues lined with overhanging trees. All down to the store to get ice cream in the dark.

Adolescent blueberry crops and sunken barns dotted the   11 fields near the bay, where the air had the taste of salt and tar, and small spruce trees seemed constantly filled with wind; where, by August, the water shimmered and even the small white lobster boats smelled of autumn, as did the ripples that moved them.

In the autumn the leaves were red, of course, and the earth,   12 by Thanksgiving, became hard as a dull turnip. Ice formed in the ditches and shallow streams. The fields became yellow and stiff. The sounds of rifle shots from men hunting deer echoed faintly away, while women walked in kerchiefs and coats to 7 o'clock mass, and the air felt heavy and leaden. Winter coming on again.

Now the town is three times as large, and fast-food franchises   13 and malls dot the roadside where there were once fields and lumberyards. There is a new process at the mill, and much of the wood is clear-cut so that huge acres lie empty and desolate, a redundancy of broken and muted earth. The river is opened all winter by an ice-breaker, so no trucks travel across the ice, and the trains, of course, are gone. For the most part the station is empty, the tracks fiercely alone in the winter sun.

The theatre is gone now, too. And those thousands of movies   14 showing us, as children filled with happy laughter someplace in Canada, what we were not, are gone as well. They have given way to videos and satellite dishes and a community that is growing slowly farther and farther away from its centre. Neither bad nor good, I suppose—but away from what it was.

UNDERSTANDING DETAILS

1. Why does Richards call the Miramichi "a great working river"?
2. Where are the points of difference between what the author saw in movies as a youth and what he knew in his own life? Why might this variance in perception have been a motivation to write?
3. How does Newcastle today differ from the town of Richards' youth?

ANALYZING MEANING

1. Life in small towns is never the simplistic picture that the media seem to show. What points in Richards' essay indicate that the texture of life in his boyhood may have been no less complex and interesting than it might have been in a city?
2. What descriptive details indicate that there was a real and vital quality to both the industrial and nature-based lives of the town of Newcastle? Does the author give a sense of a sort of reasonable coexistence of the two lives?
3. Do you agree with Richards' final statement about the Newcastle of today, that the changes which have come are "neither bad nor good" (paragraph 14)? Do you think that he is so neutral in his feelings? What specifically in this essay prompts your response?

DISCOVERING RHETORICAL STRATEGIES

1. "My Old Newcastle" as a descriptive essay demonstrates the use of a chronological method of structuring its episodes. Describe the framework of the author's pattern of organization. How does this pattern draw the reader through time? What elements in the final paragraph link back to the body of the essay?
2. Details strongly tied to our senses are frequently the most effective in communicating strong impressions. Richards uses vital visual, tactile, and olfactory descriptions, as well as direct and earthy figures of speech. Why might such strong and basic writing be suitable to his subject? Which details and similes stand out most strongly to you and why?
3. What is the effect on you as a reader of the author's alternation of short and longer sentences? How do the author's sentences,

and his choice of words, change in the final two paragraphs? Why?

1. Richards writes with a passion about the land where he grew up and spent many years living. How does his attitude toward his subject matter compare to that of Lesley Choyce ("Thin Edge of the Wedge") or Tomson Highway ("What a Certain Visionary Once Said")?
2. David Adams Richards, in writing about Newcastle, is reflecting on his childhood memories much as Ray Guy does in "When Jannies Visited." Whose childhood seems more appealing to you? Why?
3. Newcastle has changed significantly since Richards' childhood. How does the present-day Newcastle that Richards describes compare to the place portrayed by Will Ferguson ("The Sudbury Syndrome")? What do you think Ferguson would say about Newcastle?

IDEAS FOR DISCUSSION/WRITING

Preparing to Write

Try a "freewriting experiment" with a specific location where you grew up as subject. Write at the top of the page the name of a place where you spent at least several years of your childhood or your teenage years. Now, allowing yourself to play with your ideas and strongest memories, try "free associating" and simply write uninterruptedly anything that comes to mind for 10 minutes. If you hit a blank, skip to the next idea that comes along or write something like "I don't know what to say," but don't stop writing.

Next, look at what you've written, and list words or thoughts that seem to form a pattern. What memories returned to you the most strongly? Why? Do you remember people or places or activities, or a mixture of all three? How do you feel about what you remember at this stage in your life?

Choosing a Topic

1. Write a descriptive essay in the form of a letter to a friend or a relative who shared a part and a place in your earlier life with

you. Neither of you lives there any longer, but you have just returned from a visit. Describe your reactions to any changes you see, and to things and people that will interest both you and your reader. Be sure to give your essay a clear pattern of organization.

2. Using both memory and imagination, take a journey back to a particular moment or event in your past. Write an essay in which you describe in the clearest and strongest possible detail what you felt, saw, smelled, tasted, and touched at that time. What exactly were you doing? How did you feel? Who was with you? What is the strongest thing about this event that you are trying to convey?

3. What were your favourite games or activities as a child? Why? At what times of the year did you do these things? Describe these to your classmates so that you recapture for them some of the attraction, some of the reasons why you found these things such a pleasure. The order in which you place these in your essay depends on whether you wish to offer "the best first," or save it for the end.

WEB SITES

www.gov.nb.ca/royal/apr29/d3mira.htm
This is the Miramichi homepage.

degaulle.hil.unb.ca/library/archives/richards/dar.html
Here you will find David Adams Richards' fonds in the University of New Brunswick Archives and Special collections.

Sally Armstrong
1943–

■ ■ ■

P4W

Why would the editor-in-chief of a nice, respectable family magazine like *Homemaker's* write an impassioned essay about the hideous realities of women's prisons? Sally Armstrong is certainly a highly successful career journalist and editor, but her interests and productions demonstrate a deep concern for human rights and difficult social issues. Armstrong was born in Montreal and graduated from McGill University with a bachelor's degree in physical education. She began to work as a freelance writer in the mid-1970s. Much of her working career has been in Toronto, first as a contributing editor with *Canadian Living* magazine from its launch in 1975 until 1982, then as its associate editor for the next five years. In 1988 Armstrong was chosen by the new publisher to take on the role of editor as *Homemaker's* was relaunched. Armstrong has distinguished herself at *Homemaker's* with her stories that Jennifer Foster, in the *Ryerson Review of Journalism,* characterizes as "current, hard-hitting and thought-provoking pieces about the lives of women across the country and, two or three times a year, from around the world."

Concurrent with her activities at *Homemaker's* has been her work as a co-producer of video documentaries on notably gritty subjects and hot issues of human rights and social abuses. Her video documentary works include *Reason to Live* (1987), *Human Rights–Human Wrongs* (1987), and *Broken Trust* (1988). In 1994 Armstrong won a gold award in the category of public issues from the National Magazine Awards Foundation for her story "Eva: Witness for Women" about one Balkan region woman who was a victim of mass gang rape. She is also the author of a biography of Mila Mulroney, *Mila* (1992).

Preparing to Read

"P4W" looks like a puzzling code; in fact, the essay's title refers to Kingston Ontario's Prison for Women. This grim, run-down institution and the sad lives of its inmates are the little-publicized subject of Sally Armstrong's 1991 article. "Women in Prison" used to be a kind of B-movie title, but the phrase describes a tragic and ugly dilemma in the Canadian judicial system. How many of us have considered what imprisonment would feel like? What would day-to-day existence be like? How much discipline is involved in prison life? How much rehabilitation occurs? How difficult is it to endure incarceration? Who goes to what type of prison and why? Is prison a trap or does it refit inmates for a useful life in society?

Suddenly, a scream. A hollow-sounding scream, filled with de- 1
spair, that bounces off the walls and burns its way into the
conscience. Everyone stops talking, glances furtively around, and
then, as if order and action can somehow erase the haunting sound,
they return to whatever they're doing. Minutes later, the prison
grapevine begins circulating the story. One woman, held in segregation—known as "the hole"—tried to hang herself. The guards
cut her down in time and she's on her way to the hospital.

The pressure, palpable in this place, is winched up another 2
notch. The Prison for Women at Kingston, Ont., better known
as P4W, is at a flashpoint. Despair creeps through the prison like
fog, swirling around your ankles here, engulfing you there, and
from time to time dissipating so that you catch a glimpse of calm.
Then, invariably, the screw tightens again, and anger, frustration
and, ultimately, despair consume the population.

There's something very wrong at P4W. Although prison 3
reform through the '70s and '80s has improved human rights in
the prison, and a federal task force has announced that this place
must be closed and replaced with more suitable facilities, an
insidious air of failure to succeed is thriving inside its walls. Five
women hanged themselves in the last 2 1/2 years. Inmates predict
more women will end their lives in this place. Consequences for
misbehaviour include segregation, lockdown (when all inmates
are locked in their cells at once) and cancelled family visits. The
correction officers feel their danger level is at an all-time high
because of the drugs that invariably get in and create havoc with
the prisoners.

The four-year timetable for closure is unacceptable. The plan 4
for regional facilities may not even be workable. The situation
is desperate. Although there's a powerful commitment from Ole
Ingstrup, commissioner of the Correctional Service of Canada,
and Jane Miller-Ashton, national coordinator of the Federally
Sentenced Women Initiative, to right the wrongs, there's little
evidence that the 111 women serving their time today will benefit.

Getting to the truth is a daunting task: on the one hand, 5
manipulation and deceit have been survival tools for many of
the inmates; on the other hand, the staff are selective about the
information they'll disclose. Moreover, there is a nearly
impenetrable barrier between the forces for punishment and the
proponents of rehabilitation. Many correction officers see therapy
as a lot of hooey that stirs up trouble in prison, and many
therapists see the environment as an almost impossible place in

which to heal. The sobering fact—even for those with hearts of stone—is that if the inmates are denied rehabilitation, society is denied as well.

"You can't heal in this place," says Debbie, 38, a Torontonian 6 serving a 13-year term for second-degree murder. Like most women in here, Debbie had been sexually abused before her lifestyle went off the rails and she got involved in crime. "When people treat you like a piece of sh—, you soon start feeling like sh—," she says.

No one is suggesting that these women should not take 7 responsibility for their crimes and make appropriate changes in their behaviour, but the task is complicated by a number of factors. Consider the population at P4W: 70 per cent have an alcohol or drug problem, 40 per cent are functionally illiterate, the majority have little or no job skills. Ninety per cent of the native women and 80 per cent of the non-native women have been physically or sexually abused. That's a lot of baggage to carry when a woman is trying to go straight. Small wonder the recidivism rate is 52 per cent.

Anyone arriving at P4W has heard the horrible rumours 8 about beatings, riots, rape. A lifer from British Columbia says, "It's all true. Stealing, ratting and partner conflict are the main reasons for the beatings. The riots start when a shipment of drugs comes in; the girls take them all at once and go crazy."

P4W opened in 1934. Four years later, the Archambault 9 Commission described it as unfit, even for animals, and demanded that it be closed. Eight more commissions have since condemned this place. The problems begin with the physical plant. Fifty per cent of the women live in six- by 10-foot windowless cells with bars for doors, open toilets and little or no privacy. The cells are arranged in double tiers on either side of the building. Known as "the range," they have poor temperature control and ceilings so high, they sound like echo chambers.

Jocelyn (not her real name), 27, from Ontario, who's serving 10 25 years for first-degree murder, says, "There was a riot three weeks after I arrived. You can't imagine what it was like: TVs smashing into walls and exploding, the sound of boots stomping when Rambo-like goon squads came up the stairs, the noises echoing off the walls. I was under my bunk, terrified, bawling my eyes out. I knew I couldn't live on the range."

The other 50 per cent of the women live on "the wing," a 11
less harsh set-up of single bedrooms with windows looking out
on the exercise yard, doors that close for privacy, and some
freedom to move around within the locked area. Correction
officer Jaclyn Maxam says to stay on the wing, "You have to be
free of internal charges: no stealing, no contraband, no fighting
or disobeying for three months. I'm not here to judge—they've
been judged. I'm here to see that they serve their sentences as
easily as possible."

P4W's problems are much greater than an out-of-date 12
building. It's a maximum security institution, even though more
than 90 per cent of its inmates don't need such oppressive
security. And while prison reform has seen vastly improved
programs and conditions for men, the women's programs lag
far behind.

A few basic facts: a prison sentence of two years or more is 13
served in a federal prison; less than two years, a provincial prison.
There are approximately 260 federally sentenced women in
Canada (about half are out on parole and a few others are serving
their time in other institutions) and 11,300 federally sentenced
men. These numbers create the too-few-to-count syndrome. Since
there's only one prison for women, it's maximum security. The
42 facilities for men are located in regions across the country and
have a variety of security levels: maximum, medium and
minimum. Because they are closer to home, the men can be
visited by their families. Most women are too far away from their
families to see them at all.

Additional inequities arise. Men can earn the right to move 14
from maximum security to the less harsh medium or minimum
security institutions. Once there, if something goes wrong, the
prisoner responsible is moved back. "For us, there's no place to
move, no incentive to behave—it's just punishment, punishment,
all the goddamn way," says Debbie. "And if one person screws
up, everyone pays. The whole place goes into lockdown."

As well, while men have access to kitchenettes at many of 15
the institutions, the women don't at P4W. Brandy, a lifer from
Toronto, says, "Debbie was going to teach me to cook but we're
not allowed to have a stove—they're afraid we'll throw boiling
water at each other. The men have after-shave, but we can't have
hair spray, nail polish remover or perfume—they think we'll
drink it."

On a more painful level, a man generally has a woman on   16
the outside who brings his children to visit him. A woman,
however, is generally the sole support for her children. She not
only can't see them because they're too far away, she usually
loses them to foster care in the process. "The emotional rigours
of this place are so overwhelming, the women have to shut down
emotionally just to survive," says Bonnie Diamond, the executive
director of the Canadian Association of Elizabeth Fry Societies.
The association visits women in prison, lobbies for change and
stands with women before the courts, as at least half of the
women have no legal counsel.

Sitting in the warm summer sunshine at a picnic table on a   17
patch of grass between two rows of cells on the wing, the daily
lives of the inmates receive a caustic, cynical review. You can
hear the traffic outside the 30-foot wall on Sir John A. Macdonald
Blvd., and the birds swoop in and out of the yard. But there's
no mistaking that this is a house of detention.

Everyone works—in the kitchen, in the canteen, in the   18
cleaning department. They earn $1.60 per day to a maximum of
$69 every two weeks. The money is used to buy cigarettes,
shampoo, hair conditioner, coffee, creamer, sugar, all their
personal supplies. On this morning, the smokers are rationing
cigarettes; it's payday and everyone is short on tobacco. Still,
when the guard tells a visitor there's no coffee, Debbie is up on
her feet instantly, preparing a cup from her own meagre rations.

"The programs here are a joke," says Debbie. "It sounds good   19
to the public that we're doing woodworking, sewing and
hairdressing, but the fact is, we're making picture frames and
towels, and the hairdressing certificate won't get you a job on
the outside. I used to work with a computerized cash register in
a hardware store. In here, I used a 1961 adding machine in the
canteen. After 10 more years, how do you think I'll be able to
find work and support myself out there?"

Although some inmates are enrolled in literacy classes and   20
some are taking correspondence courses at Queen's University
and Waterloo University (eight women have graduated), many
others would prefer hands-on training courses. At the prison in
Burnaby, B.C., for example, there's a dog-training course. "Why
can't we have that in here?" Debbie asks. "We could even make
money by learning to do dog grooming."

While Deputy Warden Donna Morrin says the idea is worth   21
looking into, there seems to be a lack of will to really make

change—as is the case with many hot points in the prison. Examples of this are everywhere. When Jocelyn's brother drove with his wife across the country to visit his sister for a five-day pass in the "little house" (a two-bedroom bungalow within the prison walls that can be used for family visits six times a year), he was received at the reception area and told, "You're too early, come back at 2 p.m."

Eric says, "I was told to be here at 12:30, and every minute 22 counts."

Tough.   23

Jocelyn was inside crying because she'd just found out that 24 their visit was cut from five days to four days due to an error in scheduling.

Tough.   25

Later, inside the little house, Jocelyn is angry, sad, 26 disappointed, furious. But she can't linger with her feelings—the clock is already ticking. Instead, they try to obtain normalcy as quickly as possible: preparing marinade for the steaks they'll barbecue later, watching video footage of the trip from Calgary, exchanging news about family.

One change that has come about at P4W is the addition of a 27 native sweat lodge. Florence, 21, a Soto Indian from Manitoba who's serving 3 1/2 years for aggravated assault and forcible confinement, is chairperson of the Native Sisterhood. On the way to the sweat lodge she explains the spiritual purification it offers the 17 native women at P4W.

"We put white-hot rocks that represent our grandfathers in 28 the centre of the lodge [a tarpaulin over a frame of poles]; then water, the blood of mother earth, is splashed over the rocks, and with the front of the lodge sealed shut, the steam puffs throughout the lodge while we pray." This ancient tradition, used to cleanse the soul, occurs once a week, but Florence feels they need it every day. "Native women aren't treated fairly here," she says. "We're supposed to have our own programs, but they're always threatening to cancel them and making racist cracks to us about our ways."

Whether the weekly sweat lodge ceremony is lip service to an 29 escalating militancy among the native people or an honest effort to alleviate the pain and sorrow and promote healing is anyone's guess. Sadly, it would appear to be the former.

Bucking the system isn't a good idea at P4W. The consequences 30 are usually segregation, which is a collection of cells where inmates

are incarcerated 23 hours a day, deprived of personal effects, and
if they are deemed suicidal, their clothing and sheets as well (paper
nightgowns and stiff blankets that can't be torn and used as a
noose—or to wrap themselves in against the cold—are provided).

"Can you imagine the sensory deprivation?" asks Bonnie   31
Diamond. "No natural light or air, surrounded by stone and iron
in a colourless dungeon because you're feeling suicidal or acting
out in rage. We badly need change."

Jo-Ann, 48, is from Nova Scotia and has spent most of the   32
6 1/2 years of her life sentence struggling for change. Today, she's
in the newly opened minimum security house across the street
from P4W. Beautifully decorated in soft pastel colours, it's more in
line with the prison reform one would expect of the decade. Jo-
Ann jabs out her cigarette, and her soft smile evaporates when
she describes the conditions that existed when she arrived at P4W
and the pitifully few changes that have been made since. But first
she chronicles the path to hell that brought her here.

"I'm a very middle-class woman. I'm also an alcoholic. After   33
my children were born, I had postpartum depression. The doctor
put me on Valium and I never got off. My husband was a very
successful man. He was president of the Chamber of Commerce.
He was also drinking too much. The drinking and the dysfunction
in our family kept escalating. Something was bound to happen to
one of us. We had a rifle because we lived on a farm. That
afternoon, we were both drunk. He became abusive, and I got
the rifle and shot him. He'd been my boyfriend, my lover and
my best friend. We'd been married for 22 years. Our daughters
were 17 and 21 years old at the time. Nothing anyone ever does
will punish me as much as I've punished myself."

In the ensuing months, Jo-Ann had her first-ever look at a   34
forensic science centre, a psychiatric hospital, a jail, and finally,
the infamous P4W. "I felt like Alice in Wonderland and I'd fallen
down the rabbit hole. I was numb. After about three weeks here,
I received a fairly moderate beating because I asked a woman
to turn down the TV. I also had death threats from other inmates.
By then I knew you couldn't talk about anyone hurting you. I
was becoming paranoid, so afraid of everything, I didn't know
where I was safe. One day, I was moved to the wing and when I
couldn't work the taps I broke down and started to cry. They
moved me to the Regional Treatment Centre in K.P. [the wing
of the Kingston Penitentiary where psychiatric counselling is
offered and the sex offenders are housed]."

The treatment centre is like something out of a Dickens novel: 35
windows so old you can hardly see through them, black bars on
dilapidated cells, paint peeling from walls, unpleasant odours.
The exercise yard, which is not much bigger than a dog run, can
be seen from the men's yard; consequently, offensive, abusive
remarks are aimed like missiles at the women when they're
outside. Oddly enough, in spite of the ghastly surroundings,
there's a spirit of peace in this tiny corner of the prison.

Head nurse Nancy Fudge glances at the cell block from the 36
office (the first cell in the row) that she shares with five other
members of the nursing staff and says, "It takes a lot of energy to
put this aside and care for these women, many of whom are very
psychologically damaged. In spite of that, and in spite of windows
being smashed on occasion and the broken glass being thrown in
your face, we do good work here."

Diana, a skinny, sparrow-like woman of 28 from Montreal, is 37
here because she can't function at P4W. Her arms and neck are
covered in scars from slashing (a common behaviour among
women at P4W, slashing isn't a suicide attempt, it's a tension
release, as is head banging). Diane's hands tremble when she tells
the story of her miserable childhood on the streets of Montreal,
and ultimately, of stabbing someone to death—a person, she says,
she didn't even know. Now she talks of becoming a serial killer.

"My nickname is Lecter [after the character in *The Silence of* 38
the Lambs] because I like blood and guts." But after shocking you
with her intentions, she says quietly, "I'm scared to leave here. I
need rehabilitation. They try to help me and for a while it works,
but then I start slashing and head banging again. I can't help it."
Monitored constantly on closed-circuit TV, she presents a heart-
wrenching image of distress as she paces up and down her tiny cell.

Christine, 25, also from Montreal and serving four years for 39
fraud, asked to be transferred to the treatment centre because
she's getting out of prison soon and says she needs to learn
coping skills for the outside. "I'm a high-profile prisoner,
rebellious, I never give in to the system. But I'm fed up with
living like this. I was tired of seeing the slashings and hangings.
I freaked when the woman in the cell beside me hanged herself.
Everyone started blaming each other—the staff, the inmates, the
warden. No one wanted to look at each other's side.

"This place may not be very nice, but it's nicer than P4W. 40
There's peace here, it's quiet, there aren't as many head games.
Over there, everyone is telling you how to live your life. Here, the

staff are supportive and caring. The psychologist is good, honest, straightforward."

Psychologist Fred Tobin says, "Although the parole board   41 feels the treatment these women are receiving is working, jails are punitive in nature, and punishment doesn't teach behaviour, it only suppresses it."

So, what's to be done? Certainly another minimum security   42 house must be opened. Certainly there has to be an end to segregation as a means of dealing with suicidal inmates. And then there's the promise of regional centres. Most women don't believe they'll ever open. Some worry that if their concerns aren't heard now when there are 111 inmates, they'll never be heard when the numbers are cut to less than 30. Several women would like to see wings built onto the men's penitentiaries so that they can serve their time and take advantage of the programs and trades the men have. Several others have considered transferring to a provincial penitentiary on a special arrangement.

Bonnie Diamond says the task force considered all of these   43 options and there are problems with each of them. "A lot of abused women here would be terrified to be in an institution with men, and we only have one shot at this reform. Whatever we decide on has to last for another 50 years. As for the provincial option, there's an even bigger shortage of programs."

Jane Miller-Ashton is convinced that the best approach is   44 four regional facilities and a healing lodge. "It's difficult," she admits, "because we're not just building a building, we're creating a program. The function is going to dictate the form. We don't want to be locked into what it will look like, we want to concentrate on what we will do in this place." That includes family visits, children staying with their mothers, a dynamic or staff support security system rather than a static or cage-style security system, and a healing rather than a punitive approach. "We're not excusing their crimes," says Miller-Ashton, "we're assisting them to return to society."

Fran, a Cree woman from Saskatchewan, was a prisoner   45 when she was asked to be on the task force. Today, after serving her seven-year sentence, she's part of a working group to establish a native healing lodge as one of the five centres, and she's increasingly concerned about the timetable. "I've written the vision statement, we have the location criteria, if we were given the initiative, we could open it in one year.

"My theory is that crisis after crisis begets violence and 46
violence begets more violence. I know that because I raised sh—
when I was in there, and spent almost a year of my seven years
in segregation."

Jan Heney is one of the five prison psychologists (two full- 47
time, three part-time) who struggles with old correctional
philosophies and new therapies for a very needy prison
population. She was hired by the prison to do a study on self-
injurious behaviour and then asked to stay on to implement one
of her recommendations—peer support counselling. Peer support
counselling provides in-depth training initially, plus ongoing
weekly sessions to enhance the training so that the inmates on the
support team can assist other inmates in times of crisis or need.

"When a woman has been sexually abused as a child, she's 48
going to behave in certain ways as an adult," says Heney. She'll
have problems with trust, with feelings of personal control. She
tends to take responsibility for everything that goes on around
her, assuming it's her fault and she's bad. She'll have incredibly
low self-esteem, and may self-injure. She's at a high risk for
suicide.

"Imagine what lockdown and segregation are like for a 49
woman like that. Whenever there's a crisis in the prison, such
as lockdown or a hanging, we have to put long-term counselling
on hold and do crisis intervention. We walk the range, trying to
give the women information about how long it will last and
what's happening in the prison. What we end up doing in many
cases is Band-Aid work. Any healing we can create is done in
spite of the realities of prison life."

Fran cuddles her 15-month-old baby and in a voice choking 50
with emotion says, "A woman's power and self-esteem are so
desecrated in there, despair takes over. You can't see around it or
over it or through it."

There's got to be a better way. 51

UNDERSTANDING DETAILS

1. What are the penalties for misbehaviour in P4W?
2. Why is it difficult to get reliable information about the problems so apparent in the Women's Prison?
3. Outline some of the details of the living conditions in P4W.

ANALYZING MEANING

1. What is the source of the scream with which the essay opens? What do the inmates' reactions tell the reader about their state of mind?
2. Why is therapy or rehabilitation such a problematic issue for both prison officials and for inmates? Is it usually successful?
3. Do the views expressed by inmates and officials support the statement of the psychologist who says "jails are punitive in nature, and punishment doesn't teach behaviour, it only suppresses it" (paragraph 41)?

DISCOVERING RHETORICAL STRATEGIES

1. In "P4W," the author alternates between vivid emotional and physical descriptions of prison life and hard numerical facts and statistics about her subject. Is it possible to discern the writer's own viewpoint? Explain.
2. Which of Armstrong's descriptive passages use details related to the senses? How do the statistical and numerical details affect the reader? Do details in quotations reach the reader's emotions most directly and why? Do these uses of detailing have anything in common in this essay?
3. "P4W" uses the rhetorical strategy of comparison/contrast in several instances. Where do you find instances of ideas or subjects compared according to some common issue? Does the use of this supporting technique add to the descriptive power of the essay? Why?

MAKING CONNECTIONS

1. Armstrong's focus in this essay, as in most of her work, is the "bettering of lives of women." How do you think Gloria Steinem ("The Politics of Muscle") would react to the discrepancies in treatment between men and women in the Canadian prison system?
2. Robert Fulford ("The Fading Power of the Written Word") says, "… literature remains the core of civilized life precisely because it is the only reliable antidote to everything in our existence that diminishes us." What might Fulford conclude from the fact that 40 percent of the inmates at P4W are functionally illiterate?
3. Armstrong says that 90 percent of the native women and 80 percent of the non-native women have been physically or sexually

abused (paragraph 7). Laura Robinson ("Starving for the Gold") also portrays a group of women who have been abused. Compare and contrast the effects of abuse on the women depicted in these two essays.

IDEAS FOR DISCUSSION/WRITING

Preparing to Write

Write freely in sentences or write down a series of words that come to mind when you hear the word "prison." Look for links or connections between the ideas you come up with. What would you most fear about imprisonment? How close are prisons to other institutions we experience in everyday life? Are there conflicts common to any situation where people must be looked after in large numbers? How do we handle ourselves in difficult situations? Do we grow or retreat in fear? Do men and women experience imprisonment differently? Why?

Choosing a Topic

1. Write an essay describing an experience in your life that you found particularly hard to endure. Why was it so difficult to get through? Explain where you felt the sources of the problem might have lain. Were they in your background or were they external and part of the situation? How did you resolve or grow past your problem?
2. Write a letter to a friend you know especially well. Imagine that this person has been sentenced to prison for a year. What do you expect the greatest difficulties will be?
3. Armstrong's essay is a vivid description of the problems within the prison system. In a descriptive essay, give your own views on what you feel are the most significant issues concerning prisons in the 1990s. You may wish to support your argument with specific examples drawn either from "P4W" or from current news items.

WEB SITES

www.sgc.gc.ca/EFact/ewomen.htm
This is a federal government fact sheet about women in prison in Canada.

www.igc.apc.org/prisons/pubs/pns/
The *Prison News Service* has some articles about P4W.

Lesley Choyce
1951–

■ ■ ■

Thin Edge of the Wedge

Lesley Choyce is a Renaissance man with a multitude of jobs: Choyce teaches English at University of Dalhousie, he hosts a television show called *Choyce Words*, he runs a literary publishing house called Pottersfield Press, he is a musician with a band called The Surf Poets, but he is best known as a writer. After having his first book published by Fiddlehead Press in 1980, he has written more than 40 books representing a range of genres including poetry, young adult fiction, and science fiction and appealing to a variety of audiences. In addition, Choyce is an accomplished surfer as evidenced by his winning of the Men's Open Canadian National Surfing Championship in 1995.

Choyce was born in New Jersey and immigrated to Nova Scotia in 1979. His stories are often set around Lawrencetown where he now lives, and tell the stories of people, most often young adults, who share his passions.

Preparing to Read

Environmentalists tell us that we are not separate from nature, that we are part of a greater biological pattern. Our lives affect, and are affected by the total health and energy of the world around us. Lesley Choyce's essay "Thin Edge of the Wedge," first published in the spring of 1997 in *Canadian Geographic*, describes the dynamic life of an island in Nova Scotia. Interspersed between geological descriptions of the changes being wrought on this small piece of land, is the portrayal of the human experience of this territory. The vivid passages show Choyce's intense fascination with his subject. As you read "Thin Edge of the Wedge," think about an island, a park, a beach, or some natural environment you know well. How has time changed this place? Does it have a rhythm, a life of its own? What patterns in your place's life belong to the cycles of nature, and what changes have people made?

■ ─── ■

Wedge Island is barely discernible on a road map of Nova 1
Scotia because there are no roads leading there. Although it is not truly an island, its tether to the eastern shore is so tenuous that it remains remote and seemingly adrift. Eroded by the forces of the North Atlantic, it is a mere fragment of what was once a formidable headland. Within a lifetime, it will most likely be

reduced to a rubble of stone, an insignificant reef at high tide. But for now, the Wedge exists, a reminder that nothing is permanent on this shore. Geologists define it as a "drowned coast" because the sea is gradually engulfing it. It has been for a long time.

Something like a dinosaur's bony spine of boulders leads a 2 wary hiker from the salt-bleached fish shacks on the mainland to the Wedge. If it's a fine July day—blue sky, big and bold above— the hiker might slide his hand along the silky beards of sea oats as he leaves solid land, then dance from rock to rock. Low tide is the best bet to make it there in one piece. Still, waves will spank the rocks from both sides, slap cold saltwater on his shoes and spit clean, frothy Atlantic into his face.

Wedge Island is a defeated drumlin, a dagger-shaped 3 remnant of land stretching a good kilometre out to sea. Smashed lobster traps, shreds of polypropylene rope as well as bones of birds and beasts litter the rocks near the shore. Thirty metres up the red dirt cliff sits a parliament of herring gulls peering down at a rare visitor with some suspicion. If the visitor scurries up the side of crumbling dirt, the gulls will complain loudly at his intrusion, then take to the sky and let him pass.

At the top is a grassy peninsula a mere 60 centimetres wide 4 where both sides have been sculpted away by rains and pounding seas. It's a place of vertigo and lost history. The land widens as it extends seaward onto this near-island of bull thistles, raspberry bushes and grass that seems cropped short as a putting green.

Farther out, at the very tip of the island, bare ribs of bedrock 5 protrude into the sea. This is the same rock you'd find if you could make one giant leap from here across the Atlantic and step ashore on the edge of the Sahara. It is the very rock that was once part of the super-continent that drifted north to crash into this coast, then drag itself away to form Africa.

This island is a forgotten domain on the edge of the continent. 6 It is easy to imagine that no man has ever been here before. But on the way back to the mainland, the truth reveals itself on the western shore. Not three metres from the edge of a cliff eight storeys high is a circle of lichen-covered rocks in the grass. A man-made well. The water is deep and long-legged insects skim along its obsidian surface. The well is full, nearly to the brim—it seems impossible given its elevation on this narrow wedge of land.

Nearby are two dents in the ground, as if some giant had 7 punched down into a massive surface of dough. Those two dents were once the foundations of a farmhouse and barn. Nearby fields sprouted cabbage and turnips. A family lived on vegetables from the stony soil, cod and mackerel from the sea. There were no roads, no cars, nothing but boats for commerce with Halifax. A way of life long gone.

The rains and seas will continue to conspire to undo the 8 ribbon of land left between the well's fresh water and the sky. The well's stone walls will collapse. The drumlin's cliff will be pried by ice, and pocked by pelting rain. The sea will slip out stones from beneath the hill, the turf up above will tumble, and eventually the water of the farmer's well will gush out of the heart of the headland and race down to meet the sea.

UNDERSTANDING DETAILS

1. What does Choyce predict will happen to Wedge Island? When?
2. How do geologists define Wedge Island? Why?
3. What is Wedge Island? What evidence is there of human habitation of the island?

ANALYZING MEANING

1. How does Choyce feel about his subject? How do you know this?
2. What is Choyce's thesis, and how does the description of the disappearance of Wedge Island develop his thesis?
3. What is the "truth (that) reveals itself on the western shore" in paragraph 6?

DISCOVERING RHETORICAL STRATEGIES

1. Choyce's essay contains several relatively unusual verbs that make his description particularly vivid. Find five examples of such verbs and explain why they are effective choices.
2. There are several striking similes and metaphors in Choyce's descriptive passages. The waves "spank the rocks," "slap cold saltwater on his shoes and spit clean, frothy Atlantic into his face" (paragraph 2) and the grass "seems cropped short as a putting green" (paragraph 4). What does Choyce's use of these figures of speech show the reader about the author's view of his subject? How does it contrast with Choyce's use of scientific details?

3. Choyce frequently uses alliteration in "Thin Edge of the Wedge." Identify five examples of alliteration and explain how this figure of speech enhances Choyce's description.

MAKING CONNECTIONS

1. Like Tomson Highway ("What a Certain Visionary Once Said") Lesley Choyce is describing an environment he knows well. Compare and contrast the attitudes of these two writers to their subjects.
2. Lesley Choyce employs sentence fragments and several short, simple sentences in this essay. How is his style similar to, or different from that of Joe Fiorito ("Breakfast in Bed")?
3. In "Images of Canada," Laura Millard describes the various images depicted on our banknotes. Which of the sets of images would Choyce's image best fit into? Why?

IDEAS FOR DISCUSSION/WRITING

Preparing to Write

Write freely about a place in the natural environment that you have known for some time. Why is it special to you? How long have you been familiar with this place? How often do its natural features change, and what causes these changes? What details stand out most clearly in your mind, and why? Do you see echoes of, or similarities to your experience of life's patterns in any aspects of your special place?

Choosing a Topic

1. Basing your essay on specific sense details, describe your special place to a friend who has never been there. Decide on the main reason why your place is so meaningful to you, and try to communicate this dominant impression of your place as clearly as possible.
2. Are cities or towns as alive as a beach or a forest? Why? Using a logical order for arranging your arguments, describe exactly to someone whose point of view is not known which aspects of city or natural life make either or both living entities.
3. Using your imagination, travel backward in time to view and describe your special place as it might have been 500 years ago. What would be different from the way it looks today? Write an essay that describes the differences and similarities in the

two visions. Compare what your imagination's eye sees to what you see today, and decide on your point of view in the comparison.

WEB SITES

www.chebucto.ns.ca/Culture/WFNS/Writers/lchoyce.html
See the Writers Federation of Nova Scotia site for Lesley Choyce.

fox.nstn.ca/~nbarkhou/aboutlesleychoyce.html
A biography of Lesley Choyce has been prepared by students at Atlantic View Elementary School.

www.swifty.com/twuc/choyce.htm
Here you will find the Writers Union of Canada biography of Choyce.

Tomson Highway
1951–

■ ■ ■

What a Certain Visionary Once Said

In the following essay, Tomson Highway presents a loving and vibrant description of the region of Canada where he comes from. The eleventh of twelve children in his family, Highway was born and raised on the Brochet Reserve in northern Manitoba. Highway's first language was Cree, and he didn't begin learning English until he was six years old. As a child, Highway was sent away to a Catholic boarding school, and later went to high school in Winnipeg. He graduated from the University of Western Ontario with a B.A. in music and English, and began writing at about age 30. Now a resident of Toronto, Highway is the founder and, from 1986–1992, was director of the Native Earth Performing Arts Theatre, and has received wide acclaim for the plays that he has written and produced. Honours Highway has won include the Dora Mavor Moore Award and the Chalmers Canadian Play Award in 1986 for *The Rez Sisters* and again in 1990 for *Dry Lips Oughta Move to Kapuskasing*, the Toronto Arts Award (1990), and the Wang International Festival of Authors Award (1989).

In an article in *The Toronto Sun*, John Coulbourn described Highway's "gentle, quiet humour, his great but unassuming pride, his passion and the dignity and strength of his spirit ..." These qualities are undoubtedly among those that contributed to Highway being made a Member of the Order of Canada in 1994 and being chosen by *Maclean's* magazine as one of the 100 most important Canadians in history.

In 1997 Highway published his first novel, *Kiss of the Fur Queen*, a largely autobiographical story about two Cree brothers. He is currently at work on *Rose*, a full-length musical sequel to *The Rez Sisters* and *Dry Lips*.

This essay first appeared as an insert in *The Bank of Montreal Annual Report (1992)*.

Preparing to Read

The following essay is a vivid description of a part of the country Tomson Highway respects and admires. Before reading, think about the Canadian North. In your mind, travel north from the 49th parallel. How does the weather change as you progress? What do you notice about the landscape and the terrain? What happens to the population? What observations do you make about the vegetation? What about the wildlife? Are there any assumptions that you make about the seasons? Does your mode of transportation change as you travel north? What colours stand out to you? Are there any distinctive smells? What sounds do you hear? What sounds do you not hear?

As you travel north from Winnipeg, the flatness of the prairie   1
begins to give way. And the northern forests begin to take
over, forests of spruce and pine and poplar and birch. The northern rivers and northern rapids, the waterfalls, the eskers, the northern lakes—thousands of them—with their innumerable islands
encircled by golden-sand beaches and flat limestone surfaces that
slide gracefully into water. As you travel farther north, the trees
themselves begin to diminish in height and size. And get smaller,
until, finally, you reach the barren lands. It is from these reaches
that herds of caribou in the thousands come thundering down
each winter. It is here that you find trout and pickerel and pike
and whitefish in profusion. If you're here in August, your eyes
will be glutted with a sudden explosion of colour seldom seen in
any southern Canadian landscape: fields of wild raspberries, cloud-
berries, blueberries, cranberries, stands of wild flowers you never
believed such remote northern terrain was capable of nurturing.
And the water is still so clean you can dip your hand over the side
of your canoe and you can drink it. In winter, you can eat the
snow, without fear. In both winter and summer, you can breathe,
this is your land, your home.

Here, you can begin to remember that you are a human   2
being. And if you take the time to listen—really listen—you can
begin to hear the earth breathe. And whisper things simple men,
who never suspected they were mad, can hear. Madmen who
speak Cree, for one, can in fact understand the language this
land speaks, in certain circles. Which would make madmen who
speak Cree a privileged lot.

Then you seat yourself down on a carpet of reindeer moss   3
and you watch the movements of the sky, filled with stars and
galaxies of stars by night, streaked by endlessly shifting cloud
formations by day. You watch the movements of the lake which,
within one hour, can change from a surface of glass to one of
waves so massive in their fury they can—and have—killed many
a man. And you begin to understand that men and women can,
within maybe not one hour but one day, change from a mood
of reflective serenity and self-control to one of depression and
despair so deep they can—and have—killed many a man.

You begin to understand that this earth we live on—once   4
thought insensate, inanimate, dead by scientists, theologians and
such—has an emotional psychological and spiritual life every
bit as complex as that of the most complex, sensitive and
intelligent of individuals.

And it's ours. Or is it?   5

A certain ancient aboriginal visionary of this country once   6
said: "We have not inherited this land, we have merely borrowed
it from our children."

If that's the case, what a loan!   7

Eh?   8

UNDERSTANDING DETAILS

1. For Highway, what is the essential appeal of the North?
2. In contrast to the view of traditional scientists and theologians,
   how does Highway characterize the earth? In your own words,
   characterize Highway's attitude towards the earth.
3. How many senses does Highway invoke in this description?
   Give one example of each from this essay.

ANALYZING MEANING

1. What is Highway's purpose in writing this description? Who is
   he writing it for?
2. In paragraph 2, Highway refers to madmen. Who are these
   madmen and why does Highway label them this way? Does
   he really believe that they are mad?
3. Explain Highway's conclusion. Why does he end on a questioning note?

DISCOVERING RHETORICAL STRATEGIES

1. Is this description objective or subjective? Explain. How might
   a land surveyor's description of this area differ from Highway's?
2. How many times does the writer use the words "north" or
   "northern" in this essay? What effect does this have on the reader?
   How would more specific place names change the impression?
3. Does "What a Certain Visionary Once Said" contain the four
   fundamental qualities of descriptive essays that are outlined at
   the beginning of this chapter? Support your answer with specific
   details.

MAKING CONNECTIONS

1. Neil Bissoondath ("Pieces of Sky") describes sitting by a blazing
   fire at night under a sky filled with stars (paragraphs 11–12).
   Does this experience have the same effect on Bissoondath that
   it has on Highway? Explain why or why not.
2. In "Teeth," Brian Lewis writes about the attitude of white men
   toward Ottochie, a native Canadian. How does this attitude

compare to Highway's comments about perceptions of people who can "understand the language the land speaks"?

3. Tomson Highway refers several times to the place he has journeyed to as "home." What does he value in his home? How do these things compare to the things that Allen Abel values in his "A Home at the End of the Journey"?

IDEAS FOR DISCUSSION/WRITING

Preparing to Write

Write freely about weather. How would you describe the climate of Canada generally? How would you describe the region where you live? What accommodations have you made in your life for the weather you experience? What kind of weather do you most enjoy? How does the weather influence your mood? Why is the weather such a common topic of conversation?

Choosing a Topic

1. In an essay for newcomers to your region of the country, describe your favourite season. Focus on the natural physical aspects of that season, as well as the effects they have on you and your community.

2. Three contemporary television programs are set in northern towns: *Northern Exposure* (in America), and *The Rez* and *North of 60* (in Canada). If you have seen any of these shows, write an essay in which you discuss how their depiction of the northern communities has either confirmed or changed your impressions.

3. Highway obviously feels very strongly about the place he describes. Write a short essay in which you describe a place that you very strongly dislike. Provide enough detail so that your audience will be sure to avoid this spot.

WEB SITES

nativeauthors.com/search/bio/biohighway.html
Here you can find biographical information about Tomson Highway.

www.puc.ca/playwrights/text/t_highwa.html
The Writers Union of Canada has a biography for Highway.

www.nativeweb.org
Native Web is a collection of links to sites related to native issues and indigenous peoples.

Ray Guy
1939–

■ ■ ■

When Jannies Visited

Ray Guy's memories of childhood in the small town of Arnold's Cove, Placentia Bay, Newfoundland, give his essays and newspaper columns amusingly authentic and deftly apt details of a life most Canadians only occasionally consider. He attended Memorial University in St. John's and Ryerson Polytechnic Institute in Toronto, and is an award-winning freelance journalist who lives today in St. John's, Newfoundland. He is also the author of a play, and in the great Newfoundland "story-spinning" tradition, of a collection of radio monologues. A glance at the titles of some of his published works confirms his decided preference for a humorous tone: *You May Know Them As Sea Urchins Ma'am* (1975), *Outhouses of the East* (1978), *This Dear and Fine Country* (1985), and a collection of essays, *Ray Guy's Best* (1987). His skill as a comic writer won him the Stephen Leacock Medal in 1977, and his continuing loyalty to the voice and story of his native province resulted in the Newfoundland Arts Council Award in 1985.

Preparing to Read

This essay first appeared in *Canadian Geographic* magazine in November/December 1993. Here Ray Guy evokes images associated with Christmas in his childhood home. Particularly strong is the image of the "dreadful" masked jannies that would come to each home and dance and wreak havoc before moving on. As Guy explains, their power resided primarily in their anonymity. What other festivities or events are characterized by masks or disguises? What effects does anonymity have on people's behaviour? What is the difference between a costume and a disguise? In what situations do people assume each? What famous characters can you think of who wore masks or disguises to hide their true identity?

Jannies didn't spoil Christmas for me but they surely put a crimp in it. I was terrified of them. Even when I was old enough to be one myself there was still something dreadful about jannies. 1

On Boxing Day after supper at about eight there would come a heavy rapping at the door. Nobody else ever knocked, they just stamped snow off their boots on the porch in winter or 2 cleared their throats in the summer. Nobody ever knocked except strangers … and jannies!

Christmas 1947 stands out more than any before or since,   3 perhaps because I was eight that year. When you get to be eight a good many things clang into focus, the pieces of the great jigsaw seem to have grown larger, you can count past 10 without taking off your socks. So I knew, by then, that jannies, or mummers, were really only people.

Still, there was that gut-flopping dread. Someone went out   4 onto the dark porch and opened the door and you heard the King Jannie speak in a harsh, gabbling rasp of words made while sucking the breath in: "Any jannies in tonight?"

"Yes. OK. But …" There'd be a feeble attempt to set   5 conditions. Not too much noise, granny wasn't well. Not too rowdy, the youngsters were scared. But nothing short of a deathbed constrained them.

Out of the dark and the frosty air they blundered and   6 bumped and bundled, into the heat of the kitchen and the soft light of the kerosene lamp, roistering, hulking, tripping, stomping, lurching. They were big and bloated and mostly mute.

They had grotesque humps on their backs or obscenely   7 protruding bellies, sometimes both at once. Their faces were mummified with scraps of old lace curtains or masked blank with cardboard that had torn-out holes for eyes. They stank, they reeked.

A raw sheepskin hung over this one's deformed back, cow's   8 horns attached to a piece of bloody skull were lashed to that one's head. Another wore a jouncing girdle of fox pelts, two or three were in oilskins turned inside out, putrid with bilge water and week-old fish.

They danced a lumpish dance, shuddering the floorboards,   9 trembling the teapot atop the stove, flaring the lamp in its wall bracket, led in their floundering by a mouth organ crudely played by one of their number through its soggy mouth cloth.

The only game to it was to guess who they were. If a jannie   10 was guessed he had to unmask on the spot, which drained the dread away and destroyed the whole mob of them. But although there were fewer than 200 people in the whole village of Arnold's Cove, Newfoundland, jannies' identities were seldom guessed.

They carried staves or hook-tipped gaffs, and if you tugged   11 at their disguises they hit, not with raps or taps, but with bruising, bone-deadening clouts. Even your father, gamely smiling, gave off a fear of them.

They might lunge and seize anyone and drag them into their 12 ogreish dance, prodding and fumbling them in a most improper way. Or they might spitefully smash a bowl or upset a water bucket. At some unseen signal they all moved to leave, were offered a shot of rum or a tumbler of water, and blundered and reeled off into the night.

Two or three other gangs of jannies might show up before 13 the night was over, or on any night of the twelve days of Christmas, between December 26 and Old Christmas Day on January 6.

There seemed little reason to tolerate this mummering except 14 that it was the "done thing" and had been since time out of mind. Later, when I was old enough to join in the jannying, I glimpsed a dark attraction—the power of being that capricious Unknown, and feared.

Compared to jannies, most else about Christmas then was 15 bright and beautiful. For instance, snotty var. It was the very essence of the season and still is the most powerful trigger of memory.

At school in the first week of Advent, the teacher began 16 shoring up our spiritual foundations. We were catechized after morning prayer with questions like: "What is the first thing that must come to our minds when we think of Christmas?"

She asked again, this time ending the word "Christmas" with 17 a definite hiss. "Please, Miss," said one of the Bigger Boys, Leonard, I'd guess, "Snotty var, Miss." She twisted both his ears until they stayed red for an hour.

He'd been guilty of insolence, blasphemy and lapsing into 18 the local dialect, his mother tongue. Teachers strove to knock all three out of you, especially the latter. There was a whole dictionary full of punishable words, and on top of that a tireless knuckle-rapping campaign against wrong pronunciation of right words.

In 30 years, had he lived that long, Leonard might have said 19 that the first thing that came to his mind when he thought of Christmas was the pungent tang of balsam fir sap. Not snotty var. By then he might have learned the new language in which emmets were ants, dumbledores were bees, piss-a-beds were dandelions and a merrybegot was an illegitimate child.

But schooling then was like that. Now that I was eight I knew　20
that the green light said "go" and how to spell "squirrel"
although there was neither one nor the other within a hundred
miles. I could draw a soldier of the Roman legions and we sent
coded notes to each other in the Phoenician alphabet. But it was
long after I'd finished 17 years of schooling that I learned that
John Guy, merchant adventurer out of Bristol, had met the
Beothuks on a beach just over the hill. In 1612.

Or that my mother's people lived across the harbour at a　21
place known as "Burdle," but which was once a French plantation
called Bordeaux.

My hometown of Arnold's Cove (nobody named "Arnold"　22
lived there) lies on the eastern shore of Placentia Bay,
Newfoundland's largest bay, a great triangle 80 miles long and 60
miles across at its southern base. Its three main landmarks are
Cape St. Mary's, Chapeau Rouge, and, at its northern point, Pipers
Hole. Arnold's Cove is about 10 miles south of Pipers Hole.

The village was on a low, treeless peninsula a couple of miles　23
long and a quarter mile wide, and the wind roared across it from
every direction. It was like a monstrous raft at sea. But at its
western end the peninsula rose up to become the High Head
with cliffs that dropped straight down 250 feet to the ocean.

One day in June when I was eight the Bigger Girls came to　24
borrow me. While you were still in short pants the Bigger Girls
seemed to like minding you. After that you were allowed to hang
around in places where the men worked.

They were taking me, they said, to pick crowberries behind　25
the old graveyard, but we went much farther than that. We went
along the goat path through the bogs and by the low cliffs to the
Otter Rub, where the Americans had watched for submarines.
Beyond that, we went on and on …

Then, scrambling up through the scrubby spruce and the dusty　26
rockslides, we came out at the top of the High Head. Here was
my sudden enlightenment of a lifetime. Down in the village, the
line of sight of an eight-year-old extended from the cat in the shade
of the dooryard rhubarb to a glimpse of blue hills an improbable
distance away. But now I could see where I was in the world.

There were the islands of the bay, Long Island, Red Island,　27
Iona, Merasheen. On them were villages like Jean de Gaunt and
Peaches Cove, Harbour Buffett and Tacks Beach, Rose au Rue
and Haystack. The islets of Bread and Cheese, the next cove north

from us, called Come By Chance. And Bay Bulls Arm across the narrow Isthmus of Avalon in Trinity Bay, where John Guy first met "ye savages of ye clime."

I could see now where the fishing boats went after they 28
thumped away around the point in the early morning to the fishing grounds, as well known to them as the fertile patches of a farmer's field: The Jerseyman, called "Jasmin," Burdle Banks, Goose Island Ground, The Pancake, the Big Neverfail and the Little Neverfail.

That was all full and plenty, but then one of the Bigger Girls 29
said: "There's only one salt water in the world, you know, and it goes on and on and on. To China and to where the King lives. To where the cowboys is in the States, even!" I wanted to run headlong down from the High Head to the beach away below and throw so big a rock in the water as would make waves that might go to China. To where the palm trees were. I reserved doubts about the cowboys.

This great enlightenment from the top of the High Head all 30
went to make me especially remember 1947 and the Christmas of it.

Christmas then seemed like a test or a statement of readiness; 31
all was as ready as could or would be to face the winter to come. In the weeks before Christmas the stacked firewood on the back porch rose toward the ceiling, enough to last those 12 work-free days of the season. Most of it was dry, had seasoned for a few years, but some was raw green fir, oozing sap and covered with turpentine blisters, and used to damp the kitchen stove when a winter's gale drew the fire like a blacksmith's forge and the stovepipe glowed dangerously hot. Potatoes gathered in mid-October were heaped in earthen root cellars, and by the end of November all the animals for killing had been killed and their carcasses hung at the back of fish sheds built on stilts over the water.

Each family had a dozen or more sheep; nearly everyone 32
had a pony to plow the potato fields in May and to haul firewood throughout the winter. There were hens, ducks and occasionally geese. And there was a pig or two to rend the still fall air on its fatal day.

You knew it was pig day when the advisory went around 33
for women and children to stay indoors. A monstrous cauldron used for tanning nets was lugged up from the beach, set over a fire by the pig pen and set steaming. Soon, the loud and

prolonged squeals of the pig arouse. I was eight and convinced they were boiling it to death. Granny reassured me: "That's only the way pigs are, 'tis a pig's nature to make a great fuss over every sort of little thing."

The Bigger Boys claimed the pig's bladder, which was 34 inflated and covered in sail canvas and used in great formless games of football, played during Christmas before the heavy snows of January set in.

A few people kept cows so there might be a calf or two for 35 slaughter, and the larder was further stocked with game: moose, caribou, rabbits, ducks and ptarmigan. In December there was a secure feeling of sufficiency and just a tinge of trepidation about "the long and hungry month of March." The basic, rock-bottom ration against a shortfall in that lean time at the end of the winter was the setting aside of one barrel of potatoes and one barrel of salted herring for each family member.

A Newfoundland fishing village at that time had a 36 subsistence economy in which broody hens, spavined ponies and haystacks had as important a part as salt cod, dories and a following sea. Which is probably why a Quebec farm journal, *The Family Herald and Weekly Star*, was the journal of choice all over the island.

A mini-ritual sometime in mid-December was "The Opening 37 of The Gaps." Gaps in the maze of fences that enclosed potato fields, hay meadows and cabbage patches were opened up to create a new road cutting through them all—the winter road, the slide path.

As soon as the ice on the ponds was thick enough, a caravan 38 of ponies in jingling harness set out in the morning for the firewood places beyond the railway tracks—stands of spruce and fir that were hereditary and had names like Whiffen's Droke, The Level Brook, The Place Where Poor Bill Lost The Pocketknife or The Pond Where Uncle Steve Caught The Otter.

They filed back in the early winter dusk, slides loaded with 39 firewood for the insatiable kitchen stoves, a boat knee (the rib of a boat) or a stem of larchwood on top that might have been noticed 10 or 15 years before for its unusual shape, a brace or two of partridge or rabbits swinging from the slide, harness bells jingling, steam wafting from the pot-bellied ponies, sparks from the runners where the winter road was bare.

Sometimes at Christmas a dozen or more men were missing. 40 The herring fishery was the last of the year. The boats went out

10 miles or more to a reach between islands in the bay where the shoals of herring appeared. They stayed away for a fortnight ... and hoped for "light nights" (nights when the moon shone clear and bright) at Christmas.

If the nights were moonless or stormy, the herring couldn't see 41 the nets, the catch was abundant, and even Christmas was no excuse to leave such bounty and come home. But if it chanced that there were light nights, the boats came back for a day or two.

That Christmas of 1947 when I was eight there was a full 42 moon, but dark and heavy clouds night after night. On December 23 the sky cleared and the moon and stars glared down. As the church bell rang near midnight on Christmas Eve, the boats were heard coming far off, and they rounded the point into the cove, their masts hung with lanterns and green boughs. As they came they made a trail of stars on the black glass of the water.

Not only had the herring men brought themselves back in 43 good time, they'd met a moonshiner among the islands who was freshly back from St. Peter's—as they called the French island of Saint-Pierre. So there was tobacco and a better-quality spirit to enliven that Christmas.

What other rum there was for Christmas, Easter, weddings 44 and wakes, was called swish. Fisherman were entitled to the thick-staved puncheons that brought undiluted rum from the West Indies. These were sawed in two and used as tubs for salting fish.

But if three or four gallons of water were poured into these 45 empty casks and let stand for a week and the casks rolled back and forth to swish it around, it was the Wedding in Cana all over again. The staves gave up their essence and you had three or four gallons of the best Demerara rum.

So then it was Christmas. The church decorated all up and 46 down the lamp posts with balsam fir and tissue-paper roses. Socials, dances, soup suppers, "meat teas," concerts in the school every other night. Card games and singing and stories and midnight "scoffs" in the houses and ... jannies.

That year I got an orange, a fifty-cent piece, an American 47 chocolate bar, a prayer book and a new pair of mitts in my stocking, but the big thing was my father had made me a slide out of a salt pork barrel and it went like billy-be-damned down the hill in our meadow along the icy winter road.

Since there were 12 days of yuletide—and all the baking 48 done as well as the firewood laid in—there seemed to be no frantic festive pace, just that assured and designated time in the darkest part of the year when people came to your house every night or you went to theirs.

It was an obvious portion of the year. Between pig-killing 49 time and Candlemas Day, February 2, when the lamps were not lit until after supper. Then to the middle of February when the bleating of new lambs was added to the evening's sounds and on to early March, when the hammering to repair the boats on the beaches began.

Thirty-five years later I was living in a St. John's suburb with 50 cable TV and a microwave oven. One evening in early January two station wagons stopped out front. A mob of mummers debouched.

By now, jannies, like much else, had gone full circle and 51 beyond, from being a base embarrassment, a low practice from the past, to being folkloric and historic and a piece of precious heritage. The two-faced Roman god, Janus, had been brought into the picture, an actual script of the mummer's play had been reconstituted, there were elaborate costumes and the university crowd delighted in floating a revival.

They banged on the door. They said, "Any jannies in 52 tonight?"

"No," I said. I was a big boy, now.   53

UNDERSTANDING DETAILS

1. What are jannies and at what time of year do they typically appear?
2. Why do people tolerate the mummers?
3. What is snotty var? Why is one of the boys punished for saying that this was the first thing that came to his mind when he thought about Christmas?

ANALYZING MEANING

1. In paragraph 3, Guy says, "When you get to be eight a good many things clang into focus ..." and later he speaks of the great enlightenment he experienced the year he was eight. What is it that "clangs into focus" for Guy in 1947?
2. What is the role of the jannies in the community that Guy is evoking in the reader's mind's eye? How does their role change by the time Guy opens his door to them in St. John's 35 years later?

3. Characterize the community in which Guy grew up. What things dominate the lives of the inhabitants of Arnold's Cove? What influences seem particularly strong in the lives of these people?

DISCOVERING RHETORICAL STRATEGIES

1. Guy's essay is a series of snapshots of a time and place from his experience. What unifies the incidents and images that he describes?
2. Guy uses many specific place names in his description of his childhood in Arnold's Cove. Why does he choose to include these specific details? What do these names add to Guy's description?
3. Reread the description of the jannies that Guy recalls from his childhood (paragraphs 6–12) and keep track of all of the verbs used to describe their actions. What is the effect of Guy's word choices here? What language might the jannies themselves use to describe their antics?

MAKING CONNECTIONS

1. While Ray Guy writes about jannying, Alfred LeBlanc's "The Reel Thing" describes another ritual of maritime life. Compare and contrast LeBlanc's and Guy's attitudes toward these rituals.
2. How do you think Stephen King ("Why We Crave Horror Movies") would explain the appeal of jannying? What role does it play in Guy's society?
3. Ray Guy gives us a vivid description of childhood in a part of Atlantic Canada. How does this compare to Richards' childhood in Newcastle? How does it compare to your own memories of childhood?

IDEAS FOR DISCUSSION/WRITING

Preparing to Write

Write freely about an experience that you found frightening or intimidating when you were young. What made it unsettling? How did you respond? Did others share your feelings? Did your reaction to it change as you grew up?

Choosing a Topic

1. Choose a particular event or activity to which your reaction has changed over time. Describe your experience of that event so that your initial feelings about it are apparent to your audience both through the details that you include and the language choices you make.

2. Write an essay describing the three most memorable people you have met in your life. Why did you choose these particular people? Do they have qualities in common? Where and how did you meet each one? Remember to link the sections of your essay and to choose a logical order for presentation of your characters.

3. The dialect of Arnold's Cove is one of the elements in Guy's description that makes it vivid. Choose a familiar scene that involves interaction between people and write a script for this scene in which you pay particular attention to making the dialogue realistic. Your scene might be a family meal, a child asking permission to use the car, explaining why you got home late, or the half-time or intermission conversation at a sporting event you are attending with your friends.

WEB SITES

www.greendome.org/archives/mummer1/aboutmum.html
www.algonet.se/%7Ebernadot/christmas/16.html
These sites will provide more information about the Newfoundland tradition of mummering.

www.cangeo.ca
Canadian Geographic is the source of Guy's essay.

CHAPTER 2

NARRATION

Telling a Story

A good story is a powerful method of getting someone's attention. The excitement that accompanies a suspenseful ghost story, a lively anecdote, or a vivid joke easily attests to this effect. In fact, narration is one of the earliest verbal skills we all learn as children, providing us with a convenient, logical, and easily understood means of sharing our thoughts with other people. Storytelling is powerful because it offers us a way of dramatizing our ideas so that others can identify with them.

Defining Narration

Narration involves telling a story that is often based on personal experience. Stories can be oral or written, real or imaginary, short or long. A good story, however, always has a point or purpose. It can be the dominant mode (as in a novel or short story), supported by other rhetorical strategies, or it can serve the purpose of another rhetorical mode (as in a persuasive essay, a historical survey, or a scientific report).

In its subordinate role, narration can provide examples or explain ideas. If asked why you are attending college, for instance, you might turn to narration to make your answer clear, beginning with a story about your family's hardships in the past. The purpose of telling such a story would be to help your listeners appreciate your need for higher education by encouraging them to understand and identify with your family history.

Unlike description, which generally portrays people, places, and objects in *space*, narration asks the reader to follow a series of actions through a particular *time* sequence. Description often complements the movement of narration, though. People must be depicted, for instance, along with their relationships to one another, before their actions can have any real meaning for us; similarly, places must be described so that we can picture the setting and understand the activities in a specific scene. The organization of the action and the time spent on each episode in a story should be based principally on a writer's analysis of the interests and needs of his or her audience.

To be most effective, narration should prolong the exciting parts of a story and shorten the routine facts that simply move the reader from one episode to another. If you were robbed on your way to work, for example, a good narrative describing the incident would concentrate on the traumatic event itself rather than on such mundane and boring details as what you had for breakfast and what clothes you had put on prior to the attack. Finally, just like description, narration *shows* rather than *tells* its purpose to the audience. The factual statement "I was robbed this morning" could be made much more vivid and dramatic through the addition of some simple narration: "As I was walking to work at 7:30 a.m., a huge and angry-looking man ran up to me, thrust a gun into the middle of my stomach, and took my money, my new wristwatch, all my credit cards, and my pants— leaving me penniless and embarrassed."

The following paragraph written by a student recounts a recent parachuting experience. As you read this narrative, notice especially the writer's use of vivid detail to *show* rather than *tell* her message to the readers.

I have always needed occasional "fixes" of excitement in my life, so when I realized one spring day that I was more than ordinarily bored, I made up my mind to take more than ordinary steps to relieve that boredom. I decided to go parachuting. The next thing I knew, I was stuffed into a claustrophobically small plane with five other ter- rified people, rolling down a bumpy, rural runway, droning my way to 3,500 feet and an exhilarating experience. Once over the jump area, I waited my turn, stepped onto the strut, held my breath, and then kicked off into the cold, rushing air as my heart pounded heavily. All I could think was, "I hope this damn parachute opens!" The sen- sation of falling backward through space was unfamiliar and dis- concerting till my chute opened with a loud "pop," momentarily pulling me upward toward the distant sky. After several minutes of floating downward, I landed rudely on the hard ground. Life, I remembered happily, could be awfully exciting. And a month later, when my tailbone had stopped throbbing, I still felt that way.

Thinking Critically by Using Narration

Rhetorical modes offer us different ways of perceiving reality. Narration is an especially useful tool for sequencing or putting details and information in some kind of logical order, usually chronological. Working with narration helps us see clear sequences separate from all other mental functions.

Practising exercises in narrative techniques can help you see clear patterns in topics you are writing about. Although narration is usually used in conjunction with other rhetorical modes, we are going to isolate it here so that you can appreciate its specific mechanics separately from other mental activities. If you feel the process of narration in your head, you are more likely to understand exactly what it entails and thus to use it more effectively in reading other essays and in organizing and writing your own essays.

For the best results, we will once again single out narration and do some warm-up exercises to make your sequencing perceptions as accurate and successful as possible. In this way, you will actually learn to feel how your mind works in this particular mode and then be more aware of the thinking strategies available to you in your own reading and writing. As you become more conscious of the mechanics of the individual rhetorical modes, you will naturally become more adept at combining them to accomplish the specific purpose and the related effect you want to create.

The following exercises, which require a combination of thinking and writing skills, will help you practise this particular strategy in isolation. Just as in a physical workout, we will warm up your mental capabilities one by one as if they were muscles that can be developed individually before being used together in harmony.

1. Make a chronological list of the different activities you did yesterday, from waking in the morning to sleeping at night. Randomly pick two events from your day, and treat them as the highlights of your day. Now, write freely for five minutes, explaining the story of your day and emphasizing the importance of these two highlights.

2. Recall an important event that happened to you between the ages of five and ten. Brainstorm about how this event made you feel at the time it happened. Then, brainstorm about how this event makes you feel now. What changes have you discovered in your view of this event?

3. Create a myth or story that illustrates a belief or idea that you think is important. You might begin with a moral that you believe in and then compose a story that "teaches" or demonstrates that moral.

Reading and Writing Narrative Essays

To read a narrative essay most effectively, you should spend your time concentrating on the writer's main story line and use of details. To create an effective story, you have some important decisions to make before you write and certain variables to control as you actually draft your narrative.

During the prewriting stage, you need to generate ideas and choose a point of view through which your story will be presented. Then, as you write, the preliminary decisions you have made regarding the selection and arrangement of your details (especially important in a narrative) will allow your story to flow more easily. Carefully controlled organization, along with appropriate timing and pacing, can influence your audience's reactions in very powerful ways.

How to Read a Narrative Essay

Preparing to Read. As you prepare to read the narratives in this chapter, try to guess what each title tells you about that essay's topic and about the author's attitude toward that topic: Can you tell, for example, what Evelyn Lau's attitude toward her subject is from her title in "I Sing the Song of My Condo" or how Abel feels about Canadian citizenship in "A Home at the End of the Journey"? Also, scan the essay and read its synopsis in the Rhetorical Table of Contents to help you anticipate as much as you can about the author's purpose and audience.

The more you learn from the biography about the author and the circumstances surrounding the composition of a particular essay, the better prepared you will be to read the essay. For a narrative essay, the writer's point of view or perspective toward the story and its characters is especially significant. From the biographies, can you determine something about Karen Connelly's view of Thailand in "Touch the Dragon" or Brian Lewis's reason for writing his essay? What do you learn about Steven Heighton's views about war in "Elegy in Stone"? Last, before you begin to read, answer the Preparing to Read questions and then try to generate some of your own inquiries on the general subject of the essay: What do you want to know about health and living conditions among Native Canadians in the Arctic (Lewis)? What are your thoughts about Canadian citizenship (Abel)? What do you think about the value of owning a home (Lau)?

Reading. As you read a narrative essay for the first time, simply follow the story line and try to get a general sense of the narrative and of the author's general purpose. Is Lewis's purpose to make us feel sympathetic or annoyed about the responses of the bureaucrats to the needs of the Inuit people? Is Steven Heighton trying to encourage us to visit the monument at Vimy Ridge or is he simply trying to show us more about the nature of Canada? Record your initial reactions to each essay as they occur to you.

Based on the biographical information preceding the essay and on the essay's tone, purpose, and audience, try to create a context for the narrative as you read. How do such details help you understand your reading material more thoroughly? A first reading of this sort, along with a survey of the questions that follow the essay, will help prepare you for a critical understanding of the material when you read it for the second time.

Rereading. As you reread these narrative essays, notice the author's selection and arrangement of details. Why does Abel organize his essay one way and Lewis another? What effect does their organization create? Also pay attention to the timing and the pacing of the story line. What do the detailed descriptions of the land add to Connelly's narrative? What does the quick pace of Abel's "A Home at the End of the Journey" communicate?

In addition, consider at this point what other rhetorical strategies the authors use to support their narratives. Which writers use examples to supplement their stories? Which use definitions? Which use comparisons? Why do they use these strategies?

Finally, when you answer the questions after each essay, you can check your understanding of the material on different levels before you tackle the discussion/writing topics that follow. For a general checklist of reading guidelines, please see pages 15–16 of the Introduction.

How to Write a Narrative Essay

Preparing to Write. First, you should answer the prewriting questions to help you generate thoughts on the subject at hand. Next, as in all writing, you should explore your subject matter and discover as many specific details as possible. (See pages 17–19 of the Introduction for a discussion of prewriting techniques.) Some writers rely on the familiar journalistic checklist of Who, What, When, Where, Why, and How to make sure they cover all aspects of their narrative. If you were using the story of a basketball game at your college to demonstrate the team spirit of your school, for example, you might want to consider telling your readers *who* played in the game and/or *who* attended; *what* happened before, during, and after the game; *when* and *where* it took place; *why* it was being played (or *why* these particular teams were playing each other or *why* the game was especially important); and *how* the winning basket was shot. Freewriting, or a combination of freewriting and the journalistic questions, is another effective way of getting ideas and story details on paper for use in a first draft.

Once you have generated these ideas, you should always let your purpose and audience ultimately guide your selection of details, but the process of gathering such journalistic information gives you some material from which to choose. You will also need to decide whether to include dialogue in your narrative. Again, the difference here is between *showing* and *telling*: Will your audience benefit from reading what was actually said, word for word, during a discussion, or will a brief description of the conversation be sufficiently effective? In fact, all the choices you make at this stage of the composing process will give you material with which to create emphasis, suspense, conflict, and interest in your subject.

Next, you must decide upon the point of view that will most readily help you achieve your purpose with your specific audience. Point of view includes the (1) person, (2) vantage point, and (3) attitude of your narrator. *Person* refers to who will tell the story: an uninvolved observer, a character in the narrative, or an omniscient (all-knowing) narrator. This initial decision will guide your thoughts on *vantage point*, which is the frame of reference of the narrator: close to the action, far from the action, looking back on the past, or reporting on the present. Finally, your narrator will naturally have an *attitude,* or *personal feeling,* about the subject: accepting, hostile, sarcastic, indifferent, angry, pleased, or any of a number of similar emotions. Once you adopt a certain perspective in a story, you must follow it for the duration of the narrative. This consistency will bring focus and coherence to the story.

Writing. After you have explored your topic and adopted a particular point of view, you need to write a thesis statement and to select and arrange the details of your story coherently so that the narrative has a clear beginning, middle, and end. The most natural way to organize the events of a narrative, of course, is chronologically. In your story about the school basketball game, you would probably narrate the relevant details in the order in which they occurred (i.e., sequentially, from the beginning of the game to its conclusion). More experienced writers may elect to use flashbacks: An athlete might recall a significant event that happened during the game, or a coach might recollect the contest's turning point. Your most important consideration is that the elements of a story follow some sort of time sequence, aided by the use of clear and logical transitions (e.g., "then," "next," "at this point," "suddenly") that help the reader move smoothly from one event to the next.

Rewriting. As you reread the narrative you have written, pretend you are a reader and make sure you have told the story from the most effective point of view, considering both your purpose and your audience:

1. Is your purpose (or thesis) clearly stated?
2. Who is your audience?
3. To what extent does this narrator help you achieve your purpose?

Further, as you reread, make certain you can follow the events of the story as they are related:

1. Does one event lead naturally to the next?
2. Are all the events relevant to your purpose?
3. Do you show rather than tell your message?

For more advice on writing and editing, see pages 26–27.

Student Essay: Narration at Work

The following essay characterizes the writer's mother by telling a story about an unusual family vacation. As you read it, notice that the student writer states her purpose clearly and succinctly in the first paragraph. She then becomes an integral part of her story as she carefully selects examples and details that help convey her thesis.

A Vacation With My Mother

First-person narrator <u>I had an interesting childhood</u>—not because of where <u>I</u> grew up General subject and not because <u>I</u> ever did anything particularly adventuresome or thrilling. In fact, I don't think my life seemed especially interesting to me at the time. But now, telling friends about my supposedly ordinary childhood, I notice an array of responses ranging Specific subject from astonishment to hilarity. <u>The source of their surprise and amusement is my mother</u>—gracious, charming, sweet, and totally out of synchronization with the rest of the world. <u>One strange</u> Thesis statement <u>family trip we took when I was eleven captures the essence of her zaniness.</u>

Narrator's attitude My two sets of grandparents lived in Calgary and Regina, respectively, and my parents decided we would spend a few weeks driving to those cities and seeing all the sights along the relaxed and rambling way. <u>My eight-year-old brother, David, and I had some serious reservations</u>. If Dad had ever had Mom drive him to school, we reasoned, he'd never even consider letting her help drive us anywhere out of town, let alone out of Vancouver. If we weren't paying attention, we were as likely to end up at her office or the golf course as we were to arrive at school. Sometimes she'd Examples drop us off at a friend's house to play and then forget where she'd left us. The notion of going on a long trip with her was really unnerving.

Transition <u>How can I explain my mother to a stranger?</u> Have you ever watched reruns of the old *I Love Lucy* with Lucille Ball? I did as a child, and I thought Lucy Ricardo was normal. I lived with somebody a lot like her. Now, Mom wasn't a redhead (not usually, Narrator's vantage point anyway), and Dad wasn't a Cuban nightclub owner, but <u>at home we had the same situation of a loving but bemused husband trying to deal with the off-the-wall logic and enthusiasm of a frequently exasperating wife. We all adored her, but we had to admit it: Mom was a flaky, absent-minded, genuine eccentric.</u>

Transition

As the first day of our trip approached, David and I reluctantly said good-bye to all of our friends. Who knew if we'd ever see any of them again? Finally, the moment of our departure arrived, and we loaded suitcases, books, games, some camping gear, and a tent into the car and bravely drove off. We bravely drove off again two hours later after we'd returned home to get the purse and traveler's cheques that Mom had forgotten.

Careful selection of details

Use of dialogue

David and I were always a little nervous when using gas station bathrooms if Mom was driving while Dad napped: "You stand outside the door and play lookout while I go, and I'll stand outside the door and play lookout while you go." I had terrible visions: "Honey, where are the kids?" "What?! Oh, gosh . . . I thought they were being awfully quiet. Uh . . . Lethbridge?" We were never actually abandoned in a strange city, but we weren't about to take any chances.

Examples

Transition

On the fourth or fifth night of the trip, we had trouble finding a motel with a vacancy. After driving futilely for an hour, Mom suddenly had a great idea: Why didn't we find a house with a likely-looking back yard and ask if we could pitch our tent there? To her, the scheme was eminently reasonable. Vowing quietly to each other to hide in the back seat if she did it, David and I groaned in anticipated mortification. To our profound relief, Dad vetoed the idea. Mom never could understand our objections. If a strange family showed up on her front doorstep, Mom would have been delighted. She thinks everyone in the world is as nice as she is. We finally found a vacancy in the next town. David and I were thrilled—the place featured bungalows in the shape of tepees.

Passage of time

Example

Transition

The Native motif must have reminded my parents that we had not yet used the brand-new tent, Coleman stove, portable mattress, and other camping gear we had brought. We headed to a national park the next day and found a campsite by a lake. It took

Chronological order

hours to figure out how to get the tent up: It was one of those deluxe models with mosquito-net windows, canvas floors, and enough room for three large families to sleep in. It was after dark before we finally got it erected, and the night had turned quite cold. We fixed a hurried campfire dinner (chicken burned on the outside and raw in the middle) and prepared to go to sleep. That was when we realized that Mom had forgotten to bring along some important pieces of equipment—our sleeping bags. The four of us huddled together on our thin mattresses under the carpet from the station-wagon floor. That ended our camping days. Give me a stucco tepee any time.

Careful selection of details

We drove through three provinces and saw lots of interesting sights along the way: a working mine, a logging camp, caves, Examples mountains, waterfalls, even a haunted house. David and I were (spatial order) excited and amazed at all the wonders we found, and Mom was just as enthralled as we were. Her constant pleasure and sense of the world as a beautiful, magical place was infectious. I never realized until I grew up how really childlike—in the best sense of the word—my mother actually is. She is innocent, optimistic, and always ready to be entertained.

Transition <u>Looking back on that long-past family</u> vacation, <u>I now realize</u> Narrator's <u>that my childhood was more special because I grew up with a</u> attitude <u>mother who wasn't afraid to try anything and who taught me to</u> <u>look at the world as a series of marvelous opportunities to be</u> <u>explored</u>. What did it matter that she thought England was bordered by Germany? We were never going to try to drive there. So Examples what if she was always leaving her car keys in the refrigerator or Concluding some other equally inexplicable place? <u>In the end, we always got</u> remark <u>where we were going—and we generally had a grand time along</u> <u>the way</u>.

Student Writer's Comments

I enjoyed writing about this childhood vacation because of all the memories it brought back. I knew I wanted to write a narrative to explain my mother, and the word zany immediately popped into my mind. So I knew what my focus was going to be from the outset. My prewriting started in my head as soon as I found this angle. So many thoughts and memories rushed into my head that I couldn't even get to a piece of paper to write them down before I lost some of them. But there were way too many to put into one essay. The hardest part of writing this narrative was trying to decide what material to use and what to leave out. Spending a little more time before writing my first draft proved to be a good investment in this case. I got a clean piece of paper and began freewriting, trying to mould some of my scattered ideas from brainstorming into a coherent, readable form. During this second stage of prewriting, I remembered one special vacation we took that I thought might capture the essence of my mother——and also of my family.

My first draft was about three times the length of this one. My point of view was the innocent participant/observer who came to know and love her mother for her absent-mindedness. I had really developed my thesis from the time I got this writing assignment. And I told my story chronologically, except for looking back in the last paragraph, when I attempted to analyze the entire experience. I had no trouble showing rather than telling because all of the details were so vivid to me——as if they had happened yesterday. But that was my downfall. I soon realized that I could not possibly include everything that was on the pages of my first draft.

The process of cranking out my rough draft made my point of view toward life with my mother very clear to me and helped me face the cutting that was ahead of me. I took the raw material of a very lengthy first draft and forced myself to choose the details and examples that best characterized my mother and what life was like growing up under the care of such a lovely but daffy individual. The sense of her being both "lovely" and "daffy" was the insight that helped me the most in revising the content of my essay. I made myself ruthlessly eliminate anything that interfered with the overall effect I was trying to create——from extraneous images and details to words and phrases that didn't contribute to this specific view of my mom.

The final result, according to my classmates, communicated my message clearly and efficiently. The main criticism I got from my class was that I might have cut too much from my first draft. But I think this focused picture with a few highlights conveys my meaning in the best possible way. I offered enough details to show rather than tell my readers what living with my mother was like, but *not too many to bore them. I was also able to take the time in my essay to be humorous now and then ("David and I reluctantly said good-bye to all of our friends. Who knew if we'd ever see any of them again?" and "Give me a stucco tepee any time."), as well as pensive and serious ("I now realize that my childhood was more special because I grew up with a mother who wasn't afraid to try anything and who taught me to look at the world as a series of marvelous opportunities to be explored."). Even though in looking at the essay now I would tamper with a few things, I am generally happy with the final draft. It captures the essence of my mother from my point of view, and it also gave my class a few laughs. Aren't the readers' reactions the ultimate test of a good story?*

Some Final Thoughts on Narration

Just as with other modes of writing, all decisions regarding narration should be made with a specific purpose and an intended audience constantly in mind. As you will see, each narrative in this section is directed at a clearly defined audience. Notice, as you read, how each writer manipulates the various features of narration so that the readers are simultaneously caught up in the plot and deeply moved to feel, act, think, and believe the writer's personal opinions.

Narration in Review

Reading Narrative Essays

Preparing to Read

1. What assumptions can you make from the essay's title?
2. Can you guess what the author's mood is?
3. What is the essay's purpose and audience?
4. What does the synopsis in the Rhetorical Table of Contents tell you about the essay?
5. What can you learn from the author's biography?
6. Can you guess what the author's point of view toward the subject is?

7. What are your responses to the Preparing to Read questions?

Reading

1. What is the essay's general story line?
2. What is the author's purpose?
3. Did you preview the questions that follow the essay?

Rereading

1. What details did the author choose and how are they arranged?
2. How does the author control the pace of the story?
3. What other rhetorical modes does the author use to support the essay's purpose?
4. What are your responses to the questions after the essay?

Writing Narrative Essays

Preparing to Write

1. What are your responses to the Preparing to Write questions?
2. What is your purpose?
3. Who is your audience?
4. What is your narrator's point of view—including person, vantage point, and attitude toward the subject?

Writing

1. What is your thesis?
2. What details will best support this thesis?
3. How can you arrange these details most effectively?
4. Do you *show* rather than *tell* your story?
5. Does your narrative essay follow a time sequence?

Rewriting

1. Is your purpose (or thesis) clearly stated?
2. Who is your audience?
3. To what extent does your narrator help you achieve your purpose?
4. Does one event lead naturally to the next?
5. Are all the events relevant to your purpose?
6. Do you *show* rather than *tell* your message?

Allen Abel
1950–

■ ■ ■

A Home at the End of the Journey

Born in Brooklyn, New York, Allen Abel was probably a fan of the legendary Brooklyn Dodgers in the 1950s. He did, in fact, grow up to be a sports writer in his early years as a newspaper journalist. Now a resident of Toronto, he is a writer and broadcaster of wide-ranging interests and talents. After receiving a Bachelor of Science degree in 1971 from Rensselaer Polytechnic in New York State, Abel's focus of activities took an abrupt turn into a career as a sports journalist for several upstate New York papers, where he won a number of journalism awards. He moved to Toronto in the late 1970s, and became a well-known sports columnist for *The Globe and Mail* from 1977 until 1983. Abel has also worked as a sports commentator for CFRB and was the writer of a documentary called *The Game of Her Life* about the Canadian women's Olympic hockey team going to the Nagano Olympics. Abel's *Globe* columns always revealed an intelligent and ironic style, and often some more "serious" interests, which may have resulted in an extraordinary career shift for the author: The *Globe* made him their Peking correspondent in 1983 and in 1986 he became a reporter and producer of CBC-TV's *The Journal* for eight years. His career as a political observer has also led him into the production of documentary films of international interest, including *The Price of Freedom* (about East Germany) and *The Fires of Kuwait*. Allen Abel is the author of several books, including *But I Loved It Plenty Well* (1983), *Scaring Myself to Death: Adventures of a Foreign Correspondent* (1992), and *Flatbush Odyssey: A Journey to the Heart of Brooklyn* (1995). Most recently, Abel has been made a columnist for the *National Post*.

Preparing to Read

"A Home at the End of the Journey" first appeared in *Maclean's* magazine in January of 1995. In this narrative essay Abel relates the experience of becoming a Canadian citizen, and particularly the citizenship ceremony in which he participated. Before you read about Abel's experience, think about the concept of citizenship. What does it mean to be a citizen of a country? What rights and responsibilities accompany citizenship? How do these obligations and opportunities vary from one country to another? What difference is there between being a citizen of a country by birth and being a citizen of that country through choice? What do people need to do to become citizens of Canada?

On an early winter evening in the bottomlands of Toronto's 1 untamed River Don, 70 would-be Canadians file into a blinding bright conference room and take their seats in the alphabetical order of their mutually incomprehensible names. Outside, a first frosting has rendered this quadrant of the city even more picturesque than usual. The coatracks are crammed like Tokyo commuters; overshoes slump limply on the floor.

The 70 are to take the Oath of Citizenship, pledging allegiance 2 to the woman in England—and her lovelorn son and *his* son and so forth forever—who still embodies the vast, infant Canadian state. In front of the oath-takers, a speaker's podium has been set up, and there is a small desk on which are piled the certifying documents, emblazoned with Lion and Unicorn, that each new citizen will receive. I'm a little nervous, my throat a bit dry. I am one of the 70.

Now the clerk of the court comes out, a tall, energetic woman 3 in billowing robes, dashing around like a refugee claimant from the cast of *Sister Act 2*. The ceremony will begin soon, she announces. When the oath has been sworn, she instructs, we new Canadians are to proceed from our seats in a seamless serpentine to shake the hand of the presiding judge and then, doing a single axel in front of the podium, we are to return immediately to our assigned chairs. All of this is to be accomplished swiftly, to leave more time for speeches.

Photography is permitted, the clerk says, but not during the 4 swearing of the oath itself. This act, it seems, is as sacred as the fox dance of the British Columbia Musqueam, and snapshots would defile the affair. But Beta cameramen from local television stations are here, and they will roll right over the taboo, and no one will complain or try to halt them.

It is International Human Rights Week, so the ceremony is to 5 include more ceremony than usual. Decorated dignitaries from various ethnic communities of Metro Toronto have been invited to witness the swearing-in and then—it is a lovely touch—they are to reaffirm their own loyalty to Crown and Canada by taking the oath themselves. A red-coat Mountie stands at crisp attention, and officers of the Canadian Jewish Congress warmly greet each immigrant family. It is they who are hosting this group naturalization, here at their modern headquarters in this snowbound suburban vale.

I study my fellow foreigners as they arrive, and I try to guess 6 which ones are war orphans and day laborers and entrepreneurs, and which ones are gangsters and welfare cheats. Tonight's new Canadians, we are informed, have come from 27 countries, borne by the strange and sweeping currents of life to reunite, for this brief instant, in the saying of 43 words. Then, we will scatter into the infinite city, to meet again in fear or fellowship only at bus shelters, and some other less Toronto-centric place. But around me now, as the presiding judge arrives and the crowded room falls to a hush, I see the faces I have faced as a foreign correspondent in the refugee camps of Kurdistan, the back alleys of Havana, the cages of Hong Kong that hold escaped Vietnamese. It is a swirling sensation—that I have been sent from this city to their worlds and now their worlds have joined with mine.

(An hour earlier, I had thought: this is the night I finally 7 leave Brooklyn, my home town, behind me. But then, my wife and I had jumped into a taxi to make the ceremony on time and it had been outfitted with a bullet-proof partition between driver and passenger, an emblem of the new urban Canada. No one spoke; I stared glumly at the snow. Brooklyn had followed me north.)

The presiding judge greets us. An immigrant herself from 8 some European duchy, I cannot locate her accent—Latvia? Luxembourg?—she has performed this procedure manifold times but her voice still swells with proud anticipation. We are gaining a new country, she tells us. The gifts of this land will be limited only by the capacity of our hearts.

We stand at the clerk's command and begin the affirmation, 9 some of us mumbling, some nearly shouting, others utterly lost in the antiquated Anglophile creed ("I will be faithful and bear true allegiance..."). The cameras are on us. We will observe the laws of Canada, we utter. We will fulfil our duties. We will remain standing and do it all over again, says the presiding judge—in French.

The slow parade to the podium begins. I clasp the judge's 10 hand, receive my Commemoration of Canadian Citizenship. Now, the Canadians who have been citizens for longer than six minutes are invited to restate their vows. In the peanut gallery to my right, I see my Canadian wife with her right hand raised, serenely chanting along. But I am already contemplating the fruits of my neonate heritage: seats on royal commissions; diplomatic postings to warm, benign republics; poets' allowances;

jury duty. Shaking me from this reverie, *O Canada* begins, sung by two young stars of *Miss Saigon*.

The ceremony is over. We take our coats and re-enter the intemperate night. Shivering, our teeth playing marimba melodies, we give up on the bus after a couple of minutes and hail another cab. I slide in, expecting more anticrime plastic, more mistrust, more silence. 11

Instead there is a slim, blushing Arab in the driver's seat and a giggling Chinese woman right beside him. They both are in their 20s, lost in laughter. Turning east on Sheppard, skating sideways on the pond, the pilot turns around to shake my hand and to introduce his companion. 12

"Don't be afraid," the driver says. "This is my girlfriend." 13

"Congratulations!" I tell him. I'm thinking: Maybe this place 14
can work.

UNDERSTANDING DETAILS

1. Abel is relating an event in which there are many participants. What is his relationship to the participants of this citizenship ceremony?
2. What does Abel mean when he says "Brooklyn had followed me north"?
3. Explain the significance of the ceremony that Abel is depicting in this essay. How might the importance of this ceremony vary for the range of participants that Abel describes?

ANALYZING MEANING

1. What is Abel's thesis in this essay? What specific examples does he include that develop this central idea?
2. How many different nationalities or cultures does Abel refer to in "A Home at the End of the Journey"? Why does he include such a variety of references?
3. Characterize Abel's tone in this essay. What does the tone convey about the author's attitude toward his subject?

DISCOVERING RHETORICAL STRATEGIES

1. Abel uses many stylistic devices to make his writing interesting and effective. Find examples of similes, metaphors, personification, and alliteration in this essay.

2. How is Abel's past experience as a foreign correspondent and a sports writer reflected in the details and images he chooses to include in this essay?
3. How does Abel give his narrative a sense of completion? How does the conclusion of his essay link back to the introduction?

MAKING CONNECTIONS

1. The citizenship ceremony described in "A Home at the End of the Journey" has made Abel a Canadian. How does Abel's view of what is a Canadian compare to the view of Bissoondath ("Pieces of Sky")?
2. Both Diane Francis and Allen Abel have come to Canada from the United States. Francis gives us a vivid image of Canada in her essay, "Once a Kinder and Gentler Nation". Do you think Abel would agree or disagree with Francis's portrayal of Canada? Explain your answer with specific examples.
3. Steven Heighton ("Elegy in Stone") conveys a sense of pride in Canada for the understatement, quiet dignity, and reluctance to glorify war that he finds reflected in the park at Vimy Ridge. How do you think Allen Abel would react to this little piece of Canada in France?

IDEAS FOR DISCUSSION/WRITING

Preparing to Write

Before you begin writing, think of a ceremony in which you have participated that stands out in your mind. It might have been a graduation or a wedding or a coming-of-age ceremony such as a Bar or Bat Mitzvah, or it might have been a citizenship ceremony such as Abel's. What do you remember about the event? Who attended? What rituals were involved? How did you feel about the ceremony beforehand? Did you feel differently during the event? After it was over, what emotions do you recall experiencing? Did your participation in that ceremony give you any particular understanding about the world or the people in it?

Choosing a Topic

1. Abel uses his narrative to make a point about the multicultural nature of Canada. Choose a particular incident or event in which you have participated or that you have witnessed that illustrates

your view about this aspect of Canada. Write a narrative essay in which you recreate that incident or event and link it clearly to your view about multiculturalism in Canada.

2. Choose an incident or event from your life that has given you particular insight into human nature. Relate the event in a narrative essay with a clear thesis.

3. Ceremonies often change to adapt to a progressive world. Write a narrative essay in which you describe one ceremony you have attended or participated in that in some way did not follow tradition or convention. Use your essay to show how our world is changing. Make it clear through your choice of details and language whether you consider this change positive or negative.

WEB SITES

www.macleans.ca
Abel's article first appeared in *Maclean's* magazine.

www.nationalpost.com/commentary.asp?s2=columnists
Abel is a columnist for the *National Post*. Click on his picture to read his latest column.

Steven Heighton
1961–

■ ■ ■

Elegy in Stone

"If being a poet is possessing a heightened sense of perception, then in his latest collection of essays, *The Admen Move on Lhasa: Writing and Culture in a Virtual World*, Steven Heighton is every inch a poet. Here he is sometimes chatty, even wistful; at other times, wholly serious, even lamenting; and at others still, lyrical, poetic. But whatever voice he assumes, he is sure to hold your attention."

So opens L. Brent Robillard's review in the *Backwater Review* of Heighton's collection of essays from which the selection here is taken. *The Admen Move on Lhasa: Writing and Culture in a Virtual World* (1997) follows the publication of three collections of poetry: *Stalin's Carnival* (1989), *Foreign Ghosts* (1989) and *The Ecstasy of Skeptics* (1994); and two books of fiction: *Flight Paths of the Emperor* (1992) and *On earth as it is* (1995). Steven Heighton has consistently been recognized for his writing with awards including The Canadian Authors Association Air Canada Award for most promising young writer in 1989, The Gerald Lampert Memorial Award (1990), and a National Magazine Award gold medal for fiction in 1992. In addition, Heighton's *Flight Paths of the Emperor* was a Trillium Book Award finalist in 1993 and *On earth as it is* was nominated for the Governor General's Award for poetry in 1995.

Steven Heighton was born in Toronto in 1961 and grew up there and in Red Lake in Northern Ontario. After graduating from Queen's University in 1986 with a B.A. and an M.A. in English, he spent time teaching in Japan and then returned to Kingston where he became editor of *Quarry* magazine. He has also lived in Alberta and British Columbia, and now lives and works as a writer, with his family, in Kingston, Ontario.

Preparing to Read

"Elegy in Stone" is taken from a collection of essays entitled *The Admen Move on Lhasa* (1996). In this essay Steven Heighton relates his visit to the national park and monument at Vimy Ridge in France. Before reading Heighton's essay, think about war and the attitudes toward war. What images are evoked by the terms honour, valour, and bravery? How have attitudes toward war changed with new technologies that change the way wars are fought? How has increased understanding about the psychological effects of war on survivors (e.g., post-traumatic stress syndrome) changed our attitudes about war?

Vimy Ridge, April 1992

The park's entrance—a border crossing, really—was modest 1
enough: a small sign you could easily miss if you were driving past. But we were on foot. And though it turned out to be a
much longer walk than we'd expected, it was a good place to walk,
the fields along the road billowing with mustard, wheat, and poppies, the oaks and maples fragrant with new growth. We could
be in Canada, I thought—then remembered that, for official purposes, we were.

The wind as we neared the ridge grew chilly, the sky grey.   2

Before long the road passed through a forest of natural 3
growth and entered an old plantation of white pines, thick and
towering, a spacious colonnade receding in the gloom. Fences
appeared along the road, then signs warning us not to walk
among the trees where sheep foraged above grassed-in trenches,
shell holes, unexploded mines. In the blue-green, stained-glass
light of the forest, the near-silence was eerie, solemn, as in the
cathedral at Arras.

Finally we heard voices, saw a file of parked cars ahead 4
through the trees and came out at the main exhibit site of the
park, some distance below the monument that crowns Vimy
Ridge. Here, in 1917, from a line of trenches now preserved in
concrete and filled daily with French tourists, the Canadian troops
had launched their attack. Preserved likewise is the first obstacle
they had met: the front-line German trench, barely a grenade's
throw away. This whites-of-their-eyes proximity surprised us
and made stories of verbal fraternization between the lines—of
back and forth banter in broken English and German—all the
more plausible, and poignant.

A few years after the end of the First World War the 5
government of France gave Canada a sizeable chunk of the
cratered, barren terrain around Vimy Ridge, where 20,000
Canadians fell before the ridge was finally taken on 12 April
1917. Today many Canadian visitors to France pass the memorial
park en route to Arras or Lille without realizing the site is
officially a small piece of Canada. Though "plot" might be a
better word, for although the trenches where Canadian and Allied
soldiers lived and died during their siege have healed over, the
fields are scarred with cemeteries and the woodlots filled with
unmarked graves.

We'd arrived the night before in nearby Arras, finding a 6
hotel and visiting the town's medieval cathedral. The hotel
manager had elaborately regretted that we hadn't come two
weeks earlier, on Easter Monday, when French President François
Mitterand and Prime Minister Brian Mulroney and a handful of
Vimy veterans had arrived for the seventy-fifth anniversary of the
ridge's fall. I told the manager that I'd read about the ceremony
back home, but felt the park was probably best experienced
without the crowds and fanfare of an official visit. I could have
said more but didn't trust my French enough to try explaining
how disturbed I'd been by photographs of those heads of states
and their aides beaming glibly among the hunched veterans,
whose nation-building sacrifice was clearly far from the
politicians' minds.

Nation-building sacrifice sounds far too much like the kind of 7
pious, pushy rhetoric I've learned to mistrust and fear, yet for
years the bloody achievement of the Canadians on Vimy Ridge
did stand, like the ridge itself, as a landmark, a high point around
which the idea of a distinct Canadian identity could form.

"C'est magnifique," the manager told us when we explained 8
we wanted to go. "Magnifique."

At the park's main exhibit site we went into a small, 9
undistinguished brick building to see about a tour of the tunnel
system under the trenches. The young guides, in Parks Canada
uniforms, explained that we'd just missed the tour and
unfortunately would have to wait for the next. But as we turned
and went outside to confer, they must have noticed the small
Canadian flag sewn onto my backpack, because one of them
came out after us and beckoned us toward the tunnels. "You
should have told us you're Canadian," he said with a soft
Manitoba-French accent. "We don't get all that many."

The low-ceilinged, labyrinthine "subways"—where men ate 10
and slept before the attack and couriers ran with their messages
and sappers set charges under the German lines—have been
carefully restored, but more or less unembellished. The
impression, as above in the trenches, was sobering. I was relieved
that this sad, clammy underworld had not been brightened up
into some gaudy monument to Our Glorious Past; I was relieved
that it still looked, and felt, like a tomb. It reminded me of the
tunnels of the besieged Huguenots under the cathedral in Arras.

It was good to get back up into the daylight. We agreed to 11
meet Mario and the other guides for a beer that night in town.

We followed the road up the last part of the ridge to the   12
monument, wind blowing over the bare fields in a steady barrage.
Seventy-five years before, the Canadians had advanced at dawn
through driving sleet and snow, and now, nearing the exposed
crown of the ridge, we could see how weather of that intensity
must be quite common. The monument stands atop Hill 145, the
Canadians' final objective and the highest point for miles
around—but on the morning of the attack it must have been
invisible through the snow and the timed barrage behind which
the men were advancing.

Before the hilltop and the monument came in sight I'd felt   13
uneasy, recalling the many monuments I had seen that stylized
or made over the true face of war so as to safeguard an ideology,
to comply with aesthetic conventions, or to make life easier for the
recruiters of future wars. But as we neared the monument—two
enormous white limestone pillars that meet at the base to form a
kind of elongated U—I was impressed. And, as before, relieved.
I'd first become anxious when the hotel keeper had told us to
expect something "magnifique," but now I saw that in a sense
he was right, for here was something magnificent in its simplicity,
its solemnity, its understatement. And brilliant in its implication,
because the pillars did not quite form a triumphant V, as you
might expect, but a shape uncannily resembling the sights
mounted on machine guns of the First World War—the kind that
claimed tens of thousands of Canadian lives in the war and
several thousand on the morning of the attack.

I don't believe such resemblances can be assigned to chance.   14
An artist's hand is always guided in large part by the
subconscious. I don't know whether the architect of the Vimy
monument was ever asked about his intentions, conscious or
subconscious, but in a sense they're no longer the point; unlike so
many other old monuments, Walter Seymour Allward's is
strikingly modern because of the way it surpasses, or second-
guesses, all conventional intent.

We drew closer. Our feeling that this monolith was more a   15
cenotaph, a vast elegy in stone instead of petrified hot air, grew
stronger. And with it a feeling of pride. But a kind of pride very
different, I think, from the tribal, intolerant swagger so many
monuments have been built to inspire. A shy pride in our
country's awkwardness at blowing its own horn—because sooner
or later every country that does blow its own horn, with
flamboyance, starts looking for somebody else to outblow. A

pride in our reluctance—our seeming inability—to canonize
brave, scared, betrayed adolescents as bearded heroes of mythic
dimension, larger than life. Unreal.

And the monument is a cenotaph: we find its base inscribed   16
with the names of the 11,285 Canadians whose final resting place
is unknown. Blown to pieces. Lost in the mud, or buried
anonymously in the graveyards below the ridge. The parade of
names marches on and on, a kind of elegy whose heartbreaking
syllables are English- and French-Canadian, Ojibway, Ukrainian,
Dutch, German, Italian, Japanese ...

Many are the names of our own distant relations.   17

The figures carved on and around the monument, though   18
dated in style, are not blowing trumpets or beating breasts or
drums. They seem instead to grieve. We round the monument
and the Douai Plain fans out below us: another figure, much
larger, cloaked, stands apart at the edge of the monument
overlooking the plain. Behind her a sparely worded inscription,
in English and French, tells of the ridge's fall.

The figure, we will learn later that night, is Canada,   19
"mourning her lost sons."

Tonight in Arras we'll learn other things as well from the   20
Canadian guides we meet for a beer. That the whole park is
planted with shrubs and trees from Canada. That 11,285 pines
were planted after the war for every lost man whose name appears
on the monument. That the prime minister's Easter visit was
indeed a grand and lavish affair—everything the monument itself
is not—but that the old soldiers on display carried themselves
with dignity and a quiet, inconspicuous pride. And it's that feeling
we end up coming back to towards the end of the night when
the drinks have made us a bit more open and, I suppose,
sentimental. Because we learn that these young expatriates have
all felt just as we have about the austerity of the Vimy
monument—and, by implication, the Canadian tendency to
downplay the "heroism" of our achievements, to refuse to idealize,
poeticize, and thus censor an obscene, man-made reality.

Or am I wrong to offer Canada these drunken toasts on a   21
virtue that's largely a matter of historical and political necessity?
Perhaps what I'm trying to say is that Canadians are lucky to
have been spared, so far, that sense of collective power combined
with intense tribal identity that makes every imperial nation so

arrogant, competitive, and brutal. And as our friends guide us
back to our hotel, I wonder if Canadians will ever stop berating
themselves for not believing—as too many other nations have
believed, and keep on believing—that they're better than others,
that they're the chosen, the elect, the Greatest Nation on Earth,
with God on their side.

"Make sure to let people back home know about the   22
memorial," Mario calls out as we enter our hotel. And I reflect
that a visit to the monument and the many battlefields around it
might help convince some Canadians that there are worse things
than uncertainty and understatement.

And if the monument doesn't convince them, or the   23
battlefields, then surely the graveyards will. In the park or within
walking distance lie thirty cemeteries where the remains of over
7,000 Canadians are buried. They are peaceful places,
conscientiously tended. Flowers bloom over every grave. Many
are poppies. The paint on the crosses is fresh, a dazzling white in
the April sun. Here, no doubt, many of the boys whose names
appear on the monument are actually buried, beneath long files
of anonymous crosses, or stones ranked like chairs in a vast,
deserted cathedral. Another endless parade, this time of the
nameless—though here and there we do find stones inscribed
with a name, an age. David Mahon, 1901–1917. IN MEMORY
OF OUR DEAR AND ONLY CHILD.

We recite the words aloud, but this time the feeling they   24
inspire has little to do with pride. The huge limestone gunsight
looms above us on the ridge as we enter yet another aisle, and
read, yet again:

A SOLDIER OF THE GREAT WAR   25
A Canadian Regiment   26
Known Unto God   27

UNDERSTANDING DETAILS

1. What is the significance of Vimy Ridge? Explain why there is a
   park situated here.
2. What does the monument Heighton finds in the park look like?
   Draw a picture of the monument incorporating as many details as possible. When was it built? By whom?
3. What is the role of Mario in Heighton's essay?

ANALYZING MEANING

1. According to Heighton, what aspects of Canada do the monument and park at Vimy Ridge reflect? Does Heighton see these aspects as positive or negative?
2. Why is Heighton glad he missed the Prime Minister's visit?
3. Describe Heighton's reaction to all that he finds at Vimy Ridge. Why is he "relieved that this sad, clammy underworld had not been brightened up into some gaudy monument to Our Glorious Past; I was relieved that it still looked, and felt, like a tomb" (paragraph 10)?

DISCOVERING RHETORICAL STRATEGIES

1. What is the dominant tone of Heighton's essay? How does this tone suit the purpose of the essay?
2. Heighton incorporates many figures of speech into this essay. Find examples of alliteration, metaphor, simile, and personification. What is the effect of each of these on Heighton's essay?
3. While narration is the primary rhetorical strategy used in Heighton's essay, he also writes very descriptively. Find examples in "Elegy in Stone" of particularly vivid descriptive images or passages. How do these enhance Heighton's narration?

MAKING CONNECTIONS

1. Heighton's essay is largely about war and the ways that citizens of different countries view war. Barbara Ehrenreich ("The Ecstasy of War") summarizes different theories about the way wars are waged. What do you think Heighton's "theory of war" would be?
2. Both Steven Heighton and Neil Bissoondath are writing about the national character of Canada and Canadians. Whose view do you agree with more strongly? Why?
3. In "Images of Canada," Laura Millard discusses various portrayals of Canada through different series of banknotes issued between 1935 and 1986. What image or theme for a series of images would effectively convey Heighton's image of Canada? Do you think that Heighton would argue for or against the depiction of the monument at Vimy Ridge on one of Canada's banknotes? Explain your response.

IDEAS FOR DISCUSSION/WRITING

Preparing to Write

Write freely about monuments constructed to remember people or events. What purpose do monuments serve? Who builds them? Who maintains them? What kinds of monuments are public? Which are personal? What monuments are you familiar with? What kinds of emotions do they evoke?

Choosing a Topic

1. Write an essay in which you describe a place that is a good representation of Canada's identity or reflection of values. Link the aspects of the place clearly with the qualities you believe they represent.
2. Write a narrative essay about a visit you have made to some site of historical significance. Why did you go there? What was your predominant impression of this place?
3. Monuments are sometimes built in recognition of people who have been killed in some tragic way. Choose a situation such as a specific natural disaster and then outline, in a descriptive essay, what kind of monument you would design to recognize and remember this person or people.

WEB SITES

 scream.interlog.com/93/heighton.html
You will find some biographical information about Steven Heighton at the Scream in High Park Web site.

 www.swifty.com/twuc/heighton.htm
The Writers Union of Canada has a biography of Steven Heighton.

 www.vac-acc.gc.ca/memorials/vimy/vindex.htm
You can see pictures of the places Heighton describes at this Canadian government site about the Vimy Ridge memorial.

Evelyn Lau
1972–

■ ■ ■

I Sing the Song of My Condo

In *Reference West: A Monthly Review of Books for BC Readers*, Robin Skelton said that each of Lau's books merits "attention for its artistry, its vision, and its pure intelligence." An online profile by Anders Blichfeldt identifies "the soul-mark of Evelyn Lau's writing: poignancy and a sense of deep emotional disorientation, at once subtle and nightmarish." Lau has typically focused her artistry, her vision, and her poignant portrayals of characters and situations on the dark fringes of society but she says, "I have always wanted to move from the 'margin' to the 'centre' in my writing; I want to train my powers of observation and imagery on more 'normal' lives that I have previously been able to chronicle." Perhaps the essay included here is one such attempt to shift to the "centre."

The hard, gritty details of Evelyn Lau's life first became familiar to many with the success of her book, *Runaway: Diary of a Street Kid*, published in 1989. This autobiographical work that was, five years later, made into a television movie, chronicles Lau's experiences as a 14-year-old runaway who became a prostitute and a junkie on the way to becoming a writer. She has since published three books of poetry, including *Oedipal Dreams* (1992)—which made her the youngest nominee ever for the Governor General's Award for poetry—a book of short stories entitled *Fresh Girls and Other Stories* (1983), and a novel, *Other Women* (1985). A collection of six short stories and a novella entitled *Choose Me* is scheduled for publication in 1999.

Preparing to Read

This article from *The Globe and Mail* in June of 1995 appeared in a column entitled "Middle-Class Dreams." From Lau's previous work she might not seem an obvious choice as a writer for this column, but here Lau relates an experience familiar to many middle-class Canadians: that of purchasing her first home. It may be fitting that this piece comes from a writer who first made her mark writing about running away from home.

Here Lau explains why she decided to take this step, pulls us through the range of emotions that she experienced, and introduces us to the variety of people who decorated the path to eventual home ownership. The rough and marginal characters of much of Lau's work are replaced here by the Vancouver real estate agents and young married couples with new babies whose lives cross hers in her search for a place in the carefree "world of mortgage brochures."

Before reading about Lau's experience, think about buying a home and the dream of home ownership that dominates many lives. What role do real estate agents play in the search for a home? How does a real estate agent differ from a salesperson selling you any other product or service? What image do you have of real estate agents? If you have ever purchased a home, what about the process stands out in your mind?

■_____■

Late in the spring of last year, my fancy turned to thoughts of real estate and I joined the growing ranks of Canadians in their 20s who were looking for their first homes. 1

I had been a renter since I was 16 and I never wanted to deal with a landlord again. Instead, I wanted to know what it was like to worry if I spilled wine on my carpet, to agonize over the exact placement of a picture before pounding a nail in my wall, to open a closet door or rest my forehead against a kitchen cabinet and think, "I own this." 2

I went to the bank with a bundle of tax returns under my arm to prequalify for a first mortgage. After a long meeting during which the bank manager and I peered morosely at a computer screen and juggled numbers for savings, RRSPs and a writer's erratic income into a yearly figure, I walked out with a brochure titled Information for First Home-buyers in my hand. 3

The people depicted in the brochures were not like anyone I knew. The women were blond, with sunny smiles, and their husbands looked both chiselled and paternal. They were engaged in chummy family activities, like washing the dog or puttering in the garden, with the help of their model children. A white picket fence stood in soft focus in the background. 4

I knew then I wanted to live in the world of the mortgage brochures, which never showed these middle-class people lying awake among twisted sheets in their new master bedrooms or throwing up into their ceramic sinks from panic at hefty mortgages and rising interest rates. I wanted to sing the love song of the middle class. I wanted this to be the song of myself—a litany of mortgage payments and car payments, the weeping and gnashing at tax time, maximum RRSP payments and mutual funds, credit cards and credit's twin, debt. 5

Laura Cavanagh, the real-estate agent I acquired through a friend's connections, was an outgoing woman with tanned skin, long hair and hips so slim it seemed impossible she had two 6 teenaged children. The male realtors we met in front of apartment buildings always held her hand for a beat too long and fastened their eyes upon hers with much intent and private meaning.

Together we toured a depressing number of 500-square-foot 7 one-bedrooms listed by young married couples who had just had their first baby. Their apartments smelled of sour milk and spoiled food, and in the bedrooms a crib took up whatever space the double bed did not already occupy. The vendor's agent would gamely point out that new carpets weren't that expensive, really, and if I enlisted the help of friends I could easily strip away the velvet-textured and dung-coloured wallpaper. He would flick on all the light switches and then exclaim, "And look at how bright this unit is!"

I became increasingly dejected at what my savings could 8 afford in Vancouver, when I knew the same amount could buy a house, with acreage attached, in Saskatoon. Laura, however, remained true to her business card's slogan—"The realtor with a positive attitude"—and came to my apartment several times a week to show me yet another suite.

Over the months I grew fond of her. She was different from 9 some of the other agents we encountered, who drove gold Mercedes and who staggered about in high heels and silk scarves, arrived late for appointments and then whipped us through the apartment while their pagers and cell phones incessantly beeped and rang. Laura held my hand when I made my first offer—and my second, third and fourth, all unsuccessfully—and comforted me after I had spent another sleepless night over interest-rate calculations.

As summer passed into fall, I discovered that acquiring a 10 real-estate agent was like acquiring a stray kitten or a runaway child—it was a lifetime commitment. She reminded me of little Gertrude in John Cheever's *The Country Husband*, with her uncanny knack of showing up in places I did not expect. I would open my front door on a Saturday morning to pick up the paper and there she would be, showered and perfumed, standing in the hallway and proffering the latest figures on a suite in which I had expressed a moment's interest. See, here's its sales history, its current assessment. Would I like to see it in 15 minutes? She would be wearing such a brave smile that I could only admire her and never find it in my heart to turn her away.

Meanwhile, my friends, who were older and therefore 11 wealthier, were actually buying places. I went to a friend's house-warming party with a smile of congratulations on my face and envy in my heart. My former foster parent bought a penthouse with 12-foot ceilings in a new building; another friend purchased an actual house with the help of his well-off parents. I went to a cocktail party at his parents' home, where a hundred guests fit neatly into the kitchen. I was surrounded by half a dozen empty bedrooms, Jacuzzis and soaker tubs and murderous chandeliers in the marble foyer. Resentment blazed in me.

Now when I walked the streets of Vancouver, I glared up at   12 the high windows of the condominiums and felt the owners were not as special as me, nor as deserving. When I gave poetry readings, I looked out at the audience and wondered how many of them owned their own homes. It came to me that I had rarely wanted anything this much before.

One afternoon Laura took me to the opening of a converted   13 building where she said the suites were priced below market value. Balloons were tied to the gates and hedges, and dozens of would-be buyers stood about the grounds, gazing up at the suites with their brochures shielding their eyes.

The display suite was bustling with activity—realtors wearing   14 suits and flustered smiles, the women with green eye-shadow and trailing a scent of White Shoulders. They paced back and forth with their clients, pulling out calculators to demonstrate price per square foot and the amount of monthly payments. Even as I sat there, someone called out that suite 312 had just been sold and 105 down the hall, and they were expecting an offer on 210.

The cell phones rang and rang and the anxiety of the buyers   15 became a frenzy of panic. It was a fever that sparked smiles on the faces of the realtors. Offers were recklessly written, and a slim-waisted woman in a floral dress who represented the financing company stepped forward to give or withhold her approval.

I was tempted by the display suite, which was small but fully   16 renovated, boasting a marble fireplace and slate tiles. Loden wallpaper in the bathroom was printed with female Greek statues clutching scraps of fabric to their breasts. I realized that the suite was a good bargain, but as I sat on the rented leather couch I found I could not pull out my chequebook and write an offer, not without at least a night's reflection.

"In all good conscience, I can say you aren't going to lose   17 money on this one," Laura said, but I was immobilized with terror. An hour later she drove me home. I spent the evening drinking heavily and calculating my finances.

The suite was priced within my range, and by the light of   18
morning I had decided I would make my move. I went back to
the suite where I had sat on the couch and looked around my
new home—this was where I would put my desk, my bed. I
approached the sales agent—a beefy, blond man with a distracted
air and an incessantly warbling pager—and said I would buy
the display suite.

"Oh. That was sold yesterday," the man said, already turning   19
away.

I surprised myself with my own reaction—it was grief. I very   20
nearly heard the crack of my heart breaking. This was not the
relief I felt when one of my previous offers had fallen through;
this was my *home* being taken away.

I stumbled out in a daze and walked the three kilometres   21
home, wiping away tears with the back of my hand the whole
way. It seemed my song would be a different one after all, it
would be the song of Rainer Maria Rilke's *Autumn Day*:
"Whoever has no house now will never have one." It was all
very well for Rilke—he had owned houses. He had written his
famous elegies while staying in Princess Marie von Thurn and
Taxis-Hohenloe's castle. I wished bankruptcy, illness and death
upon whoever had bought my suite.

What surprised me for weeks afterward was how entirely   22
alike this feeling of bereftness was to losing the person you love.
Somehow the real, intelligent, sensible desire to buy a first home
and stop paying rent had mutated over the months into an
obsession that was like a woman's obsession for a man who had
deserted her, whom she could love only at a distance.

When I slept I was tortured by dreams in which I walked   23
through beautiful apartments that were within my price range,
then just as I pulled out my chequebook I would wake up. Several
times I dreamed I bought an apartment with three balcony doors
but no balconies, and I knew that one day I would open the
doors, step out and fall to my death. In another, I had just moved
into a new condominium and discovered that with the removal
of the previous owner's furniture and pictures, I could see that the
walls were pocked with holes the size of my fist.

Over the course of a year, my realtor and I saw 50 suites. I sat   24
on 50 strangers' sofas, looked into their cupboards, sniffed inside
their refrigerators, inspected their drapes and light switches. I
checked the drains in their balconies and flushed their toilets. I

looked for my own books on their bookshelves and was dismayed
by the rows of American bestsellers or educational texts I found
there. I peered into their closets and discovered if the owners were
people who shopped in vintage stores or Sears or Holt Renfrew.

Once I saw the apartment of a little old lady whose obsession 25
was turtles—troops of ceramic, glass and jade turtles filed across
every available counter and desktop. She owned an aquarium
of turtles, posters of turtles, a bedspread with a turtle stitched
on it.

After 12 months of searching, I no longer believed I would 26
purchase anything soon. I had visions of my realtor and me setting
out at the turn of the millennium to look at our 300th suite.

When at last I found the right place, it happened so suddenly 27
that the frustrations of the year vanished overnight. I went to an
open house on Sunday and on the Monday Laura presented my
offer. It was accepted that afternoon. She stopped by to give me
the news and when she came down the hallway her eyes were
shining.

"You have a home now," she said.   28

The rest of the week flashed by in a blur of telephone calls 29
and meetings with the bank manager. I signed contracts, read
by-laws and city council meeting minutes and certified deposit
cheques. It was so stressful that I felt disconnected from reality.
I vacillated between happiness, numb panic and a great, swelling
pride. I had never been in debt for anything before, had never
even owned a car or a computer, and now here I was committing
myself to a $100,000 mortgage for 650 square feet. I had made a
decision that was going to affect the rest of my life.

I take possession of the suite at the end of June, just days 30
before my 24th birthday. I may never sleep again. But at last I'm
a homeowner.

UNDERSTANDING DETAILS

1. Why has Lau decided to purchase a home at this stage in her
   life?
2. Describe Lau's feelings about the process of purchasing her
   first home. How does Lau react to the prospect of this commitment?
3. Describe Laura Cavanagh. How is she different from the other
   real estate agents?

ANALYZING MEANING

1. How does Lau characterize the real estate sales people she meets as she searches for her home? Why does she give us these details about them?
2. What does Lau believe that home ownership will bring to her life? In your opinion, is she being realistic?
3. What are the effects on Lau of this experience of purchasing a home? Contrast Lau's reactions to discovering that the display suite was already sold, and her actual purchase.

DISCOVERING RHETORICAL STRATEGIES

1. Explain the title of Lau's essay. Where in her essay is the idea of a song repeated?
2. Identify the details that Lau has chosen that particularly effectively *show* you her experience rather than *tell* about it?
3. Where does Lau use figurative language to help convey her experience vividly to her readers?

MAKING CONNECTIONS

1. In "I Sing the Song of My Condo," Lau references two other writers, John Cheever and Rainer Maria Rilke, and also tells her readers about her reaction to the books on the shelves of the 50 strangers whose homes she looked at. How do you think Lau would respond to Fulford's essay about the importance of literature?
2. Karen Connelly ("Touch the Dragon") and Evelyn Lau each experienced initial success with the publication of first-hand accounts of their teenage experiences and have since gone on to publish books of poetry. What aspects of their essays reflect their poetic interests?
3. One of Natalie Goldberg's ("The Rules of Writing Practice") rules for writers is to "be specific" (paragraph 16). Has Lau followed this rule? Give specific examples to support your answer.

IDEAS FOR DISCUSSION/WRITING

Preparing to Write

Write freely about the biggest purchase you have ever made. Like Lau, this might have been a home, or it might have been a car, a computer, a college or university education, a stereo, or a special outfit. What motivated you to make this purchase? How did you feel at the time? Did you save money beforehand or did you buy on credit and pay off the debt later? Would you make the same choices about your purchase if you had it to do over again?

Choosing a Topic

1. Lau tells us that in 1994 she "joined the growing ranks of Canadians in their 20s who were looking for their first homes." Write an article for your college/university or community newspaper in which you explain to young Canadians the advantages of owning a home over renting. What motivations to purchase can you supply that will outweigh the hesitation that most people feel about making such a large financial commitment?

2. Before becoming a homeowner, Lau describes the extreme disappointment she felt when the display suite she decided to purchase was no longer available. Write an essay in which you describe a major disappointment that you have experienced at some time in your life. What anticipation led up to this disappointment? What went wrong? How did you deal with the letdown when your hopes or expectations were not fulfilled?

3. Is home ownership a realistic dream for most young Canadians? Write an essay in which you argue either that Lau's experience is one within the reach of others like herself, or that it is an unreachable dream for most of her peers.

WEB SITES

www.mwsolutions.com/canlit/authors/lau.asp
You can find biographical information about Evelyn Lau in the Northwest Passages profile by Anders Blichfeldt at this site.

www.globeandmail.ca
The Globe and Mail is the source of Lau's essay.

www.vancouverstyle.com/thearts/lau.html
Oana Avasilichioaei's interview with Evelyn Lau can be found here.

www.nt.sympatico.ca/Features/Books/lau.html
Evelyn Lau's book recommendations can be found at this site.

Brian Lewis

■■■

Teeth

Originally from Wales, Brian Lewis came to Canada for a year of peace and quiet, and stayed. After working as a high school teacher in Wales, Lewis began teaching in British Columbia and then moved to Baffin Island in 1963 to teach English as a second language.

In 1968 Lewis published an arctic reading series in Inuktitut, the Inuit language, and in 1970 he completed his M.A. thesis at the University of Toronto on teaching English to Canadian "Eskimos." More recently Lewis served two terms as a member of the Legislative Assembly of the Northwest Territories. Lewis writes as a hobby to keep himself amused and occupied. Other articles by Lewis about life in the north have appeared in *Up Here*, where this piece was found.

Preparing to Read

"Teeth" appeared first in *Up Here* magazine in 1990. Brian Lewis relates a story from just after World War II about an aged Inuit hunter's experiences with Canadian bureaucracy. Ottochie, the main character, had a straightforward solution to the problem of losing his teeth. His dentures became the focus of fascination to representatives of medicine, religion, law enforcement, business, and the army. Ottochie's reactions to his new city-made dentures puzzles his audience of officials as well. As you read Lewis's account of the incident and its resolution, consider your own reactions to governments and other dispensers of "rules and regulations." How often are the authorities' judgments "a good fit"? How much or how little do most Canadians know about Northern Aboriginal People? How many assumptions do we make based on ignorance of our own country and its varied peoples? How often are native people seen as "museum artifacts" or media stereotypes?

■_____■

In Norman Wells this past winter, Ipellie Kilabuk, the MLA from Pangnirtung, complained to the Legislative Assembly of the Northwest Territories about the declining quality of dentures supplied through the Northern Health Service.   1

Joe Arlooktoo, MLA from Lake Harbour, agreed with him.   2

It seems dentists nowadays no longer provide their patients with heavy-duty false teeth, which Inuit need to masticate large   3 quantities of meat. Even moderate chewing pressure makes today's dentures crack.

The two experienced legislators from Nunavut wondered 4 whether young dentists assume Northern diets now consist exclusively of Kraft dinner.

A story that dates from the early years of dental practice on 5 Baffin Island suggests diet has too often been ignored in the design of Northern dentures.

During the Second World War, the sea often threw pieces of 6 metal flotsam onto the Arctic shore. One summer an old hunter named Ottochie, who was sadly lacking in teeth, found a promising piece of aluminum on a beach in Foxe Strait. With infinite care, he carved himself a set of dentures from the metal.

This was at a time when all ships had been pressed into war 7 duty and Northern supply and service had been reduced to a trickle. But after the war the Government of Canada resumed its Arctic patrol, checking into the health and living conditions of the Inuit. When the *Nascopie* arrived at Cape Dorset fresh from its triumphs on the Murmansk run, there was a young dentist aboard. He set directly to work.

One of the cabins in the *Nascopie* had been fixed up as a 8 dentist's office. Passengers, including an Anglican missionary, a Bay clerk, a Mountie and a retired colonel were sitting around the edge of the cabin like villagers watching a road repair gang at work.

The dentist whirled Ottochie around in the antique dentist's 9 chair, holding the gleaming jaws ajar for everyone to see.

"Beautiful set," exclaimed the missionary, who had never 10 been heard to utter a discouraging word.

"Must have taken a long wee while to make," added the Bay 11 clerk, in his cautious, ever-calculating manner.

Through an interpreter, the dentist explained how he would 12 make Ottochie a proper set of dentures. But he really had to have those home-made ones.

Reluctantly, Ottochie parted with his teeth and grimaced at 13 the thought of gumming it through a long Arctic winter.

The young dentist promised he'd return with some real 14 dentures the following August. Ottochie said he'd be waiting.

To the watching passengers, it was a wonderful thing to see 15 the State once more assuming its proper responsibilities.

"Here," declared the ever-practical Mountie, handing 16 Ottochie a black-handled pen knife. "You're going to have to cut your walrus real small."

Ottochie shook hands with everyone in the cabin and left.   17

A year later, almost to the day, the *Nascopie* anchored off   18
Kingait. Ottochie kayaked over to the ship, anxious to get his
teeth. He was the first patient into the dentist's chair. Again there
was a fringe of inquisitive passengers in the cabin, though none
of them knew the history of Ottochie's teeth: they just hung
around like gossips in a corner store, waiting to hear something
sensational.

When the young dentist revealed with a flourish the finest   19
dentures money could buy, the passengers sensed they were
witnessing something special. They ooh'd and aah'd at the
blushing pink gums and the dainty porcelain sheen of the teeth.

Ottochie also sensed the occasion as the dentist stood over   20
him holding the dentures like an Archbishop holding a coronet
waiting to crown him king. The fringe of passengers moved
strategically closer.

"There," said the dentist, inserting the dentures. "How does   21
that feel?"

"Qannohitppa?" the missionary asked Ottochie.   22

"Taikoa piuniqsaulausingmamatik," responded Ottochie,   23
clearly distraught.

"What did he say?" asked the dentist querulously, fearing   24
the worst.

"The ones he used to have were better."   25

"Oh," said the dentist, devastated. He motioned Ottochie to   26
open his mouth and smile into a small hand-held mirror.

Ottochie obliged, but it was a glum smile. He gave a mutter   27
only the missionary could understand.

"He wants his old teeth back," said the missionary. "Where   28
are they?"

"In the Smithsonian," gulped the dentist. "In the United   29
States. For the world to see."

There was a brief exchange between Ottochie and the   30
missionary.

"What was that about?" asked the dentist, his anxiety turning   31
to suspicion.

"Ottochie can't imagine why people would go all the way   32
to the United States just to see a set of false teeth on a shelf. He
says teeth should be in a mouth."

The dentist shrugged.   33

Ottochie carefully extracted the dentures from his mouth 34
and returned them to the young dentist. The gesture held
profound sadness. He moved among the passengers, shaking
hands. Then he began wandering around the cabin, examining
windows and cupboards.

"He's reluctant to leave," observed the dentist. 35

"I do believe he's looking for another piece of metal," said the 36
missionary. "Something malleable."

UNDERSTANDING DETAILS

1. What was Ottochie's response to the type and quality of dentures supplied to him? Why would the dentist find it necessary to replace the hunter's handmade set?
2. Why is it necessary for the Northern Health Service to supply a different type of false teeth to inhabitants of the Arctic?
3. How do people's differing reactions to Ottochie's aluminum teeth compare to the hunter's responses to the professionally made dentures?

ANALYZING MEANING

1. Why is the young dentist so determined to take away Ottochie's aluminum dentures? Does his estimated replacement date of "the following August" seem reasonable?
2. What does Ottochie's opinion about the proper place for a set of false teeth tell you about the Inuit approach to life?
3. What does Ottochie's ritual gesture of handshaking at the end of the two meetings suggest about both the meetings and about the hunter's innate sense of behaviour?

DISCOVERING RHETORICAL STRATEGIES

1. What is the writer's purpose in relating a story he did not experience personally? Why do you think that he begins with more contemporary statements from Native Canadian politicians?
2. Which descriptive details best illustrate the author's sympathies? How are Ottochie's reactions described? How are those of the observers described?
3. Lewis tells Ottochie's story in a two-part anecdote divided by a year's passage of real time. Which aspects of the two parts of

the story are similar, or parallel, and which differ? Why? What device links the beginning and end of the essay?

MAKING CONNECTIONS

1. Brian Lewis opens his essay with an anecdote about the needs of Inuit people being ignored by the Northern Health Services. How is this similar to the stories Armstrong ("P4W") tells of the native women in Kingston's Prison for Women?
2. Cecil Foster ("Why Blacks Get Mad") writes about preconceived notions affecting people's behaviour and attitudes. How do the preconceived ideas of the young dentist affect the way he treats Ottochie? What would Foster say about the treatment of Ottochie in this essay?
3. Charlotte Gray ("The Temple of Hygiene") and Brian Lewis both incorporate languages other than English into their essays although it is unlikely that the majority of their readers will understand Inuktitut or Japanese. What is the purpose of this technique? Do you find it effective? Why or why not?

IDEAS FOR DISCUSSION/WRITING

Preparing to Write

How have government legislation or bureaucratic rules made your life more difficult, or easier, and why? Have you ever felt that a judgment or rule that originated in the government or some other policy-setting body made no sense to a situation in your own life? Did you believe that such rules may have been created without any consultation of those most directly concerned? Whose welfare seems to be at stake in the situations where you find such regulations to be impediments?

Choosing a Topic

1. For your college newspaper, write a narrative article describing a mix-up or misunderstanding in your own life that involved dealing with authority figures and rules. Describe and evaluate your reaction to the results of your dilemma as they affected your life.
2. Write a narrative essay in the form of a letter to your Member of Parliament that explains why you feel that government-

sponsored health care is a good or a bad thing. Use examples taken from your or your family's lives to show why you feel as you do.

3. Write a letter to an imagined penpal in a different part of Canada, in which you explain aspects of your everyday life which you believe that the reader would find different or re-markable. Why have you chosen such incidents or behaviour? How would they differ from things "normal" to an inhabitant of another region?

WEB SITES

 arcticcircle.uconn.edu/
The Arctic Circle Home Page.

Karen Connelly
1969–

■ ■ ■

Touch the Dragon

In 1993, at the age of 24, Karen Connelly won the Governor General's Award for nonfiction for *Touch the Dragon: A Thai Journal*, an account of a year she spent in Thailand as an exchange student. This book spent several months on the best-seller lists and has been reprinted six times. Connelly has also published three books of poetry: *The Small Words in My Body* (1990), for which she won the Pat Lowther Memorial Award, *This Brighter Prison: A Book of Journeys* (1993) and *The Disorder of Love* (1997). Connelly's recent work, *One Room in a Castle: Letters from Spain, France & Greece* (1995), again recounts her travels, this time in the Mediterranean. She has also served as writer in residence at Okanagan University College, the University of New Brunswick, and the University of British Columbia's Green College. Karen Connelly now lives in Greece and is working on a novel, entitled *Dawn Without Breaking*, about the life of a Burmese songwriter who has been imprisoned for political reasons.

Preparing to Read

Karen Connelly wrote *Touch the Dragon* as an account of her year in Thailand as a Rotary Club exchange student when she was 17. The excerpt here comes from the beginning of her book and describes her arrival in Thailand and her initial impressions of the land, the people, and the culture. Connelly describes it as "a record of living in a place that awakened every possibility of growth in me." Before reading this selection think about what you know of Thailand. What images come to mind? What associations do you have with this part of the world? Have you ever had the experience of travelling to a culture far different from your own? What parts of that experience stand out in your memory?

A ugust 21, 1986

Leaving Canada. A view of the body of mountains: deep   1
sockets of aquamarine, blue veins slipping over cliff-sides, stone
edges splintering from the earth like cracked bones.

When I think of the span of countries, when I run my fingers   2
over the skin of a map, I get dizzy. I am too high up now—I
should have glided into this journey on a boat. As the country

pulls out from under me, I overturn like a glass on a yanked table-cloth, I spill. Land steadies people, holds them, even if they imagine they control it. Land owns and defines us. Without it, we become something else.

After refuelling in Kyoto, we are moving again, rising into 3 another time zone, another time. These are the first pages of a new country. There's almost nothing to write yet because I know so little. I can't even imagine where I'm going. I am utterly alone, a small bit of dust blown into Asia's deep green eye. I lean against the glass and gaze down at an emerald flood, knowing I'll never be able to soak up such radiance. It's a colour I never knew I'd see, the astonishing canvas of a dream, undreamed.

At the airport in Bangkok, a bald foreigner lugs three gallons 4 of water on his shoulder. He explains to suspicious customs officials that he has brought water from home because the water here is unsafe. There is laughter, a waving of dark arms and pale palms. I stumble through customs, crippled by luggage and jet lag. One English word rings out: taxi. The world is a wet braid of heat and flesh, glimpses of gold-studded teeth, shirts open to shining bellies, purple tattoos, wreaths of jasmine. Above the horde of cab drivers looms a hand-painted sign warning all tourists to beware of thieves, illicit business deals, drugs and fake gems. The air slides over me thick as honey. I have never felt such tropical warmth before.

Then I see a cardboard sign with my name on it bobbing up 5 in the crowd. Someone has come to get me. Someone has come to take me (farther) away.

August 22

We are driving northwards under black clouds, through 6 darkness broken by lightning. I could believe now that the earth is flat, and its far edges are sparking flame. Rice fields, tree groves, gleaming oval ponds flash out of the night. Mr. Prasit Piyachinda and Mr. Prasert Jeenanukulwong have both suggested I call them *paw* for the sake of simplicity. Paw Prasit speaks English. "We will treat you like a daughter, and you will treat us like father." The Rotary Club of Denchai has almost twenty members. I can't pronounce any of their names. "You must learn to speak Thai very quickly," Paw Prasit explains. "It will not be difficult. No one in your family speaks English. You have no choice." He turns around to smile at me. He talks about spicy food, a famous Buddhist monk who is also a great fortune-teller, the school I will go to, the people who are anxious to meet me. When I ask why these people want to meet me, he giggles. "Why, because you are a falang." A foreigner. It is my first Thai word.

Sudden light spears the heavy rain. I squint out the streaming   7
windows. The men laugh at my fascination with the countryside. "Are you afraid of the ... the ..."

"The lightning," I finish for Paw Prasit.   8

"Ah, yes, yes, are you afraid of it? My daughter, yes, is. She   9
will not look at fields at night, fields of rain." He points towards a distant clump of trees and taps at the window. "Dragons. She says they are dragons." He laughs, turns to Prasert, translates, they laugh again, then hoot more at some other joke. I peer through the glass; his daughter is right. There they are, tree-dragons, moulded by wind and shadow, heavy-skulled dinosaurs gathered under lightning at the edges of ponds. They lean down to the water, their scaled flanks gleaming with rain.

I fall asleep, sliding down onto the seat, listening to Paw   10
Prasit say, "And people will call you falang in the street because at first they will not know your name." I will be the only white person in the town. "You will be popular. Also there is a green fruit in Thailand called falang and when you eat it, everyone will laugh and say 'Falang eat falang. Hahaha. Ha ha.'" Again he translates for Paw Prasert (why are their names so similar?) and both men slap their knees at this hilarious play on words. I keep missing the jokes in everything, possibly because I'm so tired. What time is it here? What time is it in Canada? Canada? The word sounds funny. I slump down farther on the seat and listen to wheels humming and my guardians speaking Thai. It is indecipherable birdsong. They talk on, their voices climbing and sliding down the banisters of five tones and strange letters. This is not comparable to high school French.

Suddenly, inexplicably, they are standing outside the car   11
and calling me. "Kalen, Kalen, to bathroom now. We are in Phitsanulok. For pee-pee." The door is opened for me. I receive a handful of toilet paper and a gentle push in the right direction. I am disoriented, eyes salted with sleep. The young men hanging about the gas pumps stare and stare.

Once I am in the dark little washroom, reality swarms; the   12
pungent odour of urine burns the dreamy quality out of everything. I lose my footing on the wet edges of the Thai toilet and laugh, imagining the embarrassment of breaking my ankle in a toilet the very first day. This is Thailand, the land of smiles,

the Venice of the Orient, the pearl of Asia. The travel-agency phrases run off my tongue as mosquitoes settle on my thighs, arms, neck. Are they malarial or harmless? A few dark stains move up and down the walls, and my skin shivers, waiting for invasions.

Walking back across the lot, I notice small reddish lights 13 glowing behind a cage with thin bars. I walk towards them, curious, moving closer, closer, stretching out my hand ... Paw Prasit yells, "No, no!" but it's too late. All I do is touch the bars and half a dozen gibbons leap shrieking towards my hand.

I scream at their screams, the gas-station attendants come 14 loping across the lot and my Thai fathers rush forward to pull me away. I apologize to everyone. The gibbons are the ones making the fuss. Their furious bodies spring and bounce inside the cage. "You must learn to be careful, Kalen." Paw Prasit takes my arm, his glasses steamed with worry. "There are snakes, too. You know?" He stares at me for a moment, then laughs and says something in Thai, which makes Paw Prasert laugh, too. Even the gas-pumpers giggle and kick a few pebbles, looking up at me even though their heads are lowered. I open the car door and crawl in. When we drive away, the boys wave us off. I stare back at the neon lights of the station for a long time, the savage human faces of the monkeys still vivid in my mind.

We reach Denchai in the dark, so I see little, other than dogs 15 running through the beams of the headlights, barely making it. We finally stop at the last building on the street. "Liquor store," Paw Prasit says. "This is the liquor store of Paul Prasert. This is where you'll live." Prasert is already out of the car and up on a bench, stretching to press a door buzzer. As soon as his finger flexes, I hear barking and the rattling slap of a chain. The dog inside the building hurls itself against the metal door. We wait until the dog begins to whimper, then hear an old man's grunt and sniffle. There's a clatter of keys and a frightening roar of phlegm from the recesses of a throat; finally the door scrapes open along the cement floor. A balding old man beams at us. His skin is the colour and texture of a walnut, he is toothless and he wears nothing but a baggy pair of black satin trousers. Prasit says to me, "Old father is much blind." After awkward introductions, the three of them begin to speak in Thai. I smile and smile. Before coming in with us, the old man shuffles to the road and vigorously spits a small chunk of his lung into the gutter.

Inside the shop, the German shepherd once again begins to   16
bark and strain against her chain. Her lips are pulled back over
yellow teeth. Paw Prasert grins proudly, pulls up some long-
forgotten vestige of English and yells over the barking, "My
dog!" I smile back, nod. Paw Prasit adds, "But no worry, it not
hurt you." She leaps toward us again, only to be choked back
by the chain. After the old man hits her on the nose, she
whimpers and slumps to the ground, chin between her paws.
We walk deeper into the liquor store, past piles of dusty crates,
a display of Thai whisky, a television, an old desk piled with
newspapers and small bags of rice. Each of the men has one of my
suitcases and is breathing audibly under its weight, insisting
how light it is. We come to a small fridge. Paw Prasert opens it
and whispers to Paw Prasit, who turns to me. "He say you take
anything you want, you are like a daughter to him. You know?"

Thanking them, I glance into the fridge. It's full of water   17
bottles and a few pots of murky sauces or oil paints.

Up one staircase: bathroom, sister's room, children's room.   18
Paw Prasert's room. The top of another staircase brings us to an
uninhabited floor. The one bedroom is for me. "You have room
all to self." I am smiling, smiling my thanks. Now the men turn
to leave. Yes, yes, see you tomorrow, to begin learning Thai, to
begin learning, tomorrow, yes.

And the door closes. I look around: a low bed of cushions, a   19
child's desk, a small mirror, a woven straw chair. Green curtains,
green bedspread. A stark naked Thai girl with an erotic smile
stares down from a picture on the wall. This smile—she must be
kidding—does the trick. I sit on the edge of the bed, hug my
elbows and sob for everything that isn't here. I think of the
hundreds of days, the thousands of hours I have to stay here.
Everything I understand, everything I own is buried in my skull,
intangible. I am not feeling particularly brave. I'm sniffling, alone
but for a Thai porn queen and three beaten-up suitcases. This
does not feel exotic. Around me, the pool of night trembles with
crickets and frogs, breaks with the distant bark of dogs, and
slowly, slowly, closes over my head.

UNDERSTANDING DETAILS

1. To what country has Connelly come to live? What part of this
   country will she be staying in? How did she get there from
   Canada?

2. What language does Connelly need to learn in her new home? What is the first word that she learns?
3. Animals and insects figure largely in Connelly's initial impressions of Thailand. List the various creatures she sees in her first two days and explain how she reacts to them.

ANALYZING MEANING

1. What are Karen Connelly's feelings about the place where she has come to live? Do they change from August 21 to August 22? In what ways?
2. Explain why Connelly says the word Canada, in paragraph 10, sounds funny.
3. How does Connelly react to the climate and the land in Thailand? Give specific examples of the details that recreate her experience of each so vividly.

DISCOVERING RHETORICAL STRATEGIES

1. The use of figurative language is one of the qualities that makes Connelly's narrative distinctive and memorable. Find specific examples of similes and metaphors that contribute to her vivid description.
2. Connelly frequently mentions the colours in this new land she has come to. What colour predominates? Cite the specific places where she mentions it. What other colours contribute to her image of Thailand?
3. Connelly's description of her Thai adventure originated as a collection of letters and journal entries that were later edited for her book, *Touch the Dragon*. The dedication at the front of the book says, "This book is for the people of Thailand ..." Who is her intended audience?

MAKING CONNECTIONS

1. Karen Connelly and Charlotte Gray ("The Temple of Hygiene") both write about travelling to an Asian country. How are their experiences similar? Have your travel experiences been more like Gray's or more like Connelly's?
2. Seven rules for writing are outlined in Natalie Goldberg's essay ("The Rules of Writing Practice"). Which of these rules has Connelly followed? Given that this selection comes from an

edited, published work, is it possible to evaluate it against all of Goldberg's rules? Which ones work and which ones don't?

IDEAS FOR DISCUSSION/WRITING

Preparing to Write

Brainstorm or make a list of the trips you've taken in your life. What are the first words and thoughts and feelings that come to mind about each? Are there connections between any of these patterns of words? What ideas or sensations appear frequently in your prewriting exercise? Would you try to experience any of these things on future travels? Do you enjoy travelling? How much do you enjoy new and different experiences? What sorts of things do we learn from travelling?

Choosing a Topic

1. Recall a time when you faced a significant new experience. Write a narrative essay in which you recreate the events and your feelings about them for your audience.
2. Choose a trip, real or imagined, and write a promotional article for your college newspaper about it. What might make readers want to visit your location(s), and why? How can you best make your ideal holiday appealing to this audience?
3. Connelly's book began as a series of journal entries and letters detailing her day-to-day experiences. Write an essay in which you discuss why people keep journals. What kind of information goes into journal entries? How does journal writing differ from letter writing or essay writing?

WEB SITES

scream.interlog.com/96/connelly.html
Connelly performed at the Scream in High Park in 1998.

www.swifty.com/lc/linktext/direct/connelly.htm
Connelly is a member of the Canadian League of Poets.

www.lonelyplanet.com.au/dest/sea/thai.htm
Learn more about Thailand at the Lonely Planet site.

CHAPTER 3

EXAMPLE

■ ■ ■

Illustrating Ideas

Citing an example to help make a point is one of the most instinctive techniques we use in communication. If, for instance, you state that being an internationally ranked tennis player requires constant practice, a friend might challenge that assertion and ask what you mean by "constant practice." When you respond "about three hours a day," your friend might ask for more specific proof. At this stage in the discussion, you could offer the following illustrations to support your statement: When not on tour, Martina Hingis practises three hours per day; Pete Sampras, four hours; and Michael Chang, two hours. Your friend's doubt will have been answered through your use of examples.

Defining Examples

Well-chosen examples and illustrations are an essay's building blocks. They are drawn from your experience, your observations, and your reading. They help you *show* rather than *tell* what you mean, usually by supplying concrete details (references to what we can see, smell, taste, hear, or touch) to support abstract ideas (such as faith, hope, understanding, and love), by providing specifics ("I like chocolate") to explain generalizations ("I like sweets"), and by giving definite references ("Turn left at the second stoplight") to clarify vague statements ("Turn in a few blocks"). Though illustrations take many forms, writers often find themselves indebted to description or narration (or some combination of the two) in order to supply enough relevant examples to achieve their rhetorical intent.

As you might suspect, examples are important ingredients in producing exciting, vivid prose. Just as crucial is the fact that carefully chosen examples often encourage your readers to feel one way or another about an issue being discussed. If you tell your parents, for instance, that living in a college dormitory is not conducive to academic success, they may doubt your word, perhaps thinking that you are simply attempting to coerce money out of them for an apartment. You can help dispel this notion, however, by giving them specific examples of the chaotic nature of dorm life: the party down the hall that broke up at 2 a.m. when you had a chemistry exam that same morning at 8 o'clock; the stereo next door that seems to be stuck on its highest decibel level at all hours of the day and night; and the new "friend" you recently acquired who thinks you are the best listener in the world—especially when everyone else has the good sense to be asleep. After such a detailed and well-documented explanation, your parents could hardly deny the strain of this difficult environment on your studies. Examples can be very persuasive.

The following paragraphs, written by a student, use examples to explain how he reacts to boredom in his life. As you read this excerpt, notice how the writer shows rather than tells the readers how he copes with boredom by providing exciting details that are concrete, specific, and definite:

> We all deal with boredom in our own ways. Unfortunately, most of us have to deal with it far too often. Some people actually seek boredom. Being bored means that they are not required to do anything; being boring means that no one wants anything from them. In short, these people equate boredom with peace and relaxation. But for the rest of us, boredom is not peaceful. It produces anxiety.
>
> Most people deal with boredom by trying to distract themselves from boring circumstances. Myself, I'm a reader. At the breakfast table over a boring bowl of cereal, I read the cereal box, the milk carton, the wrapper on the bread. (Have you ever noticed how many of those ingredients are unpronounceable?) Waiting in a doctor's office, I will gladly read weekly news magazines of three years ago, a book for five-year-olds, advertisements for drugs, and even the physician's odd-looking diplomas on the walls. Have you ever been so bored you were reduced to reading through all the business cards in your wallet? Searching for names similar to yours in the phone book? Browsing through the *National Enquirer* while waiting in the grocery line? At any rate, that's my recipe for beating boredom. What's yours?

Example 133

Thinking Critically by Using Examples

Working with examples gives you yet another powerful way of processing your immediate environment and the larger world around you. It involves a manner of thinking that is completely different from description and narration. Using examples to think critically means seeing a definite order in a series of specific, concrete illustrations that are related in some way that may or may not be immediately obvious to your readers.

Isolating this rhetorical mode involves playing with related details in such a way that they create various patterns that relay different messages to the reader. Often, the simple act of arranging examples helps both the reader and the writer make sense of an experience or idea. In fact, ordering examples and illustrations in a certain way may give one distinct impression, while ordering them in another way may send a completely different message. Each pattern creates a different meaning and, as a result, an entirely new effect.

With examples, more than with description and narration, patterns need to be discovered in the context of the topic, the writer's purpose, and the writer's ultimate message. Writers and readers of example essays must make a shift from chronological to logical thinking. A writer discussing variations in faces, for example, would be working with assorted memories of people, incidents, and age differences. All of these details will eventually take shape in some sort of statement about faces, but these observations would probably not follow a strictly chronological sequence.

The exercises here will help you experience the mental differences among these rhetorical modes and will also prepare you to make sense of details and examples through careful arrangement and rearrangement of them in your essay. These exercises will continue to give you more information about your mind's abilities and range.

1. For each sentence below, provide two to three examples that would illustrate the generalization:
   a. I really liked (disliked) some of the movies released this year.
   b. Many career opportunities await a college graduate.
   c. Some companies make large sums of money by selling products with the names of professional sports teams on them.
2. Give an example (as specific as possible) of each item listed here: car, pizza, song, musician, event, friend, emotion, vacation, plant.

3. Jot down five examples of a single problem on campus that bothers you. First, arrange these examples in an order that would convince the president of your school that making some changes in this area would create a more positive learning environment. Second, organize your five examples in such a way that they would convince your parents that the learning environment at your current school cannot be salvaged and you should immediately transfer to another school.

Reading and Writing Essays That Use Examples

A common criticism of college-level writers is that they often base their essays on unsupported generalizations, such as "All sports cars are unreliable." The guidelines discussed in this introduction will help you avoid this problem and use examples effectively to support your ideas.

As you read the essays in this chapter, take time to notice the degree of specificity the writers use to make various points. To a certain extent, the more examples you use in your essays, the clearer your ideas will be and the more your readers will understand and be interested in what you are saying.

Notice also that these writers know when to stop—when "more" becomes too much and boredom sets in for the reader. Most college students err by using too few examples, however, so we suggest that, when in doubt about whether or not to include another illustration, you should go ahead and add it.

How to Read an Essay That Uses Examples

Preparing to Read. Before you begin reading the essays in this chapter, take some time to think about each author's title: What can you infer about Lynn Coady's attitude toward her subject from her title "Genius or Madness?"? What do you think Cecil Foster's view is of blacks in Canadian society? In addition, try to discover the writer's audience and purpose at this point in the reading process. Scanning the essay and surveying its synopsis in the Rhetorical Table of Contents will provide you with useful information for this task.

Also important as you prepare to read is information about the author and about how a particular essay was written. Most of this material is furnished for you in the biography preceding each essay. From it, you might learn why Lynn Coady is qualified to write about "anti-social behaviour" or why Diane Francis published "Once a Kinder and Gentler Nation."

Example 135

Finally, before you begin to read, take time to answer the Preparing to Read questions and to make some associations with the general subject of the essay: What do you want to know about infomercials (Mark Kingwell)? What are some of your opinions on the role of music in a community (Alfred LeBlanc)?

Reading. As you first read these essays, record any thoughts that come to mind. Make associations freely with the content of each essay, its purpose, its audience, and the facts about its publication. For example, try to determine why Cecil Foster writes about black discontent in Canadian society or why Diane Francis titles her essay "Once a Kinder and Gentler Nation." At this point, you will probably be able to make some pretty accurate guesses about the audience each author is addressing. Creating a context for your reading—including the writer's qualifications; the essay's tone, purpose, and audience; and the publication information—is an important first step toward being able to analyze your reading material in any mode.

Finally, after you have read an essay in this section once, preview the questions after the selection before you read it again. Let these questions focus your attention for your second reading.

Rereading. As you read the essays in this chapter for a second time, focus on the examples each writer uses to make his or her point: How relevant are these examples to the thesis and purpose of each essay? How many examples do the writers use? Do they vary the length of these examples to achieve different goals? Do the authors use examples their readers can easily identify with and understand? How are these examples organized in each case? Does this arrangement support each writer's purpose? For example, how relevant are Lynn Coady's examples of famous people's behaviour to her central idea? How many examples does Francis use to make each point? Does Cecil Foster vary the length of each of his examples to accomplish different purposes? How does Mark Kingwell organize his examples? Does this arrangement help him accomplish his purpose? In what way? Does Cecil Foster use examples that blacks, as well as people of other races, can identify with? How effective are his examples? How effective are LeBlanc's examples?

As you read, consider also how other rhetorical modes help each writer accomplish his or her purpose. What are these modes? How do they work along with examples to help create a coherent essay?

Last, answering the questions after each essay will help you check your grasp of its main points and will lead you from the literal to the analytical level in preparation for the discussion/writing assignments that follow.

For a thorough summary of reading tasks, you might want to consult the checklists on pages 15–16 of the Introduction.

How to Write an Essay That Uses Examples

Preparing to Write. Before you can use examples in an essay, you must first think of some. One good way to generate ideas is to use some of the prewriting techniques explained in the Introduction (pages 17–19) as you respond to the Preparing to Write questions that appear before the writing assignments for each essay. You should then consider these thoughts in conjunction with the purpose and the audience specified in your chosen writing assignments. Out of these questions should come a number of good examples for your essay.

Writing. In an example essay, a thesis statement or controlling idea will help you begin to organize your paper. (See page 22 for more information on thesis statements.) Examples become the primary method of organizing an essay when they guide the readers from point to point in reference to the writer's thesis statement. The examples you use should always be relevant to the thesis and purpose of your essay. If, for instance, the person talking about tennis players cited the practice schedules of only unknown players, her friend certainly would not be convinced of the truth of her statement about how hard internationally ranked athletes work at their game. To develop a topic principally with examples, you can use one extended example or several shorter examples, depending on the nature and purpose of your assertion. If you are attempting to prove that Canadians are more health conscious now than they were 20 years ago, citing a few examples from your own neighbourhood will not provide enough evidence to be convincing. If, however, you are simply commenting on a neighbourhood health trend, you can legitimately refer to these local cases. Furthermore, always try to find examples with which your audience can identify so that they can follow your line of reasoning. If you want your parents to help finance an apartment, citing instances from the lives of current rock stars will probably not prove your point, because your parents may not sympathize with these particular role models.

Example 137

The examples you choose must also be arranged as effectively as possible to encourage audience interest and identification. If you are using examples to explain the imaginative quality of Canada's Wonderland, for instance, the most logical approach would probably be to organize your essay by degrees (i.e., from least to most imaginative or most to least original). But if your essay uses examples to help readers visualize your bedroom, a spatial arrangement of the details (moving from one item to the next) might be easiest for your readers to follow. If the subject is a series of important events, like graduation weekend, the illustrations might most effectively be organized chronologically. As you will learn from reading the selections that follow, the careful organization of examples leads quite easily to unity and coherence in your essays. *Unity* is a sense of wholeness and interrelatedness that writers achieve by making sure all their sentences are related to the essay's main idea; *coherence* refers to logical development in an essay, with special attention to how well ideas grow out of one another as the essay develops. Unity and coherence produce good writing—and that, of course, helps foster confidence and accomplishment in school and in your professional life.

Rewriting. As you reread your example essays, look closely at the choice and arrangement of details in relation to your purpose and audience:

1. Have you included enough examples to develop each of your topics adequately?
2. Are the examples you have chosen relevant to your thesis?
3. Have you selected examples that your readers can easily understand?
4. Have you arranged these examples in a logical manner that your audience can follow?

For more detailed information on writing, see the checklists on pages 26–27 of the Introduction.

Student Essay: Examples at Work

In the following essay, a student uses examples to explain and analyze her parents' behaviour as they prepare for and enjoy their grandchildren during the Christmas holidays. As you read it, study the various examples the student writer uses to convince us that her parents truly undergo a transformation each winter.

Mom and Dad's Holiday Disappearing Act

<u>Often during the winter holidays, people find surprises</u>: Children discover the secret contents of brightly wrapped packages that have teased them for weeks; cooks are astonished by the wealth of smells and memories their busy kitchens can bring about; workaholics stumble upon the true joy of a few days' rest. My surprise over the past few winters has been the personality transformation my parents go through around mid-December as they change from Dad and Mom into Poppa and Granny. Yes, <u>they become grandparents and are completely different from the people I know the other eleven and a half months of the year.</u>

General topic

Details to capture holiday spiri

Background information

Thesis statement

<u>The first sign of my parents' metamorphosis is the delight they take in visiting toy and children's clothing stores.</u> These two people, who usually despise anything having to do with shopping malls, become crazed consumers. While they tell me to budget my money and shop wisely, they are buying every doll, dump truck, and velvet outfit in sight. And this is only the beginning of the holidays!

First point

Examples relevant to thesis

<u>When my brother's children arrive</u>, Poppa and Granny come into full form. <u>First they throw out all ideas about a balanced diet for the grandkids.</u> While we were raised in a house where everyone had to take two bites of broccoli, beets, or liver (foods that appeared quite often on our table despite constant groaning), the grandchildren never have to eat anything that does not appeal to them. Granny carries marshmallows in her pockets to bribe the littlest ones into following her around the house, while Poppa offers "surprises" of candy and cake to them all day long. Boxes of chocolate-covered cherries disappear while the bran muffins get hard and stale. The kids love all the sweets, and when the sugar revs up their energy levels, Granny and Poppa can always decide to leave and do a bit more shopping or go to bed while my brother and sister-in-law try to deal with their supercharged, hyperactive kids.

Transition

Second poi

Humorous examples (organized from most t least healthy

<u>Once the grandchildren have arrived, Granny and Poppa also seem to forget all of the responsibility lectures I so often hear in my daily life.</u> If little Tommy throws a fit at a friend's house, he is "overwhelmed by the number of adults"; if Mickey screams at his sister during dinner, he is "developing his own personality"; if Nancy breaks Granny's vanity mirror (after being told twice to put it down), she is "just a curious child." But, if I track mud into the house while helping to unload groceries, I become "careless";

Transition

Third point

Examples ir the form of comparison

Example 139

if I scold one of the grandkids for tearing pages out of my calculus book, I am "impatient." If a grandchild talks back to her mother, Granny and Poppa chuckle at her spirit. If I mumble one word about all of this doting, Mom and Dad reappear to have a talk with me about petty jealousies.

When my nieces and nephews first started appearing at our home for the holidays a few years ago, I probably was jealous, and I complained a lot. But now I spend more time simply sitting back and watching Mom and Dad change into what we call the "Incredible Huggers." They enjoy their time with these grandchildren so much that I easily forgive them their Granny and Poppa faults.

I believe their personality change is due to the lack of responsibility they feel for the grandkids: In their role as grandparents, they don't have to worry about sugar causing cavities or temporary failures of self-discipline turning into lifetime faults. Those problems are up to my brother and sister-in-law. All Granny and Poppa have to do is enjoy and love their grandchildren. They have all the fun of being parents without any of the attendant obligations. And you know what? I think they've earned the right to make this transformation—at least once a year.

[Margin annotations: Transition to conclusion; Writer's attitude; Writer's analysis of situation; Concluding remark; Specific reference to introduction]

Student Writer's Comments

To begin this essay, I listed examples of my parents' antics during the Christmas holidays as parents and as grandparents and then tried to figure out how these examples illustrated patterns of behavior. Next, I scratched out an outline pairing my parents' actions with what I thought were the causes of those actions. But once I sat down to write, I was completely stumped. I had lots of isolated ideas and saw a few patterns, but I had no notion of where this essay was going.

I thought I might put the theory that writing is discovery to the ultimate test and sit down to write out a very rough first draft. I wanted the introduction to be humorous, but I also wanted to maintain a dignified tone (so I wouldn't sound like a whiny kid!). I was really having trouble getting started. I decided to write down anything and then come back to the beginning later on. All of the examples and anecdotes were swimming around in my head wanting to be committed to paper. But I couldn't make sense of many of them, and I still couldn't see where I was headed. I found I needed my thesaurus and dictionary from the very beginning; they helped take the pressure off me to come up with the perfect word every time I was stuck. As I neared the middle of the paper, the introduction popped into my head, so I jotted down my thoughts and continued with the flow of ideas I needed for the body of my essay.

Writing my conclusion forced me to put my experiences with my parents into perspective and gave me an angle for revising the body of my essay. But my focus didn't come to me until I began to revise my entire paper. At that point, I realized I had never really tried to analyze how I felt toward my parents or why they acted as they do during the Christmas holidays. I opened the conclusion with "I believe their [my parents] personality change is due to" and sat in one place until I finished the statement with a reason that made sense out of all these years of frustration. It finally came to me: They act the way they do during the holidays because they don't have primary responsibility for their grandkids. It's a role they have never played before, and they are loving it. (Never mind how it is affecting me!) This basic realization led me to new insights into the major changes they go through during the holidays and ended up giving me a renewed appreciation of their behavior. I couldn't believe the sentence I wrote to close the essay: "I think they've earned the right to make this transformation——at least once a year." Holy cow! Writing this essay actually brought me to a new understanding of my parents.

Example 141

Revising was a breeze. I felt as if I had just been through a completely draining therapy session, but I now knew what I thought of this topic and where my essay was headed. I dropped irrelevant examples, reorganized other details, and tightened up some of the explanations so they set up my conclusion more clearly. Both my parents and I were delighted with the results.

Some Final Thoughts on Examples

Although examples are often used to supplement and support other methods of development—such as cause/effect, comparison/contrast, and process analysis—the essays in this section are focused principally on examples. A main idea is expressed in the introduction of each, and the rest of the essay provides examples to bolster that contention. As you read these essays, pay close attention to each author's choice and arrangement of examples; then, try to determine which organizational techniques are most persuasive for each specific audience.

Example in Review

Reading Example Essays

Preparing to Read

1. What assumptions can you make from the essay's title?
2. Can you guess what the general mood of the essay is?
3. What is the essay's purpose and audience?
4. What does the synopsis in the Rhetorical Table of Contents tell you about the essay?
5. What can you learn from the author's biography?
6. Can you guess what the author's point of view toward the subject is?
7. What are your responses to the Preparing to Read questions?

Reading

1. What general message is the author trying to convey?

2. Did you preview the questions that follow the essay?

Rereading

1. What examples help the author communicate the essay's general message?

2. How are these examples organized?

3. What other rhetorical modes does the author use to support the essay's purpose?

4. What are your responses to the questions after the essay?

Writing Example Essays

Preparing to Write

1. What are your responses to the Preparing to Write questions?

2. What is your purpose?

3. Who is your audience?

4. What is the message you want to convey?

Writing

1. What is your thesis or controlling idea?

2. Do the examples you are choosing support this thesis?

3. Are these examples arranged as effectively as possible?

4. What is your point of view toward your subject?

5. How do you achieve unity and coherence in your example essay?

Rewriting

1. Have you included enough examples to develop each of your topics adequately?

2. Are the examples you have chosen relevant to your thesis?

3. Have you arranged these examples in a logical manner that your audience can follow?

Lynn Coady
1970–

■■■

Genius or Madness?

In 1998 Lynn Coady received national recognition for her first novel, *Strange Heaven*, with a nomination for the Governor General's Award for fiction and the Canadian Authors Association's Air Canada award for the most promising writer under 30.

Lynn Coady comes from Cape Breton, Nova Scotia, but, after receiving a B.A. from Carleton University in Ottawa and living in New Brunswick, she moved to British Columbia to study creative writing at the University of British Columbia. Now living in Vancouver, Coady has been publishing short stories since 1992 and is also a playwright. Her play, *Monster*, was a finalist in Theatre BC's 1996 National Playwriting Competition. A collection of Coady's stories entitled *Play the Monster Blind* is scheduled for publication in 2000.

Preparing to Read

This essay originally appeared in *The Globe and Mail* as part of an advertisement for Chapters bookstore. This ad was part of a series of essays by notable Canadian writers, musicians, and thinkers. In "Genius or Madness?" Lynn Coady writes about the fine line between unconventional behaviour that is admired and that which is viewed negatively. Before reading Coady's essay, think about people who are considered geniuses. In what ways are they exceptional? In what way do their lives differ from those of everyone else? Who decides that an individual is a genius? At what point in a person's life is the designation of genius typically applied?

■ _____ ■

In my hometown, perhaps small towns in general, it's easy to   1
be crazy. As an adolescent, I didn't talk much and liked to read books in my room. That was all it took. Other people were crazy for different reasons. There were a couple of other kids who stayed in their rooms and played guitar (or oboe, or drums ...). Someone else was a vegetarian and an environmentalist—this in a town whose lifeblood consisted of the pulp of razed forests. Then there was the elementary school art teacher who wore high-heels, chunky jewelry, and low-cut tops. He also had a big, fluffy white

mat he liked to lounge on during class, making us kids fidget uncomfortably on the minuscule carpet-samples he provided for us.

In the glare of small-town scrutiny, any deviation from the   2 norm stands out wildly. The art teacher, because he was an adult, and well-established in the community, was treated with a faux-friendly indulgence that in any modern city would instantly be recognized for the covert bigotry it was. In our town it passed for tolerance. Weirdo adolescents, however, were less kindly-indulged—the assumption always being that teenagers exist in a developmental limbo with no solid values or proclivities of their own, and can, therefore, with firm guidance, easily be molded into well-adjusted citizens.

As it turned out, the conformity expected in my hometown   3 actually served as a handy preview of what was to come—the larger-scale conformity that defines the urban adult. Like many a small-town girl, I lived in the hope of getting out and going where not talking much and reading books was even a marginally acceptable pastime and I wouldn't be considered crazy anymore. Off I went to the big city. All I've learned in the ten year interim since is that reading books is *okay*, in moderation, but not wanting to talk remains a no-no. Small town hicks and urban sophisticates alike can't help but take it personally. People harangue me for never answering my phone, for example. But I don't like answering my phone. "But it's *anti-social*," they warn, ominously.

This is the crux of crazy, apparently. *Anti-social behavior* is   4 our euphemism for everything from the dabblings of people like the Unabomber, to that hairy street-wanderer who talks and titters to himself as he makes ready to pee on the sidewalk, to Emily Dickinson, in near-obscurity, penning some of the most shattering verse ever written. If you believe what people tell you, it's all the same, and it's all bad. There was probably much concern and consternation over Emily's doings at the time, existing in a cocoon of grief and isolation, only rousing herself to scribble her terse, morbid observations of the world. Anti-social? Definitely. Crazy? According to some, yes. There's one important thing to keep in mind, however. She was also ground-breaking.

Society is not so much afraid of full-blown chemically-   5 imbalanced madness as it is of non-conformity. To not conform to societal norms is to insult the painstaking codes of conduct enshrined by our ancestors so that we could live in civilization. The dilemma has always been that a civilization can never move forward until some nut-job flouts one or two of its standards, with the ultimate aim of toppling them. This scares the bejeezus out of people, particularly those who may have spent their lives upholding such precarious tenets. Thus when Socrates starts advising the youth of Athens to question everything around them, the citizens get a bit squirrelly. When Hamlet expresses his rampant disgust at the world and humanity, Elizabethans pop a collective garter. When the young Holden Caulfield denounces his clean-cut compatriots as phonies and whores, post-war America recoils.

You would think by now that we would see the need for this 6 kind of crazy, after centuries of conformity and blind obedience leading us over cliffs. Yet even today, we dare not step out of line. Try not answering your phone for an afternoon.

UNDERSTANDING DETAILS

1. Describe the kind of town where Coady grew up.
2. In her essay Coady cites several examples of people who might have been considered crazy. Who are these people? Why has she chosen these particular examples?
3. Why does Coady not answer her phone? What conclusion does this lead people to draw about her?

ANALYZING MEANING

1. Why are people afraid of nonconformity? Compare and contrast the reaction of adults and adolescents to nonconformist behaviour.
2. In paragraph 2 Coady contrasts covert bigotry and tolerance. Explain the difference between the two.
3. This essay appeared as an advertisement in *The Globe and Mail* for Chapters bookstore. Why would a bookstore pay for a full-page ad of this type in a national newspaper? Why do you think this topic was chosen for this audience? Explain where you think Coady would position herself on the spectrum of conformity / nonconformity.

DISCOVERING RHETORICAL STRATEGIES

1. Where in this essay do you find Coady's purpose most clearly stated? How does the organization of the major examples in this essay demonstrate the author's thesis statement?

2. Coady makes some careful language choices in this essay. Explain the effectiveness of her introduction of the elementary school teacher (paragraph 1). Why has Coady alternated between fairly sophisticated vocabulary (e.g., "To not conform to societal norms is to insult the painstaking codes of conduct enshrined by our ancestors so that we could live in civilization." paragraph 5) and very informal word choices (e.g., "nut-job," "bejeezus," "squirrelly," and "pop a collective garter" in paragraph 5)?
3. Although the author's dominant rhetorical method is the use of example, what other strategies has Coady used to organize her information? Give examples of these strategies.

MAKING CONNECTIONS

1. In a review of Coady's novel, *Strange Heaven*, in *The New Brunswick Reader*, the reviewer makes the following comment:

   > *Strange Heaven* is a very funny novel, a very light novel in spite of its often dark subject matter, and a pleasure to read. With her fine ear for speech and keen understanding of character, of true strength and common weakness, Lynn Coady is bound to be compared to Atlantic Canada's other master of the light-dark tale, David Adams Richards.

   Compare and contrast Coady's style in this essay with Richards' style in "My Old Newcastle."
2. Stephen King ("Why We Crave Horror Movies"), like Lynn Coady, explores the division between the emotions that society accepts and fosters and those that are viewed as unacceptable or indicative of insanity. How do the views of these two writers compare? How would King characterize Coady's antisocial behaviour?
3. Lynn Coady was the 1998 recipient of the Canadian Authors Association's Air Canada award for the most promising writer under 30. This award was won in previous years by Karen Connelly ("Touch the Dragon"), Steven Heighton ("Elegy in Stone"), and Evelyn Lau ("I Sing the Song of My Condo"). Choose one of these essays and identify any similarities between their writing and Coady's that may have made the Canadian Authors Association choose them as recipients of this award.

IDEAS FOR DISCUSSION/WRITING

Preparing to Write

Write freely about a particular person who is or was considered a genius. What is his or her special area of expertise? What makes this person so remarkable? What do you most admire about this person? Is this person a nonconformist in any way? Is this behaviour considered an asset or a liability?

Choosing a Topic

1. Write an essay about one area of life in which nonconformity is applauded. Is this always the case or are there specific conditions that make this nonconformity positive?

2. Choose a particular award and nominate your candidate. You might focus on an award in your school or community; an industry award such as the Juno Awards for Canadian music or the Academy Awards for movies; or an international organization award such as the Nobel Prize for Literature, Peace, or Science. Select the individual who you believe is the most deserving recipient and write your nomination piece, giving the selection committee plenty of specific examples that set your candidate apart from the other contenders and demonstrate why he or she is the obvious choice.

3. Are all geniuses or heroes a little eccentric? What makes anyone unique or special? Are we all a little odd? Are our odd qualities or apparent weaknesses sometimes assets? Using examples drawn from your own experience, write a character portrait of someone who seems unique to you.

WEB SITES

www.mwsolutions.com/canlit/titles/summary/strangeheaven.asp
You can read a profile of Lynn Coady's *Strange Heaven* at the Northwest Passages site.

www.canadacouncil.ca/ccnews/co9828-e.htm
Lynn Coady was nominated for the 1998 Governor General's Award for fiction.

ChaptersGlobe.com/
The Chapters Online bookstore.

Alfred LeBlanc

■■■

The Reel Thing

Alfred LeBlanc is a freelance writer from Toronto whose work has appeared in *Equinox* and *The Financial Post*. He is now editor at *Policy Options Politiques* in Montreal. This essay appeared in the September / October 1994 issue of *Equinox*.

Preparing to Read

In "The Reel Thing," Alfred LeBlanc visits Cape Breton Island in Nova Scotia to explore the traditional fiddle music of the area. What images come to mind when you think of fiddle music? Who plays the fiddle? Where do you envision the fiddle being played? How do people respond to the sound of fiddle music? Can you think of any particular musicians who are associated with fiddle music?

The Saturday square dances in West Mabou, on the southwest coast of Cape Breton Island, Nova Scotia, would be enough to make poor old Father Kenneth MacDonald turn over in his grave. A century ago, the local priest fought to stamp out fiddle music for its devilish influence. Judging from the action tonight in this community hall, the music still has the power to possess. 1

As fiddler Kinnon Beaton powers into Michael Rankin's Reel, a yelp of glee comes from the floor. "It's a sin to miss a dance," says 70-year-old Donnie MacDougall from nearby Inverness, sweat pouring from the last set. "I'm at every dance, and I never miss a set." In the third figure of the square set, the men and women peel away from each other, forming facing lines the length of the hall. Then there's the swoosh and tap of shoes on worn plywood as partners stepdance back to each other. After the set, the dancers clear space for Margie and Dawn Beaton, 9- and 12-year-old sisters from Mabou, to show off their steps. They finish to a loud cheer and give way to 22-year-old Rodney MacDonald, who dances to spirited versions of "Miss Lyle," "Devil in the Kitchen," and other classic strathpeys and reels. After a little coaxing, even 50-year-old Alex Hughie MacDonald from Judique gets up and has a go. 2

Traditional Celtic-style fiddling, piping, and stepdancing are 3 thriving arts in Cape Breton. In the summers, there are hundreds of square dances, concerts, and ceilidhs (parties) scattered about the island. The Ceilidh Trail, running along the west coast, likely boasts more musicians per capita than anywhere else in Canada. It is a rich cultural soil that has nurtured such musical greats as The Rankin Family, recent winners of four Juno Awards, and 19-year-old Ashley MacIsaac, an innovative young fiddler just starting a recording career that could push the Cape Breton sound onto the world stage and into the 21st century. So strong is the local tradition that the island's musicians are often invited to give workshops in Scotland to coach the founders in their own lost arts.

For every Cape Breton star who travels the world, there are 4 dozens more musicians who stay home and play a vital role in local life. To an area that has been economically depressed for generations, the Cape Breton fiddler brings self-forgetting joy. The unique driving pulse of the music leads irresistibly to the dance, which sets spirits free. "We live in the dark ages," says Patsi Palmer, who fell in love with Cape Breton's music and life and moved here from upstate New York. "This music cheers people up. This music is the doctor."

Cape Breton's Celtic music has a long history—and a resilient 5 spirit that has seen it through some rough times. Many of the tunes played by a fiddler such as 38-year-old Kinnon Beaton were imported by his forefathers when they first came from Scotland to Cape Breton during the Highland Clearances (the forced expulsion of sharecroppers) in the early 1800s, then passed down through the generations. (Beaton's grandfather, Angus Ronald, and father, Donald Angus, were both great fiddlers.) But during Beaton's own youth, fiddling became unfashionable. As I witnessed myself while growing up in the late 1960s and early 1970s in Margaree Forks, television and rock 'n' roll seemed to be getting the upper hand. The CBC made it official in a 1971 documentary lamenting "The Vanishing Cape Breton Fiddler."

"That show got a few of us mad," recalls Father John Angus 6 Rankin, one of the music's biggest supporters in recent years. "There were still many fiddlers around," he continues, "but they were in the woods. It was just a matter of getting in touch with them." To prove his point, Rankin got 100 fiddlers on stage for the first Glendale Fiddle Festival in 1973. Since then, the music has made a comeback, slowly at first, then exploding in the past 10 years.

"When I started, you were made fun of if you played," says Beaton with a chuckle. "Now you are made fun of if you can't play."

To sample the surviving heart and soul of the classic Cape   7
Breton fiddling style, you could do no better than drop by one Thursday night at a tiny white parish hall at Glencoe Mills. It is to this isolated spot that Cape Bretoners drive for miles, the last 10 along a dirt road, to catch Hugh "Buddy" MacMaster play. Dressed typically in slacks and a dress shirt, 69-year-old Buddy shows little emotion as he looks over his fiddle at a swirl of happy faces dripping with sweat. Though he has performed throughout North America and Europe—and has even taught at the Valley of the Moon School of Scottish Fiddling in California—this is his home turf; he has been working his magic here for 30 years.

Before this evening is over, Buddy will have played 150 tunes.   8
He couldn't tell you how many he knows in total; there are simply too many. In her book, *Traditional Celtic Fiddle Music of Cape Breton*, author Kate Dunlay ranks Buddy as "one of the greatest Scottish fiddlers ever to have lived." Buddy's own assessment is typically modest: "There are so many good fiddle players around today, they wouldn't miss me if I stopped playing."

What makes a great Cape Breton player? It's a combination   9
of precise tricks with the bow, a rock-solid sense of rhythm that is perfect for the dance, and a rich repertoire of old Scottish tunes and Scottish-style compositions by Cape Breton composers. While contemporary Scottish and Irish fiddlers are given to slurring the bow, Buddy executes more notes with single, or articulated, bow strokes. He bounces his bow to produce several distinct notes without reversing direction, or replaces some single notes with three "cuts" executed by rapid changes in bow direction. "That's not written in the music, you know," says Buddy of the manoeuvres he picked up from older players when he was growing up. Old-time Cape Breton fiddlers will also play notes to sound like bagpipes or play the same note on two strings at once to give a fuller sound. The result is music with great drive and lift. "If you're not dancing, you'd better pinch yourself, because you're probably dead," says fiddler and Iverness native Sandy MacIntyre.

Buddy fell in love with the music as a child, he says, listening   10
in on visiting fiddlers at "kitchen rackets," or ceilidhs, in his parents' home, then going to bed jigging (mouthing) tunes to himself. After starting to play at the age of 11, he soon advanced

to performing at weddings and parties, and at 14 played his first dance for money. As an adult, Buddy spent 45 years working as a CN stationmaster, but music was his life. "Even while I was at work, music was on my mind all the time." He has played regularly since 1949, in summer sometimes almost every night for weeks on end. Despite decades of persuasion by friends and recording studios, he waited 50 years before putting out a tape: "I didn't think I could. I never had the urge to record. I was just satisfied to play."

In the hall at Glencoe Mills, Buddy is part way through John   11 Morris Rankin's "The Way to Mull River Reel" when a slight smile of satisfaction crosses his face. He has noticed 6-year-old fiddler Robbie Fraser sitting at the edge of the stage, looking up admiringly at his hero. Fifteen years ago, Carmelita and Angus MacIsaac brought their 4-year-old son, Ashley, to soak up Buddy's music in this same hall. I still recall attending a dance there some nine years later. A new set was starting. The music was good, but it wasn't Buddy. I looked up to see a little fellow with curly brown hair, hardly big enough to hold the fiddle and looking awkward bowing with his left hand. It was Ashley—a future great fiddler pumping away for all he was worth.

If Buddy is all that Cape Breton fiddling has been, Ashley is   12 poised to become its somewhat controversial future. He was raised as solidly as Buddy in the traditional style—stepdancing as a small child, taking up the fiddle at the age of 8, and practising like a fiend, sometimes till midnight. But he also received some formal music training, made his first recording at 16, and moves readily from traditional duets with a pianist to more raucous experiments fronting a rock 'n' roll band. (During a typically furious performance in Halifax, he shocked purists by smashing and stepdancing on his fiddle.) While the music is everything for Buddy and he keeps his own presence small, Ashley seems to know instinctively that the music will get him only so far. "All I want to do is entertain people," he says—and if that means changing the music, it's okay by him. "If you pick it up for the crowd in Chéticamp, they love it. If that is a cop-out, so be it. I'd rather have people be entertained."

"Picking it up" is what Ashley is doing the afternoon of   13 Christmas Eve at Le Gabriel Lounge in the bustling Acadian village of Chéticamp. Ashley is sweating profusely, both feet pounding the floor and his body lurching. There is a loud cheer as he slips a few bars from a Christmas carol into a traditional fiddle tune. I can see why his father says, "He kills his piano players, because he never stops." When he has worn out a few stepdancers who come forward, he gets up and stepdances to his own playing.

Ashley got his big break when he came to the attention of 14 theatre director JoAnne Akalaitis and her husband, New York avant-garde composer Philip Glass, who have summered in Cape Breton for years. "The music was flowing out of him as if it was the most natural thing in the world," recalls Glass of his first listen to Ashley. He and Akalaitis were putting together a production of George Büchner's *Woyzeck* for the Joseph Papp Public Theater in New York and decided they wanted Ashley to fiddle and stepdance in it. "It was a big decision for us to let him go [to New York]," says his mother. That move and the friendship he formed with Glass opened up new possibilities. He has already made two appearances at Carnegie Hall and has recorded with the likes of Paul Simon. This fall, Ashley will release his own first major-label recording on A&M.

Some Cape Bretoners consider Ashley's new popularity a 15 mixed blessing, fearing that foreign influences will corrupt Cape Breton's old-style fiddling. "They're after changing the music," says 79-year-old Joe Kennedy, as he takes a break from playing me some tunes in his cluttered house deep in the woods near Inverside. Kennedy also objects to the flamboyant body language of fiddlers such as Ashley in full-flight performance. "The old fellows would stand right steady," he says. "Now their bodies swing every way, so wild. Pounding away with their feet. They're making too much noise with their feet."

Beyond the obvious theatrics, the younger generation of Cape 16 Breton fiddlers are also changing the music in subtler ways. Many now read music, and even more of them greatly emphasize precise technique and tonal clarity in their playing. "With the modern ear, there has been some streamlining of the music," observes author Dunlay. And because of the easy access to other music through recordings and travel, Cape Breton fiddlers now measure themselves against the international community and are more apt to pick up outside influences. Irish fiddling, which can be very fast, has great impact. Noting the foreign feel of some of the playing of his talented niece, Natalie, Buddy MacMaster says, "She has been in with some Irish players."

An overarching concern of the purists is that the newer 17 players are losing the ineffable sense of rhythm that makes Cape

Breton fiddling perfect for the dance. "The timing is getting ruined," worries Father John Angus Rankin. "People are playing for the money. If a lot of people follow Ashley, they'll all get faster and eventually the timing will get lost."

Sitting in a hotel restaurant in Toronto, Ashley sips a Coke 18 and shifts about like a puppy, as if to shake off the criticism. "Those people who think I play too fast should listen to some of the old recordings, especially those of Angus Chisholm," he says, referring to a giant in the tradition. And after all, Ashley is hardly the first revolutionary. Winston "Scotty" Fitzgerald, whose Cape Breton fiddler's credentials are impeccable, had a lot of people in Inverness County talking when he first came on the scene from White Point in neighbouring Victoria County. He added guitar to the conventional piano-fiddle combinations and played a lot cleaner, more precise style, with crisper grace notes and livelier, faster rhythms.

Fiddler Alasdair Fraser, a native of Scotland now living in 19 California, says evolution is natural. "What was unique was the way Cape Breton managed to hold onto its music for so long. Now that they have joined the rest of the world like everyone else, they will have to find a balance." More than anything, he adds, it is the dance that will keep the evolution authentic: "A good rooted way to know when things are working is if it gets the feet going."

For all his innovations that are helping expand the audience 20 for Cape Breton fiddling, young Ashley MacIsaac may well stay faithful to the dance as a touchstone of integrity. He says he's enjoying all the attention he's getting now and reasons: "I'm only going to be young for a few more years. Might as well make hay while the sun shines." But despite all the hype, Ashley still earns most of his money playing for square dances. And he knows that whenever the sun stops shining on his mainstream career, he will always have the music of his home and heart. "I'll be playing dances in West Mabou long after I've stopped playing rock gigs at the Palladium in Toronto."

The night is drawing on now in the hall in Mabou. As Kinnon 21 Beaton rosins the bow for another set, Connie MacEachen turns to me and insists, "You can't come to West Mabou and not dance. Put that pen and paper away, and let's get on the floor." My feet, which have been helpless to resist all evening, are finally set free to go where the magic of the music would take them.

UNDERSTANDING DETAILS

1. Buddy MacMaster and Ashley MacIsaac are two of the fiddlers mentioned in LeBlanc's essay. Explain the differences between them.
2. How are younger fiddlers changing traditional fiddle music? How are these changes being received? How does recognition by a broader audience both reflect and contribute to the changes?
3. Many consider Ashley MacIsaac's fiddling controversial. Describe MacIsaac's attitude toward the music he plays.

ANALYZING MEANING

1. What is LeBlanc's thesis in "The Reel Thing"? How does he develop this point of view?
2. Draw a timeline, and on it plot the range of attitudes and opinions about Cape Breton fiddling music. Include the names of specific individuals on this spectrum. What conclusions about LeBlanc's subject can you draw from this chart?
3. Explain the role of fiddle music in the Cape Breton community.

DISCOVERING RHETORICAL STRATEGIES

1. How has LeBlanc created unity in his essay? What is the relationship between the introduction and the conclusion of "The Reel Thing"?
2. What rhetorical modes has LeBlanc used in addition to example? Where in his essay do you see evidence of these rhetorical strategies?
3. LeBlanc uses many examples to illustrate the changes in Cape Breton music. Which are the strongest examples? What makes them particularly effective or memorable?

MAKING CONNECTIONS

1. Lynn Coady ("Genius or Madness?") and Alfred LeBlanc both depict characters from Nova Scotia's Cape Breton. Are the portrayals of people from this region consistent? Ashley MacIsaac's behaviour is often unconventional. Do you think Coady would consider him a genius or a madman?

2. LeBlanc writes about the importance of tradition as well as the necessity of change and progress. How does the evolution of Cape Breton fiddle music compare to the tradition of jannying (Ray Guy, "When Jannies Visited")?

3. Alfred LeBlanc and Sally Armstrong ("P4W") have both written essays about communities in which they are visitors. Compare and contrast the strategies they use to give credibility to the points they make and the observations they relate.

IDEAS FOR DISCUSSION/WRITING

Preparing to Write

Write freely about the development or progression that has happened in some form of art or entertainment. You might consider a type of music, a form of dance, a school of visual art, or a genre in film-making. When and where did this activity originate? How has it changed? How has the change been received? Are there particular individuals who are associated with these changes? Do you believe the change is good or not?

Choosing a Topic

1. Write an essay in which you focus on one individual as an innovator in his/her field. Your subject might be from the world of sports, entertainment, fashion, or business. What has this person contributed to his/her field and how have others responded?

2. In paragraph 19 Alasdair Fraser says, "evolution is natural." Write an essay about the positive aspects of evolution in some particular realm of life. Use specific examples to make your argument clear and strong.

3. You are the judge of a competition, with clear specific rules. One of the competitors performs superbly, but also breaks some of the rules with a new, innovative approach to this activity. Do you reward this competitor for his/her creativity and innovation or do you penalize him/her for not following the established guidelines? Write an essay for the local paper in which you justify your response to this situation.

WEB SITES

www.capebretonet.com/
The Cape Breton Showcase includes a section on Cape Breton music and profiles of some of the musicians mentioned in LeBlanc's essay.

Cecil Foster
1954–

■ ■ ■

Why Blacks Get Mad

Cecil Foster is a journalist and novelist who lives in Toronto with his wife and two sons. Foster immigrated to Canada in 1979 from Barbados. He has worked in a variety of journalistic positions both in Barbados and in Canada. The former editor of *Contrast*, a Toronto black community newspaper, Foster has also worked as a senior editor at *The Financial Post*, the host of a talk show on CFRB radio, special advisor to Ontario's Progressive Conservative minister of culture, and teacher of journalism at Ryerson University and Humber College. Foster's first novel, *No Man in the House*, was published in 1991 and was written for his children to help them understand one aspect of the experience of immigration. It was followed in 1995 by *Sleep on Beloved*, the award-winning *A Place Called Heaven* (1996), *Slammin' Tar* (1998), and most recently, a memoir entitled *Island Wings* (1998). Foster can also be heard occasionally on CBC radio.

Preparing to Read

In this article from *Chatelaine* magazine, Foster examines the problem of racism in Canada. Before reading Foster's views, think about racism. What is racism? What distinguishes racism from other forms of discrimination? Have you ever been subjected to racism? Do you consider yourself racist? What examples of racism have you observed in Canada? What causes racism? How can racism be overcome or eliminated?

■ ─────────────────────────────── ■

I felt totally helpless the night of May 4, as I sat in front of my 1
television set watching Toronto's Yonge Street reduced to skirmishes between the police and angry, alienated young people—many of them black.

Only a few nights earlier, my wife, Glenys, and I had been 2
glued to the set while youths across the United States torched sections of Los Angeles, Atlanta and New York. The Rodney King verdict, which exonerated L.A.'s finest in a monstrous beating of a black man, had triggered the worst outbreak of violence since the Watts riots of 1965.

Now, it was Toronto's turn, and those of us in the black 3
community who had predicted such an eruption for years could

only agonize about what we were witnessing. Glenys and I thought about our two sons, Munyonzwe, 10, and Michello, 9, sleeping upstairs. Would they feel compelled to take to the streets in another six or seven years?

This clash between black and white was particularly poignant 4 for middle-class blacks like Glenys and me. In our late 30s, with a fairly comfortable home and jobs—I am a senior editor at *The Financial Post* and a novelist, Glenys owns a Pizza Pizza franchise in Toronto—we may be said to have achieved many of the dreams we brought with us from Barbados in the '70s. But when the rampage started, we understood its roots as no white viewer could, because we too know the bitterness and frustration blacks experience every day in white society.

We didn't expect it to be this way. When I was growing up 5 in Barbados, I believed that, if I got myself an education, I would achieve success as a writer. Later on, I believed that, if I immigrated to Canada and did well, I would find acceptance in a multicultural society.

As it turned out, I did work hard, did achieve success, but 6 acceptance is another matter. The worst thing about racism in Canada is that it is not open but subtle. I can't remember anybody ever calling me nigger and yet I feel the pain of racism in the way people talk to me, handle me or just simply assume I am up to no good. It's what blacks call white stereotypical expectations.

I first encountered this stereotyping when I visited Canada in 7 1976, the year of the Montreal Olympics. I was still living in the West Indies and preparing to study mass communications at the Jamaican campus of the University of the West Indies on a scholarship later that year. I had saved every penny for almost two years to get to Montreal, see the Olympics and spend three weeks with my girlfriend, Glenys, also from Barbados.

I arrived at Mirabel airport with all my papers in order but, 8 while white passengers were processed quickly, I was held back for questioning. Would I be looking for a job? Would I take a job—even part-time—if offered?

I had been warned to expect this by Barbadians who had 9 visited Canada earlier. The immigration officer, they told me, would automatically assume I planned to be an illegal immigrant.

Three years later, in 1979, aged 24, I did immigrate—legally— 10 and joined Glenys, whom I had known since high school. She had taken the gamble in 1975 of coming to Montreal to study secretarial science at the then Sir George Williams University.

We were planning to marry and we chose Toronto as our future home, lured by the promise of economic improvement and of raising our kids in an environment that would allow them to develop to the best of their ability.

Finding a job was a problem at first. I remember being at a   11
Friday night dominoes session at a friend's house when the question of a job came up. I said my only skill was reporting. "Reporting!" a friend echoed. "Look at that television and tell me what you see." There was a Stanley Cup game on the screen. "That is Canada there. All white. If you see a black face, it must be a Buffalo station."

I was living in my brother Errol's apartment at this time. To   12
cover my living expenses, I became a bad telephone salesman for Grolier at night, hawking encyclopedias, and by day editing *Contrast*, the now-defunct black newspaper. I also started university courses at York, eventually completing two B.A. degrees in administrative studies and economics.

One day, as I was walking to a West Indian store to buy some   13
week-old Barbadian newspapers, a young white policeman pulled up on a motorcycle. An interrogation began: Who was I? Did I have any identification? Was I a legal immigrant in the country? I was frightened. My voice broke when I answered. No, I didn't have any I.D. I had neglected my brother's advice— never go out without a passport. And I became very conscious of the gun on this policeman's hip. In Barbados, policemen don't carry guns.

Finally, he said I could go; he was on the lookout for someone   14
just like me. My friends laughed at this when I told them. "He didn't mistake you. He just wanted to stop you."

During those early days, I left applications and résumés at   15
every Toronto media house. My hopes rose when I learned there was an opening at The Canadian Press news agency. Believing my experience at Reuters and the Caribbean News Agency would be an asset, I asked for the editor concerned. The man said he would be delighted to chat with me. He told me his desk was right across from the elevator, so he would see me when I got off. I should bring my clippings.

The conversation sounded so promising, but when I got off   16
the elevator, the man at the nearest desk checked his watch and frowned. I waited. Eventually, he said, "Are you Mr. Foster?" He apologized for promising me an interview. He should have known it was going to be a busy day and he wouldn't have time for a

longish chat. In any case, the opening he had in mind was filled, but he'd keep me in mind. He never looked at my clippings.

But I did get a job in late 1979 at *The Toronto Star*. I now had 17
a regular paycheque, but this did not save me from stereotyping. One day, I went to interview the head of a volunteer group for some charity. She had told me to come to the back of her affluent home in North Toronto, as she was having renovations made to the front. As I walked around piles of gravel and sand, I heard a woman shout angrily from the doorway, "So now you decide to show up? Do you know how long I've been waiting for you?"

"Didn't we agree on 10 o'clock?"   18

"Who are you?"   19

"The reporter from *The Star*."   20

"Oh, my God," she said. In spite of my jacket and briefcase, 21
one glance had been enough for her to classify me as a construction worker. It was not the only time someone has assumed that a reporter with an anglicized name at a major newspaper must be white. This is one reason we gave our sons African first names.

In 1980, Glenys and I were married and went to live in the St. 22
James Town apartment complex in downtown Toronto. It was our first home together. I was working steadily and attending college at night, she was working as a secretarial clerk in a freight-forwarding company. Life was looking better, and we started to plan for our own family. The next year, Glenys became pregnant with our first son.

But however positive we felt about our new life, the racist 23
undercurrent remained. By this time, I was working for *The Globe and Mail's Report on Business*. I was assigned to interview the executive director of some business association. As I waited in his outer office, I could see the executive through the glass. He was on the phone, and his assistant put a note on his desk, informing him of my arrival. The man got off the phone, took up some papers, looked at his watch and did some more work. Then, he made more phone calls. One of them, I learned later, was to my office, asking why I had not arrived. Finally, I asked the assistant to find out when he would see me.

The executive came out, very apologetic. He had not read 24
the note, he said, had assumed I was someone seeing his assistant. Now, it was too late for the interview.

Blacks put up with such incidents in the name of our 25
paycheques, but they frustrate and anger us.

In 1983, our second son, Michello, was born, and over the next 26
several years, Glenys and I worked hard to build the kind of life
we'd dreamed about in Barbados. As well as working as a reporter
by day and studying by night, I started writing fiction, as a means
of escape. *No Man in the House,* my first novel, was published in
Canada in 1991 and was well received. This fall, it is being released
in the U.S.

In 1989, we were able to take out a mortgage on a small house 27
in the suburbs. At about that time, Glenys realized a dream she
had had from the time when she used to help her brother with his
grocery store in Barbados. She had always wanted to run her
own business and, when the chance came to buy into a Pizza
Pizza franchise, she took the plunge.

She enjoys the work, but stereotyping is routine. White 28
customers often bypass her to speak to white employees. Once,
two yuppies saw her sweeping up and offered her a job cleaning
their homes.

"I don't try to explain anymore," Glenys says. "Being black 29
and a woman, they just don't expect me to be the owner."

Because Glenys and I are adults, we can laugh about these 30
incidents, but they are not funny when they affect our kids. Four
years ago, our son Michello, then 5, faced his first racist incident.

We knew something was up when he ran home from school 31
and burrowed under his brother's bedcover. A classmate had
not invited him to her birthday party. Her parents didn't like
blacks, she told him. My son believed that, if he slept in his
brother's bed under his cover, he would become like him—fairer-
skinned—and get the invitation.

We were devastated. What could we tell him? That it 32
wouldn't happen again? We knew it would. But why should a kid
so young be robbed of his innocence?

He's older now, and racist taunts in the schoolyard are 33
common. He tries to give as good as he gets, but "How many
times can I call them 'vanilla'?" he asks us. "They have so many
names for me: 'brown cow,' 'peanut butter,' 'chocolate cookie.'"

We encourage him to be tolerant but as peer pressure grows, 34
he may try his own solutions. In fact, at about the time of the
Yonge Street incidents, the principal sent home a note saying
my son had hit someone in the mouth.

Anger, like racism, starts young. And it builds up, fueled by 35
successive slights. "You go into work on Monday morning and
you hear everybody in the office talking about the party, the picnic

over the weekend or the invitations to the cottage, and you say to yourself, why wasn't I invited?" says my friend Lloyd, a midmanagement worker at a trust company. It should surprise no one when rage erupts, as it did recently in Toronto, Montreal and Halifax. Blacks have felt for too long that they are not invited to the party.

The riots last May told us just how desperate young blacks 36 feel about their prospects. But if the violence jolted the whites, there was also a shock in store for middle-class blacks. We discovered that these youths believe that middle-class blacks are as big a problem as white supremacists.

Pioneer blacks who have become doctors, chartered 37 accountants, journalists, bank managers, even elected politicians are perceived not as role models but as sellouts, Uncle Toms, house niggers, Oreos (black outside, white within). We are accused of failing to confront racism, of swallowing our anger and being too careful not to rock the boat.

Blacks have a term for this: white burnout. It comes when 38 you give up trying to fight the system. Austin Clarke, an outstanding novelist, also from Barbados, who used to speak out vehemently, now says, "I had two daughters at The Bishop Strachan School [an expensive private school]. I found it easier to pay the fees working inside the system than outside."

There is also the fear that, if we do fight the system, we 39 endanger our jobs.

As middle-class blacks watch violence erupt, a kind of 40 paralysis sets in. We know we must support the kids on the streets and help them build a secure future—but we also know that because of the deep resentment they feel toward us we aren't any damn use at this point.

So, whites who expect "role model" blacks to act as 41 intermediaries between them and militant youths should look elsewhere. Role model blacks are too busy patching things up with their fellow blacks.

As Austin Clarke told me the day after the riots, "I remember, 42 back in the '60s, saying the next generation of blacks is not going to stand for this shit. The next generation has now grown up."

And what the new generation sees is discouraging. Look at 43 Toronto blacks: our unemployment rate is high, and 87 percent make less than $25,000 annually. Single parent homes are three times more common among black families, and 25 per cent of these families rely on government for all income.

The result is hopelessness, and the result of that has now   44
become clear to everyone: I haven't met any black community
leader who doesn't anticipate more violence. If our kids'
frustrated rage is to be replaced by a new sense of hope, we will
need to reform the place where most of their problems have their
roots—the educational system. At present, 60 percent of black
youths in Toronto do not finish high school. But kids must remain
in school if they are to get the tools to prepare themselves for
better jobs and escape the poverty cycle. A college degree will
go a long way toward instilling confidence in young people,
even when facing the most bigoted employer. An educated kid
knows about antidiscrimination laws and regulations and will
use them to battle overt racism. More than that, he or she will
have choices in employment.

Meanwhile, governments must act fast to open up institutions   45
to blacks. This means continuing to put pressure on government
agencies such as the police and the judicial system who deal
daily with blacks. Professions such as law and medicine must
reexamine their entry criteria to rid them of racial biases.

But perhaps the best thing the wider society can do is simply   46
to let blacks feel that we belong, that there's a place for us in the
schools, in politics, the arts and, most importantly, in the work
force. Simply put, that we are Canadians and equal. Society has
brought pressure to bear on smoking, drunk driving and sexism
in the workplace. Now, it must make people equally
uncomfortable about stereotyping blacks.

At the same time, there is a lot of work to be done by the black   47
community. Not only must we create the peer pressure to make our
kids want to stay in school, but more adults must be willing to
sacrifice time, effort and even money to guide them. We have to
teach them how to live in a racist society and, hard as it is, we
cannot afford to appear to be losing hope. We must encourage
youths to dream, to believe they can bring about changes.

And it must be done fast. Already, too many blacks believe   48
they will always be on the outside looking in. Too many blacks
feel betrayed by Canadian schools, churches, human-rights
commissions, law courts and police. And too many blacks already
believe this society isn't worth maintaining and are willing to
try to destroy it.

The prospects are that bleak.   49

UNDERSTANDING DETAILS

1. In what aspects of his life has Foster experienced racism?
2. Why did Foster and his wife, Glenys, give their sons African names?
3. What does Foster believe governments should do to overcome racism? What about professions? Wider society? The black community?

ANALYZING MEANING

1. Why did Foster immigrate to Canada? Have his expectations been fulfilled? Explain.
2. "Anger, like racism, starts young" (paragraph 35). Explain this statement with specific examples you have experienced or observed.
3. Define the following terms and give specific examples to help differentiate between them: discrimination, racism, stereotyping.

DISCOVERING RHETORICAL STRATEGIES

1. How has Foster organized his examples? Is this pattern effective? Why or why not?
2. Describe the tone that Foster creates in this article. How does he establish this tone? Is this tone appropriate for his intended audience?
3. Foster's examples come from his own experience. What effect does this have on the readers?

MAKING CONNECTIONS

1. Allen Abel finishes his essay ("A Home at the End of the Journey") with the comment, "I'm thinking: Maybe this place can work." How do you think Foster would respond to Abel's story of his citizenship ceremony and his concluding comment about Canada?
2. Drew Hayden Taylor ("Pretty Like a White Boy") and Cecil Foster both write about the difficulties of being judged on their appearance and "not looking the part" but their essays have very different tones. While Hayden Taylor uses humour, Foster is very serious. Which approach do you find more effective? Explain why.

3. Foster uses personal experience to make his point about discrimination. Compare and contrast this strategy to that chosen by Judy Rebick in "Kick 'Em Again".

IDEAS FOR DISCUSSION/WRITING

Preparing to Write

Write freely about expectations. What expectations do you have for your life? What things do you hope to achieve? What goals have you set? To what degree are your expectations shaped by others in your family, your peer group, or your community? How is your behaviour influenced by the expectations of those around you?

Choosing a Topic

1. "Overall, Canada is a good country in which to live." Write an essay in which you support this statement with plenty of specific examples.
2. Foster discusses the problem of feeling caught in the middle that many middle-class blacks face in Canada. Write an essay in which you describe an experience of feeling "caught in the middle." Use specific, detailed examples to convey your position clearly.
3. Write an essay for a college-educated audience in which you claim that your school or your community is either more racist or less racist than it used to be. Specific examples will help you to build a convincing argument.

WEB SITES

www.canoe.ca/JamBooksReviews/foster_rev.html
You can find a review of Foster's book *Sleep on Beloved* here.

www.edu.yorku.ca/~WIER/foster.html
Foster is a participant in the Writers in Electronic Residence program.

Diane Francis
1946–

■ ■ ■

Once a Kinder and Gentler Nation

Well-established as a Canadian business and financial writer, Diane Francis holds definite and factually supported views of our political and economic environment. Francis is a native of Chicago who began her postsecondary education at the University of Illinois, then attended Sheridan College in Oakville, Ontario. She has written on business and political subjects for *The Toronto Star* and *The Sun*, her columns have appeared often in *Maclean's* and other Canadian magazines, and from 1979 to 1981, she was contributing editor for *Canadian Business Magazine*. Frequently heard on Peter Gzowski's *Morningside* program, she was editor of *The Financial Post* and is also a business commentator on CFRB. While readers may disagree with Francis's views on her subjects, her knowledge of financial matters and expertise in communicating that information is substantiated by her having received The Royal Bank Business Writing Award in 1982 and The Canadian Public Accountants Business Writing Award three times. In 1992, Francis was named *Chatelaine*'s Woman of the Year. Francis serves on many advisory boards and is the author of *Controlling Interest: Who Owns What?* (1986), *Contrepreneurs* (1988), *The Diane Francis Inside Guide to Canada's 50 Best Stocks* (1990), *Underground Nation: The Secret Economy and the Future of Canada* (1994), *Fighting for Canada* (1996), and *Bre X: The Inside Story (1998).* A formidable investment advisor and an accomplished writer, Francis currently lives in Toronto.

Preparing to Read

"Once a Kinder and Gentler Nation" originally appeared in *Maclean's* in September 1990. This essay uses former U.S. President George Bush's phrase to reproach Canadians for our current abuses of our economic benefit systems and for our tax evasion tactics. Francis draws support for her examples from factual statistics on government spending as well as from specific personal experiences. As you begin to read this essay, spend some time considering your own attitudes towards provincial health insurance, welfare programs, the GST, Unemployment Insurance, and even cross-border shopping. Do we as Canadians take for granted government coverage of our most basic needs? Where does the funding for such programs as student loans come from? Granted, no one enjoys paying extra taxes on every item purchased, but could you afford to pay for every visit to the doctor's office? Do we as individuals perpetuate a "me first" attitude that ignores the long-term financial consequences? Is this how Canadians want the world to see them?

Every society has its unique morality which influences individ- 1
ual behaviour and shapes its economy and politics. And it was
a pleasant surprise for me, as an American immigrant coming to
Canada in 1966, to find such a fair and generous society north of the
border. The United States is a great place to live, providing you
are not poor, sick, old or black. In contrast, Canada generously
provided the essentials, medical and educational opportunities for
all, thus breaking the poverty cycle and allowing the cream to rise
to the top. But it is a paradox that Canada's unselfish society has led
to a selfish one. Canadians are increasingly asking not what they can
do for their country, but what their country can do for them.

The welfare state seeps into every crevice of this country and 2
has evolved into the politics of envy, no matter who is in power.
The manifestations are everywhere. Provinces vie for federal
money. Some demand special privileges over others. The three
richest provinces—Ontario, British Columbia and Alberta—
recently took Ottawa to court and stopped the federal
government from capping massive transfer payments, even
though most people agree that spending restraint is needed. To
buy votes, virtually all governments continue to build
unnecessary schools, prisons, museums or roads. Politicians of
every stripe hand out grants and goodies galore. The latest
available figures show that in 1984 Canadian governments gave
$8.1 billion in grants to businesses while the Americans gave
somewhat more, $10.6 billion, even though their economy is 12
times larger than ours.

Of course, Canadians get the politics they deserve. Everybody 3
wants something for nothing. Fat-cat corporations line up for
grants. Multicultural groups demand that other taxpayers
contribute towards keeping alive cultures they left behind.
Aboriginals break the law, and cost taxpayers a fortune to uphold
their "rights." Car workers and other powerful unions hold a
gun to employers' heads, demanding overly generous
compensation for inflation even though such compensation forces
up inflation for the rest of us. Senators and aldermen alike award
themselves huge raises. The result of such selfishness is to
sandbag honest workers with soaring taxes and soaring interest
rates, which are the result, in great measure, of soaring
government debts.

I still believe most Canadians are honest and don't abuse 4
government largesse, but the rationalizations of the welfare state
increase. "If I don't get that government grant, somebody else

will," is a common refrain. Others include: "I paid into it for years so why shouldn't I collect," "The government's budgeted for it," "Everybody does it," "Canada's a rich country," "Why should Quebec get it all?" "Nobody cares," or that irrational, and self-fulfilling, old saw "The government will waste the money anyway."

Look around for examples. I have a neighbour whose son 5 works outdoors during warm months and collects Unemployment Insurance Commission benefits during the four coldest ones. Meanwhile, want ads for unskilled workers like himself, in his wage range, bulge in local newspapers every winter. His mother is disgusted, but still he collects because rules allow him to refuse a job if it is not exactly what he wants, where he wants to go and at the salary he expects. Another friend got a grant to pay for research he would have been willing to pay for himself if no grant had been available. Then there's an electrician I know who lives on disability benefits even though he could support himself if he retrained in another, unphysical line of work. It's all perfectly legal, but should not be.

There's also out-and-out crookery: Tradesmen who ask you 6 if you want an invoice made out to a company so work or services can be unfairly written off against corporate profits; cleaning ladies who only take cash because they don't pay taxes on their income; or wealthy businessmen who go out for dinner and claim it as a business expense. Still others do not need rent, legal aid or day care subsidies but claim them anyway.

Such people take and never want to give. Case in point is 7 the debate over the looming Goods and Services Tax. Critics fail to mention that the amount the tax will generate will not be more than what is being collected now from a hidden manufacturers tax. Also missing from the debate is the fact that the estimated proceeds, about $19 billion, is far short of the $27.3-billion federal contribution towards two beloved benefits, medical insurance and old-age security payments.

Instead, increasing numbers of Canadians use such taxes as 8 an excuse for indulging in the despicable practice of border shopping in the United States. They buy goods that are cheaper there because taxes are lower due, in large part, to less generous social benefits. A friend of mine is typical and buys groceries, clothing, gasoline, and other items south of the border all the time. She never declares goods at the border or pays duty on them even though she is a cancer patient who has had treatments and operations that have probably cost the rest of us hundreds of thousands in medical costs. I don't begrudge paying for her medical services, but she and others who shop south of the border are tax evaders who get benefits and do not pay their fair share of the taxes that must be raised to pay for those benefits.

What happened to Canada? When did a thrifty, generous 9 and hardworking society turn into a selfish collection of pressure groups who craftily win concessions from spineless politicians at the expense of others? When did Canada's generous-spirited intention of helping the helpless turn into a race for hand-outs paid for by others? It is more than just a disappointment. This society's selfishness speeds us towards economic oblivion, and we need answers. Perhaps politicians should only be allowed one, seven-year term to remove re-election bribery. Perhaps referendums should be mandatory on all major public expenditures, as is often the case at the state level in the United States, to control costs. Perhaps we should label things properly. How about redubbing the GST the Health Care Charge? I suggested this recently to Finance Minister Michael Wilson and he said, "Canadians understand the links already." I wish he was right. But I don't think he is.

UNDERSTANDING DETAILS

1. Why, according to Francis's personal experience, might she have chosen her title to describe her first perceptions of Canadians? What is the paradox the author sees in Canadian society?
2. What details does the author use to justify her statement that "everybody wants something for nothing" (paragraph 3) in our society? Do you agree with all her statements?
3. What does the author foresee as the final result of "society's selfishness" (paragraph 9)? What are the major contributing factors to this result? What solutions does Francis propose for each?

ANALYZING MEANING

1. Why does the author call Canada a "welfare state" which has seeped "into every crevice of this country" (paragraph 2)? Why does Francis use the phrase "the politics of envy"?
2. What are the examples of cheating the economic system that Francis cites? Are all these instances equally unethical? Why or why not, in your view?

3. Do you agree that Canadians have "turned into a selfish collection of pressure groups" in a "race for handouts paid for by others" (paragraph 9)? Which of the author's statements do you most agree or disagree with?

DISCOVERING RHETORICAL STRATEGIES

1. What factor in Francis's personal history affects her point of view on her subject? Who is her intended audience, and how could this factor affect the reading audience?
2. What headings would you give to the author's groups of examples in this essay? Does the order in which she places her examples persuade you more or less of her main points? Why?
3. Diane Francis makes her points partly through her choice of very strongly coloured words. Such words as "selfishness" and "crookery" clearly convey her attitude of disapproval on both an ethical and economic basis. How do such forthright and repeated statements of bias on the part of an author make the essay more or less effective? Give examples from this essay to support your answer.

MAKING CONNECTIONS

1. Neil Bissoondath ("Pieces of Sky") defines a number of typically Canadian behaviours. Which of these do you think Francis would agree with? Which would she dismiss as inaccurate?
2. Francis portrays Canadian society as "a selfish collection of pressure groups who craftily win concessions from spineless politicians at the expense of others." (paragraph 9). How would Allen Abel ("A Home at the End of the Journey") respond to this characterization? What about Steven Heighton ("Elegy in Stone")?
3. Judy Rebick ("Kick 'Em Again") argues that Canadians on welfare are discriminated against. Is this consistent with Diane Francis's argument? Do you agree with Rebick's position on income-based discrimination or Francis's view?

IDEAS FOR DISCUSSION/WRITING

Preparing to Write

Write freely about Canadians and our dependence on social, medical, and educational support programs. From which of these have you or your family most benefited? How is this program financially supported? Do we "understand the links" between many of the taxes we pay and the support systems we may take for granted? Which government program could you not do without? How much can any of us resist the temptations of cross-border shopping? On which issues are personal ethics and national economics at odds? Are there solutions?

Choosing a Topic

1. Write an essay for the general-interest reader in which you define and support your point of view on avoiding the GST by paying for goods and services in cash. Is it an unethical and erosive form of tax evasion or an unavoidable fact of financial survival in the 1990s? Support your main thesis with examples drawn from your own experience and from your interpretation of news reports.

2. Are Canadians more greedy, selfish, and lazy than Americans or other nationalities? Write a letter to the editor of *Maclean's* magazine that responds to the allegations made in Diane Francis's article. Base your response on specific issues raised in this essay and be sure to support your arguments with sufficient details to persuade your readers of your point of view.

3. Write an essay based on the use of examples for your English class. The subject of this essay is an unpleasant one: Taxes. Select a specific form of taxation, whether personal, like the GST, or more general, such as income tax, and discuss your understanding of the necessity, or lack thereof, for such collection systems. What does this tax pay for? Could Canadians find an alternative way to subsidize what it provides?

WEB SITES

www.macleans.ca
Francis's article comes from *Maclean's* magazine.

www.nationalpost.com/financialpost.asp?s2=opinion&s3=columnists
Francis is a contributing editor at *The Financial Post*. Click on her picture to read her latest column.

Mark Kingwell
1963–

■ ■ ■

Not Available in Stores

In a column in The Toronto Star, Jim Coyne adamantly declares that he hates Kingwell and calls Kingwell "the purple loosestrife of pop-cult pundits." Hardly a flattering description, Coyne's point is that Kingwell seems to be everywhere, and that has created some resentment. Douglas Bell, however, goes further in examining the reasons for Kingwell's huge appeal. Kingwell views his nonacademic writing as serious but accessible and Michael Ignatieff points out that Kingwell is "... interesting because he seems to know things about popular culture while also knowing something about Aristotle [and] ... he has a sense of humour." For a variety of reasons Kingwell is being called on from all sides for comments, reactions, ideas, and commentary on topics ranging from the nature of happiness to the appeal of Melrose Place; from Princess Diana's death to the millennium.

Kingwell was born in Toronto and grew up primarily in Winnipeg, southwestern Ontario, and Prince Edward Island. He graduated from the University of Toronto with a B.A., went to the University of Edinburgh for a Master's degree in literature and philosophy and then earned a Ph.D. in philosophy at Yale. Since his graduation from Yale, Kingwell has taught at Yale, York University, and Scarborough College at the University of Toronto, where he was made Assistant Professor of Philosophy in 1993. Kingwell's academic writing has been published in several journals including the *Journal of Philosophy*, the *Journal of Speculative Philosophy*, *International Philosophical Quarterly*, *Ethics*, and the *Yale Journal of Law and the Humanities*. In addition he is television columnist for *Saturday Night*, the ideas columnist for the *University of Toronto Magazine*, and a contributing editor to *Descant*, *Shift*, and *Gravitas*. His writing can also be found in a variety of other periodicals including *Adbusters*, *The Globe and Mail*, *The Toronto Star*, *The Canadian Forum*, and *Harper's*. Kingwell has also published three books: *A Civil Tongue: Justice, Dialogue, and the Politics of Pluralism* (1995), *Dreams of Millennium: Report from a Culture on the Brink* (1996), and *Better Living: In Pursuit of Happiness from Plato to Prozac* (1998). Kingwell also speaks frequently on television and radio on cultural and political issues.

Preparing to Read

"Not Available in Stores" is an essay that first appeared as a column in *Saturday Night* magazine in 1998. Kingwell, as a well-known popular culture commentator here discusses the appeal and success of infomercials as well as the trends that are changing the genre of infomercials. Before reading Kingwell's essay, think about television advertising. Do you sit and watch television commercials or do you use them as a chance to get a snack or check what is on on other channels? What is your favourite television commercial? Your least favourite? Do you ever make a point of watching infomercials?

■──■

It begins like one of those cosy Women's Television Network   1
chat shows, complete with bad lighting, fuzzy lenses, and warm looks. The host is an attractive, soft-spoken woman of a certain age. She purrs at the camera. She and her guests are here to tell you about what she chucklingly calls "Hollywood's breast-kept secret." Yes, it's true: Accents, the Plasticine bust enhancers favoured by movie stars and models alike, are now available to you, the lowly viewer. No surgery. No hideous contraptions. You don't even have to leave home to get them.

And what a difference they make! Soon a line-up of gorgeous   2
but slightly flat-chested women are being transformed before your eyes into jiggly supermodels or "Baywatch" lifeguards. These flesh-coloured slabs of silicone gel that "fit into any underwire bra" and "within minutes warm to your natural body temperature" can actually be used in the swimming pool! At the end of the half-hour, the ever-smiling host and her guests admit that *they are all wearing Accents themselves*! Well, shut my mouth.

"Accents" is only the most outrageous of the current crop   3
of television infomercials: those over-the-top attempts to hawk make-up, cleaning products, and ab-flexers under the guise of a genial talk show ("Kathie Lee Talks") or breathless science programme ("Amazing Discoveries!"). Turn on your television late at night or on a weekend afternoon—even, these days, at midmorning—and the good-natured hosts, a has-been actress (Ali McGraw) or never-was celeb (Ed McMahon), are touting cosmetics or miracle car wax as if they are doing us a public service. Information + commercial = infomercial. Line up the word, and the phenomenon, next to those long advertising features in newspapers and magazines, often slyly imitating the publication's actual typeface and design, known as "advertorials."

Patently absurd, maybe, but if emerging trends continue,   4
infomercials will not remain what they have been so far: a marginal and benign, if irritating, television presence. With the loosening of CRTC regulations, the explosion of cable channels, and the crude economics that can make them more lucrative than

regular programming for network affiliates, infomercials are showing up in more and more places on the TV schedule, elbowing aside such popular quality fare as Sunday-afternoon sports, syndicated comedies, and old movies. They are also getting more and more sophisticated, as big-name companies with mainstream products—Ford Motor Co., Procter & Gamble, Apple Canada—enter the infomercial market.

And if, as enthusiasts in the business press insist, this is the future of TV advertising, then that is very bad news indeed for television and its viewers. But not because there is anything inherently wrong with infomercials, at least not as they have existed until now. The delicate pact between ads and shows that makes television possible has always been able to withstand the amateurish, ad-becomes-show genre they represent. But when infomercials are everywhere, and especially when they go high market, that pact is in danger of being overturned, and the thin line between entertainment and pitch may be erased for good. 5

Blame Ron Popeil. Blame him a lot, and at length. Blame him until his smiling, trout-like face is imprinted on your mind as the fount of all evil. Because Popeil is the one who started the sort of television hard sell that reaches its tacky terminus in today's infomercials. Founder of Ronco, restless inventor of the Popeil Pocket Fisherman, the Patti-Stacker, and other cheesy "labour-saving" devices too numerous to mention, Popeil is the guy who all but invented television shopping. In the 1970s he discovered that people got very excited, and very willing to spend, at the thought that you need never leave your couch to have the entire Ronco or K-Tel product line delivered to your home. His favourite author was the guy who came up with *Call this toll-free number now*. 6

Popeil has recently come out from behind the camera to appear in his own convection-oven and pasta-machine infomercials. Looking like an also-ran from a professional tanning competition, he slops flour and water into slowly spinning machines that disgorge brightly coloured goo for thirty minutes. Your own fresh pasta every night! Operators are standing by! 7

It isn't hard to decipher what makes these and other low-end infomercials so successful. Potential buyers are never made to feel bad, even as their baser desires are being pandered to. For example, we are told at least four times that Accents "are shipped confidentially" and arrive at your door in (get this) "a beautiful designer chest that will look great on your vanity." The 8

Accents people even muster expert opinion, the *sine qua non* of the TV hard sell. In this case, it's a panel of Hollywood make-up artists and photographers. "I tried everything," says one. "Foam pads, wires, push-up bras, duct tape. Nothing works like Accents." (Duct tape?)

The same forms of reassurance are visible on all the successful 9 infomercials now airing, from The Stimulator to the Ab-Roller Plus. The Stimulator—a small syringe-like device that is supposed to kill pain by means of mild electric shock, a sort of mini stun gun—also produces what has to be the funniest infomercial moment of all time. Evel Knievel, the all-but-forgotten daredevil of the 1970s, shares, over footage of his famous Caesars Palace motorcycle crash, his belief in the pain-relieving properties of The Stimulator. "If it hepped me," Knievel twangs, "it can hep you." Now that's expert opinion.

This is so silly that it is easy to imagine a kind of self-parody 10 operating, of the sort in the hilarious "Money Show" spots on CBC's "This Hour Has 22 Minutes": "Gus, I want to pay less in taxes, but I'm not sure how." "Marsha, it couldn't be easier; stop filing your returns!" But that would misread the intentions of the makers—and the attitudes of the audience, whose response to infomercials has been wholehearted. Canadians spent $100-million on infomercial products in 1995, up thirty-four per cent from 1994. One Ontario company, Iona Appliances Inc., quadrupled annual sales of its "dual-cyclonic" vacuum cleaner when it started marketing via infomercial.

In fact, the point of infomercials has so far been their lack of 11 sophistication. The niche is still dominated by the charmingly inept likes of Quality Special Products, the Canadian company responsible for such thoroughly trailer-park items as the Sweepa ("The last broom you'll ever have to buy!") and the Sophist-O-Twist hair accessory ("French braids made easy!").

Most current efforts eschew the cleverness and quality visible 12 on more traditional commercial spots in favour of the low-ball aesthetic of public-access cable. Instead of competing with shows for our attention—and therefore being pushed to find better writing, multimillion-dollar budgets, and gilt-edged directorial talent—infomercials become the shows. Yet they do so in ways so obviously half-hearted that nobody, not even the quintessential couch-potato viewer, could actually be fooled. The talk-show cover story is really nothing more than a tacit agreement between marketer and viewer that they're going to spend half an hour in each other's company, working over a deal.

And this is what many critics miss: most infomercials, as 13 they now appear, aren't really trying to dupe the viewer. They are instead the bottom-feeding equivalent of the irony observable in many regular commercials. Bargain-basement infomercials offer a simpler form of customer complicity than the crafty self-mockery and self-reference that appeals to young, kitsch-hungry viewers. Infomercials are a pure game of "let's pretend," taken straight from the carnival midway.

That's why the entry of high-end marketers into the field is 14 so alarming. Big-money companies are not content to maintain the artless façade that now surrounds infomercials. They break the carny-style spell of cheap infomercials, where we know what we see is fake, but we go along anyway, and offer instead the high production quality, narrative structure, and decent acting of actual shows.

A recent Apple Canada effort, for example, which aired last 15 year in Toronto, Calgary, and Vancouver, is set up as a saccharine half-hour sitcom about a white-bread family deciding to buy a home computer ("The Marinettis Bring Home a Computer"). It is reminiscent of "Leave It To Beaver" or "The Wonder Years," complete with Mom, Pop, Gramps, the family dog, and an annoying pre-teen narrator named TJ. Gramps buys the computer, then bets grumpy Pop that the family will use it enough to justify the expense. Soon TJ is bringing up his slumping math grades, Mom is designing greeting cards for profit, and Gramps is e-mailing fellow opera buffs. It's nauseating, but effective. Heather Hutchison, marketing communications manager for Apple Canada, explains the company's decision to enter the infomercial universe this way: "Having produced something of higher quality," she says, "there's a recognition at—I hesitate to use the word 'subconscious,' but at a lower level—that it says something about the quality of the product. The Canadian market responds well to this kind of softer sell."

We all know that television, as it now operates, is primarily 16 a vehicle for the delivery of advertising. That is, we know that if it weren't for ads, nobody would get to spend a million dollars on a single episode of an hour-long drama or employ some of the best dramatic writers and directors now working. True, this symbiosis is uneasy at best, with good shows all but free-riding on the masses of dreck that keep the advertisers happily reaching their targets. That's fine—or at least not apocalyptic. We can accept that advertising is the price we have to pay (every seven minutes) for good television.

But slick infomercials, unlike their cheapo forbears, threaten to   17 destroy this shaky covenant. Only a moron could mistake a low-end infomercial for a real show. (And only a condescending jerk could think that all people who buy Sweepas and Abdomenizers are, in fact, morons.) Up-market infomercials have a much greater potential to muddy the waters between advertising and programming. It may be that, without the cheesy aesthetics and side-show barker style, these new infomercials won't find an audience. But it's more likely that big companies with big budgets and top advertising talent will be able to suck even non-morons into these narrative ads that masquerade as entertainment. The new corporate offerings, in other words, may actually do what Ron Popeil couldn't: strip TV of extraneous effects like quality programming so that it finally reveals its essential nature—selling things, selling things, and selling things.

When that's true, maybe it's time to turn the damn thing off   18 for good.

UNDERSTANDING DETAILS

1. What recent trend in infomercials does Kingwell identify? Why is this happening? How does Kingwell feel about this trend?
2. Who is Ron Popeil? Why is he significant in the world of infomercials?
3. What makes traditional low-end infomercials successful?

ANALYZING MEANING

1. How does Kingwell feel about the change that is happening in the world of infomercials?
2. What is Kingwell's thesis? How is it revealed in the examples that he relates in his essay?
3. Characterize Kingwell's attitude toward traditional infomercials? How does this compare to his attitude toward the "new, slick" infomercials?

DISCOVERING RHETORICAL STRATEGIES

1. The use of examples to illustrate his point characterizes Kingwell's essay. How many examples of infomercials does Kingwell include? Which example do you find the most effective?

2. In paragraph 9, Kingwell illustrates his point about the use of "expert opinions" with a quotation from Evel Knievel. Why does Kingwell deliberately misspell words in this quotation? How does this reinforce his point about traditional infomercials?
3. Kingwell's essay finishes with a very short final paragraph. Explain how this serves as an effective conclusion to "Not Available in Stores."

MAKING CONNECTIONS

1. Jennifer Cowan ("TV Me Alone") writes about the pervasiveness of television in our society. How do you think that Cowan would respond to Kingwell's points about infomercials and the essential nature of television?
2. Mark Kingwell's sense of humour is apparent in "Not Available in Stores" although he is making some serious points. Compare Kingwell's use of humour to that of Drew Hayden Taylor ("Pretty Like a White Boy"), Evan Solomon ("The Babar Factor"), or David Suzuki ("The Right Stuff").
3. Kingwell outlines the evolution of infomercials into something quite threatening. Tony Leighton ("The New Nature") talks about the technological evolution of image manipulation and the effect that this evolution is having on our society. Evan Solomon ("The Babar Factor") discusses the changes in children's entertainment from traditional storybooks to contemporary video games. Outline the development of one other thing that has progressed from being relatively benign to threatening.

IDEAS FOR DISCUSSION/WRITING

Preparing to Write

Brainstorm or make a list of the products you've seen advertised in infomercials. What are the first words and thoughts and images that come to mind about each? Are there connections between any of these patterns of words? Why do people watch infomercials? What sustains a whole channel of infomercials (The Home Shopping Network)? Have you ever purchased anything after watching an infomercial for it? If so, what convinced you to purchase it? Were you satisfied with your purchase? Why or why not?

Choosing a Topic

1. Advertisements pervade all aspects of our lives, sometimes blatantly and other times more subtly. As advertisers continue to look for new and innovative ways to promote their products, advertisements appear in more and more unusual places including the doors of washroom stalls, computer screen savers, on people's bodies in the form of temporary tattoos, on stickers on produce in the supermarket, and in strategic product placement in movies. A story by Mordecai Richler, published in *Saturday Night* magazine (from which Kingwell's essay comes), was laid out on the page in the shape of an Absolut Vodka bottle and carried the caption, "Absolut Mordecai." Write an essay in which you argue for or against three of the more unusual places you have seen ads.

2. Write a script for an infomercial for a product or a service of your choice. Decide whether you are going to follow a traditional infomercial approach or employ the more recent stylistic trends. Make sure you include specific details to make your product/service appealing.

3. Things do not always turn out to be as they initially appear. Products and services may be presented appealingly in advertisements but don't always fulfill our expectations. Write a letter to the company from which you purchased a product or service that didn't turn out to be as it originally appeared. Remember to be specific about your dissatisfaction and the course of action you expect from the vendor.

WEB SITES

www.scar.utoronto.ca/acad/humanities/Philosophy/Kingwell.htm
Mark Kingwell's homepage.

www.davidlavin.com/kingwell.html
You will find a profile of Kingwell at this David Lavin Agency site.

www.amazon.com/exec/obidos/show
There is an interview with Mark Kingwell at the Amazon Online bookstore site.

CHAPTER 4

PROCESS ANALYSIS

■ ■ ■

Explaining Step by Step

Human nature is characterized by the perpetual desire to understand and analyze the process of living well. The best-seller list is always crowded with books on how to know yourself better, how to be assertive, how to become famous, how to avoid a natural disaster, or how to be rich and happy—all explained in three easy lessons. Open almost any popular magazine, and you will find numerous articles on how to lose weight, how elections are run in this country, how to dress for success, how political rallies evolved, how to gain power, or how to hit a successful topspin backhand. People naturally gravitate toward material that tells them how something is done, how something happened, or how something works, especially if they think the information will help them improve their lives in a significant way.

Defining Process Analysis

A *process* is a procedure that follows a series of steps or stages; *analysis* involves taking a subject apart and explaining its components in order to better understand the whole. Process analysis, then, explains an action, a mechanism, or an event from beginning to end. It concentrates on either a mental or a physical operation: how to solve a chemistry problem, how to tune up your car, how the Canadian Senate is formed, how the Internet works. In fact, the explanation of the writing process, beginning on page 16 of this book, is a good case in point: It divides writing into three interrelated verbal activities and explains how they work—separately and together.

A process analysis can take one of two main forms: (1) It can give directions, thereby explaining how to do something (directive), or (2) it can give information about how something happened (informative). The first type of analysis gives directions for a task the reader may wish to attempt in the future. Examples include how to make jelly, how to lose weight, how to drive to Saskatoon, how to assemble stereo equipment, how to make money, how to use a microscope, how to knit, how to resuscitate a dying relationship, how to win friends, how to discipline your child, and how to backpack.

The second type of analysis furnishes information about what actually occurred in specific situations. Examples include how Hiroshima was bombed, how certain rock stars live, how the tax system works, how *Titanic* was filmed, how Mario Lemieux earned a place in the Hockey Hall of Fame, how gold was first discovered in the Yukon, how computers work, how a kibbutz functions, and how the Gulf War began. These subjects and others like them respond to a certain fascination we all have with mastering some processes and understanding the intricate details of others. They all provide us with opportunities to raise our own standard of living, either by helping us directly apply certain processes to our own lives, or by increasing our understanding of how our complex twentieth-century world functions.

The following student paragraph analyzes the process of constructing a garden compost pit. Written primarily for people who might wish to make such a pit, this piece is directive rather than informative. Notice in particular the amount of detail the student calls upon to explain each stage of the process and the clear transitions she uses to guide us through her analysis.

> No garden is complete without a functioning compost pit. Here's a simple, inexpensive way to make your garbage work for you! To begin with, make a pen out of hog wire or chicken wire, four feet long by eight feet wide by four feet high, splitting it down the middle with another piece of wire so that you end up with a structure that looks like a capital "E" on its side. This is a compost duplex. In the first pen, place a layer of soda ash, just sprinkled on the surface of the dirt. Then, pile an inch or so of leaves, grass clippings, or sawdust on top of the soda ash. You're now ready for the exciting part. Start throwing in all the organic refuse from your kitchen (no meat, bones, or grease, please). After the food is a foot or so deep, throw in a shovelful of steer manure, and cover the entire mess with a thin layer of

dirt. Then water it down. Continue this layering process until the pile is three to three-and-a-half feet high. Allow the pile to sit until it decomposes (from one month in warm climates to six months in colder weather). Next, take your pitchfork and start slinging the contents of pen one into pen two (which will land in reverse order, of course, with the top on the bottom and the bottom on the top). This ensures that everything will decompose evenly. Water this down and begin making a new pile in pen one. That's all there is to it! You now have a ready supply of fertilizer for your garden.

Thinking Critically by Using Process Analysis

Process analysis embodies clear, careful, step-by-step thinking that takes one of three different forms: chronological, simultaneous, or cyclical. The first follows a time sequence from "first this" to "then that." The second forces you to deal with activities or events that happen or happened at the same time, such as people quietly studying or just getting home from work when the major 1994 earthquake hit Los Angeles. And the third requires you to process information that is continuous, like the rising and setting of the sun. No other thinking pattern will force you to slow down as much as process analysis, because the process you are explaining probably won't make any sense if you leave out even the slightest detail.

Good process analysis can truly help your reader see an event in a totally new light. An observer looks at a product already assembled or at a completed event and has no way of knowing without the help of a good process analysis how it got to this final stage. Such an analysis gives the writer or speaker as well as the observer a completely new way of "seeing" the subject in question. Separating process analysis from the other rhetorical modes lets you practice this method of thinking so that you will have a better understanding of the various mental procedures going on in your head. Exercising this possibility in isolation will help you feel its range and its intricacies so that you can become more adept at using it, fully developed, in combination with other modes of thought.

1. List as many examples of each type of process (chronological, simultaneous, and cyclical) that you can think of. Share your list with the class.
2. Write out the process of tying a shoe step by step. Have another person follow your steps exactly to test how well you have analyzed this process.

3. Write a paragraph telling how *not* to do something. Practise
   your use of humour as a technique for creating interest in the
   essay by emphasizing the "wrong" way, for example, to wash
   a car or feed a dog.

Reading and Writing Process Analysis Essays

Your approach to a process analysis essay should be fairly
straightforward. As a reader, you should be sure you understand
the author's statement of purpose and then try to visualize each
step as you go along. As a writer, you need to adapt the mechanics
of the way you normally write to the demands of a process
analysis paper, beginning with an interesting topic and a number
of clearly explained ideas or stages. As usual, the intended
audience determines the choice of words and the degree of detail.

How to Read a Process Analysis Essay

Preparing to Read. Preparing to read a process analysis essay
is as uncomplicated as the essay itself. The title of Paul
Quarrington's essay in this chapter, "Home Brew," tells us exactly what we're going to learn about. Maureen Littlejohn's
phrase "You are a contract painkiller, code name ASA" describes
clearly what her article will teach us about. Scanning each selection to assess the author's audience will give you an even better idea of what to expect in these essays, while the synopsis of
each in the Rhetorical Table of Contents will help focus your
attention on its subject.

Also important as you prepare to read these essays are the
qualifications of each author to write on this subject: Has he or she
performed the task, worked with the mechanism, or seen the
event? Is the writer's experience firsthand? When Paul
Quarrington tells us about making beer at home, is he actually
writing from personal experience? Has Maureen Littlejohn
actually experienced the effect of ASA on pain or fever? What
is Jessica Mitford's experience with mortuaries? How does she
know what goes on "Behind the Formaldehyde Curtain"? The
biography preceding each essay will help you uncover this
information and find out other publication details that will
encourage you to focus on the material you are about to read.

Finally, before you begin reading, answer the prereading
questions, and then do some brainstorming on the subject of the
essay: What do you want to know about the evolution of

carnivorous plants (Forsyth)? How much do any of us really know about the funeral industry and the embalming process, and why might we want to know more?

Reading. When you read the essays in this chapter for the first time, record your initial reactions to them. Consider the preliminary information you have been studying in order to create a context for each author's composition: Why did Maureen Littlejohn write "You Are a Contract Painkiller"? What circumstances prompted Mitford's "Behind the Formaldehyde Curtain"? Who do you think is Fiorito's target audience in "Breakfast in Bed"?

Also determine at this point whether the essay you are reading is *directive* (explaining how to do something) or *informative* (giving information about how something happened). This fundamental understanding of the author's intentions, along with a reading of the questions following the essay, will prepare you to approach the contents of each selection critically when you read it a second time.

Rereading. As you reread these process analysis essays, look for an overview of the process at the beginning of the essay so you know where each writer is headed. The body of each essay, then, is generally a discussion of the stages of the process.

This central portion of the essay is often organized *chronologically* (as in Quarrington's and Mitford's essays), with clear transitions so that readers can easily follow the writer's train of thought. Other methods of organization are *cyclical* (such as the process of convergent evolution described by Forsyth), describing a process that has no clear beginning or end, and *simultaneous* (such as the effects of ASA outlined in Littlejohn's essay), in which many activities occur at the same time with a clear beginning and end. Most of these essays discuss the process as a whole at some point. During this second reading, you will also benefit from discovering what rhetorical modes each writer uses to support his or her process analysis and why these rhetorical modes work effectively. Do the historic examples that Littlejohn uses add to our understanding of the process she is explaining? What do Paul Quarrington's step-by-step instructions, complete with scientific data and cause-and-effect explanations of results, add to his essay on beer-making? And how do the descriptions in Mitford's essay on mortuaries heighten the horror of the North American mortuary business? How do all the rhetorical modes in each essay help create a coherent whole?

After reading each essay for a second time, answer the questions that follow the selection to see if you are understanding your reading material on the literal, interpretive, and analytical levels before you take on the discussion/writing assignments.

For an overview of the entire reading process, you might consult the checklists on pages 15–16 of the Introduction.

How to Write a Process Analysis Essay

Prewriting. As you begin a process analysis assignment, you first need to become as familiar as you can with the action, mechanism, or event you are going to describe. If possible, try to go through the process yourself at least once or twice. If you can't actually carry out the procedure, going through the process mentally and taking notes is a good alternative. Then, try to read something about the process. After all this preparation (and careful consideration of your audience and purpose), you should be ready to brainstorm, freewrite, cluster, or use your favourite prewriting technique (see pages 17–19 of the Introduction) in response to the prewriting questions before you start composing your paper.

Writing. The essay should begin with an overview of the process or event to be analyzed. This initial section should introduce the subject, divide it into a number of recognizable steps, and describe the result once the process is complete. Your thesis in a process essay is usually a purpose statement that clearly and briefly explains your approach to the procedure you will discuss: "Building model airplanes can be divided into four basic steps" or "The American courts follow three stages in prosecuting a criminal case."

Next, the directive or informative essay should proceed logically through the various stages of the process, from beginning to end. The parts of a process usually fall nicely into chronological order, supported by such transitions as "at first," "in the beginning," "next," "then," "after that," and "finally." Some processes, however, are either simultaneous, forcing the writer to choose a more complex logical order for the essay (such as classification), or cyclical, requiring the writer to choose a starting point and then explain the cycle stage by stage. Playing the guitar, for example, involves two separate and simultaneous components that must work together: holding the strings against the frets with the fingers of one hand and strumming with the other hand. In analyzing this procedure, you would probably want to describe both parts of the process and then explain how the hands work together to produce music. An example of a cyclical process would be the changing of the seasons. To explain this concept to a reader, you would need to pick a starting point, such as spring, and describe the entire cycle, stage by stage, from that point onward.

In a process paper, you need to be especially sensitive to your intended audience, or it will not be able to follow your explanation. The amount of information, the number of examples and illustrations, and the terms to be defined all depend on the prior knowledge and background of your readers. A writer explaining to a group of amateur cooks how to prepare a soufflé would take an entirely different approach to the subject than he or she would if the audience were a group of bona fide chefs hoping to land jobs in elegant French restaurants. The professional chefs would need more sophisticated and precise explanations than their recreational counterparts, who would probably find such an approach tedious and complicated because of the extraneous details.

The last section of a process analysis paper should consider the process as a whole. If, for example, the writer is giving directions on how to build a model airplane, the essay might end with a good description or drawing of the plane. The informative essay on our legal system might offer a summary of the stages of judging and sentencing a criminal. And the essay on cooking a soufflé might finish with a photograph of the mouth-watering dish.

Rewriting. In order to revise a process analysis essay, first make sure your main purpose is apparent throughout your paper:

1. Have you written a directive or an informative essay?
2. Is your purpose statement clear?

Next, you need to determine if your paper is aimed at the proper audience:

1. Have you given your readers an overview of the process you are going to discuss?
2. Do you go through the process you are explaining step by step?
3. At the end of the essay, do you help your readers see the process as a complete entity?

The checklists on pages 26–27 will give you further guidelines for writing, revising, and proofreading.

Student Essay: Process Analysis at Work

The student essay that follows analyzes the process of using a "home permanent" kit. Notice that, once the student gives an overview of the process, she discusses the steps one at a time, being careful to follow a logical order (in this case, chronological) and to use clear transitions. Then, see how the end of the essay shows the process as a whole.

Follow the Simple Directions

Although fickle hairstylists in Paris and Hollywood decide what is currently "in," many romanticists disregard fashion and yearn for a mane of delicate tendrils. <u>Sharing this urge but resenting the cost, I opted for a "home perm" kit</u>. Any literate person with normal dexterity could follow illustrated directions, I reasoned, and the eight easy steps would energize my limp locks in less than two hours. "Before" and "after" photos of flawless models showed the metamorphosis one might achieve. Confidently, I assembled towels, rollers, hair clips, waving lotion, neutralizer, end papers, and a plastic cap. <u>While shampooing</u>, I chortled about my ingenuity and economy.

<u>After towel-drying my hair, I applied the gooey, acidic waving lotion thoroughly. Then I wrapped an end paper around a parted section and rolled the first curl ("securely but not too tightly")</u>. Despite the reassuring click of the fastened rollers, as I sectioned each new curl the previous one developed its own volition and slowly unrolled itself. Resolutely, I reapplied waving lotion and rewound—and rewound—each curl. <u>Since my hair was already saturated, I regarded the next direction skeptically: "Apply waving lotion to each curl."</u> Faithfully, however, I complied with the instructions. <u>Ignoring the fragile state of the fastened rollers, I then feigned assurance and enclosed my entire head in a plastic cap</u>. In forty minutes, chemical magic would occur.

Restless with anticipation, I puttered about the house; while absorbed in small chores, I felt the first few drops of lotion escape from the plastic tent. Stuffing wads of cotton around the cap's edges did not help, and the small drops soon became rivulets that left red streaks on my neck and face and splattered on the floor. (Had I overdone the waving lotion?) Ammonia fumes so permeated each room that I was soon asked to leave. Retreating to the bathroom, I opened the window and dreamed of frivolous new hairstyles.

Margin notes:

Purpose statement for informative process analysis

Overview

First step (chronological order)

Second step

Third step

Transition

Fourth step

Transition

Fifth step

Transition   <u>Finally, the waving time had elapsed; neutralizing was next</u>. I removed my plastic cap, carefully heeding the caution: "Do not   Sixth step disturb curlers as you rinse waving lotion from hair." With their usual impudence, however, all the curlers soon bobbed in the sink; undaunted, I continued. "This next step is critical," warned the instructions. Thinking half-hearted curls were better than no curls Transition at all, I poured the entire bottle of neutralizer on my hair. <u>After a drippy ten-minute wait, I read the next step: "Carefully remove</u> Seventh step <u>rollers." As this advice was superfluous, I moved anxiously to the</u> Transition <u>finale: "Rinse all solution from your hair, and enjoy your curls."</u>   Eight step

     Lifting my head from the sink and expecting visions of Final Aphrodite, I saw instead Medusa's image in the mirror. Limp product question-mark spirals fell over my eyes, and each "curl" ended in an explosion of steel-wool frizz. Reflecting on my ineptitude, I knew why the direction page was illustrated only with drawings. After washing a large load of ammonia-scented towels, I took two aspirin and called my hairdresser. <u>Some repair services are cheap</u> Concluding <u>at any price</u>.   remark

Student Writer's Comments

Any person with normal dexterity probably could do a successful perm! But I sure had trouble. And I decided I wanted to communicate that trouble within my process analysis essay. When I was given this writing assignment, I knew immediately that I wanted to explain how to do a perm. But I didn't know how to handle the humour that had resulted from my misguided attempt to administer a perm to myself. Part of my response to this assignment resides deep within my personality (I'm a closet comedian), but part of it simply has to do with the relationship between me and permanents (actually, anything having to do with cosmetics). But as I started out on this project, I had no idea if I could mold the comedy into a step-by-step analysis of a process.

First, I went to the store and bought a brand-new home perm, so I could review the guidelines step by step. On a piece of paper, I listed the procedures for giving myself a

perm. On another sheet of paper, I wrote down any stories or associations I had with each stage of the process. Some of the notes on the second sheet of paper took the form of full paragraphs, others a list of words and phrases, and still others a combination of lists and full sentences. I found myself laughing aloud at some of the memories the home perm directions triggered.

I knew I was writing a directive essay for someone who might actually want to try a home perm. After making my preliminary lists of ideas, I just let my natural sense of humour direct my writing. My overview and purpose statement came easily. Next, I went through the directions one by one, laughing at myself and the process along the way. Before I knew it, I found myself writing, "After washing a large load of ammonia-scented towels, I took two aspirin and called my hairdresser"——the perfect end, or so I thought, to my comedy of errors. I had written the whole first draft from start to finish without once surfacing for air.

When I reread my draft, I realized that the approach I had taken to this process analysis assignment was a satirical one. It allowed me to go through the proper procedure of giving myself a home perm while simultaneously poking fun at myself along the way. As I revised my essay, I tried to exaggerate some of the humourous sections that demonstrated my ineptness or my failure to follow the directions correctly, hoping they would communicate the true ridiculousness of this entire situation. After omitting some details and embellishing others, I came up with the current last sentence of the essay: "Some repair services are cheap at any price." This new concluding remark took the edge off the whiny tone of the previous sentence and brought the essay to an even lighter close than before. I ended up liking the way the humour worked in the essay, because besides accurately capturing my most recent *process analysis experience, it made a potentially dull essay topic rather entertaining. My only problem now is that I'm still not sure I got all the frizz out of my hair!*

Some Final Thoughts on Process Analysis

In this chapter, a single process dictates the development and organization of each of the essays. Both directional and informational methods are represented here. Notice in particular the clear purpose statements that set the focus of the essays in each case, as well as the other rhetorical modes (such as narration, comparison/contrast, and definition) that are used to help support the writers' explanations.

Process Analysis in Review

Reading Process Analysis Essays

Preparing to Read

1. What assumptions can you make from the essay's title?
2. Can you guess what the general mood of the essay is?
3. What is the essay's purpose and audience?
4. What does the synopsis in the Rhetorical Table of Contents tell you about the essay?
5. What can you learn from the author's biography?
6. Can you guess what the author's point of view toward the subject is?
7. What are your responses to the Preparing to Read questions?

Reading

1. Is the essay *directive* (explaining how to do something) or *informative* (giving information about how something happened)?
2. What general message is the author trying to convey?
3. Did you preview the questions that follow the essay?

Rereading

1. Does the author furnish an overview of the process?

2. How is the essay organized—*chronologically, cyclically,* or *simultaneously?*

3. What other rhetorical modes does the author use to support the essay's purpose?

4. What are your responses to the questions after the essay?

Writing Process Analysis Essays

Preparing to Write

1. What are your responses to the Preparing to Write questions?

2. What is your purpose?

3. Who is your audience?

4. Are you as familiar as possible with the action, mechanism, or event you are going to explain?

Writing

1. Do you provide an overview of the process at the beginning of the essay?

2. Does your first paragraph introduce your subject, divide it into recognizable steps, describe the result once the process is complete, and include a purpose statement?

3. Is your process analysis essay either *directive* or *informative?*

4. Do you proceed logically through the various steps of the process?

5. Are the essay's details organized *chronologically, simultaneously,* or *cyclically?*

6. What is your audience's background?

7. Does your essay end considering the process as a whole?

Rewriting

1. Have you written a *directive* or an *informative* essay?

2. Is your purpose statement clear?

3. Have you given your readers an overview of the process you are going to discuss?

4. Do you go through the process you are explaining step by step?

5. At the end of the essay, do you help your readers see the process as a complete entity?

Adrian Forsyth
1951–

■ ■ ■

Little Plants of Horror

Adrian Forsyth is a biologist and writer from southeastern Ontario. As well as being a contributing editor at *Equinox* magazine, Forsyth has contributed to *Harrowsmith* and *Owl Magazine*, which is for children. He was born in Ottawa and received his B.Sc. from Queen's University in Kingston in 1974. In 1978 Forsyth graduated from Harvard with a Ph.D. and went on to become an associate professor in the biology department back at Queen's. He was married in 1980 and currently lives in Elgin, Ontario. Forsyth has written books for children and adults, including *Tropical Nature* (1984), *Mammals of the Canadian Wild* (1985), *A Natural History of Sex: The Ecology and Evolution of Sexual Behaviour* (1986), and *Exploring the World of Birds* (1990). The essay included here appeared in one of Forsyth's regular columns in *Equinox*.

Preparing to Read

In this essay Forsyth discusses the evolution of a unique kind of plant. Before you begin to read, think about plants. What place do plants have in the natural world? Why do people grow gardens or house plants? Where would you position plants in the food chain? Are plants benign or dangerous? What characteristics make something belong to the broad category of plant?

L anding on the rubbery red lip, the fly walks forward, tasting   1
the sweet surface with its feet. As the insect hungrily moves ahead into the open gullet, however, the sugary surface abruptly becomes waxy and slick, and the fly loses its footing. Instinctively, it beats its wings, but before it can rise, the insect has fallen into a watery pool. The clear liquid is almost soapy, with no surface tension to support the struggling fly, and when it attempts to clamber up the wall, a phalanx of downward pointing spines prevents its escape. Slowly, the fly drowns.

So begins a meal for the northern pitcher plant (*Sarracenia*   2
purpurea), which attracts, captures and eats animals. Usually, it consumes insects and spiders, but sometimes, the trumpetlike pitcher plant traps something more substantial, such as a frog.

Meat-eating plants strike us as bizarre, the stuff of science   3
fiction and horror shows. We learn in school that plants
photosynthetically manufacture their own food from carbon
dioxide and water. It is tempting, then, to consider carnivorous
plants as freaks of nature and to leave it at that. Yet a Darwinian
would be intrigued, as indeed Darwin was, to know that there are
hundreds of very different plant species which supplement their
diet by carnivory. They include sundews, butterworts,
bladderworts, pitcher plants, Venus's-flytraps and certain species
in other families, such as the bromeliads. What makes the
phenomenon particularly fascinating to ecologists is that
unrelated plant families, repeatedly and independently, have
evolved the same meat-eating habit all around the world.
Furthermore, many carnivorous plants are specialized in
remarkably similar ways, and that specialization is worth
examining before we address just why the carnivory evolved.

Let us begin with the northern pitcher plant, which is found   4
in abundance in low-lying bogs near my home in eastern Ontario.
The species grows as a rosette, a ring of pitchers reaching up
and out, each adorned with a bold flag patterned with reddish
pigment. The plant appears wholly designed for carnivory—
indeed it lacks any flat green leaves associated with conventional
sunlight-harvesting plants—and it is eminently successful in its
pursuit of flesh. In high summer, tipping or flushing out the
contents of a pitcher yields not just one or two victims but a thick
slurry of dozens of ants, deer flies, spiders and other arthropods
in various stages of degradation.

Yet pitcher plants are more than death traps, and ironically,   5
much of the interest they hold for naturalists is found in the life
they sustain, not destroy. Although pitcher plants excrete a
variety of enzymes that attack the tissues of the animals they
capture, they also play host to communities of insects and other
arthropods which have evolved an immunity to such digestive
juices. The pitcher-plant mosquito lays its eggs inside the pitcher
plant, and the larvae feed on the teeming protozoa in the fluid. A
type of midge breeds exclusively in pitcher plants; its larvae
mine and wriggle in the detritus that accumulates in the bottom
of the pitcher. On the surface of the pool, large white maggots of
a specialized flesh fly rip apart the newly captured insect
carcasses with tearing mouth hooks and battle with each other for
sole possession of the fertile foraging spot. Also, certain species
of mites and rotifers are found only inside the pitchers.

The relationship between a plant and its arthropod guests 6 may have evolved to be mutually beneficial. There is some evidence, for example, that the guests may accelerate the growth of the pitcher plant by mechanically breaking down and consuming prey captured by the plant and then excreting highly soluble, nitrogen-rich digestive wastes.

Such remarkable adaptations developed by the pitcher plants 7 of North America and their symbiotic associates are so specialized that one might think the assemblage is a unique phenomenon. Unlikely as it may seem, however, another set of pitcher plants has evolved in the rainforests of Southeast Asia, a habitat as geographically and biotically distinct from an eastern Ontario wetland as can be imagined. Yet the Asian pitcher plants, belonging to the genus *Nepenthes*, which is in no way evolution-arily related to the North American pitcher plants, are nonetheless astonishingly similar to them.

I recently encountered my first Asian pitcher plants on a 8 mountain in Sulawesi, Indonesia, in a towering rainforest that recalled nothing of an Ontario bog. In the treetops were troops of orange-eyed black macaque monkeys and massive toucan-like birds called hornbills. Lily flowers the size of watermelons and stinking like carrion erupted from the soil. Audacious and rapacious leeches sat on understorey leaves, stretching up, waving from side to side or inching along in active pursuit of blood. And there, in the midst of it all, were pitcher plants that looked nearly identical to the *Sarracenia* plants from home—upright rosettes of green- and red-flagged trumpets full of water, dead ants and wiggling mosquito larvae. Only a botanist examining the minutiae of flower anatomy would know that the two plants were unrelated.

It is not shared ancestry but shared ecology that brought 9 about the resemblance. For all their differences, bogs and tropical rainforests do share some features that have proved critical in the evolutionary sculpting of the resident flora. The soils in both habitats, for example, are very wet, extremely acidic and low in nitrates and other soil nutrients. And since every plant's metabolic machinery depends on enzymes and other molecules which contain nitrogen, harvesting that element becomes a top priority for each plant. In both rainforest and bog, pitcher plants have adopted the habit of devouring protein-rich insects to obtain their supply.

The distributional and the physical resemblance between 10
these two unrelated groups is explained by what ecologists call
"convergent evolution," or the tendency for unrelated organisms
to converge on the same solution when confronted with similar
selection pressures. If one considers the overriding importance of
nitrogen-poor, waterlogged acidic soils, it is possible to see why
both tropical rainforests and Canadian bogs should be rich in
insect-eating plants. Also, that such similar structures as the
pitcher-shaped water traps should have evolved more than once
is not entirely unexpected.

Clearly, rooted and immobile as they are, plants have a 11
limited number of capturing devices that they might evolve. The
most specialized and active predatory plants, the Venus's-flytraps
and bladderworts, have complicated traps with moving parts,
devices that evolved only once. But the sticky traps of the
sundews and butterworts, which consist of resin-tipped hairs
on the leaves, or the water-filled pitchers of the pitcher plant,
which are merely folded leaves, are examples of simple
rearrangements of existing plant features, rearrangements that
have been repeatedly exploited by different plants.

When the demanding conditions of natural selection are the 12
same, living organisms of even very different ancestry often end
up looking alike—porpoises and fish, for instance. Convergences
such as that of the pitcher plant confirm that even the most
bizarre inhabitants of this planet are not simply historical
accidents or random quirks of creation. They are the results of an
evolutionary process that works in Sulawesi just as it does in
Ontario.

As one might expect, it was Charles Darwin who did the 13
first good work both on convergent evolution and on carnivorous
plants. He seems to have studied almost every important
phenomenon, and biologists, humbled and astonished by his
achievements, often wonder about his unwavering devotion to his
work. Perhaps, though, we can sense a little of the motivating
force when we look closely at what caught and held his attention.
Convergent forms and carnivorous plants can be explained, and
they are all the more marvellous for it. I know that on the
mountain in Sulawesi with my first *Nepenthes* in hand, I felt the
reward that Darwin's view allows us. There is a fundamental
pleasure in seeing connection and pattern amid the diversity,
and the unity, of life on Earth.

UNDERSTANDING DETAILS

1. How might you recognize a carnivorous plant if you came across one?
2. How common are carnivorous plants? Why can't they be dismissed as "freaks of nature"?
3. What ecological conditions have contributed to the development of carnivory in unrelated plants?

ANALYZING MEANING

1. The writer of this article is trained as a biologist, but here he is writing for a lay audience. How does Forsyth make his subject understandable and interesting to his readers?
2. Describe the writer's attitude toward his subject, using specific examples as evidence.
3. In your own words, explain the term "convergent evolution." Can you think of an example other than the ones that Forsyth uses?

DISCOVERING RHETORICAL STRATEGIES

1. Is the title of this piece appropriate? What allusion is Forsyth making with this title?
2. While the primary rhetorical mode is process analysis, Forsyth also effectively uses other techniques. Find two examples of other strategies that he employs.
3. In this essay Forsyth outlines both the process of a carnivorous plant consuming a meal and the process of evolution that has created carnivorous plants. Use two different colours of highlighters to trace the steps in each process. What does this show you about Forsyth's method of organization?

MAKING CONNECTIONS

1. Forsyth, a trained biologist, is writing on a topic about which he has a high level of expertise. Michael Clugston ("Twice Struck") also is presenting information to a lay audience on a topic about which he is highly knowledgeable. Compare and contrast the strategies that each of these writers uses to make their information accessible and interesting to an audience that does not share the author's level of expertise.
2. Forsyth is one of many authors writing about nature and natural phenomena. How does Forsyth's focus compare to that of

Tomson Highway ("What a Certain Visionary Once Said"), Lesley Choyce ("Thin Edge of the Wedge") or Michael Clugston ("Twice Struck")?

3. Part of the effectiveness of Forsyth's essay is contributed by the vivid descriptions he incorporates into his process analysis. How does the use of description by Forsyth, Karen Connelly ("Touch the Dragon") and Jessica Mitford ("Behind the Formaldehyde Curtain") enhance their essays? Which of these authors uses description most effectively in their essays? Explain.

IDEAS FOR DISCUSSION/WRITING

Preparing to Write

Write freely about the ways in which living things adapt to their surroundings. What reasons do things have for adapting? What examples of adaptation can you see among humans? Among animals? Among plants? What problems do we experience as the result of other species adapting to conditions that we create?

Choosing a Topic

1. People immigrating to a new country have to adapt in many ways. Using specific examples, write an essay in which you analyze this process of acculturation. Decide on your intended audience and your purpose before you begin to write.

2. Humans are constantly inventing tools to help them adapt to a changing environment. Think of one particular technological advance of the late twentieth century and then project yourself back in time to the beginning of the century. Explain to the people of the early 1900s the process of change in this realm of life.

3. Forsyth talks about the surprise of finding similar adaptation in plants growing in very different and distant parts of the world. Describe the experience of going to a new place and finding something unexpectedly familiar.

WEB SITES

randomaccess.unm.edu/www/cp/cparchive.html
The Carnivorous Plant Archive Server links to a large range of information concerning carnivorous plants.

Paul Quarrington
1953–

■ ■ ■
Home Brew

Fly fisherman, beermeister, rock musician, and acclaimed young Canadian novelist: meet Paul Quarrington. Quarrington, whose brother the fellow brewer, is a musician with the Toronto Symphony, grew up in suburban Toronto. A brief stint in academia at the University of Toronto may have proved a bit confining for the prolific and lively writer-to-be, because, although he exited short of a degree, he published his first novel, *The Service* (1978), at twenty-five. If beer is one of Quarrington's consuming interests, as he suggests, then rock music—beer's inevitable companion—has been another amusing sideline in his career. He has played bass and co-produced LPs performed with yet another Quarrington brother as part of the satirically tempered group, Joe Hall and the Continental Drift, during the heyday of Toronto's Queen Street night culture. Quarrington's interest in rock gave him the subject of another of his best-selling novels, *Whale Music* (1989), which concerns itself with a fictionalized version of the reclusive Brian Wilson of the Beach Boys. This novel won Quarrington the Governor General's Award for fiction in 1990. His ability to make stories out of his interests produced three novels about sports: *Home Game* (1983), *King Leary* (1987), and *Hometown Heroes* (1988), a collection of stories edited by Quarrington entitled *Original Six: True Stories from Hockey's Classic Era* (1996), and a work of nonfiction, *Fishing With My Old Guy* (1995). In addition, Quarrington has written screenplays for popular television shows *Due South, Once a Thief,* and *Power Play*. Quarrington lives in Toronto, where he pursues other interests, including fly-fishing, and apparently, sausage-making. His latest book is *The Boy on the Back of the Turtle* (1997), a nonfiction book about travelling through the Galapagos Islands with his seven-year-old daughter and his seventy-three-year-old father.

Preparing to Read

Paul Quarrington's lively tribute to "Home Brew," which first appeared in *Harrowsmith* magazine in the spring of 1992, presents this young writer's adventures with the pleasures and problems of making Canada's favourite beverage at home. The contents of the ubiquitous brown and green bottles have been brewed by humans since the beginning of civilization. But does this mean that making beer is an easy process? As you prepare to try "Home Brew," think of what might motivate you to try to make "homemade anything": Would it be your fondness for that product? Would it be the chance to save money? Would it be the challenge of trying to better a commercial product? Or would you be driven by curiosity about the process of making something yourself? Could you then teach someone else to follow your procedure successfully?

The first thing I must explain is that my brother helped me with 1
this project. We share certain traits my brother and I, and chief
among them is a fondness, nay an *over*-fondness for beer. We have
even developed a Trivial Pursuit-type game featuring questions
about beer. Indeed, every question can be answered by bellowing, "Beer!" My brother and I take a foolish delight in ordering
drinks in the same fashion, screaming out "Beer!" at helpful bar-
tenders and waiters, deviating from this only to the extent of making it "More beer!" as the evening progresses.

At any rate, when asked by this fine journal if I would look 2
into the making of beer—home brewing—my brother stepped
into the breach (I could not stop him), and his presence shall
make itself known. For example, at one point during the
procedure, I took to ruminating aloud. "Making beer," I mused,
"is as natural as childbirth."

"True," agreed my brother, "but the child could be a 3
homicidal maniac."

By which my brother made oblique reference to the truly 4
vile bogswill that people had forced upon us in days long gone
by, bottles filled half with a dull, cloudy liquid, half with some
other-worldly sludge. It used to be that no words filled me with
as much dread as "homemade beer." But I have learned much—
the aforementioned bogswill was likely the doing of "the wild
yeasties"—and, while learning, have tasted many exceptional
beers. My brother and I are very pleased with our own batch
and have spent several lovely evenings in his living room,
occasionally glancing up at each other and bellowing, "Beer!"

But let us get down to basics; let us make sure we all know 5
exactly what is going on here. Beer is a beverage that is fermented
from cereals and malt and flavoured with hops. From this simple
statement, all else shall follow, so it is good to fix it in your mind,
to repeat it inwardly a couple of times. (Or, put as a question in
our game: What beverage is fermented from cereals and malt
and flavoured with hops? Answer: Beer!)

The first significance arising from the statement is that beer 6
is made with cereals rather than with fruit as is, say, wine. The
process of fermentation occurs when a molecule of sugar splits,
creating two molecules of carbon dioxide (CO_2) and two molecules
of ethyl alcohol (C_2H_5OH). Starch, such as that found in those
cereals, cannot be converted into alcohol. This would be extremely
bad news for us beer lovers, except for a vegetable enzyme called
amylase. You see, starch is, chemically speaking, a long chain of

molecules ($C_6H_{10}O_5$, et cetera, et cetera). Amylase breaks up the chain, pairs the molecules and adds a water molecule, thus creating $C_{12}H_{22}O_{11}$, which is a maltose sugar molecule that can thence undergo fermentation, praise the Lord. It is this process that is carried out at malting houses, which is why we begin our beermaking with a large can of malt extract (usually hopped malt extract) rather than with a bucketful of barley.

I will abandon the pseudoscientific tone now. It is bound to   7 go down in flames right around the time I try to throw in the scientific name for the yeast used to make lager beers, *Saccharomycescarlsbergensis*. That yeast, you see, was named for the place where it was discovered, and do not be embarrassed if you, too, failed to realize that there are all sorts of different yeasts with all sorts of fancy names—not to mention those unruly thugs and hooligans, the wild yeasties. Yeast is what does the actual work of fermentation. It is a plant organism, a living thing; and when it dies, it sinks to the bottom and forms sludge.

Malt and yeast are all you truly need to make beer, and   8 humankind has been making it for something like 8,000 years. (Q: What has humankind been making for 8,000 years? A: Beer!) Hops did not appear on the European scene until the 12th century, and even at that time, there was resistance in the form of laws forbidding their use. Hops are the flowers of the female hop vine (an aggressive spreader, it has earned the lovely nomenclature *Humulus lupulus* and is also known as the "wolf of the willows"), and their resins and oils impart flavour of a slightly bitter nature to the beer.

There are many different kinds of hops; they all have different   9 names (Cluster, Fuggles, Tetenang), and they come in either pellet or leaf form. It really is quite mind-boggling. That is why it is important to have a firm grip on the basics. (Q: Combine malt, hops, yeast and water, and in time, you will have what? A: Beer!) This is no more mysterious than, say, the baking of bread. Not coincidentally, the Old English *breowan* gives us both "brew" and "bread."

The first step in making beer at home is to leave it—your   10 home, that is—and hie down to a specialty shop. We chose a Wine-Art/Brewers-Art store (in Toronto) because it happened to be closest, but Wine-Art/Brewers-Art stores also have a reputation for helpfulness, and many of the home brewers I spoke with steered me in that direction. And indeed, we were greeted by a friendly sort, Martin Jordan (manager), who spent a long time explaining things. The process detailed below is, in fact, Martin's Improved Method.

You need to acquire some basic equipment: a primary   11
fermenter, a secondary fermenter and a siphoning hose. This should run you somewhere between $30 and $40. Allow me a moment to deal with the financial advantages of home brewing. Clearly, home brew is a lot less expensive than buying beer at the beer store. This seems to me, however, to be one of the least noble reasons for undertaking the endeavour. You will encounter people who brew because it is cheap, and they usually give themselves away by saying something like, "And the beer is just as good as the stuff you buy."

These people are missing the point, I think. The great thing   12
about home brewing is that you can make some really wonderful beers, you can alter recipes to suit your individual taste and if it ends up being economical, that is a fact to be savoured rather than gloated over. Besides, it may not be all that economical: although the three items listed above are all you really need, they are not all you will end up carting out of the store.

You will want a hydrometer to measure specific gravity (I will   13
explain in a moment). You will want a vapour lock, and you will want a plastic J-tube which is crooked at the bottom so that you don't have to stand there holding the siphoning hose. You will want a hose clamp for when you are bottling, which reminds me— you need some bottles. And caps. And a capper. And you will want some potassium metabisulphite crystals to cleanse and disinfect all that stuff.

The primary fermenter is typically a large plastic pail—   14
preferably a food-grade pail, but nothing used for oils or vinegars— with a tight-fitting lid. The secondary fermenter is typically a large glass bottle (such as might contain a genie). These are called, for reasons that have not been explained to my satisfaction, carboys. They come in two sizes, 19 and 23 litres. Those are the two quantities you make beer in, 19 and 23 litres. We are going to be making 23 litres.

Now that you have your basic equipment, you need to   15
purchase the ingredients for the wort. The wort is the combination of malt, grains and hops whence flows your batch of beer. My brother and I chose to make an English-style bitter and purchased a can of hopped malt extract with the word BITTER printed on it. You could purchase Brown Ale, American Light, Stout, Pale Ale, et cetera. Each can contains 1.5 kilograms of hopped malt extract,

yeast and instructions, and costs around $15. One could make a batch of beer just by using the stuff in the can (actually, you need some corn sugar), but Martin Jordan suggested that we also purchase some roasted barley and bittering hops. This we did, because he said the resulting beer would taste like Smithwick's, a statement that had my brother and me leaping about the store like puppies.

So now you are all loaded up, and it cost approximately $75, of 16 which perhaps $55 was a one-time investment. Therefore, for about $20, you are going to get 23 litres of beer. (I find it hard not to get excited.)

The first step takes place in the kitchen, where you cook up 17 the wort in a huge pot. To begin, you bring four to six litres of water to a boil. You add the bittering hops. The hops look like rabbit pellets, which is a bit off-putting. Martin Jordan suggested that in the course of cooking the wort, you occasionally take a single hop and fling it with a certain élan into the mixture. I think this is sage advice. I doubt that a single hop affects the flavour much, but it does help the novice brewmaster to relax.

At any rate, you let the hops boil for 15 to 20 minutes, at which 18 point you add the sugar. Let that boil for another five minutes, then add the crushed malt grains. (Take a pinch and eat them; you'll be surprised how good they taste.) Let that simmer for five minutes, then add the malt extract, which you will discover is a thick, glutinous syrup with the consistency of molasses. Return the mixture to a low simmer.

While the wort is cooking (and whenever you are not flinging 19 hop pellets into it) is a good time to clean and disinfect your primary fermenter—or, in my case, a good time to discover that your brother has an obsessive-compulsive personality disorder. I counsel thoroughness rather than monomania. For instance, if, having disinfected your primary fermenter, you then pick it up to move it closer to the stove, it is not necessary—although my brother found it so—to redisinfect where the offending fingers were placed. It is a good idea to mark the 23-litre level on the inside of the container.

Now put some cold water in that primary fermenter. (A tip 20 from Mr. Jordan: You might draw the water the day before and let it sit overnight, which helps get rid of the chlorine taste.) You now strain the wort into it. You stir and then add more water until you reach the 23-litre mark. You pitch the yeast, which is less strenuous than it sounds, adding it when the mixture is between 70 and 80 degrees F. (Warning: If it is too hot, you will kill the yeast.)

Now, ahem, allow me to get a little scholarly here. The 21
specific gravity of water is 1.000. Liquids containing sugar have
a higher specific gravity because they are denser. Alcohol is
lighter than water. Therefore, during fermentation, the specific
gravity of your brew will drop as more and more of the sugar
is converted into alcohol. Some of the malt will not convert (which
is what gives beer its taste), so although the final specific gravity
will approach 1.000 again, it will never truly arrive.

A rule of thumb is that when the specific gravity stops 22
dropping, fermentation is complete. Got it? For this reason, we
now take our hydrometer, which looks like a futuristic fishing
float, and place it in our beer-to-be. It might read, say, 1.046. The
higher the figure, the more potential alcohol, and some recipes
will even say, "At this point, your starting s.g. should be 1.048,"
in which case you would add more malt and / or sugar until that
level is attained.

All right now. Fermentation splits a molecule of sugar into 23
ethanol and carbon dioxide. The latter is gas, gas that is exuded
with a series of very satisfying mulching galoomps. So we need
to let the gas escape. But if we leave the container uncovered,
guess what's going to get into it? The wild yeasties! For even
though many yeasts are civilized and gentrified, there are unruly
yeasts floating about in the air, little gangs of them just looking
to mess up somebody's beer. To get into it and produce *off
flavours*. That is Martin Jordan's way of saying the wild yeasties
will make, you know, bogswill. You therefore cover your primary
fermenter very securely, having purchased a lid for that purpose.
You will notice that the lid has a largish hole dead centre, which
seems foolish until you see that your fermentation lock's rubber
stopper will plug it admirably. The fermentation lock is a twisted
piece of tubing, half-filled with water, which will let out the CO_2,
and vent the last gasps of expiring yeast without admitting the
dreaded hordes.

You then move down to the basement, especially if you are 24
attempting to make a lager. Lager, derived from the German for
"storage," cannot be properly made when the weather is too
warm, so if you are doing this in the summer, you had best make
an ale. Ale is fermented at higher temperatures, which causes
most of the yeast to rise to the top. Ale is thus a top-fermenting
brew, lager a bottom-fermenting brew. And there, at last, we
know the difference between the two.

You can relax now for approximately five days. It should be 25 easy to determine whether fermentation is taking place (bubbles in the vapour lock), although our brew appeared strangely inactive. Martin Jordan suggested that the gas was probably escaping from somewhere else, perhaps from around the lid rather than through the vapour lock, and by taking a series of readings with the carefully sterilized hydrometer, we were able to determine that all was as it should be.

On day five, you siphon into the secondary fermenter. Your 26 primary fermenter will have developed a sludgy bottom layer made up of yeast corpses, and although the siphoning tube has a crook at the bottom, hopefully raising it above it all, great care should be taken not to transfer the sludge. By the way, you realize I am assuming that all of this stuff has been cleansed and sterilized. Any slip-up on the sanitation front could result in *off flavours*, so never let down your guard. (While we were making our beer, a number of bad batches were reported to Martin Jordan at his store, as if the wild germs and yeasties had gone on a citywide rampage. Beware.)

On day 15, you add the "finings," commonly isinglass, which 27 is made from the scrapings of sturgeons' swim bladders. This makes your beer less cloudy. Don't ask how, just do it.

On day 20, you bottle. Beer's effervescence is created from 28 extra fermentation at the end of the process, so you now add a little more corn sugar or finishing malt. You could add about half a teaspoon of sugar per bottle, although the sensible thing to do is add 1-1/4 cups to the 23-litre carboy. Siphon off some beer, dissolve the sugar in it, then reintroduce it to the brew. Don't start stirring in your carboy, lest you disturb the sludge.

My brother and I bottled in plastic litre bottles with screw-on 29 plastic caps, which I realize is cheating, but I thought it worked wonderfully. A potential downside is that you need to drink a litre whenever you want a beer, but my brother and I conceived of this as *no big problem*. You might choose to bottle the standard 341-millilitre size, which you would then cap in the traditional manner. My big tip here is to purchase a clamp for the end of your siphoning tube, a simple device that stops the flow momentarily as you move from bottle to bottle.

If you are still in the basement at this point, it might be an idea 30 to move your lot upstairs where it is warmer to sort of kick-start this last bit of fermentation. Five days later, you should return your beer to a cool place, and five days after that, you could drink one.

Which is to say, it is the earliest you should drink one, but time will only improve your beer. Many claim it is best in three months.

Perhaps the diciest aspect of home brew comes with the 31
actual drinking. That final bit of fermentation produced bubbles, a little more alcohol and some dead yeast cells, which are now lying on the bottom of the bottle. When pouring the beer, it is best to hold the bottle in front of a light so that you can view the sludge's advent toward the neck. The trick is to avoid dead yeast without leaving behind half a bottle of beer. And once you have poured the beer, rinse out the bottle immediately, because as the remaining liquid evaporates, the sludge will adhere to the inside and render it useless as a beer receptacle.

So there you have it. The procedure is simple, virtually idiot- 32
proof—nothing can stop those yeasts from splitting up sugar molecules—and also educational.

Q: What beverage contains pelletized wolf of the willows and 33
sturgeon swim bladder scrapings?

A: You got it.   34

UNDERSTANDING DETAILS

1. What are the constituent parts of the recipe for beer? What role does each play in making the finished beverage?
2. What living ingredient plays a vital role in the fermentation of beer? How does it work? Why might it sometimes produce "vile bogswill," or a brewed offspring which is "a homicidal maniac"?
3. Describe the preparation of wort. What must be added to wort to produce beer? What is the function of each added ingredient?

ANALYZING MEANING

1. Has Quarrington convinced you that making your own beer is "simple" and "virtually idiot-proof"? Which of his instructions seems the easiest to follow, and which the most difficult? Why?
2. With which characteristics of the author do you identify? Where do you find evidence of such in the essay? Do these aspects of his personality make him more or less credible as someone writing a real set of instructions?
3. Quarrington's essay contains several sidetrips into what he calls "the pseudoscientific tone," passages that explain the chemical aspects of beer production. Are these passages clear and understandable to you? Explain why or why not.

DISCOVERING RHETORICAL STRATEGIES

1. Although "Home Brew" is very clearly both a directive and descriptive piece of process writing, other rhetorical strategies are used. Giving details from the essay to support your answer, explain which other rhetorical forms you discover.

2. Humour in writing often deflates the importance of the speaker, or discounts the seriousness of what is said. Is this true of Paul Quarrington's use of humour? What comic concept does he use as a unifying thematic link throughout the essay?

3. In spite of the writer and his brother being portrayed to some degree as "Garth and Wayne," there are clear evidences of Quarrington's fondness for using new and delightful words. Where do you find examples of interesting word use? How do these shifts in diction affect you as a reader? What do they add to your perception of the writer? How do they affect the overall tone of the essay?

MAKING CONNECTIONS

1. Paul Quarrington, like Joe Fiorito ("Breakfast in Bed") is basing his essay on a recipe. Explain how each of these authors makes a recipe interesting and entertaining to read.

2. Quarrington, like Drew Hayden Taylor ("Pretty Like a White Boy") and Susan Swan ("Nine Ways of Looking at a Critic"), is noted for the humour that characterizes his writing. How do each of these writers achieve a humorous tone in their respective essays?

3. In this essay, Quarrington incorporates stories of his family members. Compare the effect of this personalization to Ray Guy's ("When Jannies Visited") use of family anecdotes in his essay.

IDEAS FOR DISCUSSION/WRITING

Preparing to Write

Write freely about one of your more memorable experiments with trying to make something on your own for the first time. What were you trying to make? Why? Had you been given any prior instructions? Were you trying your "recipe" alone, or with someone else? What were the results of your first "do it yourself" attempt? Were they humorous at the time? Were the results a success, or even usable? What happens when you try to show someone else how to do something you do well?

Choosing a Topic

1. Your school newspaper has just asked you to write the first column in a "Student Cooking" series. Write an article based on the process format in which you tell readers who have cooking skills similar to yours, how to make a dish you've learned to cook. Include such information as why this dish is suitable to student cooking abilities, available equipment and facilities, how many it will serve, and what it would cost.

2. Using your own experience with a hobby or with making something which others might buy from a store, write a process essay that persuades the reader to try this "do it yourself" project. Explain your reasons for finding the activity and the end-product valuable and enjoyable as you give detailed instructions for making the same thing.

3. Beer, cola, wine, mineral water, coffee: We all have favourite beverages. Explain in a process essay why your favourite drink holds such appeal to you. What do you know about this beverage that will interest your readers? Choose a tone and clear points of detailing that will be most interesting to your audience.

WEB SITES

www.quarrington.org/
This is an excellent site with extensive information about Quarrington.

us.imdb.com/Name?Quarrington,+Paul
The Internet Movie Database Ltd. has a filmography and biography for Paul Quarrington.

realbeer.com/
This extensive beer site includes the following sections: brew tour, breweries, links, brew 'zines, burp me, notes, events, patrons, games, brew travels, authors, and retail.

pekkel.uthscsa.edu/beer.html
Eric's beer and homebrewing page.

Jessica Mitford
1917–1996

■ ■ ■

Behind the Formaldehyde Curtain

Once called "Queen of the Muckrakers" in a *Time* magazine review, Jessica Mitford has written scathing exposés of the Famous Writers' School, American funeral directors, television executives, prisons, a "fat farm" for wealthy women, and many other venerable social institutions. She was born in England into the gentry, immigrated to the United States, and later became a naturalized American citizen. After working at a series of jobs, she achieved literary fame at age forty-six with the publication of *The American Way of Death* (1963), which relentlessly shatters the image of funeral directors as "compassionate, reverent family-friends-in-need." Before her death in 1996, Mitford was nearing completion of an updated edition of this work. *The American Way of Death Revisited* was published posthumously in 1998. Her other major works include *Kind and Unusual Punishment: The Prison Business* (1973); *Poison Penmanship: The Gentle Art of Muckraking* (1979), an anthology of Mitford's articles in *The Atlantic Monthly, Harper's,* and other periodicals covering a twenty-two-year time span; two volumes of autobiography, *Daughters and Rebels* (1960) and *A Fine Old Madness* (1977); *Faces of Philip: A Memoir of Philip Toynbee* (1984); *Grace Had an English Heart: The Story of Grace Darling, Heroine and Victorian Superstar* (1988); and *The American Way of Birth* (1992). Superbly skilled in the techniques of investigative reporting, satire, and black humour, Mitford was described in a *Washington Post* article as "an older, more even-tempered, better-read Jane Fonda who has maintained her activism long past middle age."

Preparing to Read

The following essay, taken from *The American Way of Death,* clearly illustrates the ruthless manner in which Mitford exposes the greed and hypocrisy of the American mortuary business. As you prepare to read this article, think for a few minutes about funeral customs in our society: Have you attended a funeral service recently? Which rituals seemed particularly vivid to you? What purpose did these symbolic actions serve? What other interesting customs are you aware of in American society? What purpose do these customs serve? What public images do these customs have? Are these images accurate? Do you generally approve or disapprove of these customs?

The drama begins to unfold with the arrival of the corpse at the   1
mortuary.

Alas, poor Yorick! How surprised he would be to see how   2
his counterpart of today is whisked off to a funeral parlor and is
in short order sprayed, sliced, pierced, pickled, trussed, trimmed,
creamed, waxed, painted, rouged and neatly dressed—
transformed from a common corpse into a Beautiful Memory
Picture. This process is known in the trade as embalming and
restorative art and is so universally employed in the United States
and Canada that the funeral director does it routinely, without
consulting corpse or kin. He regards as eccentric those few who
are hardy enough to suggest that it might be dispensed with.
Yet no law requires embalming, no religious doctrine commends
it, nor is it dictated by considerations of health, sanitation, or
even of personal daintiness. In no part of the world but in
Northern America is it widely used. The purpose of embalming
is to make the corpse presentable for viewing in a suitably costly
container; and here too the funeral director routinely, without
first consulting the family, prepares the body for public display.

Is all this legal? The processes to which a dead body may be   3
subjected are after all to some extent circumscribed by law. In
most states, for instance, the signature of next of kin must be
obtained before an autopsy may be performed, before the
deceased may be cremated, before the body may be turned over
to a medical school for research purposes; or such provision must
be made in the decedent's will. In the case of embalming, no
such permission is required nor is it ever sought. A textbook,
The Principles and Practices of Embalming, comments on this: "There
is some question regarding the legality of much that is done
within the preparation room." The author points out that it would
be most unusual for a responsible member of a bereaved family
to instruct the mortician, in so many words, to "*embalm*" the body
of a deceased relative. The very term "embalming" is so seldom
used that the mortician must rely upon custom in the matter.
The author concludes that unless the family specifies otherwise,
the act of entrusting the body to the care of a funeral
establishment carries with it an implied permission to go ahead
and embalm.

Embalming is indeed a most extraordinary procedure, and   4
one must wonder at the docility of Americans who each year
pay hundreds of millions of dollars for its perpetuation, blissfully
ignorant of what it is all about, what is done, how it is done. Not

one in ten thousand has any idea of what actually takes place. Books on the subject are extremely hard to come by. They are not to be found in most libraries or bookshops.

In an era when huge television audiences watch surgical 5 operations in the comfort of their living rooms, when, thanks to the animated cartoon, the geography of the digestive system has become familiar territory even to the nursery school set, in a land where the satisfaction of curiosity about almost all matters is a national pastime, the secrecy surrounding embalming can, surely, hardly be attributed to the inherent gruesomeness of the subject. Custom in this regard has within this century suffered a complete reversal. In the early days of American embalming, when it was performed in the home of the deceased, it was almost mandatory for some relative to stay by the embalmer's side and witness the procedure. Today, family members who might wish to be in attendance would certainly be dissuaded by the funeral director. All others, except apprentices, are excluded by law from the preparation room.

A close look at what does actually take place may explain 6 in large measure the undertaker's intractable reticence concerning a procedure that has become his major *raison d'être*. Is it possible he fears that public information about embalming might lead patrons to wonder if they really want this service? If the funeral men are loath to discuss the subject outside the trade, the reader may, understandably, be equally loath to go on reading at this point. For those who have the stomach for it, let us part the formaldehyde curtain. ...

The body is first laid out in the undertaker's morgue—or 7 rather, Mr. Jones is reposing in the preparation room—to be readied to bid the world farewell.

The preparation room in any of the better funeral 8 establishments has the tiled and sterile look of a surgery, and indeed the embalmer-restorative artist who does his chores there is beginning to adopt the term "dermasurgeon" (appropriately corrupted by some mortician-writers as "demisurgeon") to describe his calling. His equipment, consisting of scalpels, scissors, augers, forceps, clamps, needles, pumps, tubes, bowls and basins, is crudely imitative of the surgeon's, as is his technique, acquired in a nine- or twelve-month post-high-school course in an embalming school. He is supplied by an advanced chemical industry with a bewildering array of fluids, sprays, pastes, oils, powders, creams, to fix or soften tissue, shrink or distend it as needed, dry it here, restore the moisture there. There are cosmetics, waxes and paints to fill and cover features, even plaster of Paris to replace entire limbs. There are ingenious aids to prop and stabilize the cadaver: A Vari-Pose Head Rest, the Edwards Arm and Hand Positioner, the Repose Block (to support the shoulders during the embalming), and the Throop Foot Positioner, which resembles an old-fashioned stocks.

Mr. John H. Eckels, president of the Eckels College of Mortuary Science, thus describes the first part of the embalming procedure: "In the hands of a skilled practitioner, this work may be done in a comparatively short time and without mutilating the body other than by slight incision—so slight that it scarcely would cause serious inconvenience if made upon a living person. It is necessary to remove the blood, and doing this not only helps in the disinfecting, but removes the principal cause of disfigurements due to discoloration." 9

Another textbook discusses the all-important time element: "The earlier this is done, the better, for every hour that elapses between death and embalming will add to the problems and complications encountered. ..." Just how soon should one get going on the embalming? The author tells us, "On the basis of such scanty information made available to this profession through its rudimentary and haphazard system of technical research, we must conclude that the best results are to be obtained if the subject is embalmed before life is completely extinct—that is, before cellular death has occurred. In the average case, this would mean within an hour after somatic death." For those who feel that there is something a little rudimentary, not to say haphazard, about this advice, a comforting thought is offered by another writer. Speaking of fears entertained in early days of premature burial, he points out, "One of the effects of embalming by chemical injection, however, has been to dispel fears of live burial." How true; once the blood is removed, chances of live burial are indeed remote. 10

To return to Mr. Jones, the blood is drained out through the veins and replaced by embalming fluid pumped in through the arteries. As noted in *The Principles and Practices of Embalming*, "every operator has a favorite injection and drainage point—a fact which becomes a handicap only if he fails or refuses to forsake his favorites when conditions demand it." Typical favorites are the carotid artery, femoral artery, jugular vein, subclavian vein. There are various choices of embalming fluid. If 11

Flextone is used, it will produce a "mild, flexible rigidity. The skin retains a velvety softness, the tissues are rubbery and pliable. Ideal for women and children." It may be blended with B. and G. Products Company's Lyf-Lyk tint, which is guaranteed to reproduce "nature's own skin texture...the velvety appearance of living tissue." Suntone comes in three separate tints: Suntan; Special Cosmetic Tint, a pink shade "especially indicated for young female subjects"; and Regular Cosmetic Tint, moderately pink.

About three to six gallons of a dyed and perfumed solution 12 of formaldehyde, glycerin, borax, phenol, alcohol and water is soon circulating through Mr. Jones, whose mouth has been sewn together with a "needle directed upward between the upper lip and gum and brought out through the left nostril," with the corners raised slightly "for a more pleasant expression." If he should be bucktoothed, his teeth are cleaned with Bon Ami and coated with colorless nail polish. His eyes, meanwhile, are closed with flesh-tinted eye caps and eye cement.

The next step is to have at Mr. Jones with a thing called a 13 trocar. This is a long, hollow needle attached to a tube. It is jabbed into the abdomen, poked around the entrails and chest cavity, the contents of which are pumped out and replaced with "cavity fluid." This done, and the hole in the abdomen sewn up, Mr. Jones's face is heavily creamed (to protect the skin from burns which may be caused by leakage of the chemicals), and he is covered with a sheet and left unmolested for a while. But not for long—there is more, much more, in store for him. He has been embalmed, but not yet restored, and the best time to start the restorative work is eight to ten hours after embalming, when the tissues have become firm and dry.

The object of all this attention to the corpse, it must be 14 remembered, is to make it presentable for viewing in an attitude of healthy repose. "Our customs require the presentation of our dead in the semblance of normality...unmarred by the ravages of illness, disease or mutilation," says Mr. J. Sheridan Mayer in his *Restorative Art.* This is rather a large order since few people die in the full bloom of health, unravaged by illness and unmarked by some disfigurement. The funeral industry is equal to the challenge: "In some cases the gruesome appearance of a mutilated or disease-ridden subject may be quite discouraging. The task of restoration may seem impossible and shake the confidence of the embalmer. This is the time for intestinal fortitude and determination. Once the formative work is begun and affected tissues are cleaned or removed, all doubts of success vanish. It is surprising and gratifying to discover the results which may be obtained."

The embalmer, having allowed an appropriate interval to 15 elapse, returns to the attack, but now he brings into play the skill and equipment of sculptor and cosmetician. Is a hand missing? Casting one in plaster of Paris is a simple matter. "For replacement purposes, only a cast of the back of the hand is necessary; this is within the ability of the average operator and is quite adequate." If a lip or two, a nose or an ear should be missing, the embalmer has at hand a variety of restorative waxes with which to model replacements. Pores and skin texture are simulated by stippling with a little brush, and over this cosmetics are laid on. Head off? Decapitation cases are rather routinely handled. Ragged edges are trimmed, and head joined to torso with a series of splints, wires and sutures. It is a good idea to have a little something at the neck—a scarf or a high collar— when time for viewing comes. Swollen mouth: Cut out tissue as needed from inside the lips. If too much is removed, the surface contour can easily be restored by padding with cotton. Swollen necks and cheeks are reduced by removing tissue through vertical incisions made down each side of the neck. "When the deceased is casketed, the pillow will hide the suture incisions. ... As an extra precaution against leakage, the suture may be painted with liquid sealer."

The opposite condition is more likely to present itself—that 16 of emaciation. His hypodermic syringe now loaded with massage cream, the embalmer seeks out and fills the hollowed and sunken areas by injection. In this procedure the backs of the hands and fingers and the under-chin area should not be neglected.

Positioning the lips is a problem that recurrently challenges 17 the ingenuity of the embalmer. Closed too tightly, they tend to give a stern, even disapproving expression. Ideally, embalmers feel, the lips should give the impression of being ever so slightly parted, the upper lip protruding slightly for a more youthful appearance. This takes some engineering, however, as the lips tend to drift apart. Lip drift can sometimes be remedied by pushing one or two straight pins through the inner margin of the lower lip and then inserting them between the two front upper teeth. If Mr. Jones happens to have no teeth, the pins can just as easily be anchored in his Armstrong Face Former and

Denture Replacer. Another method to maintain lip closure is to dislocate the lower jaw, which is then held in its new position by a wire run through holes which have been drilled through the upper and lower jaws at the midline. As the French are fond of saying, *il faut souffrir pour être belle*.

If Mr. Jones had died of jaundice, the embalming fluid will 18 very likely turn him green. Does this deter the embalmer? Not if he has intestinal fortitude. Masking pastes and cosmetics are heavily laid on, burial garments and casket interiors are color-correlated with particular care, and Jones is displayed beneath rose-colored lights. Friends will say "How *well* he looks." Death by carbon monoxide, on the other hand, can be rather a good thing from the embalmer's viewpoint: "One advantage is the fact that this type of discoloration is an exaggerated form of a natural pink coloration." This is nice because the healthy glow is already present and needs but little attention.

The patching and filling completed, Mr. Jones is now shaved, 19 washed and dressed. Cream-based cosmetic, available in pink, flesh, suntan, brunette and blond, is applied to his hands and face, his hair is shampooed and combed (and, in the case of Mrs. Jones, set), his hands manicured. For the horny-handed son of toil special care must be taken; cream should be applied to remove ingrained grime, and the nails cleaned. "If he were not in the habit of having them manicured in life, trimming and shaping is advised for appearance—never questioned by kin."

Jones is now ready for casketing (this is the present participle 20 of the verb "to casket"). In this operation his right shoulder should be depressed slightly "to turn the body a bit to the right and soften the appearance of lying flat on the back." Positioning the hands is a matter of importance, and special rubber positioning blocks may be used. The hands should be cupped slightly for a more lifelike, relaxed appearance. Proper placement of the body requires a delicate sense of balance. It should lie as high as possible in the casket, yet not so high that the lid, when lowered, will hit the nose. On the other hand, we are cautioned, placing the body too low "creates the impression that the body is in a box."

Jones is next wheeled into the appointed slumber room where 21 a few last touches may be added—his favorite pipe placed in his hand or, if he was a great reader, a book propped into position. (In the case of little Master Jones a Teddy bear may be clutched.) Here he will hold open house for a few days, visiting hours 10 a.m. to 9 p.m.

All now being in readiness, the funeral director calls a staff 22
conference to make sure that each assistant knows his precise
duties. Mr. Wilber Kriege writes "This makes your staff feel that
they are a part of the team, with a definite assignment that must
be properly carried out if the whole plan is to succeed. You never
heard of a football coach who failed to talk to his entire team
before they go on the field. They have drilled on the plays they
are to execute for hours and days, and yet the successful coach
knows the importance of making even the bench-warming third-
string substitute feel that he is important if the game is to be
won." The winning of *this* game is predicated upon glass-smooth
handling of the logistics. The funeral director has notified the
pallbearers whose names were furnished by the family, has
arranged for the presence of clergyman, organist, and soloist,
has provided transportation for everybody, has organized and
listed the flowers sent by friends. In *Psychology of Funeral Service*,
Mr. Edward A. Martin points out: "He may not always do as
much as the family thinks he is doing, but it is his helpful
guidance that they appreciate in knowing they are proceeding
as they should. ...The important thing is how well his services
can be used to make the family believe they are giving unlimited
expression to their own sentiment."

The religious service may be held in a church or in the chapel 23
of the funeral home; the funeral director vastly prefers the latter
arrangement, for not only is it more convenient for him but it
affords him the opportunity to show off his beautiful facilities
to the gathered mourners. After the clergyman has had his say,
the mourners queue up to file past the casket for a last look at
the deceased. The family is *never* asked whether they want an
open-casket ceremony; in the absence of their instruction to the
contrary, this is taken for granted. Consequently, well over 90
percent of all American funerals feature the open casket—a
custom unknown in other parts of the world. Foreigners are
astonished by it. An English woman living in San Francisco
described her reaction in a letter to the writer:

> I myself have attended only one funeral here—that of an elderly 24
> fellow worker of mine. After the service I could not understand why
> everyone was walking towards the coffin (sorry, I mean casket), but
> thought I had better follow the crowd. It shook me rigid to get there and
> find the casket open and poor old Oscar lying there in his brown tweed
> suit, wearing a suntan makeup and just the wrong shade of lipstick. If

I had not been extremely fond of the old boy, I have a horrible feeling that I might have giggled. Then and there I decided that I could never face another American funeral—even dead.

The casket (which has been resting throughout the service 25 on a Classic Beauty Ultra Metal Casket Bier) is now transferred by a hydraulically operated device called Porto-Lift to a balloon-tired, Glide Easy casket carriage which will wheel it to yet another conveyance, the Cadillac Funeral Coach. This may be lavender, cream, light green—anything but black. Interiors, of course, are color-correlated, "for the man who cannot stop short of perfection."

At graveside, the casket is lowered into the earth. This office, 26 once the prerogative of friends of the deceased, is now performed by a patented mechanical lowering device. A "Life-time Green" artificial grass mat is at the ready to conceal the sere earth, and overhead, to conceal the sky, is a portable Steril Chapel Tent ("resists the intense heat and humidity of summer and the terrific storms of winter...available in Silver Grey, Rose or Ever-green"). Now is the time for the ritual scattering of earth over the coffin, as the solemn words "earth to earth, ashes to ashes, dust to dust" are pronounced by the officiating cleric. This can today be accomplished "with a mere flick of the wrist with the Gordon Leak-Proof Earth Dispenser. No grasping of a handful of dirt, no soiled fingers. Simple, dignified, beautiful, reverent! The modern way!" The Golden Earth Dispenser (at $5) is of nickel-plated brass construction. It is not only "attractive to the eye and long wearing"; it is also "one of the 'tools' for building better public relations" if presented as "an appropriate non-commercial gift" to the clergyman. It is shaped something like a saltshaker.

Untouched by human hand, the coffin and the earth are now 27 united.

It is in the function of directing the participants through the 28 maze of gadgetry that the funeral director has assigned to himself his relatively new role of "grief therapist." He has relieved the family of every detail, he has revamped the corpse to look like a living doll, he has arranged for it to nap for a few days in a slumber room, he has put on a well-oiled performance in which the concept of *death* has played no part whatsoever—unless it was inconsiderately mentioned by the clergyman who conducted the religious service. He has done everything in his power to make the funeral a real pleasure for everybody concerned. He and his team have given their all to score an upset victory over death.

UNDERSTANDING DETAILS

1. List the major steps of the embalming process that the author reveals in this essay.
2. Why, according to Mitford, do funeral directors not want to make public the details of embalming? To what extent do you think their desire for secrecy is warranted?
3. Why isn't the permission of a family member needed for embalming? From Mitford's perspective, what does this custom reveal about Americans?
4. In what ways has embalming become the undertaker's *raison d'être*? How do American funeral customs encourage this procedure?

ANALYZING MEANING

1. What is Mitford's primary purpose in this essay? Why do you think she has analyzed this particular process in such detail?
2. Explain the title of this essay.
3. Do you think the author knows how gruesome her essay is? How can you tell? What makes the essay so horrifying? How does such close attention to macabre detail help Mitford accomplish her purpose?
4. What does Mitford mean when she argues that the funeral director and his team "have given their all to score an upset victory over death" (paragraph 28)? Who or what is "the team"? Why does Mitford believe death plays no part in American burial customs?

DISCOVERING RHETORICAL STRATEGIES

1. Why does Mitford begin her essay with a one-sentence paragraph? Is it effective? Why or why not?
2. A euphemism is the substitution of a deceptively pleasant term for a straightforward, less pleasant one. In what way is "Beautiful Memory Picture" (paragraph 2) a euphemism? How are we reminded of this phrase throughout the essay? What other euphemisms can you find in this selection?
3. What tone does Mitford establish in the essay? What is her reason for creating this particular tone? What is your reaction to it?
4. What other rhetorical strategies does Mitford use besides gruesome examples and illustrations to make her point? Give examples of each of these different strategies.

MAKING CONNECTIONS

1. Imagine that Stephen King ("Why We Crave Horror Movies") has just read Mitford's essay on funeral customs. According to King, what would be the source of our fascination with these macabre practices? Why do essays like Mitford's both intrigue and repulse us at the same time?

2. Compare and contrast Mitford's use of examples with those used by Trina McQueen ("Why We Crave Hot Stuff") or Sally Armstrong ("P4W"). How often does each author use examples? What is the relationship between the frequency of examples in each essay and the extent to which you are convinced by the author's argument?

3. "Stand Tall, and Pass the Ammunition" (Gerald W. Paul) is obviously a rebuttal to pieces like the one Mitford has written. What makes Mitford's essay so effective that people like Paul feel it necessary to refute her argument?

IDEAS FOR DISCUSSION/WRITING

Preparing to Write

Write freely about a particularly interesting custom in Canada or in another country: Why does this custom exist? What role does it play in the society? What value does it have? What are the details of this custom? In what way is this custom a part of your life? Your family's life? What purpose does it serve for you? Is it worth continuing? Why or why not?

Choosing a Topic

1. In a process analysis essay directed to your classmates, explain a custom you do not approve of. Decide on your tone and purpose before you begin.

2. In a process analysis essay directed to your classmates, explain a custom you approve of. Select a specific tone and purpose before you begin to write.

3. You have been asked to address a group of students at a college of mortuary science. In this role, you have an opportunity to influence the opinion of these students concerning the practice of embalming. Write a well-reasoned lecture to this group, arguing either for or against the process of embalming.

WEB SITES

 www.funeral.net/info/default2.html
Armstrong Funeral Home.

 www.ofsa.org/wiaf.htm
The Ontario Funeral Service Association.

www.nfda.org/
The National Funeral Directors Association.

www.mitford.org/index.html
The Jessica Mitford Memorial Site.

Maureen Littlejohn

■ ■ ■

You Are a Contract Painkiller

For a writer, "it is important to listen and never assume" as well as to "ask a lot of questions" according to Maureen Littlejohn, a journalist who has specialized in pop culture for about 15 years. Littlejohn, who is now Entertainment/Lifestyles features writer at the *Winnipeg Free Press*, began her journalistic career working on *Campus Digest* (now *Campus Canada*) after graduating with an honours B.A. (General Arts) from the University of Toronto and completing the magazine journalism program at Ryerson Polytechnic Institute. While at U of T, Littlejohn, who always wanted to go into the field of communications, worked at the *Varsity* campus newspaper as a writer and typesetter. Later, Littlejohn further developed her writing skills through participating in the Banff Publishing Workshop. Littlejohn also worked as an on-air music critic for Global TV for three years and edited *Network* magazine for six years.

Articles Littlejohn has written have appeared in a variety of publications including the *Financial Post* magazine, *Flare* magazine, the Canadian Airlines in-flight magazine, *The Music Scene*, *CARAS News*, *Canadian Musican*, *Network*, and *Equinox*, where the piece included here was first published.

Preparing to Read

ASA or aspirin is a medication that is readily available and familiar to most of us. In this essay, Maureen Littlejohn outlines the process by which ASA works to relieve our pain and the process through which ASA was developed. Before reading this essay, think about familiar medications. What do you typically keep stocked in your medicine cabinet at home? Do you ever use aspirin? When? Why? What other nonprescription medications do you use? Do you favour medications available from pharmacies or more natural remedies? Why?

■_____■

You are a contract painkiller, code name ASA, also known to   1
your clients as aspirin. Pain is your gain—Canadians swallow almost one billion of your agents each year. You have achieved renown by destroying headaches but you are equally effective in countering sprains, burns, or blows. You stop swelling and reduce fever and research suggests you may even help prevent heart attacks and stroke.

On your latest mission, your client has just had a fight with   2
her boss, and her head is pounding. Involuntary muscle
contractions on her scalp and at the back of her neck, triggered by
the argument, are now causing swelling and throbbing. In
reaction, her body has produced an enzyme called prostaglandin,
which is sensitizing the nerve endings in her scalp, especially
around her temples and sending a message of pain to her brain.   3

Taken with a modest stream of water or ginger ale, your
chalky, round self begins the mission by moving through the
host's esophagus, into the stomach, then the upper small intestine,
where you are dissolved and passed into the bloodstream. There,
you slop into a molecular chain of events and disable the enzyme
that converts the acid in cell membranes into prostaglandins.
The nerve endings are now desensitized, that pain message to
the brain is stopped, and your host is smiling again.

You reduce fever in a similar way. If your host were suffering   4
from the flu, her white blood cells would be fighting the virus
by producing prostaglandins that, in turn, cause the body's
temperature to rise. You head off the prostaglandins and bring the
fever down.

You are not the only pain relieving agent at work. Ibuprofen   5
and other aspirinlike drugs known as nonsteroidal anti-
inflammatory drugs (NSAIDs) do much the same thing. You all
share possible side effects—in 2 to 6 percent of your clients, you
cause stomach irritation and possibly bleeding and, in extreme
cases, kidney failure. Prostaglandins help maintain the integrity
of the stomach lining, and in their absence, the acidic NSAIDs
give the host a queasy feeling.

As a tonic for hire, you have been around for a century, but   6
your family tree goes back much further. In ancient Greece,
Hippocrates noted that chewing on willow leaves reduced fever.
In the 1800s, two Italian chemists confirmed that willow bark
contains one of your main ingredients, the antipyretic (fever-
reducing) salicin. A Swiss pharmacist then found that
meadowsweet, a shrub in the spirea family, has even more of
the magic substance than willow bark. And while experimenting
with salicin, a German chemist created salicylic acid (the SA of
ASA). He called it *Spirsäure* after spirea, hence the "spirin" part
of your name. The "a" was added for "acetyl," the substances—
including a salt—that made the SA easier on the stomach. In
1893, Felix Hoffmann at the Bayer AG Chemical Works in
Germany purified and stabilized you, and that's when you first

claimed celebrity status as one of the world's most popular, inexpensive pain relievers. Today you are synthesized from coal tar or petroleum instead of plants.

Beyond garden-variety aches and pains, you are prescribed   7 as a remedy for arthritis because of your genius for blocking prostaglandins that trigger the pain and swelling of joints. Your most recent prostaglandin-fighting potential is to prevent heart attack and stroke. There is even talk that you may help ward off cancer and senility. Mission impossible? We'll see.

UNDERSTANDING DETAILS

1. What is ASA made from? What does ASA stand for?
2. When was ASA invented? By whom?
3. Explain how ASA works to relieve pain and reduce fever.

ANALYZING MEANING

1. Why has ASA become so popular over time? What do you anticipate its status will be in the future?
2. Describe Littlejohn's attitude toward her subject. What specific examples contribute to this impression?
3. Explain why ASA is now synthesized from coal tar or petroleum. Why have we moved beyond simply ingesting willow leaves and meadowsweet?

DISCOVERING RHETORICAL STRATEGIES

1. Littlejohn uses second person to detail the history and the effect of ASA. What is the effect of casting the reader in the role of an ASA tablet? Why has she chosen this strategy? How effective is her choice to address the inanimate subject of her essay directly?
2. In this essay Littlejohn uses an extended metaphor. To what does she compare ASA? List five examples where she makes this connection.
3. Is this essay a directive or a descriptive process analysis? Why is this an appropriate strategy for this topic?

MAKING CONNECTIONS

1. Littlejohn uses an extended metaphor in this essay to make her subject more interesting and easier to understand. Explain how

her use of metaphor compares to that of Lesley Choyce ("Thin Edge of the Wedge") or Karen Connelly ("Touch the Dragon").

2. "You are a Contract Painkiller" addresses the reader directly as "you" and, in fact, casts the reader as the subject of the essay. How is this approach similar to that of Joe Fiorito's "Breakfast in Bed"? How is the role of the reader different in these two essays?

3. Maureen Littlejohn is presenting scientific information in this essay and incorporating terminology that may initially be unfamiliar to her readers. What strategies has she used to make this subject accessible and interesting to her audience? How does her approach compare to that of Adrian Forsyth ("Little Plants of Horror") or Tony Leighton ("The New Nature")?

IDEAS FOR DISCUSSION/WRITING

Preparing to Write

Write freely about common pain medications with which you are familiar. What do you do if you burn yourself on an iron? How do you remedy a headache? What do you do for bee stings? What is the best way to relieve sunburn pain? How do you treat a sprain? How did you learn about these treatments? How do you gauge their effectiveness?

Choosing a Topic

1. Think of a practice that was once commonly accepted for treating some ailment. It might be the use of mustard plasters or cod liver oil to cure or prevent colds, electric shock therapy to treat psychological problems, amputation to prevent the spread of infection, or lobotomies to cure psychological disorders. In a short essay, explain how and why this practice fell out of favour.

2. There are many things that we may find disagreeable but that we do because we recognize the benefits that they offer. This might include getting our teeth cleaned at the dentist's, exercising, or cleaning the bathroom. Describe one such process, focusing on its positive aspects.

3. Taking medication is one response to relieving pain but many people are resistant to taking medications such as ASA. Write an essay in which you present some alternative responses to treating a headache or other "garden-variety aches and pains."

WEB SITES

www.geocities.com/SunsetStrip/Balcony/3582/story.html
or
www.tabbweb.com/thehip/text/network.txt
Read Maureen Littlejohn's essay about Gord Downie of The Tragically Hip.

www.nursespdr.com/members/database/ndrhtml/acetylsalicylic acid.html
Read the entry on ASA from the *Nurse's PDR Handbook*.

www.bayerus.com/aspirin/main.html
Visit Bayer's Aspirin site to play the Aspirin trivia game, see how Bayer Aspirin advertising has changed, and to read more about the research linking aspirin to the prevention of stroke and heart attacks.

Joe Fiorito
1948–

■ ■ ■

Breakfast in Bed

Originally from Thunder Bay, Ontario, Joe Fiorito now lives in Montreal, Quebec, where he has worked as a columnist for *The Montreal Gazette* and now contributes regular columns to Air Canada's *En Route* magazine and the *National Post*. He has worked for CBC radio, where he produced "The Food Show," and he is also a published poet. His book *Comfort Me With Apples* (1994) is a collection of essays that originally were published as a weekly column in *Hour* magazine. While Fiorito has no formal journalism training, in 1996 he won a national newspaper award for his *Gazette* columns. A collection of these profiles, or "people pieces," has now been published in a book entitled *Tango On the Main*.

Preparing to Read

While "Breakfast in Bed" is taken from *Comfort Me With Apples*, it originally appeared in *Hour* magazine in 1993. In this short essay, Fiorito gives the reader a recipe and a reason for making popovers. Before you begin to read, think about the importance of smell in your life. What is the difference between a smell and a scent? What about an odour? What smells do you find appealing? What smells are repulsive or annoying? Do you have a favourite perfume or cologne? What is it? How would you describe its scent?

The Inuit greet face to face, but they don't rub noses, exactly, and you shouldn't call it kissing. It is a form of greeting every bit as intimate as a kiss, but it goes deeper than that; it's a way for friends to take in each other's smell. It's how friends fill the empty places caused by absence. 1

Smell is fundamental to happiness. I know a man who travels with a piece of his wife's clothing sealed in a plastic bag. When the separation is too much to bear, he opens the bag and breathes. 2

Traces of this signature mark our sheets and pillows; this is what makes crawling into bed on a cold night such a comfort. 3

Smell is one of the many nameless things you miss when love goes wrong. That smell will linger, it will haunt you and exhaust you long after your lover has gone. 4

Think I'm exaggerating? Wake early one Sunday and smell 5
the person sleeping next to you. Do it. Lean over. The side of the
neck will do, just below the ear. Take a deep breath. The
knowledge of this scent is lodged in the deepest part of your
brain. Breathe deeply, if only to remind yourself of why you are
where you are, doing what you're doing.

Now go to the kitchen. Throw two eggs into a bowl with a 6
cup of milk and a cup of flour. Add a quarter teaspoon of salt
and a tablespoon of melted butter. Mix until smooth, but don't
overdo it.

Pour the batter into buttered muffin tins, filling the cups no 7
more than half full. Put the tins in a cold oven. Turn on the heat
to 450°F. After fifteen minutes, turn the oven down to 350°F.
Wait fifteen minutes more.

This recipe comes from the *Fannie Farmer Baking Book* by 8
Marion Cunningham. It's an important book, with clear recipes
and much new thinking. For example, prior to Marion, popovers
were always started in a hot oven. This is a small thing, but one
which changed my life.

While you're changing yours, make some coffee and squeeze 9
a couple of oranges. Do what you want with a pear or a
pineapple. Get a tray ready to take back to bed.

Now open the oven. It will make you smile. They don't call 10
these things popovers for nothing. They look like little domes,
golden brown and slightly crisp on the outside. The texture inside
is as soft as your partner's neck. The smell is just as warm and
every bit as earthy.

Take them out of the muffin tins and put them in a basket. 11
They'll steam as you break them open. Eat them with a little
butter and the best jam or honey in the cupboard. A soft
camembert isn't out of place if you have it.

Breakfast together is the second- or third-most intimate thing 12
you can share. If someone new is sleeping over and you want
to make an impression, make these. If you're worried about what
to talk about while you're eating, remember what Oscar Wilde
said. Only dull people are brilliant at breakfast.

If you haven't got a partner, make popovers anyway. It's 13
easy enough to cut this recipe in half. It's good practise. It's its
own reward. The butter melts into the jam and the sun pours
onto your breakfast bed. And you have another way to fill the
emptiness caused by absence.

UNDERSTANDING DETAILS

1. How does Fiorito suggest that one can fill the emptiness that results from loneliness?
2. What process is Fiorito explaining in this essay?
3. What are popovers? How did they get their name?

ANALYZING MEANING

1. Explain the relationship between smell and memory.
2. What does Fiorito mean when he says that smell is fundamental to happiness?
3. Explain why, in Fiorito's estimation, breakfast together is such an intimate experience.

DISCOVERING RHETORICAL STRATEGIES

1. In this essay, Fiorito is giving the readers a recipe. How does it differ from the way a popover recipe might be written in *The Joy of Cooking* or any other cookbook?
2. How does Fiorito link the beginning and the end of his essay? Does he have an effective introduction and conclusion?
3. Describe Fiorito's tone in this essay. Use specific examples to show how his style (use of language) creates this tone.

MAKING CONNECTIONS

1. Fiorito and Carol Krenz ("Food for Sloth") both discuss the associations that food carries in its smell. Compare and contrast their theories about the link between food and memory.
2. Joe Fiorito's writing is distinguished by a conversational tone and an informal style. Compare his style to that of Laura Robinson ("Starving for the Gold") or Tony Leighton ("The New Nature"). Whose style do you find more effective? Why?
3. Fiorito takes a subject that seems relatively simple and potentially boring and creates interest through the incorporation of specific detail. Explain how this approach makes his topic interesting and entertaining.

IDEAS FOR DISCUSSION/WRITING

Preparing to Write

Write freely about your favourite food. What do you know about its national origins or about the history of its preparation? Where and when do you eat this food? Do you associate it with any particular events or people in your life? Could you write a recipe for this food yourself? What ingredients does it contain? Is your favourite food healthy and nutritious, junk food, or a bit of both?

Choosing a Topic

1. Write an essay in which you include a recipe for one of your favourite foods that is fairly simple to prepare. Instead of writing it in "cookbook instruction style," present the information in a narrative like Fiorito did, in which you also provide a context and some subjective information about this dish. Make sure that you provide enough detail that your reader will be able to follow your recipe.

2. In "Breakfast in Bed" Fiorito says that breakfast together is one of the most intimate experiences you can share. Think of some particular ritual that you share with others that involves food. This might be preparing or eating a family meal, preserving fruit or vegetables, making wine or beer, or going out for a drink after work. How often does this ritual happen? Who participates? Where does this ritual fall on the intimacy scale? Write an essay in which you describe this event in a descriptive process analysis.

3. In "Breakfast in Bed" Fiorito cites Oscar Wilde as saying, "Only dull people are brilliant at breakfast." Write an essay in which you explain to your audience how to appear brilliant at any meal you choose.

WEB SITES

 food.epicurious.com/g_gourmet/g02_cookbooks/jun94/g_review.html
Learn more about the Fannie Farmer Baking Book from *Choosing a Kitchen Bible*, by Anne Mendelson (Gourmet).

 www.epicurious.com/db/dictionary/terms/p/popover.html
Epicurious dictionary: popover.

armen-info.com/hol/066-01b.htm
"Armenia home to 300,000 refugees" is one of Fiorito's articles from *The Montreal Gazette*.

www.edibleplanet.com/1997.08/features/sushi.html
Here you can read one of the essays from *Comfort Me With Apples*.

www.nationalpost.com/commentary.asp?s2=columnists
Fiorito is now a columnist at the *National Post*. Click on his name to read his latest column.

CHAPTER 5

DIVISION / CLASSIFICATION

■ ■ ■

Finding Categories

Both division and classification play important roles in our everyday lives: Bureau drawers separate one type of clothing from another; kitchen cabinets organize food, dishes, and utensils into proper groups; grocery stores shelve similar items together so shoppers can easily locate what they want to buy; school notebooks with tabs help students divide up their academic lives; newspapers classify local and national events in order to organize a great deal of daily information for the general public; and our own personal classification systems assist us in separating what we like from what we don't so that we can have access to our favourite foods, our favourite cars, our favourite entertainment, our favourite people. The two processes of division and classification are so natural to us, in fact, that we sometimes aren't even aware we are using them.

Defining Division/Classification

Division and classification are actually mirror images of each other. Division is the basic feature of process analysis, which we studied in the last chapter: It moves from a general concept to subdivisions of that concept or from a single category to multiple subcategories. Classification works in the opposite direction, moving from specifics to a group with common traits or from multiple subgroups to a single, larger, and more inclusive category. These techniques work together in many ways: A college, for example, is *divided* into departments (single to multiple), whereas courses are *classified* by department (multiple to single); the medical field is *divided* into specialties, whereas doctors are *classified* by a single specialty; a cookbook is *divided* into chapters, whereas recipes are *classified* according to type; and athletics is *divided* into specific sports, whereas athletes are *classified* by the sport in which they participate. Division is the separation of an idea or an item into its basic parts, such as a home into rooms, a course into assignments, or a job into various duties or responsibilities; classification is the organization of items with similar features into a group or groups, such as ordering furniture to decorate a dining room, dropping all carbohydrates from your diet, or preferring to date only tall, sun-tanned swimmers.

Classification is an organizational system for presenting a large amount of material to a reader or listener. This process helps us make sense of the complex world we live in by letting us work with smaller, more understandable units of that world. Classification must be governed by some clear, logical purpose (such as focusing on all lower-division course requirements), which will then dictate the system of categories to be used. The plan of organization that results should be as flexible as possible, and it should illustrate the specific relationship to each other of items in a group and of the groups themselves to one another.

As you already know, many different ways of classifying the same elements are possible. If you consider the examples at the outset of this chapter, you will realize that bureau drawers vary from house to house and even from person to person; that no one's kitchen is set up exactly the same way as someone else's; and that grocery stores have similar but not identical systems of food classification. (Think, for instance, of the many different schemes for organizing dairy products, meats, diet foods, etc.) In addition, your friends probably use a method different from yours to organize their school notebooks; different newspapers vary their presentation of the news; and two professors will probably teach the same course material in divergent ways. We all have distinct and uniquely logical methods of classifying the elements in our own lives.

The following student paragraph about friends illustrates both division and classification. As you read it, notice how the student writer moves back and forth smoothly from general to specific and from multiple to single:

> The word friend can refer to many different types of relationships. Close friends are "friends" at their very best: people for whom we feel respect, esteem, and, quite possibly, even love. We regard these

people and their well-being with kindness, interest, and goodwill; we trust them and will go out of our way to help them. Needless to say, we could all use at least one close friend. Next come "casual friends," people with whom we share a particular interest or activity. The investment of a great amount of time and energy in developing this type of friendship is usually not required, though casual friends often become close friends with the passage of time. The last division of "friend" is most general and is composed of all those individuals whose acquaintance we have made and who feel no hostility toward us. When one is counting friends, this group should certainly be included, since such friendships often develop into "casual" or "close" relationships. Knowing people in all three groups is necessary, however, because all types of friends undoubtedly help us live healthier, happier lives.

Thinking Critically by Using Division/ Classification

The thinking strategies of division and classification are the flip sides of each other: Your textbook is *divided* into chapters (one item divided into many), but chapters are *classified* (grouped) into sections or units. Your brain performs these mental acrobatics constantly, but to be as proficient at this method of thinking as possible, you need to be aware of the cognitive activities you go through. Focusing on these two companion patterns of thought will develop your skill in dealing with these complex schemes as it simultaneously increases your overall mental capabilities.

You might think of division/classification as a driving pattern that goes forward and then doubles back on itself in reverse. Division is a movement from a single concept to multiple categories, while classification involves gathering multiple concepts into a single group. Dividing and/or classifying helps us make sense of our subject by using categories to highlight similarities and differences. In the case of division, you are trying to find what differences break the items into separate groups, while, with classification, you let the similarities among the items help you put the material into meaningful categories. Processing your material in this way helps your readers see your particular subject in a new way and often brings renewed insights to both reader and writer.

Experimenting with division and classification is important to your growth as a critical thinker. It will help you process complex information so you can understand more fully your options for dealing with material in all subject areas. Practising division and classification separately from other rhetorical modes makes you concentrate on improving this particular pattern of thinking before adding it to your expanding arsenal of critical thinking skills.

1. Study the table of contents of a magazine that interests you. Into what sections is the magazine divided? What distinguishing features does each section have? Now study the various advertisements in the same magazine. What different categories would you use to classify these ads? List the ads in each category.
2. Make a chart classifying the English instructors at your school. Explain your classification system to the class.
3. List six to eight major concerns you have about Canadian society. Which of these are most important? Which are least important? Now classify these concerns into two or three distinct categories.

Reading and Writing Division/Classification Essays

Writers of division/classification essays must first decide if they are going to break down a topic into many separate parts or group together similar items into one coherent category; a writer's purpose will, of course, guide him or her in this decision. Readers must likewise recognize and understand which of these two parallel operations an author is using to structure an essay. Another important identifying feature of division/classification essays is an explanation (explicit or implicit) of the significance of a particular system of organization.

How to Read a Division/Classification Essay

Preparing to read. As you approach the selections in this chapter, you should study all the material that precedes each essay so you can prepare yourself for your reading. First of all, what hints does the title give you about what you are going to read? To what extent does Amy Willard Cross reveal in her title her attitude toward the pace of life? Who do you think Susan Swan's audience is in "Nine Ways of Looking at a Critic"? Does David Foot's title give us any indication about his point of view in "Boomers Dance to a New Beat"? Then, see what you can learn from scanning each essay and reading its synopsis in the Rhetorical Table of Contents.

Also important as you prepare to read the essays in this chapter is your knowledge about each author and the conditions under which each essay was written: What does the biographical material tell you about William Golding's "Thinking as a Hobby"? Knowing where these essays were first published will give you even more information about each author's purpose and audience.

Finally, before you begin to read, answer the Preparing to Read questions, and then, think freely for a few minutes about the general topic: What do you want to know about the different types of money discussed by Laura Millard in "Images of Canada: Canadian Bank Notes." What are some of your own stories about living in a time-conscious society (Cross)?

Reading. As you read each essay for the first time, write down your initial reactions to the topic itself, to the preliminary material, to the mood the writer sets, or to a specific incident in the essay. Make associations between the essay and your own experiences.

In addition, create a context for each essay by drawing on the preliminary material you just read about the essay: What is David Foot telling us about the baby boom generation and why is this of interest? What is Swan saying about the role of the critic in the creative process? According to Millard, why are the designs of our bank notes significant?

Also, in this first reading, notice whether the writers divided (split up) or classified (gathered together) their material to make their point. Finally, read the questions after each essay, and let them guide your second reading of the selection.

Rereading. When you read these division/classification essays a second time, notice how the authors carefully match their dominant rhetorical approach (in this case, division or classification) to their purpose in a clear thesis. What, for example, is Millard's dominant rhetorical approach to her subject? How does this approach further her purpose? What other rhetorical strategies support her thesis? Then, see how these writers logically present their division or classification systems to their readers, defining new categories as their essays progress. Finally, notice how each writer either implicitly or explicitly explains the significance or value of his or her division/classification system.

How does Susan Swan explain her system of organization? And how does Cross give her organizing principle significance? Now, answer the questions after each essay to check your understanding and to help you analyze your reading in preparation for the discussion/writing topics that follow.

For a more complete survey of reading guidelines, you may want to consult the checklist on pages 15–16 of the Introduction.

How to Write a Division/Classification Essay

Preparing to Write. You should approach a division/classification essay in the same way you have begun all your other writing assignments—with some kind of prewriting activity that will help you generate ideas, such as the Preparing to Write questions featured in this chapter. The prewriting techniques outlined in the Introduction on pages 17–19 can help you approach these questions imaginatively. Before you even consider the selection and arrangement of details, you need to explore your subject, choose a topic, and decide on a specific purpose and audience. The best way to explore your subject is to think about it, read about it, and then write about it. Look at it from all possible angles, and see what patterns and relationships emerge. To choose a specific topic, you might begin by listing any groups, patterns, or combinations you discover within your subject matter. Your purpose should take shape as you form your thesis, and your audience is probably dictated by the assignment. Making these decisions before you write will make the rest of your task much easier.

Writing. As you begin to write, certain guidelines will help you structure your ideas for a division/classification essay:

1. First, declare an overall purpose for your classification.
2. Then, divide the item or concept you are dealing with into categories.
3. Arrange these categories into a logical sequence.
4. Define each category, explaining the difference between one category and another and showing that difference through 236 examples.
5. Explain the significance of your classification system. (Why is it worth reading? What will your audience learn from it?)

All discussion in such an essay should reinforce the purpose stated at the beginning of the theme. Other rhetorical modes—

such as narration, example, and comparison/contrast—will naturally be used to supplement your classification.

To make your classification as workable as possible, take special care that your categories do not overlap and that all topics fall into their proper places. If, for example, you were classifying all the jobs performed by students in your writing class, the categories of (1) indoor work and (2) outdoor work would probably be inadequate. Most delivery jobs, for example, fall into both categories. At a pizza parlour, a florist, or a gift shop, a delivery person's time would be split between indoor and outdoor work. So you would need to design a different classification system to avoid this problem. The categories of (1) indoor work, (2) outdoor work, and (3) a combination of indoor and outdoor work would be much more useful for this task. Making sure your categories don't overlap will help make your classification essays more readable and more accurate.

Rewriting. As you rewrite your division/classification essays, consider carefully the probable reactions of your readers to the form and content of your paper:

1. Does your thesis communicate your purpose clearly?
2. Have you divided your topic into separate and understandable categories?
3. Are these categories arranged logically?
4. Are the distinctions between your categories as clear as possible?
5. Do you explain the significance of your particular classification system?

More guidelines for writing and rewriting are available on pages 26–27 of the Introduction.

Student Essay: Division/Classification at Work

The following student essay divides skiers into interesting categories based on their physical abilities. As you read it, notice how the student writer weaves the significance of his study into his opening statement of purpose. Also, pay particular attention to his logical method of organization and clear explanation of categories as he moves with ease from multiple to single and back to multiple again throughout the essay.

People on the Slopes

When I first learned to ski, I was amazed by the shapes who whizzed by me and slipped down trails marked only by a black diamond signifying "most difficult," while others careened awkwardly down the "bunny slopes." These skiers, I discovered, could be divided into distinct categories—for my own entertainment and for the purpose of finding appropriate skiing partners.

First are the poetic skiers. They glide down the mountainside silently with what seems like no effort at all. They float from side to side on the intermediate slopes, their knees bent perfectly above parallel skis, while their sharp skills allow them to bypass slower skiers with safely executed turns at remarkable speeds.

The crazy skiers also get down the mountain quickly, but with a lot more noise attending their descent. At every hill, they yell a loud "Yahoo!" and slam their skis into the snow. These go-for-broke athletes always whiz by faster than everyone else, and they especially seem to love the crowded runs where they can slide over the backs of other people's skis. I often find crazy skiers in mangled messes at the bottoms of steep hills, where they are yelling loudly, but not the famous "Yahoo!"

After being overwhelmed by the crazy skiers, I am always glad to find other skiers like myself: the average ones. We are polite on the slopes, concentrate on improving our technique with every run, and ski the beginner slopes only at the beginning of the day to warm up. We go over the moguls (small hills) much more cautiously than the crazy or poetic skiers, but we still seek adventure with a slight jump or two each day. We remain a silent majority on the mountain.

Below us in talent, but much more evident on the mountainside, are what I call the eternal beginners. These skiers stick to the same beginner slope almost every run of every day during their vacation. Should they venture onto an intermediate slope, they quickly assume the snowplow position (a pigeon-toed stance) and never leave it. Eternal beginners weave from one side of the run to the other and hardly ever fall, because they proceed so slowly; however, they do yell quite a bit at the crazies who like to run over the backs of their skis.

Having always enjoyed people-watching, I have fun each time I am on the slopes observing the myriad of skiers around me. I use these observations to pick out possible ski partners for myself and others. Since my mother is an eternal beginner, she has more fun skiing with someone who shares her interests than with

Margin annotations:
Subject
Thesis statement
Overall purpose
First category
Definition
Supporting details
Second category
Definition
Supporting details (with humour)
Transition
Third category
Definition
Supporting details (comparative)
Fourth category
Definition
Supporting details
Transition
Significance of classification system

my dad, who is a poetic skier with solitude on his mind. After taking care of Mom, I am free to find a partner I'll enjoy. My sister, the crazy skier of the family, just heads for the rowdiest group she can find! <u>As the years go by and my talents grow, I am trusting my perceptions of skier types to help me find the right partner for life on and off the slopes. No doubt watching my fellow skiers will always remain an enjoyable pastime.</u>

Concluding remarks

Student Writer's Comments

To begin this paper——the topic of which occurred to me as I flew over snow-capped mountains on a trip——I brainstormed. I jotted down the general groups of skiers I believed existed on the slopes and recorded characteristics of each group as they came to me. The ideas flowed quite freely at this point, and I enjoyed imagining the people I was describing. This prewriting stage brought back some great memories from the slopes that cluttered my thinking at times, but in most cases one useless memory triggered two or three other details or skiing stories that helped me make sense of my division/classification system.

I then felt ready to write a first draft but was having a lot of trouble coming up with a sensible order for my categories. So I just began to write. My categories were now clear to me, even though I wanted to work a little more on their labels. And the definitions of each category came quite naturally as I wrote. In fact, the ease with which they surfaced made me believe that I really had discovered some ultimate truth about types of skiers. I also had tons of details and anecdotes to work with from my brainstorming session. When I finished the body of my first draft (it had no introduction or conclusion yet), I realized that every paragraph worked nicely by itself—— four separate category paragraphs. But these paragraphs didn't work together yet at all.

As I reworked the essay, I knew my major job was to reorganize my categories in some logical way and then smooth out the prose with transitions that would make the essay work as a unified whole. To accomplish this, I wrote more drafts of this single paper than I can remember writing for any other assignment. But I feel that the order and the transitions finally work now. The essay moves logically from type to type, and I think my transitions justify my arrangement along the way. My overall purpose came to me as I was reorganizing my categories, at which point I was able to write my introduction and conclusion. After I had put my purpose into words, the significance of my division/classification system became clear. I saved it, however, for the conclusion.

The most exciting part of this paper was realizing how often I had used these mental groupings in pairing my family and friends with other skiers. I had just never labeled, defined, or organized the categories I had created. Writing this paper helped me verbalize these categories and ended up being a lot of fun (especially when it was finished).

Some Final Thoughts on Division/Classification

The essays collected in this chapter use division and/or classification as their primary organizing principle. All of these essays show both techniques at work to varying degrees. As you read these essays, you might also want to be aware of the other rhetorical modes that support these division/classification essays, such as description and definition. Finally, pay particular attention to how these authors bring significance to their systems of classification and, as a result, to their essays themselves.

Division/Classification in Review

Reading Division/Classification Essays

Preparing to Read

1. What assumptions can you make from the essay's title?
2. Can you guess what the general mood of the essay is?
3. What is the essay's purpose and audience?
4. What does the synopsis in the Rhetorical Table of Contents tell you about the essay?
5. What can you learn from the author's biography?
6. Can you guess what the author's point of view toward the subject is?
7. What are your responses to the Preparing to Read questions?

Reading

1. What do you think the "context" of the essay is?
2. Did the author use division or classification most often?
3. Did you preview the questions that follow the essay?

Rereading

1. How does division or classification help the author accomplish his/her purpose?
2. What other rhetorical strategies does the author use to support the essay's purpose?
3. How does the writer explain the significance of his/her division/classification system?
4. What are your responses to the questions after the essay?

Writing Division/Classification Essays

Preparing to Write

1. What are your responses to the Preparing to Write questions?
2. What is your purpose?
3. Who is your audience?

Writing

1. Do you declare an overall purpose for your essay?

2. Do you divide the item or concept you are dealing with into categories?

3. Do you arrange these categories into a logical sequence?

4. Do you define each category, explaining the difference between one category and another and demonstrating that difference through examples?

5. Do you explain the significance of your division/classification system?

6. Are the categories in your essay distinct from one another so they don't overlap?

7. What rhetorical strategies support your essay?

Rewriting

1. Does your thesis communicate your purpose clearly?

2. Have you divided your topic into separate and understandable categories?

3. Are these categories arranged logically?

4. Do you explain the significance of your particular classification system?

William Golding
1911–1993

■■■

Thinking as a Hobby

Born in Cornwall, England, William Golding attended Oxford University and then followed in his father's footsteps by becoming a schoolteacher. After commanding a rocket-launching ship in the North Atlantic during World War II, he returned to his teaching career and began writing novels, the first of which was his epic allegory on human nature entitled *Lord of the Flies* (1954), which chronicles the degeneration to savagery of a group of British schoolboys stranded on an island during a nuclear war. Rejected by a total of 21 publishers before Faber & Faber accepted the manuscript, this brilliant novel was described by its author as "an attempt to trace the defects of society back to the defects of human nature." Golding followed this successful literary debut with a number of other novels, including *The Inheritors* (1955), *Free Fall* (1960), *The Spire* (1964), *Darkness Visible* (1979), *Rites of Passage* (1980), and *Fire Down Below* (1989). Awarded the Nobel prize for literature in 1983, he preferred to be known as a "craftsman" rather than an "artist." He saw himself as being "like one of the old-fashioned shipbuilders, who conceived the boat in their mind and then, after that, touched every single piece that went into the boat. They were in complete control; they knew it inch by inch, and I think the novelist is very much like that." Prior to his death in 1993, Golding described his hobbies as "thinking, classical Greek, sailing, and archaeology."

Preparing to Read

The following essay, originally published in *Holiday* magazine (August 1961), offers us some important insights into the mind of young William Golding, who depicts himself as a student in grammar school struggling to learn how to think clearly and creatively. Prior to reading this essay, consider your definition of thinking: What constitutes thinking? When do you know you are really thinking clearly? Are there different types of thinking? How is thinking different from feeling? How do you know the difference between these functions? Do thinking and feeling serve separate purposes? What are these purposes?

While I was still a boy, I came to the conclusion that there were three grades of thinking; and since I was later to claim thinking as my hobby, I came to an even stranger conclusion—namely, that I myself could not think at all. 1

I must have been an unsatisfactory child for grownups to 2
deal with. I remember how incomprehensible they appeared to
me at first, but not, of course, how I appeared to them. It was
the headmaster of my grammar school who first brought the
subject of thinking before me—though neither in the way, nor
with the result he intended. He had some statuettes in his study.
They stood on a high cupboard behind his desk. One was a lady
wearing nothing but a bath towel. She seemed frozen in an eternal
panic lest the bath towel slip down any farther; and since she
had no arms, she was in an unfortunate position to pull the towel
up again. Next to her, crouched the statuette of a leopard, ready
to spring down at the top drawer of a filing cabinet labeled A-AH.
My innocence interpreted this as the victim's last, despairing
cry. Beyond the leopard was a naked, muscular gentleman, who
sat, looking down, with his chin on his fist and his elbow on his
knee. He seemed utterly miserable.

Some time later, I learned about these statuettes. The 3
headmaster had placed them where they would face delinquent
children, because they symbolized to him the whole of life. The
naked lady was the Venus of Milo. She was Love. She was not
worried about the towel. She was just busy being beautiful. The
leopard was Nature, and he was being natural. The naked,
muscular gentleman was not miserable. He was Rodin's *Thinker*,
an image of pure thought. It is easy to buy small plaster models
of what you think life is like.

I had better explain that I was a frequent visitor to the 4
headmaster's study, because of the latest thing I had done or left
undone. As we now say, I was not integrated. I was, if anything,
disintegrated; and I was puzzled. Grownups never made sense.
Whenever I found myself in a penal position before the
headmaster's desk, with the statuettes glimmering whitely above
him, I would sink my head, clasp my hands behind my back and
writhe one shoe over the other.

The headmaster would look opaquely at me through flashing 5
spectacles.

"What are we going to do with you?" 6

Well, what *were* they going to do with me? I would writhe my 7
shoe some more and stare down at the worn rug.

"Look up, boy! Can't you look up?" 8

Then I would look up at the cupboard, where the naked lady 9
was frozen in her panic and the muscular gentleman contem-
plated the hind-quarters of the leopard in endless gloom. I had

nothing to say to the headmaster. His spectacles caught the lights so that you could see nothing human behind them. There was no possibility of communication.

"Don't you ever think at all?" 10

No, I didn't think, wasn't thinking, couldn't think—I was 11
simply waiting in anguish for the interview to stop.

"Then you'd better learn—hadn't you?" 12

On one occasion the headmaster leaped to his feet, reached 13
up and plonked Rodin's masterpiece on the desk before me.

"That's what a man looks like when he's really thinking." 14

I surveyed the gentleman without interest or comprehension. 15

"Go back to your class." 16

Clearly there was something missing in me. Nature had 17
endowed the rest of the human race with a sixth sense and left me
out. This must be so, I mused, on my way back to the class, since
whether I had broken a window, or failed to remember Boyle's
Law, or been late for school, my teachers produced me one, adult
answer: "Why can't you think?"

As I saw the case, I had broken the window because I had 18
tried to hit Jack Arney with a cricket ball and missed him; I could
not remember Boyle's Law because I had never bothered to learn
it; and I was late for school because I preferred looking over the
bridge into the river. In fact, I was wicked. Were my teachers,
perhaps, so good that they could not understand the depths of my
depravity? Were they clear, untormented people who could direct
their every action by this mysterious business of thinking? The
whole thing was incomprehensible. In my earlier years, I found
even the statuette of the Thinker confusing. I did not believe any
of my teachers were naked, ever. Like someone born deaf, but
bitterly determined to find out about sound, I watched my
teachers to find out about thought.

There was Mr. Houghton. He was always telling me to think. 19
With a modest satisfaction, he would tell me that he had thought
a bit himself. Then why did he spend so much time drinking?
Or was there more sense in drinking than there appeared to be?
But if not, and if drinking were in fact ruinous to health—and
Mr. Houghton was ruined, there was no doubt about that—why
was he always talking about the clean life and the virtues of fresh
air? He would spread his arms wide with the action of a man
who habitually spent his time striding along mountain ridges.

"Open air does me good, boys—I know it!" 20

Sometimes, exalted by his own oratory, he would leap from 21 his desk and hustle us outside into a hideous wind.

"Now, boys! Deep breaths! Feel it right down inside you— 22
huge draughts of God's good air!"

He would stand before us, rejoicing in his perfect health, an 23
open-air man. He would put his hands on his waist and take a
tremendous breath. You could hear the wind, trapped in the
cavern of this chest and struggling with all the unnatural
impediments. His body would reel with shock and his ruined
face go white at the unaccustomed visitation. He would stagger
back to his desk and collapse there, useless for the rest of the
morning.

Mr. Houghton was given to high-minded monologues about 24
the good life, sexless and full of duty. Yet in the middle of one of
these monologues, if a girl passed the window, tapping along
on her neat little feet, he would interrupt his discourse, his neck
would turn of itself and he would watch her out of sight. In this
instance, he seemed to me ruled not by thought but by an
invisible and irresistible spring in his nape.

His neck was an object of great interest to me. Normally it 25
bulged a bit over his collar. But Mr. Houghton had fought in the
First World War alongside both Americans and French, and had
come—by who knows what illogic?—to a settled detestation of
both countries. If either country happened to be prominent in
current affairs, no argument could make Mr. Houghton think
well of it. He would bang the desk, his neck would bulge still
further and go red. "You can say what you like," he would cry,
"but I've thought about this—and I know what I think!"

Mr. Houghton thought with his neck.   26

There was Miss Parsons. She assured us that her dearest wish 27
was our welfare, but I knew even then, with the mysterious
clairvoyance of childhood, that what she wanted most was the
husband she never got. There was Mr. Hands—and so on.

I have dealt at length with my teachers because this was my 28
introduction to the nature of what is commonly called thought.
Through them I discovered that thought is often full of
unconscious prejudice, ignorance and hypocrisy. It will lecture on
disinterested purity while its neck is being remorselessly twisted
toward a skirt. Technically, it is about as proficient as most
businessmen's golf, as honest as most politician's intentions, or—
to come near my own preoccupation—as coherent as most books
that get written. It is what I came to call grade-three thinking,
though more properly, it is feeling, rather than thought.

True, often there is a kind of innocence in prejudices, but in 29 those days I viewed grade-three thinking with an intolerant contempt and an incautious mockery. I delighted to confront a pious lady who hated the Germans with the proposition that we should love our enemies. She taught me a great truth in dealing with grade-three thinkers; because of her, I no longer dismiss lightly a mental process which for nine-tenths of the population is the nearest they will ever get to thought. They have immense solidarity. We had better respect them, for we are outnumbered and surrounded. A crowd of grade-three thinkers, all shouting the same thing, all warming their hands at the fire of their own prejudices, will not thank you for pointing out the contradictions in their beliefs. Man is a gregarious animal, and enjoys agreement as cows will graze all the same way on the side of a hill.

Grade-two thinking is the detection of contradictions. I 30 reached grade two when I trapped the poor, pious lady. Grade-two thinkers do not stampede easily, though often they fall into the other fault and lag behind. Grade-two thinking is a withdrawal, with eyes and ears open. It became my hobby and brought satisfaction and loneliness in either hand. For grade-two thinking destroys without having the power to create. It set me watching the crowds cheering His Majesty the King and asking myself what all the fuss was about, without giving me anything positive to put in the place of that heady patriotism. But there were compensations. To hear people justify their habit of hunting foxes and tearing them to pieces by claiming that the foxes liked it. To hear our Prime Minister talk about the great benefit we conferred on India by jailing people like Pandit Nehru and Gandhi. To hear American politicians talk about peace in one sentence and refuse to join the League of Nations in the next. Yes, there were moments of delight.

But I was growing toward adolescence and had to admit that 31 Mr. Houghton was not the only one with an irresistible spring in his neck. I, too, felt the compulsive hand of nature and began to find that pointing out contradiction could be costly as well as fun. There was Ruth, for example, a serious and attractive girl. I was an atheist at the time. Grade-two thinking is a menace to religion and knocks down sects like skittles. I put myself in a position to be converted by her with an hypocrisy worthy of grade three. She was a Methodist—or at least, her parents were, and Ruth had to follow suit. But, alas, instead of relying on the Holy Spirit to convert me, Ruth was foolish enough to open her pretty mouth in argument. She claimed that the Bible (King James Version) was literally inspired. I countered by saying that the Catholics believed in the literal inspiration of Saint Jerome's *Vulgate*, and the two books were different. Argument flagged.

At last she remarked that there were an awful lot of 32 Methodists, and they couldn't be wrong, could they—not all those millions? That was too easy, said I restively (for the nearer you were to Ruth, the nicer she was to be near to) since there were more Roman Catholics than Methodists anyway; and they couldn't be wrong, could they—not all those hundreds of millions? An awful flicker of doubt appeared in her eyes. I slid my arm round her waist and murmured breathlessly that if we were counting heads, the Buddhists were the boys for my money. But Ruth had *really* wanted to do me good, because I was so nice. She fled. The combination of my arm and those countless Buddhists was too much for her.

That night her father visited my father and left, red-cheeked 33 and indignant. I was given the third degree to find out what had happened. It was lucky we were both of us only fourteen. I lost Ruth and gained an undeserved reputation as a potential libertine.

So grade-two thinking could be dangerous. It was in this 34 knowledge, at the age of fifteen, that I remember making a comment from the heights of grade two, on the limitations of grade three. One evening I found myself alone in the school hall, preparing it for a party. The door of the headmaster's study was open. I went in. The headmaster had ceased to thump Rodin's Thinker down on the desk as an example to the young. Perhaps he had not found any more candidates, but the statuettes were still there, glimmering and gathering dust on top of the cupboard. I stood on a chair and rearranged them. I stood Venus in her bath towel on the filing cabinet, so that now the top drawer caught its breath in a gasp of sexy excitement. "A-ah!" The portentous Thinker I placed on the edge of the cupboard so that he looked down at the bath towel and waited for it to slip.

Grade-two thinking, though it filled life with fun and 35 excitement, did not make for content. To find out the deficiencies of our elders bolsters the young ego but does not make for personal security. I found that grade two was not only the power to point out contradictions. It took the swimmer some distance from the shore and left him there, out of his depth. I decided that Pontius Pilate was a typical grade-two thinker. "What is truth?" he said, a very common grade-two thought, but one that is used always as the end of an argument instead of the beginning. There is a still higher grade of thought which says, "What is truth?" and sets out to find it.

But these grade-one thinkers were few and far between. They 36 did not visit my grammar school in the flesh though they were there in books. I aspired to them, partly because I was ambitious and partly because I now saw my hobby as an unsatisfactory thing if it went no further. If you set out to climb a mountain, however high you climb, you have failed if you cannot reach the top.

I *did* meet an undeniably grade-one thinker in my first year 37 at Oxford. I was looking over a small bridge in Magdalen Deer Park, and a tiny mustached and hatted figure came and stood by my side. He was a German who had just fled from the Nazis to Oxford as a temporary refuge. His name was Einstein.

But Professor Einstein knew no English at that time and I 38 knew only two words of German. I beamed at him, trying wordlessly to convey by my bearing all the affection and respect that the English felt for him. It is possible—and I have to make the admission—that I felt here were two grade-one thinkers standing side by side; yet I doubt if my face conveyed more than a formless awe. I would have given my Greek and Latin and French and a good slice of my English for enough German to communicate. But we were divided; he was as inscrutable as my headmaster. For perhaps five minutes we stood together on the bridge, undeniable grade-one thinker and breathless aspirant. With true greatness, Professor Einstein realized that any contact was better than none. He pointed to a trout wavering in midstream.

He spoke: "*Fisch.*" 39

My brain reeled. Here I was, mingling with the great, and 40 yet helpless as the veriest grade-three thinker. Desperately I sought for some sign by which I might convey that I, too, revered pure reason. I nodded vehemently. In a brilliant flash I used up half of my German vocabulary.

"*Fisch. Ja. Ja.*" 41

For perhaps another five minutes we stood side by side. Then 42 Professor Einstein, his whole figure still conveying good will and amiability, drifted away out of sight.

I, too, would be a grade-one thinker. I was irreverent at the 43 best of times. Political and religious systems, social customs, loyalties and traditions, they all came tumbling down like so many rotten apples off a tree. This was a fine hobby and a sensible substitute for cricket, since you could play it all year round. I came up in the end with what must always remain the justification for grade-one thinking, its sign, seal and chapter. I devised a coherent system for living. It was a moral system, which was wholly logical. Of course, as I readily admitted, conversion of the world to my way of thinking might be difficult, since my system did away with a number of trifles, such as big business, centralized government, armies, marriage. . . .

It was Ruth all over again. I had some very good friends who 44 stood by me, and still do. But my acquaintances vanished, taking the girls with them. Young women seemed oddly contented with the world as it was. They valued the meaningless ceremony with a ring. Young men, while willing to concede the chaining sordidness of marriage, were hesitant about abandoning the organizations which they hoped would give them a career. A young man on the first rung of the Royal Navy, while perfectly agreeable to doing away with big business and marriage, got as red-necked as Mr. Houghton when I proposed a world without any battleships in it.

Had the game gone too far? Was it a game any longer? In 45 those prewar days, I stood to lose a great deal, for the sake of a hobby.

Now you are expecting me to describe how I saw the folly of 46 my ways and came back to the warm nest, where prejudices are so often called loyalties, where pointless actions are hallowed into custom by repetition, where we are content to say we think when all we do is feel.

But you would be wrong. I dropped my hobby and turned 47 professional.

If I were to go back to the headmaster's study and find the 48 dusty statuettes still there, I would arrange them differently. I would dust Venus and put her aside, for I have come to love her and know her for the fair thing she is. But I would put the Thinker, sunk in his desperate thought, where there were shadows before him—and at his back, I would put the leopard, crouched and ready to spring.

UNDERSTANDING DETAILS

1. What exactly is Golding classifying in this essay? Explain each part of his classification system.

2. What does the author think of each type of thinking he discusses?
3. What characterizes the relationship between Golding and his headmaster? What do they learn from each other?
4. Describe the people who represent each of Golding's categories of thinking.

ANALYZING MEANING

1. Why must Golding have been "an unsatisfactory child for grownups to deal with" (paragraph 2)? In what ways was Golding probably "unsatisfactory"?
2. What did the three statuettes in the headmaster's office represent? Why are they important to Golding's essay?
3. Why do you think so many adults asked Golding, "Why can't you think"?
4. Why does Golding call thinking his "hobby"?

DISCOVERING RHETORICAL STRATEGIES

1. In what ways does Golding use division and classification in this essay? How does he give significance or value to his system of organization? What other rhetorical techniques does he use to accomplish his purpose?
2. What distinctions does Golding make between thinking and feeling in this essay? Do you agree with these distinctions?
3. Through his style, Golding gives the impression that he is detached from his subject and is able to analyze his behaviour as well as the behaviours of others around him. How does he give his readers this impression? Do you think it is an accurate impression?
4. Why do you think Golding ends his essay with a discussion of the statuettes in the headmaster's office? What effect does this ending create? What is the significance of the new arrangement of the statuettes?

MAKING CONNECTIONS

1. William Golding relates school experiences from his childhood in developing this essay. How does Golding's description of his schooldays and his teachers compare to that of Ray Guy ("When Jannies Visited")? How do their school experiences compare to your own?

2. Compare and contrast Golding's early years, when he was learning to think clearly, with the same period in the life of Eudora Welty ("Listening"). Which author had a more stable, comfortable upbringing? How was each author influenced by these different circumstances? Whose early years were most like yours?

3. Which of the three stages of thinking does Golding spend most of his time describing? Which the least? Does Susan Swan ("Nine Ways of Looking at a Critic") or Amy Willard Cross ("Life in the Stopwatch Lane") display a similar imbalance in her division/classification essay? Why do some authors emphasize some categories more than others?

IDEAS FOR DISCUSSION/WRITING

Preparing to Write

Write freely about various types of thinking you are aware of: What are these types? How are these types of thinking represented in different kinds of behaviour? Why are different types of thinking important to your daily survival? To your progress in school? What type of thinking do you believe will bring you the most success in life? In school? In what ways is thinking different from feeling?

Choosing a Topic

1. Your English teacher has asked about your ability to think critically. Respond to this question by classifying for this teacher all the different types of thinking you do in a typical day—with your main focus on critical thinking. Remember that each thinking task you do should fit into a category. Decide on a point of view before you begin to write.

2. Speculate about the thinking activities of a close friend or relative by analyzing that person's behaviour and preferences. Remember that analysis is based on the process of division. Divide this person's behaviour and preferences into logical parts; then, study those parts so that you can better understand the person's reasoning techniques. Decide on a purpose and audience before you begin to write.

3. If the mental activities we perform say something about us, analyze yourself by writing an essay that classifies the different mental activities you have carried out in the last week. Discuss your choices as you proceed.

WEB SITES

nobel.sdsc.edu/laureates/literature-1983-1-bio.html
The Nobel Foundation biography of William Golding.

www.theinsider.com/sf/Photos/legionThinker.htm
or
**shell5.ba.best.com/~ghelms/htmlpages/about/area/peninsla/
thinker.html**
or
www.cantorfoundation.com/1.html
or
**it.ncsa.uiuc.edu/~mag/Graphics/MoreFrance/indoor-
thinker.html**
At these sites you will find pictures of Rodin's *The Thinker*.

pw1.netcom.com/~jsemrau/venus.htm
A picture of the *Venus de Milo* sculpture.

David Foot
1944–

■ ■ ■

Boomers Dance to a New Beat

David Foot is a professor of Economics at the University of Toronto who has become very well known for his work concerning the role of demographics in determining societal and economic trends. Foot's book, *Boom, Bust and Echo: How to Profit from the Coming Demographic Shift*, cowritten with Daniel Stoffman, has quickly become a best-seller and has made Foot a popular speaker and authority on future Canadian trends.

Prior to the 1996 publication of *Boom, Bust and Echo*, Foot had published two other books: *Canada's Population Outlook: Demographic Futures and Economic Challenges* (1982) and, with Blossom T. Wigdor, *The Over Forty Society* (1988). Foot's other publications are listed on his Web site (**www.footwork.com**).

David Foot was born in England, grew up in Australia where he completed an undergraduate degree, and then continued his education at Harvard University where he earned a doctorate in economics. While his writing has focused much attention on Dr. Foot, he has also been recognized for his teaching ability. He is a two-time recipient (1983 and 1992) of the University of Toronto undergraduate teaching award. As well, in 1992, he received a 3M Award for Teaching Excellence from the Society for Teaching and Learning in Higher Education, which recognizes outstanding Canadian university educators.

Preparing to Read

Before you read this essay, think about different generations. To what generation do you belong? What generation are your parents a part of? What defines a generation? What is a "generation gap"? Which generation has had the most significant impact on our society? Why?

■_____■

Cocooning is dead, the trend-spotters have proclaimed.   1

   In the eighties, North Americans hunkered down in their 2 house-fortresses with remote control to avoid an increasingly unsafe world. Now, this cocooning trend, first labelled by guru Faith Popcorn, is in reverse.

   Canadians and Americans are watching less TV and going 3 out more to movies, museums, the performing arts and restaurants. Crime rates have stopped rising and, in many jurisdictions, they are falling.

All forms of home entertainment are either stagnant or 4 declining in popularity. The Internet does not seem to be catching on as home entertainment or as a shopping vehicle. There has been a resurrection of city streets and a renewed concern for communities. According to a recent Globe and Mail article, we are rejecting the "bland fruits of wired isolation."

But is all this so surprising? A careful understanding of 5 demographic trends provides a logical and easily understood explanation. For managers and marketers, it also serves as a foundation for anticipating new trends.

In a person's teens and 20s, "action" is important. The 6 downtown core of major cities provide this action. Being "grounded" by a tough parent is real punishment; moving out, usually into a city apartment, is a common goal.

Growing up into the late 20s and early 30s often means 7 partnering and family formation. For many parents, the city core doesn't seem like a great place to raise kids, so they buy houses in the suburbs. This means a mortgage and other loans to purchase furniture, appliances and the minivan.

So it was with the baby boomer generation, which has 8 dominated, if not determined, postwar economic and social trends in North America. The 10 million boomers in Canada, born between 1947 and 1966, comprise the biggest generation in the history of this country. Watching them can provide an understanding of these trends.

The first boomer became a teen-ager in 1960. So the sixties 9 and seventies were dominated by boomers moving through their teen-age years into their 20s. They rushed into cities, stimulating massive urbanization. They rented apartments, driving down vacancies and increasing rents. They went to movies and rock concerts and they ate lots of cheap food.

In 1977, a significant event went almost unnoticed—the first 10 boomer reached the dreaded age of 30. The early boomers started buying homes in the suburbs. By the mid-eighties, the new trend became an avalanche. Suburbanization took off.

Debt levels soared and the "echo generation" was spawned. 11 Minivan sales took off. Young children and lots of debt put a damper on going out. Technology and TV in particular, including video rentals, became the main entertainment media. Cocooning was established.

So Faith Popcorn was right, but it was not because of new   12
societal values. The biggest generation in history was leaving its
action years behind and moving into its family ones. Not
surprisingly, family values emerged as a new social trend. Rental
housing, movie theatres and take-out restaurants experienced
much slower growth and, in some cases, decline.

Spending growth was focused on family and home. Pet-food   13
sales were still brisk but convenience-store sales sagged. Boomers
started paying off their loans and mortgages, leaving no cash for
luxuries or savings.

With kids to raise and careers to manage, the boomers in   14
their 30s and 40s were running "99 Lives"—another Popcorn
trend. They were trying to be good parents to their kids and
good children to their aging parents. They were working overtime
and competing for promotion to ever-fewer mid-management
positions. Woe betide any organization that wasted their time.
The "vigilante consumer" had arrived in full force.

But last year, another watershed was reached—the first   15
boomers turned 50. This is mid-life crisis time. The kids are
beginning to leave home and those sprained ligaments are taking
longer to heal.

Running shoes have become walking shoes, and the treadmill   16
purchased to replace visits to the fitness centre now induces
guilt. Resting has become a pleasurable activity, especially at the
cottage. Anyone ignorant of the power of demographics might
think values are changing again.

With lower interest rates and evaporating loans, there is   17
more discretionary income, making it possible to afford a luxury
or a sports-utility vehicle, a restaurant meal, and a show.

The teen-age or twentysomething kids don't need babysitting   18
any more, so going out is possible again. But the show is less
likely to be a movie or a rock concert unless, of course, the Rolling
Stones are back in town. Increasingly, the lavish musical, the
symphony and maybe the opera hold more attraction.

So boomers are emerging from their cocoons. Surprise! They   19
are watching less TV—home entertainment is dropping in
popularity—they are shopping in their neighbourhoods and they
are not using the Internet. Their beloved pets are aging and the
vet is becoming as familiar as the doctor.

Their parents are also getting old and mortality has come   20
closer to home. Aging has entered a deeply psychological, almost
spiritual phase. Boomers are snapping up books on the topic,

provided the print is large.

But the seven million "echo" kids are also having an impact.   21
Movie attendance is rising, mainly because of the increased
numbers of teen-agers. Similarly, the growth in confectionary,
pop and some fast-food sales has little to do with boomers trying
to relive youth. Their echo kids born in the eighties are delivering
these trends.

The marketplace of the future is becoming more complex.   22
While the leading boomers are killing cocooning, their kids are
reigniting the trends of the sixties. Rock stars have a bright future,
as does new technology. Of course, it should not be surprising to
see a reversal of the downward trend in crime rates as the echo
generation enters its prime crime-prone ages.

But will this drive the boomers back to cocoons? Hardly.   23
They are finding time to volunteer, to give to charity and to
support their communities. They are increasingly worried about
pensions, investing in the market and thinking about moving
out of the urban rat race. These are the trends of the future.

The boomer generation is predictably shifting into the next   24
phase of life: They are beginning to move from parenthood to
grandparenthood.

Managing this new trend is both a personal and a societal   25
challenge, with all the associated opportunities and tribulations.
Demographic analysis can provide us with a window to
understand these changes, to disentangle them and to predict
them. What more could the successful manager ask for?

UNDERSTANDING DETAILS

1. List the stages of the life that Foot identifies including the
   defining events and interests.
2. Who are the two groups currently impacting trends? Explain
   why.
3. Who exactly are the baby boomers and why have they had such
   a big impact on major trends in our society?

ANALYZING MEANING

1. Why is demographic analysis important?
2. What trends are likely to emerge in the next decade as a result
   of demographics, given the influences that Foot outlines?

3. "Anyone ignorant of the power of demographics might think values are changing again" (paragraph 16). Explain this quotation from Foot's essay. What is the distinction between changing values and the power of demographics?

DISCOVERING RHETORICAL STRATEGIES

1. How does Foot organize his categories in this essay? Why does he place these categories in this particular order?
2. Describe the author's intended audience. What makes you think he is directing his comments to this group?
3. What other rhetorical modes does Foot use in this essay besides division and classification? How do these other modes support the author's division/classification system?

MAKING CONNECTIONS

1. David Foot outlines how the baby boomer generation has influenced economic and societal trends in postwar North America. How might Foot explain the phenomena of television in public places (Cowan, "TV Me Alone") and the increasing homogeneity/suburbanization of places like Sudbury (Ferguson, "The Sudbury Syndrome")?
2. Amy Willard Cross ("Life in the Stopwatch Lane") is part of the boomer generation. At what stage in the boomers' lives was her essay originally published? How do you think that demographics may have contributed to the categories of time Cross has identified in her essay? If she were writing this essay today how might it be different?
3. Mark Kingwell ("Not Available in Stores") has written about infomercials and the changes that they have undergone. Based on demographics, what would you predict for the future of infomercials? For television generally?

IDEAS FOR DISCUSSION/WRITING

Preparing to Write

Write freely about your thoughts on your generation. What things define your generation? What music? What attitudes and ideas? What leisure activities? What clothing? What values identify someone of your generation? Do you like the image of your generation? Why or why not? What would you like to change about your generation?

Choosing a Topic

1. As a young entrepreneur you want to start a small business in the next decade. Explain what kind of business you believe would be successful, based on the demographic trends that are outlined in Foot's essay.
2. You are a manager of a mid-size company and you want to hire and retain the best employees. Describe what kind of working environment you will aim to establish to appeal to the workforce of the early 2000s. Where will your employees be located? What kinds of benefits will you offer them? What hours will your employees be expected to work?
3. Imagine you are contributing to the fourth edition of *Reader's Choice* in 2003. Find one new essay that you think should be included. Write a letter to the editor of this text in which you justify your choice based on its merits including its appeal to your audience.

WEB SITES

www.chass.utoronto.ca/~foot/pubs.html
A list of publications by David Foot, some with links to complete articles.

www.footwork.com/index.html
David K. Foot's Footwork Consulting Inc.

Amy Willard Cross
1960–

■ ■ ■

Life in the Stopwatch Lane

Amy Willard Cross is a writer who manages to divide her time between the stopwatch pace of the city and the more relaxed tempo of her other home "in the woods." *The Summer House: A Tradition of Leisure* (1992) is Cross's first book. In it, she examines the North American practice of escaping to the more leisurely life of a cottage or summer house. Born in Washington, D.C., Cross is currently based in Canada. Her articles can be found in *City and Country Home, The Globe and Mail*, and *Cottage Life*, and she is currently Health Editor at *Chatelaine*.

Preparing to Read

This article first appeared in *The Globe and Mail*'s "Facts and Arguments" column in 1990. In "Life in the Stopwatch Lane," Amy Willard Cross examines the trend toward dividing time into progressively smaller units and labelling different types of time. Before reading this essay, think about the concept of time and how it has changed. How is time viewed differently in different cultures? What value do you place on your time? How do you measure time and what labels do you use to identify different divisions of time?

■ _____ ■

If time is money, the rates have skyrocketed and you probably 1 can't afford it. North Americans are suffering a dramatic time shortage since demand greatly exceeds supply. In fact, a recent survey revealed that people lost about 10 hours of leisure per week between 1973 and 1987. Maybe you were too busy to notice.

Losing that leisure leaves a piddling 16.6 hours to do 2 whatever you want, free of work, dish-washing or car-pooling. In television time, that equals a season of 13 *thirtysomething* episodes, plus 3 1/2 reruns. Hardly enough time to write an autobiography or carry on an affair.

How has replacing free time with more billable hours affected 3 society? It has created a new demographic group: the Busy Class—who usurped the Leisure Class. Easy to recognize, members of the Busy Class constantly cry to anyone listening,

"I'm *soooooo* busy." So busy they can't call their mother or find change for a panhandler. Masters of doing two things at once, they eke the most out of time. They dictate while driving, talk while calculating, entertain guests while nursing, watch the news while pumping iron. Even business melts into socializing—people earn their daily bread while they break it.

In fact, the Busies must make lots of bread to maintain 4 themselves in the standard of busy-ness to which they've become accustomed. To do that, they need special, expensive stuff. Stuff like call waiting, which lets them talk to two people at once. Stuff like two-faced watches, so they can do business in two time zones at once. Neither frenzied executives nor hurried housewives dare leave the house without their "book"—leather-bound appointment calendars thick as bestsellers. Forget hi-fi's or racing cars, the new talismans of overachievers also work: coffee-makers that brew by alarm; remote-controlled ignitions; or car faxes. Yet, despite all these time-efficient devices, few people have time to spare.

That scarcity has changed how we measure time. Now it's 5 being scientifically dissected into smaller and smaller pieces. Thanks to digital clocks, we know when it's 5:30 (and calculate we'll be home in three hours, eight minutes). These days lawyers can reason in 1/10th of an hour increments; they bill every six minutes. This to-the-minute precision proves time's escalating value.

Time was, before the advent of car phones and digital clocks, 6 we scheduled two kinds of time: time off and work hours. Not any more. Just as the Inuit label the infinite varieties of snow, the Busy Class has identified myriad subtleties of free time and named them. Here are some textbook examples of the new faces of time:

Quality time. For those working against the clock, the quality 7 of time spent with loved ones supposedly compensates for quantity. This handy concept absolves guilt as quickly as rosary counting. So careerist couples dine à deux once a fortnight. Parents bond by reading kids a story after nanny fed and bathed them. When pressed for time, nobody wastes it by fighting about bad breath or unmade beds. People who spend quality time with each other view their relationships through rose-coloured glasses. And knowing they've created perfect personal lives lets the Busy Class work even harder—guilt-free.

Travel time. With an allowance of 16.6 hours of fun, the Busy 8

Class watches time expenditures carefully. Just like businesses do while making bids, normal people calculate travel time for leisure activities. If two tram rides away, a friendly squash game loses out. One time-efficient woman even formulated a mathematical theorem: fun per mile quotient. Before accepting any social invitation, she adds up travel costs, figures out the time spent laughing, drinking and eating. If the latter exceeds the former, she accepts. It doesn't matter who asks.

Downtime. Borrowed from the world of heavy equipment 9
and sleek computers, downtime is a professional-sounding word meaning the damn thing broke, wait around until it's fixed. Translated into real life, downtime counts as neither work nor play, but a maddening no-man's land where nothing happens! Like lining up for the ski-lift, or commuting without a car phone, or waiting a while for the mechanic's diagnosis. Beware: people who keep track of their downtime probably indulge in less than 16 hours of leisure.

Family time. In addition to 60-hour weeks, aerobics and dinner 10
parties, some people make time for their children. When asked to brunch, a young couple will reply, "We're sorry but that's our family time." A variant of quality time, it's Sunday afternoon between lunch and the Disney Hour when nannies frequent Filipino restaurants. In an effort to entertain their children without exposure to sex and violence, the family attends craft fairs, animated matinees or tree-tapping demonstrations. There, they converge with masses of family units spending time alone with the kids. After a noisy, sticky afternoon, parents gladly punch the clock come Monday.

Quiet time. Overwhelmed by their schedules, some people 11
try to recapture the magic of childhood when they watched clouds for hours on end. Sophisticated grown-ups have rediscovered the quiet time of kindergarten days. They unplug the phone (not the answering machine), clutch a book and try not to think about work. But without teachers to enforce it, quiet doesn't last. The clock ticks too loudly. As a computer fanatic said, after being entertained at 16 megahertz, sitting still to watch a sunset pales by comparison.

As it continues to increase in value, time will surely divide 12
into even smaller units. And people will share only the tiniest amounts with each other. Hey, brother, can you spare a minute? Got a second? A nanosecond?

UNDERSTANDING DETAILS

1. Summarize the various categories into which Cross divides time. How many categories does she believe used to exist?
2. Why do busy people divide time into so many different categories?
3. What technological innovations does Cross mention that have allowed us to "maximize our efficient use of time"?

ANALYZING MEANING

1. What is Cross's purpose in this essay? To what extent does she achieve this purpose?
2. What is responsible for our measuring time in smaller and smaller units? What implications does this have for the way that we live?
3. Why has increased efficiency resulted in less leisure time?

DISCOVERING RHETORICAL STRATEGIES

1. While Cross's main division is that of time, she also divides people into groups. On what basis has she divided each of these subjects?
2. How would you describe the tone that Cross adopts in this essay? How does she feel about the "Busy Class" and the categories of time they have created? How do you know this?
3. Humour and unexpected phrasing are used effectively in describing the people that are featured in this essay and the different categories of time. Which details are particularly effective in conveying Cross's point of view?

MAKING CONNECTIONS

1. Amy Willard Cross identifies several types of time in her essay. Imagine a conversation between Cross and Tomson Highway ("What a Certain Visionary Once Said"). Do you think these two writers would view time the same way? Explain why or why not.
2. David Foot ("Boomers Dance to a New Beat") discusses the role of demographics in societal trends. How is Cross's division of time a reflection of the generation to which she belongs?
3. Amy Willard Cross identifies each of the categories in her essay with a clear heading. How does this compare to the strategies

used by Susan Swan ("Nine Ways of Looking at Critic") and William Golding ("Thinking as a Hobby")? Why has each author chosen his or her respective approach?

IDEAS FOR DISCUSSION/WRITING

Preparing to Write

Write freely about the effects of technology. What technological developments have made us more efficient? What expectations have changed as a result of changing technology? What positive effects do you see from things such as computers, cellular telephones, and fax machines? What negative consequences have these pieces of equipment had on our lives?

Choosing a Topic

1. In a short essay outline the ways in which some technological development has changed your life. Before you start writing, make sure that you choose a purpose and a particular point of view.
2. The way time is viewed varies greatly across cultures. Write an essay, to be distributed at an international conference on education, which gives teachers from a variety of different countries an idea of how a typical North American student spends her/his time. Use a clear system of division to convey your message effectively.
3. Write an essay in which you classify the various people you know, in categories. First, decide on a principle for classification, and then use specific detail to explain where individuals are placed.

WEB SITES

www.globeandmail.ca
The Globe and Mail is the source of this article.

Laura Millard
1961–

■ ■ ■

Images of Canada: Canadian Bank Notes

Laura Millard is a visual artist who currently lives in Owen Sound, Ontario, but is originally from Calgary, Alberta. Millard's work, which includes paintings and mixed media installations, has been shown in both solo and group exhibitions across Canada and in Sweden. In addition to producing her own work, Millard has taught a variety of art courses at The Nova Scotia College of Art and Design, The Ontario College of Art, Concordia University, and The Alberta College of Art. The essay from *Border/Lines* which appears here is about the design of Canadian currency, and reflects Millard's particular interest in landscape art.

Preparing to Read

In this essay, Laura Millard examines the ways in which Canada has been represented on the various issues of bank notes that have been produced by the Bank of Canada since 1935. Before you read her essay, think about your own associations with Canada. What images do you think typify the country? What formal symbols are used to represent Canada? What informal associations are made by both Canadians and others? Are there common characteristics of these symbolic representations?

"The nature of our government, our bilingual heritage and the di- 1
versity of Canada's geography and wildlife are emphasized by the portraits, legends, landscapes, birds and national symbols which appear on every bank note."

This quotation from the display text in the "Paper Puzzles" 2 exhibition at the Currency Museum in Ottawa states that aspects of our "nature" as Canadians are emphasized through the appearance of our bank notes and suggests that every note provides a cryptic combination of elements which signify "Canada." The text goes on to say, "Bank notes are worth getting to know better—not only because of their value but because of the fascinating secrets they have to tell." The key for unlocking these secrets, however, is not provided by official texts.

Just as our nature as Canadians apparently "appears" to us 3 on our bank notes, the bank note imagery itself seems to "appear" through a conjuring act which is unfettered by accompanying explanations. The routes taken which lead to the specific images selected are not marked. The official literature does not discuss the process through which it is decided how Canada is portrayed, but states simply that Canada is portrayed. Clues to the nature of this portrayal, to the identity of this Canada, spring from the hope that a picture is indeed worth a thousand words and that an analysis of the Bank of Canada's bank note imagery from its first issue to the present will provide these clues.

The history of the Bank of Canada's control over note design   4 begins in 1935 when it struggled for the sole right to issue notes. Provincial governments and chartered banks had previously issued their own. The issue then, as now, was security and control and the newly founded Bank claimed to be better able to control counterfeiting. It set out to improve printing technology so that increasingly intricate designs could be issued to ensure its claim. The Bank of Canada pursues this endeavour to this day. Unlike the tradition of American paper currency which has not deviated from its "green-back," Canadian bank notes have undergone numerous design and imagery changes.

Through a self-propelled flurry of continuing improvement,   5 set in motion by the initial rush to prove itself to angry provincial governments and banks, the Bank of Canada now claims to have arrived at the forefront of currency design. A line is devoted in each press release to the fact that counterfeiting is not a problem in Canada, nor has it been for years. Regardless, the Bank of Canada maintains a program of deterring counterfeiting.

The pursuit of the technologically more advanced note is the   6 rationale behind the almost constant changes and plans to change our bank note design. An example of this can be seen in the creation of the new optical security device (OSD). According to a Bank of Canada press release of 1989, "Canadians can be justly proud of this technological breakthrough, which puts Canadian notes a good step ahead of advanced copying and printing techniques. Canada does not have a counterfeiting problem and the OSD will help to make sure it stays that way."

What "fascinating secret" might this aspect of bank note   7 design tell us? The preoccupation it suggests with security, control and the law, is met with the relentless pursuit of a technology that will ensure the maintenance of that preoccupation, in spite of the fact that there are no real threats or enemies to protect against. Compare this with the situation in the United States which have, according to the Currency Museum's employee, the most counterfeited currency in the world, and yet employ design technology equivalent to what ours was in 1935. Perhaps the American government is just less inclined to interrupt the cash flow of its spirited entrepreneurs, but more certainly it shows that country's own preoccupation with its history and the tradition of its "green-back."

Beginning with its first issue in 1935, which was issued in 8 separate French and English versions, the images presented on both versions were as follows:

$1.00 bill: "Agriculture allegory: Seated female with agricultural products."

$2.00 bill: "Harvest allegory: Seated female with fruits of harvest."

$5.00 bill: "Electric Power allegory: Seated male with symbols of electricity."

$10.00 bill: "Transportation allegory: Mercury with ships, trains and planes."

$20.00 bill: "Toiler allegory: Kneeling male exhibiting the produce of the field to the Spirit of Agriculture."

$50.00 bill: "Modern Inventions allegory: Seated female with symbols of radio broadcasting."

$100.00 bill: "Commerce and Industry allegory: Seated male showing ship to child, harbour scene and blast furnace in background."

The same images were used on the following 1937 bilingual 9 issue. When I first saw these images I was taken aback by how foreign they appear, slightly European but predominantly American. The promise, the optimism and the reassurance offered by the supernatural beings portrayed are not aspects of the nature of Canada as I understand it. Portrayed in these bank notes is what Gaile McGregor, in *The Wacousta Syndrome, Explorations in Canadian Landscape*, describes as the American colonist's experience of the New World environment: "Under the influence of the millennial expectations of the 17th century, the early American colonist, borrowing concepts from scriptural explication, tended to interpret the empirical environment predominantly in terms of signs or types of supernatural events." Through this association, "the entire world became charged with cosmic significance and every human life was seen as part of a cosmic conflict between the forces of Good and Evil."

The landscapes in these images have been won over by Good.   10
The landscape is set in the distance and poses no threat, only the
promise of space fully inhabitable and hospitable. It is almost
completely obscured by the archetypal and supernatural figures
which foreground and fill the frame. As allegories for the human
domination and domestication of the New World, these images
clearly present the wilderness as tamed.

In 1954, when the Bank of Canada issued its next series, it   11
did so with the stated aim of creating "a Canadian dimension"
through a complete change of these note images. Concerning the
selection of the new images, the Bank of Canada stated only that
"a prominent Canadian dimension was created by replacing the
earlier allegorical figures with Canadian landscapes." They are
described simply as a series of "realistic landscapes and
seascapes."

Clearly the Bank of Canada felt that the previous imagery   12
was not Canadian enough. The difference between the 1935
images and the 1954 images is startling. The 1954 images are as
follows:

$1.00 bill: "Prairie View Saskatchewan."
$2.00 bill: "View of Upper Melbourne, Richmond, Quebec."
$5.00 bill: "Otter Falls at Mill 996 of the Alaska Highway."
$10.00 bill: "Mount Burgess, Alberta."
$20.00 bill: "Laurentian Winter."
$50.00 bill: "Atlantic Seashore."
$100.00 bill: "Okanagan Lake, British Columbia."
$1000.00 bill: "Anse St. Jean, Saguenay River, Quebec."

It is assumed, or hoped, that the Canadian dimension that   13
these images create is self-apparent. How does this created
dimension imagine itself and how do these images locate it? The
allegory of garden paradise in the previous images is gone,
replaced by realism. This realism is attained by beginning the
image production process with a photograph of the landscape.
The photograph is then used as the source for a painted image,
a procedure also employed by many Canadian landscape painters
from Tom Thomson to Jack Chambers. The painted step in the
procedure, which brings in a "human" touch, is almost
apologized for in the Currency Museum's display text: "Because
of some of the technical and esthetic considerations of Bank note
design, the illustrations may vary slightly from the actual
locations depicted." The engraving made from the painting

renders it mechanically reproducible but so intricately detailed that it is as difficult to copy as possible. The resulting landscape has a technological esthetic, a realism devoid of subjective interpretation or of the mythicized encounter with the landscape in the 1935 series. This process of demythicizing the landscape is also commented on by McGregor: "Too extensively demythicized the environment tends simply to become a kind of void that resists all human connection. This is what happens in Canada."

What evidence of this void can be found in the Canadian 14 dimension series? Whereas all the previous issue images celebrated the inhabitable and benevolent landscape, only half of the 1954 series show any sign of a human presence at all and it is revealing to look at how this human presence is portrayed.

For example, the $1 bill presents the landscape as a vast 15 expanse under a stormy sky. Cutting through it are telephone poles, a dirt road and a barbed wire fence that recedes in one-point perspective to a distant grain elevator poised on the horizon. A large thunderhead hangs just above the tiny structure. It is a far and rather lonely cry from the Agriculture allegory seated on her throne surrounded by heaps of produce. The thin threads of transportation (road) and communication (poles) provide little reassurance against the distant storm and vast space.

The $2 bill shows three or four small farm houses and a 16 church clustered in the center of the mid-ground. The distant houses are alone and unreachable. The $1000 image is like the $2 one, showing a few structures in the mid-ground, but here the foreground is greatly reduced and mountains loom on the horizon which almost obscures the sky. The vast landscape again engulfs a few buildings. This image is also in stark contrast to its previous image of the Security allegory.

The remaining images of the 1954 series depict landscapes 17 devoid of human presence, and of these only the $100 one has a foreground which it seems possible to enter. The other images do not suggest possible passage through them, their foregrounds blocked by rapids, trees or snow. The images on the $5, $10 and $20 bills specifically appear utterly wild and alien. McGregor suggests that, "The real relevance of the wilderness mythos to Canada can be seen only if we pay attention to what its proponents show us unconsciously, rather than giving too much weight to what they say they are doing."

What do the 1954 images show us, given that they are to 18 create a dimension that is Canadian? With regard to the portrayal

of Canadians within the Canadian landscape, they un-
questionably show a great deal of It and a little of Us. We huddle
together while the landscape surrounds us and look out at a
wilderness that prohibits our entry. Northrop Frye has termed
this response to the Canadian landscape the "garrison mentality"
and McGregor has termed it the "Wacousta syndrome."

Between 1969 and 1975 a new set of images replaces the 1954   19
issue. They are as follows:

> $1.00 bill: "Parliament Hill across Ottawa River."
> $2.00 bill: "Inuit hunting scene on Baffin Island."
> $5.00 bill: "Salmon seine, Johnson Strait, Vancouver Island."
> $10.00 bill: "Polymer Corporation, Sarnia, Ontario."
> $20.00 bill: "Morraine Lake, Alberta."
> $50.00 bill: "Dome Formation, Royal Canadian Mounted Police,
>   Musical Ride."
> $100.00 bill: "Waterfront scene at Lunenburg."

These images again provide an interesting set of comparisons.   20
In this series the landscape becomes inhabitable again, but
without the assistance of supernatural beings. Technology,
government and the law are now featured and, with the exception
of the image on the $20 bill (found within the confines of a
National Park), all these new images show clear signs of human
presence. In the new $10 bill this presence overwhelms the
landscape: it presents a techno-scape where not a trace of Nature
remains. This complete reversal is all the more remarkable
because of the extremes it represents.

Into this new configuration of It and Us, a third term is   21
introduced by the first appearance of Them in Bank of Canada
notes. "They" are the Inuit pictured on the $2 bill, appearing in
the harshest of the series landscapes. With minimal (low-tech)
means, they interact with the icy environment in a nostalgic
hunting scene. Nostalgia plays a part as well in the ship-building
industry pictured on the $100 bill with its sailing ships of a
bygone era.

The government is presented on the $1 bill back and center,   22
crowning Parliament Hill and overlooking the river. The
threatening storm and the vast distances portrayed on the
previous $1 bill are replaced by an image of a log-choked river
(prosperity through natural resources), overseen by government's
central body. It is worth mentioning here that the industrial scene
on the $10 bill of this series depicts Polymer Corp., which was at

the time of issue a crown-owned company.

While the government is portrayed on the $1 bill centrally 23 placed and looking outward from its vantage on the hilltop, the law is portrayed as a ring looking inward. The R.C.M.P. Dome Formation on the $50 bill gives the unfortunate impression of a law force poised to attack itself, its weapons pointed in. The threat of the sea presented in the previous $50 bill is replaced by an image which shows the national police ceremonially closed in on itself in a circle with nothing at the center save the threat of its own spear.

The idea of generalized landscapes reemerges with the 24 current series issue. The current series began in 1986 and the Bank of Canada's decision to make the change is described as follows: "There were three principal reasons for its introduction: technological advances in printing and photocopying of coloured graphic material that made the earlier series more vulnerable to counterfeiting; the need to facilitate the operation of high-speed, note-sorting machines by means of a bar code; and the development of features to assist the visually impaired." These new notes, which come to be through "advanced Canadian technology" and make "le Canada à l'avant-garde de la conception des billets de banque" picture the Canadian landscape utterly devoid of any human presence. The word "CANADA" now fills the sky of a landscape solely inhabited by birds.

Buried under assurances that these new notes are even more 25 secure and are more helpful than before, the question that lurks is "Where did We go?" Optical security devices, electronic readers and high-speed note-sorting machines do not provide an answer. Perhaps the question is not a relevant one, the "predominantly Canadian dimension" being technology itself and not the imagistic concern of locating Us, Here.

The 1986 issue images are as follows: 26

$2.00 bill: "Robin."
$5.00 bill: "Belted Kingfisher."
$10.00 bill: "Osprey."
$20.00 bill: "Common Loon."
$50.00 bill: "Snowy Owl."
$100.00 bill: "Canada Goose."

The bird images are constructed so that they best 27 accommodate the advanced security printing technology. The design criteria state, however, that specific birds were selected because they have wide nesting ranges and would therefore be most familiar to Canadians. There is a concern, then, for recognizability.

While the birds are specifically named, the landscapes are   28 general; the wetlands, the grasslands, the northern wilderness. The specific locations of "here" in most of the previous images (Otter Falls at mile 996 on the Alaska Highway, Upper Melbourne, Richmond, etc.) is now replaced by a general image of "there." The placement of birds, large in the immediate foreground, right of center and facing left, is done for reasons concerning printing and verifiability. The landscapes are minimal, primarily to contrast the detail in the birds, and for reasons of cost. Because of this, the birds seem separate from the landscape—momentarily halted, ready to fly off again.

The Canadian landscape here is seen as utterly uninhabitable   29 and unenterable, the possibility of moving through it blocked by the apparition of its own name in huge block letters. The unconscious treatment of this landscape may be more familiar and more recognizable to Canadians than are the birds that fly in front of it. Looking out across a sparse and unlocatable land we see only the ghostly name of ourselves, a mirage which names our country but prohibits passage over its horizon.

UNDERSTANDING DETAILS

1. Give a brief term to classify each of the issues of Canadian bank notes (1935, 1954, 1969–1975, 1986).
2. Outline the stages in the depiction of the Canadian landscape on our bank notes.
3. Why has the Bank of Canada made continual design changes to its bank notes when those of other countries have remained constant?

ANALYZING MEANING

1. Why do you think that the relationship between "It" (the landscape) and "Us" (the people) has been depicted so differently through the different designs on our bank notes?
2. In what way is money a reflection of a country? What relationship does a country have to its money? Why do different countries have different forms of currency? What do you think will be the effect of the introduction of the Euro in 1999?

3. Within each bank note issue there are six or seven different designs. How do you think the decisions about specific images were made once the broader categories were established? What are the stated grounds for choice? What other unstated criteria might have been used?

DISCOVERING RHETORICAL STRATEGIES

1. In addition to classification and division, what rhetorical modes has Millard used in her exploration of the images of Canada portrayed on our bank notes?
2. How would you describe the mood or tone of this article? How does the focus reflect what you know about the writer?
3. Millard has used quotations from the exhibition at the Currency Museum in Ottawa, as well as a variety of other sources. Why has she incorporated this material? What effect does it have on the reader?

MAKING CONNECTIONS

1. Laura Millard has presented several series of "images of Canada" in her descriptions of the various Canadian bank note issues. Each series of images is governed by a prevailing concern of the time. What series of images might David Foot ("Boomers Dance to a New Beat") choose to represent Canada in 2000? What about Will Ferguson ("The Sudbury Syndrome") or Allen Abel ("A Home at the End of the Journey")?
2. The currency is one thing that graphically represents a country but nations are also represented by their stories. What image is conveyed by the Canadian news stories used as examples by Trina McQueen ("Why We Crave Hot Stuff")? How does this compare to the image conveyed by Will Ferguson ("The Sudbury Syndrome")?
3. Millard's essay highlights the importance of a country's image. What image do you think Karen Connelly ("Touch the Dragon") might choose to represent Thailand? What image might symbolize Japan for Charlotte Gray ("The Temple of Hygiene")?

IDEAS FOR DISCUSSION/WRITING

Preparing to Write

Write freely about money. What does it mean to have money? Not to have money? How do people get money? What problems does money cause? What problems does money solve? What things can money not buy? Look carefully at different kinds of currency. What makes something particularly appealing or interesting to a coin collector? How does this differ from the attraction of money to people in general? What reactions did people have to the introduction of the one- and two-dollar coins as replacements for the one- and two-dollar bills?

Choosing a Topic

1. Assume the Bank of Canada has announced a competition for designing the next issue of Canadian bank notes. Choose a unifying category and then five images that will appear to represent Canada. Outline your choices with some rationale in an essay for the judges.
2. The images of Canada presented on the various issues of bank notes are primarily visual ones. In essay form, chose a different sense, such as smell or hearing, and submit a representative collection of Canadian scents or sounds.
3. Imagine that you are a financial columnist for a general interest magazine. You have had a number of inquiries from people looking for investment options when they have received a lump sum of money. Write an article in which you outline some of the options available to them.

WEB SITES

 web.idirect.com/~mjp/mjpqna.html
Canadian paper money Q & A.

 web.idirect.com/~mjp/mjpwww.html
Paper money—WWW directory.

Susan Swan
1945–

■ ■ ■

Nine Ways of Looking at a Critic

"Swan has a gift for the provocative ..." says Joe Hooper of *Mirabella*, and in the essay that appears here, Swan does not shy away from provoking her audience.

Born in Midland, Ontario, Swan was a student at Havergal College in Toronto in the early 1960s and received a B.A. from McGill University in 1967. In the 1970s Swan became involved in theatre, both writing and performing. She is now a novelist, a journalist, a script writer, a faculty member for the Humber School for Writers' correspondence program, and a professor of Humanities at York University in Toronto.

Susan Swan's novels include *The Biggest Modern Woman in the World* (1983), the story of a giantess who exhibited with P.T. Barnum; *The Last of the Golden Girls* (1989); and *The Wives of Bath* (1993), about a murder in a girls' boarding school. Swan's most recent novel is *Stupid Boys Are Good to Relax With* (1998). While Swan has received a very positive response to her work, as evidenced by her nominations for Canada's Governor General's Award, the UK Guardian Award and Ontario's Trillium Award, she has also created controversy as sexuality figures prominently in all of Swan's novels. Suanne Kelman, in a 1994 story about "Can Lit's bad girls" from *Chatelaine* magazine, summarizes Swan's attitude as follows: "Swan writes the way she thinks: raised to be a pillar of society, she's still trying to free herself—and her readers—from what she sees as a phony concept of female virtue."

Preparing to Read

In this humorous essay, which originally appeared in *The Globe and Mail*, Susan Swan divides book reviewers into nine different categories. Before you begin reading, think about the job of a reviewer whether that person is reviewing books, movies, restaurants, concerts, or any other work or performance. Who is the audience the reviewer is targeting? What is the goal of a reviewer? Are there reviewers whose opinions you particularly value? Are there reviewers with whom you disagree? What makes a good reviewer? How do you think reviewers are perceived by those whose work they review?

As a writer, I naturally have some idealistic notions about book 1
reviewing. For instance, I admire Alexander Pope's list of necessary qualities for a critic—integrity, modesty, tact, courage and an awareness of the critic's own limitations. I also like Matthew Arnold's claim that a critic should possess an eager, open mind and the ability to rise above a sect or clique.

But a reviewer with these qualities is not a person most 2
authors get to meet very often, no matter how much we might long for an intelligent review. The more books I write and the more reviews I receive (whether good, bad or indifferent), the more I see how elusive this ideal reviewer is. What I notice instead are the clearly recognizable types of unsatisfactory reviewers no author can avoid meeting in the pages of our newspapers and magazines. I'm not talking so much about academic journals, although you can probably spot my reviewing types there too.

The following is a list of eight types of less-than-ideal 3
reviewers I've met in my 20 years of writing fiction and 30 years of reviewing.

Number one are The Masturbators, a common category. 4
These are the reviewers who feel they could have written a better book on the subject, given half the chance. In their eyes, the author got it all wrong, and the only value in the book is that it reminds the reviewers that they have superb and untested writing skills which, for one reason or another, they haven't got around to putting into practice.

Sometimes, the direction these reviewers suggest the book 5
take are strange and hilarious. For instance, G.K. Chesterton was fond of quoting the reviewer who liked Charles Dickens's novel *Martin Chuzzlewit*, but complained that it shed no light on the marital customs of Norway.

Number two are The Spankers. Canada, which has an 6
abundance of good writers, also teems with Spankers, who are out to administer discipline over anything from ill-conceived plot-lines to misplaced commas. If Spankers are male, they often display a macho zest—"a real man calls crap crap." If they are female, Spankers can indulge in a scolding, martyred tone—as in, "I have better things to do, but for the good of literature I will dirty my hands in pronouncing this book not worth the reader's time."

Once in a while, in my writerly paranoia, I think the Canadian 7
style *is* to punish and admonish. After all, Canadians tend to look suspiciously at anyone who upholds what is good. Like our

pioneers, who distrusted emotions and the body—viz French-Canadian Jansenism and English-Canadian Calvinism—we prefer the canny so-and-so who won't be fooled by what is bad.

But Spankers can be found anywhere, particularly if the book 8 tries to tackle sexuality. "D.H. Lawrence has a diseased mind. He is obsessed with sex ... we have no doubt that he will be ostracized by all except the most degenerate coteries in the literary world," an English reviewer once wrote in John Bull.

The third category, closely aligned with Spankers, is the Young 9 (and Old) Turk. This group sees the review solely as an opportunity to demonstrate its literary superiority and above-average intelligence. (Not only was I once one of these—dismissing older, established writers in a few sentences—I have been the victim of Young Turks, too. This may be my karma for assuming earlier that my limited life experience and barely developed writing skills were the very qualities that allowed me to see the tinny emptiness of the older writer's celebrity.)

It's probably a good thing Turks can sometimes leave us with 10 memorable witticisms that may be remembered long after the book they reviewed. Who can forget Oscar Wilde's riposte that it took a heart of stone to read of the death of Little Nell without laughing?

The fourth category is Gushers: They skip over discussion of 11 the book; they just want to communicate the enjoyment of reading it. The best example of Gushers can be found in the book ads of publications like The New York Times Book Review, where phrases lifted from reviews proclaim: "major"; "ground-breaking"; "compulsively readable"; "new genius that will change the face of literature"; "the first truly great novel since Tolstoy," and so on. Americans excel at the use of superlatives, trotting out for different authors the same laudatory manifestos of praise week after week. Few writers will object to this habit, for obvious reasons.

The fifth category is The Diviners, a sympathetic but 12 misguided lot. Diviners claim to know the author's reasons for writing the book. They may even deliver an up-to-the-minute and totally fabricated psychological analysis of the author as an incest victim or recovering alcoholic as evidence for their position. (Authors are wise to hold their tongues when confronted with these well-wisher divinations.)

Sixth are The Puritans, who don't like a book if they think its 13 characters have bad morals. They have trouble separating the author from the people in the story.

Seventh come The Grumps, who may like the book but   14
begrudge its author too much praise. Grumps are fond of making
congratulatory noises and then lingering for much of their review
over typos and small mistakes as if they were major boo-boos
that undermined the book's credibility. Most authors I know
would feel grateful (although embarrassed) if the reviewer
pointed out a major mistake. But to be taken to task for tiny errors
by reviewers who say they love the book is the sort of thing that
can make a writer want to take up brick-laying.

My eighth and final category—to date—is that of The Flat-   15
Earthers. These reviewers believe all fiction should be true-to-
life, relying, like non-fiction, on fact. Flat-Earthers tend to say
things like, "This would never happen so it's no good." In this
category, a film like *Thelma and Louise* would be a failure because
how often have you heard of two women driving their car over
a cliff into the Grand Canyon?

Flat-Earthers also have an astonishing ability to know what   16
life is really like. I don't mean the reviewer who is upset by a
writer sloppily sticking wrong details into a piece of fictional
realism, like putting palm trees on Baffin Island. The Flat-Earther
has more hubris than that; a book must support his or her
definition of what it's like to be alive, as he or she knows it. The
idea that fiction can present a reality altogether different from
the life the reviewer knows is unheard of to a Flat-Earther.

All right. I've told you about the types of reviewers writers   17
often meet. But if a writer like me could construct the ideal critic
the way I make up a character, what qualities would I give this
creature? First of all, most writers I know want professional
standards. Curiously enough, many reviewers aren't know-
ledgeable about literature. Nor are they experienced enough with
reviewing to know what they're doing. Would you let your child
take English lessons from somebody newly arrived from a non-
English-speaking country? Canada now has an abundance of
good writers, but the quality of our reviewers hasn't kept up
with the quality of our books. Much of the blame for this belongs
to the media, which has eliminated space for book reviews and
is still paying reviewers roughly what it did when I started
reviewing back in the late 1960s.

No other profession I know could get away with such sub-   18
standard pay. A good reviewer needs credentials and a living
wage, otherwise getting your book reviewed is like having your
teeth pulled in the Wild West. Instead of a trained dentist, you

face the equivalent of a drunken cowboy with pliers, who has the confidence to think he can do a good job. The idea that he might leave a hole in your head for the rest of your life doesn't occur.

As Pope said, a writer appreciates a reviewer who is brave 19 enough to declare a bias. Why review Jane Austen if you are a Jack Kerouac fan who hates 19th-century British writers, unless you are going to admit up front that Austen isn't your cup of tea? (Book columnists are an exception because readers get to know their taste and can put their judgments in perspective.)

"Says who?," I often think reading reviewers with no 20 particular credentials to engage the book's subject, or who lack the courage to admit that a certain style isn't their specialty.

By contrast, good reviews will represent the book (without 21 lapsing into long-winded plot summaries) so the reader gets a sense of what the book is like whether the reviewer likes it or not. And the best reviews offer an informed reading that will provide an interesting or revealing point of view from which the book can be perceived. In other words, a well-written review gives us not only the reviewer's personal reaction, it adds to our knowledge of the book.

Pure opinion is a cheat; it belongs to talk radio stations, not 22 reviews. In some ways, personal reaction is the most uninteresting thing a reviewer has to offer.

UNDERSTANDING DETAILS

1. List the nine types of critics Swan identifies. Explain the apparent contradiction between the title, which prepares you for nine groupings, and the sentence in paragraph 3 that introduces eight types of critics.
2. According to Swan, what is the difference between a good review and a bad review?
3. Into which category of reviewer does Swan put herself? Does she believe she still belongs in this category? Why or why not?

ANALYZING MEANING

1. Explain why Swan has chosen the name "The Flat-Earthers" for the category of reviewers who "believe all fiction should be true-to-life"? Is this an effective name for this group?

2. In this essay, Swan refers to a variety of people ranging from Alexander Pope to Jack Kerouac. Who are the people she mentions and why has she made reference to them in this essay?
3. Explain which of the eight types of "less-than-desirable" reviewers you think would be the worst in the opinion of most writers. Which would be the best? Why?

DISCOVERING RHETORICAL STRATEGIES

1. Why do you think that Susan Swan has written this essay? What is her purpose? Where is this made clear?
2. Who is the intended audience of this essay? Explain why you have identified this group of people.
3. Explain the effectiveness of Swan's introduction and conclusion. How has she linked the beginning and end of her essay?

MAKING CONNECTIONS

1. In this essay Swan identifies one category as being particularly Canadian and another as being typically American. How do these qualities compare to the contrasts between Canadians and Americans that are pointed out by Diane Francis ("Once a Kinder and Gentler Nation")?
2. In "The Babar Factor," Evan Solomon reviews video games by comparing them to Babar books. In Swan's terms, what category does Solomon fit into as a reviewer?
3. In "Genius or Madness?", Lynn Coady considers the opinions of others and the way that people are classified. Imagine a discussion between Coady and Swan about the role of the critic in the life of a writer. Do you think they would see the critic's role the same way? Why or why not?

IDEAS FOR WRITING/DISCUSSION

Preparing to Write

Write freely about a book you have read. What was the book about? Did you like it? What was good about it? What didn't you like? Was there anything about it that confused you? Would you read other books by the same author? What would you say to the author if you met him or her? How would you rate the book overall? Would you recommend it to others?

CHOOSING A TOPIC

1. In this essay Swan divides book reviewers into nine different categories. Write an essay in which you divide movie reviewers into a series of appropriate categories.

2. Using the Internet or periodical indices, find a review of one of Swan's books. Read the review and then decide which of Swan's nine categories the reviewer best fits. Explain why the reviewer fits the category you have chosen.

3. Stores classify their merchandise into various categories to help shoppers locate the things they are looking for. Think of a type of store where things are often difficult to find and propose a new system of classification that you think would be more effective. You might choose a music store, a grocery store, a hardware store, a department store, or some other type of store with which you are familiar.

WEB SITES

 www.sombooks.com/adult/stupid_boys/index.html
The Somerville Publishing Web site for *Stupid Boys are Good to Relax With* includes a short interview with Susan Swan.

CHAPTER 6

COMPARISON / CONTRAST

■ ■ ■

Discovering Similarities and Differences

Making comparisons is such a natural and necessary part of our everyday lives that we often do so without conscious effort. When we were children, we compared our toys with those of our friends, we contrasted our height and physical development to other children's, and we constantly evaluated our happiness in comparison with that evidenced by our parents and childhood companions. As we grew older, we habitually compared our dates, teachers, parents, friends, cars, and physical attributes. In college, we learn about anthropology by writing essays on the similarities and differences between two African tribes, about political science by contrasting the Liberal and Reform platforms, about business by comparing annual production rates, and about literature by comparing Atwood with Munro or Shakespeare with Marlowe. Comparing and contrasting various elements in our lives helps us make decisions, such as which course to take or which house to buy, and it justifies preferences that we already hold, such as liking one city more than another or loving one person more than the next. In these ways and in many others, the skillful use of comparison and contrast is clearly essential to our social and professional lives.

Defining Comparison/Contrast

Comparison and contrast allow us to understand one subject by putting it next to another. Comparing involves discovering likenesses or similarities, whereas contrasting is based on finding differences. Like division and classification, comparison and contrast are generally considered part of the same process, because we usually have no reason for comparing unless some contrast is also involved. Each technique implies the existence of the other. For this reason, the word *compare* is often used to mean both techniques.

Comparison and contrast are most profitably applied to two items that have something in common, such as cats and dogs or cars and motorcycles. A discussion of cats and motorcycles, for example, would probably not be very rewarding or stimulating, because they do not have much in common. If more than two items are compared in an essay, they are still most profitably discussed in pairs: for instance, motorcycles and cars, cars and bicycles, or bicycles and motorcycles.

An analogy is an extended, sustained comparison. Often used to explain unfamiliar, abstract, or complicated thoughts, this rhetorical technique adds energy and vividness to a wide variety of college-level writing. The process of analogy differs slightly from comparison/contrast in three important ways: Comparison/contrast begins with subjects from the same class and places equal weight on both of them. In addition, it addresses both the similarities and the differences of these subjects. Analogy, conversely, seldom explores subjects from the same class, and focuses principally on one familiar subject in an attempt to explain another, more complex one. Furthermore, it deals only with similarities, not with contrasts. A comparison/contrast essay, for example, might study two veterans' ways of coping with the trauma of the Gulf War by pointing out the differences in their methods as well as the similarities. An analogy essay might use the familiar notion of a fireworks display to reveal the chilling horror of the lonely hours after dark during this war: "Nights in the Persian Gulf were similar to a loud, unending fireworks display. We had no idea when the next blast was coming, how loud it would be, or how close. We cringed in terror after dark, hoping the next surprise would not be our own death." In this example, rather than simply hearing about an event, we participate in it through this highly refined form of comparison.

The following student paragraph compares and contrasts married and single life. As you read it, notice how the author compares similar social states and, in the process, justifies her current lifestyle:

> Recently I saw a bumper sticker that read, "It used to be wine, women, and song, and now it's beer, the old lady, and TV." Much truth may be found in this comparison of single and married lifestyles.

When my husband and I used to date, for example, we'd go out for dinner and drinks and then maybe see a play or concert. Our discussions were intelligent, often ranging over global politics, science, literature, and other lofty topics. He would open doors for me, buy me flowers, and make sure I was comfortable and happy. Now, three years later, after marriage and a child, the baby bottle has replaced the wine bottle, the smell of diapers wipes out the scent of roses, and our nights on the town are infrequent, cherished events. But that's ok. A little bit of the excitement and mystery may be gone, but these intangible qualities have given way to a sturdy, dependable trust in each other and a quiet confidence about our future together.

Thinking Critically by Using Comparison/Contrast

Comparison and contrast are basic to a number of different thought processes. We compare and contrast quite naturally on a daily basis, but all of us would benefit greatly from being more aware of these companion strategies in our own writing. They help us not only in perceiving our environment but also in understanding and organizing large amounts of information.

The basic skill of finding similarities and differences will enhance your ability to create accurate descriptions, to cite appropriate examples, to present a full process analysis, and, of course, to classify and label subjects. It is a pattern of thought that is essential to more complex thinking strategies, so perfecting the ability to use it is an important step in your efforts to improve your critical thinking.

Once again, we are going to practise this strategy in isolation to get a strong sense of its mechanics before we combine it with other rhetorical modes. Isolating this mode will make your reading and writing even stronger than they are now, because the individual parts of the thinking process will be more vigorous and effective, thus making your academic performance more powerful than ever.

1. Find magazine ads that use comparison/contrast to make a point or sell a product. What is the basis of each comparison? How effective or ineffective is each comparison?
2. Compare or contrast the experience of spending time with a special person to another type of experience (e.g., a roller-coaster ride, drowning, sleeping, or a trip across Canada). Be as specific as possible in your comparison.

3. Have you ever been to the same place twice? Think for a moment about how the first and second visits to this place differed. How were they similar? What were the primary reasons for the similarities and differences in your perceptions of these visits?

Reading and Writing Comparison/Contrast Essays

Many established guidelines regulate the development of a comparison/contrast essay and should be taken into account from both the reading and the writing perspectives. All good comparative studies serve a specific purpose. They attempt either to examine their subjects separately or to demonstrate the superiority of one over the other. In evaluating two different types of cars, for example, a writer might point out the amazing gas mileage of one model and the smooth handling qualities of the other, or the superiority of one car's gas consumption over that of the other. Whatever the intent, comparison/contrast essays need to be clear and logical and to have a precise purpose.

How to Read a Comparison/Contrast Essay

Preparing to Read. As you begin reading this chapter, pull together as much preliminary material as possible for each essay so you can focus your attention and have the benefit of prior knowledge before you start to read. In particular, you are trying to discover what is being compared or contrasted and why. What does Will Ferguson's title ("The Sudbury Syndrome") suggest to you? From the title of his essay, can you tell what John Fraser is comparing in "Save the Last Dance"? From glancing at the essay itself and reading the synopsis in the Rhetorical Table of Contents, what does Gloria Steinem's essay try to accomplish?

Also, before you begin to read these essays, try to discover information about the author and about the conditions under which each essay was written. Why is Fraser qualified to write about ballet dancers? Does he reveal his background in his essay? What is Charlotte Gray's job? To what extent do you expect this to colour her comparison of Japanese and Canadian cultures?

Finally, just before you begin to read, answer the Preparing to Read questions, and then make some free associations with the general topic of each essay. For example, what are some of the similarities and differences between Sudbury and Saint John

(Will Ferguson)? What is your general view on women's bodybuilding (Gloria Steinem)?

Reading. As you read each comparison/contrast essay for the first time, be sure to record your own feelings and opinions. Some of the issues presented in this chapter are highly controversial. You will often have strong reactions to them, which you should try to write down as soon as possible.

In addition, you may want to comment on the relationship between the preliminary essay material, the author's stance in the essay, and the content of the essay itself. For example, what motivated Solomon to write "The Babar Factor"? Who was his primary audience? What is Ferguson's tone in "The Sudbury Syndrome," and how does it further his purpose? Answers to questions such as these will provide you with a context for your first reading of these essays and will assist you in preparing to analyze the essays in more depth on your second reading.

At this point in the chapter, you should make certain you understand each author's thesis and then take a close look at his or her principal method of organization: Is the essay arranged (1) point by point, (2) subject by subject, (3) as a combination of these two, or (4) as separate discussions of similarities and differences between two subjects? (See the chart on page 288 for an illustration of these options.) Last, preview the questions that follow the essay before you read it again.

Rereading. When you read these essays a second time, you should look at the comparison or contrast much more closely than you have up to now. First, look in detail at the writer's method of organization (see the chart on page 288). How effective is it in advancing the writer's thesis?

Next, you should consider whether each essay is fully developed and balanced: Does Fraser compare similar items? Does Solomon discuss the same qualities for his subjects? Does Gray deal with all aspects of the comparison between Japanese and Canadian people? Is Steinem's treatment of her two subjects well balanced? And does Ferguson give his audience enough specific details to clarify the extent of his comparison? Do all the writers in this chapter use well-chosen transitions so you can move smoothly from one point to the next? Also, what other rhetorical modes support each comparison/contrast in this chapter? Finally, answering the questions after each selection will let you evaluate your understanding of the essay and help you analyze its contents in preparation for the discussion/writing topics that follow.

For a more thorough inventory of the reading process, you should turn to pages 15–16 in the Introduction.

How to Write a Comparison/Contrast Essay

Preparing to Write. As you consider various topics for a comparison/contrast essay, you should answer the Preparing to Write questions that precede the assignments and then use the prewriting techniques explained in the Introduction to generate even more ideas on these topics.

As you focus your attention on a particular topic, keep the following suggestions in mind:

1. Always compare/contrast items in the same category (e.g., compare two professors, but not a professor and a swimming pool).
2. Have a specific purpose or reason for writing your essay.
3. Discuss the same qualities of each subject (if you evaluate the teaching techniques of one professor, do so for the other professor as well).
4. Use as many pertinent details as possible to expand your comparison/contrast and to accomplish your stated purpose.
5. Deal with all aspects of the comparison that are relevant to the purpose.
6. Balance the treatment of the different subjects of your comparison (i.e., don't spend more time on one than on another).
7. Determine your audience's background and knowledge so that you will know how much of your comparison should be explained in detail and how much can be skimmed over.

Next, in preparation for a comparison/contrast project, you might list all the elements of both subjects that you want to compare. This list can then help you give your essay structure as well as substance. At this stage in the writing process, the task may seem similar to pure description, but a discussion of two subjects in relation to one another rapidly changes the assignment from description to comparison.

Writing. The introduction of your comparison/contrast essay should (1) clearly identify your subjects, (2) explain the basis of your comparison/contrast, and (3) state your purpose and the overall limits of your particular study. Identifying your subject is, of course, a necessary and important task in any essay. Similarly, justifying the elements you will be comparing and contrasting creates reader interest and gives your audience some specifics to look for in the essay. Finally, your statement of purpose or thesis (for example, to prove that one professor is superior to another) should include the boundaries of your discussion. You cannot cover all the reasons for your preference in one short essay, so you must limit your consideration to three or four basic categories (perhaps teaching techniques, the clarity of the assignments given, classroom attitude, and grading standards). The introduction is the place to make all these limits known.

You can organize the body of your paper in one of four ways: (1) a point-by-point, or alternating, comparison; (2) a subject-by-subject, or divided, comparison; (3) a combination of these two methods; or (4) a division between the similarities and differences. (See the chart on page 288.)

The point-by-point comparison evaluates both subjects in terms of each category. If the issue, for example, is which of two cars to buy, you might discuss both models' gasoline consumption first; then, their horsepower; next, their ease in handling; and, finally, their standard equipment. Following the second method of organization, subject by subject, you would discuss the gasoline consumption, horsepower, ease in handling, and standard equipment of car A first and then follow the same format for car B. The third option would allow you to introduce, say, the interior design of each car point by point (or car by car) and then to explain the mechanical features of the automobiles (kilometers per litre, horsepower, gear ratio, and braking system) subject by subject. To use the last method of organization, you might discuss the similarities between the two models first and the differences second (or vice versa). If the cars you are comparing have similar kilometers-per-litre (km/L) ratings but completely different horsepower, steering systems, and optional equipment, you could discuss the gasoline consumption first and then emphasize the differences by mentioning them later in the essay. If, instead, you are trying to emphasize the fact that the km/L ratings of these models remain consistent despite their differences, then reverse the order of your essay.

Methods of Organization

<table>
<tr><td>

Point by Point

km/L, car A
km/L, car B

horsepower, car A
horsepower, car B

handling, car A
handling, car B

equipment, car A
equipment, car B

</td><td>

Subject by Subject

km/L, car A
horsepower, car A
handling, car A
equipment, car A

km/L, car B
horsepower, car B
handling, car B
equipment, car B

</td></tr>
<tr><td>

Combination

Interior, car A
Interior, car B

———

km/L, car A
horsepower, car A

km/L, car B
horsepower, car B

</td><td>

Similarities/Differences

similarities:
  km/L, cars A & B

differences:
  horsepower, cars A & B
  handling, cars A & B
  equipment, cars A & B

</td></tr>
</table>

When confronted with the task of choosing a method of organization for a comparison/contrast essay, you need to find the pattern that best suits your purpose. If you want single items to stand out in a discussion, for instance, the best choice will be the point-by-point system; it is especially appropriate for long essays, but has a tendency to turn into an exercise in listing if you don't pay careful attention to your transitions. If, however, the subjects themselves (rather than the itemized points) are the most interesting feature of your essay, you should use the subject-by-subject comparison; this system is particularly good for short essays in which the readers can retain what was said about one subject while they read about a second subject. Through this second system of organization, each subject becomes a unified whole, an approach to an essay that is generally effective unless the theme becomes awkwardly divided into two separate parts. You must also remember, if you choose this second method of organization, that the second (or last) subject is in the most emphatic position because that is what your readers will have seen most recently. The final two options for organizing a comparison/contrast essay give you some built-in flexibility so that you can create emphasis and attempt to manipulate reader opinion simply by the structure of your essay.

Using logical transitions in your comparison/contrast essays will establish clear relationships between the items in your comparisons and will also move your readers smoothly from one topic to the next. If you wish to indicate comparisons, use such words as *like, as, also, in like manner, similarly,* and *in addition*; to signal contrasts, try *but, in contrast to, unlike, whereas,* and *on the one hand/on the other hand*.

The conclusion of a comparison/contrast essay summarizes the main points and states the deductions drawn from those points. As you choose your method of organization, remember not to get locked into a formulaic approach to your subjects, which will adversely affect the readability of your essay. To avoid making your reader feel like a spectator at a verbal table tennis match, be straightforward, honest, and patient as you discover and recount the details of your comparison.

Rewriting. When you review the draft of your comparison/contrast essay, you need once again to make sure that you communicate your purpose as effectively as possible to your intended audience. Two guidelines previously mentioned should help you accomplish this goal:

1. Do you identify your subjects clearly?
2. Does your thesis clearly state the purpose and overall limits of your particular study?

You will also need to pay close attention to the development of your essay:

1. Are you attempting to compare/contrast items from the same general category?
2. Do you discuss the same qualities of each subject?
3. Do you balance the treatment of the different subjects of your essay?
4. Did you organize your topic as effectively as possible?
5. Does your conclusion contain a summary and analysis of your main points?

For further information on writing and revising your comparison/contrast essays, consult the checklists on pages 26-27 of the Introduction.

Student Essay: Comparison/Contrast at Work

The following student essay compares the advantages and disadvantages of macaroni and cheese versus tacos in the life of a harried first-year college or university student. As you read it, notice that the writer states his intention in the first paragraph and then expands his discussion with appropriate details to produce a balanced essay. Also, try to determine what effect he creates by using two methods of organization: first subject by subject, then point by point.

Dormitory Chef

To this day, I will not eat either macaroni and cheese or tacos. No, it's not because of any allergy; it's because during my first year at college, I prepared one or the other of these scrumptious dishes more times than I care to remember. However, my choice of which culinary delight to cook on any given night was not as simple a decision as one might imagine.

Macaroni and cheese has numerous advantages for the dormitory chef. First of all, it is inexpensive. No matter how poor one may be, there's probably enough change under the couch cushion to buy a box at the market. All that starch for only 89¢. What a bargain! Second, it can be prepared in just one pan. This is especially important given the meager resources of the average dorm kitchen. Third, and perhaps most important, macaroni and cheese is odourless. By odourless, I mean that no one else can smell it. It is a well-known fact that dorm residents hate to cook and that they love nothing better than to wander dejectedly around the kitchen with big, sad eyes after someone else has been cooking. But with macaroni and cheese, no enticing aromas are going to find their way into the nose of any would-be mooch.

Tacos, on the other hand, are a different matter altogether. For the dorm cook, the most significant difference is obviously the price. To enjoy tacos for dinner, the adventurous dorm gourmet must purchase no fewer than five ingredients from the market: corn tortillas, beef, lettuce, tomatoes, and cheese. Needless to say, this is a major expenditure. Second, the chef must adroitly shuffle

---

Margin annotations:

- Topics
- Basis of comparison
- Thesis statement: Purpose and limits of comparison
- Paragraph on Subject A: Macaroni and cheese
- Point 1 (Price)
- Point 2 (Preparation)
- Point 3 (Odour)
- Paragraph on Subject B: Tacos
- Transition
- Point 1 (Price)
- Point 2 (Preparation)

these ingredients back and forth among his very limited supply of
pans and bowls. And finally, tacos smell great. That wouldn't be Point 3
a problem if the tacos didn't also smell great to about twenty of the (Odour)
cook's newest—if not closest—friends, who appear with those
same pathetic, starving eyes mentioned earlier. When this happens,
the cook will be lucky to get more than two of his own creations.

Subject B   Tacos, then, wouldn't stand much of a chance if they didn't Transition

Paragraph outdo macaroni and cheese in one area: taste. Taste is almost— Subject A
on Point 4: but not quite—an optional requirement in the opinion of a frugal
  Taste dormitory hash-slinger. Taste is just important enough so that
tacos are occasionally prepared, despite their disadvantages.

Transition   But tacos have other advantages besides their taste. With their Subject B

Paragraph enticing, colourful ingredients, they even look good. The only
on Point 5: thing that can be said about the colour of macaroni and cheese is Subject A
  Colour that it's a colour not found in nature.

Transition   On the other hand, macaroni and cheese is quick. It can be pre- Subject A

Paragraph pared in about ten minutes, while tacos take more than twice as Subject B
on Point 6: long. And there are occasions—such as final exam week—when
  Time time is a scarce and precious resource.

Transition   As you can see, quite a bit of thinking went into my choice of Summary

Analysis food in my younger years. These two dishes essentially got me
through my first year and indirectly taught me how to make important decisions (like what to eat). But I still feel a certain revul- Concluding
sion when I hear their names today. statement

Student Writer's Comments

*I compare and contrast so many times during a typical
day that I took this rhetorical technique for granted. In
fact, I had overlooked it completely. The most difficult
part of writing this essay was finding two appropriate
subjects to compare. Ideally, I knew they should be united
by a similarity. So I brainstormed to come up with some
possible topics. Then, working from this list of potential
subjects, I began to freewrite to see if I could come up
with two topics in the same category on which I could write
a balanced comparison. Out of my freewriting came this
reasoning: Macaroni and cheese and tacos, in reality, are
two very different kinds of food from the same category.*

Proving this fact is easy and wouldn't result in an interesting essay. But their similar property of being popular dorm foods unites the two despite their differences and also gave me two important reasons for writing the comparison: to discover why they are both popular dorm delicacies and to determine which one had more advantages for my particular purposes. In proportion to writing and revising, I spent most of my time choosing my topic, brainstorming, freewriting, and rebrainstorming to make sure I could develop every aspect of my comparison adequately. Most of my prewriting work took the form of two columns, in which I recorded my opinions on the choice between macaroni and cheese versus tacos.

Sitting down to mould my lists into an essay posed an entirely new set of problems. From the copious notes I had taken, I easily wrote the introductory paragraph, identifying my topics, explaining the basis of my comparison/contrast, and stating the purpose and limits of my study (my thesis statement). But now that I faced the body of the essay, I needed to find the best way to organize my opinions on these two dorm foods: Point by point, subject by subject, a combination of these two, or a discussion of similarities and differences?

I wrote my first draft discussing my topics point by point. Even with an occasional joke and a few snide comments interjected, the essay reminded me of a boring game of table tennis with only a few attempts at changing the pace. I started over completely with my second draft and worked through my topics subject by subject. I felt this approach was better, but not quite right yet for my particular purpose and audience. I set out to do some heavy-handed revising.

Discussing my first three points (price, preparation, and odour) subject by subject seemed to work quite well.

I was actually satisfied with the first half of my discussion of these two subjects. But the essay really started to get sluggish when I brought up the fourth point: taste. So I broke off my discussion there and rewrote the second half of my essay point by point, dealing with taste, colour, and time each in its own paragraph. This change gave my essay the new direction it needed to keep the readers' attention and also offered me some new insights into my comparison. Then, I returned to the beginning of my essay and revised it for readability, adding transitions and making sure the paper now moved smoothly from one point or subject to the next. Finally, I added my final paragraph, including a brief summary of my main points and an explanation of the deductions I had made. My concluding remark ("But I still feel a certain revulsion when I hear their names today.") came to me as I was putting the final touches on this draft.

What I learned from writing this particular essay is that comparison/contrast thinking, more than thinking in other rhetorical modes, is much like a puzzle. I really had to spend an enormous amount of time thinking through, mapping out, and rethinking my comparison before I could start to put my thoughts in essay form. The results are rewarding, but I sure wore out a piece of linoleum on the den floor on the way to my final draft.

Some Final Thoughts on Comparison/Contrast

The essays in this section demonstrate various methods of organization as well as a number of distinct stylistic approaches to writing a comparison/contrast essay. As you read these selections, pay particular attention to the clear, well-focused introductions; the different logical methods of organization; and the smooth transitions between sentences and paragraphs.

Comparision/Contrast in Review

Reading Comparison/Contrast Essays

Preparing to Read

1. What assumptions can you make from the essay's title?
2. Can you guess what the general mood of the essay is?
3. What is the essay's purpose and audience?
4. What does the synopsis in the Rhetorical Table of Contents tell you about the essay?
5. What can you learn from the author's biography?
6. Can you guess what the author's point of view toward the subject is?
7. What are your responses to the Preparing to Read questions?

Reading

1. What is the author's thesis?
2. How is the essay organized: Point by point? Subject by subject? As a combination of the two? As separate discussions of similarities and differences between two subjects?
3. Did you preview the questions that follow the essay?

Rereading

1. Is the writer's method of organization effective for advancing the essay's thesis?
2. Is the essay fully developed?
3. What other rhetorical strategies does the author use to support the essay's purpose?
4. What are your responses to the questions after the essay?

Writing Comparison/Contrast Essays

Preparing to Write

1. What are your responses to the Preparing to Write questions?
2. What is your purpose?
3. Are you comparing/contrasting items in the same category (e.g., two professors, but not a professor and a swimming pool)?

4. Do you have a specific purpose or reason for writing your essay?

5. Are you going to discuss the same qualities of each subject?

6. Have you generated as many pertinent details as possible to expand your comparison/contrast and to accomplish your stated purpose?

Writing

1. Does your introduction (1) clearly identify your subjects, (2) explain the basis of your comparison/contrast, and (3) state your purpose and the overall limits of your particular study?

2. Does your thesis include the boundaries of your discussion?

3. Have you limited your discussion to three or four basic categories?

4. Is your paper organized in one of the following ways: point by point, subject by subject, as a combination of the two, or as separate discussions of similarities and differences between two subjects?

5. Does your conclusion summarize your main points and state the deductions you made from those points?

Rewriting

1. Do you identify your subjects clearly?

2. Does your thesis clearly state the purpose and overall limits of your particular study?

3. Are you attempting to compare/contrast items from the same general category?

4. Do you discuss the same qualities of each subject?

5. Do you balance the treatment of the different subjects of your essay?

6. Have you organized your topic as effectively as possible?

7. Does your conclusion contain a summary and analysis of your main points?

Charlotte Gray
1948–

■ ■ ■

The Temple of Hygiene

Charlotte Gray is a regular contributor to three magazines: Chatelaine (for which she writes a parenting column), Saturday Night (where her focus is national politics and for which she is the Ottawa editor), and the Canadian Medical Association Journal (in which she examines a wide scope of health-care-related issues). This range is testament to Gray's ability as a writer and her capacity to enable her reader to relate to many different experiences. Originally from Sheffield, UK, Gray earned her B.A. from Oxford University in 1969, and went on to work as the assistant editor and then the editor of Psychology Today (UK). She is, in addition, the author of Governor General's Award nominee Mrs. King: The Life & Times of Isabel Mackenzie King. For this book, Gray also won the Canadian Authors Association Birks Family Foundation Award for a biographical work about a Canadian by a Canadian. The mother of three children, Gray currently lives and works in Ottawa and appears periodically on radio and television speaking on political issues.

Preparing to Read

This essay first appeared in *Saturday Night* magazine in 1989, and was subsequently included in *The Saturday Night Traveller*, which is a collection of travel writing pieces. In this essay Charlotte Gray discusses a trip she took to Japan, with particular attention to her visit to a traditional Japanese bathhouse. Before reading, think about trips that you have taken and the elements of those experiences that stand out in your memory. Are the geographic details or the recollections of the people more vivid in your mind?

■——————————————————————————■

Some years ago, I bought a nineteenth-century Japanese print of a fight in a bathhouse. The snarling intensity of the naked, dishevelled women always intrigues me—it's so at odds with the impassive neatness of the ranks of workers, schoolchildren, or commuters featured in the standard documentaries about the Japanese "economic miracle." So when I arrived in Japan on a Japanese government programme for foreign journalists, I ranked a *sento* above a teahouse on the "preferred excursions" list I was told to prepare.

I made my request to Mr. Kondo, head of the foreign ministry's international press division, who processed foreigners along the conveyor belt of Constructive Japanese Experience. He listened, stony-faced. Organized tours around factories, yes. Voyeurism in the temples of hygiene—well, even an official guest and her accompanying spouse would have to organize that for themselves.

I persisted. The hospitality service of the foreign ministry   2
had provided George and me with an escort: pretty, thirty-year-old Kaoru. Beneath Kaoru's demure smile and dutiful attention to my every whim, there bubbled a nonconformist streak. She always drank coffee instead of green tea. She refused to wear a kimono at her cousin's wedding, even though the most Westernized women in her family stuck to the national dress for the rites of passage. Most seriously, she had already rejected three suitors selected by her parents because they were too traditional, and would not have permitted her to continue working after marriage. Now, Kaoru giggled, she was "Christmas cake"—Japanese shorthand for women beyond their twenty-fifth birthday, as unwanted as Christmas cake beyond December 25.

"Kaoru, please could you take us to a *sento*?" I asked. Her smile   3
froze for a second, then she replied, "Do you mean a swimming pool?" The limits of Japanese nonconformity began to show. I insisted that I wanted to visit an authentic bathhouse—not a swimming pool, or a gussied-up version in which Westerners outnumbered residents. We sparred for five minutes, then Kaoru got out her little notebook. The previous time the notebook had appeared was when I had asked to visit the gate of Tokyo's Imperial Palace so I could see the crowds of tiny, bent old women keeping a death watch on the occupant of the Chrysanthemum Throne. Kaoru had found that expedition a little tacky: foreign television cameras outnumbered well-wishers during most of my visit. Nevertheless, she had written down the request and taken me.

The bathhouse opportunity finally arose in Kyoto. The ancient   4
capital of Japan is now a badly planned, crowded city. Buddhist temples, Zen gardens, and ancient palaces are pools of serenity amongst bleak modern buildings. We were staying in a *ryokan*—a Japanese inn where smiling women in kimonos served us an elaborate meal at the traditional knee-level table in our own room. "Maybe tonight we'll visit a *sento*?" Kaoru suggested out of the blue. I uncurled from a cartilage-cracking kneel with enthusiasm. Kaoru summoned a cab, which ferried us through the "night area" of Kyoto—an exuberant bustle of bars, nightclubs, and restaurants.

Through the cab windows we saw the same kinds of street   5
scenes that had fascinated us in Tokyo. Clutches of neatly
groomed men, wearing navy suits and carrying briefcases,
strolled along, often propping up one of their number who was
swaying like a stage lush. These "sararimen" (salary-men) had
been male-bonding over beer or Scotches before lurching home
to their wives. I had spent an afternoon with a sarariman's wife
in a Tokyo suburb. Mrs. Hama's life had horrified me: she was
trapped at home with only a microwave, electric bread maker,
electric rice steamer, and koto (long harplike instrument) for
company. Her days appeared to be spent ferrying her twelve-
year-old daughter and sixteen-year-old son between schools and
cramming classes. Once a week, she joined a group of other
housewives for a gym class. She never knew when her husband
would come home.

Mrs. Hama obviously found my life equally horrifying—   6
though the merest shadows of shock flitted across her permanent
smile. Why did I need to work if my husband was a government
sarariman? What was I doing leaving my three little boys with
someone who was looking after them only for money? Wasn't I
worried that, in a country like Canada, they might marry
somebody from a different background—even a different race?
As Kaoru escorted me home after the visit, her self-control
dissolved. "I thought she would choke you when you ate a grape
whole, without removing the skin," she giggled, overcome by the
hilarious culture clash between two forty-year-old mothers. "And
then, when you told her that your seven-year-old rarely has
homework ..."

The cab finally dropped Kaoru, George, and me at the end of   7
an unlit lane. Towels in hand, we walked past the back doors of
noodle shops and brightly lit windows with metal grilles in front
of them. The bathhouse looked like a shabby municipal office.
People scurried in and out, some wearing baggy pyjamas. A lick
of hot, damp air curled round the door as we entered—George to
the right and Kaoru and I to the left. We walked straight into a
large, tiled locker room, with the inevitable row of neatly paired
shoes by the entrance. A curtain separated the men's and
women's changing rooms. A watchful attendant in a navy apron
was seated at a raised counter which straddled the changing
rooms. We paid her our 240 yen (about two dollars) each and
went over to a bank of lockers.

Through a glass wall directly in front of us, I could see naked 8
figures moving in clouds of steam. Around me, six women were
silently getting dressed or undressed, another was drying her
hair at a long horizontal mirror. A naked septuagenarian in a
brown leather armchair grunted with concentration—the chair
appeared to be some kind of La-Z-Boy back-massager and she
was rhythmically squirming against a set of rollers behind her.
On a high shelf stood a row of twenty-five plastic bowls, neatly
tied up in pink, blue, or purple gauze scarves. These contained the
washing equipment of the regulars. The whole place looked
entirely functional—a human laundrette rather than a health spa.

On the way over, Kaoru admitted that she had visited a 9
bathhouse only once before; her family had always had their
own bathroom. Once, communal bathhouses had been the centre
of community life. In feudal Japan, there was a clear bathhouse
pecking order: the samurai families used the bathhouses in the
mornings, when the water was cleanest; the merchants in the
afternoon; the peasants, workers, and household servants in the
evening after they had toiled in fields and kitchens. As recently
as ten years ago, more households had colour televisions than
had bathtubs. But a twentyfold increase in GNP since the war
has allowed the Mrs. Hamas of this world to have baths as well
as bread makers (and, inevitably, reinforced their isolation). Only
the poor continue to rely on bathhouses. Most of the women
around Kaoru and me in the changing room seemed to be
students or grannies.

It was hard to take the scene in, however, because bathing 10
meant business. Kaoru didn't waste a second as she stripped
and scuttled towards the door into the inner sanctum—the
bathhouse proper. I was so busy keeping up that I forgot to pick
up my *oke*, or water scoop, on my way through. A lady who had
appeared oblivious to my presence caught my arm as I opened
the big door and handed me one. If this had been a fancy Tokyo
bathhouse, now geared to tourists and joggers, it would have
been a beautifully turned little pail made of cypress wood, bound
with copper hoops. What I was handed, however, was a
utilitarian blue plastic bowl.

There were four separate baths in the bathhouse: a large 11
Jacuzzi that could accommodate about eight people; a whirlpool
in which six people could sit; a smaller tub filled with freezing
cold water; and another tub filled with hot water that I didn't

immediately see anything special about. Each bath was sunk into the floor, close to the wall, and covered in white tile. At two-foot intervals along the wall between the baths, and along a low wall down the middle of the room, were taps about eighteen inches off the ground.

Over each tap was a mirror with an advertising slogan pasted 12 across it, for soft drinks including Coca-Cola and one unfortunately named Sweat, for different kinds of soap, and for electrical equipment. I could recognize the brand names, which were in the Roman alphabet (*romaji*), though the other words were all indecipherable to me. A few were in *kanji*, the elaborate Chinese pictographs that the Japanese adopted between the fourth and the ninth centuries; most were in *hiragana*, the much simpler, abbreviated system of forty-eight phonetic symbols that the Japanese evolved from the ninth century onwards. (Japanese schoolchildren are expected to master all three scripts by the age of eight—a feat that makes the challenge of bilingualism look Mickey Mouse.) Painted on the tile of the end wall was a large landscape, filled with the familiar clichés of a Hokusai print: a lavender Mount Fuji hovered in the distance; black-jacketed peasants in coolie hats toiled on the left; foam-tipped waves curled over on the right.

Kaoru bustled over to a tap, squatted in front of it, and hid 13 her self-consciousness in the ferocity of her ablutions. Occasionally she gave me a slightly conspiratorial smile, as I followed her example. We soaped all over, then scrubbed with the long cotton cloths we had brought with us, then poured bowls of hot water over ourselves. We repeated the ritual three times. The seven other women in the bathhouse appeared completely indifferent to us as we soaped, even though I was as inconspicuous as a yellow Labrador in a cluster of Siamese cats. After a while, I noticed suspicious glances reflected in the mirrors, so I rubbed with ostentatious fervour. Kaoru had warned me that Japanese people don't trust Westerners in their bathhouses: they find our predilection for wallowing in our own dirty water disgusting.

One woman sat in the Jacuzzi, her eyes closed, her knees 14 bunched up, her chin resting on her fist. Two other women squatted by the central row of taps, holding an animated conversation while one energetically scrubbed the other's back pink with a bristle brush. Another washed her hair with furious energy, creating bowlfuls of lather which she sluiced off and down the drain that circled the room. One crouched figure stared intently at her face in a mirror. She appeared to be stroking her forehead and cheeks: after a few minutes I realized that she was methodically shaving every inch of her face, except for her carefully outlined eyebrows.

All the bodies around me were virtually hairless (except for 15 pubic hair). They were also far firmer than the bodies that surround me on Canadian beaches every summer. Not a ripple of cellulite ruffled the surface of thighs or buttocks—not even on a couple of thickset, middle-aged women. Western women would die for such marble-smooth agelessness. Yet nearly every body in a fashion magazine or face on a store mannequin was Occidental. "Why don't I ever see Japanese women in commercials?" I asked Kaoru. "Because your people are more beautiful than us," she replied firmly.

After taking the top layer of my skin off with merciless 16 scrubbing, I did the rounds of the baths. My gasp of shock when I moved from the heat of the Jacuzzi to the icy cold bath triggered smiles from fellow bathers. I was quite startled: by now I'd become accustomed to the studied indifference to foreigners that the Japanese exhibit (partly through respect for privacy, partly through fear of "getting involved" and actually having to take responsibility for a stranger). The impenetrability of the language, combined with Japanese *enryo* (usually translated as reserve or restraint), often made me feel I was knocking against a locked and soundproofed glass door. But for a moment, the door opened. The Rodin thinker in the Jacuzzi opened her eyes and asked Kaoru where I was from. When Kaoru replied "Canada," a few more faces turned towards me. One of the two back scrubbers nodded vigorously. "Ben Johnson," she sang out, and assumed an expression of condolence. There was a muted chorus of sympathetic "Aaahs," then everyone returned to her own bath business.

The real shock came in the fourth, "mystery" bath. It was 17 rectangular in shape, and had yellow panels with pinholes in them on the two long sides. I slid in at one end, and cautiously stuck my foot into the hot water between the two panels. An electric shock immediately zapped my calf. The current seemed to vary: sometimes it just tingled, other times, especially when I stood between the panels, it was torture. It was the perfect therapy for muscles aching from all the unaccustomed kneeling in teahouses, private homes, and the *ryokan*.

We'd arranged to meet George outside at ten o'clock. I rose 18
from the electric-shock bath, where I'd given my neck a last zap,
and carelessly draped myself in the nice fluffy towel I'd brought
from the *ryokan*, as though I'd just finished swimming. Another
breach of bathhouse etiquette—the patrons didn't go in for big
fluffy towels. They patted themselves dry with the thin white
cloth, then draped that in front of themselves as their only
concession to modesty when they left the bathhouse area.

Back in the changing room I watched with covert fascination 19
as one woman dressed in three layers of underwear, including
thermal long johns, before donning the regulation dark skirt and
polyester blouse that is the universal attire of middle-aged
women. No wonder domestic energy consumption in Japan is
one-quarter the level in Canada. Underwear is their primary
heating source.

George emerged a few minutes after us. His side of the 20
bathhouse had been more crowded and sociable. Bull-shaped
men had roared at each other across the waters, while a couple of
crones moved around, cleaning the place. But the bathing had
been equally purposeful and thorough. He had not exchanged
a word with his fellow bathers, and they had studiously ignored
him. Even in the steamy intimacy of the *sento*, we had been firmly
kept at arm's length. Only a mention of our Olympic steroid-
user, who had committed the unforgivable sin (in Japanese eyes)
of disgracing his family and his nation, had broken through the
enryo.

UNDERSTANDING DETAILS

1. What are some of the specific areas in which Gray points out differences between Japan and Canada? Which traditions, customs, and institutions, and which other aspects of life does Gray
   mention? How do these differences affect people in the essay?
2. How is Kaoru's nonconformity as a young Japanese woman illustrated? Give specific examples.
3. Gray uses several Japanese words or expressions in this essay.
   Explain the following terms that appear in "The Temple of
   Hygiene": Christmas cake, *sento*, *ryokan*, *sararimen*, *enryo*. What
   effect does Gray hope to achieve by using Japanese words such
   as *sento* and *enryo* rather than English translations of these terms?

ANALYZING MEANING

1. Why is Kaoru reluctant to take her guests to the bathhouse? How does she demonstrate this reluctance? What does Kaoru's reluctance about taking her guests to the bathhouse indicate about Japanese attitudes toward this institution?
2. How would you summarize Gray's view of the Japanese people and Japanese life? Which of Gray's examples best demonstrate her perception of the Japanese people and Japanese life? Does she only point out differences or are there also similarities?
3. The use of the word temple in the title suggests ritual. What ritual patterns do you see in the actions of the people in the bathhouse? What does this attitude toward a bath suggest to you about Japanese life?

DISCOVERING RHETORICAL STRATEGIES

1. What is the point of view of the narrator of this essay? In what context has Gray made this trip to Japan? How does this influence her experience and her perspective? What is the purpose of Gray's trip?
2. In this essay, Gray compares and contrasts aspects of Japanese life and Canadian life. What specific details or examples does she use to make the differences vivid and memorable? Which specific paragraphs of detailed description give you the clearest pictures of Gray's reactions to her unique Japanese experience? Why?
3. Gray has used a metaphor to highlight the difference between herself and the other women in the bathhouse in paragraph 13. Explain what makes this metaphor effective. Identify other metaphors, similes, or analogies that Gray has used in this comparison and contrast.
4. The structure of Gray's essay follows the progress of a miniature journey, with Kaoru as the guide. Using specific examples, trace the progress of the trip or journey in the essay, and identify the primary method of organization Gray has used. Why do you think Gray might have selected this pattern?

MAKING CONNECTIONS

1. Charlotte Gray and Allen Abel ("A Home at the End of the Journey") both consider what it means to be Canadian by contrasting Canadians and Canadian experience with people and

experiences from other countries. In your view, what does it mean to be Canadian? How are Canadians and how is Canada different from at least one other specific country?

2. Charlotte Gray introduces some Japanese vocabulary into her essay just as Brian Lewis ("Teeth") incorporates some Inuktitut phrases into his. Explain why these authors have added bits in languages that the majority of their readers are unlikely to know? What effect does this create for their readers?

3. "Touch the Dragon" (Karen Connelly) and "The Temple of Hygiene" (Charlotte Gray) both relate experiences of Canadians travelling to parts of the far east. How are Connelly and Gray's observations consistent? Where do they differ? How does each of their situations affect their experience of this foreign place?

IDEAS FOR DISCUSSION/WRITING

Preparing to Write

Write freely about Japan. What associations do you have with this country? What images come to mind when you think about Japan? How have these impressions been developed? What different sources have contributed to your overall view of Japan and of Japanese people? Which of your impressions are objective and which are subjective? What Japanese products are you familiar with? What Japanese personalities or public figures can you name?

Choosing a Topic

1. As people travel more frequently and more easily, aspects of different cultures and countries blend. Which aspects of the Japanese society that Gray describes do you see as desirable to introduce into Canada? Are there any aspects that you would not want to see merged into Canadian society? Are there any examples of Japanese influence already in Canada that you have observed?

2. *It's a Small World* travel magazine has asked you to write an essay about a trip you have taken or another place you have lived. In your essay compare another city, province, or country to the one you live in now. Focus on specific elements so you can provide substantial detail.

3. Gray questions Kaoru about the lack of Japanese women in advertisements and is firmly told that "Your people are more beautiful than us." What gives Kaoru this impression? How are general standards of beauty established? Maintained?

WEB SITES

www.cs.washington.edu/homes/notkin/jstories/node3.html
Dave Notkin's and Cathy Tuttle's Japan Stories—*Sentos, Yokohama and the Matsumotos.*

www.inter-g7.or.jp/g7/wabisabi/konpal/enjoy-e.html
How to take a bath in Ginza.

www.cyber-bp.or.jp/japan/living/bath.html
The public bath—an illustrated step-by-step guide.

John Fraser
1944–

■■■

Save the Last Dance

Born in Montreal, John Fraser is a respected Canadian journalist who is a Master at Massey College. After attending high school at private boys' schools in Ontario, Fraser went to Memorial University in Newfoundland (B.A., 1969), and then to Exeter College, Oxford (University Diploma, 1970), and the University of East Anglia (M.A., 1971). Married in 1975, Fraser has three daughters and currently lives in Toronto.

Fraser has held a wide range of journalistic positions, including that of editor of *Saturday Night* magazine, and dance critic and feature writer for *The Globe and Mail*, as well as Peking bureau chief for that newspaper from 1977 to 1979. His published books, including *The Chinese: Portrait of a People* (1980), *Kain and Augustyn: A Photographic Study, Stolen China: A Novel* (1996) and *Saturday Night Lives!: Selected Diaries* (1996), reflect his varied experience and interests. In this article Fraser focuses on the similarities and differences between Rudolph Nureyev and Mikhail Baryshnikov. The latter was the subject of Fraser's 1988 book, *Private View: Inside Baryshnikov's American Ballet Theatre.*

Preparing to Read

John Fraser compares and contrasts Rudolph Nureyev and Mikhail Baryshnikov in the following essay from *Saturday Night* (1993). Both men are Soviet defectors who have become recognized around the world as exceptional artists in the ballet world, and yet they have led very different lives. As you prepare to read this article, think about ballet and ballet dancers. What typical characteristics come to mind? What accounts for the appeal of ballet across continents and why does it remain so popular? What other ballet dancers can you name?

■   ■

Mikhail Baryshnikov came back to dance in Toronto just a month before Rudolf Nureyev died in Paris on January 6. Baryshnikov was at the O'Keefe Centre, the theatre where he orchestrated his dramatic leap to the West in 1974 (and which he still lists as one of the worst performing houses in all of North America). Nureyev died in the city in which he made his own leap to a new life in the West in 1961. His memorial service was held in the ornate Paris Opera, a house he adored and where he often left dancers in tears, so outrageous were some of his harangues when he presided over the ballet company there in the 1980s.

Both men sported the news-wire sobriquet "Soviet defector," 2 a special category of performing artist that will soon mean very little except as a historical footnote. Next to their obvious talent, however, it used to mean half of their mystique, half of *everything*: exoticism, artistic distinction, aloofness, unique star quality, being set apart from all Western-trained male dancers. Their overt sexuality on stage, differently expressed, was the other half. Critics were rarely explicit in discussing this, yet potency positively radiated from them during performances—from their costumes, mannerisms, athleticism, studied stage glances, even their curtain calls. Their artistry has formed the definition of male dancing for the last half of the twentieth century, but it was sex appeal that shot them both into the highest stratosphere of stardom.

Nureyev was gay and died of AIDS. Baryshnikov is straight 3 and is still fathering children; he has had two with his companion, Lisa Rinehart. (An older child is the daughter of the film actress Jessica Lange.) Nureyev was promiscuous, almost to the end; Baryshnikov has settled down, though it was not so long ago that he led a merry chase through the ranks of ballerinas and movie stars where the risk of cross-sexual infection from the terrible disease is far more real than in, say, the middle-class enclaves of north Toronto. Many heterosexuals in North America still don't take the risk of AIDS very seriously. Not so in the world of the performing arts. Especially not so in the world of ballet. Safe sex is a contradiction in terms. Baryshnikov knows that; Nureyev laughed at it.

At the outset of his career in the West, Nureyev had two 4 noble relationships with people older than himself that provided emotional and perhaps sexual stability. The first was with Dame Margot Fonteyn, the great English prima ballerina, and the other was with Erik Bruhn, the brilliant Danish dancer who loved him deeply. In each case, Nureyev gave generously of himself and extended his partner's performing career. In his fashion, he remained loyal to both, but his libido was restless and he was notorious for seeking out anonymous, dispensable lovers. This aroused endless pop-psychological speculation. Craig Dodd, the author and ballet critic who knew Nureyev in the sixties, argued that this was his way of meeting people "on as nearly equal terms as anyone as famous as him is likely to do." Writing after Nureyev's death in London's *Sunday Telegraph*, Nicholas Farrell reported that some of the dancer's colleagues felt that "perhaps it could even have been a defiance of death—a sort of danse macabre."

What we do know is this: at the same age (their late thirties),   5 Nureyev and Baryshnikov took dramatically different paths in their personal lives. Nureyev lingered on in dangerland and Baryshnikov headed straight for middle-class domesticity. And the impact of those personal decisions and directions has had a profound effect on their art.

When I was a dance critic at the dawn of time, nearly a   6 quarter-century ago, I had my problems with Nureyev. I admired him enormously, of course. Only a fool wouldn't. He electrified every stage he danced on. Kid critics nevertheless had a responsibility for making sure the reading public didn't think we were overly awed by superstars like Nureyev, and I took my responsibilities as a *Canadian* kid critic very seriously in those days. After paying due attention to Nureyev's particular genius for three or four years, especially after he chose the National Ballet of Canada to be a handsome backdrop to his own expensive productions (his *Sleeping Beauty*, which reeked of dollars spent in the six figures, was notorious), I decided he wasn't sufficiently appreciative of the opportunities Canada had provided him. I detected unpleasant proof that the National Ballet was giving up too much of its mandate just for the thrill of having a soon-forgotten summer season at the Met in New York. I expatiated on all this, somewhat more pointedly than I am doing here, in the pages of the Sunday *New York Times*, where readers cared a lot more about Nureyev than about the future of Canadian ballet.

What a lot of fuss and bother ensued. By the time the dust   7 and chicken feathers had settled, I'd managed to add to my list of blood enemies the legendary dancer/choreographer Martha Graham, the *New York Times* dance critic Clive Barnes, all the principal dancers of the National Ballet, and at least one American balletomane who took the trouble to mail me faecal material in a plastic bag. The article was published about the same time Baryshnikov defected in Toronto, so it was a wild time in my life. Curiously, the one person I didn't make an enemy of—in the long term, anyway—was Nureyev himself. After he had whipped everyone up into a frenzy of loyalty oaths and assured himself that the kid critic spoke for no one but himself, we collaborated on a book about the Canadian dancers Karen Kain and Frank Augustyn (I did the legwork, he did the foreword.) During the course of this little collaboration, we agreed that we both listened to too much idle gossip. And then we gossiped idly and amiably through an affectionately remembered dinner and past all the damage we had tried to inflict on each other.

How I loved Nureyev after that, although I never really got 8 close to him. Not close in the way I got to Baryshnikov, who walks on golden pathways as far as I'm concerned, and who understands human nature, and his own, in ways Nureyev could never have begun to plumb. You could see the proof of this in the dancing they both did after they had passed their prime. Nureyev clung to all the old forms. As he went on refusing to retreat from a field fit only for young men at their peak, he became for some a sad and desperate figure who allowed himself to be tricked out in his old costumes, half-dancing his former roles of glory. I caught one of these events in upstate New York. (He rarely took such efforts to main stages.) At first I was embarrassed for his sake and then I had a change of heart and thought the spectacle poignant and even beautiful in a weird way. For Nureyev, being on stage—any stage—was synonymous with being alive. I think it was as simple as that.

It's not all that simple for Baryshnikov. He takes the business 9 of aging very seriously. A far better technician than Nureyev, he always seemed to soar twice as high. The problem here, though, was that he lit twice as hard and the damage to his legs over the years has been considerable. Unlike Nureyev, he has never had any interest in trying to perpetuate a former self. If he was middle-aged, dammit, he would dance middle-aged. His performances with Twyla Tharp in Toronto were a triumph: witty, sophisticated, but, most of all, wise. In Tharp, he has latched onto a choreographer/dancer who manages to confirm every dark, paranoid suspicion of the young Generation X feeling endlessly shafted by the hegemony of the baby boomers. Where once only youth was allowed to adorn the dance stage, Tharp and Baryshnikov announced that today's audiences don't really need the callow perspective of the under-thirty crowd. Here was a postmenopausal romp that embodied female independence, comfortable male self-acceptance, and a knowing deference to the realities and complications of relationships. Baryshnikov works around his game leg, makes a virtue of it, in fact, and,

once he and Tharp established the new rules and conventions
of the game, they had us all cheering.

I suppose he can go on like this for a long time and we may   10
yet see him do a dance based on *The Old Man and the Sea*. He
probably won't, though, because he is riddled through and
through with common sense and a concept of decorum that is
as natural to him as it was alien to Nureyev. This is not to detract
from Nureyev. He was what he was and gave immense pleasure
to millions of people. Anyone who saw him dance, particularly
when he was in top form, is marked for life; to have known him,
even fitfully, was an honour.

In private, he wasn't particularly nice about Baryshnikov—   11
professional jealousy was as much a part of his personality as
was generosity to young artists—but, like dominant predators
who understand their mutual powers, they sniffed each other
out early on and more or less kept to separate territories. And
Baryshnikov, for his part, always understood Nureyev's appeal.
"He had the charisma and simplicity of a man of the earth,"
Baryshnikov said after Nureyev's death, "and the untouchable
arrogance of the gods." Those Russians! Those Soviet defectors!

UNDERSTANDING DETAILS

1. What things do Baryshnikov and Nureyev share? In what ways
   are they similar?
2. What are the main ways in which these two men differ? At
   what point in their lives did they begin to follow significantly
   different paths?
3. To what does Fraser attribute the appeal and success of these
   two dancers? Identify at least three distinct points.

ANALYZING MEANING

1. What is Fraser's purpose in this essay? In your opinion does
   he achieve this purpose? Why or why not?
2. What is Fraser's personal bias in discussing this subject? How
   is it revealed to you? At what point in the essay does Fraser
   disclose his partiality?
3. How would you explain Fraser's final lines "Those Russians!
   Those Soviet defectors!"? What characteristics, personal and
   political, do those labels encompass?

DISCOVERING RHETORICAL STRATEGIES

1. Which of the four main methods of organizing a comparison and contrast essay does Fraser use?
2. How does Fraser give his essay cohesiveness? What details link the conclusion back to the beginning of the essay?
3. What details does Fraser include to give his point of view credibility? What is the purpose of telling the story of his review in *The New York Times*?

MAKING CONNECTIONS

1. Lynn Coady ("Genius or Madness?") outlines different reactions to people who behave in ways outside the mainstream. Where on her spectrum of genius and madness do you think Nureyev and Baryshnikov should be placed? Do you think that Fraser would agree with your assessment? Explain why or why not.
2. Imagine that John Fraser and David Foot ("Boomers Dance to a New Beat") are having a conversation about the appeal of Baryshnikov's dancing past the traditional dancer's prime and into his middle age. How do you think they would explain his continued appeal? Would Fraser and Foot agree on this topic or not?
3. Fraser contends that, "it was sex appeal that shot them both (Baryshnikov and Nureyev) into the highest stratosphere of stardom." How do you think David Suzuki ("The Right Stuff") would react to this claim? How universal is sex in generating interest in an audience?

IDEAS FOR DISCUSSION/WRITING

Preparing to Write

Write freely about a well-known entertainer such as an actor/actress, a sports figure, a musician, or a dancer. What do you know about that person's life? Is there a relationship between the personal life and the performer that you see "on stage"? Why are we interested in the details of celebrities' lives?

Choosing a Topic

1. In his essay Fraser includes information about the very physical demands of dancing and the athleticism of dancers. Write an

essay in which you compare ballet with a sport such as football, competitive swimming, tennis, or ice skating. What things do these activities have in common? In what ways are they different?

2. Fraser links his two subjects as "Soviet defectors." They, along with many other high-profile Soviet citizens, chose to leave their communist-ruled homes to live in North America. What do you think was the appeal of North America that made them change their lives so radically? Do you think that the reality of life in North America was what they expected? Give specific examples to support your point of view.

3. The reactions to aging of Nureyev and Baryshnikov are highlighted in "Save the Last Dance." Nureyev is described as "a sad and desperate figure who allowed himself to be tricked out in his old costumes, half-dancing his former roles of glory." In contrast, Fraser says that Baryshnikov, "... never had any interest in trying to perpetuate a former self. If he was middle-aged, dammit, he would dance middle-aged." Choose an aging rock star such as Mick Jagger, Tina Turner, Neil Young, or Sting, and compare him/her to the dancer whose attitude towards aging seems compatible.

WEB SITES

www.celebsite.com/people/mikhailbaryshnikov/index.html
Learn more about Mikhail Baryshnikov.

www.abt.org/archives/choreographers/nureyev_r.html
or

www.abt.org/no_javascript/archives/choreographers/nureyev_r. html
This site contains biographical information about Rudolf Nureyev.

cgi.pathfinder.com/people/daily/96back/960626.html
An article about Nureyev from *People* magazine.

Will Ferguson

■■■

The Sudbury Syndrome

Originally from Fort Vermilion in northern Alberta, Will Ferguson has lived and worked in a wide variety of places both in Canada and abroad, including five years in Japan. These experiences provide the basis for the books he has written and the commentary he occasionally provides on CBC radio. Ferguson's *I Was a Teenage Katima-Victim* (1998) is a memoir of the period he spent participating in the national Katimavik volunteer program that brought together young people from across the country to work on various projects in different communities. *Hokkaido Highway Blues: Hitchhiking Japan* (1998) is an account of Ferguson's 1996 hitchhiking trip of the length of Japan, which he undertook after a stint as an English language teacher there, and *The Hitchhiker's Guide to Japan* (1998) is a budget-focused travel guide to Japan. The book from which the selection here was taken is *Why I Hate Canadians* (1997), a humorous analysis of what Canada is and the meaning of being Canadian. A graduate of York University with a B.F.A. in film studies, Ferguson now lives in New Brunswick.

Preparing to Read

In this essay, Ferguson introduces Sudbury as one of Canada's "scars" rather than one of its "smiles". Before you read Ferguson's essay, think about a specific place that you would characterize as a "scar" instead of a "smile". Why is it a scar? What specific details illustrate its ugliness or lack of appeal? Does it have any redeeming qualities? Does it seem to be improving or getting worse?

■

So far we have been discussing Canada largely in the abstract. 1 Let's now take a closer look at some of the places and spaces we occupy. Canada on the street corner of a specific town or city is far different from the Canada of the imagination. With that in mind, I give you the city of Sudbury. And remember as you read this that (A) I love Sudbury, and (B) our scars define us every bit as much as our smiles, and our *collective* scars define us even further. Plastic surgery is *not* the answer.

England may have the White Cliffs of Dover, but Canada 2 has the Black Cliffs of Sudbury. And unlike the cliffs of Dover, which are really more of an *off*-white, the cliffs of Sudbury are black. Even better, they are man-made.

You see the cliffs as you drive into town, Sudbury's slag-pile 3 glaciers, the scorched tailings of the city's infamous nickel mines. Rail-cars roll up to the edge, then pause, tilt and pour out the molten slag, casting an orange echo against the sky, like the castle defences of a medieval siege. The slag cools into a crust, then blackens, and is in turn covered.

No animal can live off its own waste. This is a basic rule of 4 biology, and yet Sudbury, a city of 90,000 in the scrub-backed land of the Canadian Shield, seems to defy this. Folk singer Murray McLaughlin called it a "hard-rock town." Others have been less charitable. But if Sudbury has a bad reputation, it came by it honestly. It may be ugly, but it was a damn sight uglier and nastier just a few years ago. (*Suggested town motto*: You think it stinks now, you should have seen it before!)

Sudbury started in 1883 as a muddy, backwoods rail town at 5 the junction of two main lines. With the discovery of the world's richest nickel deposits came an economic boom. Two companies blasted their way to the top of the slag pile and stayed there: Falconbridge Mines and the almighty American-based International Nickel Company, now known simply as INCO.

INCO ruled Sudbury for almost eighty years. As final courts 6 of appeal, there was God, Ottawa and INCO, but not necessarily in that order. As late as 1964, the mayor of Sudbury was cheerfully informing newcomers to the city: "INCO calls the shots around here, and don't ever forget it."

> Oh the girls are out to bingo,
>   and the boys are gettin' stink-o,
> And we'll think no more of INCO
>   on a Sudbury Saturday night.

So sang Stompin' Tom Connors, and the words ring true of 7 a company town that ate its own. The pollution was horrific. Every dollar earned was wrestled from the earth, carved, blasted, crushed, melted down and skimmed off. For miles around the vegetation was dead, the land was barren and sullied. Lung cancer, acid rain, lakes turned to vinegar, bedrock torched bare: Sudbury had it all. It was—and still is—a hard-drinking, blue-collar place, with a rowdy mix of French and English. An archetypal mining town, a sorrowful and sickly place.

And yet never were a people so proud of their town. The 8

good citizens of Sudbury will defend their rocky home amid the smokestacks with the same fierce stubbornness that a parent defends a particularly ugly child. It's a town with a chip on its shoulder, and so it should. If you were the brunt of innumerable jokes, if in high school you were always voted most likely to die of industrial disease, you too would get pissed off at writers like me who come into town, shake their heads and declare it a "sorrowful and sickly place."

Later, INCO built Superstack, the tallest chimney in the 9 world, to throw the emissions out higher and over a larger area. This massive, spewing smokestack is a symbol of Sudbury as much as the Giant Nickel on the road into town. (In his travel book *Last Train to Toronto*, Terry Pindell recalls meeting Miss Nude Canada, the amply endowed Kathy Stack, in her home town of Sudbury. Her stage name was XTC, but everyone around town called her Superstack, though I believe this nickname may not have been in reference to the INCO chimney.)

The glory of nude dancing aside, Sudbury went into free- 10 fall sometime around 1980 and just kept tumbling. A series of bitter strikes and layoffs was followed hard by recession and terminal unemployment and the apocalyptic INCO strike. The picket lines, the cutbacks, the false minibooms that came and went like death spasms, all weighed heavy on the City That Nickel Built.

The story of Sudbury doesn't end there, though by all logic 11 it should; it was a one-industry town and its time had run out. But then, like a minor miracle, the clouds broke and the Sudbury Renaissance began. A streak of civic pride, as deep as any nickel core, saved them. (That and millions of dollars in federal and corporate aid.) The strategy was simply, the mantra short: diversify or die.

And what do you think they decided to base their recovery 12 on? You'll never guess. Never. They decided to make Sudbury a centre for *tourism*. That's right, tourism. "I don't know, honey, this year it's either Paris or Sudbury, I just can't decide." The crazy thing is, it worked. Tourism is now a major, multimillion-dollar industry in Sudbury and one of the cornerstones of the city's recovery plan.

INCO donated $5 million towards the construction of Science 13 North, a tourist-orientated interactive centre. It was the biggest single corporate donation to a community project in Canadian history—something which INCO never tires of pointing out.

Science North is "science beyond the classroom." The   14
buildings are designed in the shape of snowflakes, *stainless steel*
snowflakes, that are connected via bedrock tunnels. And how
do they entice you to come to the complex? With the promise
that you will *"Pet a tarantula! Hold a porcupine! and lie on a bed of
nails!"* Tarantulas? Bed of nails? Just how does this tour end? Do
they poke you in the eye with a stick and set your hair on fire? In
fact, Science North is a lot of fun. And yes, as I discovered, you
can pet a porcupine. His name is Ralf, he likes to have his belly
rubbed, and no, his quills don't come off. Unless he's angry. So
you should try to stay on his good side.

Sudbury has reinvented itself, and with tourism now   15
booming, people are actually ending up in Sudbury *on purpose*!
The city's concentrated tree-planting and beautification project
finally paid off when *Chatelaine* magazine—that purveyor of
good taste—ranked Sudbury as one of the ten best Canadian
cities to live in. *Crowds cheer! Balloons fly! Parades parade!*

Now then, let's not go overboard. Sudbury, no matter how   16
many trees you plant is still, well, Sudbury. Many of the newly
built and much ballyhooed residential complexes were really
just the generic Canadian Suburb transplanted whole into what
was once, and still is, a rough northern town. All the trees by
the side of the road are not going to hide the rock and refineries.
(*Suggested Motto:* As far as industrial wastelands go, we're not
that bad!)

It's true, the United Nations Environment Committee has   17
applauded Sudbury's urban renewal efforts. (*Crowds cheer,
balloons fly*, etc. etc.) Do you remember back in grade school,
when the teacher used to give special silver stars to that slow
kid who tried really, really hard but was still a bit thick? They
called the award Most Improved. Well, Sudbury is that student,
and she wears her star proudly.

From the top of the hill, beside the giant stainless steel nickel,   18
she proclaims, like Scarlett O'Hara in *Gone with the Wind*, "As
God as my witness, I will never be ugly again!"

And on the other side, across the hill, the slag cars rumble   19
and roll, pouring the fire that slides down like lava and cools
into blackness on the edge of town.

Tucked in within Sudbury's Copper Cliff townsite is a place   20
called Little Italy. Built by migrant workers to resemble the
mountain villages of their native land, it is a small enclave of
narrow random streets and oddly angled houses. From Little

Italy to the Giant Nickel, from the Black Cliffs to the Superstack itself, Sudbury has stories to tell. Love her or hate her, there is no place quite like her. Sudbury *is* ugly. It is a city with a past, a city covered with scars, but it is also a city with that elusive quality we call *character*, and character is not something you can buy. But it is something you can lose.

Every time you pass through Sudbury, you will notice the 21 encroaching sameness of suburbia. It is happening across Canada. I call it the Sudbury Syndrome: the desire to eradicate the scars and birthmarks of a place and import instead the shiny surfaces and retail clones of a common urban/suburban culture. It is nothing short of the Blanding of Canada. Local character and diversity is slowly being watered down, and our cities and towns are fast becoming as interchangeable as shopping malls.

The town of Sudbury, with its gritty working-class roots and 22 nickel-plated pride, epitomizes this. A campaign has been under way since the early 1990s to change Sudbury's image, to make it more like every other town, to make it as innocuous as possible. To make it as nice as everybody else.

Let me take you now to Saint John, New Brunswick, or, as I 23 like to call it, Sudbury-by-the-sea. Living as I do in the fey little town of St. Andrews, I have come to rely on Saint John (population: 79,000) as my pipeline to consumer goods, import foods, cinemas, and adult sex shoppes (*sic*).

St. Andrews, with a population less than 1,300 has a mind- 24 boggling variety all its own, a riffraff collection of greying hippies, faded back-to-the-landers, imported salmon researchers, restless college kids, price-gouging landlords, wealthy elders and assorted craftspeople. The town has also, wisely and with more than a little smugness, decided to resist the drift towards mass commercialization. The town stewards have kept fast-food chains and discount department stores at bay and the result is an expensive but largely unspoiled town. Quaint. Historic. Narcoleptic.

The city of Saint John, an hour and a half down the road, is 25 a world away from St. Andrews, and the two coexist like a dowager aunt and a tattooed dock-worker: uneasily.

Let's be frank. Saint John is a functionally illiterate city. 26 Trying to find a decent used bookstore in Saint John is like trying to find a decent restaurant in Regina. Much like Sudbury, Saint John is a blue-collar, gaseous, foul-smelling, knocked-about town. And just as Sudbury has been cursed and blessed—but to my mind, mostly cursed—by the presence of INCO, so has Saint John suffered at the hands of its own capitalist overlords: the Clan Irving.

To me, the Irvings have always seemed to be old-school 27 caricatures: cigar-smoking, round-bellied, union-busting capitalists of nineteenth-century America. Except it isn't the nineteenth century any more (a fact which no one has had the nerve to tell the Irvings) and Saint John remains a city in thrall.

Have you ever started packing to move, and you start out 28 by boxing and labelling everything and then arranging them carefully by content and size, but by the time you are done you are throwing things into boxes and shoving them wherever the hell they can fit? Well, it's the same with Saint John. There may have been a plan way back when, but the city is now a stack of random boxes jumbled along the bedrock, wedged in among highway overpasses and Irving shipyards. With its one-way streets and sadistic bypasses, Saint John is an unforgiving city; take a wrong turn and it's *Hello Moncton!*

And yet, for all that—because of that—I love Saint John. It's 29 a great place. The Old City is filled with surprises and the people are as raw and real as they come. Whether you're eating the meatloaf sandwich and spicy fries at Reggie's Diner or waiting for the Reversing (yawn) Falls to do their stench-side trick, it is hard not to feel a begrudging admiration for Saint John. Like Sudbury, it has a character all its own. Which makes it all the more depressing that it was in Saint John that I experienced my worst case of Urban Amnesia ever.

Fredericton, meanwhile, is a government town. Inhabited 30 largely by bureaucrats, poets and students, Fredericton can't quite make up its mind if it wants to be eccentric or snooty and has settled on a kind of eccentric snootiness that puzzles as much as it captivates. Like most Canadian cities, Fredericton (population: 45,000) is inflicted with a perimeter rim of shopping malls and fast-food emporiums. Like Saint John, Fredericton is about an hour and a half from St. Andrews.

Where Saint John is pure grit, Fredericton is pampered and 31 refined. Where Saint John is masculine, Fredericton is feminine. Where Saint John is dark, Fredericton is light. It's yin, it's yang. It's the fiddle vs. the violin. It's diner coffee vs. cappuccino. Saint John is unforgiving, Fredericton is welcoming.

The two cities are as different as any two could be, and yet, 32 during a grey winter outing as I wandered down a hermetically sealed shopping mall corridor, I suddenly lost all sense of place. I couldn't remember if I was in Saint John or Fredericton. Everything was completely familiar—and yet I had absolutely no idea where I was. It must be the way a victim of amnesia feels.

Which city was I in? Fredericton? Saint John? There was 33 nothing to distinguish it either way. Shopping malls, like suburbs, have no character. They are, by their very nature, generic.

It turned out I was in Saint John, which I discovered only 34 after I stopped someone and asked. (And boy, did I get a funny look.) It was a heart-sinking moment to realize just how standardized modern Canadian culture has become. It is cheerful and clean and comfortable. And soulless.

What this country needs is more Sudburys and fewer 35 shopping malls.

UNDERSTANDING DETAILS

1. How has Sudbury changed between the 1980s and the late 1990s when Ferguson's essay was written? Give specific examples that show the progression.
2. How are Saint John and Fredericton similar? In what ways do they differ?
3. What force has been primarily responsible for the establishment and development of Sudbury?

ANALYZING MEANING

1. In this essay Ferguson introduces a trend he labels the "(b)landing of Canada." Explain exactly what "the blanding of Canada" is. What is Ferguson's attitude toward this trend?
2. How does Ferguson feel about his hometown of St. Andrew's, New Brunswick? Is his attitude consistent with the characteristics he uses to introduce St. Andrew's? Explain the apparent contradiction in Ferguson's approach.
3. Ferguson concludes his essay with a call for more Sudburys and fewer shopping malls. Explain why Ferguson sees this as the ideal.

DISCOVERING RHETORICAL STRATEGIES

1. Which of the four patterns of organization has Ferguson chosen in this essay?

2. Reading reviews of *Why I Hate Canadians*, in which this essay first appeared, shows that Ferguson offends many readers with his views about Canada and Canadians. The tone that Ferguson uses and his tendency to exaggerate to make a point may exacerbate this reaction. Explain why Ferguson hasn't adopted a more diplomatic, even tone in conveying the ideas he has about his subject matter.

3. Ferguson uses many metaphors and similes to make his writing interesting and vivid. Find four examples of Ferguson's use of these figures of speech. Which do you find the most effective? Why?

MAKING CONNECTIONS

1. Ferguson concludes his essay by saying that "(w)hat this country needs is more Sudburys and fewer shopping malls." Imagine that Ferguson is having a conversation about Canada with Neil Bissoondath ("Pieces of Sky"), Laura Millard ("Images of Canada: Canadian Bank Notes") and Tomson Highway ("What a Certain Visionary Once Said"). Who in this group do you think would agree with Ferguson? Who would disagree? Who would you most closely agree with?

2. In "My Old Newcastle," David Adams Richards writes about his New Brunswick hometown. How does Richards' depiction of Newcastle compare to Ferguson's depiction of St. Andrews? Would Richards describe Newcastle as a "scar" or a "smile" on the face of Canada?

3. Ferguson uses an informal and humorous tone in this essay. Identify the specific techniques he employs to achieve this tone. How do those techniques compare to the strategies used by Drew Hayden Taylor ("Pretty Like a White Boy")?

IDEAS FOR DISCUSSION/WRITING

Preparing to Write

In "The Sudbury Syndrome" Ferguson writes about the value of character in a place. Write freely about a place you know that has character. What makes this place unique? Is it generally viewed positively or negatively? Why? Are the elements of character valued? How has this place changed over time? Has that enhanced its character or diminished it?

Choosing a Topic

1. Think about a city or town you know well. Compare and contrast what that place is like today with what it was like when you first knew it. Using specific examples, show how it has changed. In your view, has the change been an improvement or a deterioration?

2. Ferguson laments the uniformity and consistency of shopping malls and the lack of unique character that they possess. Using specific examples with which you are familiar, write an essay in which you either advance Ferguson's view or counter it with a defence of shopping malls.

3. Choose two people who work in the same field and compare and contrast their approaches to the job. You might consider two teachers, two newscasters, two DJs, two store clerks, two servers in a restaurant, or two politicians.

WEB SITES

region.sudbury.on.ca/
The Region of Sudbury Web site.

sciencenorth.on.ca/
Learn more about Science North.

www.chaptersglobe.com
Find information on and reviews of the books Ferguson has written.

Gloria Steinem
1934–

■ ■ ■

The Politics of Muscle

Once described as a writer with "unpretentious clarity and forceful expression," Gloria Steinem is one of the foremost organizers and champions of the modern women's movement. She was born in Toledo, Ohio, earned a B.A. at Smith College, and pursued graduate work in political science at the universities of Delhi and Calcutta in India before returning to America to begin a freelance career in journalism. One of her earliest and best-known articles, "I Was a Playboy Bunny," was a witty exposé of the entire Playboy operation written in 1963 after she had worked undercover for two weeks in the New York City Playboy Club. In 1968 she and Clay Felker founded *New York* magazine; then, in 1972, they started *Ms* magazine, which sold out its entire 300,000-copy run in eight days. Steinem's subsequent publications have included *Outrageous Acts and Everyday Rebellions* (1983), *Marilyn: Norma Jean* (1986), *Bedside Book of Self-Esteem* (1989), and *Moving Beyond Words* (1994). She has also written several television scripts and is a frequent contributor to such periodicals as *Esquire, Vogue, Cosmopolitan, Seventeen,* and *Life.* An articulate and passionate spokesperson for feminist causes, Steinem has been honoured nine times by the *World Almanac* as one of the 25 most influential women in America.

Preparing to Read

Taken from the author's newest book, *Moving Beyond Words,* "The Politics of Muscle" is actually an introduction to a longer essay entitled "The Strongest Woman in the World," which celebrates the virtues of women's bodybuilding champion Bev Francis. In this introductory essay, Steinem examines the sexual politics of women's weight lifting and the extent to which a "new beauty standard" has begun to evolve because of pioneers in the sport like Francis. As you prepare to read this essay, examine for a few minutes your own thoughts about the associations people make with weakness and strength in both men and women: Which sex do you think of as stronger? In our society, what does strength have to do with accomplishment? With failure? Do these associations vary for men and women? What does weakness suggest in North American culture? Do these suggestions vary for men and women? What are the positive values North Americans associate with muscles and strength? With helplessness and weakness? What are the negative values North Americans associate with muscles and strength? With helplessness and weakness? What connections have you made from your experience between physical strength and gender roles?

I come from a generation who didn't do sports. Being a cheer- 1
leader or a drum majorette was as far as our imaginations or
role models could take us. Oh yes, there was also being a strut-
ter—one of a group of girls (and we were girls then) who marched
and danced and turned cartwheels in front of the high school band
at football games. Did you know that big football universities actually gave strutting scholarships? That shouldn't sound any more
bizarre than football scholarships, yet somehow it does. Gender
politics strikes again.

But even winning one of those rare positions, the stuff that 2
dreams were made of, was more about body display than about
the considerable skill they required. You could forget about trying
out for them if you didn't have the right face and figure, and my
high school was full of girls who had learned to do back flips
and twirl flaming batons, all to no avail. Winning wasn't about
being the best in an objective competition or achieving a personal
best, or even about becoming healthy or fit. It was about *being
chosen*.

That's one of many reasons why I and other women of my 3
generation grew up believing—as many girls still do—that the
most important thing about a female body is not what it does
but how it looks. The power lies not within us but in the gaze
of the observer. In retrospect, I feel sorry for the protofeminist
gym teachers who tried so hard to interest us in half-court
basketball and other team sports thought suitable for girls in my
high school, while we worried about the hairdo we'd slept on
rollers all night to achieve. Gym was just a stupid requirement
you tried to get out of, with ugly gym suits whose very freedom
felt odd on bodies accustomed to being constricted for viewing.
My blue-collar neighborhood didn't help much either, for it
convinced me that sports like tennis or golf were as remote as
the country clubs where they were played—mostly by men
anyway. That left tap dancing and ballet as my only exercise,
and though my dancing school farmed us out to supermarket
openings and local nightclubs, where we danced our hearts out
in homemade costumes, those events were about display too,
about smiling and pleasing and, even during the rigors of ballet,
about looking ethereal and hiding any muscles or strength.

My sports avoidance continued into college, where I went 4
through shock about class and wrongly assumed athletics were
only for well-to-do prep school girls like those who brought their
own lacrosse sticks and riding horses to school. With no sports

training to carry over from childhood—and no place to become childlike, as we must when we belatedly learn basic skills—I clung to my familiar limits. Even at the casual softball games where *Ms.* played the staffs of other magazines, I confined myself to cheering. As the *Ms.* No Stars, we prided ourselves on keeping the same lineup, win or lose, and otherwise disobeying the rules of the jockocracy, so I contented myself with upsetting the men on the opposing team by cheering for their female team members. It's amazing how upset those accustomed to conventional divisions can become when others refuse to be divided by them.

In my case, an interest in the politics of strength had come not 5 from my own experience but from observing the mysterious changes in many women around me. Several of my unathletic friends had deserted me by joining gyms, becoming joggers, or discovering the pleasure of learning to yell and kick in self-defense class. Others who had young daughters described the unexpected thrill of seeing them learn to throw a ball or run with a freedom that hadn't been part of our lives in conscious memory. On campuses, I listened to formerly anorexic young women who said their obsession with dieting had diminished when they discovered strength as a third alternative to the usual fat-versus-thin dichotomy. Suddenly, a skinny, androgynous, "boyish" body was no longer the only way to escape the soft, female, "victim" bodies they associated with their mothers' fates. Added together, these examples of before-and-after strength changes were so dramatic that the only male analogues I could find were Vietnam amputees whose confidence was bolstered when they entered marathons in wheelchairs or on artificial legs, or paralyzed accident survivors whose sense of themselves was changed when they learned to play wheelchair basketball. Compared to their handicapped female counterparts, however, even those men seemed to be less transformed. Within each category, women had been less encouraged to develop whatever muscle and skills we had.

Since my old habits of ignoring my body and living inside my 6 head weren't that easy to break, it was difficult to change my nonathletic ways. Instead, I continued to learn secondhand from watching my friends, from reading about female strength in other cultures, and from asking questions wherever I traveled.

Though cultural differences were many, there were political 7 similarities in the way women's bodies were treated that went as deep as patriarchy itself. Whether achieved through law and social policy, as in this and other industrialized countries, or by way of tribal practice and religious ritual, as in older cultures, an individual woman's body was far more subject to other people's rules than was that of her male counterpart. Women always seemed to be owned to some degree as the means of reproduction. And as possessions, women's bodies then became symbols of men's status, with a value that was often determined by what was rare. Thus, rich cultures valued thin women, and poor cultures valued fat women. Yet all patriarchal cultures valued weakness in women. How else could male dominance survive? In my own country, for example, women who "belong" to rich white men are often thinner (as in "You can never be too rich or too thin") than those who "belong" to poor men of color; yet those very different groups of males tend to come together in their belief that women are supposed to be weaker than men; that muscles and strength aren't "feminine."

If I had any doubts about the psychological importance of 8 cultural emphasis on male/female strength difference, listening to arguments about equality put them to rest. Sooner or later, even the most intellectual discussion came down to men's supposedly superior strength as a justification for inequality, whether the person arguing regretted or celebrated it. What no one seemed to explore, however, was the inadequacy of physical strength as a way of explaining oppression in other cases. Men of European origin hadn't ruled in South Africa because they were stronger than African men, and blacks hadn't been kept in slavery or bad jobs in the United States because whites had more muscles. On the contrary, males of the "wrong" class or color were often confined to laboring positions precisely because of their supposedly greater strength, just as the lower pay females received was often rationalized by their supposedly lesser strength. Oppression has no logic—just a self-fulfilling prophecy, justified by a self-perpetuating system.

The more I learned, the more I realized that belief in great 9 strength differences between women and men was itself part of the gender mind-game. In fact, we can't really know what those differences might be, because they are so enshrined, perpetuated, and exaggerated by culture. They seem to be greatest during the childbearing years (when men as a group have more speed and upper-body strength, and women have better balance, endurance, and flexibility) but only marginal during early childhood and old age (when females and males seem to have about the same degree of physical strength). Even during those middle years, the range of difference *among* men and *among* women is far greater than the generalized difference *between* males and females as groups. In multiracial societies like ours, where males of some races are smaller than females of others, judgments based on sex make even less sense. Yet we go right on assuming and praising female weakness and male strength.

But there is a problem about keeping women weak, even in   10 a patriarchy. Women are workers, as well as the means of reproduction. Lower-class women are especially likely to do hard physical labor. So the problem becomes: How to make sure female strength is used for work but not for rebellion? The answer is: Make women ashamed of it. Though hard work requires lower-class women to be stronger than their upper-class sisters, for example, those strong women are made to envy and imitate the weakness of women who "belong" to, and are the means of reproduction for, upper-class men—and so must be kept even *more* physically restricted if the lines of race and inheritance are to be kept "pure." That's why restrictive dress, from the chadors, or full-body veils, of the Middle East to metal ankle and neck rings in Africa, from nineteenth-century hoop skirts in Europe to corsets and high heels here, started among upper-class women and then sifted downward as poor women were encouraged to envy or imitate them. So did such bodily restrictions as bound feet in China, or clitoridectomies and infibulations in much of the Middle East and Africa, both of which practices began with women whose bodies were the means of reproduction for the powerful, and gradually became generalized symbols of femininity. In this country, the self-starvation known as anorexia nervosa is mostly a white, upper-middle class, young-female phenomenon, but all women are encouraged to envy a white and impossibly thin ideal.

Sexual politics are also reflected through differing emphases   11 on the reproductive parts of women's bodies. Whenever a patriarchy wants females to populate a new territory or replenish an old one, big breasts and hips become admirable. Think of the bosomy ideal of this country's frontier days, or the *zaftig*, Marilyn Monroe–type figure that became popular after the population losses of World War II. As soon as increased population wasn't desirable or necessary, hips and breasts were deemphasized. Think of the Twiggy look that arrived in the 1960s.

But whether bosomy or flat, *zaftig* or thin, the female ideal 12
remains weak, and it stays that way unless women ourselves
organize to change it. Suffragists shed the unhealthy corsets that
produced such a tiny-waisted, big-breasted look that fainting
and smelling salts became routine. Instead, they brought in
bloomers and bicycling. Feminists of today are struggling against
social pressures that exalt siliconed breasts but otherwise stick-
thin silhouettes. Introducing health and fitness has already led to
a fashion industry effort to reintroduce weakness with the waif
look, but at least it's being protested. The point is: Only when
women rebel against patriarchal standards does female muscle
become more accepted.

For these very political reasons, I've gradually come to believe 13
that society's acceptance of muscular women may be one of the
most intimate, visceral measures of change. Yes, we need progress
everywhere, but an increase in our physical strength could have
more impact on the everyday lives of most women than the
occasional role model in the boardroom or in the White House.

UNDERSTANDING DETAILS

1. According to Steinem, what is "gender politics" (paragraph 1)?
2. In what ways does Steinem equate "winning" with "being chosen" (paragraph 2)? Why is this an important premise for her
   essay?
3. What does Steinem mean when she says, "Oppression has no
   logic" (paragraph 8)? Explain your answer in detail.
4. In what ways does "power" lie with the observer rather than
   within the female?

ANALYZING MEANING

1. Why does Steinem call the female body a "victim" body (paragraph 5)? What did girls' mothers have to do with this association?
2. Do you agree with the author that a woman's body is "far more
   subject to other people's rules than [is] that of her male counterpart" (paragraph 7)? Explain your answer giving examples
   from your own experience.
3. What is Steinem implying about the political overtones connected with female weakness and male strength? According to
   Steinem, why are these judgments so ingrained in North
   American social and cultural mores?

4. What are Steinem's reasons for saying that "Society's acceptance of muscular women may be one of the most intimate visceral measures of change" (paragraph 13)? Do you agree with
this statement or not? Explain your reaction in detail.

DISCOVERING RHETORICAL STRATEGIES

1. Who do you think is Steinem's intended audience for this essay?
On what evidence do you base your answer?
2. In your opinion, what is Steinem's primary purpose in this
essay? Explain your answer in detail.
3. How appropriate is the title of this essay? What would be some
possible alternate titles?
4. What rhetorical modes support the author's comparison/con-
trast? Give examples of each.

MAKING CONNECTIONS

1. To what extent would Laura Robinson ("Starving for the Gold")
agree with Gloria Steinem's assertion that "the most important
thing about a female body is not what it does but how it looks"
(paragraph 3)? Do you agree or disagree with this assertion?
Give at least three reasons for your opinion.
2. If Steinem is correct that American women have not traditionally found power in their muscles, where have they found it? If
you were able to ask Naheed Mustafa ("My Body Is My Own
Business") or Michele Lemon ("Understanding Does Not
Always Lead to Tolerance") this same question, what do you
think their answers would be? With whom would you agree
most? Explain your answer.
3. Steinem's essay explores women in a realm that is traditionally male-dominated. How does her presentation of the experience of women in bodybuilding compare to Sally Armstrong's
("P4W") exploration of women in a world (that of prison) that
is traditionally male-dominated? What elements make a difference in these experiences?

IDEAS FOR DISCUSSION/WRITING

Preparing to Write

Write freely about the definition and role of strength and
weakness in North American society: What does strength

generally mean in our society? What does weakness mean? What association do you have with both modes of behaviour? Where do these associations come from? What are the political implications of these associations? The social implications? In what ways are strength and weakness basic to the value system in North American culture?

Choosing a Topic

1. Compare two different approaches to the process of succeeding in a specific job or activity. Develop your own guidelines for making the comparison; then write an essay for your fellow students about the similarities and differences you have observed between these two different approaches. Be sure to decide on a purpose and a point of view before you begin to write.

2. Interview your mother and father about their views on physical strength in their separate family backgrounds. If you have grandparents or stepparents, interview them as well. Then compare and contrast these various influences in your life. Which of them are alike? Which are different? How have you personally dealt with these similarities and differences? Be sure to decide on a purpose and a point of view before you begin to write.

3. In her essay, Steinem argues that "an increase in our [women's] physical strength could have more impact on the everyday lives of most women than the occasional role model in the boardroom or in the White House" (paragraph 13). Do you agree with the author? Write an essay to be published in your local newspaper explaining your views on this issue.

WEB SITES

www.greatwomen.org/stnem.htm
Find biographical information about Steinem at the National Women's Hall of Fame.

www.thomson.com/gale/cwh/steinem.html
You will find a detailed account of Steinem's life and accomplishments at this Encyclopedia of World Biography site.

catalog.com/arts/amazon.htm
Form Follows Function—All-Natural Amateur Women's Bodybuilding photo essay by Joseph Levy.

www.femalemuscle.com/home.html
Lori Victoria Braun's musclezine focuses on athletic and powerful women.

Evan Solomon
1968–

■ ■ ■

The Babar Factor

A graduate of McGill University with degrees in English literature and religious studies, Evan Solomon is the cofounder and executive editor of *Shift* magazine, a freelance journalist, and a fiction writer. For four years he was the host of a weekly show on *Newsworld* called "Futureworld" and he is now the host of *Newsworld*'s "Hot Type." He has also worked as a reporter for *The South China Morning Post* and is a regular contributor to CBC's *The National*, as a guest host and a contributor of cultural essays. Solomon's success is evidenced, in part, by the fact that he has received three Gemini nominations for "Futureworld." His first novel, *Crossing the Distance*, the story of two brothers, was published in the spring of 1999.

Preparing to Read

"The Babar Factor" first appeared in *Shift* magazine in the spring of 1994. In this essay Evan Solomon looks at the distinctions between the stories of childhood and the enormously popular video games that have made a fairly recent appearance. In preparing to read this essay think about the stories that you remember from your own childhood. Do you remember reading books or having them read to you? Were stories told to you by the adults in your life? Are there characters from traditional stories that you can recall? Do you remember any specific stories that you particularly liked? What role did stories and books play in your childhood?

■   ■

People come from all over the world to Celesteville-on-the-Sea. It has 1
the most beautiful beach in the land of the elephants.

And so begins another adventure with Jean de Brunhoff's 2
noble elephant-king Babar. Remember him? He was a great hero.
So were Curious George, Madeline, Mike Mulligan and his steam
shovel Mary Anne. This is a memorial to them. This is a memorial
to popular stories without interactive characters.

Super Mario sets foot in the door . . . 3

Accompanied by a catchy digital melody, these lines begin 4
another adventure in the ongoing saga of that noble video game
plumber Mario. Do you know him? Apparently, he's a great hero.

So is Sonic the Hedge Hog and Dino man. This is a memorial to them. This a memorial to popular video game characters who have yet to be forgotten.

Listen: 5

Two very interesting documents were recently made public. 6 One is called the Nintendo Co. 1993 *Annual Report* and the other is the year-end numbers for Sega Canada. Both are filled with extraordinary figures like this:

1. Over 75% of the 9.9 million households in Canada own video games.
2. The video game market is worth $400 million in Canada and $6 billion worldwide.
3. Nintendo has sold more than 100 million Mario video games worldwide.

Dazzling figures. So dazzling that they induce me to throw 7 away my Luddite bias and embark on a quest to understand why video games are popular.

Because my background is filled with books rather than video 8 games, I decide to measure the quality of the games by the Babar factor. Is a game more interesting than a story about Babar? Are the graphics more compelling than Jean de Brunhoff's famous watercolours? Is there more action, are the characters better developed? In short, what would I rather do, play with a game, or read a Babar?

I begin by playing those games which boil CRTC chief Keith 9 Spicer's lobster. First there's Night Trap, an adventure where vampire-like gentlemen in black costumes stalk women and suck out their blood. Called a "live action game" because it contains video images complete with incredibly bad acting, this beauty is now available from 3DO. Translation: The company 3DO uses better graphics than the much touted 16-bit machines from Sega and so the women's blood is more visible.

Cheers from the vidiots, jeers from the worry-warts. 10 Summary: an altogether dreary game with less graphic violence than the Ren and Stimpy show (stay with me now as I connect with these cultural touchstones). Definitely less interesting than a Babar story—even those which focus too much on Babar's pesky nephew Arthur—but only slightly more sexist.

Then there's the controversial Mortal Kombat, details of which 11 I will spare you, but needless to say, it revolves around a tournament where players fight to the death. With a multi-cultural cast of sadistic characters, this action-packed thriller is clearly fluent in the vernacular of fun.

Home versions of the game don't allow players to see 12 essentials like blood spurting from a decapitated corpse, and that has some customers crying foul. But what these customers don't realize is that every home unit of the Sega system is, in fact, secretly encoded with a way to unleash Mortal Kombat's gory potential. Here is that secret code. Move your joy stick in the following sequence: Down, Up, Left, Left, press button A, then Right, and finally Down. Now, I'm no expert in mnemonics, but there is an easy way to remember the code. The first letters spell the word DULLARD. Go check. Is this a profound semiotic irony or merely hacker humour that I don't get? I decide to rate Mortal Kombat highly. While not as strong on narrative as Brunhoff's work, the game is far more compelling. Just think, if only Celeste had ripped out Babar's tusks in a bloody domestic dispute. What a read! And those would have been watercolours worth saving.

But enough of the violent games. What of Mario and Sonic, 13 the real driving forces behind the video game explosion? Getting to know them is slightly more difficult. First Mario. Resides in Brooklyn. Plumber. First appeared as "Jumpman" in the 1981 version of Donkey Kong. Nimble of foot. On a mission to save one of his three lovers. Last year Mario slipped the surly bonds of the video game world and become a movie star. Played by the irrepressible Bob Hoskins, Mario emerges as a bumbling fool with a good heart. Bob did such a fine job effacing any nuance in Mario's character that children went wild and a sequel went into production.

And then Sonic, Sega's champion character. Sonic: video 14 game star, Saturday morning cartoon hero, leader of an interactive video empire worth an estimated 3.5 billion dollars. And the recent Q-score independent research ratings in the States concluded that Sonic is more recognizable than Mickey Mouse. Hmm, makes you look twice at this hedgehog.

And if you do look twice, here is what you will find. Not 15 only are Mario and Sonic childishly underdeveloped characters, they do not even function within a narrative framework. But because of a sophisticated marketing campaign, the lines between story and game have become blurred. And so we mistake these exercises in hand-eye coordination for valuable narratives.

The campaign to blur these lines begins in promotional 16 literature. "Fun is an international language," a Nintendo report says, and then continues, "and Mario helps kids experience fun." Loaded words like "language" and "experience" are used to enrich the basic idea of fun, while positive characteristics such as bravery and loyalty are grafted onto one-dimensional game characters. By dressing up chase-games in the garb of story, marketing possibilities are exponentially greater. After all, it's easier to sell a person than a pixel.

And so, Mario the game piece becomes Mario the lovable 17 hero, and Sonic the blue graphic becomes Sonic the precocious child. Now they can be sold as role models. It's interactive literature, the press releases say, and the kids relate to it, don't you see? I, for one, don't see. Because despite the cartoons, the movies, and the proliferation of games, no real narrative structure exists at all. And everyone in the industry knows it.

"Mario is goofy and awkward, but he works hard and thus 18 can do superhuman things like flying and leaping over buildings," says Nintendo marketing vice president Peter Main, desperate to give Mario some depth. Notice how Main is not compelled to justify Mario's actions in a coherent way. Rather, the *non sequitur*—"he works hard therefore he can fly"—suffices. It suffices because the games move too fast for anyone to notice.

But contrast this shallow imaginative universe to that of 19 Babar. Babar, whose mother is tragically gunned down in front of him. Babar, who unites the elephants after the old king dies from poison. Babar who builds a city, fights enemies and teaches his children valuable, hard-learned lessons.

Because video games have no story, they are unable to create 20 or sustain dramatic tension. The excitement generated by overcoming obstacles is not dramatic because players can always replay the game if they fail. Nothing of value is ever won or lost. In Babar, on the other hand, there is always the potential for tragedy. Each story is compelling because we rely on the eminently mortal Babar to save the situation. But in video games, the "Play Again" factor is the prevailing eschatology, dulling the pleasures derived from emotional uncertainty.

Ultimately, this debases our understanding of the heroic. 21 Mario and Sonic are no more than Pavlovian dogs, conditioned to either pursue or retreat. Nothing they do requires risk or choice. The fact that Pavlov's bell has been substituted by a quarter and the dog biscuit by a princess should not fool us. Mario and Sonic are neither heroes nor role models, they are cute exercise tools that amuse, distract and ultimately bore.

As video games continue to grow in popularity, our 22
imaginative universe continues to shrink. While classic forms of
entertainment like Babar demand a willing suspension of
disbelief, video games only demand a willing suspension—that
is to say, the choice to believe or disbelieve is irrelevant because
there is nothing to believe or disbelieve in. With no context, there
is no way to explore the heights and depths of human experience,
which, after all, is the fundamental task of stories. In the end, all
there is left to do is unplug the mind, plug in the game and play. 23

I don't like to wax nostalgic for books. I keep up with
developments in CD-ROMs. Heck, I just recently got myself an e-
mail address. But when it comes to Mario and Sonic, I have
simple advice: turn back from these wicked ways and read your
holy Babar.

UNDERSTANDING DETAILS

1. What is Solomon comparing and contrasting a) specifically and
   b) generally?
2. Who is Babar? Who are Super Mario and Sonic?
3. Why does Solomon choose to measure the appeal of video
   games against a story about Babar?

ANALYZING MEANING

1. What is the essential difference between video games and
   stories?
2. Explain the popularity of video games such as Mortal Kombat
   and Super Mario.
3. Explain Solomon's conclusion. What do books have to offer
   that video games do not?

DISCOVERING RHETORICAL STRATEGIES

1. Describe Solomon's tone in this essay. Point out specific examples that create this tone.
2. In addition to comparison and contrast, what rhetorical modes
   has Solomon used in "The Babar Factor"?
3. Explain what strategies Solomon uses to make his introduction
   particularly effective.

MAKING CONNECTIONS

1. Evan Solomon and Will Ferguson ("The Sudbury Syndrome") are contemporaries who are both writing about change. In both cases they conclude that the original is preferable to the newer, although many people see the newer form (video games or shopping malls) as more desirable. Why do these writers advocate for resisting the change and returning to what has gone before? Do you agree with their positions?

2. Solomon's conclusion ultimately favours literature over video games. How does Solomon's view compare to that of Robert Fulford ("The Fading Power of the Written Word")? What do you see as the role of literature in our society?

3. Much of Solomon's essay considers the impact of new technology. Imagine a conversation between Evan Solomon and Tony Leighton ("The New Nature") about the significance of the impact of new technology on our society. How do the views of these two men compare? Do you believe they would essentially agree or disagree? How does your view fit into the conversation?

IDEAS FOR DISCUSSION/WRITING

Preparing to Write

In this essay Solomon cites statistics that demonstrate the overwhelming popularity of video games. Write freely about the role that video games play in our lives. Who plays video games? When and where are they played? What is their appeal? What accounts for their success? Do you think that their popularity will last?

Choosing a Topic

1. Choose two forms of entertainment and write an essay in which you compare and contrast them. Use your examination of their similarities and differences to determine which is the better option.

2. Choose a character from a story that you think resembles you or someone you know in appearance and/or character. You might choose a childhood story or one that you have read as an adult. Write an essay in which you describe the similarities between your two subjects.

3. Your student council is going to purchase a new video game for the student lounge at your school. Write an essay in which you compare and contrast two of the available games in order to make a recommendation about which one they should purchase.

WEB SITES

www.Shift.com/Shift/shift.shtml
Shift online—this essay comes from *Shift*.

rat.org/sonic/merchandise.html
Find out more about Sonic the Hedgehog.

newsworld.cbc.ca/programs/sites/hottype_about.html
Solomon is the host of *Newsworld*'s "Hot Type."

www.speakers.ca/esolomon.html
Solomon is featured at Speaker's Spotlight.

CHAPTER 7

DEFINITION

■ ■ ■

Limiting the Frame of Reference

Definitions help us function smoothly in a complex world. All effective communication, in fact, is continuously dependent on our unique human ability to understand and employ accurate definitions of a wide range of words, phrases, and abstract ideas. If we did not work from a set of shared definitions, we would not be able to carry on coherent conversations, write comprehensible letters, or respond to even the simplest radio and television programs. Definitions help us understand basic concrete terms (such as automobiles, laser beams, and the gross national product), discuss various events in our lives (such as snow skiing, legal proceedings, and a New Year's celebration), and grasp difficult abstract ideas (such as the concepts of democracy, ambition, and resentment). The ability to comprehend definitions and use them effectively helps us keep our oral and written level of communication accurate and accessible to a wide variety of people.

Defining Definition

Definition is the process of explaining a word, object, or idea in such a way that the reader (or listener) knows as precisely as possible what we mean. A good definition sets up intellectual boundaries by focusing on the special qualities of a word or phrase that set it apart from other similar words or phrases. Clear definitions always give the writer and the reader a mutual starting point on the sometimes bumpy road to successful communication.

Definitions vary from short, dictionary-length summaries to longer, "extended" accounts that determine the form of an entire essay. Words or ideas that require expanded definitions are usually abstract, complex, or unavoidably controversial; they generally bear many related meanings or many shades of meaning. Definitions can be *objective* (technically precise and generally dry) or *subjective* (coloured with personal opinion), and they can be used to instruct or entertain, or to accomplish a combination of these two fundamental rhetorical goals.

In the following excerpt, a student defines "childhood" by putting it into perspective with other important stages of life. Though mostly entertaining, the paragraph is also instructive as the student objectively captures the essence of this phase of human development:

> Childhood is a stage of growth somewhere between infancy and adolescence. Just as each developmental period in our lives brings new changes and concerns, childhood serves as the threshold to puberty—the time we learn to discriminate between good and bad, right and wrong, love and lust. Childhood is neither a time of irresponsible infancy nor responsible adulthood. Rather, it is marked by duties that we don't really want, challenges that excite us, feelings that puzzle and frighten us, and limitless opportunities that help us explore the world around us. Childhood is a time when we solidify our personalities in spite of pressures to be someone else.

Thinking Critically by Using Definition

Definitions are building blocks in communication that help us make certain we are functioning from the same understanding of terms and ideas. They give us a foundation to work from in both reading and writing. Definitions force us to think about meanings and word associations that make other thinking strategies stronger and easier to work with.

The process of thinking through our definitions forces us to come to some understanding about a particular term or concept we are mentally wrestling with. Articulating that definition helps us move to other modes of thought and higher levels of understanding. Practising definitions in isolation to get a feel for them is much like separating the skill of peddling from the process of riding a bike. The better you get at peddling, the more natural the rest of the cycling process becomes. The following exercises ask you to practise definitions in a number of different ways. Being more conscious of what definition entails will make it more useful to you in both your reading and your writing.

1. Define one of the concrete words and one of the abstract words listed here in one or two sentences. What were some of the differences between the process you went through to explain the concrete word and the abstract word? What can you conclude from this brief exercise about the differences in defining abstract and concrete words? Concrete: *cattle, book, ranch, water, gum.* Abstract: *freedom, progress, equality, fairness, boredom.*

2. Define the word "grammar." Consult a dictionary, several handbooks, and maybe even some friends to get their views on the subject. Then, write a humorous definition of grammar that consolidates all these views into a single definition.

3. In what ways can you "define" yourself? What qualities or characteristics are crucial to an understanding of you as a person?

Reading and Writing Definition Essays

Extended definitions, which usually range from two or three paragraphs to an entire essay, seldom follow a set pattern of development or organization. Instead, as you will see from the examples in this chapter, they draw on a number of different techniques to help explain a word, object, term, concept, or phenomenon.

How to Read a Definition Essay

Preparing to Read. As you begin to read each of the definition essays in this chapter, take some time to consider the author's title and the synopsis of the essay in the Rhetorical Table of Contents: What is Michael Clugston's attitude toward lightning in "Twice Struck"? What do you sense is the general mood of Neil Bissoondath's "Pieces of Sky"?

Equally important as you prepare to read is scanning an essay and finding information from its preliminary material about the author and the circumstances surrounding the composition of the essay. What do you think is Carol Krenz's purpose in her definition of comfort food? And what can you learn about Drew Hayden Taylor and his qualifications for writing "Pretty Like a White Boy"?

Last, as you prepare to read these essays, answer the prereading questions before each essay, and then, spend a few minutes thinking freely about the general subject of the essay at hand: What role does comfort food play in your life (Krenz)? What information do you need about being a "banana" (North American of Chinese ancestry) (Wayson Choy)? What values do you consider distinctively Canadian (Bissoondath)?

Reading. As you read a definition essay, as with all essays, be sure to record your initial reactions to your reading material. What are some of your thoughts or associations in relation to each essay?

As you get more involved in the essay, reconsider the preliminary material so you can create a context within which to analyze what the writer is saying: Who do you think is Taylor's primary audience? Do you think his essay will effectively reach that group of people? In what ways is Wayson Choy qualified to write about being a "banana"?

Also, determine at this point whether the author's treatment of his or her subject is predominantly objective or subjective. Then, make sure you understand the main points of the essay on the literal, interpretive, and analytical levels by reading the questions that follow.

Rereading. When you read these definition essays for a second time, check to see how each writer actually sets forth his or her definition: Does the writer put each item in a specific category with clear boundaries? Do you understand how the item being defined is different from other items in the same category? Did the author name the various components of the item, explain its etymology (linguistic origin and history), discuss what it is not, or perform a combination of these tasks?

To evaluate the effectiveness of a definition essay, you need to reconsider the essay's primary purpose and audience. If Taylor is trying to get the general reader to understand the experience of not "looking the part," how effective is he in doing so? In like manner, is Clugston successful in explaining the nature of lightning and humans' understanding of it? Especially applicable is the question of what other rhetorical strategies help the author communicate this purpose. Through what other modes does Bissoondath define what it is to be Canadian?

For an inventory of the reading process, you can review the guidelines on pages 15–16 of the Introduction.

How to Write a Definition Essay

Preparing to Write. As with other essays, you should begin the task of writing a definition essay by answering the prewriting questions featured in this text and then by exploring your subject and generating other ideas. (See the explanation of various prewriting techniques on pages 17–19 of the Introduction.) Be sure you know what you are going to define and how you will approach your definition. You should then focus on a specific audience and purpose as you approach the writing assignment.

Writing. The next step toward developing a definition essay is usually to describe the general category to which the word belongs and then to contrast the word with all other words in that group. To define *exposition*, for example, you might say that it is a type of writing. Then, to differentiate it from other types of writing, you could go on to say that its main purpose is to "expose," or present information, as opposed to rhetorical modes such as description and narration, which describe and tell stories. In addition, you might want to cite some expository methods, such as example, process analysis, division/classification, and comparison/contrast.

Yet another way to begin a definition essay is to provide a term's etymology. Tracing a word's origin often illuminates its current meaning and usage as well. *Exposition*, for example, comes from the Latin *exponere*, meaning "to put forth, set forth, display, declare, or publish" (*ex* = out; *ponere* = to put or place). This information can generally be found in any good dictionary or in a good encyclopedia.

Another approach to defining a term is to explain what it does *not* mean. For example, *exposition* is not creative writing. By limiting the readers' frame of reference in these various ways, you are helping to establish a working definition for the term under consideration.

Finally, rhetorical methods that we have already studied, such as description, narration, example, process analysis, division/classification, and comparison/contrast, are particularly useful to writers in expanding their definitions. To clarify the term *exposition*, you might **describe** the details of an expository theme, **narrate** a story about the wide use of the term in today's classroom, or **give examples** of assignments that would produce good expository writing. In other situations, you could **analyze** various writing assignments and discuss the **process** of producing an expository essay, **classify** exposition apart from creative writing and then **divide** it into categories similar to the headings of this book, or **compare** and **contrast** it with creative writing. Writers also use definition quite often to support other rhetorical modes.

   Rewriting. Reviewing and revising a definition essay is a relatively straightforward task:

1. Have you chosen an effective beginning for your paper?
2. Did you create a reasonable context for your definition?
3. Have you used appropriate rhetorical strategies to develop your ideas?
4. Have you achieved your overall purpose as effectively as possible?

   Other guidelines to direct your writing and revising appear on pages 26–27 of the Introduction.

Student Essay: Definition at Work

In the following essay, a student defines "the perfect yuppie." Notice how the writer puts this term in a category and then explains the limits of that category and the uniqueness of this term within the category. To further inform her audience of the features of "yuppiedom," the student calls on the word's etymology, its dictionary definition, an itemization of the term's basic characteristics, a number of examples that explain those characteristics, and, finally, a general discussion of causes and effects that regulate a yuppie's behaviour.

The Perfect Yuppie

Etymology/dictionary definition Many people already know that <u>the letters YUP stand for "young urban professional."</u> *Young* in this context is understood to mean thirtyish; *urban* often means suburban; and *professional* means most *Subject* definitely college-educated. Double the *P* and add an *I* and an *E* at the end, and you get *yuppie*—that 1980s bourgeois, the marketers' darling, and the 1960s' inheritance. But let's not generalize. <u>Not *Limitations set* every thirty-year-old suburban college graduate qualifies as a yuppie. Nor is every yuppie in his or her thirties.</u> True yuppiness involves much more than the words that make up the acronym. *Writer's credibility* Being the little sister of a couple of yups, I am in an especially good position to define the perfect yuppie. I watched two develop.

   The essence of yuppiness is generally <u>new money</u>. In the yuppie's defense, I will admit that most yuppies have worked hard

General category of word being defined

Why the dictionary definition is inadequate

General characteristic

Cause/ Effect for their money and social status. Moreover, the baby boom of which they are a part has caused a glut of job seekers in their age bracket, forcing them to be competitive if they want all the nice things retailers have designed for them. But with new money comes *General character- istic* an interesting combination of wealth, naiveté, and pretentiousness.

Specific example   For example, most yuppies worthy of the title have long ago traded in their fringed suede jackets for fancy fur coats. Although they were animal rights activists in the 1960s, they will not notice *Cause/ effect* the irony of this change. In fact, they may be shameless enough to parade in their fur coats—fashion-show style—for friends and *Specific example* family. Because of their "innocence," yuppies generally will not see the vulgarity of their actions.

General character- istic   Because they are often quite wealthy, yuppies tend to have a lot of "things." They are simply overwhelmed by the responsibil- ity of spending all that money. For example, one yup I know has *Specific example* fourteen pairs of sunglasses and seven watches. She, her husband, and their three children own at least twenty collections of every- *Specific example* thing from comic books to Civil War memorabilia. Most yuppies have so much money that I often wonder why the word "yuppie" does not have a dollar sign in it somewhere.

    Perhaps in an effort to rid themselves of this financial burden, *Cause/ effect* *General character- istic* all good yuppies go to Europe as soon as possible. Not Germany or France or Portugal, mind you, but Europe. They do not know what they are doing there and thus generally spend much more *Cause/ effect* money than they need to—but, after all, no yuppie ever claimed to *General character- istic* be frugal. Most important, they bring home slides of Europe and show them to everyone they know. A really good yuppie will for- get and show you his or her slides more than once. Incidentally, when everyone has seen the slides of Europe twice, the yuppie's next stop is Australia.

General character- istic   A favorite pastime of yuppies is having wine-tasting parties for their yuppie friends. At these parties, they must make a great *Specific example* to-do about tasting the wine, cupping their faces over the glass with their palms (as if they were having a facial), and even sniff- ing the cork, for goodness sake. I once knew a yuppie who did *Specific example* not understand that a bottle of wine could not be rejected simply *Specific example* because he found he "did not like that kind." Another enjoyed making a show of having his wife choose and taste the wine oc- casionally, which they both thought was adorable.

What it is not   Some yuppie wanna-be's drive red or black BMWs, but don't let them fool you. A genuine, hard-core yuppie will usually own a gold or silver Volvo station wagon. In this yuppie-mobile, the *General characteristic* yuppie wife will chauffeur her young yupettes to and from their modeling classes, track meets, ballet, the manicurist, and boy scouts, for the young yuppie is generally as competitive and socially active as his or her parents. On the same topic, one particularly annoying trait of yuppie parents is bragging about their yupettes. You will know yuppies by the fact that they have the smartest, most talented children in the world. They will show you their kids' report cards, making sure you notice any improvements from last quarter.

Specific examples

General characteristic

Specific example

Perhaps I have been harsh in my portrayal of the perfect yuppie, and, certainly, I will be accused by some of stereotyping. But consider this: I never classify people as yuppies who do not so classify themselves. The ultimate criterion for being yuppies is that they will always proudly label themselves as such.

Division/ classification

General characteristic and concluding statement

Student Writer's Comments

The most difficult part about writing this definition essay was choosing a topic. I knew it had to be a word or phrase with different shades of meaning, but it also had to be either something I knew more about than the average person or something I had an unusual perspective on. I figured yuppie was a good word, not only because it has different meanings for different people, but also because it is an acronym, and acronyms tend to be greater than the sum of their parts.

I started by looking the word up in the dictionary and writing down its etymology (which I later referred to in my opening sentence). I then used freewriting to record the various meanings and natural associations I have with the word yuppie, which helped me discover relationships between these meanings and associations. I felt my mind wandering freely over all aspects of this word as I filled up pages and pages of freewriting. I then felt as if I had enough material to work with, so I began to write a draft of my essay.

I started writing the essay from the beginning, a process that was a real novelty for me. After citing the etymology of my word and placing it in a general category, I explained why the dictionary definition was inadequate. Then, I let the general characteristics I associate with the word take me step by step through the essay. As I wrote, I found myself mentally reorganizing my prewriting notes so that I could stay slightly ahead of my actual writing. I kept looping back and forth into my notes, looking for the next best characters to introduce, then writing, then going back to my notes again. I generated my entire first draft this way and revised the order only slightly in my final draft.

As I reworked my essay before handing it in, I added some humour from my own experience with my older sisters and looked closely at other rhetorical modes I had used to support my definition. Naturally, I had scattered examples throughout my essay and had discussed causes and effects quite openly. I revised my paper to make some of the connections I had had in mind clearer by either adding transitions or explaining the relationships in other words. I found that this process lengthened my essay quite a bit as I revised. I also worked on the essay at this point to bring out a secondary point I had had in mind, which is that some yuppies have lost the 1960s values they once had but often don't even realize it.

I spent the remainder of my time on my conclusion, which I rewrote from scratch four times. I finally ended up directly addressing the classification of yuppies, at which point I stumbled on the ultimate criterion for being a yuppy: "They will always proudly label themselves as such." When I reached this insight, I knew my paper was finished, and I was content with the results. I also realized that rewriting the conclusion so many times had given me a headache, but the pain was worth it.

Some Final Thoughts on Definition

The following selections feature extended definitions whose main purpose is to explain a specific term or idea to their readers. Each essay in its own way helps the audience identify with various parts of its definitions, and each successfully communicates the unique qualities of the term or idea in question. Notice what approaches to definition each writer takes and how these approaches limit the readers' frame of reference in the process of effective communication.

Definition in Review

Reading Definition Essays

Preparing to Read

1. What assumptions can you make from the essay's title?
2. Can you guess what the general mood of the essay is?
3. What is the essay's purpose and audience?
4. What does the synopsis in the Rhetorical Table of Contents tell you about the essay?
5. What can you learn from the author's biography?
6. Can you guess what the author's point of view toward the subject is?
7. What are your responses to the Preparing to Read questions?

Reading

1. Have you recorded your reactions to the essay?
2. Is the author's treatment of the subject predominantly subjective or objective?
3. Did you preview the questions that follow the essay?

Rereading

1. How does the author lay out the definition?
2. What is the essay's main purpose and audience?
3. What other rhetorical strategies does the author use to support the essay's purpose?
4. What are your responses to the questions after the essay?

Writing Definition Essays

Preparing to Write

1. What are your responses to the Preparing to Write questions?
2. Do you know what you are going to define and how you will approach your topic?
3. Who is your audience?

Writing

1. Does the beginning of your essay suit your purpose?
2. Do you use effective strategies to define your word or concept?
3. What rhetorical strategies do you use to expand your definition essay?

Rewriting

1. Have you chosen an effective beginning for your paper?
2. Did you create a reasonable context for your definition?
3. Have you used appropriate rhetorical strategies to develop your ideas?
4. Have you achieved your overall purpose as well as possible?

Carol Krenz
1949–

■ ■ ■

Food for Sloth

Currently writing a novel involving George Gershwin and living in Montreal with her husband and her cat, Carol Krenz writes articles on fashion and popular culture for publications including *The Montreal Gazette, Flare, Today's Woman,* and *Panache.* She is also the author of several children's books as well as *Audrey: A Life In Pictures* (1997) (a biography of Audrey Hepburn), and she was a regular contributor to *The Globe and Mail*'s now defunct *Montreal Magazine.* The selection that is included here reflects Krenz's humour, which is evident in much of her writing.

Preparing to Read

This article first appeared in Carol Krenz's column in *Montreal Magazine* in 1990. In "Food for Sloth" Krenz writes about one of the determining factors in our food choices. In defining comfort food Krenz enables us to laugh at some of our own idiosyncrasies. Before beginning to read, think generally about the role that food plays in your life. What foods do you particularly like? Dislike? Are there any foods you ever crave? What associations do you have with food, both positive and negative? How do the appearances, smells, and textures of food contribute to your reactions to particular types of food?

■───■

Comfort foods are humankind's way of fighting back against the cruel realities of cold temperatures and blah days. 1

Although anthropologists might disagree about humans' relationship to bears, physicians and psychologists attest to the fact that we are all prone to hibernation activities from the first November slushfests to May's crocuses. We tend to grow sluggish and stupid. We grumble and growl a lot. A large majority of *homo erectus urbanus* views with mock horror the folds of loose fat that begin to dangle from our midriffs around March. 2

Our greatest winter pleasure appears to be eating, then heavy sleeping followed by more eating. (Unlike bears, however, we have masochistic tendencies that occasionally take over in this period, forcing us to sit in front of the television, awash in winter pounds and lethargy, watching finely honed bodies leap after a 3 football or execute *grand jetés*.)

Instinctively we reach for foods loaded with simple sugars 4
and complex carbohydrates—something we've been doing for
centuries without question—only now we have medical science
confirming that hearty bowls of bean and barley soup or mounds
of pasta will actually make us feel sedated, fuzzy about the edges
and blissfully sleepy.

There are no distinct separations between hibernation foods 5
and comfort foods, but you could regard comfort foods as year-
round pacifiers while hibernation edibles are great in cold
weather. Case in point: a hot chocolate fudge sundae. It's
adaptable. You could eat it anytime. (Mind you, chocolate
anything needs no *raison d'être*.) However, Irish stew, shepherd's
pie and homemade macaroni and cheese seem more appropriate
in winter. Same for apple dumplings, blinis, rice-packed cabbage
rolls, fresh baked strudel, roasted or baked potatoes, baked beans
and molasses.

But one person's comfort food might be another's poison, at 6
least psychologically speaking. The aim of comfort foods is to
soothe, to make us retreat into childhood memories of warmth
and security. If you look back, no matter how trauma-filled your
early life might have been, there were times when you looked
to food for solace. As Rhoda Morgenstern observed in the
seventies, "The first thing I remember liking that liked me back
was *food*." Ergo, you may long for baked custard sprinkled with
nutmeg, I might hanker for blancmange or junket. A friend with
a remarkable long-term memory reaches for Pablum when the
going gets rough, and one chap I know thinks that toasted rye
with peanut butter, sweet gherkins and mayonnaise is the answer.
One might ask, how could his mother have allowed this? Which
is the whole point. Comfort foods don't have to make nutritional
sense (or be politically correct)!

Sandra P., a mother of three grown daughters, can be spotted 7
at the Atwater Steinberg checking out low-fat milk, alfalfa
sprouts, tofu and seven-grain bread. As she nears the cashier
with her healthy selections, she steals a furtive glance around,
then quickly reaches under her coat to produce five Tootsie Rolls,
one box of Kraft dinner, and a Monarch chocolate sponge
pudding cake. She explodes with a sigh of relief when the items
are finally secreted in (non-biodegradable) white plastic bags.
But Sandra P. has it all wrong. Comfort foods are in. They should
be flaunted. They should not be a source of guilt.

The instinctive desire to hibernate through winter with loads   8
of comfort foods is understandable. Most of us are not descended
from Norse gods who lounged naked around frigid fjords, ice
fishing after their saunas, drinking steaming bowls of cinnamon-
laced grog. We're a bunch of wimps, and we'll take our grog
indoors, thank you very much.

The carbohydrate component to our food choices offers new   9
evidence of chemical alteration of the body's brain. Rather than
giving us energy, carbohydrates slow people down, and can even
decrease reaction time and alertness. According to *Psychology
Today*, unbalanced carbohydrates—high amounts of sugars and
starches without accompanying protein—accomplish this quickly,
but are blocked somewhat when even the smallest amount of
protein is added. Armed with this information, you may want
to avoid eating pure carbs during a mentally taxing business
day. On the other hand, try reaching for the Sugar Pops when
you have to visit the dentist. What better time to feel spaced out
and dopey?

Medical research into unbalanced carbohydrates began in   10
the early seventies. Experiments on rats at the Massachusetts
Institute of Technology proved that higher levels of serotonin,
a brain chemical that affects sleep, pain perception and motor
activity, are the end result of carbohydrate consumption.
According to neuroscientist Richard Wurtman, chemicals in the
bloodstream compete for access to the brain. Tryptophan, an
amino acid is converted into serotonin once inside the brain. By
eating carbohydrates we make tryptophan the odds-on favourite
among its competitors for brain entry. But it's not because carbs
contain tryptophan. Rather, carbohydrates distract the
competition by stimulating the release of insulin, which moves
the other chemicals into muscles. The tryptophans, like
conquering heroes, march unchallenged into the brain, change
into serotonin and mellow us out.

So when Mom gave us a bowl of warm milk with wisps of   11
white bread drenched in sugar, she may have insisted it was
easy to digest, but we now know it was loaded with both
tryptophan (in the milk) and carbohydrates or insulin releasers.

It is therefore not surprising that most comfort foods are   12
riddled with complex and simple carbohydrates. Physically and
psychologically, they soothe us. So if it's February and you have
this mad urge to consume mashed potatoes and turnips, take
comfort. Get thee to a den and hibernate.

UNDERSTANDING DETAILS

1. In your own words explain what comfort foods are.
2. What is Krenz's distinction between hibernation foods and comfort foods?
3. In what ways do comfort foods satisfy us?

ANALYZING MEANING

1. What is Krenz's purpose? Is she attempting to instruct or entertain or both? Is she successful?
2. Is the title "Food for Sloth" an appropriate one? Explain your response.
3. Explain why we turn to food for comfort. What are your comfort foods?

DISCOVERING RHETORICAL STRATEGIES

1. Is the language that Krenz uses consistent in its level of formality? Support your response with specific examples. What effect does this have on the reader?
2. Would you categorize Krenz's definition as objective or subjective? What leads you to this conclusion?
3. Identify any metaphors or similes that Krenz uses. How do these help to make her definition clear?

MAKING CONNECTIONS

1. Krenz uses specific techniques to effectively explain to her audience the biological effect of certain foods on humans. Maureen Littlejohn ("You Are a Contract Painkiller") similarly makes a scientific process accessible and interesting to a lay audience. Compare and contrast the strategies that these two writers have used to make their essays effective.
2. Compare and contrast the ways in which Carol Krenz, Wayson Choy ("I'm a Banana and Proud of It"), and Michael Clugston ("Twice Struck") begin their definition essays. Which do you think is the most effective introduction? Why?
3. Explain the allusion with which Carol Krenz concludes her essay. How is her conclusion similar to that of Evan Solomon ("The Babar Factor")? Is this an effective closing to her essay? Why or why not?

IDEAS FOR DISCUSSION/WRITING

Preparing to Write

Write freely about positive images that you associate with childhood. These may include smells, textures, sounds, sights, and tastes. What emotions do you connect to these images? Are there any of these reminders that you try to recreate in your current life? Are there particular people with whom you associate these images?

Choosing a Topic

1. Foods play different roles in different cultures. Write an essay for someone from a different cultural background than your own that defines the function of food in your culture.

2. Choose a term that is familiar to you but that is not in common usage. This may be a family idiom or an expression that is used among your friends. In essay style write a definition of this term so that its meaning is clear to outsiders.

3. In essay style, write a column for a general interest magazine in which you define one of the following terms: status symbol, peaceful place, lucky charm, relaxing holiday. Think about your audience and decide whether you want your column to be entertaining, informative, or both. Use specific examples to illustrate your definition.

WEB SITES

 www.epicurious.com/
Epicurious is a great food site.

 www.foodserviceworld.com/cuisine/home.html
Cuisine Canada's mission is "to actively promote the growth and study of our distinctly Canadian food culture."

Drew Hayden Taylor
1962–

■ ■ ■

Pretty Like a White Boy:
The Adventures of a Blue Eyed Ojibway

Living in Toronto but originally from the Curve Lake Reserve near Peterborough, Ontario, Drew Hayden Taylor is quoted in a profile from *The Montreal Gazette* as follows: "I hate the technical part of writing ... I hate it with a passion." And yet he had achieved enviable success by his early thirties—as a writer.

Since graduating from the broadcasting program at North York, Ontario's, Seneca College, Taylor has worked as a radio reporter, a sound recordist for a film company, a trainee producer with the CBC, a promoter at the Canadian Native Arts Foundation, and a freelance writer. In addition to articles and stories that have appeared in *Maclean's*, *The Globe and Mail*, *This magazine*, *Anishinabek News*, *Cinema Canada*, and *Windspeaker*, Taylor has written episodes for *The Beachcombers* and *Street Legal*. He is also an award-winning playwright who has acted as the writer-in-residence for the Native Earth Performing Arts Theatre. His published works include several plays (*Toronto at Dreamer's Rock Bootlegger Blues, Someday*, and *Only Drunks and Children Tell the Truth*), a collection of essays (*Funny, You Don't Look Like One: Observation from a Blue-Eyed Ojibway*) and, most recently, a book of short stories (*Fearless Warriors*). His most recent theatre production is *The Baby Blues*.

Taylor brings a strong sense of humour to his work, which centers primarily around native issues. One of his aspirations is described in a quotation from a profile in *Windspeaker*: "With Native People writing their own stories, Canadians and people in other countries may get a more accurate view of (our people)," says Taylor. "It may help abolish the popular concept that Indians are all the same ..." The essay "Pretty Like a White Boy: Adventures of a Blue Eyed Ojibway" conveys Taylor's frustrating experiences of not "looking the part."

Preparing to Read

In this essay, Drew Hayden Taylor presents examples from his own life that illustrate the problems that occur as we categorize and define people by their heritage and appearance. Taylor's definition of a new term that accurately defines who he is provides a concluding summary to his discussion of stereotypes and the difficulties of not fitting neatly into the already existing categories. As you prepare to read, consider the terms "Indians," "Native People," and "white man." What associations do you have with each of these? Are they positive labels or negative ones? How do you distinguish people from these groups? What does an Indian look like? In what way does a white person differ in appearance? What does the title of this essay tell you about the author's attitude toward his topic?

■───■

In this big, huge world, with all its billions and billions of people, it's safe to say that everybody will eventually come across personalities and individuals that will touch them in some peculiar yet poignant way. Individuals that in some way represent and help define who you are. I'm no different, mine was Kermit the Frog. Not just because Natives have a long tradition of savouring Frogs' legs, but because of his music. If you all may remember, Kermit is quite famous for his rendition of 'It's Not Easy Being Green.' I can relate. If I could sing, my song would be 'It's Not Easy Having Blue Eyes in a Brown Eyed Village.'

Yes, I'm afraid it's true. The author happens to be a card-carrying Indian. Once you get past the aforementioned eyes, the fair skin, the light brown hair, and noticeable lack of cheekbones, there lies the heart and spirit of an Ojibway storyteller. Honest Injun, or as the more politically correct term may be, honest aboriginal.

You see, I'm the product of a white father I never knew, and an Ojibway woman who evidently couldn't run fast enough. As a kid I knew I looked a bit different. But, then again, all kids are paranoid when it comes to their peers. I had a fairly happy childhood, frolicking through the bullrushes. But there were certain things that, even then, made me notice my unusual appearance. Whenever we played cowboys and Indians, guess who had to be the bad guy, the cowboy.

It wasn't until I left the Reserve for the big bad city, that I became more aware of the role people expected me to play, and the fact that physically I didn't fit in. Everybody seemed to have this preconceived idea of how every Indian looked and acted. One guy, on my first day of college, asked me what kind of horse I preferred. I didn't have the heart to tell him 'hobby.'

I've often tried to be philosophical about the whole thing. I have both white and red blood in me, I guess that makes me pink. I am a 'Pink' man. Try to imagine this, I'm walking around on any typical Reserve in Canada, my head held high, proudly announcing to everyone 'I am a Pink Man.' It's a good thing I ran track in school.

My pinkness is constantly being pointed out to me over and 6
over and over again. 'You don't look Indian?' 'You're not Indian,
are you?' 'Really?!?' I got questions like that from both white
and Native people, for a while I debated having my status card
tattooed on my forehead.

And like most insecure people and specially a blue eyed 7
Native writer, I went through a particularly severe identity crisis
at one point. In fact, I admit it, one depressing spring evening, I
dyed my hair black. Pitch black.

The reason for such a dramatic act, you may ask? Show 8
Business. You see, for the last eight years or so, I've worked in
various capacities in the performing arts, and as a result I'd
always get calls to be an extra or even try out for an important
role in some Native oriented movie. This anonymous voice would
phone, having been given my number, and ask if I would be
interested in trying out for a movie. Being a naturally ambitious,
curious, and greedy young man, I would always readily agree,
stardom flashing in my eyes and hunger pains from my wallet.

A few days later I would show up for the audition, and that 9
was always an experience. What kind of experience you may
ask? Picture this, the picture calls for the casting of seventeenth-
century Mohawk warriors living in a traditional longhouse. The
casting director calls the name 'Drew Hayden Taylor' and I enter.

The casting director, the producer, and the film's director 10
look up from the table and see my face, blue eyes flashing in
anticipation. I once was described as a slightly chubby beachboy.
But even beachboys have tans. Anyway, there would be a quick
flush of confusion, a recheck of the papers, and a hesitant 'Mr.
Taylor?' Then they would ask if I was at the right audition. It
was always the same. By the way, I never got any of the parts I
tried for, except for a few anonymous crowd shots. Politics tells
me it's because of the way I look, reality tells me it's probably
because I can't act. I'm not sure which is better.

It's not just film people either. Recently I've become quite 11
involved in Theatre, Native theatre to be exact. And one cold
October day I was happily attending the Toronto leg of a
province-wide tour of my first play, *Toronto at Dreamer's Rock*.
The place was sold out, the audience very receptive and the
performance was wonderful. Ironically one of the actors was
also half white.

The director later told me he had been talking with the actor's 12
father, an older Non-Native type chap. Evidently he had asked a

few questions about me, and how I did my research. This made the director curious and he asked about his interest. He replied 'He's got an amazing grasp of the Native situation for a white person.'

Not all these incidents are work related either. One time a   13 friend and I were coming out of a rather upscale bar (we were out YUPPIE watching) and managed to catch a cab. We thanked the cab driver for being so comfortably close on such a cold night, he shrugged and nonchalantly talked about knowing what bars to drive around. 'If you're not careful, all you'll get is drunk Indians.' I hiccuped.

Another time this cab driver droned on and on about the   14 government. He started out by criticizing Mulroney, and eventually to his handling of the Oka crisis. This perked up my ears, until he said 'If it were me, I'd have tear-gassed the place by the second day. No more problem.' He got a dime tip. A few incidents like this and I'm convinced I'd make a great undercover agent for one of the Native political organizations.

But then again, even Native people have been known to look   15 at me with a fair amount of suspicion. Many years ago when I was a young man, I was working on a documentary on Native culture up in the wilds of Northern Ontario. We were at an isolated cabin filming a trapper woman and her kids. This one particular nine-year-old girl seemed to take a shine to me. She followed me around for two days both annoying me and endearing herself to me. But she absolutely refused to believe that I was Indian. The whole film crew tried to tell her but to no avail. She was certain I was white.

Then one day as I was loading up the car with film   16 equipment, she asked me if I wanted some tea. Being in a hurry I declined the tea. She immediately smiled with victory crying out 'See, you're not Indian, all Indians drink tea!'

Frustrated and a little hurt I whipped out my Status card   17 and thrust it at her. Now there I was, standing in a Northern Ontario winter, showing my Status card to a nine-year-old non-status Indian girl who had no idea what one was. Looking back, this may not have been one of my brighter moves.

But I must admit, it was a Native woman that boiled   18 everything down in one simple sentence. You may know that woman, Marianne Jones from 'The Beachcombers' television series. We were working on a film together out west and we got to gossiping. Eventually we got around to talking about our respective villages. Hers on the Queen Charlotte Islands, or Haida Gwaii as the Haida call them, and mine in central Ontario.

Eventually childhood on the Reserve was being discussed 19 and I made a comment about the way I look. She studied me for a moment, smiled, and said 'Do you know what the old women in my village would call you?' Hesitant but curious, I shook my head. 'They'd say you were pretty like a white boy.' To this day I'm still not sure if I like that.

Now some may argue that I am simply a Métis with a Status 20 card. I disagree, I failed French in grade 11. And the Métis as everyone knows have their own separate and honourable culture, particularly in western Canada. And of course I am well aware that I am not the only person with my physical characteristics.

I remember once looking at a video tape of a drum group, 21 shot on a Reserve up near Manitoulin Island. I noticed one of the drummers seemed quite fairhaired, almost blond. I mentioned this to my girlfriend of the time and she shrugged saying 'Well, that's to be expected. The highway runs right through the Reserve.'

Perhaps I'm being too critical. There's a lot to be said for 22 both cultures. For example, on the left hand, you have the Native respect for Elders. They understand the concept of wisdom and insight coming with age.

On the white hand, there's Italian food. I mean I really love 23 my mother and family but seriously, does anything really beat good Veal Scallopini? Most of my aboriginal friends share my fondness for this particular brand of food. Wasn't there a warrior at Oka named Lasagna? I found it ironic, though curiously logical, that Columbus was Italian. A connection I wonder?

Also Native people have this wonderful respect and love for 24 the land. They believe they are part of it, a mere chain in the cycle of existence. Now as many of you know, this conflicts with the accepted Judeo-Christian i.e. western view of land management. I even believe somewhere in the first chapters of the Bible it says something about God giving man dominion over Nature. Check it out, Genesis 4:?, 'Thou shalt clear cut.' So I grew up understanding that everything around me is important and alive. My Native heritage gave me that.

And again, on the white hand, there's breast implants. Darn 25 clever them white people. That's something Indians would never have invented, seriously. We're not ambitious enough. We just take what the Creator decides to give us, but no, not the white man. Just imagine it, some serious looking white man, and let's face it people, we know it was a man who invented them, don't we? So just imagine some serious looking white doctor sitting around in his laboratory muttering to himself, 'Big tits, big tits, hmmm, how do I make big tits?' If it was an Indian, it would be 'Big tits, big tits, white women sure got big tits' and leave it at that.

So where does that leave me on the big philosophical 26 scoreboard, what exactly are my choices again; Indians—respect for Elders, love of the land. White people—food and big tits. In order to live in both cultures I guess I'd have to find an Indian woman with big tits who lives with her grandmother in a cabin out in the woods and can make Fettucini Alfredo on a wood stove.

Now let me make this clear, I'm not writing this for 27 sympathy, or out of anger, or even some need for self-glorification. I am just setting the facts straight. For as you read this, a new Nation is born. This is a declaration of independence, my declaration of independence.

I've spent too many years explaining who and what I am 28 repeatedly, so as of this moment, I officially secede from both races. I plan to start my own separate nation. Because I am half Ojibway and half Caucasian, we will be called the Occasions. And I of course, since I'm founding the new nation, will be a Special Occasion.

UNDERSTANDING DETAILS

1. Does Drew Hayden Taylor affiliate himself more closely with Native or white culture? Give specific examples to support your answer.
2. What advantages does Taylor associate with being Native? What advantages does Taylor link with being white?
3. According to Taylor, why would he make a great undercover agent for a Native political organization?

ANALYZING MEANING

1. What is the author's purpose in this essay? Does he take an objective or a subjective approach in defining his subject?
2. Explain why Drew Hayden Taylor does not consider himself to be Métis.
3. Why do you think that Taylor did not get the parts in the films for which he auditioned?

DISCOVERING RHETORICAL STRATEGIES

1. What tone is established in this essay? How does Taylor create this tone? Is it effective?
2. What rhetorical strategies is Taylor employing in this essay in addition to definition? Give specific examples to support your answer.
3. Why does Taylor settle on the term "Special Occasion" rather than "Pink Man" as a way to define himself? What definition strategy has resulted in his final title?

MAKING CONNECTIONS

1. Drew Hayden Taylor credits Tomson Highway ("What a Certain Visionary Once Said") with "helping him to get his feet wet" in native theatre. What similarities are there between Taylor's essay and Highway's?
2. Imagine Cecil Foster ("Why Blacks Get Mad") and Drew Hayden Taylor having a conversation about their experiences of being judged based on their appearance. In what respects are their experiences similar? How do they differ? Do the two respond to appearance-based judgment in the same way? Give specific examples to support your answer.
3. Drew Hayden Taylor has chosen humour as a vehicle for making a difficult subject more palatable to his readers. Compare this strategy to that of Laura Robinson ("Starving for the Gold"). Explain which you think is the more effective approach.

IDEAS FOR DISCUSSION/WRITING

Preparing to Write

Write freely about your ethnic background, race, or heritage. How would you define yourself? Do existing categories work for you or do you feel the need to create a new category to capture who you are? What physical characteristics define you as part of the group you have identified? What personality characteristics affiliate you with this group? How would you categorize children of mixed heritage?

Choosing a Topic

1. Think of a term to define yourself in a way that reflects various aspects of your heritage/background. Others may belong to

this group, but focus on the aspects that make you unique from other, already existing categories. Write an essay for a general interest magazine in which you define your term using examples from your own life to make your definition clear.

2. Often our expectations are not borne out by reality. Write an essay for college students in which you define a particular job or profession based on your knowledge of someone in that position.

3. In paragraph 1, Taylor refers to "individuals that in some way represent and help define who you are." Describe one such individual in your life and explain how he or she has contributed to making you who you are.

WEB SITES

www.nativeweb.org/
Native Web is a collection of links to sites related to Native issues and Indigenous Peoples.

Wayson Choy
1939–

■ ■ ■

I'm a Banana and Proud of It

Now a teacher of English at Toronto's Humber College, Wayson Choy was born and raised in British Columbia. He won the 1995 Trillium Award and the 1995 Vancouver City Book Award for his first novel, *The Jade Peony*, which is about Vancouver's Chinatown during the Depression and World War II.

Preparing to Read

In this essay, which first appeared in *The Globe and Mail*'s Facts and Arguments column, Wayson Choy proudly defines himself as a "banana," an affectionate nickname for integrated North American children of Chinese parents. Before reading this essay think about nicknames and the role that they play in our lives. Who assigns nicknames? Who uses them? What makes some nicknames stick and others fade? Are nicknames positive or negative? Do you have a nickname? Do you like it? Does it appropriately reflect who you are?

■_____■

Because both my parents came from China, I took Chinese. But I cannot read or write Chinese and barely speak it. I love my North American citizenship. I don't mind being called a "banana," yellow on the outside and white inside. I'm proud I'm a banana. 1

After all, in Canada and the United States, native Indians are "apples" (red outside, white inside); blacks are "Oreo cookies" (black and white); and Chinese are "bananas." These metaphors assume, both rightly and wrongly, that the culture here has been primarily anglo-white. Cultural history made me a banana. 2

History: My father and mother arrived separately to the B.C. coast in the early part of the century. They came as unwanted "aliens." Better to be an alien here than to be dead of starvation in China. But after the Chinese Exclusion laws were passed in North America (late 1800s, early 1900s), no Chinese immigrants were granted citizenship in either Canada or the United States. 3

Like those Old China village men from *Toi San* who, in the   4
1850s, laid down cliff-edge train tracks through the Rockies and
the Sierras, or like those first women who came as mail-order
wives or concubines and who as bond-slaves were turned into
cheaper labourers or even prostitutes—like many of those men
and women, my father and mother survived ugly, unjust times.
In 1917, two hours after he got off the boat from Hong Kong, my
father was called "chink" and told to go back to China. "Chink"
is a hateful racist term, stereotyping the shape of Asian eyes: "a
chink in the armour," an undesirable slit. For the Elders, the past
was humiliating. Eventually, the Second World War changed
hostile attitudes toward the Chinese.

During the war, Chinese men volunteered and lost their lives   5
as members of the American and Canadian military. When
hostilities ended, many more were proudly in uniform waiting to
go overseas. Record Chinatown dollars were raised to buy War
Bonds. After 1945, challenged by such money and ultimate
sacrifices, the Exclusion laws in both Canada and the United
States were revoked. Chinatown residents claimed their
citizenship and sent for their families.

By 1949, after the Communists took over China, those of us   6
who arrived here as young children, or were born here, stayed.
No longer "aliens," we became legal citizens of North America.
Many of us also became "bananas."

Historically, "banana" is not a racist term. Although it clums-   7
ily stereotypes many of the children and grandchildren of the Old
Chinatowns, the term actually follows the old Chinese tendency to
assign endearing nicknames to replace formal names, semicomic
names to keep one humble. Thus, "banana" describes the
generations who assimilated so well into North American life.

In fact, our families encouraged members of my generation   8
in the 1950s and sixties to "get ahead," to get an English education, to get a job with good pay and prestige. "Don't work like
me," Chinatown parents said. "Work in an office!" The *lao wah-
kiu* (the Chinatown old-timers) also warned, "Never forget—you
still be Chinese!"

None of us ever forgot. The mirror never lied.   9

Many Chinatown teen-agers felt we didn't quite belong in   10
any one world. We looked Chinese, but thought and behaved
North American. Impatient Chinatown parents wanted the best
of both worlds for us, but they bluntly labelled their children
and grandchildren *"juk-sing"* or even *"mo no."* Not that we were

totally "shallow bamboo butt-ends" or entirely "no brain," but we had less and less understanding of Old China traditions, and less and less interest in their village histories. Father used to say we lacked Taoist ritual, Taoist manners. We were, he said, "*mo li*."

This was true. Chinatown's younger brains, like everyone 11 else's of whatever race, were being colonized by "white bread" U.S. family television programs. We began to feel Chinese home life was inferior. We co-operated with English-language magazines that showed us how to act and what to buy. Seductive Hollywood movies made some of us secretly weep that we did not have movie-star faces. American music made Chinese music sound like noise.

By the 1970s and eighties, many of us had consciously or 12 unconsciously distanced ourselves from our Chinatown histories. We became bananas.

Finally, for me, in my 40s or 50s, with the death first of my 13 mother, then my father, I realized I did not belong anywhere unless I could understand the past. I needed to find the foundation of my Chinese-ness. I needed roots.

I spent my college holidays researching the past. I read 14 Chinatown oral histories, located documents, searched out early articles. Those early citizens came back to life for me. Their long toil and blood sacrifices, the proud record of their patient, legal challenges, gave us all our present rights as citizens. Canadian and American Chinatowns set aside their family tongue differences and encouraged each other to fight injustice. There were no borders. "After all," they affirmed, "*Daaih ga tohng yahn … We are all Chinese!*"

In my book, *The Jade Peony*, I tried to recreate this past, to 15 explore the beginnings of the conflicts trapped within myself, the struggle between being Chinese and being North American. I discovered a truth: these "between world" struggles are universal.

In every human being, there is "the Other"—something that 16 makes each of us feel how different we are to everyone else, even to family members. Yet, ironically, we are all the same, wanting the same security and happiness. I know this now.

I think the early Chinese pioneers actually started "going 17 bananas" from the moment they first settled upon the West Coast. They had no choice. They adapted. They initiated assimilation. If they had not, they and their family would have starved to death. I might even suggest that all surviving Chinatown citizens eventually became bananas. Only some, of course, were more ripe than others.

That's why I'm proudly a banana: I accept the paradox of   18
being both Chinese and not Chinese.

Now at last, whenever I look in the mirror or hear ghost   19
voices shouting, "You still Chinese!", I smile.

I know another truth: In immigrant North America, we are all   20
Chinese.

UNDERSTANDING DETAILS

1. What does the term "banana" mean? How is this different from
   "apple" and "Oreo cookie"?
2. Describe the experience of Choy's parents coming to Canada.
3. What motivated Choy to research the past? What type of
   research did he do? Did he find what he was looking for?

ANALYZING MEANING

1. Choy differentiates between racist terms and nicknames. What
   is the difference between them? Can a term be both a racist
   term and a nickname? Can it move from being one to the other?
2. In the '50s and '60s, why did Chinatown parents encourage
   their children to assimilate?
3. Explain Choy's discovery of the "… truth [that] these 'between
   world' struggles are universal" (paragraph 15).

DISCOVERING RHETORICAL STRATEGIES

1. Choy centres his essay around the use of the term "banana."
   How does he extend this metaphor in his essay?
2. What is Choy's thesis? Where is it found?
3. Who is Choy's intended audience?

MAKING CONNECTIONS

1. Choy defines the term "banana" as an affectionate nickname
   which he groups with the metaphors "apple" and "Oreo
   cookie." Imagine Choy is having a conversation with Cecil
   Foster ("Why Blacks Get Mad") about the use of these terms. On
   what points would the two agree? Are there areas where they
   would disagree?
2. Choy's essay is one of self-definition. In what ways is "I'm a
   Banana and Proud of It" similar to Drew Hayden Taylor's
   "Pretty Like a White Boy"? What differences do you find in the

strategies these two writers use to define themselves?

3. In "I'm a Banana and Proud of It," Wayson Choy talks about the importance of understanding the past. Steven Heighton ("Elegy in Stone") also recognizes value in understanding the past. Why is an understanding of our history important to our sense of belonging in the present? How does the larger context enrich our lives in the present?

IDEAS FOR DISCUSSION/WRITING

Preparing to Write

Wayson Choy talks in this essay about what the Chinatown parents wanted for their children. Write freely about parental aspirations or dreams for their children. What dreams did your parents have for you as you were growing up? Were these messages conveyed explicitly or implicitly? Did you share these aspirations? What hopes would you have for your children if you were a parent?

Choosing a Topic

1. Think of a nickname you have now or have had in the past, and write an essay in which you explain how this nickname defines you.

2. Wayson Choy, in writing *The Jade Peony* as an exploration of his roots, discovered the combination in every human being of "the Other" and the desire for the same security and happiness. Using your own personal history, write a narrative essay showing this combination of elements in a person or people you know.

3. In this essay, Wayson Choy introduces a food metaphor that defines many North Americans. Write an essay in which you use an animal metaphor to describe the various members of your family. Make sure you keep your metaphor consistent.

WEB SITES

www.amazon.com/exec/obidos/ASIN/0312155565/ ref=sim_books/t/002-5741453-0968065
The Amazon.com listing of Wayson Choy's novel *The Jade Peony* includes several reviews.

www.ccnc.ca/
The Chinese Canadian National Council.

Michael Clugston

■ ■ ■

Twice Struck

A Canadian journalist, Michael Clugston has had articles published in a variety of magazines, including *Equinox*, from which this essay was taken; *Reader's Digest*; *The Globe and Mail*'s *Destinations*; and *Canadian Geographic*, where he was an editor until 1996. Clugston is now living and working in Tokyo, Japan.

Preparing to Read

In *Equinox*, where "Twice Struck" originally appeared in 1991, Clugston's essay is accompanied by a picture of a spectacular bolt of lightning. Before you begin reading, think about lightning and thunderstorms. How do you feel about thunderstorms? Have you ever been frightened by a crack of thunder or a flash of lightning? What kind of emotions do thunder and lightning typically evoke in people? In animals? What associations do you have with thunder and lightning in movies you have seen or stories you have read? What gives Clugston's subject its lasting appeal and interest?

■_____■

Tennyson called it a "flying game." Benjamin Franklin termed 1 it a "sudden and terrible mischief." In Roman mythology, the god Jupiter used spiky thunderbolts as letters to the editor when he chose to show displeasure with the poor mortals below.

By whatever name, lightning is a spectacular natural event. 2 Captured in photographs, its grandeur and beauty are safely petrified in static portraits of primal energy. In reality, at 24,000 to 28,000 degrees C, it is four times hotter than the surface of the sun. It can vaporize steel, plough up fields, shatter giant trees and scatter livid incendiary sparks over vast forests. Each day, it kills 20 people.

Its horror is the haphazard nature of its violence, a random 3 Russian-roulette threat beyond control. If you are caught out in the open during a thunderstorm, it can look like oncoming headlights of celestial chaos. Lightning can terrify you, charm you with its beauty, fry you, or, prosaically enough, bring on asthma, drowsiness and other discomforting side effects from the ionized air it creates.

Ask a scientist what lightning is, and he or she will most 4 likely remind you of the electric kiss you get indoors on a dry winter day when you walk across a carpet and then touch an electric switch or another person. That nasty little jolt is the micro version of the heaven-sent tracery that can look as delicate as needlepoint while travelling between 100,000 and 300,000 kilometres per second.

But the scientist will also tell you that there is still a 5 considerable mystery to lightning. "In some areas, we really don't know what's happening up there," says Andrew Podgorski, a senior research officer at the National Research Council of Canada in Ottawa and head of the Electromagnet Interference/ Electromagnetic Compatibility Programme. "It's very difficult to predict where the lightning is being initiated and how the lightning channels are defined. Nor do we know how the lightning bolt itself can grow so quickly to the huge channel that we perceive."

What is known, though, is fascinating enough. If nature 6 abhors a vacuum, electricity abhors imbalance. Like water, which seeks its own level, electricity tries to even out the imbalance on charges between two neighbouring bodies by leaping the gap with a bright spark. However, when we see that spark in the form of lightning, what we see is not what we think we see.

The colossal structures we know as thunderheads are giant 7 electrical generators. They occur when weather conditions create rapid updrafts of warm, moist air that travel high in the atmosphere. Furious updrafts and downfalls of water and ice particles create regions of positive and negative charge. Lightning can travel between the opposite charges within the clouds or between the cloud and ground. The negative base of a thunderhead creates a positive charge in the ground immediately below and sets the scene for the gaudy short circuits overhead.

Majestic bolts such as those pictured here were probably 8 preceded by a weak electrical spark that descended from the negatively charged clouds to the positively charged earth. The weak spark is called the "stepped leader," named for its rootlike branchings. Near the earth, the spindly leader intersects with a shorter leader rising from the ground to meet it. This creates a conductive pathway of ionized air—a bridge of ions from heaven to earth. The stage is then set for the real business to begin.

A few millionths of a second later, a bright channel of light 9
and heat—a lightning bolt—leaps back up the bridge, but the
human eye is not fast enough to distinguish the leader from the
bolt. If lightning appears to be branched downward, it is because
the upward-moving charge flows through all the ionized side
routes established by the leader. It is the return stroke that causes
most of the thunder we hear.

Last year, Podgorski conducted lightning experiments inside 10
the top of Toronto's CN Tower during a thunderstorm. "I thought
about Ben Franklin while I was up there," he says. "But the tip is
protected by metal, so I didn't even realize lightning was striking
the tower while I was inside."

Franklin, the Philadelphian Renaissance man, flew his famous 11
kite in 1752 to prove that clouds were electrified, an experiment
which led him to the invention of lightning rods. By 1782, the
only building in Philadelphia that did not sport one of Franklin's
rods was the French Embassy. One official died when it was
struck by lightning that year.

Ever since Franklin's experiment and well into the 1800s, 12
lightning, and protection against it, has caught the public
imagination. For a few years, people could be seen carrying
lightning-rod umbrellas, which lofted a sharp metal rod on top
and trailed ground wires behind them.

While we may think of such a device as a silly momentary 13
fad, it was a big step forward in understanding from the Middle
Ages in Europe. Then people believed that ringing church bells
in thunderstorms kept the lightning from striking nearby
buildings. In this way, the call of duty sent hundreds of bell
ringers on sudden ascensions to heaven before the curious custom
belatedly became unpopular. The words *fulgura frango* ("I break
the lightning") can still be found on some medieval bells.

We still cannot "break" lightning, but we can study it. 14
Experiments have shown that lightning saturates the air with
positive ions—atoms that have lost one or more electrons. The
heat of lightning produces ions by searing electrons away from
the atoms in its path. For some people, these can bring on a host
of unpleasant effects. "Weather-sensitive people have reported
insomnia, irritability, tension, chills, sweats, dizziness and loss of
balance, migraines and other types of headaches, visual
disturbances, nausea and vomiting," writes bacteriologist Julius
Fast in his book of reactions.

But whatever the folklore or science of the day, our 15
perception of lightning remains rooted in the universal reactions
of wonder and respect.

UNDERSTANDING DETAILS

1. In your own words, define lightning.
2. List the various effects that lightning can have.
3. Explain the words "fulgura frango" that can be found on some
   medieval church bells.

ANALYZING MEANING

1. In "Twice Struck," Clugston cites scientific knowledge about
   lightning as well as folklore on this subject. What is the relationship between these two realms of understanding our world?
2. Explain why Clugston says that wonder and respect are universal reactions to lightning.
3. In the Middle Ages people rang church bells to ward off lightning; in the 1800s they carried lightning rod umbrellas. What do
   people in the 1990s do to protect themselves against the "flying
   flames"? Are these practices based on science or folklore?

DISCOVERING RHETORICAL STRATEGIES

1. Is Clugston's definition objective or subjective? Explain your
   answer.
2. In his essay, Clugston cites Benjamin Franklin, Andrew
   Podgorski, Julius Fast and Alfred Lord Tennyson. Who is each
   of these people and why is each mentioned in "Twice Struck"?
3. Reread paragraph 3 of "Twice Struck." Identify all the examples of figurative language that you can find in this paragraph.
   What effect do these uses of language have on you as a reader?

MAKING CONNECTIONS

1. Michael Clugston cites many people in his essay as do Carol
   Krenz ("Food for Sloth") and Sally Armstrong ("P4W"). Explain
   why these authors have incorporated quotations from others
   into each of their essays.
2. In "Twice Struck" Clugston describes a particular natural phenomenon and our reactions to it. How do the responses to
   lightning that Clugston details compare to the reactions to other

natural processes such as that described by Lesley Choyce ("Thin Edge of the Wedge")?

3. Michael Clugston says that wonder and respect are universal reactions to lightning. How do you think Tomson Highway ("What a Certain Visionary Once Said") would respond to this assertion? Explain your answer.

IDEAS FOR DISCUSSION/WRITING

Preparing to Write

Write freely about the weather. In what ways does the weather affect your life? How are our lives generally governed by weather? What is the most severe storm you have ever experienced? How did you react to it? Why do we consider weather predictions important? What need sustains whole television stations devoted to weather?

Choosing a Topic

1. While science has come a long way in explaining lightning, there are still some things we don't know. Traditionally, myths and legends have been invented to explain events that we don't entirely understand. Write a myth to explain a particular weather phenomenon.

2. Write an essay in which you explain how the weather that you experience in your region of the country has contributed to defining you as a person.

3. Weather is often said to influence people's behaviour in fairly significant ways. This might be an ongoing condition like Seasonal Affective Disorder (SAD) or it might be a more specific behaviour related to a dramatic change in temperature or humidity or a phase of the moon. Write an essay in which you explore the connection between people's behaviour and the weather.

WEB SITES

www.horsburgh.com/h_bolt.html
or

cirrus.sprl.umich.edu/wxnet/media.html
Impressive photographs of lightning.

sln.fi.edu/franklin/rotten.html
The world of Benjamin Franklin.

Neil Bissoondath
1955–

■■■

Pieces of Sky

Neil Bissoondath is the Trinidadian-born Canadian author of three novels and two collections of short stories. Known internationally for his fiction, Bissoondath has probably become best known in Canada for his contentious views on multiculturalism as put forth in his first nonfiction book, *Selling Illusions: The Cult of Multiculturalism in Canada.* "Pieces of Sky," which appeared in *The Globe and Mail*'s "National Values" column in May 1995, is drawn from *If You Love This Country: 15 Voices for a Unified Canada,* an anthology of essays by Canadians concerned about the possible outcome of the then-approaching October 1995 referendum and published by Penguin Books Canada Limited.

Preparing to Read

In this selection, Bissoondath discusses the values that he sees as uniquely Canadian and why values are important. Before reading Bissoondath's essay, think about Canadian values. What makes Canadians distinctive as a people? What distinguishes Canadians from Americans? From people of other nationalities? How is the Canadian culture a unique one? Which values are national and which are regional?

■ ■

*W*e are what the geography of the country has made us ... That is 1 why we are, in a sense, nearer to English Canadians than to Frenchmen. After a month in Paris, which I loved with all my heart, I just the same got very lonesome for our trees, and the sight of the Laurentides and the horizon of Quebec. I felt lonesome for the Canadian sky so vast and so grandiose. In Paris, you have pieces of sky.*

> —Rodger Lemelin, Quebec novelist,
> from a letter written in English, 1950.

It has become popular in recent years for many, in both 2 public and private life, to insist that there are no such things as Canadian values and, by extension, a Canadian culture. This is a peculiar notion in a country that has existed as a political entity for almost 130 years and as a historical one for even longer. It is a way of saying that Canada and Canadians have no reality.

But the nation, fractious and uneasy as it frequently is, does   3
exist, and so do its values. They may not always be readily
identifiable, they may not always be easily defined, but their
effect can be sniffed in the very air that surrounds us. Canada
may physically resemble the United States in many ways, but
when I cross the border I know immediately that I am in a foreign
land. The psychic electricity is different, alien. It tells me that I am
no longer at home.

Principles, values and beliefs—words used by Pierre Elliott   4
Trudeau in a statement of affirmative values attached to the
Charter of Rights and Freedoms—are the playthings of moral
philosophers, the rallying cries of religious fundamentalists, the
linguistic torches of politicians seeking a tone of higher order.
They have also become concepts of battle plans in a Canada
profoundly shaped by the ideas of Mr. Trudeau.

They say there was a time when you could tell the Canadian   5
easily; he was the one who would stuff empty candy wrappers
and gnawed apple cores into his pockets until he came to a
garbage can. Then he'd stand there as if in holy communion,
muttering phrases that ended with "… eh?" and making offerings
at the altar of civic pride.

We have always defined our pride differently. But this   6
particular trait was set on the path to a slow death by the advent
some years ago of the word "biodegradable." Silently assuring
ourselves that nature would take care of it, Canadians began
acquiring new abilities; surreptitious flicks of the wrist and—
"Nice lookin' clouds up there, eh?"—eyes that wandered
resolutely away from the flight paths of balled paper or empty
cigarette packs. Today, the Canadian litters with the best of them.
Specificity, it must be said, may be dwindling.

And yet, they say, the Canadian continues to reveal himself   7
most readily in other ways, with an overheated politeness. For
instance: Tread accidentally on a Canadian's foot, and he falls all
over himself apologizing to you. Many view this as a silly trait. I
do not. In some parts of the world, you'd be lucky to get away
with just a scowl. In others, you'd be lucky to get away with your
life. The Canadian's urge to apologize for having got his shoe
under yours strikes me as endearing and eminently civilized.

We cannot trust stereotype, of course. The best it can offer is   8
general direction. But this part is, I hope, true. For it suggests the
principles, values and beliefs that define the character of a people.
So just what, at this time in our history, are Canadians' values?

This is a question often posed by those who would deny 9
their existence. Instead, the very asking of the question tends to
be an attempt to belittle the notion itself, as if the identification
of a value as Canadian is somehow meant to deny it to others. But
of course this is not so.

I suspect we glimpsed one such value in the thousands of 10
get-well messages Bloc Québécois Leader Lucien Bouchard
received from Canadians outside Quebec during his life-
threatening illness: To abhor the man's political dream is not
necessarily to abhor the man. Values such as this—the recognition
that the human being is worth more than political principle—
lend texture to a society. Such an attitude is not exclusive to
Canada, but I would suggest that its being shared by others does
not make it less Canadian.

A blazing campfire late at night, beneath a sky luminous 11
with more stars than the mind could comfortably conjure:
nature's way, you think, of dwarfing the human imagination,
not into insignificance but into a proper perspective of its place
in the larger world. Like the prairie sky, perhaps, or the reach
of the Rockies, which have a way of dampening arrogance, of
imposing a vital modesty.

Way up there, in a sky so large it defies the mind to go 12
beyond cliché, a single tiny light cuts a rapid course through the
glittering darkness, the satellite's path somehow deepening the
silence that is already as profound, as all-encompassing, as that
of the world before time. You feel yourself alone despite the
companionship of neighbouring campfires lit by people—
anglophone, francophone—who offer little more than a smile, a
nod, a wave: No more is required, no more expected. The
communality of purpose is sufficient. The experience we are
sharing goes beyond words or invitations or the usual
requirements of social convention.

It was the writer Margaret Visser who pointed out to me that 13
camping—this safest of engagements with the natural world—can
justly be viewed as a Canadian ritual. And ritual, let us
remember, is the physical representation of values. To sit there,
then, between campfire and tent, in the utter safety of a national
park, is to feel the self part of a larger, miraculous whole. It is
to immerse yourself, however fleetingly, in the power of a social
value rarely seen as such to understand the modesty for which
Canadians are justly known.

It was Prime Minister John Diefenbaker who, in protest   14
against apartheid at the 1961 Commonwealth Conference,
arranged the expulsion of South Africa from the organization.
And it was Prime Minister Brian Mulroney, who many years
later at another Commonwealth Conference, earned the enmity
of British Prime Minister Margaret Thatcher by leading the battle
for the imposition of severe trade sanctions against the
government in Pretoria.

The battle against racism by Canadians may be imperfect—   15
here at home, for instance, discomfort can be found in attitudes
toward blacks and Asians, and in conditions on numerous Native
reserves—but it has been many decades since the principle of
racial segregation has found any public favour in this country.
Individuals continue to struggle with their own racism, trying
to bridge the chasm between the heart—which has been taught
racial distrust—and the mind, which has recognized the evil of it.

And yet …   16

Even as apartheid slides steadily into the history books, even   17
as South Africa under the leadership of Nelson Mandela struggles
to achieve a society free of racial segregation, we here in Canada
are seeing it take root—in the name of equality. In Ontario,
demands are made for the public funding of segregated schools.
In British Columbia, a Chinese parents' association is set up. The
Writers' Union of Canada funds a racially segregated conference,
and governments across the country implement hiring policies
based partly on race.

A queer thing is happening, then, to this value so long   18
cherished. It is not so much slipping away as metamorphosing
into an ugly version of itself, acquiring the justification that the
founders of apartheid once used for that abhorrent system: that,
somehow, separate could also mean equal.

The difference between innocence and naiveté is not always   19
clear, yet the former can be seen as a positive trait—as in the
innocence of children—while the second is reviled as being a
small step away from stupidity. Innocence implies having a
trusting nature, while naiveté implies simplemindedness.

And so I opt for the word "innocence" to describe what seems   20
to constitute an enduring and laudable Canadian quality. Indeed, so
ingrained is it that I would go so far as to call it a Canadian value.

Consider, for instance, the public outrage that met the   21
broadcast of videotapes from the Canadian Airborne Regiment.
What those tapes offered were the antics of brutes who happened

to be Canadian. To anyone who has seen Gwynne Dyer's superb documentary series, *War*, the behaviour on our television screens was distressing but hardly surprising.

We found it distressing because this is not how we see 22 ourselves. We believe in our own clean-cut, good-guy image. And even if we know that the military does not aim to create Boy Scouts, even if we know that the ultimate goal of military training is to produce efficient killers, we still want them to reflect our image of ourselves: We want our killers clean-cut, polite and well-behaved.

It was suggested to me at the time that the outrage merely 23 revealed the profound naiveté of the Canadian public. On reflection, I agreed, but suggested the word "innocence" instead. I did not see this as condemnation. Instead, I thought it a becoming innocence, heartening proof of how seriously we take our notions of goodness. I saw it as a confirmation of idealism.

Five or six years ago, my companion and I were on vacation 24 in France. Wandering around Nice one morning, we spotted on a deserted street two 500-franc notes (about $250 in all), one lying on the sidewalk, the other under a parked car. With visions of some frantic pensioner in our heads, we entered a nearby bank in the hopes that a customer may have reported their loss.

We were met with utter incredulity. As we stood there, the 25 bills held uneasily in our hands, they asked where we were from, and on being told, mumbled, "*Ahh, les gentils Canadiens ...*" in a way that you knew stories would be told of the innocent Canadians, that we would be objects of mirth. And yet, for once, condescension did not rankle. After all, in the larger scheme of things it was not a bad image to leave behind.

We took our leave, feeling a little silly, a little guilty—and, as 26 far as I was concerned, glad to be innocent Canadians in a world that saw naiveté in simple honesty.

Innocence, naiveté: Call it what you will. But to give up on it 27 is to surrender our essential idealism. We seem at times to be in danger of doing just that. The signs are there: in those, for instance, who would break Quebec away from Canada as well as in those who, through weariness or short-sightedness, would allow Quebec to break away; in a willingness to sacrifice the unfortunate of our society in the name of fiscal responsibility; and in marvelling at the multiplicity of languages on European cereal boxes while raging at the other official language printed on our own.

Principles, values and beliefs are big words easily tossed 28
around. Politicians and philosophers believe they give them
weight, but they rarely ever do; they merely make evident the
weight with which they have already been invested by the public.
And it is our little actions that give them weight, lend them
meaning; that give us as a people, anglophone and francophone,
a specific personality that is not always easily perceived but that
is there nonetheless, shaping us and being shaped by us in an
act of mutual and ongoing creation.

Canada has always been an act of faith—and acts of faith 29
depend on idealism. To give up on our innocence is to give up
on our idealism, is to give up on ourselves. It is to stigmatize our
eyes, so that what we see is not the whole sky but just pieces of it.

UNDERSTANDING DETAILS

1. In the stereotype cited by Bissoondath, what traits would identify a Canadian in the past? Are these still characteristic behaviours today?
2. Explain the difference between innocence and naiveté. Which
   does Bissoondath see as a Canadian quality?
3. What, at this time in our history, are Canadian values, according to Bissoondath? Do you agree with him? Are there other
   values that you would add to the list that are definitively
   Canadian?

ANALYZING MEANING

1. Bissoondath's view of employment equity and multiculturalism programs has been the subject of much debate. How does
   he regard such programs? Why?
2. Explain the importance of principles, values, and beliefs in
   defining a nation.
3. Bissoondath says that the writer Margaret Visser pointed out to
   him that camping is a Canadian ritual. Why has camping become so important to Canadians? What values are reflected in
   this pastime?

DISCOVERING RHETORICAL STRATEGIES

1. Is Bissoondath's definition primarily an objective or a subjective
   one? Explain your conclusion.

2. Bissoondath refers to several politicians in the course of this essay. Why does he mention all of these people? How do these references help Bissoondath accomplish his purpose?
3. In this essay Bissoondath uses a variety of rhetorical modes to help him define distinctive Canadian values. Explain what other rhetorical modes Bissoondath has employed in "Pieces of Sky."

MAKING CONNECTIONS

1. Imagine a conversation among Diane Francis ("Once a Kinder and Gentler Nation"), Will Ferguson ("The Sudbury Syndrome"), and Neil Bissoondath about characteristic Canadian values. On which points would these three writers agree? On which would they disagree? With whom do you identify most closely on this subject?
2. Cecil Foster ("Why Blacks Get Mad") and Neil Bissoondath both write about racism in Canada. Compare and contrast their views on this topic.
3. Wayson Choy ("I'm a Banana and Proud of It") identifies himself as a "banana," the child of Chinese parents, who has assimilated well into North American life. How would Bissoondath react to this characterization and to this metaphor representing one who is "yellow on the outside and white inside"?

IDEAS FOR DISCUSSION/WRITING

Preparing to Write

Bissoondath says that rituals are the physical representation of values. What rituals are important in your life? How were those rituals established? How are they maintained? Who else partakes in the rituals of your life? What underlying values are represented by those rituals? List the five most important values in your life, or principles that guide you in your life. Where did those values come from? Have they changed over time?

Choosing a Topic

1. Write an essay for a newspaper or magazine outside Canada in which you define what a Canadian is. Make sure that you provide specific examples to make your definition clear to your readers.

2. Choose a group to which you belong and write a definition of that group, based on the common values, beliefs, or rituals that unite its members and distinguish them from other similar groups. The group might be your family; a sports club or team to which you belong; members of the congregation of your synagogue / church / temple / mosque, etc.; a group of volunteers for some cause, event, or organization; a gang; or a group of students with whom you particularly identify.

3. Canadians have an easier time travelling internationally than people with passports from many other countries. Write an essay explaining why travelling Canadians generally get a warm reception from most other countries.

WEB SITES

 www.theglobeandmail.ca
This excerpt from Bissoondath's book originally appeared in *The Globe and Mail*.

 www.citytv.com/theoriginals/seriesiitext.html#neil
A bit of biographical information about Bissoondath.

 www.chaptersglobe.com
Use the Search function on the ChaptersGLOBE Web site to look for all the books written by Bissoondath.

CHAPTER 8

CAUSE / EFFECT

■ ■ ■

Tracing Reasons and Results

Wanting to know why things happen is one of our earliest, most basic instincts: Why can't I go out, Mommy? Why are you laughing? Why won't the dog stop barking? Why can't I swim faster than my big brother? These questions, and many more like them, reflect the innately inquisitive nature that dwells within each of us. Closely related to this desire to understand *why* is our interest in *what* will happen in the future as a result of some particular action: What will I feel like tomorrow if I stay up late tonight? How will I perform in the track meet Saturday if I practise all week? What will be the result if I mix together these two potent chemicals? What will happen if I turn in my next English assignment two days early?

A daily awareness of this intimate relationship between causes and effects allows us to begin to understand the complex and interrelated series of events that make up our lives and the lives of others. For example, trying to understand the various causes of the conflict in the Persian Gulf teaches us about international relations; knowing our biological reactions to certain foods helps us make decisions about what to eat; understanding the interrelated reasons for the outbreak of World War II offers us insight into historical trends and human nature; knowing the effects of sunshine on various parts of our bodies helps us make decisions about how much ultraviolet exposure we can tolerate and what suntan lotion to use; and understanding the causes of Canada's most recent recession will help us respond appropriately to the next economic crisis we encounter. More than anything else, tracing causes and effects teaches us how to think clearly and react intelligently to our multifaceted environment.

In college, you will often be asked to use this natural interest in causes and effects to analyze particular situations and to discern general principles. For example, you might be asked some of the following questions on essay exams in different courses:

Anthropology: Why did the Mayan culture disintegrate?

Psychology: Why do humans respond to fear in different ways?

Biology: How do lab rats react to caffeine?

History: What were the positive effects of building the Trans-Canada Highway?

Business: Why did so many computer manufacturing companies go bankrupt in the early 1980s?

Your ability to answer such questions will depend in large part on your skill at writing a cause/effect essay.

Defining Cause/Effect

Cause/effect analysis requires the ability to look for connections between different elements and to analyze the reasons for those connections. As the name implies, this rhetorical mode has two separate components: cause and effect. A particular essay might concentrate on cause (Why do you live in a dorm?), on effect (What are the resulting advantages and disadvantages of living in a dorm?), or on some combination of the two. In working with causes, we are searching for any circumstances from the past that may have caused a single event; in looking for effects, we seek occurrences that took place after a particular event and resulted from that event. Like process analysis, cause/effect makes use of our intellectual ability to analyze. Process analysis addresses *how* something happens, whereas causal analysis discusses *why* it happened and *what* the result was. A process analysis paper, for example, might explain how to advertise more effectively to increase sales, whereas a cause/effect study would discover that three specific elements contributed to an increase in sales: effective advertising, personal service, and selective discounts. The study of causes and effects, therefore, provides many different and helpful ways for humans to make sense of and clarify their views of the world.

Looking for causes and effects requires an advanced form of thinking. It is more complex than most rhetorical strategies we have studied because it can exist on a number of different and progressively more difficult levels. The most accurate and effective causal analysis accrues from digging for the real or ultimate causes or effects, as opposed to those that are merely superficial or immediate. Actress Angela Lansbury would have been out of work on an episode of the television show *Murder, She Wrote*, for example, if her character had stopped her investigation at the immediate cause of death (slipping in the bathtub) rather than searching diligently for the real cause (an overdose of cocaine administered by an angry companion, which resulted in the slip in the tub). Similarly, voters would be easy to manipulate if they considered only the immediate effects of a tax increase (a slightly higher tax bill) rather than the ultimate benefits that would result (the many years of improved education that our children would receive because of the specialized programs created by such an increase). Only the discovery of the actual reasons for an event or an idea will lead to the logical and accurate analysis of causes and effects important to a basic understanding of various aspects of our lives.

Faulty reasoning assigns causes to a sequence of actions without adequate justification. One such logical fallacy is called *post hoc, ergo propter hoc* (after this, therefore because of this): The fact that someone lost a job after walking under a ladder does not mean that the two events are causally related; by the same token, if we get up every morning at 5:30 a.m., just before the sun rises, we cannot therefore conclude that the sun rises *because* we get up (no matter how self-centred we are!). Faulty reasoning also occurs when we oversimplify a particular situation. Most events are connected to a multitude of causes and effects. Sometimes one effect has many causes: A student may fail a history exam because she's been working two part-time jobs, she was sick, she didn't study hard enough, and she found the instructor very boring. One cause may also have many effects. If a house burns down, the people who lived in it will be out of a home. If we look at such a tragic scene more closely, however, we may also note that the fire traumatized a child who lived there, helped the family learn what good friends they had, encouraged the family to double their future fire insurance, and provided the happy stimulus that they needed to make a long-dreamed-of move to another city. One event has thus resulted in many interrelated effects. Building an argument on insecure foundations or oversimplifying the causes or effects connected with an event will seriously hinder the construction of a rational essay. No matter what the nature of the cause/effect analysis, it must always be based on clear observation, accurate facts, and rigorous logic.

In the following paragraph, a student writer analyzes some of the causes and effects connected with the controversial issue of euthanasia. Notice how he makes connections and then analyzes those connections as he consistently explores the immediate and ultimate effects of being able to stretch life beyond its normal limits through new medical technology:

> Along with the many recent startling advances in medical technology have come a number of complex moral, ethical, and spiritual questions that beg to be answered. We now have the ability to prolong the life of the human body for a very long time. But what rights do patients and their families have to curtail cruel and unusual medical treatment that stretches life beyond its normal limits? This dilemma has produced a ripple effect in society. Is the extension of life an unquestionable goal in itself, regardless of the quality of that life? Modern scientific technology has forced doctors to reevaluate the exact meaning and purpose of their profession. For example, many medical schools and undergraduate university programs now routinely offer classes on medical ethics—an esoteric and infrequently taught subject only a few years ago. Doctors and scholars alike are realizing that medical personnel alone cannot be expected to decide on the exact parameters of life. In like manner, the judicial process must now evaluate the legal complexities of mercy killings and the rights of patients to die with dignity and without unnecessary medical intervention. The insurance business, too, wrestles with the catastrophic effects of new technology on the costs of today's hospital care. In short, medical progress entails more than microscopes, chemicals, and high-tech instruments. If we are to develop as a thoughtful, just, and merciful society, we must consider not only the physical well-being of our nation's patients, but their emotional, spiritual, and financial status as well.

Thinking Critically by Using Cause/Effect

Thinking about causes and effects is one of the most advanced mental activities that we perform. It involves complex operations that we must think through carefully, making sure all connections are reasonable and accurate. Unlike other rhetorical patterns, cause/effect thinking requires us to see specific relationships between two or more items. To practise this strategy, we need to look for items or events that are causally related—that is, one that has caused the other. Then, we can focus on either the causes (the initial stimulus), the effects (the results), or a combination of the two.

Searching out causes and effects requires a great deal of digging that is not necessary for most of the other modes. Cause/effect necessitates the ultimate in investigative work. The mental exertion associated with this thinking strategy is sometimes exhausting, but it is always worth going through when you discover relationships that you never saw before or you uncover links in your reasoning that were previously unknown or obscure to you.

If you've ever had the secret desire to be a private eye or an investigator of any sort, practising cause/effect reasoning can be lots of fun. It forces you to see relationships among multiple items and then to make sense of those connections. Completing exercises in this skill will help you perfect the logistics of cause/effect thinking before you mix and match it with several other thinking strategies.

1. Choose a major problem you see in our society, and list what you think are the main causes of this problem on one side of a piece of paper and the effects on the other side. Compare the two lists to see how they differ. Then, compare and contrast your lists with those written by other students.

2. What "caused" you to become a student? What influences led you to this choice at this point in your life? How has being a student affected your life? List several overall effects.

3. List the effects of one of the following: getting a speeding ticket, winning an Olympic medal, graduating from college, or watching TV till the early hours of the morning.

Reading and Writing Cause/Effect Essays

Causal analysis is usually employed for one of three main purposes: (1) to prove a specific point (such as the necessity of stricter gun control), in which case the writer generally deals totally with facts and with conclusions drawn from those facts; (2) to argue against a widely accepted belief (for example, the assertion that cocaine is addictive), in which case the writer relies principally on facts, with perhaps some pertinent opinions; or (3) to speculate on a theory (for instance, why the crime rate is higher in most major cities than it is in rural areas), in which case the writer probably presents hypotheses and opinions along with facts. This section will explore these purposes in cause/effect essays from the standpoint of both reading and writing.

How to Read a Cause/Effect Essay

Preparing to Read. As you set out to read the essays in this chapter, begin by focusing your attention on the title and the synopsis of the essay you are about to read and by scanning the essay itself: What do you think Stephen King is going to talk about in "Why We Crave Horror Movies"? What does the synopsis in the Rhetorical Table of Contents tell you about Laura Robinson's "Starving for the Gold"?

Also, at this stage in the reading process, you should try to learn as much as you can about the author of the essay and the reasons he or she wrote it. Ask yourself questions like the following: What is King's intention in "Why We Crave Horror Movies"? Who is John Gray's intended audience in "You're Thinking of Getting a *What*?" And what is Trina McQueen's point of view in "Why We Crave Hot Stuff"?

Finally, before you begin to read, answer the prereading questions for each essay and then consider the proposed essay topic from a variety of perspectives: For example, concerning Gray's topic, do you have any tattoos? Do you read tabloid news stories? Have you participated in competitive sports? Was it a positive or negative experience? What do you want to know about digital manipulation of photographs from Tony Leighton?

Reading. As you read each essay in this chapter for the first time, record your spontaneous reactions to it, drawing as often as possible on the preliminary material you already know: What do you think of horror movies (King)? Why did Robinson choose the title she did? What is McQueen suggesting about "hot stuff" stories? Whenever you can, try to create a context for your reading: What is the tone of Gray's discussion about tattooing? How does this tone help him communicate with his audience? What do you think Robinson's purpose is in her essay on athletes and eating disorders? How clearly does she get this purpose across to you?

Also, during this reading, note the essay's thesis and check to see if the writer thoroughly explores all possibilities before settling on the primary causes and/or effects of a particular situation; in addition, determine whether the writer clearly states the assertions that naturally evolve from a discussion of the topic. Finally, read the questions following each essay to get a sense of the main issues and strategies in the selection.

Rereading. When you reread these essays, you should focus mainly on the writer's craft. Notice how the authors narrow and focus their material, how they make clear and logical connections between ideas in their essays, how they support their conclusions with concrete examples, how they use other rhetorical modes to accomplish their cause/effect analysis, and how they employ logical transitions to move us smoothly from one point to another. Most important, however, ask yourself if the writer actually discusses the real causes and/or effects of a particular circumstance: What does King say are the primary reasons people crave horror movies? What does McQueen consider the main cause of the appeal of "hot stuff" stories? How does the ability to manipulate photographs with ease change the way we view the world, according to Leighton? What are the primary causes and effects of wearing a tattoo?

For a thorough outline of the reading process, consult the checklist on pages 15–16 of the Introduction.

How to Write a Cause/Effect Essay

Preparing to Write. Beginning a cause/effect essay requires—as does any other essay—exploring and limiting your subject, specifying a purpose, and identifying an audience. The Preparing to Write questions before the essay assignments, coupled with the prewriting techniques outlined in the Introduction, encourage you to consider specific issues related to your reading. The assignments themselves will then help you limit your topic and determine a particular purpose and audience for your message. For cause/effect essays, determining a purpose is even more important than usual, because your readers can get hopelessly lost unless your analysis is clearly focused.

Writing. For all its conceptual complexity, a cause/effect essay can be organized quite simply. The introduction generally presents the subject(s) and states the purpose of the analysis in a clear thesis. The body of the paper then explores all relevant causes and/or effects, typically progressing either from least to most influential or from most to least influential. Finally, the concluding section summarizes the various cause-and-effect relationships established in the body of the paper and clearly states the conclusions that can be drawn from those relationships.

The following additional guidelines should assist you in producing an effective cause/effect essay in all academic disciplines:

1. Narrow and focus your material as much as possible.

2. Consider all possibilities before assigning real or ultimate causes or effects.

3. Show connections between ideas by using transitions and key words—such as *because, reasons, results, effects,* and *consequences*— to guide your readers smoothly through your essay.

4. Support all inferences with concrete evidence.

5. Be as objective as possible in your analysis so that you don't distort logic with personal biases.

6. Understand your audience's opinions and convictions, so that you know what to emphasize in your essay.

7. Qualify your assertions to avoid overstatement and oversimplification.

These suggestions apply to both cause/effect essay assignments and exam questions.

Rewriting. As you revise your cause/effect essays, ask yourself the following important questions:

1. Is your thesis stated clearly at the outset of your paper?

2. Does it include your subject and your purpose?

3. Do you accomplish your purpose as effectively as possible for your particular audience?

4. Do you use logical reasoning throughout the essay?

5. Do you carefully explore all relevant causes and/or effects, searching for the real (as opposed to the immediate) reasons in each case?

6. Do you state clearly the conclusions that can be drawn from your paper?

More specific guidelines for writing and revising your essays appear on pages 26–27 of the Introduction.

Student Essay: Cause/Effect at Work

In the following essay, the student writer analyzes the effects of contemporary TV soap operas on young people: Notice that she states her subject and purpose at the beginning of the essay and then presents a combination of facts and opinions in her exploration of the topic. Notice also that, in her analysis, the writer is careful to draw clear connections between her perceptions of the issue and various objective details in an attempt to trace the effects of this medium in our society today. At the end of her essay, look at her summary of the logical relationships she establishes in the body of the essay and her statements about the conclusions she draws from these relationships.

Distortions of Reality

Background Television's contributions to society, positive and negative, have been debated continually since this piece of technology invaded the average Canadian household in the 1950s. Television has brought an unlimited influx of new information, ideas, and cultures into our homes. However, based on my observations of my thirteen-year-old cousin, Katie, and her friends, I think we need to take a closer look at the effects of soap operas on adolescents today. The distortions of reality portrayed on these programs are frighteningly misleading and, in my opinion, can be very confusing to young people.

Thesis statement

Transition   During the early 1990s, the lifestyle of the typical soap opera "family" has been radically transformed from comfortable pretentiousness to blatant and unrealistic decadence. The characters neither live nor dress like the majority of their viewers, who are generally middle-class Canadians. These television families live in large, majestic homes that are flawlessly decorated. The actors are often adorned in beautiful designer clothing, fur coats, and expensive jewellery, and this opulent lifestyle is sustained by people with no visible means of income. Very few of the characters seem to "work" for a living. When they do, upward mobility—without the benefit of the proper education or suitable training—and a well-planned marriage come quickly.

First distortion of reality

Concrete examples

Transition   From this constant barrage of conspicuous consumption, my cousin and her friends seem to have a distorted view of everyday economic realities. I see Katie and her group becoming obsessed

First effect

with the appearance of their clothes and possessions. I frequently
Concrete examples hear them berate their parents' jobs and modest homes. With noticeable arrogance, these young adolescents seem to view their
parents' lives as "failures" when compared to the effortless, luxurious lifestyles portrayed in the soaps.

Transition   One of the most alluring features of this genre is its masterful use
of deception. Conflicts between characters in soap operas are based
on secrecy and misinformation. Failure to tell the truth and to per-
Concrete examples form honorable deeds further complicates the entangled lives and
love affairs of the participants. But when the truth finally comes out *Second distortion of reality*
and all mistakes and misdeeds become public, the culprits and
offenders hardly ever suffer for their actions. In fact, they appear
to leave the scene of the crime guilt-free.

Transition   Regrettably, Katie and her friends consistently express alarming
Concrete examples indifference to this lack of moral integrity. In their daily viewing, they
shrug off underhanded scenes of scheming and conniving, and they
marvel at how the characters manipulate each other into positions
of powerlessness or grapple in distasteful love scenes. I can only *Second effect*
conclude that continued exposure to this amoral behaviour is eroding the fundamental values of truth and fidelity in these kids.

Transition   Also in the soaps, the powers-that-be conveniently disregard *Third distortion of reality*
any sense of responsibility for wrongdoing. Characters serve jail
Concrete examples terms quickly and in relative comfort. Drug or alcohol abuse does
not mar anyone's physical appearance or behaviour, and poverty
is virtually nonexistent. Usually, the wrongdoer's position, wealth,
and prestige are quickly restored—with little pain and suffering.

     Adolescents are clearly learning that people can act without re- *Third effect*
gard for the harmful effects of their actions on themselves and
others when they see this type of behaviour go unpunished. Again,
I notice the result of this delusion in my cousin. Recently, when a
businessman in our community was convicted of embezzling large
sums of money from his clients, Katie was outraged because he
Concrete examples was sentenced to five years in prison, unlike her daytime TV
"heartthrob," who had been given a suspended sentence for a
similar crime. With righteous indignation, Katie claimed that the
victims, many of whom had lost their entire savings, should have
realized that any business investment involves risk and the threat
of loss. Logic and common sense evaded Katie's reasoning as she
insisted on comparing television justice with real-life scruples.

     The writers and producers of soap operas argue that the shows
are designed to entertain viewers and are not meant to be reflections of reality. Theoretically, this may be true, but I can actually

see how these soap operas are affecting my cousin and her crowd. Although my personal observations are limited, I cannot believe they are unique or unusual. <u>Too many young people think that they can amass wealth and material possessions without an edu-</u><u>cation, hard work, or careful financial planning; that material goods are the sole measure of a person's success in life; and that honesty and integrity are not necessarily admirable qualities.</u> Ultimate
effect

Proposed
solution <u>Soap operas should demonstrate a realistic lifestyle and a re-</u><u>sponsible sense of behaviour.</u> The many hours adolescents spend in front of the television can obviously influence their view of the world. As a society, we cannot afford the consequences resulting from the distortions of reality portrayed every day in these shows.

Student Writer's Comments

In general, writing this essay was not as easy as I had anticipated during my prewriting phase. Although I was interested in and familiar with my topic, I had trouble fitting all the pieces together: matching causes with effects, examples with main points, and problems with solutions.

My prewriting activities were a combination of lists and journal entries that gave me loads of ideas and phrasing to work with in my drafts. From this initial thinking exercise, I made an informal outline of the points I wanted to make. I played with the order of these topics for a while and then began to write.

Because I had spent so much time thinking through various causal relationships before I began to write, I generated the first draft with minimal pain. But I was not happy with it. The examples that I had chosen to support various points I wanted to make did not fit as well as they could, and the whole essay was unfocused and scattered. Although all writing requires support and focus, I realized that a cause/effect essay demands special attention to the relationship between specific examples and their ultimate causes and/or effects. As a result, I had to begin again to revise my sprawling first draft.

I spent my first revising session on the very sloppy introduction and conclusion. I felt that if I could tighten up these parts of the essay, I would have a clearer notion of my purpose and focus. I am convinced now that the time I spent on the beginning and ending of my essay really paid off. I rewrote my thesis several times until I finally arrived at the statement in the draft printed here. This final thesis statement gave me a clear sense of direction for revising the rest of my paper.

I then worked through my essay paragraph by paragraph, making sure that the examples and illustrations I cited supported as effectively as possible the point I was making. I made sure that the causes and effects were accurately paired, and I reorganized sections of the essay that didn't yet read smoothly. I put the final touches on my conclusion and handed in my paper——with visions of causes, effects, and soap opera characters still dancing around in my head.

Some Final Thoughts on Cause/Effect

The essays in this chapter deal with both causes and effects in a variety of ways. As you read each essay, try to discover its primary purpose and the ultimate causes and/or effects of the issue under discussion. Note also the clear causal relationships that each author sets forth on solid foundations supported by logical reasoning. Although the subjects of these essays vary dramatically, each essay exhibits the basic elements of effective causal analysis.

Cause/Effect in Review

Reading Cause/Effect Essays

Preparing to Read

1. What assumptions can you make from the essay's title?

2. Can you guess what the general mood of the essay is?

3. What is the essay's purpose and audience?

4. What does the synopsis in the Rhetorical Table of Contents tell you about the essay?

5. What can you learn from the author's biography?

6. Can you guess what the author's point of view toward the subject is?

7. What are your responses to the Preparing to Read questions?

Reading

1. What is the author's thesis?

2. What are the primary causes and/or effects in the essay?

3. Did you preview the questions that follow the essay?

Rereading

1. How does the writer narrow and focus the essay?

2. Does the writer make clear and logical connections between the ideas in the essay?

3. What concrete examples support the author's conclusions?

4. Does the writer discuss the real causes and effects?

5. What are your responses to the questions after the essay?

Writing Cause/Effect Essays

Preparing to Write

1. What are your responses to the Preparing to Write questions?

2. What is your purpose?

3. Who is your audience?

Writing

1. Do you narrow and focus your material as much as possible?

2. Do you consider all possibilities before assigning real or ultimate causes or effects?

3. Do you show connections between ideas by using transitions and key words?

4. Do you support all inferences with concrete evidence?

5. Are you as objective as possible in your analysis so that you don't distort logic with personal biases?

6. Do you understand your audience's opinions and convictions, so that you know what to emphasize in your essay?

7. Do you qualify your assertions to avoid overstatement and oversimplification?

Rewriting

1. Is your thesis stated clearly at the outset of your paper?

2. Does it include your subject and your purpose?

3. Do you accomplish your purpose as effectively as possible for your particular audience?

4. Do you use logical reasoning throughout the essay?

5. Do you carefully explore all relevant causes and/or effects, searching for the real (as opposed to the immediate) reasons in each case?

6. Do you state clearly the conclusions that can be drawn from your paper?

Stephen King
1947–

■ ■ ■

Why We Crave Horror Movies

"People's appetites for terror seem insatiable," Stephen King once re-marked, an insight which may help justify his phenomenal success as a writer of horror fiction since the mid-1970s. His books have sold over one hundred million copies, and the movies made from them have gen-erated more income than the gross national product of several small countries. After early jobs as a janitor, a laundry worker, and a high school English teacher in Portland, Maine, King turned to writing full time following the spectacular sales of his first novel, *Carrie* (1974), which focuses on a shy, socially ostracized young girl who takes revenge on her cruel classmates through newly developed telekinetic powers. King's subsequent books have included *The Shining* (1976), *Firestarter* (1980), *Cujo* (1981), *The Dark Tower* (1982), *Christine* (1983), *Pet Sematary* (1983), *Misery* (1987), *The Stand* (1990), *Four Past Midnight* (1990), *The Waste Lands* (1992), *Delores Claiborne* (1993), *Insomnia* (1994), *Rose Madder* (1995), *Desperation* (1996), and *Bag of Bones* (1998). Asked to explain why readers and moviegoers are so attracted to his tales of horror, King told a *Chicago Tribune* interviewer that most people's lives "are full of fears—that their marriage isn't working, that they aren't going to make it on the job, that society is crumbling all around them. But we're really not supposed to talk about things like that, and so they don't have any outlets for all those scary feelings. But the horror writer can give them a place to put their fears, and it's ok to be afraid then, because nothing is real, and you can blow it all away when it's over." A cheerful though somewhat supersti-tious person, King, who now lives in Bangor, Maine, admits to doing most of his best writing during the morning hours. "You think I want to write this stuff at night?" he once asked a reviewer.

Preparing to Read

As you prepare to read this article, consider your thoughts on Canada's emotional condition: How emotionally healthy are Canadians? Were they more emotionally healthy twenty years ago? A century ago? What makes a society emotionally healthy? Emotionally unhealthy? How can a society maintain good health? What is the relationship between emo-tional health and a civilized society?

I think that we're all mentally ill; those of us outside the asylums 1
only hide it a little better—and maybe not all that much better,
after all. We've all known people who talk to themselves, people
who sometimes squinch their faces into horrible grimaces when
they believe no one is watching, people who have some hysterical
fear—of snakes, the dark, the tight place, the long drop ... and, of
course, those final worms and grubs that are waiting so patiently
underground.

When we pay our four or five bucks and seat ourselves at 2
tenth-row center in a theater showing a horror movie, we are
daring the nightmare.

Why? Some of the reasons are simple and obvious. To show 3
that we can, that we are not afraid, that we can ride this roller
coaster. Which is not to say that a really good horror movie may
not surprise a scream out of us at some point, the way we may
scream when the roller coaster twists through a complete 360 or
plows through a lake at the bottom of the drop. And horror
movies, like roller coasters, have always been the special province
of the young; by the time one turns 40 or 50, one's appetite for
double twists or 360-degree loops may be considerably depleted.

We also go to reestablish our feelings of essential normality; 4
the horror movie is innately conservative, even reactionary. Freda
Jackson as the horrible melting woman in *Die, Monster, Die!*
confirms for us that no matter how far we may be removed from
the beauty of a Robert Redford or a Diana Ross, we are still light-
years from true ugliness.

And we go to have fun.   5

Ah, but this is where the ground starts to slope away, isn't it? 6
Because this is a very peculiar sort of fun, indeed. The fun comes
from seeing others menaced—sometimes killed. One critic has
suggested that if pro football has become the voyeur's version
of combat, then the horror film has become the modern version
of the public lynching.

It is true that the mythic, "fairy-tale" horror film intends to 7
take away the shades of gray .... It urges us to put away our
more civilized and adult penchant for analysis and to become
children again, seeing things in pure blacks and whites. It may be
that horror movies provide psychic relief on this level because this
invitation to lapse into simplicity, irrationality, and even outright
madness is extended so rarely. We are told we may allow our
emotions a free rein ... or no rein at all.

If we are all insane, then sanity becomes a matter of degree. 8
If your insanity leads you to carve up women, like Jack the Ripper
or the Cleveland Torso Murderer, we clap you away in the funny
farm (but neither of those two amateur-night surgeons was ever
caught, heh-heh-heh); if, on the other hand, your insanity leads
you only to talk to yourself when you're under stress or to pick
your nose on your morning bus, then you are left alone to go
about your business … though it is doubtful that you will ever be
invited to the best parties.

The potential lyncher is in almost all of us (excluding saints, 9
past and present; but then, most saints have been crazy in their
own ways), and every now and then, he has to be let loose to
scream and roll around in the grass. Our emotions and our fears
form their own body, and we recognize that it demands its own
exercise to maintain proper muscle tone. Certain of these
emotional muscles are accepted—even exalted—in civilized
society; they are, of course, the emotions that tend to maintain the
status quo of civilization itself. Love, friendship, loyalty,
kindness—these are all the emotions that we applaud, emotions
that have been immortalized in the couplets of Hallmark cards
and in the verses (I don't dare call it poetry) of Leonard Nimoy.

When we exhibit these emotions, society showers us with 10
positive reinforcement; we learn this even before we get out of
diapers. When, as children, we hug our rotten little puke of a sister
and give her a kiss, all the aunts and uncles smile and twit and cry,
"Isn't he the sweetest little thing?" Such coveted treats as chocolate-
covered graham crackers often follow. But if we deliberately slam
the rotten little puke of a sister's fingers in the door, sanctions
follow—angry remonstrance from parents, aunts and uncles;
instead of a chocolate-covered graham cracker, a spanking.

But anticivilization emotions don't go away, and they demand 11
periodic exercise. We have such "sick" jokes as, "What's the
difference between a truckload of bowling balls and a truckload
of dead babies?" (You can't unload a truckload of bowling balls
with a pitchfork … a joke, by the way, that I heard originally
from a ten-year-old.) Such a joke may surprise a laugh or a grin
out of us even as we recoil, a possibility that confirms the thesis:
If we share a brotherhood of man, then we also share an insanity
of man. None of which is intended as a defense of either the sick
joke or insanity but merely as an explanation of why the best
horror films, like the best fairy tales, manage to be reactionary,
anarchistic, and revolutionary all at the same time.

The mythic horror movie, like the sick joke, has a dirty job to   12
do. It deliberately appeals to all that is worst in us. It is morbidity
unchained, our most base instincts let free, our nastiest fantasies
realized … and it all happens, fittingly enough, in the dark. For
those reasons, good liberals often shy away from horror films.
For myself, I like to see the most aggressive of them—*Dawn of
the Dead*, for instance—as lifting a trap door in the civilized
forebrain and throwing a basket of raw meat to the hungry
alligators swimming around in that subterranean river beneath.

Why bother? Because it keeps them from getting out, man. It   13
keeps them down there and me up here. It was Lennon and
McCartney who said that all you need is love, and I would agree
with that.

As long as you keep the gators fed.   14

UNDERSTANDING DETAILS

1. Why, in King's opinion, do civilized people enjoy horror
   movies?
2. According to King, in what ways are horror movies like roller
   coasters?
3. According to King, how are horror films like public lynchings?
4. What is the difference between "emotions that tend to maintain the status quo of civilization" (paragraph 9) and "anticivilization emotions" (paragraph 11)?

ANALYZING MEANING

1. How can horror movies "reestablish our feelings of essential
   normality" (paragraph 4)?
2. What is "reactionary, anarchistic, and revolutionary" (paragraph 11) about fairy tales? About horror films?
3. Why does the author think we need to exercise our anticivilization emotions? What are some other ways we might confront these emotions?
4. Explain the last line of King's essay: "As long as you keep the
   gators fed" (paragraph 14).

DISCOVERING RHETORICAL STRATEGIES

1. What is the cause/effect relationship King notes in society between horror movies and sanity?

2. Why does King begin his essay with such a dramatic statement as "I think that we're all mentally ill" (paragraph 1)?
3. Who do you think is the author's intended audience for this essay? Describe them in detail. How did you come to this conclusion?
4. What different rhetorical strategies does King use to support his cause/effect analysis? Give examples of each.

MAKING CONNECTIONS

1. Apply Stephen King's definition of "horror" to such horrific experiences as a stay in P4W (Sally Armstrong, "P4W"), and/or the preparation of a dead body for a funeral (Jessica Mitford, "Behind the Formaldehyde Curtain"). In what way is each of these events "horrible"? What are the principal differences between watching a horror movie and living through a real-life horror like being confined to prison?
2. In this essay, King gives us important insights into his own writing process, especially into how horror novels and movies affect their audiences. Compare and contrast his revelation of the techniques of his trade with those advanced by Natalie Goldberg ("The Rules of Writing Practice"). Whose advice is most helpful to you? Explain your answer.
3. Compare King's comments about "fear" with similar insights into fear by such other authors as Laura Robinson ("Starving for the Gold"), Lynn Coady ("Genius or Madness?"), and Ray Guy ("When Jannies Visited"). How would each of these writers define the term differently? With which author's definition would you most likely agree? Explain your answer.

IDEAS FOR DISCUSSION/WRITING

Preparing to Write

Write freely about how most people maintain a healthy emotional attitude: How would you define emotional well-being? When are people most emotionally healthy? Most emotionally unhealthy? What do your friends and relatives do to maintain a healthy emotional life? What do you do to maintain emotional health? What is the connection between our individual emotional health and the extent to which our society is civilized?

Choosing a Topic

1. Think of a release other than horror films for our most violent emotions. Is it an acceptable release? Write an essay for the general public explaining the relationship between this particular release and our "civilized" society.
2. If you accept King's analysis of horror movies, what role in society do you think other types of movies play (e.g., love stories, science fiction, and comedies)? Choose one type, and explain its role to your college composition class.
3. Your psychology instructor has asked you to explain your opinions on the degree of sanity or insanity in Canada at present. In what ways are we sane? In what ways are we insane? Write an essay for your psychology instructor explaining in detail your observations along these lines.

WEB SITES

 www.acs.appstate.edu/~pl7714/sking_html/
Stephen King on the Web.

 wwwcsif.cs.ucdavis.edu/~pace/king.html
Stephen King Web site.

Trina McQueen

■■■

Why We Crave Hot Stuff

Trina McQueen is now the president of the Discovery Channel after working at the CBC for 25 years in positions ranging from on-air reporter and program host to director of news and current affairs. McQueen also serves as the chair of the Action Group on Violence in Television and sits on the boards of the Banff Television Foundation, the World Wildlife Fund and the Canadian Journalism Foundation. The essay that appears here was published in *The Globe and Mail* and is an adaptation of a piece that appears in a collection of essays entitled *Journalism in the New Millennium*, published to commemorate the opening of the University of British Columbia's Sing Tao School of Journalism.

Preparing to Read

In this essay, Trina McQueen considers the role of journalism in our lives and presents an argument for the appeal of "tabloid" news stories. Before you begin reading, consider the appeal of stories about people such as Bill Clinton, O.J. Simpson, Princess Diana, Pamela Anderson, and Gillian Guess. Why are we fascinated by the lives of people who are "beset with extremely interesting personal demons"? What kinds of items in the news catch your attention? What kinds of items do you ignore?

■

Journalism about ethics reminds me of those "thin book" jokes. 1 There isn't much of it. Even when an event seems to have a moral centre, journalists will report around, over, under and through the moral issue.

One case in point: the controversy over providing financial 2 aid to people who had contracted hepatitis C from tainted blood. The controversy was hugely reported. The facts of the matter were well documented. There was extensive background analysis of surrounding issues. What got very little ink and air time were the principles that a society might use in deciding whether compensation was justified. Much was made of the tears streaming down the face of a dissident Liberal who voted with the government. But how had she come to her original decision that compensation was a moral duty? And how had she balanced those principles against the principles used in deciding her political duty? In mainstream journalism, the moral issues were mostly edited out or weren't even there to be edited.

But before we consider what's left out, let's consider what 3 is lately there: Princess Diana, Bill Clinton, Margaret Trudeau, O.J. Simpson, Mr. and Mrs. Matthew Barrett, Pamela Anderson. Beautiful, rich and sensational, their characters are redolent of power and sexuality, and all are beset by extremely interesting personal demons.

Many academics and journalists wonder why there is so 4 much in newspapers, magazines and television about these folks and so little about Chiapas and hydroelectric restructuring. They argue about it at conferences; they write books and columns and theses. It's called the "tabloidization of news." Some of this tabloidization is wild rumour and some of it is outright lies. It is acknowledged that this is deplorable. It is also agreed that some tabloid journalism is true but there is too much of it.

Today, tabloid journalism may have reached terminal 5 velocity. The next U.S. president, for example, cannot reasonably be expected to provide the wealth of embarrassingly riveting intimate material that the current one does. Yet we can predict that attempts will be made and that the coverage of them will be exuberant.

What distresses some media thinkers about tabloid news is 6 that it fits uncomfortably into the usually accepted noble purposes of news. The word "noble" is not being used sarcastically here. The practice of journalism has, in most democracies, special protections and rights because it is one of the people's defences against tyranny and injustice. Tabloid stories—let's call them hot-stuff stories—are not likely to inspire the people to rise against their oppressors.

So hot stuff is not part of the core competencies of journalism: 7 politics and business. It has no advice for us on our democratic responsibilities and duties. It may tell us something of the character of powerful people, but it is silent on the systems and processes that rule us. It deep-backgrounds not nor does it spin.

Nor is hot stuff related to another accepted use of journalism: 8 to determine whether we are safe. Stories about war, crime, disasters and the environment are all said to answer these important questions. Is my family safe? Is my community safe? Is my world safe? But few of us can learn much that we did not know about safety from Diana's death. We had already decided whether to do up our seat belts and ask our chauffeurs to slow down in Paris tunnels.

Hot stuff is not "news you can use," as are stories about 9 health, consumerism, hobbies and education. And I would argue that hot stuff is not truly human interest, as are features about feisty centenarians and champion pumpkin carvers. The characters in hot stuff are truly characters; the demonic killers, the fabulous babes, the hot commander-in-chief and the angelic princess. They are dramatis personae.

Hot stuff certainly fills one of the chief purposes of 10 journalism, which is to sell copies and increase ratings. The *Columbia Journalism Review,* in an issue devoted to what it calls "money lust," opines that "more so than at any other moment in journalism's history, the news product that lands on newsstands, doorsteps and television screens is hurt by a heightened, unseemly lust at many companies for ever greater profits." The periodical warns that today's "diminished and deracinated journalism ... could lead to a fatal erosion of the ancient bond between journalists and the public."

Certainly if profits are the question, hot stuff is one terrific 11 answer. In the past five years, hot stuff has produced all the ecstatic revenue moments of the news business. From the first shot of the white Bronco on the freeway, O.J. drove CNN ratings, revenue and stock prices. *Time* and *Newsweek* covers on Diana— two each in a row—produced the biggest newsstand sales in the magazines' histories. CBC Newsworld drew huge audiences even at midnight the night Diana died. The numbers for her funeral service were as much as 60 times higher than normal.

The Diana phenomenon was the breathtaking culmination 12 of a change in news choices that had begun years before. The *Times* of London probably shows that change most dramatically. *The Economist* has noted that in a newspaper historically celebrated for its international news (Stanley finds Livingstone, the Charge of the Light Brigade), the *Times'* front page recently had only one foreign piece: it was about Leonardo DiCaprio's new girlfriend.

Rupert Murdoch—he of Fox TV and sensational tabloids— 13 had a heretical vision. Like many other heretical visions, it has become commonplace. The Project for Excellence in Journalism analyzed stories on television, newsmagazines and front pages and concluded that stories of celebrity, gossip and scandal took up 43 per cent of the total space—three times more than 20 years ago. It all seems to have worked out nicely. Profits at most newspaper chains are showing healthy gains, and television news departments have become profit centres.

None of these choices and changes would have been made if 14 the public had not responded. Hot stuff sells. Right now I'm reading every word of *The Globe and Mail*'s comprehensive and straight-faced coverage of the trial of a dominatrix in Richmond Hill, Ont.

There are many theories about why scandal and gossip are so 15 popular.

Margaret Thatcher said "there is no such thing as society: 16 only individuals and their families." In her time, politicians, associations and even nation states began to be seen as ineffective and even irrelevant (incorrectly seen so, in my view). Philosopher Mark Kingwell in his book *Better Living* says this is an age in which "the individual is granted an unprecedented moral, political and epistemological influence." So it is hardly surprising that the intensely personal becomes an important subject of journalism.

A simpler theory is that ordinary people are rather stupid, 17 moving their lips as they read the latest about Brad Pitt. Although there is a definite bozo factor in the population, it is my experience that most people want to expand their experience. Working at the Discovery Channel, where a hot-stuff story is the uncovering of a new dinosaur skeleton, I'm constantly humbled by the knowledge and the intelligence of our public. But Discovery Channel's ratings hit their lowest the week of Aug. 31, 1997. Our viewers had the same fascination for the Diana story as everyone else.

And it was a Story. That is the attraction of hot stuff. Most of 18 it has the pure and elemental force of story. There is a narrative; there are characters. Storytelling is simply the most powerful form of human communication. We are wired to absorb and comprehend the world through constructing, telling and hearing stories.

But journalism is more than storytelling. It is about witnessing 19 faithfully and intelligently, it is about recording carefully, it is about hard questioning and intense listening, and it is about skepticism and empathy. But when all of that is done, there is still a story to tell. And in most traditional journalism, from daily news to documentaries, this is the element most forgotten.

There are dangers to journalistic storytelling: Sometimes the 20
facts won't fit a neat narrative; bits have to be crammed in or
left out. But the story rules, and unless journalists are willing to
study the craft of storytelling so they can apply it to subjects that
are difficult and foreign but relevant, they will fight a losing
battle against the natural story. And why should the Devil have
all the good tunes?

It is important to consider also that hot-stuff journalism 21
brings the storyteller and audience directly together. Political,
business or labour reporters all want and need the respect of
those about whom they write. The result is often a kind of insider
writing that puts the onus on the viewer or reader to fight his
or her way into the inner sanctum where the reporter and subject
live. In much of hot-stuff reporting, that's not so. No journalist
really cared what Monica Lewinsky or Louise Woodward thought
about their press. The reporters were free to think only about
the viewers and their needs.

Hot stuff, however, has another appeal: the moral questions 22
it raises. When I was a young journalist, idealistic, arrogant and
hopeful, I thought my profession might change the world—
expose injustice, inspire citizenship, provoke thought, preserve
democracy, increase decency.

I have read a survey of people who described the uses they 23
made of journalism. They found news to be very important in
their lives, but they did not say they used it to help them fulfill
the duties of citizenship or to decide their economic courses of
action or to galvanize themselves into political action. They used
the news as something to talk about. How trivial, I thought,
raging. They see the world as small talk.

I now think that using the news as something to talk about is 24
terribly important. I think it may even be the way of linking
information to personal decisions, what U.S. cultural critic Neil
Postman might call adding wisdom to data.

And I suspect that one of the appeals of hot-stuff journalism 25
is that it gives people a simple and effective opportunity to
explore and discuss morals and ethics, to test their own standards
and principles, to answer Socrates' question, "What is the life
that is worth living?"

We make many more ethical decisions than we do political 26
ones. We will be called on to vote perhaps once a year. But every
day we face moral decisions, big and small: Should I give money
to a squeegee kid? Should I walk back four blocks to return the

extra $10 the cashier gave me? Is that man lying on the street drunk or sick? And there are horrific dilemmas: My unborn child is deformed; my dying father begs me to help him go sooner. Or how do we deal with a nasty neighbour, a daughter-in-law of a different religion, a drug-addicted friend? What does it mean to be a good parent, spouse, child or employee? Perhaps when we gather in the lunchroom to discuss O.J. or Paul Bernardo or Paula Jones or Alan Eagleson or Diana, we are really discussing our moral options and ourselves.

There is a paradox here: People clearly seek out and desire   27
information about morality; and they are just as clearly rejecting more of the traditional sources of that information.

But mainstream journalism is curiously absent from this   28
arena. It offers "news you can use" on almost every subject: RRSPs, removing stains, starting a neighbourhood action group, writing a résumé, taking vitamins. It educates us endlessly on politics, personal finance and health. But on ethics and spirituality, the great presses and the great networks can offer only whispers. There are a few religion columns and essays. Business ethics receive some attention, and journalistic ethics are covered. CBC Newsworld, in fact, will begin airing a new program titled *The Moral Divide* in the new year. It is probably the first of its kind. Perhaps it is the first of a trend.

It makes me squeamish to try to "sell" journalism about ethics,   29
but I think it is possible to find utility as well as virtue in the subject.

The more we consider the importance—the value and the   30
wonderful stories of moral and ethical decisions—the more curious the lack of their presence in journalism is. The Greeks had a word for those unacquainted with ethics: *idiot*.

UNDERSTANDING DETAILS

1. Explain the term "tabloidization of news" (paragraph 4).
2. What are the noble purposes of journalism identified by McQueen? What element does she say is forgotten (paragraph 19)? How has her view of the profession of journalism shifted over time?
3. In McQueen's opinion, what is the attraction of "hot stuff" stories?

ANALYZING MEANING

1. McQueen repeatedly uses the example of Princess Diana in her essay. Why is this example particularly significant?

2. Describe McQueen's attitude toward journalistic storytelling. Do you agree with her position?
3. To what extent do you think news stories shape behaviour and public opinion on socially relevant issues? According to McQueen, why is journalism about ethics so rare (paragraph 22)?

DISCOVERING RHETORICAL STRATEGIES

1. In this essay McQueen uses many examples to illustrate the points she is making. Why has she employed so many examples in her essay? Which examples are the most effective?
2. Characterize the tone McQueen uses in this essay. Why has she made this choice? How is the tone appropriate for the subject matter and the audience she is addressing?
3. Explain McQueen's conclusion to this essay. What comment is she making about the importance of ethics in our lives?

MAKING CONNECTIONS

1. McQueen's title has obvious similarities to the title of Stephen King's essay ("Why We Crave Horror Movies"). What do the topics they have chosen to write about have in common?
2. McQueen attributes some of the attraction of "hot stuff" to the appeal of story. How would Eudora Welty ("Listening") respond to McQueen's position? What about Evan Solomon ("The Babar Factor")?
3. Imagine a conversation between Trina McQueen and David Foot ("Boomers Dance to a New Beat"). How do you think Foot would account for the appeal and the growing prevalence of "hot stuff" stories? On what points do you think McQueen and Foot would agree? Where might they disagree? Whose view is closer to your own?

IDEAS FOR DISCUSSION/WRITING

Preparing to write

Write freely about a major news topic that has captured your attention over the last year. How much detail do you have about this topic? What about it attracted your attention? What retained your interest? What made it a "news-worthy" event? Did your friends or family members share your interest in this story? Why or why not?

Choosing a topic

1. Editors and producers of news stories constantly have decisions to make about what kinds of stories to pursue and report on as well as what angle should be taken on a story. Write an essay for your school newspaper in which you discuss the role you believe that journalism should play in our society.

2. McQueen suggests that using the news as something to talk about may be a way of exploring personal morals and ethics. Choose a well-known news story such as that of Monica Lewinsky, Alan Eagleson, or Albert Walker, and write an essay in which you discuss how you support the behaviour of one of the participants in the story, or argue that he or she should have behaved differently.

3. One of the questions McQueen poses in her essay is "What does it mean to be a good parent, spouse, child, or employee?" Choose one of these roles and write an essay in which you answer this question. Include specific details and examples to support your argument.

WEB SITES

www.interlog.com/~crailer/etr/4/403.htm
Here you will find an article about Trina McQueen and the Discovery Channel from *Electronic Times Report.*

Laura Robinson
1958–

■ ■ ■

Starving for the Gold

A former member of Canada's national cycling and nordic skiing teams, Laura Robinson is known for her articles on sports and recreation, and particularly women athletes. Her commentaries have appeared in *The Toronto Star, The Globe and Mail, Canadian Living, Toronto Life, Saturday Night, NOW Magazine,* and *Up Here.* She has also published *She Shoots, She Scores: Canadian Perspectives on Women in Sport* (1997) and, most recently, *Crossing the Line: Sexual Assault in Canada's National Sport* (1998), a book that details the abuse in the world of minor league hockey. Robinson no longer participates in sports competitively. Instead, she enjoys recreational ski racing and cycling. In this article Robinson portrays a frightening picture of the way young female athletes are treated by their male coaches.

Preparing to Read

As you prepare to read think about competitive sports and athletes. What does it take for someone to become a top athlete? How does pursuing this level of achievement influence the lives of those athletes? What is the appeal of competitive sports, both to the participants as well as to the observers? What benefits does one enjoy as a top athlete? What disadvantages or drawbacks might there be? In international competitions, such as the Olympic Games, why are some countries consistently winners in particular sports? Think specifically of sports such as gymnastics and figure skating, where many young women compete. As either a participant or a spectator, what role do you see coaches playing in competitive sports?

Imagine for a moment you are an Olympic athlete. If you   1
pictured a male athlete, try again. Actually, you are a woman, engaged in rigorous year-round training. Now, imagine that your body-fat percentage is less than half the average for a reasonably active woman your age. As a result, your menstrual cycle has stopped; you no longer have a period. You are a textbook case of anorexia nervosa, obsessed with weight and body shape. Perhaps you are bulimic, and resort to compulsive binge eating, followed

by violent purging—vomiting, fasting or the taking of laxatives and diuretics. If you are a junior athlete, in your early teens, you are effectively delaying the onset of puberty and stunting normal growth.

A rational observer would conclude that you are seriously ill. 2 A rational observer would not suspect that you had been driven to these life-threatening disorders by your coach.

According to five women, former members of Canada's 3 national sports teams, their coaches' insistence on excessive thinness threatened their physical health. The athletes' identities have been disguised for reasons that will presently be made clear.

The first woman, while still a junior, was told by her coach 4 that she should "think about" losing weight. "I was 5-foot-5 and weighed 135, but he said, 'Look, all the top women, all the senior women are thin.' So I thought, 'Maybe I am a little chubby.' I started to train for the Calgary Olympics. By late 1987, I weighed less than 110. I was constantly hungry, but I told myself, 'This is a good feeling.' I lost another five pounds the week before our qualifying competition, but I felt extremely weak and didn't make the team." Her standing began to suffer, and two years later she retired from active competition.

Says another woman, "Looking back, I can see how stupid it 5 was. The coaches were saying, 'Hey, we've got the thinnest team around, the girls are looking great.' We didn't have great results, but that didn't seem to matter. I was just a teenager, and a coach's attitude means everything when you're young. Now, I'm angry. They screwed up my mind, and I'll never be able to look at food again the way I did before."

A third athlete, now attending university, wrote in a study of 6 athletic amenorrhea (cessation of the menstrual period): "Pressure was always felt to be lean, and considerable emphasis was placed on being beneath 12 per-cent body fat. It seemed that the primary goal was to maintain a low body-fat composition. Often, it was felt this was more important than actual performance."

This pressure was applied in unmistakable ways. One coach 7 held contests to see who could leave the most food uneaten on her plate at training camp. Yet another athlete experienced anxiety attacks over the caliper tests and pool dunking (total submersion in order to accurately gauge a subject's body fat). "After the tests, we'd compare results," she says. "Our coach would announce at dinner who had the lowest fat percentage, and the roller-coaster eating would start all over again."

One's first reaction to these charges is a measure of disbelief. 8
We hesitate to think that coaches would do such things—but not
so long ago, our athletes were supplied with anabolic steroids
because it was "necessary" in order to win, because "everyone
else did it." A conspiracy of silence surrounded these activities.
Ben Johnson's and Angella Issajenko's physiques were obviously
artificial: the changes in their bodies couldn't be attributed to
natural causes. Every athlete, every sports journalist and sports
official had ample cause for suspicion. No one spoke up.

Next, one might ask: Where are the women coaches, who 9
presumably wouldn't participate in this nonsense? An answer
is suggested by the dismissal in February of Ken Porter, Athletics
Canada's former director of track and field technical programs.
Mr. Porter claimed that he was fired in part because he wished to
promote black and women coaches, and deplored the relegation
of women to "a ghetto-type position as team chaperone."

Third, why hasn't coaching malfeasance come to light? Well, 10
it has. The Dubin Report, commissioned after Ben Johnson tested
positive for anabolic steroids at the 1988 Seoul Olympics,
concluded that coaches must assume responsibility for the "health,
welfare, moral education and preparation for life of the athlete."
Since then, another report, prepared for the federal Minister of
Fitness and Amateur Sport, found that athletes feel they are
coerced into "harmful practices . . . and believe their concerns on
the subject of personal harm are ignored." A third report,
undertaken on behalf of the same ministry, is due within the next
month. It is said to address the issue of physical and sexual abuse.

The reports stack up, the problems are studied to death, and 11
the bad-apple coaches are seldom weeded out.

According to Marion Lay, manager of the Women's Program 12
at Sport Canada (the funding agent for our national teams),
"Coaches who manipulate through food and body image are
robbing women of their self-esteem and self-respect. But what
safe place is there for an athlete who feels abused?"

The women who confided in me asked for anonymity 13
because some of them intend to work within the system; but
even those who maintain only a casual interest fear that if they
speak out they will be perceived as "traitors" to sport. Ms. Lay's
reaction says it all: "Of course, they can't reveal their identities.
There's no mechanism to protect them."

Why this particular form of abuse? Helen Lenskyj, a sports 14
sociologist at the Ontario Institute for Studies in Education, cites

the emergence during the 1970s of a prepubescent body type—
the very young, very thin gymnast, minus hips and breasts,
whose appearance continues to influence judges when it comes
to awarding points for artistic merit in the so-called esthetic
sports. As a result, coaches everywhere decided that their athletes
should look like Soviet gymnast Olga Korbut. In fact, leanness is
a factor in both esthetic and endurance sports—to a point.
Athletes shouldn't carry extra pounds. The trouble is that not
everyone is prepubescent and can't possibly look that way, no
matter what she does.

Another factor, according to Marion Lay, is simply resistance 15
to change. The last two decades have seen a dramatic increase
in the number of female competitors. Ms. Lay feels that often
coaches haven't come to terms with this fact: "There's an attitude
of, 'Yes, we'll let you in, but you have to play the game our way,
look the way we want you to look.' Women have to give things
up in order to enter sports." In other words, the predominant
view (because men control sports) is that sports are male. If a
woman is going to take part, she'd better resemble a man. If she's
got womanly hips, she can't really be an athlete, because real
athletes aren't women—and so on, all round the vicious circle.

Little wonder that even so cautious an organization as the 16
Coaching Association of Canada (CAC) raises the shocking notion
that nearly one-third of all women athletes have some sort of
eating disorder. This figure, culled from unspecified studies,
appears in the National Coaching Certification Program's Level
III Course—mandatory at a national-team level. The course
describes the symptoms of anorexia and bulimia, and provides
checklists for their detection, but assumes that the person
studying the materials isn't the source of the difficulty. According
to Tom Kinsman, the CAC's executive director, "These are
problems that weren't talked about before, so we didn't write
about them. I hope a new awareness will go a long way in helping
people raise the issues with dignity and security. But I can tell you
the process won't be nice, clean and clear-cut."

Apparently not. In fact, these issues were under discussion 17
when I began competing over 20 years ago. One of the problems
has always been, as Mr. Kinsman admits, if a coach acts
improperly, it's up to the sport's governing body, not the CAC,
to discipline him—an unlikely scenario if athletes are too
intimidated to lodge complaints, and "believe their concerns are
ignored" when and if they do so.

It is important not to trivialize the issue here. Demeaning 18 comments and sexist behaviour aren't confined to the world of sports. Yes, it's crude and counterproductive to criticize an athlete in front of her peers. If a coach's first reaction to every woman who passes by is "What a lardass," the message sinks in. These things are wounding, but women everywhere face similar indignities daily. Nor do I suggest that every coach is like Charlie Francis, Ben Johnson's steroid supplier.

A skeptic would argue that plenty of non-athletic teenagers 19 are anorectic, that countless women punish their bodies for doubtful ends (silicone implants and face-lifts spring to mind), that a certain number of women athletes would succumb to eating disorders even with the most supportive and caring coach. As well, an athlete places such extraordinary demands on her body that it's hard to pinpoint cause and effect.

All this may be so. But it can't be denied that Canada's most 20 senior coaches are exacerbating—if not creating—a problem of terrible magnitude.

With devastating results. First, long-term amenorrheics are 21 susceptible to a loss in bone density or osteoporosis (abnormally porous or weakened bones). If these conditions persist, one in three such athletes will suffer a fracture. A 1985 study found that even athletes with irregular (as opposed to nonexistent) periods were nearly four times more prone to stress fractures than those whose periods were uninterrupted.

Next, and more serious, is the fact that athletes engage in 22 regular aerobic activity, which reduces low-density lipoprotein-cholestrol. So far, so good—LDL-C is a contributing factor in coronary ailments. But because an amenorrheic woman's estrogen secretions are low, this positive effect is reversed. Up go the LDL-C levels; up goes the risk of heart disease.

Lastly, it's been predicted that almost 15 per cent of anorectics 23 and bulimics will die over the course of 30 years as a direct result of their disorders. There hasn't been a verifiable instance yet among Canadian athletes—but these are early days.

So the question remains. Why would a coach encourage such 24 dangerous behaviour? Anorectic athletes are too unhealthy to do well over the long haul; you can't compete at the international level if you're starving yourself. Many athletes eventually break down and disappear from view. Unless they're household names, no one notices. They're interchangeable, there are plenty more where they came from.

One answer has been suggested by Ms. Lenskyj, the OISE 25
sports psychologist: it's imitative crime. In addition to underage
gymnasts like Olga Korbut, a fair number of older European athletes
are much too thin. I could name an entire cycling team whose
members are plainly anorectic. They're fast on the road, but they're
burning out even faster. Watch for them at the Barcelona Olympics,
because they won't be competing in a couple of years.

But Marion Lay's comments earlier about forced make-overs 26
may be closer to the mark. Notes Karin Jasper, a Toronto
psychotherapist, "The athletic look is lean with narrow hips, and
we have learned that women dislike the size of their hips,
stomachs and thighs, those areas most connected with
pregnancy." Constant harping on these areas—the first ones to
catch a male coach's eye—is enough to stir up instant insecurity.
"The ideal male athlete has narrow hips, but that's not normal for
women," says Ms. Lenskyj. "Dieting can't change skeletal
structure. Only a few girls have bodies that correspond to a male's
in terms of leanness. If coaches use weight and fat percentages as
a tool to manipulate athletes, it is a form of sexual abuse."

The inescapable conclusion is that the coach, unused to 27
women in sport, wants them to look like boys. Or, failing that, like
little girls. This syndrome assumes even more ominous overtones
when you consider the inordinate number of women athletes
and coaches who wind up as romantic items. I remember a
Canadian national team where every member was living with
or married to her coach or technical adviser. One hesitates to
speculate on these unions. According to Karin Jasper, an
unfortunate side-effect of self-starvation is often a loss of sexual
drive. The coach gets less than he bargained for in that
department. The other possibility is that his fondest wish has
come true—he has found someone who's lost all outward signs
of womanhood—no breasts, no hips, no period. It makes you
wonder whether he might not be happier coaching little boys.

The real imperative here is obviously control over someone 28
less powerful, someone malleable and eager to please. Given
that girls begin their athletic careers very young, they don't get
a chance to develop into well-rounded human beings in any
sense. I personally believe that many male coaches don't like,
and are ill-equipped to deal with, grown women. There's no
other explanation for the ceaseless humiliation and ridicule—
the construction of a closed system where trauma becomes a tool
to produce great-looking girls, the thinnest team around.

Is change possible in the world of organized sports? Let's 29 give coaches the benefit of the doubt. Maybe they think that all these things will actually help us bring home lots of medals. Remember the outcry when Canada's skaters "failed" to win Gold and had to "settle for" Bronze. Third-best in the world translated as "not good enough." (The logical extension of this sort of thinking is that, whatever an athlete's body is like, it's never right. It's too fat, too thin, too this or too that.)

When our athletes, being human, made mistakes, they were 30 savagely criticized by the media. As a result, every athlete, man or woman, becomes a performance machine. Karin Jasper is not surprised: "We talk to girls and women about overcoming perfectionism, about not basing their evaluation of themselves on all-or-nothing standards. But athletes are taught to see themselves this way. Either they win, or they don't. When their entire value is based on performance, they won't be viewed as a whole person, they're one-dimensional."

Under these conditions, even an influx of women coaches 31 would do little good. Until the system asks what's best for a given person, not an athlete, it's stuck in the all-or-nothing groove. For male coaches to change, they'd have to re-examine their priorities, their own sexuality, their entire basis for coaching. That's not going to happen.

The real tragedy is that sports can feel so good, so refreshing 32 and exciting and freeing. I entered organized sports when I was 14. I was lucky. I had people who made sure I got to the races on time, but also gave me plenty of books to read. Still, I couldn't help but be affected to some degree. I was obsessed with exercise; I overtrained. That was my response to the pressure, and it wasn't healthy. Even now, I tend to avoid scales. I have to think twice if someone asks me if I consider myself thin. I escaped the worst of it, but my attitudes remain.

One of the women whose own sad story I recounted earlier 33 has started to coach girls between the ages of 12 and 16. "They ask me if they're overweight," she says, "and I tell them, 'If you think you can work with your weight, then you're fine. This is the body God has given you, so enjoy it.'" That's encouraging, as far as it goes—although the fact that 12-year-old athletes anguish about their weight is food for thought. But, because of her experiences, this woman is incapable of saying, "This is the body God has given me, so I'll enjoy it." That has been taken from her and nothing can compensate her for such a loss.

UNDERSTANDING DETAILS

1. Why, in Robinson's opinion, are male coaches starving their female athletes?
2. Why don't the athletes challenge the coaches about their food consumption?
3. According to Robinson, what is necessary for this unhealthy pattern to be broken?

ANALYZING MEANING

1. What does the title tell you about the tone of this article?
2. Do you agree that the use of weight and fat percentages as a tool to manipulate athletes is a form of sexual abuse (paragraph 26)? Why or why not?
3. In her discussion of this problem, Robinson identifies a chain of reaction. She considers both the causes and effects of the coaches' behaviour, as well as the causes and effects of the athletes' behaviour. Rank these four categories according to the amount of attention Robinson gives to each. Which ranks the highest? Why has Robinson chosen this focus?

DISCOVERING RHETORICAL STRATEGIES

1. What is Robinson's main purpose in this essay? Has she achieved her goal? Explain.
2. Describe Robinson's intended audience.
3. At what points in this essay does Robinson analyze the causes of this problem? When does she study the effects? Is a pattern apparent?

MAKING CONNECTIONS

1. Imagine a conversation between Gloria Steinem ("The Politics of Muscle") and Laura Robinson about the role of sport in women's lives. On what points do you think they would agree? Where might they disagree? Whose view would you most closely agree with?
2. Laura Robinson and Naheed Mustafa ("My Body Is My Own Business") both discuss body image in their essays. Compare and contrast the views of these two writers.
3. In this essay Laura Robinson discusses her own experience but she also includes many quotations from others and cites many

experts in the field of sports psychology, coaching, and psychotherapy. How does this approach compare to that used by Cecil Foster ("Why Blacks Get Mad") and Sally Armstrong ("P4W")?

IDEAS FOR DISCUSSION/WRITING

Preparing to Write

Write freely about participation in sports. Do you participate in any sports? If so, what sports? Do individual sports or team sports hold more appeal? Would you rather be involved in sports recreationally or competitively? What sports do you like to watch? Do sports play a role in your school life now? Should participation in sports be mandatory in elementary school? In secondary school? Why or why not?

Choosing a Topic

1. In an article for a fashion magazine, promote participation in sports for the beneficial effects that it can have. Provide specific examples to generate a convincing argument.
2. Body image is a major concern, particularly for young women. Why do females, especially, work so hard to achieve a certain prescribed image? What effects does this obsession with appearance have? Write an essay for teenagers that points out the problems of striving to be something that does not come naturally.
3. Think of a situation in which your behaviour was influenced either positively or negatively by the expectations of another individual, such as a parent, friend, teacher, or other relative. Write an essay for that person in which you outline and explain the effects of those expectations.

WEB SITES

www.competitor.com/
Competitor is an online, interactive sports magazine.

www.sfwed.org/top.htm
"Something Fishy" eating disorder site provides extensive information on various eating disorders.

John Gray
1946–

■ ■ ■

You're Thinking of Getting a *What?*

Writer and broadcaster Vicki Gabereau, in a column in *Chatelaine,* described John Gray as follows: "playwright, man of letters, civilized husband and childlike father of two boys ... the man is a delightful ranter. He
can talk about anything; if it's something he knows little about, he just
makes it up on the spot, thereby entertaining a nation or a dinner party
with equal enthusiasm." Gabereau isn't the only one enchanted by Gray.
He has received a Governor General's Award, a Golden Globe Award,
a National Magazine Award, nominations for a first novel award, and
the Stephen Leacock Prize for Humour. Gray's works include the play
Billy Bishop Goes to War, and a novel entitled *Dazzled.* Gray can be seen
periodically on CBC television's *The National* and heard on CBC radio.

Preparing to Read

The title of Gray's 1995 book from which this selection is taken (*I Love
Mom: An Irreverent History of the Tattoo*) makes his subject obvious. Before
you begin reading this selection, think about tattoos. Do you have a tattoo? Do you know anyone else who does? What is your impression of
tattoos? Of the people who have tattoos? Do you think of tattoos as traditionally masculine or feminine? Why do people choose to be tattooed?
What distinguishes tattoos from other ways of decorating our bodies?

■

Nothing evokes that superior shudder, that anal-retentive cluck   1
of civilized disapproval, quite like a tattoo.

Find out for yourself: in casual conversation with a relative   2
or colleague mention casually, as though an afterthought, "By
the way, I'm thinking of acquiring a tattoo."

After the pause you will hear something like "What are you   3
thinking of doing *that* for?", murmured with the inflection of
"Why would you want to pull out all your teeth?"

Now switch to a neutral topic—a recent movie or the price of   4
real estate. Note the lingering chill in the basement of the
conversation, a vaguely sectarian distance, as though you had
just declared yourself a Scientologist.

To complete the experiment you will need a point of   5
comparison, a control. Try this:

Under similar circumstances, turn to a family member or 6
business associate and declare, "I'm thinking of having a surgeon
slice the pouches from under my eyes," or "I want to have bags
of silicone sewn into my breasts."

Quite another response: concern about your self-esteem, 7
perhaps; or reassurance as to the state of your pouches or bustline;
be yourself, beauty only skin deep, etc. Even when laced with
contempt (vanity, vanity), the reaction will not vibrate with that
hum of theological alarm that accompanied the subject of tattooing.

While having animal tissue injected into one's lips with a 8
needle the size of a bug sprayer, or artificial hairs poked into
one's skull may not receive enthusiastic applause, these urges
are treated as symptoms of a mild psychological crisis, endearing
evidence of a vulnerable, insecure nature.

A tattoo, however, is a threat.   9

Unlike cosmetic-surgery enthusiasts, tattoos seek not to 10
conform to a conventional standard of beauty, but to distance
themselves from the rest of us, to join an alien opposition.

People either have tattoos or they do not. A tattoo does not 11
win friends among the untattooed majority. A tattoo is no way to
get ahead.

A Dirty Business

Tattooing has always emitted an unsavory aura in Western 12
culture—a whiff of the criminal, the carnival sharp, the fallen
woman, and the unhygienic lover.

"Tattooed Thracians are not well-born," sniffed Herodotus, 13
the father of history, in the fifth century B.C. (According to
Plutarch, Thracian women acquired tattoos as a souvenir of
Orpheus, whom they tore to pieces in a fit of pique over his
homosexual preferences.)

"Well-born" indeed! Today, tattoos are a common fetish of 14
the shave-and-puncture subculture, to go with the radiation-
victim haircuts and multiple rings of surgical steel in nostrils
and nipples—visual codes, no doubt, for unseemly sexual
enthusiasms.

According to the media, tattooing is about to go permanently 15
mainstream. Don't believe it. Rumours of imminent respectability
have been chasing the tattoo for a century. When respectable
people acquire tattoos, and they do, it's not because the practice
has become respectable, it's because the recipient wishes inwardly
to be *not* respectable, seeking out acts of private outrage that
won't adversely affect the career path.

It doesn't matter what the tattoo is—a dedication ("I Love 16
Mom"), a motto ("Death Before Dishonor"), a vow ("Property
of Vito"), a warning ("Fuck Off"), a death symbol, predatory or
mythical animal, flower, patriotic gesture, cartoon character,
pinup girl, automotive logo, or primitive tribal scrawl. It's not
the subject but the *fact* of a tattoo that contains its stigma and
appeal. The tattooee has chosen to have an image indelibly
stamped on his or her hide for no apparent reason other than a
desire to be different.

What's wrong with the rest of us? Who do they think they are? 17

For a quasi-medical practice that entails injecting a foreign 18
substance into a wound, the tattoo parlor is a breathtakingly
unregulated industry. Although the city health inspector may
call now and then to update the crumbling certificate on the wall,
only the tattooist's personal ethic prompts him or her to maintain
sanitary premises, wear surgical gloves, use new needles, and
learn the medical effects of the various pigments. (It is not
unknown for amateurs and semiprofessional "bootleggers" to
use house paint!)

Given the Darwinian, *laissez-faire* nature of the craft, it's a 19
testament to human probity that there exist any standards at all:
that most tattooists turn away clients who are drunk, stoned,
warped, or underage; refuse to mark "public skin" (above the neck
or below the waist); and usually refuse racist slogans, Nazi emblems,
ill-advised vows, and obscenities. Such restraints are voluntary,
however, and like most discretionary industrial standards of
safety and cleanliness, apt to slip during an economic downturn.

In addition to medical qualms, there is every reason to fret 20
about aesthetic standards, for nothing publicly or professionally
identifies the impeccable craftsman or incompetent scratcher.
Tattooists earn no degrees or fellowships; no magazine critics
review their work. For the buyer there is no trial period, no
guarantee, no five-year warranty on parts or labor.

Not that the average patron is fussy. Statistically, the majority 21
of tattoos result from a momentary, possibly drunken, impulse
(although the desire may have been present for some time), and
tattoo parlors are chosen primarily on the basis of geographical
convenience. As a rule, more thought goes into the purchase of
a stereo than a tattoo.

With predictable results. Face it—most tattoos look dreadful. 22
A few years after application, these ill-considered icons of crude
personal symbolism have blurred into dirty blobs of ink with

hairs growing from them, as meaningful and attractive as a large strawberry mole.

Oh, What the Hell

Despite these obvious drawbacks, approximately ten percent of 23
the adult population choose to have themselves marked for life.

Why would they do that?   24

It's inadequate, though tempting, to dismiss them as mildly 25
insane. Although psychiatrists usually view tattoos as symptoms
of mental trouble, inmates of mental institutions have fewer
tattoos than do the outside population. (On the other hand, it
has been said that the three traits common to psychopathic serial
killers is that they are male and white and they possess a tattoo.)

While it is no great challenge to understand why a person 26
would not acquire a tattoo, the reasons why people *do* are
interesting, contradictory, and elusive.

Like other persistent cultural practices just outside publicly 27
acknowledged art, such as circuses, soap operas, and rock and
roll, tattooing draws from deep wells in the collective and
subjective consciousness. A cultural weed growing without
encouragement, it is nourished by primitive needs. To frighten off
an attacking enemy. To invoke magic or borrow power from
another being. To ward off evil. To attract good fortune. To draw
attention and sexual respect by means of an exaggerated
plumage. To declare oneself different from, or part of, a tribe.
To make permanent a decision or rite of passage. Tattooing is a
complex act—social, sexual, mystical, and cosmetic.

The one fact about a tattoo that never varies is its 28
permanence. There's no such thing as a temporary tattoo. Yes,
tattoos can indeed be erased, but the resulting patch of scar tissue
is as conspicuous as the mark it replaced.

People receive a tattoo *because* of its permanence. All tattoos 29
represent a desire for a reality that endures despite our wrinkling
skin and mutating identities. All tattoos, ugly or beautiful, Jesus
Christ or Tweety Bird, represent the same urge: to transcend.

Subconsciously, in an absurd, naive, slapstick fashion, people 30
who receive tattoos are searching for God.

Think about it: a prominent 1930s tattooist named Jack 31
Redcloud displayed a large bust of Jesus, complete with bleeding
crown of thorns, *upon his bald head.*

UNDERSTANDING DETAILS

1. Explain why people get tattoos. In what ways is getting a tattoo different from getting a facelift or hair implants? Consider both the motivations that lead people to have each type of procedure done and the effects that their changed appearance has.
2. Why does Gray refer to tattooing as "a dirty business"?
3. What are typical or common tattoo images? List some of the popular categories of tattoos.

ANALYZING MEANING

1. What details does Gray give to support his characterization of the tattoo industry as "breathtakingly unregulated"? What is it about this industry that might lead to the lack of standards that Gray describes?
2. Summarize Gray's attitude toward his subject. Do you think that Gray is likely to ever get a tattoo? Why or why not?
3. How do you interpret Gray's comment in paragraph 30 that, "(s)ubconsciously . . . people who receive tattoos are searching for God."

DISCOVERING RHETORICAL STRATEGIES

1. Identify Gray's purpose in writing this piece about tattoos. Who is his intended audience?
2. Gray's essay is only 5 pages long, but it has 31 paragraphs and is also characterized by sentence fragments. What effect do these short paragraphs and choppy sentence fragments have? Is this effect suitable for the subject of tattoos?
3. Characterize Gray's tone. What language choices contribute towards conveying this tone?

MAKING CONNECTIONS

1. John Gray's discussion of tattoos deals with body image and the effect of one's appearance on others. Imagine a discussion between John Gray and Jill Leslie Rosenbaum and Meda Chesney-Lind ("Appearance and Delinquency: A Research Note"). Would these writers agree about the effects of tattoos?
2. John Gray's writing style is similar in many respects to that of Joe Fiorito ("Breakfast in Bed"). Describe the style of each of these writers, using specific examples, with particular attention to characteristics that are shared by the two.

3. John Gray suggests many reasons why people choose to get tattoos. Do you agree with his views? Why or why not? Do you think that David Foot ("Boomers Dance to a New Beat") would account for this behaviour in the same way? Explain.

IDEAS FOR DISCUSSION/WRITING

Preparing to Write

Tattooing is one form of body ornamentation. Write freely about the various forms of body decoration that you can think of. This might include piercing different parts of the body, painting body parts, scarification, and cutting one's hair in a particular style. Which of these are permanent? Which are temporary? Do you decorate yourself in any of these ways? Why or why not? Are some forms of body decoration specific to males or females? Are some forms typical of people in a particular age group? What motivates people to choose the forms of body ornamentation that they do? What are the effects of these forms of decoration?

Choosing a Topic

1. Write an essay in which you either encourage your readers to get a tattoo or dissuade them from getting one. Make sure you give specific reasons why your audience should take your advice in this matter.
2. Gray has focused his discussion on tattooing. Write an essay in which you focus on another form of body ornamentation. Consider both the causes or motivations for people choosing this form or decoration, as well as the effects of this ornamentation. In your essay use your choices of language and detail to convey your attitude toward your subject.
3. Tattoos are considered by some a form of art. Write an essay in which you discuss what constitutes art. Do tattoos fit into your definition? Make your explanation clear with specific examples.

WEB SITES

tattoos.com/
A tattoo site with articles, convention information, galleries, contests, and extensive links to other tattoo-related sites.

www.zelacom.com/~nyctattoo/welcome.html
New York City Style Tattoos: This page has been created as an introduction to the upcoming book, *New York City Tattoo: The Oral History of a Forgotten Past.*

Tony Leighton
1954–

■ ■ ■

The New Nature

Tony Leighton is a writer from Guelph, Ontario, whose work can be found in *Harrowsmith*, *Canadian Geographic*, *The Globe and Mail*'s *Report on Business*, and *Equinox*, where "The New Nature" was first published late in 1994. Leighton was also the editor of the Bank of Montreal's customer newsletter, *Possibilities*.

Preparing to Read

"The New Nature" is an exploration of the growing industry of digital imaging, a process that is, in many ways, replacing traditional photography. Before reading Leighton's essay, think about photographs and the role that they play in our lives. What role do photographs play in newspapers and magazines, in conveying news stories, and in providing us with memories of specific events and people? It is often said that "a picture is worth a thousand words." Can you think of any other sayings about pictures? How reliable are pictures? Can you always believe your eyes?

O f all the media coverage that has whirled around O.J.   1
Simpson's indictment for murder, one image has had lingering impact. Shortly after Simpson's arrest on June 17, the Los Angeles Police Department released a now infamous photograph that appeared on the covers of both *Time* and *Newsweek*. It's not a particularly striking image. Simpson is being arraigned at a courthouse. He is obviously tired and shaken. What's significant is what *Time* did to it. The magazine's art department used a computer to "process" the image digitally, darkening Simpson's features and his day-old beard and making the background details appear indistinct and shadowy. The result is unmistakably sinister. *Time*'s Simpson looked more threatening than *Newsweek*'s.

Once discovered, *Time*'s use of computer manipulation was   2
hotly criticized as a cheat on an unsuspecting public. But it's more than that. The Simpson episode reflects a broad trend in contemporary media that's giving rise to a new ethical debate.

Thanks to the revolution of digital technology, the original source materials of many cultural media, including photographs, films, and recordings, can now be reshaped with amazing—and some say alarming—felicity. Reality can be transfigured with a few swift strokes of a keyboard. And it can be done with such skill that the difference between an authentic image or sound and a digitized fake is no longer recognizable.

For those who work in the fantasy business producing 3 movies, commercials, pop records, or fine art, digital manipulation offers cost savings and enhanced creative power. But when it is used to alter, say, news photography, it has much darker implications. It can be argued that for every advancement of technology, there is a price to pay. With the digitization of photography, the price is veracity. We can no longer believe what we see.

"It's that old thing about 'photography never lies,'" says 4 Doug Smith, a computer-support specialist at The Banff Centre for the Arts in Alberta, where resident artists are taught digital photography. "We know that photography lies, but we still rely on newspapers, television, and magazines for truthful information. I guess we have to trust somebody. If we know they are manipulating images, it becomes just another of the many things we have to mistrust."

Learning to mistrust may soon be a survival skill for the 5 customers of media, one that forces us to break some very old habits of mind. "For a century and a half ... photographs appeared to be reliably manufactured commodities, readily distinguishable from other types of depictions," wrote William J. Mitchell, a professor of architecture and media arts at the Massachusetts Institute of Technology (MIT), in the February 1994 issue of *Scientific American*. "The emergence of digital imaging has irrevocably subverted these certainties, forcing us all to adopt a far more wary and vigilant interpretive stance ... We will have to take great care to sift the facts from the fictions and falsehoods."

Anyone who doubts the urgency of the issue need only 6 consider a handful of classic digital ploys. Last February, *New York Newsday* showed Olympians Tonya Harding and Nancy Kerrigan skating "together" shortly after the famous bashed-knee incident. The photo was a composite, with the skaters stitched in place electronically. In the musical realm, Frank Sinatra sang "duets" on a recent compact disc with artists he never met, their voices recorded digitally, some transmitted with flawless clarity over telephone lines. In Hollywood, John Candy's last movie, *Wagons East*, unfinished at the time of his death, was completed with digitally cloned images of the actor inserted into essential scenes.

Historically, of course, the media have always been able to   7
manipulate source materials one way or another. American Civil War battlefields were rigged with "dead" bodies by photographers drumming up sympathy for the Union's cause. Trying to rewrite history, Stalin had Trotsky expunged from a 1920 photograph that showed him at Lenin's side. What's the difference today? Those who altered photographs in the '20s used knives, light, silver-halide paper, and darkrooms, and only a handful of skilled specialists could work such magic. Today, with an hour of practice, you and I could do a much better job in a few minutes on a desktop computer.

Of all media, photography provides the most instructive look   8
at both the seductive power and the haunting price of the new digital technology. When the content of a conventional photograph is stored as digital code, it is transformed from a static reflection of reality frozen on film and paper to a fluid bit stream that is as alterable as a fantasy. In fact, most of what you see in newspapers, magazines, and books these days are no longer photographs at all. They are digital images.

Put most simply, digital code is a binary, or "on-off"   9
language, a kind of simplified alphabet with only two characters, O and I. Any computer program is a huge script of these two characters strung together into large, meaningful patterns that ultimately command a word-processing program to place letters on a screen, a spreadsheet to calculate, or a design program to display an automobile part in three dimensions.

Photographs enter the digital realm by way of a tool called a   10
scanner. With a bar of intense light, it moves across a photograph, reading colours and details, breaking down the original image into thousands of tiny "picture elements," or "pixels," that are like the dots that make up a television screen. Pack together enough dots in sufficient density, and you have a picture. Once digitized, an image can be redescribed at will. In other words, it can be copied, transmitted, or altered with utter mathematical precision.

Working conventionally, a photographer must labour for   11
hours in a darkroom to alter what a camera and film captured in the field. It is fussy, messy work to isolate certain elements in

a photograph and then "dodge" them (deny them light) to darken them in the final print or "burn" them (expose them to more light) to lighten them. Elaborate composites or montages used to require multiple exposures and manual contrivances, to say nothing of all the paper and caustic chemicals devoured in the process. "Now," says Doug Smith, "you can do and undo experimental changes ad infinitum without being in a darkroom, without expending materials, and without standing on your feet for hours and hours."

If you pay any attention to the popular media, you've 12 probably seen the products of digital imaging. Practised photo manipulators have worked some cheeky digital deceptions: Hillary Rodham Clinton's head on the barely dressed body of a voluptuous young model (on the cover of Spy magazine). Arnold Schwarzenegger and Queen Elizabeth as black people and black director Spike Lee with white skin and green eyes (in Colors, a magazine published by Italian clothier Benetton). And Marilyn Monroe flirting arm-in-arm with Abraham Lincoln (on the cover of Scientific American). These images are astonishing and stand as the comic beginning of revolution in image control.

No organization has been quite as engaged in this tech- 13 nological leap as photographic giant Eastman Kodak Company of Rochester, New York. Kodak recently hired chief executive officer George Fisher, who aims to find a new way for the company synonymous with the old way of taking pictures, the analogue way. Fisher's strategy is to focus Kodak's energies on the highly competitive fray of consumer electronics (copiers, printers, Photo CD players) and, of course, to transform Kodak into the company synonymous with digital imaging. In the lobby of Kodak Canada's corporate offices in Toronto's west end, the writing is literally on the wall. The company's business lines are inscribed proudly on several mounted plaques: Printing and Publishing Imaging, Office Imaging, Professional Imaging, Consumer Imaging, Motion Picture and Television Imaging. Nowhere is the word "photography" used.

When asked whether photography is as good as dead, Neil 14 Buchanan, the national sales manager of Kodak Canada's Digital Imaging Group, says no, conventional silver-halide photography will coexist with digital imaging for many years to come. "Technologies don't get displaced," he says. "They just reinvent themselves."

But at the very moment Buchanan is explaining film's 15 importance, one of his colleagues in the same room is downloading an image that was captured moments ago on perhaps the single most subversive tool of the digital age: the filmless camera. Kodak's DCF 420 camera looks like a normal 35 mm model that a professional photographer might use. (And indeed, the main part of the body is a standard Nikon N90.) But inside it is the future of photography—a "charge-coupled device," or CCD array. A CCD is a chip composed of millions of microscopic light-sensing cells that generate millions of little electrical charges in proportion to the intensity of light that strikes them through the camera's lens. The charges are converted to numbers. The numbers describe pixels. In essence, the CCD snatches an image straight from the ether. The electronic image is then stored on a credit-card-sized cartridge that fits in an extension at the base of the camera. It can be downloaded directly to a computer or stored for later use.

The DCF 420 is not for you and me. It costs around $15,000. 16
The image it currently produces is not quite as sharp as a photograph, but it's not far off. And it's getting better with each new version of the camera.

The CCD is a key component in a whole digital desktop 17
system contained in Kodak's demonstration room that can, in minutes, convert what we see around us into a finished colour print. No film. No chemicals. No monopolistic middlemen. No waiting. The system includes a Macintosh computer loaded with Adobe Photoshop software for altering digital images, a "continuous-tone digital-output device" for printing colour images straight from the computer, and if you want to store the images for later retrieval, Kodak's remarkable Photo CD technology that digitally encodes dozens of pictures on a compact disc.

Products such as Kodak's Photo CD and Adobe System's 18
Photoshop are technological watersheds. They have, within the past five years or so, vaulted the entire field of image capture and manipulation through a critical barrier. Granted, not many photographers are working extensively in the medium just yet, considering the cost factors and the leap of faith involved in leaving silver and celluloid behind. But those who have gone digital are proving its huge potential.

"This is about creative control," says Burton Robson, 19
Canadian director of Adobe Systems. "It's putting creative control in a photographer's hands or a designer's hands. Photographers can now provide concepts in advertising and promotions that couldn't be done before."

Toronto photographer Philip Rostron's advertising work is 20 a case in point. He estimates that about 70 percent of his photography is now altered with digital-imaging software, gaining him a creative and financial edge. His work on a Chrysler Canada ad for instance, featured a photograph of a car apparently roaring around a turn in an attractive rural landscape. But it is a landscape of deception. The grassy fields in the background, originally a limp grey-green, were warmed up in Photoshop with the roasted autumnal tones of a chaparral. The sky, in reality a thin blue, was dramatized with beguiling purple. The car, actually photographed when stationary but jacked up on one side to suggest motion, was touched up with a slight digital blur at its back end to create the illusion of speed. Its paint job was raised to the high lustre of polished lacquer. And to finish things off, an intrusive-looking lamp post was simply vaporized. "You could stay on location for two years and not see that landscape," says Rostron. "And it's very hard to justify $20,000 of location photography with no guarantee that God will cooperate."

Rostron says he still works hard to take the best possible 21 photographs. "The stronger the image that goes into the system," he says, "the better the final product that comes out." But he can rest a lot easier these days if a sky is pale or a model has a pimple. The computer will forgive the imperfections.

Digital technology has had a similar effect on Louis Fishauf, 22 a partner in Reactor Art & Design, one of Toronto's best-known graphic-design studios. Fishauf works exclusively on a Macintosh, frequently in Photoshop, and increasingly with Kodak's Photo CD. "The major change," says Fishauf, "has been that the whole process of design can now be telescoped into days, even hours, and be accomplished by one person."

Canada Post Corporation recently hired Reactor to create a 23 stamp and commemorative booklet to honour the 125th anniversary of The T. Eaton Company Limited. With access to a vast trove of Eaton's memorabilia from the Archives of Ontario, Fishauf and his associate, Stephanie Power, decided to do both the stamp and booklet in collage style, displaying as many old photos and illustrations as possible. They selected more than 300 items from the archives and had them photographed on 35 mm slides. All 300 images were then digitized onto Photo CDs.

"It was a great way of organizing so many images," says 24 Fishauf. "With an electronic collage, if you make a mistake or change your mind, you can reuse the same source elements, go back and make it bigger or smaller, change the colour balance, make it transparent, change the brightness or the contrast. You have all kinds of capabilities for manipulating imagery that don't exist in the real world."

The enthusiasm of users such as Rostron and Fishauf is not 25 universally shared. Some critics worry that the greater ease offered by digital technology will seduce us into modifying images without due reflection on a variety of ethical questions. This was a theme at a conference called Ethics, Copyright, and the Bottom Line: A Symposium on Digital Technologies and Professional Photography, held in 1992 at the Center for Creative Imaging in Camden, Maine. One of the speakers, Fred Ritchin, director of photography at *The New York Times Magazine*, summarized the double-edged nature of digital imagery. "As we applaud the technology—as we should," he said, "I think we have to simultaneously ask, 'Is this helping us to see, to understand the world?' You have this impulse to make it bigger, make it smaller, make it pink, because it is so easy. This is what some people have called the God Complex."

The God Complex may be harmless enough in the hands of 26 an artist retouching a mole on the cheek of a *Vogue* cover model, but what about when it crosses over into photography that we are conditioned to trust as documentary evidence? Ritchin gave the example of a Swedish plane that crashed in Finland. No photographer was present, so a newspaper interviewed three eyewitnesses and created a composite image of a plane crash, which it ran as a "news photo."

As Ritchin and others point out, historically we have relied 27 on the accuracy of photography (and film and video) to get the truth—about Tiananmen Square, the Rodney King incident, Gary Hart, and Marion Barry. Or for that matter, about the Civil War, Auschwitz, Hiroshima, and the assassination of JFK. But when truth can so easily be falsified and news travels so rapidly and completely around the world through huge, centralized news organizations or courtesy of the Pentagon, can we believe what we see any more? Will photography ever be taken seriously as evidence again? Will powerful people still need to be "afraid of photographs," as Ritchin puts it?

All of this is good cause for soul-searching among 28 professional image makers. "I think there is a moral decision we have to make," says Nancy Shanoff, another Toronto-based commercial photographer. "We have to think about what engages our minds. If I want to create a photographic illusion, that's one thing, but manipulating a photograph in a news context, that seems to me totally void of morality. Just because we have the technological ability to do something, does that exonerate people from moral obligation? I don't think so."

Olusegun Olaniyan, a Montreal graphic designer who teaches 29 digital imaging to photographers, gives a qualified endorsement to photo manipulation. "I personally have no problem with it, as long as I'm told. As humans, we have a need to know what reality is. When our reality is being played around with, it puts us in a shaky position. It's a state of mind."

If the ethics of current digital developments are difficult to 30 wrestle with, the future looks even more unsettling. As Ritchin said in his conference talk: "We now have something called a range-camera, which is a 360-degree scan that is being developed at the MIT Media Lab. So you could basically encode George Bush's data from any angle, and then you could reconstruct the image from any angle you want any time you wanted, with any stop, with any depth of field, any focus, any lighting, any people next to him that you want. Basically what you end up with is that you no longer need the photographer there."

There's also a persuasive argument to be made that computer 31 images have retarded creativity at least as much as they have advanced it. If ad agencies are now content with digital cut-and-pastes that avoid the high cost of putting a photographer in front of the Eiffel Tower or the Grand Canyon, will professionals become lastingly complacent? "Will we any longer be the originators of images?" asks Shanoff. "Or will we be reduced to image makers who supply pieces of images? This background, this person—like sampling music or actors?"

Shanoff is not an unschooled technophobe. Like Rostron, she 32 has spent hundreds of hours working with Photoshop. For clients who prefer their images in digital format, she now delivers her work on magnetic disk. Yet she is a reluctant participant. She doesn't alter her own images. She has hired an operator to use the computer in her studio. "I am a middle-aged woman, and I decided a long time ago I wasn't going to be left behind. [But conventional photography] is the craft I have spent my life training for, and there is an intrinsic human thing that doesn't want to let go of that."

In the long run, the impact of digital imaging on our culture 33 may be profound. The cognitive consequence of altering reality is dissonance, the uncomfortable befuddlement we feel when our anchor points are uprooted and there's nothing left to hang onto. News as entertainment does this to us. Television does it in general. Digitally altered photographs do it. As Marshall McLuhan said, "We become what we behold," and "We shape our tools, and afterwards, our tools shape us."

Lewis H. Lapham, the editor of *Harper's*, recounted these   34
words of McLuhan's in a recent editorial. Lapham believes that in the here-there-and-everywhere universe of modern media, "a world in which the stars of daytime soap opera receive 10,000 letters a week from fans who confess secrets of the heart that they dare not tell their husbands, their mothers, or their wives," our perceptions are being perilously reshuffled. As he argues it, we are moving intractably from the pre-electronic straight lines of intellectual cause and effect to nonlinear ways of thinking based on emotions, impressions, sensations—things that invite manipulation. When we allow our tools to shape us, he concludes, we "deconstruct the texts of a civilization" and "nothing necessarily follows from anything else."

The same can be said very specifically for rearranging our   35
photographic reality. If all things are digitally fluid, nothing necessarily follows from anything else. A photograph no longer tells the truth. It only suggests a possibility.

UNDERSTANDING DETAILS

1. What effect has the advent of digital imaging had on traditional photography? Give specific examples to support your answer.
2. How does the ability to manipulate photographs digitally differ from the manipulation of photographs practised earlier in this century?
3. Summarize the benefits that digital imaging can offer. What negative effects counter these positives?

ANALYZING MEANING

1. According to the various people cited in Leighton's article, what reaction to this new technology is now required from consumers? Why?
2. What has been the impact of digital imaging on the way that people view the world? Explain what ethical issues it raises.

3. Where is the line drawn between appropriate and inappropriate use of this form of new technology? Does everyone agree on what is acceptable? Whose view is closest to your own? Explain why.

DISCOVERING RHETORICAL STRATEGIES

1. Reread Leighton's introduction to this essay. What rhetorical technique has he used to introduce his topic and get his audience's attention? Is it effective? Why or why not?
2. Paragraph 20 has several good examples of words that have been carefully chosen for their connotations. List the words or phrases that emphasize the negative impression of the real and those that highlight the positive attitude toward the illusion.
3. Identify Leighton's intended audience in this essay. How has he tailored his discussion of digital imaging to suit this group of readers?

MAKING CONNECTIONS

1. Evan Solomon ("The Babar Factor") concludes his essay by choosing old technology over new. Do you think that Leighton views the new technology that he describes as positive or negative? Explain. What is your position on new technologies such as digital enhancement of photographs?
2. Trina McQueen ("Why We Crave Hot Stuff") alerts us to some of the dangers of journalistic storytelling. How would the information and examples in Tony Leighton's essay support McQueen's caution?
3. Several of the authors represented in *Reader's Choice* give vivid descriptions of places they know. Would the essays of Tomson Highway ("What a Certain Visionary Once Said"), Lesley Choyce ("Thin Edge of the Wedge"), Karen Connelly ("Touch the Dragon"), and Will Ferguson ("The Sudbury Syndrome") be enhanced by photographs of their subjects? Why or why not? If photographs were to accompany their essays do you think that any of them would want to use digitally enhanced photographs? Explain your answer.

IDEAS FOR DISCUSSION/WRITING

Preparing to Write

Write freely about the reliable sources of information in your life. How do you obtain information on news items in your community? National events? International happenings? Historical events? How do you know that those sources are accurate? Who can you count on to tell you the truth? Have you ever found a reliable source to be inaccurate? Do newspaper or television reporters ever misrepresent a story? Do stories get different coverage by different reporters or by different media? Also consider information about personal matters. How have you learned about your family and your ancestors? What do you know about your friends? How do you know what they have told you is true?

Choosing a Topic

1. Many of the people cited in Leighton's essay discuss the situations where digital manipulation of photographs is and is not appropriate. What is your position on the use of digital imaging? What limits, if any, should restrict the use of this technology?
2. Find a picture of yourself that was taken at least five years ago, preferably at some memorable or significant event (e.g., a wedding, a party, a vacation, a holiday celebration). What does it convey about the reality of where and who you were at that time? If you could, is there anything about this picture that you would change? Explain why or why not.
3. In "The New Nature" Leighton quotes Marshall McLuhan as saying, "We shape our tools, and afterwards, our tools shape us." In a short essay, discuss the truth of this statement with reference to at least one specific example of a "tool" that you use in your life.

WEB SITES

www.bmo.com/newsltr/gendernmoney.html
or
www.bmo.com/newsltr/10reasons.html
Here you can read other articles by Tony Leighton from the Bank of Montreal's *Possibilities* newsletter.

s9000.furman.edu/~eharmon/team2/issues.html
Issues and Ethics Involved in Photojournalism.

CHAPTER 9

ARGUMENT/PERSUASION

■ ■ ■

Inciting People to Thought or Action

Almost everything we do or say is an attempt to persuade. Whether we dress up to impress a potential employer or argue openly with a friend about an upcoming election, we are trying to convince various people to see the world our way. Some aspects of life are particularly dependent upon persuasion. Think, for example, of all the television, magazine, and billboard ads we see urging us to buy certain products, or of the many impassioned appeals we read and hear on such controversial issues as school prayer, abortion, gun control, and nuclear energy. Religious leaders devote their professional lives to convincing people to live a certain way and believe in certain religious truths, whereas scientists and mathematicians use rigorous logic and natural law to convince us of various hypotheses. Politicians make their living persuading voters to elect them and then support them throughout their terms of office. In fact, anyone who wants something from another person or agency, ranging from federal money for a research project to a new bicycle for Christmas, must use some form of persuasion to get what he or she desires. The success or failure of this type of communication is easily determined: If the people being addressed change their actions or attitudes in favour of the writer or speaker, the attempt at persuasion has been successful.

Defining Argument/Persuasion

The terms *argument* and *persuasion* are often used interchangeably, but one is actually a subdivision of the other. Persuasion names a purpose for writing. To persuade your readers is to convince them to think, act, or feel a certain way. Much of the writing you have been doing in this book has persuasion as one of its goals: A description of an African tribe has a "dominant impression" you want your readers to accept; in an essay comparing various ways of celebrating the New Year, you are trying to convince your readers to believe that these similarities and differences actually exist; and in writing an essay exam on the causes of the strife in the Middle East, you are trying to convince your instructor that your reasoning is clear and your conclusions sound. In a sense, some degree of persuasion propels all writing.

More specifically, however, the process of persuasion involves appealing to one or more of the following: to reason, to emotion, or to a sense of ethics. An *argument* is an appeal predominantly to your readers' reason and intellect. You are working in the realm of argument when you deal with complex issues that are debatable; opposing views (either explicit or implicit) are a basic requirement of argumentation. But argument and persuasion are taught together because good writers are constantly blending these three appeals and adjusting them to the purpose and audience of a particular writing task. Although reason and logic are the focus of this chapter, you need to learn to use all three methods of persuasion as skillfully as possible to write effective essays.

An appeal to reason relies upon logic and intellect and is usually most effective when you are expecting your readers to disagree with you in any way. This type of appeal can help you change your readers' opinions or influence their future actions through the sheer strength of logical validity. If you wanted to argue, for example, that pregnant women should refrain from smoking cigarettes, you could cite abundant statistical evidence that babies born to mothers who smoke have lower birth weights, more respiratory problems, and a higher incidence of sudden infant death syndrome than the children of nonsmoking mothers. Because smoking clearly endangers the health of the unborn child, reason dictates that mothers who wish to give birth to the healthiest possible babies should avoid smoking during pregnancy.

Emotional appeals, however, attempt to arouse your readers' feelings, instincts, senses, and biases. Used most profitably when your readers already agree with you, this type of essay generally validates, reinforces, and/or incites in an effort to get your readers to share your feelings or ideas. In order to urge our lawmakers to impose stricter jail sentences for alcohol abuse, you might describe a recent tragic accident involving a local twelve-year-old girl who was killed by a drunk driver as she rode her bicycle to school one morning. By focusing on such poignant visual details as the condition of her mangled bike, the bright blood stains on her white dress, and the anguish on the faces of parents and friends, you could build a powerfully persuasive essay that would be much more effective than a dull recitation of impersonal facts and nationwide statistics.

An appeal to ethics, the third technique writers often use to encourage readers to agree with them, involves cultivating a sincere, honest tone that will establish your reputation as a reliable, qualified, experienced, well-informed, and know-ledgeable person whose opinions on the topic under discussion are believable because they are ethically sound. Such an approach is often used in conjunction with logical or emotional appeals to foster a verbal environment that will result in minimal resistance from its readers. Ed McMahon, Johnny Carson's congenial announcer on the *Tonight Show* for many years and the host of *Star Search*, was an absolute master at creating this ethical, trustworthy persona as he coaxes his television viewers to purchase everything from dog food to beer. In fact, the old gag question "Would you buy a used car from this man?" is our instinctive response to all forms of attempted persuasion, whether the salesperson is trying to sell us Puppy Chow or gun control, hair spray or school prayer. The more believable we are as human beings, the better chance we will have of convincing our audience.

The following student paragraph is directed primarily toward the audience's logical reasoning ability. Notice that the writer states her assertion and then gives reasons to convince her readers to change their ways. The student writer also brings both emotion and ethics into the argument by choosing her words and examples with great precision.

> Have you ever watched a pair of chunky thighs, a jiggling pos-terior, and an extra-large sweatshirt straining to cover a beer belly and thought, "Thank God I don't look like that! I'm in pretty good shape ... for someone my age." Well, before you become too smug and self-righteous, consider what kind of shape you're really in. Just because you don't look like Shamu the Whale doesn't mean you're in good condition. What's missing, you ask? Exercise. You can diet all day, wear the latest slim-cut designer jeans, and still be in worse

shape than someone twice your age if you don't get a strong physical workout at least three times a week. Exercise is not only good for
you, but it can also be fun—especially if you find a sport that makes
you happy while you sweat. Your activity need not be expensive:
Jogging, walking, basketball, tennis, and handball are not costly, unless you're seduced by the glossy sheen of the latest sporting fashions
and accessories. Most of all, however, regular exercise is important for
your health. You can just as easily drop dead from a sudden heart attack in the middle of a restaurant when you're slim and trim as when
you're a slob. Your heart and lungs need regular workouts to stay
healthy. So do yourself a favour and add some form of exercise to
your schedule. You'll feel better and live longer, and your looks will
improve, too!

Thinking Critically by Using Argument/Persuasion

Argument and persuasion require you to present your views on
an issue through logic, emotion, and good character in such a
way that you convince an audience of your point of view. This
rhetorical mode comes at the end of this book because it is an
extremely complex and sophisticated method of reasoning. The
more proficient you become in this strategy of thinking and
presenting your views, the more you will get what you want out
of life (and out of school). Winning arguments means getting
the pay raises you need, the refund you deserve, and the grades
you've worked so hard for.

In a successful argument, your logic must be flawless. Your
conclusions should be based on clear evidence, and your evidence
must be organized in such a way that it builds to an effective,
convincing conclusion. You should constantly have your purpose
and audience in mind as you build your case; at the same time,
issues of emotion and good character should support the flow
of your logic.

Exercising your best logical skills is extremely important to
all phases of your daily survival—in and out of the classroom.
Following a logical argument in your reading and presenting a
logical response to your course work are the hallmarks of a good
student. Right now, put your best logic forward and work on
your reasoning and persuasive abilities in the series of exercises
below. Isolate argument and persuasion from the other rhetorical
strategies so that you can practise it and strengthen your ability
to argue before you combine it with other methods.

1. Bring to class two magazine ads—one ad that tries to sell a product and another that tries to convince the reader that a particular action or product is wrong or bad (unhealthy, misinterpreted, politically incorrect, etc.). How does each ad appeal to the reader's logic? How does the advertiser use emotion and character in his or her appeal?

2. Think of a recent book you have read. How could you persuade a friend either to read or not to read this book?

3. Fill in the following blanks: The best way to _____ is to _____ . (For example, "The best way to lose weight is to exercise.") Then, list ways you might persuade a reader to see your point of view in this statement.

Reading and Writing Persuasive Essays

Although persuasive writing can be approached essentially in three different ways—logically, emotionally, and/or ethically—our stress in this chapter is on logic and reason, because they are at the heart of most college writing. As a reader, you will see how various forms of reasoning and different methods of organization affect your reaction to an essay. Your stand on a particular issue will control the way you process information in argument and persuasion essays. As you read the essays in this chapter, you will also learn to recognize emotional and ethical appeals and the different effects they create. In your role as writer, you need to be fully aware of the options available to you as you compose. Although the basis of your writing will be logical argument, you will see that you can learn to control your readers' responses to your essays by choosing your evidence carefully, organizing it wisely, and seasoning it with the right amount of emotion and ethics—depending on your purpose and audience.

How to Read Persuasive Essays

Preparing to Read. As you prepare to read the essays in this chapter, spend a few minutes browsing through the preliminary material for each selection: What does Judy Rebick's title, "Kick 'Em Again," prepare you for? What can you learn from scanning Gerald W. Paul's essay, "Stand Tall, and Pass the Ammunition," and reading its synopsis in the Rhetorical Contents?

Also, you should bring to your reading as much information as you can from the authors' biographies: Why do you think Jennifer Cowan writes about keeping television out of public places in "TV Me Alone"? Does she have the appropriate qualifications to teach us about the proper time and place for TV? What is the source of David Suzuki's interest in "The Right Stuff"? For the essays in this chapter that present two sides of an argument, what biographical details prepare us for each writer's stand on the issue? Who were the original audiences for these pro and con arguments?

Last, before you read these essays, try to generate some ideas on each topic so that you can take the role of an active reader. In this text, the Preparing to Read questions will ready you for this task. Then, you should speculate further on the general subject of the essay: Do you believe that the collection of personal data is dangerous or desirable (Lawrence Solomon, "Too Much Privacy Can Be Hazardous to the Person")? What do you want to know from Paul about the funeral business?

Reading. Be sure to record your spontaneous reactions to the persuasive essays in this chapter as you read them for the first time: What are your opinions on each subject? Why do you hold these opinions? Be especially aware of your responses to the essays representing opposing viewpoints at the end of the chapter; know where you stand in relation to each side of the issues here.

Use the preliminary material before an essay to help you create a framework for your responses to it: Who was Jennifer Cowan's primary audience when her essay was first published? In what ways is the tone of her essay appropriate for that audience? What motivated Paul to publish his arguments on the value of the funeral business? Why is Suzuki so interested in the high school science curriculum? Which argument do you find most convincing?

Your main job at this stage of reading is to determine each author's primary assertion or proposition (thesis statement) and to create an inquisitive environment for thinking critically about the essay's ideas. In addition, take a look at the questions after each selection to make sure you are picking up the major points of the essay.

Rereading. As you reread these persuasive essays, notice how the writers integrate their appeals to logic, to emotion, and to ethics. Also, pay attention to the emphasis the writers place on one or more appeals at certain strategic points in the essays: How does Cowan integrate these three appeals in "TV Me Alone"? Which of these appeals does she rely on to help bring her essay to a close? How persuasive is her final appeal? What combination of appeals does Rebick use in "Kick 'Em Again"? In what ways does the tone of her writing support what she is saying? How does she establish the tone?

Also, determine what other rhetorical strategies help these writers make their primary points. How do these strategies enable each writer to establish a unified essay with a beginning, a middle, and an end?

Then, answer the questions after each reading selection to make certain you understand the essay on the literal, interpretive, and analytical levels in preparation for the discussion/writing assignments that follow.

For a list of guidelines for the entire reading process, see the checklists on pages 15–16 of the Introduction.

How to Write Persuasive Essays

Preparing to Write. The first stage of writing an essay of this sort involves, as usual, exploring and then limiting your topic. As you prepare to write your persuasive paper, first try to generate as many ideas as possible—regardless of whether they appeal to logic, emotion, or ethics. To do this, review the prewriting techniques in the Introduction and answer the Preparing to Write questions. Then, choose a topic. Next, focus on a purpose and a specific audience before you begin to write.

Writing. Most persuasive essays should begin with an assertion or a proposition stating what you believe about a certain issue. This thesis should generally be phrased as a debatable statement, such as, "If the national government instituted a guaranteed income supplement for seasonal workers, it would provide security for workers in the natural resource sectors of the economy and minimize the draw on the Employment Insurance Fund." At this point in your essay, you should also justify the significance of the issue you will be discussing: "Such a program would help to support workers in industries vital to Canada's economy, would help to maintain the EI fund for people who become unexpectedly out of work, and would improve the image of seasonal workers among Canadians."

The essay should then support your thesis in a variety of ways. This support may take the form of facts, figures, examples, or opinions by recognized authorities, case histories, narratives/anecdotes, comparisons, contrasts, or cause/effect studies. This evidence is most effectively organized from least to most important when you are confronted with a hostile audience (so that you can lead your readers through the reasoning step by step) and from most to least important when you are facing a supportive audience (so that you can build on their loyalty and enthusiasm as you advance your thesis). In fact, you will be able to engineer your best support if you know your audience's opinions, feelings, and background before you write your essay, so that your intended "target" is as clear as possible. The body of your essay will undoubtedly consist of a combination of logical, emotional, and ethical appeals—all leading to some final summation or recommendation.

The concluding paragraph of a persuasive essay should restate your main assertion (in slightly different terms from those in your original statement) and should offer some constructive recommendations about the problem you have been discussing (if you haven't already done so). This section of your paper should clearly bring your argument to a close in one final attempt to move your audience to accept or act on the viewpoint you present. Let's look more closely now at each of the three types of appeals used in such essays: logical, emotional, and ethical.

To construct a *logical* argument, you have two principal patterns available to you: inductive reasoning or deductive reasoning. The first encourages an audience to make what is called an "inductive leap" from several particular examples to a single, useful generalization. In the case of a guaranteed income supplement, you might cite a number of examples, figures, facts, and case studies illustrating the effectiveness of a guaranteed income supplement plan, thereby leading to your firm belief that implementation of this program is essential to the survival of many of Canada's core industries. Used most often by detectives, scientists, and lawyers, the process of inductive reasoning addresses the audience's ability to think logically by moving it systematically from an assortment of selected evidence to a rational and ordered conclusion.

In contrast, deductive reasoning moves its audience from a broad, general statement to particular examples supporting that statement. In writing such an essay, you would present your thesis statement about a guaranteed income supplement first and then offer clear, orderly evidence to support that belief. Although the mental process we go through in creating a deductive argument is quite sophisticated, it is based on a three-step form of reasoning called the *syllogism*, which most logicians believe is the foundation of logical thinking. The traditional syllogism has:

a major premise: Seasonal workers are essential to the Canadian economy;

a minor premise: All workers must make enough money, through wages and / or supplements, to support themselves year round;

and a conclusion: Therefore, for the survival of the Canadian economy, seasonal workers need to receive enough money, through wages and / or supplements, to live adequately for the entire year.

As you might suspect, this type of reasoning is only as accurate as its original premises, so you need to be careful with the truth of the premises as well as with the logical validity of your argument.

In constructing a logical argument, you should take great care to avoid the two types of fallacies in reasoning found most frequently in college papers: giving too few examples to support an assertion and citing examples that do not represent the assertion fairly. If you build your argument on true statements and abundant, accurate evidence, your essay will be effective.

Persuading through *emotion* necessitates controlling your readers' instinctive reactions to what you are saying. You can accomplish this goal in two different ways: (1) by choosing your words with even greater care than usual and (2) by using figurative language whenever appropriate. In the first case, you must be especially conscious of using words that have the same general denotative (or dictionary) meaning but bear decidedly favourable or unfavourable connotative (or implicit) meanings. For example, notice the difference between *slender* and *scrawny*, *patriotic* and *chauvinistic*, or *compliment* and *flattery*. Your careful attention to the choice of such words can help readers form visual images with certain positive or negative associations that subtly encourage them to follow your argument and adopt your opinions. Second, the effective use of figurative language—especially similes and metaphors—makes your writing more vivid, thus triggering your readers' senses and encouraging them to accept your views. Both of these techniques will help you manipulate your readers into the position of agreeing with your ideas.

Ethical appeals, which establish you as a reliable, well-informed person, are accomplished through (1) the tone of your essay and (2) the number and type of examples you cite. Tone is created through deliberate word choice: Careful attention to the mood implied in the words you use can convince your readers that you are serious, friendly, authoritative, jovial, or methodical—depending on your intended purpose. In like manner, the examples you supply to support your assertions can encourage readers to see you as experienced, insightful, relaxed, or intense. In both of these cases, winning favour for yourself will usually also gain approval for your opinions.

Rewriting. To rework your persuasive essays, you should play the role of your readers and impartially evaluate the different appeals you have used to accomplish your purpose:

1. Is your thesis statement clear?
2. Is the main thrust of your essay argumentative (an appeal to reason)?
3. Will the balance of these appeals effectively accomplish your purpose with your intended audience?
4. Does your conclusion restate your argument, make a recommendation, and bring your essay to a close?

You should also look closely at the way your appeals work together in your essay:

1. When you use logic, is that section of your paper arranged through either inductive or deductive reasoning?
2. Is that the most effective order to achieve your purpose?
3. In appealing to the emotions, have you chosen your words with proper attention to their denotative and connotative effects?
4. Have you chosen examples carefully to support your thesis statement?
5. Are these examples suitable for your purpose and your audience?

Any additional guidance you may need as you write and revise your persuasive essays is furnished on pages 26–27 of the Introduction.

Student Essay: Argument/Persuasion at Work

The following student essay uses all three appeals to make its point about the power of language in shaping our view of the world. First, the writer sets forth her character references (ethical appeal) in the first paragraph, after which she presents her thesis and its significance in paragraph 2. The support for her thesis is a combination of logical and emotional appeals, heavy on the logical, as the writer moves her paragraphs from general to particular in an effort to convince her readers to adopt her point of view and adjust their language use accordingly.

The Language of Equal Rights

Ethical appeal Up front, I admit it. <u>I've been a card-carrying feminist since junior high school. I want to see an Equal Rights Amendment to the U.S. Constitution, equal pay for equal—and comparable—work, and I go dutch on dates. Furthermore, I am quite prickly on the subject of language. I'm one of those women who bristles at terms like lady doctor (you know they don't mean a gynecologist), female policeman (a paradox), and mankind instead of humanity (are they really talking about me?).</u> Emotional appeal

Many people ask "How important are mere words, anyway? You know what we really mean." A question like this ignores the symbolic and psychological importance of language. <u>What words "mean" can go beyond what a speaker or writer consciously intends, reflecting personal and cultural biases that run so deep that most of the time we aren't even aware they exist. "Mere words" are incredibly important: They are our framework for seeing and understanding the world.</u> Assertion or thesis statement

Significance of assertion

Logical appeal <u>Man, we are told, means woman as well as man, just as mankind supposedly stands for all of humanity.</u> In the introduction of a sociology textbook I recently read, the author was anxious to demonstrate his awareness of the controversy over sexist language and to assure his female readers that, despite his use of non-inclusive terms, he was not forgetting the existence or importance of women in society. He was making a conscious decision to continue to use man and mankind instead of people, humanity, etc., for ease of expression and aesthetic reasons. "Man" simply sounds better, he explained. I flipped through the table of contents and found "Man and Society," "Man and Nature," "Man and Technology," and, near the end, "Man and Woman." <u>At what point did Man quit meaning people and start meaning men again?</u> The writer was obviously unaware of the answer to this question, because it is one he would never think to ask. Having consciously addressed the issue only to dismiss it, he reverted to form. Examples organized deductively

Emotional appeal

Logical appeal <u>The very ambiguity of man as the generic word for our species ought to be enough to combat any arguments that we keep it because we all "know what it means" or because it is both</u>

traditional and sounds better. And does it really sound all that much better, or are we just more used to it, more comfortable? Our own national history proves that we can be comfortable with [Examples organized deductively] a host of words and attitudes that strike us as unjust and ugly today. A lot of white folks probably thought that Negroes were getting pretty stuffy and picky when they began to insist on being called blacks. After all, weren't there more important things to [Emotional appeal] worry about, like civil rights? But black activists recognized the emotional and symbolic significance of having a name that was parallel to the name that the dominant race used for itself—a name equal in dignity, lacking that vaguely alien, anthropological sound. After all, whites were called *Caucasians* only in police reports, text-books, and autopsies. *Negro* may have sounded better to people in the bad old days of blatant racial bigotry, but we adjusted to the word *black* and have now moved on to African American, and more and more people of each race are adjusting to the wider implications and demands of practical, as well as verbal labels.

[Logical appeal] In a world where *man* and *human* are offered as synonymous terms, I don't think it is a coincidence that women are still vastly underrepresented in positions of money, power, and respect. Children grow up learning a language that makes maleness the norm for anything that isn't explicitly designated as female, giving little girls a very limited corner of the universe to picture themselves in. Indeed, the language that nonfeminists today claim to be inclusive was never intended to cover women in the first place. [Examples organized deductively] "One man, one vote" and "All men are created equal" meant just that. Women had to fight for decades to be included even as an afterthought; it took constitutional amendments to convince the government and the courts that women are human, too.

[Conclusion/restatement] The message is clear. We have to start speaking about people, not men, if we are going to start thinking in terms of both women and men. A "female man" will never be the equal of her brother.

Student Writer's Comments

The hardest task for me in writing this essay was trying to come up with a topic! The second hardest job was trying to be effective without getting preachy, strident, or wordy. I wanted to persuade an audience that would no doubt include the bored, the hostile, and the indifferent, and I was worried about losing their attention.

I chose my topic after several prewriting sessions that generated numerous options for me to write about. I stumbled on the idea of sexist language in one of these sessions and then went on to generate new material on this particular topic. Eventually satisfied that I had enough ideas to stay with this topic, I doubled back and labeled them according to each type of appeal.

Even before I had written my thesis, I had a good idea of what I wanted to say in this essay. I began working from an assertion that essentially remained the same as I wrote and revised my essay. It's more polished now, but its basic intention never changed.

To create my first draft, I worked from my notes, labeled by type of appeal. I let the logical arguments guide my writing, strategically introducing emotional and ethical appeals as I sensed they would be effective. I appealed to ethics in the beginning of the essay to establish my credibility, and I appealed to the readers' emotions occasionally to vary my pace and help my argument gain momentum. I was fully aware of what I was doing when I moved from one appeal to another. I wrote from a passionate desire to change people's thinking about language and its ability to control our perceptions of the world.

Next, I revised my entire essay several times, playing the role of different readers with dissimilar biases in each case. Every time I worked through the essay, I made major changes in the introduction and the conclusion as well. At this point, I paid special attention to the denotation, connotation, and tone of my words (especially highly charged language) and to the examples I had chosen to support each point I decided to keep in my argument. Though I moved a lot of examples around and thought of better ones in some cases, I was eventually happy with the final product. I am especially pleased with the balance of appeals in the final draft.

Some Final Thoughts on Argument/Persuasion

As you can tell from the selections that follow, the three different types of persuasive appeals usually complement each other in practice. Most good persuasive essays use a combination of these methods to achieve their purposes. Good persuasive essays also rely on various rhetorical modes we have already studied—such as example, process analysis, division/classification, comparison/contrast, definition, and cause/effect—to advance their arguments. In the following essays, you will see a combination of appeals at work and a number of different rhetorical modes furthering the arguments.

Argument/Persuasion in Review

Reading Argument and Persuasion Essays

Preparing to Read

1. What assumptions can you make from the essay's title?
2. Can you guess what the general mood of the essay is?
3. What is the essay's purpose and audience?
4. What does the synopsis in the Rhetorical Table of Contents tell you about the essay?
5. What can you learn from the author's biography?
6. Can you guess what the author's point of view toward the subject is?
7. What are your responses to the Preparing to Read questions?

Reading

1. What is the author's main assertion or thesis?
2. What are the primary appeals at work in the essay?
3. Did you preview the questions that follow the essay?

Rereading

1. How does the writer integrate the appeals in the essay?
2. What is the tone of the essay? How does the author establish this tone?
3. What other rhetorical strategies does the author use to support the essay's purpose?

4. What are your responses to the questions after the essay?

Writing Argument and Persuasion Essays

Preparing to Write

1. What are your responses to the Preparing to Write questions?
2. Do you narrow and focus your material as much as possible?
3. What is your purpose?
4. Who is your audience?

Writing

1. Is your thesis a debatable question?
2. Do you justify the organization of your essay?
3. Is your essay organized effectively for what you are trying to accomplish?
4. Does the body of your essay directly support your thesis?
5. Do you understand your audience's opinions, convictions, and backgrounds so that you know what to emphasize?
6. Does your conclusion restate your main intention and offer some constructive recommendations?

Rewriting

1. Is your thesis statement clear?
2. Is the main thrust of your essay argumentative (an appeal to reason)?
3. Will the balance of these appeals effectively accomplish your purpose with your intended audience?
4. Does your conclusion restate your argument, make a recommendation, and bring your essay to a close?
5. When you use logic, is that section of your paper arranged through either inductive or deductive reasoning? Is that the most effective order to achieve your purpose?
6. In appealing to the emotions, have you chosen your words with proper attention to their denotative and connotative effects?
7. Have you chosen examples carefully to support your thesis statement?
8. Is this tone suitable for your purpose and your audience?

Jennifer Cowan
1965–

■ ■ ■

TV Me Alone

Jennifer Cowan has spent more than a decade as a pop culture commentator, writer, director, and producer. Since graduating with a journalism degree from Carleton University in Ottawa, Cowan has become a regular contributor to *Wired*, CBC Stereo's *Realtime*, and *Shift*, from which this selection was taken. Also, in 1995 Cowan produced and directed the documentary, *Douglas Coupland: Close Personal Friend*, which has been broadcast and screened at festivals across North America and Europe. Cowan's advice for writers: Have fun, be nice, and do good work.

Cowan's television experience has included work on *mediatelevision*, *Girltalk*, *ENG*, and *Wired for Sex* (a CBC "Witness" documentary). Cowan makes television, but in "TV Me Alone," she argues for keeping TV out of public places.

Preparing to Read

Jennifer Cowan's essay first appeared in *Shift* in the summer of 1995. Written on an overnight flight from Los Angeles to Toronto, in "TV Me Alone" Cowan argues that television does not belong in public places. Before reading her argument, think about television and the role that it plays in your life. What do you watch on TV? What is your favourite program? What do you like least on TV? When do you watch television? Where do you watch it? What do you think of television in public places? Could you live without television?

■─────────────────────────────■

I recently had the scrumptious opportunity to take the red-eye from Los Angeles to Toronto. Buoyed by the three-hour stopover in Chicago, I swiped a mini-puft-pillow and set out to catch some sleep in the departure lounge. Sadly, the hum of 5 a.m. airport traffic was drowned out by the incessant loop of CNN airport television. Instead of some much needed zzzzs, I was repeatedly subjected to life-enhancing information on the nutritional value of stamps (two to eight calories per lick if you must know) and tips for the solo traveller (when in San Francisco rent a car and drive down the coast).

TV in public and quasi-public places has become as 2

ubiquitous. Flight attendants no longer demo oxygen masks or point out exits with choreographed precision. Instead, pop-out screens serve up sanitized corporate videos with a unisexual Benetton cast. And while you have to pony up a few bucks to see an inflight movie, you can freely access the ABC and NBC news-feeds on short hauls.

Airports are not the only venue plagued by monitor 3 multiplication. Try banks. If being watched by their security cameras while picking underwear out of your bum wasn't enough media scrutiny, now financial institutions want to watch you as you watch them. So during the recent RSP blitz, they played video loops of sailing, sunset strolls on the beach and other dishy retirement options for the canny investor.

At the HMV music stores, the garish interiors and sadistic 4 display practices aren't the only consumer bonus. Toronto's Yonge Street mausoleum is fronted by a 20-foot video wall programmed with HMV's promotional choices of the moment.

Nary a retail space is free of TV. Used to be if you wanted to 5 watch TV in a department store, you had to go to the home entertainment section. Now a detour through the men's wear in Eaton's includes a how-to-open-an-umbrella TV demonstration courtesy of the Totes galoshes people. No doubt the women's accessories department plugs 50 ways to use a scarf clip. There are even TVs, according to *Entertainment Tonight*, tucked into gas pumps, so you can stay tuned while filling your car. The notion that TV is mindless and relaxing, I've discovered, has become as obsolete as manual channel-changing.

Even when there's nothing to see, televisions have taken on an 6 omniscient aura, staring like a Cyclops at the cultural psyche. On a recent visit to a bar, three overhead monitors screened the film *Blood Simple,* just in case my companion failed to provide enough visual enticement. Not to be outdone, a few blocks down, at the neighbouring Bovine Sex Club (where the interior design meshes chicken wire, doll parts and TVs), four big screens emanated everything from *Much Music* and anime to *Tommy* and *Night of the Living Dead*. Bloodshot eyes were glued. Even I found myself staring lemming-like, transfixed by the stream of cathode rays.

Don't get me wrong. I'm not trying to pull a Neil Postman. I 7 don't think TV will topple civilization and make us stop reading or talking or screwing. I love TV! Hell, I make TV. But I think TV has a time and a place—a personal time and a private place. No more.

When TV left our homes and went public, something curious 8
happened. It went from home appliance to tool of compliance.
And TV continues to make inroads into the public domain
because it reinforces our commonality. Or more specifically, our
communality. This is good. I know I'm not alone in relishing
mid-*Melrose Place* phone calls from friends dissing Amanda's
roots, or Kimberly's lunacy. However, droning news packages,
investment tips and how-to-dress techniques served up in
buzzing public places don't inspire communal awe among
strangers. The only thing I had in common with my fellow
travellers at O'Hare during our airport television experience was
peckishness and crankiness. United Airlines had united us in
disdain, hardly the yummiest form of community.

Pundits keep spewing hoopla about the glowing blue future- 9
direct broadcast satellites, the 500-channel universe, video-on-
demand—and we all blink in bewilderment. But if we open our
eyes, we'll notice the 500-channel universe is already upon us,
and someone else is holding the remote control! The TV nation is
little more than a sea of TVs in every environment conceivable.

The fact is, TV should not be in airports or retail stores or 10
banks. TV should not be in doctors' waiting rooms (as the defunct
Medical News Network discovered). And there's no need for it
in supermarket checkouts. The power and wonder of TV is that
it has an ability to create a community. It gives us things to laugh
about, cry about and bitch about. But when it is forced upon us,
all the things that give it power—intimacy, insularity, intensity—
are deadened.

Moving through daily life should not be a battle to avoid the 11
relentless electronic assault. TV deserves so much more.

UNDERSTANDING DETAILS

1. List the range of public places Cowan mentions where TV can
   be found. Are there others you can add to this list?
2. What is Cowan's thesis or main point in this essay? Where in the
   essay can it be found?
3. What aspects of TV give it its power?

ANALYZING MEANING

1. How and why does television reinforce a sense of community?
   What other activities fill this role of creating and maintaining
   community?

2. Discuss the different reasons that various businesses and corporations have introduced TV into their public spaces.
3. Cowan says that the "notion that TV is mindless and relaxing... has become as obsolete as manual channel-changing" (paragraph 5). Explain what view has replaced this antiquated notion.

DISCOVERING RHETORICAL STRATEGIES

1. Explain Cowan's perspective on the subject of this essay. What credentials does she have to write this essay?
2. One strategy Cowan uses to strengthen her argument is specific, vivid examples. Identify four such examples and explain how they enhance her argument.
3. Cowan has made some careful deliberate word choices in "TV Me Alone." What is the effect of each of the following vocabulary choices: mausoleum (paragraph 4), plagued (paragraph 3), lemming-like (paragraph 6), and zzzzs (paragraph 1)?

MAKING CONNECTIONS

1. Cowan and Mark Kingwell ("Not Available in Stores") both write about the role of television in our society. On what points do they agree about the place of TV? On what points do they disagree?
2. Cowan's essay first appeared in *Shift* magazine as did "The Babar Factor" by Evan Solomon. From these two essays, what conclusions might you draw about the readers of *Shift*? What other essay in this book is also likely to appeal to this audience? Explain your answer.
3. Analyze the balance in Cowan's essay between logical, emotional, and ethical appeals. How is this balance different from that found in Judy Rebick's "Kick 'Em Again"? Which author uses more of an emotional appeal? Who uses more logic? Who relies most on ethical appeal? In what way does the mixture of appeals in each of these essays determine how convincing they are to you?

IDEAS FOR DISCUSSION/WRITING

Preparing to Write

Cowan says that one of the positive things TV has to offer is its ability to create a sense of community. Write freely about other shared aspects of life that create a sense of community. What filled this role before television was invented? What other things achieve this purpose today? How has TV contributed to the idea of the global community?

Choosing a Topic

1. Cowan loves TV, but she thinks TV has a time and a place. Write about a particular setting or time where you find television annoying. Explain clearly to your readers why television does not belong in that place or why it is not appropriate at that time.
2. In "TV Me Alone" Cowan says that TV's power is deadened when it is forced upon us. Choose another example of something that loses its power when it is forced on people, and write an essay in which you argue against its imposition.
3. TV is subject to a lot of criticism. Write an essay for *TV Guide* in which you present the benefits that TV has to offer its viewers.

WEB SITES

 www.wired.com/wired/archive/1.06/citytv.html
"The Sheer Force of Attitude," about Citytv and Moses Znaimer, is another of Cowan's articles from *Wired*.

Lawrence Solomon
1948–

■ ■ ■

Too Much Privacy Can Be Hazardous
to the Person

In addition to being the editor of *The Next City*, Lawrence Solomon has contributed to many publications including *The Globe and Mail* and the *Wall Street Journal*. Solomon's areas of expertise include public utilities, public private partnerships, and regulation. Solomon is also noted as a leading environmentalist, and in the late 1970s he was an advisor to President Carter's Task Force on the Global Environment. In addition, his work on energy deregulation, as presented in his books *Energy Shock* (1980), *Breaking Up Ontario Hydro's Monopoly* (1982), and *Power At What Cost?* (1984), has served as a model for privatization of the electricity industry in several countries, including the U.K.

Preparing to Read

"Too Much Privacy Can be Hazardous to the Person" first appeared in *The Next City*, described in its masthead as "a solutions-oriented magazine that tackles issues confronting our new urban society." In this essay, Lawrence Solomon responds to the concern shared by many that electronic data collection and storage are an undesirable invasion of our privacy. Before you begin reading, think about the idea of privacy. What things do you consider private? Do others share your opinion about what things are private? In what ways have you had your privacy invaded? Do you ever refuse to give people information that you consider to be private? What is the risk associated with having private information shared with others?

■_____■

With vast computer network data bases storing detailed information about our private lives, many of us are becoming uneasy about invasions of privacy. Already, computers track our daily activities, time-stamping every credit and debit card transaction, monitoring who we call on the telephone or visit over the World Wide Web. Many businesses snoop on their employees, many municipalities film activities on city streets to cut down on red-light runners and other violators. Soon, every highway will be tolled, recording our comings and goings; and so will every neighbourhood road—satellite technology today tracks the movement of London cabbies, the better to dispatch them; tomorrow these satellites will economically track private automobiles, the better to bill their owners.

Some privacy concerns revolve around bothersome junk mail 2 and unwanted telemarketing calls: Air mile and other cards let marketers analyze your personal shopping habits, opening you up to an avalanche of targeted offers. Other concerns— particularly access to your genetic code, which contains intimate details about you and your likely future life—are anything but frivolous. A recent study by the Federal Bureau of Investigation and the Computer Security Institute found that "most organizations are woefully unprepared ... [making] it easier for perpetrators to steal, spy, or sabotage without being noticed and with little culpability if they are." After sampling 400 sites, the study found 42 per cent had experienced an intrusion or unauthorized use over the past year. Even sophisticated agencies are vulnerable. Pentagon computers suffered 250,000 attacks by intruders in 1995, 65 per cent of whom gained entry to a computer network. That same year, the London *Sunday Times* reported that the contents of anyone's electronic health record could be purchased on the street for £150.

Because the dangers—ranging from financial exploitation 3 to, in the worst case, a police state—can be profound, legislation of various types is being proposed. Some argue that all personal information should be our own private property, to prevent marketers from storing and exchanging information about us without our consent; others would severely restrict or even prohibit the collection of sensitive personal data. These approaches miss the mark. The collection of data—the accumulation of knowledge—is almost always desirable. The relevant question is, when does the information belong in the public sphere and when in the private?

The claim that we somehow have property rights to our 4 personal information does not stand up to scrutiny. We all exchange information about others—"Did you see Andrea's new car?"; "I hear Jim got a promotion"—in our daily routines without requiring their consent, and a democratic society that respects free speech could not do otherwise. Even if we did enact laws to restrict or ban data banks from collecting information about us, it would generally backfire. Junk mail is unwanted precisely because it is indiscriminate and useless. If marketing succeeds in sending us useful, targeted information, many of us would have our goal of restricting unwanted mail. In one survey, 71 per cent of 18- to 20-year-olds wanted mail on products that interested them; in another, 52 per cent of consumers wanted to be profiled if that would lead to special offers. Those who don't want the mail or the offers will only need to make their views heard: Few companies would defy their customers by selling their names.

Valid restrictions governing free speech—such as slandering others or violating their copyright on personal works—are properly limited. But we should add one other restriction—control over the use of our genetic code, where privacy should take precedence over free speech. 5

The field of genetic information promises to be the greatest boon to science and medicine in human history. We suffer from at least 4,000 genetic diseases and conditions—everything from Huntington's disease to depression—that may one day be treated or cured as science unravels the mysteries of the human genome. Even today, reading our genes can guide us in making decisions about our future, revealing whether we have predispositions for cancers or alcoholism, medical conditions that preventative measures could ameliorate. The information in your genetic code amounts to a probabilistic future diary that describes an important part of a unique and personal character—not just about your physical and mental health but also about your family, especially your parents, siblings, and children. 6

Yet this field also promises to lead to invasions of privacy unprecedented in their nature and scale. Unlike your personal diary, in which you might reveal your innermost secrets, the information in your genetic code may become known to strangers but not to you. From our own experiences, we know that there are no shortages of people with motives to acquire such information. Insurers and employers would value this information for business purposes. Political operatives might want to discredit opponents, as might combatants in divorces or other domestic disputes. Even where stakes aren't high, people may have malicious curiosities about their friends, neighbors, co-workers, or romantic rivals. 7

Until the turn of the century, our privacy was recognized as a property right and consequently given great legal weight. Our diaries and our secrets, particularly our medical secrets, were our own, in the United Kingdom as in North America. The genetic code, the epitome of that which is personal, is both a 8 present document and a future diary. Giving each of us clear rights to our genetic code and requiring those who would use it to first obtain our consent would provide a necessary and indispensable ingredient to protecting our privacy.

Most day-to-day concerns that people have about privacy 9 will evaporate. Those who don't want consumer data collected on them can avoid air miles-type marketing. Those seeking anonymity in making a phone call or a toll road trip can purchase prepaid cards; other technologies will foil telemarketers and e-mail snoops. Those who value record keeping—primarily businesspeople who bill their time or track it for other purposes—will see this data collection as an added-value service. Most of us won't care much one way or the other.

In private spaces—banks, convenience stores, office 10 buildings—we have accepted cameras, taking little notice of them and worrying about their misuse even less. We understand the proprietor's motives—to protect his property and the security of those who use it—and accept them as valid. Though we want similar protection in our public spaces, we are less trusting here, not because we value public property and security less but because we know the proprietor—the state—may have mixed motives. Too often government officials have used privileged information—whether medical data or income tax files—for self-serving ends. We do need safeguards governing surveillance in public spaces to allay legitimate public fears over the advent of the police state. Less privacy, ironically, would be one such safeguard.

Many criminal lawyers believe the police state arrived some 11 time ago, that law enforcement authorities effectively frame individuals whom they believe to be guilty. Guy Paul Morin is a case in point: Convinced of his guilt, police fudged the facts. When conflicting evidence frustrated their efforts—Morin left work too late to have travelled the 30 miles home in time to have murdered 9-year-old Christine Jessop—police ingenuity overcame this shortcoming.

Morin has plenty of company—Donald Marshall, David 12 Milgaard, and countless others have been convicted of murder and lesser offences because they could not establish where they were at some fateful time. Put another way, they were victims of their privacy. The vacuum of reliable information about their whereabouts created the opening for overzealous or overlazy police officers and prosecutors. Overzealous and overlazy authorities will always be with us, but vacuums of reliable information are increasingly becoming scarce. Had Jessop been murdered today, and had Morin travelled along an electronically tolled road such as Ontario's Highway 407, a record of when he got on and where he got off the highway would have established his whereabouts. The injustices perpetrated by the criminal justice system on this young man would never have occurred. Highway 407 was built too late to help Morin, but not for future travellers, whose record of their comings and goings—unbeknownst to them—adds a touch of security to their lives. So do new advances in DNA analysis, which eventually proved Morin innocent, as they are now doing for others around the world who were also falsely imprisoned.

A world in which we can verify our daily movements—the 13 very world that has been unfolding for decades—diminishes the number of miscarriages of justice that can occur. To fill a void with false information has always been easy; to rewrite data showing that someone drove 30 miles at a particular time along a particular electronic toll road involves reconstructing an alternate route and time, which involves alternate billing, which involves replacing the old invoice with a new one, and on and on. The effort required to spin a web of false information and then overlay it upon an existing factual network without getting tangled up would be so daunting as to virtually never occur. The very data base networks that some fear will usher in the police state, in the end, are really the best protection against it.

UNDERSTANDING DETAILS

1. Itemize the privacy concerns that Solomon identifies in his essay. How many are there in total?
2. What is Solomon's position on the collection and sharing of personal genetic information?
3. In what ways is our daily activity monitored and tracked according to Solomon? What has led to this type of collection of information?

ANALYZING MEANING

1. Explain how Guy Paul Morin, Donald Marshall, and David Milgaard were "victims of privacy."
2. Where does Solomon draw the line between the type of information that belongs in the public sphere and that which

belongs in the private realm? Do you agree with him? Explain why or why not.

3. Explain why people are concerned about the collection of data. Are these concerns warranted? Why or why not?

DISCOVERING RHETORICAL STRATEGIES

1. In several places, Solomon uses statistics to help him advance his argument. Why does he incorporate survey and study results into his essay?
2. What is Solomon's thesis? Where in his essay does it appear? Why has he chosen to organize his argument in this way?
3. What type of appeal does Solomon primarily use in his essay? Is this an effective choice? Why or why not?

MAKING CONNECTIONS

1. Solomon discusses changes in our society that result from advances in technology. How are these changes similar to or different than the changes identified by Tony Leighton ("The New Nature")?
2. Electronic monitoring of our daily activities has the potential to affect our behaviour in many ways. How might electronic monitoring be used to combat racism (Cecil Foster, "Why Blacks Get Mad") or discrimination based on poverty (Judy Rebick, "Kick 'Em Again")?
3. Trina McQueen ("Why We Crave Hot Stuff") discusses the appeal of scandal, gossip, and stories about fascinating people. To what extent is information gathered through the types of electronic monitoring that Solomon describes fair game for media stories?

IDEAS FOR DISCUSSION/WRITING

Preparing to Write

Write freely about electronic monitoring of your daily activities. In what ways are your daily activities monitored? By whom? How do you feel about this monitoring? What are the consequences of the monitoring you have identified? Are these welcome outcomes or undesired consequences? Who should decide what activities are monitored?

Choosing a Topic

1. The electronic gathering of information about us enables marketers to send us unsolicited information or offers on various products and services. Write an essay in which you either promote the use of electronic gathering of data to support this activity or argue against the collection of this information to send "junk mail."

2. One person exercising the right to free speech may infringe on another's right to personal privacy. Write an essay in which you explain where the line should be drawn between free speech and personal privacy.

3. Solomon argues that the monitoring of our activities may protect us in many ways but he has reservations about the collection of genetic data. Write an essay in which you either support or argue against the collection of genetic data. Make sure you include specific examples to support your argument.

WEB SITES

www.nextcity.com
The Next City is the periodical in which this essay first appeared.

Judy Rebick
1945–

■■■

Kick 'Em Again

A noted feminist and political commentator, Judy Rebick can currently be seen on CBC Newsworld's *Straight From the Hip* and was previously the cohost of CBC's *Face Off,* a national debate show. In addition, Rebick has appeared on a variety of TV and radio shows including *The Journal, Prime Time News, Canada AM,* and *CBC Midday* and CBC's *Morningside.* Rebick also writes a regular political column for *Elm Street* and is the author of *Politically Speaking.*

A graduate of McGill University with a degree in psychology, Rebick worked as the Director of Special Projects for the Canadian Hearing Society. From 1990–1993 Rebick served as the President of Canada's largest women's organization, the National Action Committee on the Status of Women.

Preparing to Read

In "Kick 'Em Again," which first appeared in *Elm Street* magazine in the summer of 1998, Judy Rebick discusses the growing problem of poverty and the inappropriate response from our political leaders. Before you begin reading, think about people on welfare. What sort of people are welfare recipients? Why are they on welfare? Is welfare fraud a common problem? What can be done to get people off welfare?

Poor bashing is becoming a national sport in this country, with politicians outdoing each other in blaming welfare recipients for their own poverty. Ontario premier Mike Harris went further than most this spring when he cut the prenatal benefit to pregnant women on welfare, saying that he didn't want them to spend it on beer. Prime Minister Jean Chrétien has also equated those who don't have paid work with drunks. "In my judgment," he told a black-tie audience in 1994, "it is better to have them at 50 per cent productivity than to be sitting at home, drinking beer, at zero per cent productivity." Even NDPers have joined in. Former B.C. premier Mike Harcourt announced his welfare reforms in September 1993 by explaining: "We want to clean the cheats and deadbeats off the welfare rolls ... Where there is work and where

1

there are training programs, people who are able to work who won't take those training programs, who are taking advantage of the goodwill of British Columbians, who refuse to get into the workforce—those people will be cut off of welfare."

What's the reality of people on welfare? The highest welfare 2 fraud figure I have ever seen is 6.8 per cent. There is more fraud going on in Toronto's SkyDome on any given Saturday when businessmen take their families to tax-deductible boxes that are supposed to be for business associates than in all the welfare offices across the country.

This spring, the National Council of Welfare produced an 3 important document entitled *Profiles of Welfare: Myths and Realities*. Contrary to the notion that most welfare recipients are lazy good-for-nothing young people looking for a free ride, people under 20 living on their own account for only four per cent of welfare recipients and only another 12 per cent are between 20 and 25. Another powerful myth is that teenage women get pregnant to qualify for welfare. In fact, only three per cent of single parents on welfare are under age 20 and nearly half of all single-parent families on welfare have only one child; another 31 per cent have only two children.

Jean Swanson, former president of the National Anti-Poverty 4 Organization, now with End Legislated Poverty in Vancouver, says that poor bashing goes beyond the crass comments of politicians and media pundits. "Even the questions we ask about the poor show our prejudice," she says. "We ask: How can we help the poor? How can we get people off welfare and on to work? What we should be asking is: How can we reduce poverty? How can we get the rich to share? How can we get jobs with adequate income?"

Swanson points out that all the welfare-to-work experiments 5 are simply moving people from one form of poverty to another, because the decreasing value of minimum wage and difficulty in finding full-time work mean staying well below the poverty line even with a job. "Poor people have as much control over these experiments as lab rats," she says.

Meanwhile, social assistance is disappearing as a public issue. 6 A CBC/Environics poll in February listed a series of public policy issues and asked people to prioritize their concerns. The "welfare poor" is not even on the list, even though every person I know who lives in a big city is more and more disturbed by the extent of homelessness and despair.

A new book called *Confronting the Cuts: A Sourcebook for*   7
Women in Ontario, edited by Luciana Ricciutelli, June Larkin and
Eimear O'Neill, describes some of the impact of Mike Harris's
Ontario on women and children. After the 21.6 per cent cut to
welfare when Harris came into office, a mother of two now
receives $1,239 a month. When you consider that the cost of a
two-bedroom basement apartment in Toronto is about $800 a
month, that means struggling to survive on $4.88 a day for each
person in the family. In a recent Health Canada study, 80 per
cent of mothers reported cutting down on their own meals and
20 per cent said they went hungry for an entire day. Over half had
to give up the telephone or other basic services in order to have
money for food. According to the Daily Bread Food Bank in
Toronto, 29 per cent of mothers report that their children go
without food at least once a week. A Thunder Bay study revealed
that a couple with two young children now have to make do
with $43 a week for food after other expenses are paid. Before
the cuts, they had $104 a week.

How can anyone live on $43 a week for food for four people?   8
And this is in the province where the economy is supposed to
be booming.

In 1997 Robert Gratton, the CEO of Power Financial   9
Corporation, earned more than $27 million. Six other CEOs made
more than $10 million each.

How can a society call itself democratic when some people   10
can't afford to put food on the table and others make so much
money they couldn't spend it in 10 lifetimes?

UNDERSTANDING DETAILS

1. What is "poor-bashing"? According to Rebick, who is doing it?
2. Identify the myths and the realities about welfare that Rebick
   mentions in her essay.
3. How significant is the problem of welfare fraud?

ANALYZING MEANING

1. What is Rebick's thesis? What exactly is she advocating?
2. Why is poor-bashing becoming a national sport? Why are our
   political leaders not responding to the welfare situation with
   strategies to reduce poverty?
3. Explain Jean Swanson's comment that "Even the questions we

ask about the poor show our prejudice." Do you agree with this position? Why or why not?

DISCOVERING RHETORICAL STRATEGIES

1. What is Rebick's purpose in writing this article? Given the original source of this essay, who do you think is her intended audience?
2. In this essay, Rebick frequently uses statistics and quotations from authorities. Explain why she has incorporated these elements. How do they enhance her argument?
3. Is Rebick's essay primarily an appeal to logic, to emotion, or to ethics? Why do you think Rebick has made this choice?

MAKING CONNECTIONS

1. Diane Francis ("Once a Kinder and Gentler Nation") laments the effects of the welfare state and the changes in Canada that she sees as a result. How do you think that Francis would respond to Rebick's argument? Whose view is closer to your own?
2. Rebick and Cecil Foster ("Why Blacks Get Mad") both discuss types of social prejudice. Who or what would each of these authors say is responsible for these different prejudices? Which of these prejudices would they say is the most injurious to Canadian society and why?
3. Discuss the relative balance of the logical, emotional, and ethical appeals in the essays by Rebick and David Suzuki ("The Right Stuff") and Gerald W. Paul ("Stand Tall, and Pass the Ammunition"). Which author uses logic most? Who relies most heavily on emotion? Whose ethical appeal is the strongest? What do the dominance of these appeals have to do with the subject matter of each essay?

IDEAS FOR DISCUSSION/WRITING

Preparing to Write

Write freely about poverty. What does it mean to be poor? How can you tell if someone is poor? How much money does someone need to have or to make not to be poor? How much money makes a person rich? What are the consequences of being poor? What is the role of the government in eliminating or controlling poverty? Can someone be poor and still be happy?

Choosing a Topic

1. Write a letter to the premier of your province or the prime minister of Canada about the measures they have taken to deal with the problem of poverty. Be clear about what actions you are responding to and what you expect from your reader.

2. In your opinion, how serious is poverty in your city or town? How is it manifested? Who suffers the most from poverty? In a coherent essay, persuade your neighbours that poverty is or is not a serious social problem in your community.

3. Rebick concludes her essay with a rhetorical question: "How can a society call itself democratic when some people can't afford to put food on the table and others make so much money they couldn't spend it in 10 lifetimes?" Write an essay in which you either advance this argument or justify the inequities that Rebick identifies.

WEB SITES

newsworld.cbc.ca/programs/sites/straight_bio.html
Judy Rebick is the host of Newsworld's "Straight from the Hip."

David Suzuki
1936–

■ ■ ■

The Right Stuff

From Vancouver, British Columbia, David Suzuki is a geneticist, writer, broadcaster, educator, parent, and environmentalist. Suzuki received his university education from Amherst College, the University of Chicago, and the University of PEI. He began teaching zoology at the University of British Columbia in 1969 and has appeared on radio and television as the host of *Quirks and Quarks* and *The Nature of Things*. Suzuki's writings on science and the environment have appeared in columns in *The Globe and Mail* and *The Toronto Star* as well as many books, which include *Genethics* (1989), his *Looking at...* series for children, *It's a Matter of Survival* (1990), *Wisdom of the Elders* (1992), and *Inventing the Future* (1989), a collection of previously published essays from which "The Right Stuff" is taken.

Preparing to Read

As you prepare to read this essay, think about your associations with high school. What positive memories do you have of high school? What things would you rather not recall? What people do you remember from high school? Teachers? Friends? What was the building like? Did you attend a public school? A private school? A separate school? An alternative school? Are there any classes that stand out in your recollections? What was the most important thing that you learned in high school?

Years ago I read a marvellous book entitled *Is There Life After High School*? In spite of the title, it was a serious comparison of human relationships at different stages in life. The study revealed that impressions formed in high school are more vivid and indelible than those formed at any other time in life. The author described how people in their seventies and eighties who had difficulty remembering most of their associates in university and at work would instantly recall most of their classmates by name while leafing through their high school yearbooks. In the analysis of the author, high school society is divided into two broad categories, the innies and the outies. The innies were football and basketball players and cheerleaders who set the whole social climate of the school. The outies were all the rest, the majority of the student body, most of whom lusted to be innies. I sure hope it's different today because that description fits my recollection of high school and it was awful. But I'm getting off the point.

Those high school memories are so intense because that is the 2 time when puberty occurs. The enormous physiological changes that take place in response to the surge of new hormones through the body completely transform both anatomy and mind. I always feel kids lose about half their intelligence for a few years in response to that blast of hormones. Relationships change radically. Suddenly parents change from protective, loving gods to dictatorial wardens incessantly imposing restrictions and criticizing everything. A pubescent teenager perceives adults and members of their own age group with totally new eyes. It's not surprising then that attitudes to school, courses and studying also change dramatically.

In the early 1970s, I visited a small northern town to judge a 3 science fair. Back then, it was a tough town with a transient population of men working in the oil fields and a high proportion of Native people. The night I arrived, I dropped in to the bar of the motel and a man came over and said, "I hear you're going to talk to the students at the high school tomorrow." When I affirmed it, he shocked me by adding, "They'll kill you. I'm the science teacher there and I can tell you that all they think about is sex, drugs and cars. They'll tear you apart."

Well, he really scared me. I immediately formed images of a 4 blackboard jungle, filled with switchblades and drug-crazed hoods. The next day when I walked into that auditorium, it was with great trepidation. There were 400 teenagers in the gym, about a third of them Indians. They looked pretty normal, but I had been warned and knew they were just biding their time before turning into raving animals.

So I began by saying, "I'm a geneticist. I know that you're 5 basically walking gonads, so I'm going to talk about sex." That opener caught their attention. I started with the beginning of human life by describing eggs and sperm, talked about chromosomes and the X and Y basis for sex determination and went on from there. The kids were dead silent and attentive. I talked for about an hour and then opened it up for questions. I was astounded at the range of topics we covered. We discussed drugs and chromosomes, test-tube babies, amniocentesis and cloning. The principal finally had to step in to dismiss the group an hour and a half after that.

Science education in high school should be designed around 6
sex and human biology. It's a shock every time I hear that a
school board has caved in to pressure and kept sex education
out of schools. I am sure opponents of sex ed have no intention
of providing that information to their own children. In a time of
easy access to the most explicit films, videos, magazines and
books, who can believe it's better to keep youngsters ignorant
by denying them some accurate facts? They're going to get all
kinds of anecdotal, apocryphal stuff about sex from their peer
group, anyway.

By starting their instruction with human sexuality and 7
reproduction, teachers will be able to go on to practically every
other subject in science. It just takes a hard look from a different
perspective. After all, we are not trying to train future scientists
(only a small percentage of high school graduates will go on in
science), yet all of them will be able to use information that science
can provide for the rest of their lives. And you can bet they will
remember those lessons vividly in their life after high school.

UNDERSTANDING DETAILS

1. Why, according to Suzuki, are "impressions formed in high
   school more vivid and indelible than those formed at any other
   time in life"?
2. What is Suzuki's position on sex education in schools?
3. What changes in kids does Suzuki attribute to puberty?

ANALYZING MEANING

1. What arguments does Suzuki provide to support his position on
   high school science education? Are these arguments convincing?
   Why or why not?
2. What accounted for the reaction that Suzuki got from the students at the high school he visited? Was the science teacher
   right in saying, "all they think about is sex, drugs and cars"
   (paragraph 3)?
3. Why is sex education in schools such a controversial issue?

DISCOVERING RHETORICAL STRATEGIES

1. What do you think the writer's purpose is in "The Right Stuff"?
   Where does Suzuki state his thesis?

2. Characterize the tone that Suzuki adopts in this essay. What words and phrases does he use to create this tone?
3. What is the dominant type of appeal in this essay?

MAKING CONNECTIONS

1. Suzuki is presenting a somewhat controversial position in his essay as is Lawrence Solomon ("Too Much Privacy Can Be Hazardous to the Person"). Compare and contrast the strategies that these two writers have used to advance their positions and make their audiences more receptive to their views.
2. The incorporation of humour is one of the strategies that Suzuki uses in his essay. Compare and contrast his use of humour with that of Evan Solomon ("The Babar Factor") and Drew Hayden Taylor ("Pretty Like a White Boy").
3. Suzuki's essay presents a strategy for making scientific topics appealing and interesting to a lay audience. How do you think Maureen Littlejohn ("You are a Contract Painkiller"), Michael Clugston ("Twice Struck"), or Adrian Forsyth ("Little Plants of Horror") would respond to Suzuki's strategy?

IDEAS FOR DISCUSSION/WRITING

Preparing to Write

Write freely about learning about sex. What was your primary source of information? How did you learn about sex? What role did your parents play? Your peers? The school? The church? What did you learn from films, videos, magazines, or books? Was there anything that you learned that you discovered later to be untrue? What was the source of that information? What is your primary source of information about sex now?

Choosing a Topic

1. Write a letter to your school board either advocating or arguing against Suzuki's suggestion for high school science curriculum design.
2. Write a proposal for a department head of your old high school proposing a way to make another subject area (other than science) relevant and interesting. Make sure you explain your idea clearly and provide adequate justification to make the changes.
3. The inclusion of many works of fiction in the high school curriculum has been challenged based on the sexual content. Find

one book that has been subject to censorship challenge and write a letter to the editor of the paper expressing your views on whether or not such a book should be rejected from the classroom.

WEB SITES

www.vkool.com/suzuki/index.html
The David Suzuki Foundation home page.

www.tv.cbc.ca/nature_of_things/
David Suzuki is the host of *The Nature of Things* on CBC television.

Gerald W. Paul

■■■

Stand Tall, and Pass the Ammunition

Reverend Gerald W. Paul has worked as a miner, a soldier, an electrician, a university chaplain, and a pastor. His articles have been published in *The United Church Observer, The Christian Ministry, Canadian Geographic,* and *Canadian Funeral Director.*

Preparing to Read

This essay was originally published in *Canadian Funeral Director* in 1985. In "Stand Tall, and Pass the Ammunition" Rev. Gerald W. Paul urges funeral directors to change their traditional response to attacks on their profession. Instead of "slink[ing] away like naughty children" when attacked, Paul advocates fighting back. Before you begin reading, think about funerals and the funeral business. How is the funeral business different from other businesses connected to significant life events such as birth, or marriage? What kind of people choose to go into the funeral business? Is the funeral industry regulated by any professional associations or governing bodies? Who makes choices about an individual's funeral arrangements? How has the funeral business changed over time?

Periodically, if not perennially—especially when no hot news is 1
breaking in the nation—journalists sharpen their pencils and take another swipe at funeral directors and funerals. The latest attack on those persons and practices dealing with death (by Leslie Tarr in the *United Church Observer,* Oct. 1984) calls for "trimming down funeral traditions". Arguing that funerals are not "rooted in Judeo-Christian traditions", with the aid of loaded words like "trappings", "gaudy", "tasteless", Tarr puts down the all-too-passive funeral directors as "salesmen of merchandise" priced too high.

After 25 years of close association with funeral directors I'm 2
appalled at how easily this profession accepts the role of victim. When lawyers are attacked they use their eloquence to riddle their opponents. When clergy are attacked they use their pulpits to counterattack. When physicians are attacked they use their

mystique to ward off blows. But when funeral directors are attacked, showing no fight, they slink away like naughty children ashamed of what they've done.

I'm not saying that flight or freeze are always inappropriate 3 responses to bullies. When an attack is imminent, hares flee and grouse freeze. But funeral directors under attack not by tooth and claw but by pen and tongue should come out fighting. If you believe your business is providing a valuable and competitive service, why not say so. And not with sweet reasonableness only. But with a bit of bite as well.

Attacks on traditional funerals often focus on the casket. 4 According to the critics you save a lot by disposing of the body swiftly. Granted that a quickie private cremation or burial might save dollars, the absence of body and casket at the memorial service makes the event perfunctory rather than therapeutic. Hundreds of times I have accompanied a family into the chapel prior to visiting hours and witnessed a therapeutic shower of repressed grief. The casket and its contents acted as a grief releaser. All the pent-up emotions accumulated by weeks of hospital visiting and days of anticipating death were unleashed by the viewing of the body in the casket.

During the last few years two of my loved ones died. My 5 brother-in-law wanted no funeral. Only cremation, with dispersion of his ashes over Georgian Bay. Without casket or service there was no family rallying point, no mutual support, no sharing of hopes and memories. His death was reduced to a private affair.

My mother prearranged her funeral. It took place in 6 Powassan, Ontario at The Paul Funeral Home, in the area where she had spent both her early and later years. The family came from all over the country. Old friends shared memories of mom. Relatives gathered in groups reminiscing. Knowing we had the support of one another we expressed our deepest feelings. There were handshakes, embraces, tears. Even appropriate laughter. The open casket was both rallying point and grief releaser. A kind of symbol—like the wailing wall in Jerusalem—permitting, evoking, and supporting, the expression of our grief.

Necrophobia, it seems to me, is more evident in the speedy 7 disposal than in the traditional funeral. Shortcuts in funeral arrangements often short-circuit the grief process. Dr. Elizabeth Kübler-Ross, author of *Death & Dying* reminds us that if the bereaved are to move beyond the "denial of death" into the "acceptance" phase, it's important for the family to view the body. By privately spiriting away the body the bereaved run the risk of settling for some illusory state dangerously short of accepting the reality of death.

A second focus for attacks on the funeral business is the 8 practice of embalming. Tarr takes the Ontario Funeral Service Association to task for stating in "What Every Family Should Know" that "most of the funeral beliefs and practices observed in Canada today are rooted in Judeo-Christian traditions."

After reviewing Biblical and theological records I'm puzzled 9 at Tarr's indignation. Treatment in *The Interpreter's Bible* of accounts in Mark, Luke & John of how Jesus' body was prepared suggests the use of spices had some affinity with embalming. Henri Daniel-Rops (*Daily Life in the Time of Jesus*) describes how the dead were prepared in those days. "As soon as he was dead, his eyes were closed ... he was to be kissed with love and washed; aromatics and scents being used for this purpose."

While this was neither a true embalming in the Egyptian 10 manner nor in the modern manner, its kinship is obvious. The Christian faith provides for development and changes in funeral practices. Jacob living in Egypt was embalmed. Jesus living in Palestine was anointed with spices. Today most Canadians, Americans and Australians who die are embalmed in the modern way. Even in religion, traditional practices are not frozen; they have some flexibility.

As for the health and aesthetic reasons for embalming, funeral 11 directors need to point out the dangers to health of a decaying body; the embarrassment-potential of an unembalmed body; and the way in which the mourners' fear of the processes of putrescence are dissolved by the knowledge that the loved one is embalmed and, therefore, nothing untoward will mar the ceremony. In western society where health considerations are paramount, funeral directors who insist on embalming on the grounds of hygiene should be commended not maligned.

The third focus of attacks on funerals and directors comes 12 in the guise of economic justice. While people may surround themselves with possessions and rituals that give them special status in life, death is the equalizer. "Live high until you die," seems to be the motto for frugal funerals. Although the amount spent on weddings is considerably higher than what is spent on funerals, few condemn the materialism of weddings. People with a luxurious lifestyle, say the critics, are to be buried as paupers.

Funeral directors can fire a lot of ammunition at that 13
argument. It's unrealistic. As Huntington & Metcalf say in
Celebrations of Death, "wealth and social class will be expressed in
funerals as they are in housing, clothing and automobiles." People
will insist on deathways in keeping with lifestyles. Insistence on
equality of funerals is also undemocratic: while variety rules
when we're alive, standardization takes over as soon as we're
dead. And finally, calling for cheap and quick disposal of the
dead misplaces a legitimate concern for justice: let's stop the
greed and acquisitiveness of three score years and ten, and,
instead of fighting for justice at the end of life let's fight for it all
along.

Perhaps the best ammunition funeral directors have against 14
their opponents is a track record of providing customers not with
ultimatums but with a wide range of choices. In selecting a casket,
choices range from thrifty to expensive. If embalming is not
wanted, the customer just has to say so. If the casket is to be
closed that's the client's prerogative. Funeral directors are not
absolutists or legalists. They are business men and women who
offer a spectrum of choices. It should come as no surprise that
people want funerals to reflect their style of life. Not many dying
people find comfort in anticipating a hurried funeral reminiscent
of poet Carl Sandburg's "Junkman" taking the dead away to the
dump in his wagon.

A few generations ago people died at home. The deathbed 15
scene was the norm. The wake usually occurred in the same
building as the death. Today, people die elsewhere. Often alone.
The total (or traditional) funeral as the successor to the wake, is
part of the deathways approved by Canadian civil religion. I'm
convinced no other structure in our society provides as adequate
an expression of comfort for the bereaved, gratitude for the
deceased and hope for us all, as the traditional funeral.

P. Silverman in "Another Look at the Role of the Funeral 16
Director" says the widows she worked with in Boston "received
more help and comfort from the funeral director than from either
physician or clergyman." Stop grovelling. Defend yourselves
with dignity. Fight fairly and openly and society will recognize
who the unfair fighters really are. Speak out boldly of the
therapeutic aspects of the casket, the Christian and hygienic
dimensions of embalming, and the comforting features of a
funeral in harmony with one's style of living.

Let's hear it: Stand tall, and pass the ammunition.   17

UNDERSTANDING DETAILS

1. Why does Paul believe that funeral directors should fight back against attacks on their business? Typically, why don't they?
2. List the major areas of attack on funeral directors as outlined in Paul's essay.
3. What is necrophobia (paragraph 7)? Why does Paul say that it "is more evident in the speedy disposal than in the traditional funeral"?

ANALYZING MEANING

1. What has motivated Paul to encourage funeral directors to fight back against attacks on their profession? What is his particular interest in this topic?
2. Explain the role of the funeral in the death of a person. Are the advocates of no funeral justified in their arguments against this ceremony?
3. How are funerals "rooted in Judeo-Christian traditions" while at the same time reflecting the modern concerns of western society? Does Paul see these adaptations as an enhancement or a diminishment of the traditions? Explain.

DISCOVERING RHETORICAL STRATEGIES

1. While Paul's essay is primarily argument and persuasion, he has also used other rhetorical strategies. Identify the other strategies that Paul has employed and give examples of each one.
2. In paragraphs 5 and 6, Paul relates two personal anecdotes. Why has he chosen to include these two examples? What type of appeal is he using here?
3. Characterize Paul's tone. How does this choice of tone help him to achieve his purpose with this essay?

MAKING CONNECTIONS

1. Paul's essay is obviously a response to essays like that of Jessica Mitford ("Behind the Formaldehyde Curtain"). Which argument do you find more convincing? Why? Create a chart in which you list Paul's arguments on one side and Mitford's corresponding arguments on the other. Presented in this fashion, whose argument is more effective? Why?
2. David Foot ("Boomers Dance to a New Beat") writes about the effect of demographics on societal and economic trends. What might demographic patterns mean for the funeral business in the next decade?

3. What kind of balance does Paul achieve in his essay between logical, emotional, and ethical appeals? Contrast this balance with that reached by David Suzuki in "The Right Stuff." Which author relies more on logic? Who uses emotion more? Whose essay has the strongest ethical appeal?

IDEAS FOR DISCUSSION/WRITING

Preparing to Write

Write freely about a personal experience with death and your responses to it. This is sometimes a difficult task, since death may be the most complex subject our emotions ever approach. How did you react to the first funeral you ever attended? How might your reactions to a funeral of a more distant acquaintance have differed from how you felt when you know or loved the deceased? How does society deal with dead bodies? What do you think or know of the entire undertaking process? How do our emotions change when someone we may have known is no longer physically present?

Choosing a Topic

1. Write a narrative essay about a funeral you have attended, or about your discovery of the death of someone you knew. Specify which of the two you will describe. What was the event? What was the extent of your involvement? How did you prepare yourself? What were your actions and those of others affected? What actually occurred, and what were your feelings during each stage? Choose and arrange your steps and details in such a way that they form a clear story line.

2. Death is one of those subjects where our responses may sometimes seem inappropriate or odd to others. As well, what one culture sees as normal may seem distinctly peculiar to another. Write a narrative-style article for your college paper about some aspect of the funeral industry, or about our culture's handling of death, which you find puzzling or stupid.

3. The funeral ceremony that Paul describes in his essay is very different from typical death ceremonies in other parts of the world. Write an essay in which you defend another type of death ceremony against those who might challenge it.

WEB SITES

www.katsden.com/death/index.html
The Death, Dying, and Grief Resources site has extensive links to related sites on the WWW.

Opposing Viewpoints

Wearing the Veil

■ ■ ■

Both Naheed Mustafa and Michele Lemon chose to voice their opinions about the traditional Muslim dress for women in essays published in the "Facts and Arguments" column of *The Globe and Mail*. A graduate of the University of Toronto with a degree in political science and history, Mustafa makes the point in her essay that she grew up in Canada, although she has moved to Pakistan since her article was originally published in 1993. Also a resident of Metropolitan Toronto, Lemon is a graduate of McGill University, where she completed a Master's degree in Islamic Studies. While these two women have many things in common, their views on the acceptability and significance of the traditional costume of Muslim women vary dramatically in these two selections.

Preparing to Read

In this pair of essays, both Michele Lemon and Naheed Mustafa discuss the ways in which appearance and clothing are related to the oppression of women. Before you read their essays, think about feminism and the oppression of women. What is feminism? Do you consider yourself a feminist? Why or why not? Traditionally, what aspects of society have oppressed women? Are there still barriers that women face at the end of the twentieth century? How does the situation in Canada compare to that of other countries? What is the relationship between women's physical appearance and their oppression?

Michele Lemon

■ ■ ■

Understanding Does Not Always Lead to Tolerance

Item: A young Muslim girl in Montreal is expelled from her 1
school for wearing *hejab*, a scarf that covers the hair and neck.
The issue has become a contentious one in Quebec. Agnes Gruda,
writing in *La Presse*, notes the dilemma that faces a multicultural
society when confronted by a symbol loaded with other associations. "The Islamic veil is more than religious garb," she writes. "It
is one of the most powerful symbols of women's servitude."

I am unsure as to what Ms. Gruda means by the veil. Is a 2
head scarf really the same as a veil that covers the face?

Item: Waiting for the bus on a warm, sunny day outside a 3
grocery store in Mississauga, my musings about the difference
between a scarf and a veil are answered. I see a pre-medieval
spectre before my eyes. A woman covered from head to toe
makes for the store. On her hands in this 24-degree heat are a
woolen pair of winter gloves. The white piece of cloth covering
her face flutters ever so slightly in the breeze, but never enough
to allow for a glimpse of the person who hides behind it. All
that one sees are her eyes.

I feel I've been punched in the stomach. Her oppression, for 4
oppression it is, becomes a symbol of the difficulty all women
once faced and a startling reminder that the struggle for equality
has not ended. I understand all too well why she wears this
hideous costume, but I despise it nonetheless. How could anyone
defend the outfit as preserving anything but the low regard and
true unimportance of women, all protestations of respect to the
contrary?

This woman is a walking billboard that proclaims public 5
space is reserved for men. Her outfit proclaims a woman's place

is indoors. Even the colour of the ankle-length coat dress she wears, navy blue, is designed to make her more uncomfortable in the blazing sun and proclaims that her place of comfort is in the home. Look at photographs of women in cloaks or chadors and you will find the majority of them are black, navy, dark brown. In Saudi Arabia, that bastion of misogyny, fear and blame, men wear white and women black. So completely male is public space in Saudi Arabia that women are not even supposed to call to a friend they recognize for fear of disturbing the male by provoking thoughts of sex.

The woman before us has accepted on some level the   6
argument of those who claim that society must be protected from chaos and anarchy. One of the greatest dangers to social harmony is the temptation women present to men. The way to ensure that lust is not acted upon, runs this facile logic, is not to work on civilizing or restraining a handful of men who cannot be trusted to control themselves, but by making women believe that they are the source of evil and must be made non-existent if they wish to venture out of doors.

Hideous as the practice is, at least in the Middle East, there   7
is a cultural context into which it can be fitted. Here, instead of making this woman inconspicuous, it draws all kinds of supposedly unwanted attention to her.

Two older women at the bus stop are "tsk-tsking." One of   8
them murmurs "dreadful." The young girl standing closest to me stares off into space. Two youngish couples exchange glances and burst out laughing. I want to tell them that this is no laughing matter, that under the forbidding costume there lurks a defaced human being, but I know that in laughter there is escape.

I arrive home feeling shell shocked. I say that people who   9
want to promenade in this country as slaves should not be allowed to do so. It is an affront to the rest of us; to human dignity and self-respect. My husband is appalled at my lack of tolerance. He reminds me that non-criminal activity is permitted in this country. He notes that wearing what you choose is not against the law. I say perhaps only women can understand my discomfort and understand my very real and very visceral antipathy to the repellent straitjacket in which she is encased.

It is not the woman I despise, but her compliance in a charade   10
that can in no way be defended on religious grounds, that handy refuse of the desperate authoritarian.

Item: A few days later I see this woman again. My reaction is 11 as before. She is with two friends. One is similarly enveloped from head to toe, her ensemble completed by black woolen gloves and face veil. Another woman of about 25 walks with them. This young woman interests me. I have seen her before and recognize her now. She has on a long navy robe that reaches to the ankle. She wears a *hejab*. Today a voluminous piece of black-and-white paisley cloth is wrapped around her hair and neck. The last time I saw this woman her scarf rested on her chin. This time it has edged up. It is now level with her upper lip. I expect to see her whole face covered by month's end.

I have found my threshold of tolerance and it is lower than 12 I expected. Sikhs in Legion Halls, absolutely; turbaned Sikhs in the RCMP, why on earth not? Women in robes and head scarves, sure. Women with face veils, no. It is as if I hit a brick wall on this issue. A woman with a covered face will always be a shocking spectacle of subservience to me.

It has become accepted wisdom that if you educate people 13 and explain the meaning of certain practices, then they will understand them and their level of tolerance will necessarily increase. This is not always so, as I have found out.

I am all too aware of the reasons and rationale employed by 14 women who outfit themselves in this fashion. I know that to ask a woman who has covered her face all her life to remove her veil would be akin to asking me to walk down Yonge Street half-clothed. But I am also a woman who was brought up in an era that saw women make great strides forward and, no matter how much I may pity this creature, I have an enormously difficult time seeing her and her friends parade around a Canadian city at the end of the 20th century dressed like this. I have read too many heartrending stories by Middle Eastern women who struggled against this debasement. I have read too many soul-destroying stories about crimes of honour and young men ordering their much older female relatives about for me to look at this woman with anything even approaching equanimity.

Naheed Mustafa

■ ■ ■

My Body Is My Own Business

I often wonder whether people see me as a radical, fundamentalist 1
Muslim terrorist packing an AK-47 assault rifle inside my jean
jacket. Or maybe they see me as the poster girl for oppressed womanhood everywhere. I'm not sure which it is.

I get the whole gamut of strange looks, stares and covert 2
glances. You see, I wear the *hijab*, a scarf that covers my head,
neck and throat. I do this because I am a Muslim woman who
believes her body is her own private concern.

Young Muslim women are reclaiming the *hijab*, reinterpreting 3
it in light of its original purpose—to give back to women ultimate
control of their own bodies.

The Koran teaches us that men and women are equal, that 4
individuals should not be judged according to gender, beauty,
wealth or privilege. The only thing that makes one person better
than another is her or his character.

Nonetheless, people have a difficult time relating to me. After 5
all, I'm young, Canadian born and raised, university-educated—
why would I do this to myself, they ask.

Strangers speak to me in loud, slow English and often appear 6
to be playing charades. They politely inquire how I like living
in Canada and whether or not the cold bothers me. If I'm in the
right mood, it can be very amusing.

But why would I, a woman with all the advantages of a 7
North American upbringing, suddenly, at 21, want to cover
myself so that with the *hijab* and the other clothes I choose to
wear, only my face and hands show?

Because it gives me freedom. 8

Women are taught from early childhood that their worth is 9
proportional to their attractiveness. We feel compelled to pursue
abstract notions of beauty, half realizing that such a pursuit is futile.

When women reject this form of oppression, they face ridicule 10
and contempt. Whether it's women who refuse to wear makeup
or to shave their legs or to expose their bodies, society, both men
and women have trouble dealing with them.

In the Western world, the *hijab* has come to symbolize either 11
forced silence or radical, unconscionable militancy. Actually, it's
neither. It is simply a woman's assertion that judgment of her
physical person is to play no role whatsoever in social interaction.

Wearing the *hijab* has given me freedom from constant 12
attention to my physical self. Because my appearance is not
subjected to public scrutiny, my beauty, or perhaps lack of it,
has been removed from the realm of what can legitimately be
discussed.

No one knows whether my hair looks as if I just stepped out 13
of a salon, whether or not I can pinch an inch, or even if I have
unsightly stretch marks. And because no one knows, no one
cares.

Feeling that one has to meet the impossible male standards 14
of beauty is tiring and often humiliating. I should know, I spent
my entire teenage years trying to do it. I was a borderline bulimic
and spent a lot of money I didn't have on potions and lotions in
hopes of becoming the next Cindy Crawford.

The definition of beauty is ever-changing; waifish is good, 15
waifish is bad, athletic is good—sorry, athletic is bad. Narrow
hips? Great. Narrow hips? Too bad.

Women are not going to achieve equality with the right to 16
bare their breasts in public, as some people would like to have
you believe. That would only make us party to our own
objectification. True equality will be had only when women don't
need to display themselves to get attention and won't need to
defend their decision to keep their bodies to themselves.

UNDERSTANDING DETAILS

1. Why does Mustafa tell us that she has chosen to wear the
   "hijab"? Why does Lemon believe women wear the traditional
   Muslim clothing? What does the hijab represent to each writer?
2. How does Mustafa's outfit differ from the "hideous costume"
   that Lemon describes?
3. On what points do Lemon and Mustafa agree? Are there any
   values or beliefs they share?

ANALYZING MEANING

1. Mustafa claims that "because no one knows [details of her physical appearance], no one cares" (paragraph 13). How would
   Lemon respond to this argument?
2. What does wearing the hijab say about the respective roles of
   men and women, according to Lemon's view? What about
   Mustafa's argument?
3. Lemon tells us that she feels "shell-shocked" (paragraph 9), as
   if she had been "punched in the stomach" (paragraph 4). She
   feels pity for the women she sees "covered from head to toe,"
   and says "It is not the woman I despise, but her compliance in
   a charade that can in no way be defended on religious
   grounds ... " What reaction would Mustafa consider more
   appropriate? Why?

DISCOVERING RHETORICAL STRATEGIES

1. Each of these authors was writing for the same audience. How
   would you characterize this audience?
2. Each writer has personal characteristics that give her credibility in dealing with this subject. What aspects of Mustafa's life
   strengthen her argument? What do we know about Lemon that
   adds to her argument?
3. Each writer uses figurative language to help convey her point
   effectively. Find three examples of figurative language (e.g.,
   metaphor, simile, alliteration) in each of these essays. What effect do these language choices have on each essay?

MAKING CONNECTIONS

1. Like Lemon and Mustafa, Gloria Steinem ("The Politics of
   Muscle") and Laura Robinson ("Starving for the Gold") both
   write about aspects of the appearance of women. On what
   points do you think these writers would agree on this topic?
   On which points would they disagree? Explain your answer.
2. Drew Hayden Taylor ("Pretty Like a White Boy") and Cecil
   Foster ("Why Blacks Get Mad") frequently run into difficult
   situations as people make assumptions based on their appearance. How is their experience similar to that of Naheed Mustafa
   or the women described in Lemon's essay? How do their experiences differ?

3. Naheed Mustafa and Michele Lemon both write about some of the conflicts that arise as two cultures meet. How are the situations they describe similar to the one that Charlotte Gray presents in "The Temple of Hygiene" and that described by Wayson Choy in "I'm a Banana and Proud of It"?

IDEAS FOR DISCUSSION/WRITING

Preparing to Write

Write freely about clothing and the fashion industry. Why do we wear what we wear? What is the purpose of clothing? How do we choose the things that we wear? What does our clothing tell the world about us? Why do fashions change? Why is fashion such a major industry? What factors in our lives dictate the fashion choices we make?

Choosing a Topic

1. Lemon says that women wearing veils is where she discovered her threshold of tolerance. Write an essay in which you explain your own threshold of tolerance when it comes to practices of various nationalities, religions, or ethnicities. What practices go beyond the realm of those you consider acceptable or tolerable?
2. The imposition of the values of one culture on another is always a difficult issue. In promoting multiculturalism, many immigrants to Canada are encouraged to maintain some traditional practices and lifestyles. Which practices should be maintained from an old culture and which Canadian values should be imposed upon newcomers? Write an essay for a group of newcomers to Canada in which you explain which values or practices are appropriate to maintain, and which Canadian values or practices should replace the ones with which they are familiar. Be sure that you present your argument in a clear, tactful, and diplomatic way.
3. The clothing we choose to wear tells the world a lot about who we are. Write an essay for a fashion magazine in which you explain how the fashion choices you make reflect your lifestyle and values.

WEB SITES

www.globeandmail.com/
The Globe and Mail is where Mustafa's and Lemon's articles were
originally published.

www.altavista.com

or

www.hotbot.com

Use a search engine like Alta Vista or HotBot to see where else
Mustafa's article has been reproduced.

DOCUMENTED ESSAYS

■ ■ ■

Reading and Writing From Sources

We use sources every day in both informal and formal situations. We explain the source of a phone message, for example, or we refer to an instructor's comments in class. We use someone else's opinion in an essay, or we quote an expert to prove a point. We cite sources both in speaking and in writing through summary, paraphrase, and direct quotation. Most of your college instructors will ask you to write papers using sources so they can see how well you understand the course material. The use of sources in academic papers requires you to understand what you have read and to integrate this reading material with your own opinions and observations—a process that requires a high level of skill in thinking, reading, and writing.

Defining Documented Essays

Documented essays provide you with the opportunity to perform sophisticated and exciting exercises in critical thinking; they draw on the thinking, reading, and writing abilities you have built up over the course of your academic career, and they often require you to put all the rhetorical modes to work at their most analytical level. Documented essays demonstrate the process of analytical thinking at its best in different disciplines.

In the academic world, documented essays are also called *research papers, library papers, and term papers.* Documented essays are generally written for one of three reasons: (1) to **report**, (2) to **interpret**, or (3) to **analyze**.

The most straightforward, uncomplicated type of documented essay **reports** information, as in a survey of problems that children have in preschool. The second type of documented essay both presents and **interprets** its findings. It examines a number of different views on a specific issue and weighs these views as it draws its own conclusions. A topic that falls into this category would be whether children who have attended preschool are more sociable than those who have not. After considering evidence on both sides, the writer would draw his or her own conclusions on this topic. A documented essay that **analyzes** a subject presents a hypothesis, tests the hypothesis, and analyzes or evaluates its conclusions. This type of essay calls for the most advanced form of critical thinking. It might look, for example, at the reasons preschool children are more or less socially flexible than non-preschool children. At its most proficient, this type of writing requires a sophisticated degree of evaluation that forces you to judge your reading, evaluate your sources, and ultimately scrutinize your own reasoning ability as the essay takes shape.

Each of these types of documented essays calls for a higher level of thinking, and each evolves from the previous category. In other words, interpreting requires some reporting, and analyzing draws on both reporting and interpreting.

In the following paragraph, a student reports, interprets, analyzes, and uses sources to document the problem of solid waste in America. Notice how the student writer draws her readers into the essay with a commonly used phrase about America and then questions the validity of its meaning. The student's opinions give shape to the paragraph, while her use of sources helps identify the problem and support her contentions.

> "America the Beautiful" is a phrase used to describe the many wonders of nature found throughout our country. America's natural beauty will fade, however, if solutions to our solid waste problems are not discovered soon. America is a rich nation socially, economically, and politically. But these very elements may be the cause of Americans' wastefulness. Americans now generate approximately 160 million tons of solid waste a year—3 1/2 pounds per person per day. We live in a consumer society where convenience, ready-to-use, and throwaway are words that spark the consumer's attention (Cook 60). However, many of the products associated with these words create a large part of our problem with

solid waste (Grossman 39). We are running out of space for our garbage. The people of America are beginning to produce responses to this problem. Are we too late? A joint effort between individuals, businesses, government industries, and local, state, and federal governments is necessary to establish policies and procedures to combat this waste war. The problem requires not one solution, but a combination of solutions involving technologies and people working together to provide a safe and healthy environment for themselves and future generations.

Reading and Writing Documented Essays

Reading and writing documented essays involves the skillful integration of two complex operations: research and writing. Reading documented essays critically means understanding the material and evaluating the sources as you proceed. Writing documented essays includes reading and understanding sources on the topic you have chosen and then combining this reading with your own conclusions. The two skills are, essentially, mirror images of one another.

How to Read Documented Essays

Preparing to Read. You should approach a documented essay in much the same way that you approach any essay. First, take a few minutes to look at the preliminary material for the selection: What can you learn from scanning Barbara Ehrenreich's essay ("The Ecstasy of War") and Jill Leslie Rosenbaum and Meda Chesney-Lind's essay ("Appearance and Delinquency: A Research Note") or from reading their synopses in the Rhetorical Table of Contents? What does Marilyn Dahl's title prepare you to read? And what questions do you have about "appearance and delinquency" before you read Rosenbaum and Chesney-Lind's essay?

Also, you should learn as much as you can from the authors' biographies: What is Ehrenreich's interest in war? What biographical details prepare us for her approach to this topic? Who was the original audience for her essay? What is Dahl's background? Does she have the proper qualifications to write about the depiction of disabled people by the media?

Another important part of preparing to read a documented essay is surveying the sources cited. Turn to the end of the essay, and look at the sources. What publications do Rosenbaum and Chesney-Lind draw from? Do you recognize any of the authorities that Dahl cites? Are these books and magazines well respected?

Last, before you read these essays, try to generate some ideas on the topics so you can participate as fully as possible in your reading. The Preparing to Read questions will get you ready for this task. Then, try to speculate further on the topic of the essay: Why has the relationship between female appearance and delinquency gained so much momentum in the United States? Where will this momentum take us in the future? What is the connection for Ehrenreich between war and ecstasy? What does this relationship tell us about human nature in general? What do you want to know from Dahl about disabilities and the media? Why do you think this topic has become such a major social issue?

Reading. As you react to the material in this chapter, you should respond to both the research and the writing. Record your responses as you read the essay for the first time: What are your reactions to the information you are reading? Are the sources appropriate? How well do they support the author's main points? Use the preliminary material before each essay to help you create a framework for your responses to it: Who was Dahl's primary audience when her essay was first published? In what ways is the tone of her essay appropriate for that audience? What motivated Ehrenreich to publish her argument on war? Do you find it convincing? Your main job at this stage is to determine the author's primary assertion (thesis statement), note the sources the author cites to support this thesis, and begin to ask yourself questions about the essay so you can respond critically to your reading. In addition, take a look at the questions after the selection to make certain you are comprehending the major ideas of the essay.

Rereading. As you reread this documented essay, take some time to become aware of the difference between fact and opinion, to weigh and evaluate the evidence brought to bear on the arguments, to consider the sources the writer uses, to judge the interpretation of the facts cited, to determine what the writer has omitted, and to confirm your own views on the issues at hand. All these skills demand the use of critical thinking strategies at their most sophisticated level.

You need to approach this type of argument with an inquiring mind, asking questions and looking for answers as you read the essay. Be especially conscious of the appeals (logical, emotional, and ethical) at work in the essay (see Chapter 9), and take note of other rhetorical strategies that support the author's main argument.

Also, be aware of your own thought processes as you sort facts from opinions. Know where you stand personally in relation to each side of the issues here.

For a list of guidelines for the entire reading process, see the checklists on pages 15–16 of the Introduction.

How to Write Documented Essays

Preparing to Write. Just as with any writing assignment, you should begin the task of writing a documented essay by exploring and limiting your topic. In this case, however, you draw on other sources to help you with this process. You should seek out both primary and secondary sources related to your topic. **Primary sources** are works of literature, historical documents, letters, diaries, speeches, eyewitness accounts, and your own experiments, observations, and conclusions; **secondary sources** explain and analyze information from other sources. Any librarian can help you search for both types of sources related to your topic.

After you have found a few sources on your general topic, you should scan and evaluate what you have discovered so you can limit your topic further. Depending on the required length of your essay, you want to find a topic broad enough to be researched, established enough so that you can find sources on it , and significant enough to demonstrate your abilities to grapple with ideas and draw conclusions. The Preparing to Write questions can help you generate and focus your ideas.

Once you have established these limitations, you might try writing a tentative thesis. At this point, asking a question and attempting to find an answer are productive. But you should keep in mind that your thesis is likely to be revised several times as the range of your knowledge changes and as your paper takes different turns while you research and write. Then, decide on a purpose and audience for your essay.

Once your tentative thesis is formed, you should read your sources for ideas and take detailed notes on your reading. These notes will probably fall into one of four categories: (1) *summary—*

a condensed statement of someone else's thoughts or observations; (2) *paraphrase*—a restatement in your own words of someone else's ideas or observations; (3) *direct quotations from sources*; or (4) *a combination of these forms*. Be sure to make a distinction in your notes between actual quotations and paraphrases or summaries. Also, record the sources of all your notes—especially of quoted, summarized, and paraphrased material—that you may need to cite in your essay.

As you gather information, you should consider keeping a "research journal" where you can record your own opinions, interpretations, and analyses in response to your reading. This journal should be separate from your notes on sources. It is the place where you can make your own discoveries in relation to your topic by jotting down thoughts and relationships among ideas you are exposed to, by keeping a record of sources you read and others you want to pursue, by tracking and developing your own ideas and theories, and by clarifying your thinking on an issue.

Finally, before you write your first draft, you might want to write an informal working outline for your own information. Such an exercise can help you check the range of your coverage and the order and development of your ideas. With an outline, you can readily see where you need more information, less information, or more solid sources. Try to be flexible, however. This outline may change dramatically as your essay develops.

Writing. Writing the first draft of a documented essay is your chance to discover new insights and to find important connections between ideas that you may not be aware of yet. This draft is your opportunity to demonstrate that you understand the issue at hand and your sources on three increasingly difficult levels— literal, interpretive, and analytical; that you can organize your material effectively; that you can integrate your sources (in the form of summaries, paraphrases, or quotations) with your opinions; and that you can document (that is, cite) your sources.

To begin this process, look again at your thesis statement and your working outline, and adjust them to represent any new discoveries you have made as you read your sources and wrote in your research journal. Then, organize your research notes and information in some logical fashion.

When you begin to draft your paper, write the sections of the essay that you feel most comfortable about first. Throughout the essay, feature your own point of view and integrate summaries, paraphrases, and quotations from other sources into your analysis. Each point you make should be a section of your paper consisting of your own conclusion and your support for that conclusion (in the form of facts, examples, summaries, paraphrases, and quotations). Remember that the primary reason for doing such an assignment is to let you demonstrate your ability to synthesize material, draw your own conclusions, and analyze your sources and your own reasoning.

A documented paper usually blends three types of material:

1. *Common knowledge, such as the places and dates of events (even if you have to look them up).*

   Example: Neil Armstrong and Edwin Aldrin first walked on the moon on July 20, 1969.

2. *Your own thoughts and observations.*

   Example: Armstrong and Aldrin's brief walk on the moon's surface was the beginning of a new era in the U.S. space program.

3. *Someone else's thoughts and observations.*

   Example: President Richard Nixon reacted to the moonwalk in a telephone call to the astronauts: "For one priceless moment in the history of man all the people on this earth are truly one— one in their pride in what you have done and one in our prayers that you will return safely to earth."

Of these three types of information, you must document or cite your exact source only for the third type. Negligence in citing your sources, whether purposeful or accidental, is called *plagiarism,* which comes from a Latin word meaning "kidnapper." Among student writers, plagiarism usually takes one of three forms: (1) using words from another source without quotation marks; (2) using someone else's ideas in the form of a summary or paraphrase without citing your source; and (3) using someone else's paper as your own.

Avoiding plagiarism is quite simple: You just need to remember to acknowledge the sources of ideas or wording that you are using to support your own contentions. Acknowledging your sources also gives you credit for the reading you have done and for the ability you have developed to use sources to support your observations and conclusions.

Documentation styles vary from discipline to discipline. Ask your instructor about the particular documentation style he or she wants you to follow. The most common styles are the Modern Language Association (MLA) style, used in humanities courses, and the American Psychological Association (APA) style, used in behavioural sciences and science courses. (See any writing handbook for more details on documentation formats.)

The World Wide Web is an exciting new source of information for your research papers. Electronic sources include online journals and magazines, CD-ROMs, software programs, newsletters, discussion groups, bulletin boards, gopher sites, and e-mail. But, just as with sources in more traditional media, not all electronic sources are equally accurate and reliable. Based on your topic, you need to exercise your best judgment and get your instructor's help in assessing the most useful online sites for your purposes. If you use electronic sources in any of papers, remember that you have two goals in any citation: (1) to acknowledge the author and (2) to help the reader locate the material. Then you should check the MLA or APA Home Pages for their current guidelines for online documentation: The URL for the Modern Language Association is **www.mla.org** and for the American Psychological Association, **www.apa.org**.

Even though documentation styles vary somewhat from one discipline to another, the basic concept behind documentation is the same in all disciplines: You must give proper credit to other writers by acknowledging the sources of the summaries, paraphrases, and quotations that you use to support the topics in your documented paper. Once you grasp this basic concept and accept it, you will have no trouble avoiding plagiarism.

Rewriting. To rewrite your documented essay, you should play the role of your readers and impartially evaluate your argument and the sources you have used as evidence in that argument. To begin with, revise your thesis to represent all the discoveries you made as you wrote your first draft. Then, look for problems in logic throughout the essay; you might even develop an outline at this point to help evaluate your reasoning:

1. Are the essay's assertions clear? Are they adequately supported?
2. Are other points of view recognized and examined?
3. Does the organization of your paper further your assertions/ argument?
4. Have you removed irrelevant material?

Next, check your documentation style:

1. Is your source material (either summarized, paraphrased, or quoted) presented fairly and accurately?

2. Have you rechecked the citations for all the sources in your paper?
3. Do you introduce the sources in your paper when appropriate?
4. Are your sources in the proper format according to your instructor's guidelines (MLA, APA, or another)?

Then, proofread carefully. Finally, prepare your paper to be submitted to your instructor:

1. Have you followed your instructor's guidelines for your title page, margins, page numbers, tables, and abstracts?
2. Have you prepared an alphabetical list of your sources for the end of your paper?

Any additional guidance you may need as you write and revise your documented essays is provided on pages 26–27 of the Introduction.

Student Essay: Documentation at Work

The following student essay uses documented sources to support its conclusions and observations about our eating habits today. First, the writer creates a profile of carnivorous species in contrast to human beings. She then goes on to discuss the harsh realities connected with eating meat. After recognizing and refuting some opposing views, this student writer ends her paper with her own evaluation of the situation and a list of some famous vegetarians. Throughout the essay, the student writer carefully supports her principal points with summaries, paraphrases, and quotations from other sources. Notice that she uses the MLA documentation style and closes the paper with an alphabetical list of "Works Cited."

Food for Thought

The next time you sit down to a nice steak dinner, pause for a moment to consider whether you are biologically programmed to eat meat. Unlike carnivores, such as lions and tigers, with claws and sharp front teeth allowing them to tear and eat raw flesh, humans are omnivores, with fingers that can pluck fruits and grains and flat teeth that can grind these vegetable foods. To digest their meals, carnivores have an acidic saliva and a very strong hydrochloric acid digestive fluid. In contrast, we humans have an alkaline saliva, and

Background information

Common knowledge

Common
knowledge our digestive fluids are only one-tenth as potent as those of carnivores. Moreover, carnivores have an intestinal tract barely three
times their body length, which allows for faster elimination of rot-
ting flesh; humans have an intestinal tract eight to twelve times our
Paraphrase body length, better enabling us to digest plant nutrients. These
of secondary
source marked physiological distinctions clearly suggest that carnivorous
animals and humans are adapted to very different kinds of foods
(Diamond and Diamond, *Fit for Life II* 239). What happens, then, **Citation (ML**
form)
Thesis when we eat flesh? <u>The effects of a meat-based diet are far-reaching:</u>
<u>massive suffering of the animals killed and eaten, a myriad of dis-</u>
Student's <u>eases in humans, and a devastating effect on world ecology.</u>
first <u>The atrocities committed daily to provide meat should be</u>
conclusion <u>enough to make a meat-based diet completely unconscionable</u>.
According to Peter Singer, of People for the Ethical Treatment of **Summary of**
Animals (PETA), every year several hundred million cattle, pigs, **secondary**
source
and sheep and 3 billion chickens are slaughtered to provide food
for humans (*Animal Liberation* 92). That is equal to 6,278 animals
every minute of every day—and those are just the ones that make
it to the slaughterhouse. Over 500,000 animals die in transit each **Support for**
year (Singer, *Animal Liberation* 150). **conclusion #**

Paraphrase   A slaughterhouse is not a pretty sight. Anywhere from 50 to
of
secondary 90 percent of the cattle are slaughtered in a "kosher" manner **Summary of**
source (fact) (Robbins 142). "Kosher" sounds innocent enough, but what it ac- **secondary**
source
tually means is that the animal must be "healthy and moving" at
the time of death. This requires the animals to be fully conscious
as "a heavy chain is clamped around one of their rear legs; then
they are jerked off their feet and hang upside down" for anywhere
from two to five minutes, usually twisting in agony with a broken leg, while they are moved down the conveyer belt to be slaughtered (Robbins 140–41).

Student's   The pain doesn't start at the time of slaughter, however, for
opinion most of these animals, but rather at birth. An in-depth look at the
animal most slaughtered by people, the chicken, reveals particularly horrendous treatment. Chickens are used in two ways: for
their flesh and for their eggs. For egg manufacturers, the one-half **Examples to**
million male chicks born every day are useless, so they are im- **support**
opinion
Paraphrase mediately thrown into garbage bags and left to suffocate. When
of
secondary you consider the life of their female counterparts, however, perhaps
source such brutal treatment is a blessing (Robbins 54).
(opinion)   Chickens naturally belong to a flock with a specific pecking **Paraphrase**
order. They seem to enjoy open spaces to stretch their wings as **secondary**
source (facts
they scratch around, dust-bathe, and build nests for their eggs

Paraphrase of secondary source (facts) (Singer, *Animal Liberation* 109). Today, however, chickens are housed in wire-mesh cages suspended over a trench to collect droppings. The typical cage is 12 by 18 inches, holding four or five hens for their entire productive life, which is at least a year or more (Mason in Singer, *Defense* 91). This overcrowding results in such high levels of stress that the hens resort to pecking each other's feathers out and to cannibalism (Singer, *Animal Liberation* 98). Rather than incur the expense of increasing space to alleviate these conditions, chicken farmers have routinely adopted the practice of debeaking the hens by slicing a hot knife through their highly sensitive beak tissue (Singer, *Animal Liberation* 99). Another result of this overcrowding is that the hens' toenails get tangled in the bottom wires of the cages; after some time the flesh grows onto the wire. The solution to this problem has become to cut off the chick's toes within a day or two of birth (Robbins 61). Conditions for other farm animals are equally despicable (Singer, *Defense*).

Analysis from secondary source

Paraphrase of secondary sources (facts)

Paraphrase of secondary source (opinion)

While we would like to assume the animals we eat are healthy at the time of butchering, this is often not the case. Most veal calves, for example, are near death from anemia when sent to the butcher (Diamond and Diamond, *Fit for Life II* 238). Inspections have revealed leukosis (cancer) in 90 percent of the chickens (Robbins 67), pneumonia rates of 80 percent and stomach ulcers of 53 percent in pigs (Robbins 94). Salmonellosis is found in 90 percent of the chickens dressed and ready to be purchased (Robbins 303).

Student's opinion

Examples from secondary sources

Student's opinion

How can the factory farming industry justify its behavior? The answer boils down to money, for factory farming has become an incredibly huge business, and meat producers can't afford to be sentimental. As shown by USDA Economic Indicators for the Farm Sector, in 1988 the United States had cash receipts totaling over $150 billion from farm marketing (*State Financial Summary* 151) and nearly $80 billion from livestock and livestock products (153). As Fred Haley, head of a poultry farm with nearly 250,000 hens, has stated, "The object of producing eggs is to make money. When we forget this objective, we have forgotten what it is all about" (qtd. in Robbins 67). Cattle auctioneer Henry Pace has a similar comment about the treatment of cattle: "We believe we can be most efficient by not being emotional. We are a business, not a humane society, and our job is to sell merchandise at a profit. It's no different from selling paper clips or refrigerators" (qtd. in Robbins 104).

Paraphrase of secondary sources

Quotation from secondary source

Quotation from secondary source

Student's second conclusion

Even if we, like the industry leaders, could turn a cold heart to the plight of our fellow creatures, we would still find many reasons

to warrant a vegetarian diet, beginning with our own health.
Recapping just a few of the hundreds of studies that link diet to disease, we might consider the following:

Paraphrase   —A study of nearly 90,000 American women published in the   Support for
of   *New England Journal of Medicine* reports that daily pork, lamb, or   second
secondary   beef eaters have a 250 percent greater likelihood of developing   conclusion
sources
(facts)   colon cancer than people who consume these foods once a month
or less ("Red Meat Alert").

—The *Journal of the American Medical Association* stated that a
vegetarian diet could prevent 97 percent of coronary occlusions
(Robbins 247).

—Scientists now routinely screen cattle workers for BIV, a disease that "shares about 35 percent of its genetic makeup with
HIV," the human AIDS retrovirus ("Cattle's Link with AIDS" 19).

Other equally shocking residual health problems associated
with a meat diet are also being documented. For instance, people
tend to think that vegetarians are at high risk for pesticide poi-
Summary of   soning, but according to the EPA's *Pesticides Monitoring Journal,*
secondary   most pesticides in the American diet come from foods originat-
source   ing from animals. Studies have shown that 95 to 99 percent of
toxic chemicals in the American diet come from meat, fish, and
animal products (Robbins 315). These same pesticides are ending
up in the milk of lactating mothers. A similar study in the *New*   Paraphrase
England Journal of Medicine showed that the breast milk of vege-   secondary
sources (fact
tarian mothers has contamination levels only 1 to 2 percent of the
average (Robbins 345). Not only does vegetarian breast milk have
strikingly lower levels of contamination, it also has higher levels
of essential elements, such as selenium (Debski *et al.* 215).

Student's   But don't we need a lot of protein to be strong and healthy?
question   The RDA for protein is 56 grams (just under 2 ounces) per day   Paraphrase
secondary
(Diamond and Diamond, *Fit for Life* 88). People seem to think that   source (fact)
meat is the best (or the only) way to get protein, but think about
Paraphrase   this: Some of the world's strongest animals—elephants, horses,
of   and gorillas—eat principally fruits, grain, or grass (Diamond, *Fit*
secondary
source (fact)   *for Life* 89–90). Lest you believe that humans must eat meat to be
strong and healthy, consider the following: Edwin Moses, unde-
feated in the 400-meter hurdles for eight years, is a vegetarian;   Examples th
answer
Andreas Cahling, 1980 Mr. International Body Builder, is a vege-   protein
tarian (Robbins 160–61); and Dave Scott, Ironman Triathlon winner   question
Examples   four times (no one else has won it more than once), is a vegetarian
that answer   (Robbins 158). In study after study, the consumption of protein is
protein
question   linked not with health but with such illnesses as heart disease,

hypertension, various forms of cancer, arthritis, and osteoporosis (Diamond and Diamond, *Fit for Life* 87).

Student's third conclusion — The effects of meat diets go beyond causing human disease and death. <u>Perhaps the most frightening legacy being left by America's dietary ritual is just now being realized, and that is the profound ecological impact factory farming is having on our planet.</u> Every five seconds, one acre of forest is cleared in America, and one estimate is that 87 percent is cleared for either livestock grazing or growing livestock feed (Robbins 361). According to Christopher Uhl of the Pennsylvania State University Department of Biology and Geoffrey Parker of the Institute of Ecosystem Studies, 55 square feet of forest in Central America is lost for each hamburger eaten (642). **Support for third conclusion** · **Paraphrase of secondary sources (facts)**

Student's opinion — Forests are not all that we are sacrificing. Local governments are constantly calling for water conservation, yet over 50 percent of all water used in America goes into grain production for livestock (Robbins 367). According to one study, the water required to feed a meat eater for one day is 4,000 gallons, but it is only 1,200 gallons for a lacto-ovo (dairy and egg eating) vegetarian and 300 gallons for a vegan (one who consumes no animal-derived products) (Robbins 367). Not only is the vast amount of water wasted through a meat-based diet outrageous, but the added cost of controlling animal waste must also be taken into account. One cow produces sixteen times as much waste as one human (Robbins 372), and cattle waste produces ten times the water pollution that human waste does (Robbins 373). **Paraphrase of secondary sources (facts)**

Student's opinion — A third loss is even more serious than the losses of forests and water. This year, 60 million people will die of starvation, yet in America, we feed 80 percent of our corn and 95 percent of our oats to farm animals. The feed given to cattle alone, excluding pigs and chickens, would feed double the population of humans worldwide (Robbins 352). Three and one-quarter acres of farmland are needed to provide meat for one person per year. A lacto-ovo vegetarian can be fed from just one-half acre per year; a vegan needs only one-sixth of an acre. This means twenty vegans can eat a healthy diet for the same acreage needed to feed just one meat eater. Cutting our meat habit by only 10 percent would provide enough food for all of the 60 million people worldwide who will starve this year (Robbins 352–353). **Paraphrase of secondary sources (facts)**

Quotation from secondary source — As John Robbins, who relinquished his inheritance of the largest ice cream company in America, Baskin-Robbins, said, "We live in a crazy time, when people who make food choices that are healthy and compassionate are often considered weird, while people are considered normal whose eating habits promote disease and are dependent on enormous suffering" (305).

Student's final remarks

With all the devastation the average American diet is creating, we must begin to take responsibility for the consequences of our actions. Let us follow in the footsteps of such famous vegetarians as Charles Darwin, Leonardo da Vinci, Albert Einstein, Sir Isaac Newton, Plato, Pythagoras, Socrates, and Tolstoy (Parham 185). Every time we sit down to eat, we can choose either to contribute to or to help put an end to this suffering and destruction. Only one move matters, and that is the one we make with our forks.

Works Cited

"Cattle's Link with AIDS." *New Scientist* 8 Oct. 1987:19.

Debski, Bogdan, *et al*. "Selenium Content and Glutathione Peroxidase Activity of Milk from Vegetarian and Nonvegetarian Women." *Journal of Nutrition* 119 (1989):215–20.

Diamond, Harvey, and Marilyn Diamond. *Fit for Life*. New York: Warner, 1985.

——. *Fit for Life II, Living Health*. New York: Warner, 1987.

Parham, Barbara. *What's Wrong with Eating Meat?* Denver: Ananda Marga, 1981.

"Red Meat Alert." *New Scientist* 22/29 Dec. 1990.

Robbins, John. *Diet for a New America*. Walpole: Stillpoint, 1987.

Singer, Peter. *Animal Liberation: A New Ethics for Our Treatment of Animals*. New York: Hearst, 1975.

——, ed. *In Defense of Animals*. New York: Basil Blackwell, 1985.

State Financial Summary, 1988. Washington: Economic Indicators for the Farm Sector, 1988.

Uhl, Christopher, and Geoffrey Parker. "Our Steak in the Jungle." *Bio Science* 36 (1986):642.

Student Writer's Comments

From the moment this essay was assigned, I knew my topic would be vegetarianism, because I felt the key to a convincing argument was to select a topic I was passionate about. Since I was undertaking the task of speaking out against the time-honored American tradition of eating meat,

I knew I needed to approach the topic in as nonthreatening a manner as possible. I wanted to be graphic as I appealed to the emotions, concerns, and ethics of my audience, so that my message would not easily be forgotten, but I had to strike a careful balance, so that I would not alienate my readers by appearing preachy, accusatory, or unduly crude.

I began the process of writing this paper by going to the library every chance I had (between classes, during lunch, and at night before I went home) and collecting information on the horror stories connected with eating meat. (I had been a loyal vegetarian for years and actually wanted some concrete information on some of the choices I had made in my own eating habits.) I found plenty of horror stories, but I also uncovered some counterarguments that I hadn't been aware of. I was fascinated by the information—both facts and opinions—that I was discovering. But the material wasn't taking any shape at all yet; the only common denominator was the general topic and my interest level.

I was taking notes on notecards, so I had filled quite a stack of cards when I stopped to reread all my material to see if I could put it into any coherent categories. Happily, my notes fell quite naturally into three divisions: (1) the overwhelming cruelty to the animals that we kill and eat, (2) the diseases resulting from eating animals, and (3) the effect of this type of slaughter on world ecology. After this exercise, I could see right away that I had enough material on the suffering of the animals killed for human consumption, and my material in this area was from well-known, reputable sources. My notes on world ecology would be sufficient as well with a few more library sessions, but I had to do some serious investigation on the topic of human diseases in reference to meat eaters or else drop the topic altogether. I had some stray notes that didn't fit any of these categories, but I decided to worry about those later. I tried my hand at a thesis statement, which I think had been floating around in my head for days. Then, I wrote the paper topic by topic over a period of several days. I didn't attempt the introduction and the conclusion until I began to rewrite. As I composed the essay, I was especially aware of the types of material I had to support each of my topics. I had a good distribution of summaries, paraphrases, and quotations and had remembered to keep careful notes on my sources, so I put my source and page numbers into my first draft. I also had several examples for each of my topics and a good blend of facts and opinions.

When I rewrote, I kept in mind that I would be successful in arguing my case only if my words caused the readers to make a change, however small, in their own behavior. I reworked my research paper several times as I played different readers with various biases, during which time I paid special attention to word choice and sentence structure.

Overall, writing this paper gave me a great deal of pleasure. I feel even stronger in my determination to be a vegetarian, and now I have some concrete reasons (and their sources!) for my natural instincts.

Some Final Thoughts on Documented Essays

The essays that follow offer vigorous exercises in critical thinking. They use a combination of the three different types of persuasive appeals we studied in Chapter 9 (logical, emotional, and ethical) and draw on a wealth of rhetorical modes that we have studied throughout the book. In the first essay, Barbara Ehrenreich illustrates the Modern Language Association documentation style as she uses sources to support her thesis that people do not have a natural instinct to kill. The second essay, by Jill Leslie

Rosenbaum and Meda Chesney-Lind, explains the connection between female appearance and judgments in criminal cases; its use of sources illustrates the American Psychological Association documentation style. As you read these essays, be aware of the combination of appeals at work, the various rhetorical modes the authors use to further their arguments, and the way each author uses sources to support the topics within the argument.

Documented Essays in Review

Reading Documented Essays

Preparing to Read

1. What assumptions can you make from the essay's title?
2. Can you guess what the general mood of the essay is?
3. What is the essay's purpose and audience?
4. What does the synopsis in the Rhetorical Table of Contents tell you about the essay?
5. What can you learn from the author's biography?
6. Can you guess what the author's point of view toward the subject is?
7. What are your responses to the Preparing to Read questions?

Reading

1. What are your initial reactions to the essay?
2. What is the author's main assertion or thesis?
3. What sources does the author cite to support the thesis?
4. What questions do you have about this topic?
5. Did you preview the questions that follow the essay?

Rereading

1. How does the author use facts and opinions in the essay?
2. Are the sources the writer cites valid and reliable?
3. Are the sources cited in the essay respected in the field?
4. Does the author interpret facts accurately?
5. Has the author omitted any necessary information?

6. What are your responses to the questions after the essay?

Writing Documented Essays

Preparing to Write

1. What are your responses to the Preparing to Write questions?
2. What is your purpose?
3. Who is your audience?

Writing

1. Do you have a thesis statement?
2. Do you use both primary and secondary sources in your essay?
3. Have you organized your material effectively?
4. Have you avoided plagiarism and cited your sources correctly?
5. Do you use the appropriate documentation style?

Rewriting

1. Are the essay's assertions clear? Are they adequately supported?
2. Are other points of view recognized and examined?
3. Does the organization of your paper further your assertions/argument?
4. Have you removed irrelevant material?
5. Is your source material (whether summarized, paraphrased, or quoted) presented fairly and accurately?
6. Have you rechecked the citations for all the sources in your paper?
7. Do you introduce the sources in your paper when appropriate?
8. Are your sources in the proper format according to your instructor's guidelines (MLA, APA, or another)?
9. Have you followed your instructor's guidelines for your title page, margins, page numbers, tables, and abstracts?
10. Have you prepared an alphabetical list of your sources for the end of your paper?

Barbara Ehrenreich
1941–

■■■

The Ecstasy of War

Barbara Ehrenreich is a respected author, lecturer, and social commentator with opinions on a wide range of topics. After earning a B.A. from Reed College in chemistry and physics and a Ph.D. from Rockefeller University in cell biology, she turned almost immediately to freelance writing, producing a succession of books and pamphlets on a dazzling array of subjects. Early publications examined student uprisings, health care in America, nurses and midwives, poverty, welfare, economic justice for women, and the sexual politics of disease. Her most recent books include *The Hearts of Men: American Dreams and the Flight from Commitment* (1983), *Fear of Falling: The Inner Life of the Middle Class* (1989), and *The Worst Year of Our Lives: Irreverent Notes from a Decade of Greed* (1990)—an indictment of the 1980s that was described by the *New York Times* as "elegant, trenchant, savagely angry, morally outraged, and outrageously funny." Ehrenreich is also well known as a frequent guest on television and radio programs, including *The Today Show, Good Morning America, NightLine, Crossfire*, and *The Phil Donohue Show*. Her many articles and reviews have appeared in the *New York Times Magazine, Esquire*, the *Atlantic Monthly*, the *New Republic, Vogue, Harper's* and the *Wall Street Journal*. She has been an essayist for *Time* since 1990. Ehrenreich, whose favourite hobby is "voracious reading," lives in Syosset, New York.

Preparing to Read

Taken from *Blood Rites: Origins and History of the Passions of War* (1997), the following essay analyzes the psychology of war. Its citations and bibliography illustrate proper MLA (Modern Language Association) documentation form. As you prepare to read this article, take a few minutes to think about aggression in society today: Do you think aggression plays a significant role in North American society? In other societies? What do you think is the origin of aggression? In your opinion, what role does aggression play in war? In everyday life? How do you react to aggressive behaviour? How do people you associate with react to aggressive behaviour?

"*So elemental is the human need to endow the shedding of blood* 1 *with some great and even sublime significance that it renders the intellect almost entirely helpless*" *(Van Creveld 166).*

Different wars have led to different theories of why men 2
fight them. The Napoleonic Wars, which bore along with them
the rationalist spirit of the French Revolution, inspired the
Prussian officer Carl von Clausewitz to propose that war itself is
an entirely rational undertaking, unsullied by human emotion.
War, in his famous aphorism, is merely a "continuation of policy
... by other means," with policy itself supposedly resulting from
the same kind of clearheaded deliberation one might apply to a
game of chess. Nation-states were the leading actors on the stage
of history, and war was simply one of the many ways they
advanced their interests against those of other nation-states. If
you could accept the existence of this new superperson, the
nation, a battle was no more disturbing and irrational than, say,
a difficult trade negotiation—except perhaps to those who lay
dying on the battlefield.

World War I, coming a century after Napoleon's sweep 3
through Europe and northern Africa, led to an opposite
assessment of the human impulse of war. World War I was hard
to construe as in any way "rational," especially to that generation
of European intellectuals, including Sigmund Freud, who survived
to ponder the unprecedented harvest of dead bodies. History
textbooks tell us that the "Great War" grew out of the conflict
between "competing imperialist states," but this Clausewitzian
interpretation has little to do with the actual series of accidents,
blunders, and miscommunications that impelled the nations of
Europe to war in the summer of 1914.[1] At first swept up in the
excitement of the war, unable for weeks to work or think of
anything else, Freud was eventually led to conclude that there is
some dark flaw in the human psyche, a perverse desire to destroy,
countering Eros and the will to live (Stromberg 82).

So these are, in crude summary, the theories of war which 4
modern wars have left us with: That war is a means, however
risky, by which men seek to advance their collective interests
and improve their lives. Or, alternatively, that war stems from
subrational drives not unlike those that lead individuals to
commit violent crimes. In our own time, most people seem to
hold both views at once, avowing that war is a gainful enterprise,
intended to meet the material needs of the groups engaged in it,
and, at the same time, that it fulfills deep and "irrational"
psychological needs. There is no question about the first part of
this proposition—that wars are designed, at least ostensibly, to
secure necessaries like land or oil or "geopolitical advantage."

The mystery lies in the peculiar psychological grip war exerts on us.

In the 1960s and '70s, the debate on the psychology of war 5 centered on the notion of an "aggressive instinct," peculiar to all humans or only to human males. This is not the place to summarize that debate, with its endless examples of animal behavior and clashes over their applicability to human affairs. Here I would simply point out that, whether or not there is an aggressive instinct, there are reasons to reject it as the major wellspring of war.

Although it is true that aggressive impulses, up to and 6 including murderous rage, can easily take over in the heat of actual battle, even this statement must be qualified to take account of different weaponry and modes of fighting. Hand-to-hand combat may indeed call forth and even require the emotions of rage and aggression, if only to mobilize the body for bursts of muscular activity. In the case of action-at-a-distance weapons, however, like guns and bows and arrows, emotionality of any sort can be a distinct disadvantage. Coolness, and the ability to keep aiming and firing steadfastly in the face of enemy fire, prevails. Hence, according to the distinguished American military historian Robert L. O'Connell, the change in the ideal warrior personality wrought by the advent of guns in the fifteenth and sixteenth centuries, from "ferocious aggressiveness" to "passive disdain" (119). So there is no personality type—"hot-tempered," "macho," or whatever—consistently and universally associated with warfare.

Furthermore, fighting itself is only one component of the 7 enterprise we know as war. Wars are not barroom brawls writ large, or domestic violence that has been somehow extended to strangers. In war, fighting takes place within battles—along with much anxious waiting, of course—but wars do not begin with battles and are often not decided by them either. Most of war consists of *preparation* for battle—training, the organization of supplies, marching and other forms of transport—activities which are hard to account for by innate promptings of any kind. There is no plausible instinct, for example, that impels a man to leave his home, cut his hair short, and drill for hours in tight formation. As anthropologists Clifton B. Kroeber and Bernard L. Fontana point out, "It is a large step from what may be biologically innate leanings toward individual aggression to ritualized, socially sanctioned, institutionalized group warfare" (166).

War, in other words, is too complex and collective an activity   8
to be accounted for by a single warlike instinct lurking within
the individual psyche. Instinct may, or may not, inspire a man to
bayonet the first enemy he encounters in battle. But instinct does
not mobilize supply lines, manufacture rifles, issue uniforms, or
move an army of thousands from point A on the map to B. These
are "complicated, orchestrated, highly organized" activities, as
social theorist Robin Fox writes, undertaken not by individuals
but by entities on the scale of nations and dynasties (15). "The
hypothesis of a killer instinct," according to a commentator
summarizing a recent conference on the anthropology of war, is
"not so much wrong as irrelevant" (McCauley 2).

In fact, throughout history, individual men have gone to   9
near-suicidal lengths to avoid participating in wars—a fact that
proponents of a warlike instinct tend to slight. Men have fled
their homelands, served lengthy prison terms, hacked off limbs,
shot off feet or index fingers, feigned illness or insanity, or, if
they could afford to, paid surrogates to fight in their stead. "Some
draw their teeth, some blind themselves, and others maim
themselves, on their way to us" (Mitchell 42), the governor of
Egypt complained of his peasant recruits in the early nineteenth
century. So unreliable was the rank and file of the eighteenth-
century Prussian army that military manuals forbade camping
near a woods or forest: The troops would simply melt away into
the trees (Delbrück 303).

Proponents of a warlike instinct must also reckon with the   10
fact that even when men have been assembled, willingly or
unwillingly, for the purpose of war, fighting is not something
that seems to come "naturally" to them. In fact, surprisingly,
even in the thick of battle, few men can bring themselves to shoot
directly at individual enemies.[2] The difference between an
ordinary man or boy and a reliable killer, as any drill sergeant
could attest, is profound. A transformation is required: The man
or boy leaves his former self behind and becomes something
entirely different, perhaps even taking a new name. In small-
scale, traditional societies, the change was usually accomplished
through ritual drumming, dancing, fasting, and sexual
abstinence—all of which serve to lift a man out of his mundane
existence and into a new, warriorlike mode of being, denoted by
special body paint, masks, and headdresses.

As if to emphasize the discontinuity between the warrior   11
and the ordinary human being, many cultures require the would-

be fighting man to leave his human-ness behind and assume a new form as an animal.[3] The young Scandinavian had to become a bear before he could become an elite warrior, going "berserk" (the word means, "dressed in a bear hide"), biting and chasing people. The Irish hero Cuchulain transformed himself into a monster in preparation for battle: "He became horrible, many-shaped, strange and unrecognizable," with one eye sucked into his skull and the other popping out of the side of the face (Davidson 84). Apparently this transformation was a familiar and meaningful one, because similarly distorted faces turn up frequently in Celtic art.

Often the transformation is helped along with drugs or social   12 pressure of various kinds. Tahitian warriors were browbeaten into fighting by functionaries called Rauti, or "exhorters," who ran around the battlefield urging their comrades to mimic "the devouring wild dog" (Keeley 146). The ancient Greek hoplites drank enough wine, apparently, to be quite tipsy when they went into battle (Hanson 126); Aztecs drank pulque; Chinese troops at the time of Sun Tzu got into the mood by drinking wine and watching "gyrating sword dancers" perform (Griffith in Sun Tzu 37). Almost any drug or intoxicant has served, in one setting or another, to facilitate the transformation of man into warrior. Yanomamo Indians of the Amazon ingest a hallucinogen before battle; the ancient Scythians smoked hemp, while a neighboring tribe drank something called "hauma," which is believed to have induced a frenzy of aggression (Rolle 94–95). So if there is a destructive instinct that impels man to war, it is a weak one, and often requires a great deal of help.

In seventeenth-century Europe, the transformation of man   13 into soldier took on a new form, more concerted and disciplined, and far less pleasant, than wine. New recruits and even seasoned veterans were endlessly drilled, hour after hour, until each man began to feel himself part of a single, giant fighting machine. The drill was only partially inspired by the technology of firearms. It's easy enough to teach a man to shoot a gun; the problem is to make him willing to get into situations where guns are being shot and to remain there long enough to do some shooting of his own. So modern military training aims at a transformation parallel to that achieved by "primitives" with war drums and paint: In the fanatical routines of boot camp, a man leaves behind his former identity and is reborn as a creature of the military—an automaton and also, ideally, a willing killer of other men.

This is not to suggest that killing is foreign to human nature   14
or, more narrowly, to the male personality. Men (and women)
have again and again proved themselves capable of killing
impulsively and with gusto. But there is a huge difference
between a war and an ordinary fight. War not only departs from
the normal; it inverts all that is moral and right: In war one *should*
kill, *should* steal, *should* burn cities and farms, should perhaps
even rape matrons and little girls. Whether or not such activities
are "natural" or at some level instinctual, most men undertake
them only by entering what appears to be an "altered state"—
induced by drugs or lengthy drilling, and denoted by face paint
or khakis.

The point of such transformative rituals is not only to put   15
men "in the mood." Returning warriors may go through equally
challenging rituals before they can celebrate victory or reenter
the community—covering their heads in apparent shame, for
example; vomiting repeatedly; abstaining from sex (Keeley 144).
Among the Maori, returning warriors could not participate in
the victory celebration until they had gone through a whaka-hoa
ritual, designed to make them "common" again: The hearts of
slain enemies were roasted, after which offerings were made to
the war god Tu, and the rest was eaten by priests, who shouted
spells to remove "the blood curse" and enable warriors to reenter
their ordinary lives (Sagan 18). Among the Taulipang Indians of
South America, victorious warriors "sat on ants, flogged one
another with whips, and passed a cord covered with poisonous
ants, through their mouth and nose" (Métraux 397). Such painful
and shocking postwar rites impress on the warrior that war is
much more than a "continuation of policy ... by other means."
In war men enter an alternative realm of human experience, as far
removed from daily life as those things which we call "sacred."

Notes

1. See, for example, Stoessinger, *Why Nations Go to War*, 14–20.
2. See Grossman, *On Killing*.
3. In the mythologies of the Indo-European tradition, Dumézil
   relates, thanks "either to a gift of metamorphosis, or to a monstrous heredity, the eminent warrior possesses a veritable animal nature" (140).

Works Cited

Davidson, Hilda Ellis. *Myths and Symbols in Pagan Europe: Early Scandinavian and Celtic Religions.* Syracuse, NY: Syracuse UP, 1988.

Delbrück, Hans. *History of the Art of War, vol. 4. The Dawn of Modern Warfare.* Lincoln, U of Nebraska P, 1985.

Dumézil, Georges. *Destiny of the Warrior.* Chicago: U of Chicago P, 1969.

Fox, Robin. "Fatal Attraction: War and Human Nature." *The National Interest* (Winter 1992/93): 11–20.

Grossman, Lt. Col. Dave. *On Killing: The Psychological Cost of Learning to Kill in War and Society.* Boston: Little, Brown, 1995.

Hanson, Victor Davis. *The Western Way of War: Infantry Battle in Classical Greece.* New York: Knopf, 1989.

Keeley, Lawrence H. *War Before Civilization: The Myth of the Peaceful Savage.* New York: Oxford UP, 1996.

Kroeber, Clifton B., and Bernard L. Fontana. *Massacre on the Gila: An Account of the Last Major Battle Between American Indians, with Reflections on the Origin of War.* Tucson: U of Arizona P, 1986.

McCauley, Clark. "Conference Overview." *The Anthropology of War.* Ed. Jonathan Haas. Cambridge: Cambridge UP, 1990, 1–25.

Métraux, Alfred. "Warfare, Cannibalism, and Human Trophies." *Handbook of South American Indians,* vol. 5. Ed. Julian H. Steward. New York: Cooper Square Publishers, 1963. 383–409.

Mitchell, Timothy. *Colonizing Egypt.* Berkeley: U of California P, 1991.

O'Connell, Robert L. *Of Arms and Men: A History of War, Weapons, and Aggression.* New York: Oxford UP, 1989.

Rolle, Renate. *The World of the Scythians.* Berkeley: U of California P, 1989.

Sagan, Eli. *Cannibalism: Human Aggression and Cultural Form.* New York: Harper and Row, 1974.

Stoessinger, John G. *Why Nations Go to War.* New York: St. Martin's Press, 1993.

Stromberg, Roland. *Redemption by War: The Intellectuals and 1914.* Lawrence: U of Kansas P, 1982.

Sun Tzu. *The Art of War.* Trans. Samuel B. Griffith. London: Oxford UP, 1971.

Van Creveld, Martin. *The Transformation of War.* New York: Free Press, 1991.

UNDERSTANDING DETAILS

1. What do you think Ehrenreich's main purpose is in this essay?
2. According to Ehrenreich, what is the difference between hand-to-hand combat and fighting at a distance?
3. What does Ehrenreich say are the various components of what we call "war"?
4. In what ways do some cultures ritualize the transformation from regular citizen to warrior? Give three examples.

ANALYZING MEANING

1. Do you believe war can ever be emotionless and rational, like "a difficult trade negotiation" (paragraph 2)?
2. What do Clifton B. Kroeber and Bernard L. Fontana mean when they say "It is a large step from what may be biologically innate leanings toward individual aggression to ritualized, socially sanctioned, institutionalized group warfare" (paragraph 7)?
3. Why is "the hypothesis of a killer instinct" "not so much wrong as irrelevant" to the "anthropology of war" (paragraph 8)?
4. Are you convinced by this essay that "In war men enter an alternative realm of human experience, as far removed from daily life as those things which we call 'sacred'" (paragraph 15)?

DISCOVERING RHETORICAL STRATEGIES

1. Who do you think is Ehrenreich's main audience? How did you come to this conclusion?
2. The author begins her discussion of war with different "theories of why men fight them [wars]" (paragraph 2). Is this an effective beginning for what Ehrenreich is trying to accomplish? Explain your answer.
3. What information in this essay is most persuasive to you? What is the least persuasive?
4. What tone does the author establish by citing frequent statistics and referring to other sources in her essay?

MAKING CONNECTIONS

1. Compare and contrast Ehrenreich's insights on the psychology of war with Stephen King's theories on "Why We Crave Horror Movies." How do their ideas support one another? How do they contradict each other?

2. Compare Ehrenreich's use of examples with those of Rosenbaum and Chesney-Lind ("Appearance and Delinquency: A Research Note").
3. In a conversation between Ehrenreich and Steven Heighton ("Elegy in Stone") about the glorification of war in American society, on what points would they agree and disagree? Give examples.

IDEAS FOR DISCUSSION/WRITING

Preparing to Write

Write freely about aggression in general: Why do people fight? Why do countries go to war? What are some ways in which people take out their aggression? Have you ever noticed people fighting just for the sake of fighting? When is aggression acceptable? When is it unacceptable?

Choosing a Topic

1. Ehrenreich claims that "even when men have been assembled, willingly or unwillingly, for the purpose of war, fighting is not something that seems to come 'naturally' to them" (paragraph 10). Do you agree or disagree with this statement? Explain your reaction in a clearly reasoned argumentative essay. Cite Ehrenreich's selection whenever necessary.
2. In the last paragraph of her essay, Ehrenreich suggests that warriors often have to go through rituals to return to their civilizations. Use Ehrenreich's article as one of your sources; then read further on such transformations. Next, write a clear, well-documented argument expressing your opinion on a specific transformation. Organize your paper clearly, and present your suggestions logically, using proper documentation (citations and bibliography) to support your position.
3. Use additional sources to study the circumstances of a war you are familiar with. Then, referring to Ehrenreich's explanation of "the anthropology of war" (paragraph 8), write a well-documented argument explaining the causes and effects of the war by discussing or analyzing in depth the consequences you have discovered.

Before beginning your essay, you might want to consult the checklists on pages 501–502.

Jill Leslie Rosenbaum
1955–
and Meda Chesney-Lind
1947–

■ ■ ■

Appearance and Delinquency:
A Research Note

Jill Leslie Rosenbaum, a criminologist specializing in female crime, earned her B.A. in sociology at the University of Michigan, her M.S. in addiction studies at the University of Arizona, and her Ph.D. in criminal justice at SUNY Albany. She is currently a professor of criminal justice at California State University, Fullerton, where she has published recent articles in *Crime and Delinquency*, *Justice Quarterly*, and *Youth and Society*. In her spare time, she enjoys working out at a local gym, reading good novels, and participating in children's theatre. Her advice to students using *Reader's Choice* is to "spend lots of time writing. Write and rewrite your work until it is perfect!" Her co-author, Meda Chesney-Lind, earned her B.A. at Whitman College and her M.A. and Ph.D. at the University of Hawaii. She is currently a professor of women's studies at the University of Hawaii at Manoa, where she has published two books on women and crime—*Girls, Delinquency, and Juvenile Justice* (1992, with Randall Shelden) and *The Female Offender* (1997)—plus over 50 articles on related topics. Her recreational activities include walking and haunting thrift shops. She advises student writers "to practise, practise, practise," explaining that "you have to trust your instincts in order to become a better writer, which also requires patience, discipline, and a healthy sense of humour."

Preparing to Read

Taken from a journal entitled *Crime and Delinquency* (April 1994), the following essay explains that perceived attractiveness of female offenders plays an important part in the criminal justice system. Its citations and bibliography illustrate proper APA (American Psychological Association) documentation form. As you prepare to read this article, take a few minutes to think about the influence appearance has on your view of the world: Do you consciously think about appearance? Do someone's looks influence your professional judgment of that person? Would a defendant's appearance affect your view of his or her guilt? Does appearance play any part in how well you listen to someone or whether or not you agree with a person? How does appearance affect your opinion of a stranger?

Women are judged by culturally derived standards of attrac-   1
tiveness. These culturally created standards affect women in
all walks of life, including, it appears, the way they are treated by
the criminal justice system. Research has shown that perception of
physical appearance can have a significant impact on an individual's success in a variety of endeavors. These endeavors include
dating opportunities (Crause and Mehrabian, 1977; Stretch and
Figley, 1980; Walster, Aronson, Abrahams, and Rottman, 1966),
the initiation of relationships (Murstein and Christy, 1976; Price
and Vandenberg, 1979; White, 1980), teachers' evaluations of students (Clifford and Walster, 1973; Dion, 1973), and corporate success (Heilman and Stopeck, 1985; Heilman and Sarawatari, 1979).

The role of appearance in judgments of criminal responsibility   2
and the punishment of such behavior have also been the focus of
a variety of psychological studies (Efran, 1974; Sigall and Ostrove,
1975; Stewart, 1980). These studies consistently indicate that
physical attractiveness influences judgments of wrongdoing.
Dion (1973) found that adult judgments of children's
transgressions were affected by the attractiveness of the child.
Transgressions, both mild and severe, were perceived to be less
undesirable when committed by an attractive child than an
unattractive child. Furthermore, subjects were less likely to
attribute chronic antisocial behavior to attractive than to
unattractive children.

The work of Sigall and Ostrove (1975) suggests that the   3
sentences given to offenders are often conditioned by the
appearance of the offender. Attractive female offenders, whose
offense was not appearance-related (burglary), received greater
leniency than unattractive offenders. However, when the offense
was attractiveness-related (swindle), attractive offenders received
harsher sentences than their unattractive counterparts. These
findings are consistent with those of Efran (1974), whose work has
shown that attractive defendants are much less likely to be found
guilty than unattractive defendants. This becomes especially
pronounced when males are judging the culpability of females.
Sigall and Ostrove (1975) and Efran (1974) also indicate that when
a female offender is seen as using her attractiveness to assist in the
commission of a crime, attractive defendants were more likely
to be found guilty.

Studies of appearance also demonstrate that society has higher   4
expectations for attractive individuals; some of these expectations
pertain exclusively to women. For instance, attractive women are

assumed to be more feminine and have a more socially desirable personality, and as a result, they are assumed to have greater overall happiness in their personal, social, and professional lives (Dion, Berscheid, and Walster, 1973). It is also assumed that they are less likely to remain single, more likely to marry earlier, be better spouses, and be better sexual partners as well.

Although the lives of attractive women are assumed to be 5 far superior to those of less attractive women, some believe that attractive women have less integrity, and thus managerial opportunities for them may be hindered. In fact, Heilman and Sarawatari (1979) concluded that women with more masculine characteristics are believed to have greater ability than women with feminine characteristics. Thus, although attractive women are thought to be more feminine, they are also thought to be less well-suited for nontraditional female roles.

Finally, Emerson (1969) noted that judges and other juvenile 6 court personnel often expressed considerable interest in the appearance of girls appearing before the court he observed. He noted a judge's interest in whether runaway girls were "clean" after having been away from home for more than a day or two; the assumption was that if they were clean and/or heavily made up, they might be engaging in prostitution (1969, p. 112).

Since the establishment of the first juvenile court, there has 7 been ongoing interest by judges and other court workers in the sexual activity of girls. In the early days of the court (1899–1920), there was a clear bias against girls deemed sexually active and a harsh official response to their misbehavior. Virtually all of the girls who appeared before the first juvenile courts were charged with immorality or waywardness (Chesney-Lind, 1971; Schlossman and Wallach, 1978; Shelden, 1981; Rafter, 1990), and the response of the courts to this noncriminal behavior frequently was incarceration.

In Honolulu during 1929–1930, over half of the girls referred 8 to court were charged with immorality, which meant evidence (or inferences drawn) of sexual intercourse. In addition, another 30% were charged with waywardness. Evidence of immorality was vigorously pursued both by arresting officers and social workers through lengthy questioning of the girl and, if possible, males with whom she was suspected of having sex. Other evidence of exposure was provided by gynecological examinations, which were routinely ordered. Doctors, who understood the purpose of such examinations, would routinely note the condition of the hymen: "admits intercourse-hymen ruptured," "no laceration," and "hymen ruptured" were typical of their notations. Girls during this period were also twice as likely as boys to be detained, and they remained in detention five times as long on the average as their male counterparts. They were also nearly three times more likely to be sentenced to training schools (Chesney-Lind, 1971) where well into the 1950s they continued to be half of those committed in Honolulu (Chesney-Lind, 1973).

National statistics reflect the official enthusiasm for the 9 incarceration of girls during the early part of this century; their share of the population of juvenile correctional facilities increased from 1880 (when girls were 19% of the population) to 1923 (when girls were 28%). By 1950, girls had climbed to 34% of the total, and in 1960 they were still 27% of those in correctional facilities. By 1980, this pattern appeared to be reversed, and girls were again 19% of those in correctional facilities (Calahan, 186, p. 130), and in 1989, girls accounted for 11.9% of those held in public detention centers and training schools (Allen-Hagen, 1991, p. 4).

The decline in incarceration of juvenile females in public 10 facilities run by the juvenile justice system is directly linked to an intense debate on the issue of the institutionalization of young people, especially youth charged with noncriminal status offenses (e.g., running away from home, being incorrigible, truant, or in danger of leading a lewd and lascivious lifestyle). In particular, the Juvenile Justice and Delinquency Prevention Act (JJDPA) of 1974 stressed the need to divert and deinstitutionalize youth charged with status offenses and provided states with a number of incentives to achieve this goal.

Critical to any understanding of the dynamics of gender bias 11 in the juvenile justice system, then, is an appreciation of the gendered nature of delinquency, and particularly status offenses. It should be understood that status offenses have also served as "buffer charges" for the once historic, but now implicit, interest in monitoring girls' sexual activities and their obedience to parental authority (Gold, 1971, p. 571). In essence, modern status offense charges mask the court's historic interest in girls' propriety and obedience to parental authority (Chesney-Lind and Shelden, 1992).

Because of the recent but eroding success of the JJDPA of 12 1974, it is perhaps essential to review the dynamics of sexism within the juvenile justice system immediately prior to the passage of this act. The study reported here, although relatively modest, documents one aspect of the sexism that girls encountered as they entered institutions in the 1960s: the interest of criminal justice professionals in the physical appearance of girls.

Data and Methods

This analysis is based on the records of 159 women who, as   13
juveniles, were committed to the California Youth Authority (CYA) during the 1960s. Records were requested on all 240 of the girls who were sentenced to the CYA between 1961 and 1965 from San Francisco and the Sacramento Valley. There were 59 cases unavailable because the juvenile records had been purged and another 22 cases could not be located. For the 159 cases where data was available, the records included the complete CYA files containing all comments / reports regarding the ward and the case by CYA intake workers, counselors, teachers, living unit personnel, chaplains, social workers, and psychologists (for more information regarding data collection, see Warren and Rosenbaum, 1986).

The racial composition of these 159 cases was 51% Caucasian,   14
30% African-American, 9% Latino, and the remaining 10% were Asian or Native American. Two-thirds of the girls had been committed to the CYA for status offenses, and, more specifically, 49% were charged with running away from home, 28% for being "beyond control," 12% for "being in danger of a lewd and lascivious lifestyle," 7% for truancy, and 4% for curfew. To say that these girls were committed for status offenses actually understates the role of status offenses in their delinquency records; this group of girls committed 698 offenses prior to their commitment to the CYA. The average number of arrests was six, and over 90% of these were status offenses. There were no racial differences observed in the distribution of these offenses.

Each file was examined by two independent coders who   15
coded data on the type of offenses committed prior to CYA commitment, the gender of the social worker who did the evaluation of the ward, whether mention was made of the ward's appearance, and if so, the description given of the girl's appearance.[1] Reliability among the coders was over 96%. Because all of the girls in the sample were part of an experimental program and were randomly assigned to treatment programs, the length of their incarceration was not coded.

Findings

Female case workers did intake evaluations on 29% (46) of the 159   16
cases, whereas males were responsible for 71% (113) of them.
When female CYA personnel conducted the intake evaluation,
there was no mention of physical appearance in any of the 46
cases for which they were responsible. This was not the case
when males performed the evaluation; appearance was
mentioned in 63% (75) of the cases.

A variety of physical descriptions was recorded for the 75   17
wards whose appearance was mentioned in the files. These show
male staff concern with the physical maturity of the girls, as well
as some evidence of racial stereotyping; indeed, of those where
evaluative judgments about appearance were made, 60% were
made about minority group females. Moreover, those viewing
these young women of color adhered to "representations of race"
(hooks, 1992) that negate any beauty that does not conform to
White standards of appearance, while celebrating those images
that mimic White appearance.

From the description of the girls' appearance, four general   18
categories emerged: attractive, unattractive, plain/wholesome,
and "well-built."[2] Of the wards whose appearance was
mentioned, 26% (19) were described as attractive (e.g., "the ward
is an attractive, physically mature 13-year-old"), whereas 38%
(27) were described as unattractive (e.g., "Her appearance is
rather uninteresting and unattractive"); 19% as plain or
wholesome; and 17% (14) were described as well-built.

Differences emerged when the relationship between the type   19
of offense and the mention of appearance in the intake
evaluations was examined. About 50% (56) of the girls who had
been evaluated by a male had at least one immorality charge
against them. When females who had been charged with
immorality offenses (being in danger of leading a lewd and
lascivious life and prostitution) were compared with those who
had no such charge, differences in the mention of appearance
became especially pronounced. For instance, for those charged
with one or more counts of immorality, a physical description
was present in 93% (55) of the cases. However, when no
immorality charges were present, a physical description was
included in only 37% (20) of the cases (see Table 1). Looking at the
data from another perspective, in cases where no description of
the girl's appearance was present, 89% (34) had no charges of

immorality. As indicated in Table 1, a significant relationship ($X^2 = 37.4$) was found between having at least one immorality charge and having mention made of the girl's appearance in her file.

Table 1: Appearance by Presence of Immorality Charges

	Appearance Described	No Description Included	
Immorality charges	93 (55)	7 (4)	100 (59)
No Immorality charges	37 (20)	63 (34)	100 (54)

$X^2 = 37.4$, 1 df, significance = .000.

Differences also existed with respect to the type of offenses   20
present and the description given. All of the girls who were described as attractive and all of the girls who were described as well-built had been charged with at least one immorality offense. However, only 26% of the girls described as plain/wholesome and 34% of those described as unattractive had similar charges against them. Although these numbers are small, the magnitude of the difference is clearly significant.

More Recent Data

To assess whether or not appearance remains an issue today,   21
more recent data from the CYA was examined. In the process of collecting data from the CYA files of all girls who were wards of the CYA in 1990, close attention was paid to any mention of the girl's appearance. Similar attention was paid in a separate examination of the case files of all boys and girls who were confined in the Hawaii Youth Correctional Facility in 1989.

Although there were 214 girls who were wards of the CYA in   22
1990, comments regarding appearance were found in only eight files. All, except one who was described as slovenly and unattractive, were simply described as attractive. Five of the eight had arrests for violent crime; the other three had long records for property and drug offenses. Although the vast majority of the girls' arrests during the 1960s were for status offenses, only 4% of their 1990 counterparts' arrests were for status offenses.

Comments found in girls' files in Hawaii concerned when   23
and where they had been arrested for curfew violations. This same research effort noted that no such comments appeared in

boys' files and that a third of the girls held in training schools were being held solely for "probation violation," which is a mechanism for continuing to incarcerate status offenders (Saiki, 1990, p. 23). The Hawaii study found that roughly half of the girls incarcerated during spring 1990 were "bootstrapped" status offenders (Costello and Worthington, 1991) and even for those girls who had committed criminal offenses, their offenses were far less serious than the boys and "the bulk of their juvenile offenses consisted of status offenses" (Saiki, 1990, p. 48).

Discussion

The emphasis on physical appearance found in this small study 24 and the link between this interest in girls' appearance and their noncriminal delinquent behavior is more important than it might first seem. In essence, these observations provide a window into the worldview of the keepers of young women during the years prior to the passage of the JJDPA of 1974; sadly, they may also reflect a bias that remains in the states that have been resistant to the deinstitutionalization efforts signaled by the passage of that act. Like earlier studies, which found a large number of girls in institutions subjected to physical examinations to determine if they were virgins (see Chesney-Lind and Shelden, 1992), interest in the physical appearance of girls, and particularly their physical maturity, indicates substantial interest in the sexual behavior of girls and illuminates another important dimension of the sexual policing of girls (Cain, 1989).

Particularly troubling are the comments which indicate a 25 presumed association between "beauty," specifically male Caucasian standards of beauty, and sexual behavior. Certainly the fact that these girls were incarcerated for noncriminal offenses indicates the seriousness with which the criminal justice system viewed their transgressions. In short, these data provide some support for the notion, suggested by Sigall and Ostrove (1975), as well as that by Efran (1974), that judges, social workers, and other criminal justice professionals (particularly if they are male) may look upon attractive girls who engage in sexual "immorality" more harshly. They may also overlook some of the same behaviors in less attractive girls.

Such a fascination with appearance is also at odds with the 26 literature on street prostitutes. These studies indicate that the pace and pressure of this life does not produce "attractive" young women, but instead tends to take a physical toll on the girls engaged in the behavior (Weisberg, 1985, p. 116). Indeed, some descriptions of prostitutes describe them as unattractive, overweight, with poor complexions and bad teeth (Winick and Kinsie, 1972, p. 35).

The remarks found in the files which were made by male   27 intake workers suggest a fascination with the appearance of the girls who were charged with immorality. Clearly there was considerable concern with their physical maturity and physical attraction. The comments regarding the girls' appearance suggest that status offenses may have functioned as buffer charges for suspected sexual behavior. Although it appears that at least in California, where girls are no longer incarcerated for noncriminal offenses, this no longer seems to be a problem, national data suggest that in some states, like Hawaii, the detention and incarceration of girls for noncriminal status offenses persists; thus the concerns raised by this article may, sadly, not be of simply historic interest.

References

Allen-Hagen, B. (1991). *Children in Custody 1989*. Washington, DC: Bureau of Justice Statistics.

Cain, M. (1989). *Growing Up Good: Policing the Behavior of Girls in Europe*. London: Sage.

Calahan, M. W. (1986). *Historical Corrections Statistics in the United States 1950–1984*. Washington, DC: U.S. Department of Justice.

Chesney-Lind, M. (1971). *Female Juvenile Delinquency in Hawaii*. Master's thesis, University of Hawaii at Manoa.

—. (1973). Judicial enforcement of the female sex role. *Issues in Criminology 8*, 51–70.

Chesney-Lind, M., & Shelden, R. (1992). *Girls, Delinquency, and the Juvenile Justice System*. Pacific Grove, CA: Brooks/Cole.

Clifford, M., & Walster, E. (1973). The effect of physical attractiveness on teacher expectations. *Sociology of Education 46*, 248–258.

Costello, J. C., & Worthington, N. L. (1991). Incarcerating status offenders: Attempts to circumvent the Juvenile Justice and Delinquency Prevention Act. *Harvard Civil Rights-Civil Liberties Law Review 16*, 41–81.

Crause, B. B., & Mehrabian, A. (1977). Affiliation of opposite-sexed strangers. *Journal of Research in Personality 11*, 38–47.

Dion, K. (1973). Physical attractiveness and evaluation of children's transgressions. *Journal of Personality and Social Psychology 24*, 207–218.

Dion, K., Berscheid, E., & Walster, E. (1973). What is beautiful is good. *Journal of Personality and Social Psychology 24*, 285–290.

Efran, M. (1974). The effect of physical appearance on the judgment of guilt, interpersonal attraction, and severity of recommended punishment. *Journal of Experimental Research in Personality 8*, 45–54.

Emerson, R. (1969). *Judging Delinquents*. Chicago: Aldine.

Flanagan, T. J., & McGarrell, E. F., eds. (1986). *Sourcebook of Criminal Justice Statistics — 1985*. Washington, DC: U.S. Department of Justice.

Gold, S. (1971). Equal protection for girls in need of supervision in New York State. *New York Law Forum 17*, 570–591.

Heilman, M., & Sarawatari, L. (1979). When beauty is beastly: The effects of appearance and sex on evaluations of job applicants for managerial and nonmanagerial jobs. *Organizational Behavior and Human Performance 23*, 360–372.

Heilman, M., & Stopeck, M. (1985). Attractiveness and corporate success: Different casual attributions for males and females. *Journal of Applied Psychology 70*, 379–388.

hooks, b. (1992). *Black Looks*. Boston: South End Press.

Jamieson, K. M., & Flanagan, T., eds. (1987). *Sourcebook of Criminal Justice Statistics — 1986*. Washington, DC: U.S. Department of Justice, Bureau of Justice Statistics.

Murstein, B., & Christy, P. (1976). Physical attractiveness and marriage adjustment in middle aged couples. *Journal of Personality and Social Psychology 34*, 537–542.

Price, R., & Vandenberg, S. (1979). Matching for physical attractiveness in married couples. *Personality and Social Psychology Bulletin 5*, 398–399.

Rafter, N. (1990). *Partial Justice: Women, Prisons and Social Control*. New Brunswick, NJ: Transaction Books.

Saiki, S. (1990). Girls, double standards and status offenses in Hawaii's juvenile court. Unpublished paper. William Richardson School of Law, University of Hawaii.

Schlossman, S., & Wallach, S. (1978). The crime of precocious sexuality: Female delinquency in the progressive era. *Harvard Educational Review 48*, 65–94.

Shelden, R. (1981). Sex Discrimination in the juvenile justice system: Memphis, Tennessee, 1900–1971. In *Comparing Male and Female Offenders*, edited by M. Q. Warren. Beverly Hills, CA: Sage.

Sigall, H., & Ostrove, N. (1975). Beautiful but dangerous: Effects of offender attractiveness and nature of crime on juridic judgment. *Journal of Personality and Social Psychology 31*, 410–414.

Stewart, J. (1980). Defendant's attraction as a factor in the outcome of criminal trials: An observational study. *Journal of Applied Social Psychology 10*, 348–361.

Stretch, R., & Figley, C. (1980). Beauty and the beast: Predictions of interpersonal attraction in a dating experiment. *Psychology, a Quarterly Journal of Human Behavior 17*, 34–43.

Walster, E., Aronson, E., Abrahams, D., & Rottman, L. (1966). Importance of physical attractiveness in dating behavior. *Journal of Personality and Social Psychology 4*, 508–516.

Warren, M. Q., & Rosenbaum, J. (1986). Criminal careers of female offenders. *Criminal Justice and Behavior 13*, 393–418.

Weisberg, D. K. (1985). *Children of the Night: A Study of Adolescent Prostitution.* Lexington, MA: Lexington Books.

White, G. (1980). Physical attractiveness and courtship progress. *Journal of Personality and Social Psychology 39*, 660–668.

Winick, C., & Kinsie, P. M. (1972). *The Lively Commerce.* New York: Signet.

Notes

1. Nowhere on any of the CYA forms was there any particular place for a physical description of the ward. Comments were found throughout the narratives by the CYA personnel who became involved with the case. As far as we can tell, the issue of appearance was never discussed with regard to policy. It seemed to be merely an issue for the intake personnel.

2. These categories are broad and somewhat evasive; however, they were the factors that emerged during this analysis. It is important to remember that attractiveness is in the eye of the beholder and we, as researchers, are merely reporting the subjective assessments that we found.

UNDERSTANDING DETAILS

1. What do Rosenbaum and Chesney-Lind mean when they argue that "Women are judged by culturally derived standards of attractiveness" (paragraph 1)?
2. How does being attractive usually affect judgments in the criminal justice system?
3. What expectation does society have of attractive people? What sources do Rosenbaum and Chesney-Lind cite to verify these expectations?
4. What are "status acts"? In what ways did the Juvenile Justice and Delinquency Prevention Act (JJDPA) of 1974 affect the court's reaction to status acts?

ANALYZING MEANING

1. Can you explain the relationship the researchers found between appearance and immorality charges in California Youth Authority (CYA) females? Why do you think this relationship existed?
2. What effect do the recent data show the Juvenile Justice and Delinquency Protection Act had on immorality charges since 1990? Can you explain this change?
3. Are males ever unfairly treated because of their appearance? If so, in what situations? Explain your answer in detail.
4. Can you speculate about the future of status and immorality offences? Do you think they will continue to be connected to descriptions of appearance in female criminal records?

DISCOVERING RHETORICAL STRATEGIES

1. Who do you think is Rosenbaum and Chesney-Lind's main audience? How did you come to this conclusion?
2. The authors begin their essay by citing various professional sources that verify the connections in American society between appearance and success in various aspects of life. Is this an effective beginning for what Rosenbaum and Chesney-Lind are trying to accomplish? Explain your answer.
3. What information in this essay is most persuasive to you? Least persuasive?
4. What tone do the authors establish by citing statistics and referring to other sources in their essay?

MAKING CONNECTIONS

1. If Rosenbaum and Chesney-Lind were having a conversation about the importance of appearance with Drew Hayden Taylor ("Pretty Like a White Boy") and Gloria Steinem ("The Politics of Muscle"), what issues would the four writers agree on? What would they disagree on?

2. Compare and contrast the way Rosenbaum and Chesney-Lind use statistics and documentation in their argument with the use of this technique by Barbara Ehrenreich ("The Ecstasy of War") or Marilyn Dahl ("The Role of the Media in Promoting Images of Disability"). Which author provides such information most skillfully? Explain your answer.

3. Examine the balance in Rosenbaum and Chesney-Lind's essay among logical, emotional, and ethical appeals. Then compare and contrast it with the balance in essays by Lawrence Solomon ("Too Much Privacy Can Be Hazardous to the Person") and Judy Rebick ("Kick 'Em Again"). Which author uses the most logic? Who uses emotion the most? And whose ethical appeal is strongest? Which author do you find most convincing? Explain your answer.

IDEAS FOR DISCUSSION/WRITING

Preparing to Write

Write freely about your views on the relationship between appearance and delinquency: What role does the notion of appearance play in the justice system? Should it be a part of the system? When would it be appropriate? When would it be inappropriate? Do you find that you have certain biases regarding people's appearances? What are they? Do you know others who hold biases about attractiveness? Do the biases verge on sexism? Do they involve both males and females? What do these biases say about our society in general?

Choosing a Topic

1. Design a constructive solution to the problem of sexist criminal reports. Then, using Rosenbaum and Chesney-Lind's essay as your main source, write an argumentative essay presenting the problem as you understand it and offering a detailed solution to it. Cite Rosenbaum and Chesney-Lind's essay whenever necessary.

2. What do you think the role of appearance and behaviour should be in our judicial system? Use Rosenbaum and Chesney-Lind's article as one of your sources; then read further on the subject. Finally, write a clear, well-documented argument on what part appearance and behaviour should play in the court's judgment of criminals. Organize your paper carefully, and present your suggestions logically, using proper documentation (citations and bibliography) to support your position.
3. Choose another problem related to the justice system, and research it further. Then write a well-documented argument explaining the problem and offering a solution based on the information you have discovered.

Before beginning your essay, you might want to consult the checklists on pages 501–502.

Marilyn Dahl
1931–

■ ■ ■

The Role of the Media in Promoting Images of Disability—Disability as Metaphor: The Evil Crip

Marilyn Dahl is a western Canadian nurse educator originally from Broderick, Saskatchewan, and now living in Port Coquitlam, B.C. After graduating as an R.N. in 1953 from the Victoria Hospital School of Nursing in Prince Albert, Dahl practised nursing in a variety of settings until 1977. During this time she was married, had three children, wrote a hospital teaching video, and also wrote and produced a weekly children's television program in Medicine Hat from 1967–69. Dahl then returned to school at the University of British Columbia to get her B.Sc.N. in 1979. In the 1980s Dahl worked as an instructor at the Douglas College Faculty of Nursing and became a disabled consumer advocate in 1980. In 1985 she assumed the position of president of the Canadian Hard of Hearing Association and three years later became the vice-president of the International Hard of Hearing Federation. Dahl completed her M.A. at Simon Fraser University in 1988 with a thesis looking at how disabled role identity is culturally produced in Canadian society. Her many publications include *Caring for the Patient Who is Hard of Hearing* (1979). This article appeared in the *Canadian Journal of Communication* in 1993.

Preparing to Read

Before reading this article think about how disabilities are portrayed by the media. Brainstorm a list of movies, television shows, and books that include characters with disabilities. What disabilities do these characters have? Is the disability the focus of the story or is it an incidental characteristic? How are these people with disabilities portrayed? What do you know about the characters apart from their disabilities?

It is a commonly held theory that one cannot legislate attitude change. One can legislate behavioural change and hopefully changes in attitude will follow. Attitudes, beliefs, and misconceptions of society constitute a major barrier for people with disabilities. Attitude change can follow on heightened awareness, increased contact, and increased meaningful communication

1

between disabled and non-disabled people. Although personal interaction is the most effective medium for conveying the personal experience of disability, the mass media can be an effective vehicle for bringing about greater understanding, and a consequent gradual change in public perceptions, of people with disabilities.

Disability as a Metaphor

A review of our cultural forms of expression provides evidence 2 of the metaphoric role of disability which is deeply ingrained in our social values. It has been a convention of all literature and art that physical deformity, chronic illness, or any visible defect symbolizes an evil and malevolent nature and monstrous behaviour (Sontag, 1978). A summary look at literary distortions of handicapping conditions illustrates this point: Captain Hook (in *Peter Pan*) is intentionally an amputee with a prosthesis; Shakespeare links Richard III's hunchback to his evil lust. Somerset Maugham uses Philip's clubfoot (in *Of Human Bondage*) to symbolize his bitter and warped nature.

Occasionally a type of reaction formation is invoked and the 3 literary association to disability is instead quite sentimental. Hans Christian Andersen depicts The Little Lame Prince in maudlin tones, and some other childhood tales use the stereotype of the selfless dwarf, or the blind seer. Occasionally the protagonist copes nobly with a disability but even then it is depicted as a "curse" to bear. Cyrano de Bergerac with his grotesque nose and Quasimodo with his hunchback are remarked not for their deformity but because they are both deformed and good (as though one precludes the other). Rarely does there appear an average or ordinary person whose disability is incidental.

We are both repelled and intrigued by the cripple as 4 metaphor. Children's classics are particularly graphic and concrete in this regard. Villains are always ugly and deformed in some manner, heroes and heroines are possessed of beauty and grace. Fellini used freaks and disabilities to cue people to respond with revulsion and disgust to his film characters. Disney frequently promoted disability as metaphor. More recently, Hollywood has tended to sentimentalize the disabled with stock movies of two-dimensional characters who "learn to cope" and "live happily ever after." The deaf (*Voices*), the blind (*Ice Castles*), and quadriplegics (*The Other Side of the Mountain*) have all been treated within this formula. Film and television have also employed the metaphor of the disabled as helpless victim. Roughing up a cripple or a blind man is a device used to show a villain as a particularly evil person. At times television has tended to transform the metaphor by endowing the disabled person with superhuman characteristics, such as the Bionic Man; while in *Ironside*, the paraplegic was given a brilliant mind (Bird, Byrd, & Allen, 1977).

Research into the relationship between physical attractiveness 5 and crime in the various media found that physical ugliness and physical differences are often associated with media depictions of violence and crime. (Needham & Weiner, 1974). Horror movies make free use of this strategy. Gardner & Radel (1978), who analyzed American newspapers and television for references to disabled people, found that about one half of the items portrayed the disabled as dependent persons. A tenth of the items portrayed the disabled as being in some way deviant: "strange, antisocial or bizarre." Only about one quarter of the items portrayed the disabled as persons capable of independent living and of contributing to society. Cartoons and comic strip captions are also important carriers of prejudicial and discriminatory language and images of evil cripples. Words such as "stupid moron," "idiot," "crazy," are common jargon in strips such as *Beetle Bailey*, and the various "animal" comic strips. Everyday words which refer to specific conditions have become standardized as curse words, and stereotypes of conditions are reinforced (Weinberg & Santana, 1978).

In spite of these trends, there have been some changes in 6 American plays and films, which today present more sympathetic and romanticized views of the disabled. Gussow (1979) labelled the phenomenon "the time of the wounded hero." Some of the examples are *The Elephant Man* (congenital deformity), *Wings* (stroke), *Whose Life Is it Anyway?* (paralysis), and *Children of a Lesser God*. There have been more recent attempts to portray the disabled as "incidental" characters, neither hero nor victim. A policeman in a wheelchair on *Cagney and Lacey* portrayed an average role. The elderly, the ugly, the obese are seen more often as "normal." Marlee Matlin, as assistant district attorney in *Reasonable Doubts*, attempts to show a deaf person filling a professional role in much the same way as a hearing person. Made for television films in the 1980s have portrayed sensitive and realistic stories of schizophrenia and Alzheimer's victims. *L.A. Law* portrays a mentally handicapped man in a sensitive way, and has a lawyer who wears a hearing aid.

Effects of Media Selectivity in Describing Disability

The media promote certain images of the disabled by selectively 7
covering certain events and ignoring others. Jernigan, president
of the National American Federation of the Blind, reported that
reporters invited to a press conference on a highly political topic,
ignored the political topic and wanted instead to photograph
and report on the various walking aids, lead dogs, and other
stereotypical symbols of blindness (Bogden & Biklen, 1977). In
covering the Terry Fox story, the media focused on the "dying
hero" and the medical model of illness, ignoring the counter-
ideology issue of environmental pollution from nuclear fallout
over the area where Fox was born in the 1950s, and its
relationship to causes of cancer (Harrison, 1985).

The selective coverage of disability has led to the creation 8
of "heroes by hype." The power of the media in manipulating
public response is seen in the media coverage of the disabled
marathoners who in the 1980s were a uniquely Canadian
phenomenon (Graham, 1987). While many marathoners crossed
Canada for causes, it was only the young, attractive men with
dramatic visual disabilities (Fox, Fonyo, and Hansen) who
received orchestrated backing and media coverage. Promoters
and handlers "packaged" the young man and directed the
programs and publicity en route. A star was created. Increased
coverage pressured corporations and politicians to be seen giving
generously to the hero's cause. An exception was the "W5"
program (CTV, 1987), which presented the misgivings held by
disabled people themselves about what "disabled as superstar"
portrays to the public.

The *Disability Network* (TV Ontario) presents lifestyles of 9
people with disabilities, but most disabled people would prefer
to be shown as part of the average population. The Bay's
advertising flyer recently featured a model in a wheelchair,
McDonald's ads have included people with different types of
disabilities (King, 1992). These ads are the exception rather than
the rule. Advertisers do not seem to think in terms of disabled
people as customers—drinking beer, brushing their teeth, or
buying a car. One particularly onerous depiction of disability
remains a television regular: fund-raising telethons. The model
for this is the Jerry Lewis Telethon which presents an alliance of
business, high status public persons and service providers, plus
a disabled child who is helpless and appealing. The images equate
disability with childlike behaviour and an infantile condition, a

minor role, while the healthy normal star has the spotlight, status, and prestige. Helping the disabled becomes entertainment (Dahl, 1987).

The mass media perpetuate stereotypes of disability through   10 their portrayals of characters. But there is no evidence that the mass media have any major effect on manipulating the attitudes and opinions of its audience. Researchers state that it is difficult to discover what are the precise effects of the media on public opinion. It is possible that attitudes and opinions change dramatically as a result of what is seen or heard. There are indications of selective perception of what is viewed, namely that audiences tend to identify with that which reinforces their existing beliefs. On the whole it appears that "the potential of the mass media to create false impressions ... is tempered by the tendency of the public to neglect the mass media in favour of other sources of understanding social reality" (Howitt, 1989, p. 179). Some speculation is in order, however, on the effect of negative stereotyping on the disabled themselves, especially children with disabilities. "Self-identity is formed by what is communicated through the media as well as by interpersonal acts" (Gumpert & Cathcart, 1982, p. 13). To see oneself labelled and cast always in the role of the villain, helpless dependent, or victim is not an enviable fate.

Creating an "Average" Typification of the Disabled

Although there are no specific data showing attitude change in   11 response to media communication, people tend to believe that the manner in which characters are portrayed is important. Characters presented on screen are sociocultural stereotypes designed to appeal to the majority of viewers, and reflect widely held values (albeit mostly American). It seems apparent that the repeated presentation of images in an acceptable and palatable manner will result in those images becoming a typification of everyday existence. The media are efficient in implanting new information and contributing new ideas and values, where they are not in conflict with strongly held views. The effect of mass communication on society is often more a contributory than a sole effect (Schramm, 1973). "Media images, however, can help to shape the meanings we find directly in the situation and what we discover in the actual situation can influence the way we look at the media" (Kelly, 1981, p. 167).

The CRTC recognized the influence of broadcasting on 12
viewers in its 1986 policy statement: "Broadcasting is ... a
powerful medium to reinforce [sex-role] stereotyping and can
be equally powerful to correct it." Since 1979, the Treasury Board,
the Advertising Management Group, the CRTC, and CBC have
developed policies on the elimination of sexual stereotyping and
cultural stereotyping. The CRTC called for self-regulation by the
industry in regard to policy implementation. Guidelines are
monitored by the CRTC, the industry, and consumer groups
such as Mediawatch and Evaluation/Medias (in Quebec). The
CRTC report (December, 1986) indicated that some sensitization
to the issue of sex-role stereotyping had occurred, but significant
reductions in such stereotyping had not been achieved. No
separate set of guidelines exists with respect to persons with
disabilities; such guidelines are included under regulations
prohibiting discrimination. In 1990 the Department of Secretary
of State, Canada, published two reports: *Worthless or Wonderful*
includes recommendations on elimination of social stereotyping
of disabled persons, modelled on the guidelines for sex-role and
cultural stereotype elimination; *A Way With Words* (1990) provides
guidelines and appropriate terminology for the portrayal of
persons with disabilities.

We have moved somewhat away from the disabled as hero 13
or victim but we are still a long way from a normal depiction of
disability. Disabled people could be depicted as living and
working in a variety of situations, with a diverse range of
responsibilities, and not necessarily overcoming great odds to
achieve their status. The mass media affect public opinion and
public perception of social reality by their ability to create
typifications. Careful use of terminology and visual images of
the disabled can gradually create a more acceptable and realistic
typification of people with disabilities as "average" people.

References

Bird, E.K., Byrd, P.D., & Allen, C.M. (1977). Television
programming and disability. *Applied Rehabilitation Counselling*,
8(1), 28–32.

Bogden, Robert, & Biklen, Douglas. (1977). *Handicapism*.
Mimeographed paper, Social Policy Corporation, New York.

CRTC. (1986). *Sex role stereotyping in the broadcast media* (Report on
Industry Self-Regulation). Ottawa: Supply and Services
Canada.

CRTC. (1986). *Sex role stereotyping in the broadcast media* (Policy Statement). Ottawa: Supply and Services Canada.

Dahl, Marilyn. (1987). *The cultural production of the disabled role identity in contemporary Canadian society.* MA thesis, Simon Fraser University, Burnaby, BC.

Fiedler, Leslie. (1978). *Freaks, myths and images of the secret self.* New York: Simon & Shuster.

Gardner, J.M., & Radel, M. (1978). Portrait of the disabled in the media. *Journal of Community Psychology, 6,* 269–274.

Graham, R. (1987, January). On the road. *Saturday Night,* 102(1) 16ff.

Gumpert, Gary, & Cathcart, Robert. (1982). *Inter/media: Interpersonal communication in a media world.* New York: Oxford University Press.

Gussow, Mel. (1979, April 15). The time of the wounded hero. *The New York Times,* 11, 1–2.

Harrison, Deborah. (1985). The Terry Fox story and the media: A case study in ideology and illness. *Canadian Review of Sociology and Anthropology,* 22(4), 496–514.

Howitt, Denis. (1982). *The mass media and social problems.* Oxford: Pergamon Press.

Kelly, John. (1981). *A philosophy of communication and culture.* London: Centre for Study of Communications and Culture.

King, Marsha. (1992, February 20). Companies doing the right thing. *The Province,* p. C9.

Needleman, B., & Weiner, N. (1974). *Faces of evil: The good, the bad and the ugly.* Mimeographed paper, Oswego State College Department of Sociology, New York.

Schramm, Wilbur. (1973). *Men, messages and media.* New York: Harper & Row.

Sontag, Susan. (1978). *Illness as metaphor.* New York: Farrar, Strauss and Giroux.

Secretary of State. (1988). *Worthless or wonderful: The social stereotyping of persons with disabilities.* Ottawa: Minister of Supply and Services.

—. (1988). *A way with words: Guidelines and appropriate terminology for the portrayal of persons with disabilities.* Ottawa: Minister of Supply and Services.

Weinberg, Nancy, & Santana, Rosina. (1978, November–December). Comic books: Champions of the disabled stereotype. *Rehabilitation Literature,* pp. 11–12.

UNDERSTANDING DETAILS

1. According to Dahl, in what way does the mass media make life difficult for people with disabilities?
2. What does Dahl see as likely to cause attitude change regarding people with disabilities?
3. Why does Dahl not support fund-raising telethons for disabilities?

ANALYZING MEANING

1. Is Dahl optimistic or pessimistic about the current portrayal of people with disabilities by the mass media? Explain.
2. What is Dahl's attitude toward disabled marathoners such as Terry Fox, Steve Fonyo, or Rick Hansen?
3. Summarize the categories that Dahl establishes to organize portrayals of people with disabilities. Add one original example to each category.

DISCOVERING RHETORICAL STRATEGIES

1. From what you know about the source of this essay and the writer, describe Dahl's audience. Is this the same group that she usually addresses? How do you know this?
2. In this article is Dahl reporting, interpreting, or analyzing? How do Dahl's sources and statistics help advance her argument? What main rhetorical modes does Dahl use to state her case? Give examples of each.

MAKING CONNECTIONS

1. Dahl contends that stereotyping can be diminished through changing the images that people see in the media and that legislation can promote the changes in these images. How would Cecil Foster ("Why Blacks Get Mad") react to Dahl's position on the importance of the images that people see in the media? What is your position on this issue?
2. How does Dahl's argument about media-fed perceptions of people with disabilities support the position that Rosenbaum and Chesney-Lind ("Appearance and Delinquency: A Research Note") advance about the role of appearance in the criminal justice system? Give specific examples.
3. Imagine that Dahl is having a conversation with Cecil Foster

("Why Blacks Get Mad") and Naheed Mustafa ("My Body is My Own Business") about the effect of appearance. On what points would the three writers agree? On which would they disagree?

IDEAS FOR DISCUSSION/WRITING

Preparing to Write

Write freely about language and disability. What connotations are there to words like "maimed," "crippled," "handicapped," "physically challenged," "differently-abled," "disfigured," or "disabled"? What words are acceptable? Which ones are not? What associations do you have with the terms "retarded," "feeble-minded," and "moron"?

Choosing a Topic

1. In a letter to the organizers of one of the fundraising telethons for disabilities, explain the negative effects of their well-intentioned actions and encourage them to stop holding their telethon.
2. Dahl refers to the depiction of disabilities in fairy tales. In a well-documented essay, explore the portrayal of evil or bad characters in fairy tales. To what extent are disabilities used to reflect negative roles?
3. Using both primary and secondary sources, research the effects of including people with disabilities in advertisements. Write a well-documented essay in which you examine both the direct and indirect outcomes of this approach to advertising.

WEB SITES

www1.us.nizkor.org/~kmcvay/obc-93-recipients.html#DAHL
Dahl was a 1993 recipient of the Order of British Columbia.

www.yahoo.com/Society_and_Culture/Disabilities/
Yahoo's list of disability-related sites.

CHAPTER 11

ESSAYS ON THINKING, READING, AND WRITING

In each of the preceding chapters, we have examined a single rhetorical mode in order to focus attention on how writers use that pattern to organize their thoughts. In this final chapter, six essays on the topics of thinking, reading, and writing demonstrate a combination of rhetorical modes at work in each selection.

Our primary purpose in this text has been to show how thinking, reading, and writing work together as fine machinery to help all of us function as intelligent and productive human beings. Our introduction discusses the relationship of thinking, reading, and writing; the text itself illustrates the crucial interdependence of these skills; and this last chapter concludes the book by presenting essays by some of North America's best writers on such related topics as listening, understanding the writing process, the power of the written word, metaphorical language, and the challenge to books by electronic media.

These essays are intended for you to read and enjoy. Let your mind run freely through the material as you recall in a leisurely way what you have learned in this text. The essays bring together the theoretical framework of this text as they illustrate how thinking, reading, and writing inform each other and work interdependently to make meaning. And they integrate the rhetorical patterns in such a way that each essay is a complex blend of the various rhetorical modes discussed in the preceding chapters—a perfect summary of the topics and strategies you have been working with throughout this text.

Eudora Welty
1909–

■■■

Listening

I learned from the age of two or three that any room in our house, at any time of day, was there to read in, or to be read to. My mother read to me. She'd read to me in the big bedroom in the mornings, when we were in her rocker together, which ticked in rhythm as we rocked, as though we had a cricket accompanying the story. She'd read to me in the diningroom on winter afternoons in front of the coal fire, with our cuckoo clock ending the story with "Cuckoo," and at night when I'd got in my own bed. I must have given her no peace. Sometimes she read to me in the kitchen while she sat churning, and the churning sobbed along with *any* story. It was my ambition to have her read to me while *I* churned; once she granted my wish, but she read off my story before I brought her butter. She was an expressive reader. When she was reading "Puss in Boots," for instance, it was impossible not to know that she distrusted *all* cats. 1

It had been startling and disappointing to me to find out that story books had been written by *people*, that books were not natural wonders, coming up of themselves like grass. Yet regardless of where they came from, I cannot remember a time when I was not in love with them—with the books themselves, cover and binding and the paper they were printed on, with their smell and their weight and with their possession in my arms, captured and carried off to myself. Still illiterate, I was ready for them, committed to all the reading I could give them. 2

Neither of my parents had come from homes that could afford to buy many books, but though it must have been something of a strain on his salary, as the youngest officer in a young insurance company, my father was all the while carefully selecting and ordering away for what he and Mother thought we children should grow up with. They bought first for the future. 3

Besides the bookcase in the livingroom, which was always 4
called "the library," there were the encyclopedia tables and
dictionary stand under windows in our diningroom. Here to
help us grow up arguing around the diningroom table were the
Unabridged Webster, the Columbia Encyclopedia, Compton's
Pictured Encyclopedia, the Lincoln Library of Information, and
later the Book of Knowledge. And the year we moved into our
new house, there was room to celebrate it with the new 1925
edition of the Britannica, which my father, his face always
deliberately turned toward the future, was of course disposed
to think better than any previous edition.

In "the library," inside the mission-style bookcase with its 5
three diamond-latticed glass doors, with my father's Morris chair
and the glass-shaded lamp on its table beside it, were books I
could soon begin on—and I did, reading them all alike and as
they came, straight down their rows, top shelf to bottom. There
was the set of Stoddard's Lectures, in all its late nineteenth-
century vocabulary and vignettes of peasant life and quaint
beliefs and customs, with matching halftone illustrations:
Vesuvius erupting, Venice by moonlight, gypsies glimpsed by
their campfires. I didn't know then the clue they were to my
father's longing to see the rest of the world. I read straight
through his other love-from-afar: the Victrola Book of the Opera,
with opera after opera in synopsis, with portraits in costume of
Melba, Caruso, Galli-Curci, and Geraldine Farrar, some of whose
voices we could listen to on our Red Seal records.

My mother read secondarily for information; she sank as a 6
hedonist into novels. She read Dickens in the spirit in which she
would have eloped with him. The novels of her girlhood that
had stayed on in her imagination, besides those of Dickens and
Scott and Robert Louis Stevenson, were *Jane Eyre, Trilby, The
Woman in White, Green Mansions, King Solomon's Mines*. Marie
Corelli's name would crop up but I understood she had gone
out of favor with my mother, who had only kept *Ardath* out of
loyalty. In time she absorbed herself in Galsworthy, Edith
Wharton, above all in Thomas Mann of the *Joseph* volumes.

St. Elmo was not in our house; I saw it often in other houses. 7
This wildly popular Southern novel is where all the Edna Earles
in our population started coming from. They're all named for
the heroine, who succeeded in bringing a dissolute, sinning roué
and atheist of a lover (St. Elmo) to his knees. My mother was
able to forgo it. But she remembered the classic advice given to

rose growers on how to water their bushes long enough: "Take a chair and *St. Elmo.*"

To both my parents I owe my early acquaintance with a 8 beloved Mark Twain. There was a full set of Mark Twain and a short set of Ring Lardner in our bookcase, and those were the volumes that in time united us all, parents and children.

Reading everything that stood before me was how I came 9 upon a worn old book without a back that had belonged to my father as a child. It was called *Sanford and Merton.* Is there anyone left who recognizes it, I wonder? It is the famous moral tale written by Thomas Day in the 1780s, but of him no mention is made on the title page of *this* book; here it is *Sanford and Merton in Words of One Syllable* by Mary Godolphin. Here are the rich boy and the poor boy and Mr. Barlow, their teacher and interlocutor, in long discourses alternating with dramatic scenes— danger and rescue allotted to the rich and the poor respectively. It may have only words of one syllable, but one of them is "quoth." It ends with not one but two morals, both engraved on rings: "Do what you ought, come what may," and "If we would be great, we must first learn to be good."

This book was lacking its front cover, the back held on by 10 strips of pasted paper, now turned golden, in several layers, and the pages stained, flecked, and tattered around the edges; its garish illustrations had come unattached but were preserved, laid in. I had the feeling even in my heedless childhood that this was the only book my father as a little boy had had of his own. He had held onto it, and might have gone to sleep on its coverless face: He had lost his mother when he was seven. My father had never made any mention to his own children of the book, but he had brought it along with him from Ohio to our house and shelved it in our bookcase.

My mother had brought from West Virginia that set of 11 Dickens; those books looked sad, too—they had been through fire and water before I was born, she told me, and there they were, lined up—as I later realized, waiting for *me.*

I was presented, from as early as I can remember, with books 12 of my own, which appeared on my birthday and Christmas morning. Indeed, my parents could not give me books enough. They must have sacrificed to give me on my sixth or seventh birthday—it was after I became a reader for myself—the ten-volume set of *Our Wonder World.* These were beautifully made, heavy books I would lie down with on the floor in front of the diningroom hearth, and more often than the rest volume 5, *Every*

Child's Story Book, was under my eyes. There were the fairy tales— Grimm, Andersen, the English, the French, "Ali Baba and the Forty Thieves"; and there was Aesop and Reynard the Fox; there were the myths and legends, Robin Hood, King Arthur, and St. George and the Dragon, even the history of Joan of Arc; a whack of *Pilgrim's Progress* and a long piece of *Gulliver*. They all carried their classic illustrations. I located myself in these pages and could go straight to the stories and pictures I loved; very often "The Yellow Dwarf" was first choice, with Walter Crane's Yellow Dwarf in full color making his terrifying appearance flanked by turkeys. Now that volume is as worn and backless and hanging apart as my father's poor *Sanford and Merton*. The precious page with Edward Lear's "Jumblies" on it has been in danger of slipping out for all these years. One measure of my love for *Our Wonder World* was that for a long time I wondered if I would go through fire and water for it as my mother had done for Charles Dickens; and the only comfort was to think I could ask my mother to do it for me.

I believe I'm the only child I know of who grew up with this   13 treasure in the house. I used to ask others, "Did you have *Our Wonder World*?" I'd have to tell them *The Book of Knowledge* could not hold a candle to it.

I live in gratitude to my parents for initiating me—and as early   14 as I begged for it, without keeping me waiting—into knowledge of the word, into reading and spelling, by way of the alphabet. They taught it to me at home in time for me to begin to read before starting to school. I believe the alphabet is no longer considered an essential piece of equipment for traveling through life. In my day it was the keystone to knowledge. You learned the alphabet as you learned to count to ten, as you learned "Now I lay me" and the Lord's Prayer and your father's and mother's name and address and telephone number, all in case you were lost.

My love for the alphabet, which endures, grew out of reciting   15 it but, before that, out of seeing the letters on the page. In my own story books, before I could read them for myself, I fell in love with various winding, enchanted-looking initials drawn by Walter Crane at the heads of fairy tales. In "Once upon a time," an "O" had a rabbit running it as a treadmill, his feet upon flowers. When the day came, years later, for me to see the *Book of Kells*, all the wizardry of letter, initial, and word swept over me a thousand times over, and the illumination, the gold, seemed a part of the word's beauty and holiness that had been there from the start.

David Smith

■■■

Burying the Hatchet in Language

The following article by McGill University professor of education, David Smith, comes from the July/August 1997 issue of *Peace Magazine*, published by the Canadian Disarmament Information Service.

L inguistic research over the last quarter century has exposed 1
the influence of language on our thinking patterns and
processes. We are seldom aware that the kind of language we use
affects our behaviour in significant ways. One example of these
revelations is the militarization of English over a long period of
time. The result is that our conceptual and higher-level thinking
is shaped in ways that we might not consciously wish it to be,
and that the language we use in some cases may actually prevent us from attaining our goals.

The History of Military Metaphors

Military metaphors have become part of our language over 2
hundreds of years. This has been a normal process, since people
tend naturally to draw upon experiences in one area of life in
order to give fresh insight and understanding to experiences in
another. Think of the language that sailors have brought from
the sea to the land (Know the ropes), that urban dwellers have
adapted from farms (Put the cart before the horse), or that people
have brought home from their places of work (Strike while the
iron is hot).

Soldiers have had vivid, sometimes traumatic, experiences 3
during military duty that they have then applied to non-military
situations. Today, we may ask someone to "spearhead the
discussion" or to "get off your high horse." From marching,
someone may "get off on the wrong foot" or "mark time"; from
strategy, we might "close ranks" or "beat a hasty retreat"; from
weapons, we can "cross swords" with an adversary or "look

daggers." From the military hierarchy, we refer to "the top brass" or "the rank and file." There are literally hundreds of military metaphors used in everyday speech and writing.

One might well argue that at the relatively shallow level of 4
vocabulary, or even of metaphorical expression, the use of militaristic language is harmless and serves to make our communication more colorful, more precise and perhaps, as Aristotle claimed, to convey fresh meaning or perspective. Indeed, there are words in use that we do not link at all to their origins with the military establishment (such as "harbinger," someone who went before an army to find accommodation, especially for officers). If no violence or military meaning is associated with the word, surely its use is innocuous. But is the use of military language in our society cause for concern at a deeper level?

Metacognitive Thinking

What has concerned some linguists and philosophers is not the 5
use of military language per se, but patterns of metaphorical thinking at the metacognitive level. In their book, *Metaphors We Live By*, George Lakoff and Mark Johnson give clear examples of such metaphorical thinking. They assert that in English-speaking society, we conceive of "argument as war" as shown by the following set of conceptual metaphors:

- Your claims are *indefensible.*
- He *attacked* every point in my argument.
- I have lots of *ammunition* in my *arsenal.*
- His criticisms were right on *target.*
- I *demolished* his argument.
- If you use that *strategy*, she'll *wipe* you out.
- You disagree? Okay, *shoot.*
- He *shot down* all my arguments.

While there are many alternative metaphors, we may often 6
think of "love as war":

- She *fought* for him, but his mistress *won out.*
- He is slowly *gaining ground* with her.
- He *won* her hand in marriage.
- She is *besieged* by suitors.
- She has to *fend* them *off.*
- He made an *ally* out of her mother.
- He is known for his many *conquests.*

Both of the overriding ideas that "argument is war" and 7
"love is war" consist of coherent and consistent sets of
metaphorical expressions. Such related clusters are referred to
as structural metaphors, and it is these metaphors that may
become part of our generally unarticulated belief system.

In order to explore these ideas further over the past year, I 8
have been reading and analyzing a variety of newspaper and
magazine articles mainly in the areas of politics, economics,
environment, and health. My analysis has involved the
identification of structural metaphors and their supporting
evidence. Perhaps I can give one example from the recent federal
election campaign, as reported in the *Gazette* of February 24.
Under the headline "Charest *broadsides* Liberals," we find the
following (italics are mine):

- Charest made a *blistering attack* on the Liberal record.
- He's not *targeting* the Bloc.
- He has a *shot* at becoming prime minister.
- Federalist *forces* could easily *rally* against separatists.
- He has been an *underdog, fighting* to keep the politicians in
  Ottawa honest.
- They played the song, *Another One Bites the Dust.*
- He devoted his entire speech to *attacking* the Liberals.

In all, there were 13 military metaphors that supported the 9
structural metaphor, "electoral campaigning as war." In the same
article, there were three conceptual metaphors supporting the
structural metaphor "election campaigning is a race." The
dominant metaphor was clearly that of war.

Analysis of articles such as these yields an interesting variety 10
of structural metaphors. However, the dominant theme of war
emerges repeatedly: Politics is war, Electoral reform is war,
Improvement of the economy is a battle, Marketing is war,
Environmental protection is a battle, Medical progress is a battle,
and so on.

In their book, *Language and Peace*, Christina Schaffner and 11
Anita Wenden assert that structural metaphors like these do not
exist in our belief systems as separate ideas but are related to one
another and are systematically organized into metaphors at an
even higher, ideological level. The metaphor Life is a (an uphill)
battle would be one such ideological metaphor. In presenting the
research of linguists and philosophers over the past ten years,
the authors arrive at a number of sobering conclusions.

They conclude that the language of journalists and diplomats   12
frequently represents ideological stances that accept and promote
war as a legitimate way of regulating international relations and
settling intergroup conflict (legitimization); that language
unquestioningly promotes values, sustains attitudes, and
encourages actions that create conditions that can lead to war
(propagation); and that language itself creates the kind of enemy
image essential to provoking and maintaining hostility that can
help justify war (justification).

Critical Language Education

Recognition of the kind of metaphor contained in the language we   13
use should become part of the education of every person.
Schaffner and Wenden write about the need for critical language
education in *Language and Peace*. The elements of such education
might include the following:

1. *Develop an awareness of metaphorical language.* The study of
   metaphor could be introduced at the elementary level,
   beginning with simple examples (such as White Tiger Kung
   Fu, Blockbuster Video, Arrow Taxi, Check-Mate Investigations)
   and proceeding to more sophisticated ones at the secondary
   and tertiary levels. We already study metaphor in poetry and
   novels; to study its use in political and other discourse would
   create an understanding of the way in which language reflects
   ideologies and can influence the exercise of power.

2. *Develop skills in decoding metaphorical language.* One model of
   formal analysis is to identify conceptual and structural
   metaphors and map the latter by showing the intended
   parallels between the structural metaphor and the issues under
   discussion. This can then provide the basis for a critical
   summary of the mode of metaphorical reasoning.

3. *Recognize the limitations of metaphors.* Sure, metaphors are
   helpful in enlarging our understanding of something we may
   already be familiar with, yet the system that allows us to
   comprehend one aspect of a concept in terms of another (for
   example, argument in terms of war) will necessarily hide some
   aspects of the concept. There may well be aspects of argument
   that are inconsistent with war. We may lose sight of the
   opportunities for cooperation in an argument, of sharing
   viewpoints that do not support our own position, or of
   learning from the points raised by the other person.

4. *Become more self-critical to enhance communication skills.* Many kinds of discourse use metaphorical language that is inconsistent with the purpose of the speakers or writers. An example is the one-page article on influenza that includes 13 conceptual metaphors to support the structural metaphor, "preventing flu is war." The mental set of the person who accepts the article is to fight the flu. However, the article concludes with the contrary advice, "Finally, remember to be a nice person; studies have shown that feelings of hostility reduce immune system levels, while being at peace with your world will actually increase your body's ability to resist infection." We need to ensure that the language we use is consistent with the message we wish to convey.

5. *Encourage creativity through the use of alternative metaphors.* Suppose instead of thinking about argument in terms of war, we were to think of argument as a pleasing, graceful dance. How would such a metaphor cause us to conceptualize argument in a different way? It is initially difficult for us to accept such a creative challenge because the present cultural metaphor gets in the way of conceiving argument in terms other than war. We may even conclude that thinking of argument in terms of dance produces a concept that is not argument at all. That is precisely the power of metaphors to control and limit our thinking; yet it is also their power to create a breakthrough (military metaphor intended) to renew and reconstruct.

Robert Fulford
1932–

■■■

The Fading Power of the Written Word

In the course of a Shakespearean production in Toronto in 1987, 1 there was a moment that briefly illustrated why contemporary society desperately needs literature and the literary imagination. The moment came just after the scene in Henry V in which some soldiers, about to leave for war, tearfully said good-bye to their wives. As soon as the women were safely out of sight, martial music poured from loudspeakers, the men shouted with joy, and patriotic signs were paraded across the stage. One sign held a single word: "Gotcha!"

What was remarkable about that little piece of modernized 2 Shakespeare was that it placed, in the middle of a work from the greatest literary imagination of the ages, a graphic reminder of the 20th-century imagination at its meanest and most degraded.

Not everyone in the Canadian audience understood why 3 "Gotcha!" was there. This was the English Shakespeare Company, and the reference was to something that happened in England five years earlier. On the afternoon of May 3, 1982, west of the Falkland Islands, torpedos from a British submarine hit the General Belgrano, an Argentine cruiser. Almost immediately, the ship began to sink. When the news of this victory reached London, the *Sun*, a hugely successful tabloid, put a one-word headline on the next morning's front page: Gotcha!

This quickly became famous as a symbol of blind jingoism, 4 but it was also a spectacular instance of failed imagination. The people who put that headline on their newspaper were victims of the peculiar callousness that afflicts all of us to some degree. What they did was hideously inappropriate, but it was also in a sense consistent with the atmosphere of this period in history.

During the sinking, about 300 sailors, many of them teenage 5 conscripts, choked to death on smoke, burned to death in oil or boiling water, or sank to the bottom of the sea. The rest of the crew, 800 or so, spent 36 hours floating on rafts in icy water, praying for rescue. The appropriate response to any such event is pity and terror, but the response of the people at the *Sun* was boyish.

The *Sun* had already been treating the Falklands war as a 6 kind of video game, a clash of abstract forces with no human meaning. The ships, the submarines, the helicopters and the people on them were no more consequential than flickers of electric light on a screen.

Flickers of light are the problem—perhaps the greatest mass 7 emotional problem of our era. Flickers of light on the television screen, or the movie screen, have become our principal means of receiving information about distant reality. Television brings us close to certain forms of reality, such as war in the Persian Gulf, but it also separates us emotionally from whatever it shows us. The more we see, the less we feel. Television instructs us that one war looks much like another, one plane crash much like another; we lose our sense of the human meaning of disaster. Mass communication deadens rather than enlivens us.

In the movies, too, we learn that the death of others is 8 unimportant. For a quarter-century the movies have been teaching us that people who die by gunfire are usually only extras, or deserve to die.

Those who defend violence in entertainment are quick to 9 point out that it has always been part of drama and literature— there's violence in the Bible, in the Greek tragedies and, of course, in Shakespeare. But until our time, violence in drama and literature was given meaning. It was given weight. It was set in a context that made the appropriate response—pity and terror— possible. In Shakespeare, no one dies without a purpose. One moral of the Shakespeare history plays is that those who kill their kings will live to rue it. Certainly those plays tell us, again and again, that the results of killing are never negligible—and that they will be felt for generations.

On the other hand, the editor who wrote: "Gotcha!" later 10 said, "I agree that headline was a shame. But it wasn't meant in a blood-curdling way. We just felt excited and euphoric. Only when we began to hear reports of how many men died did we begin to have second thoughts." There speaks a sadly crippled imagination, desperately in need of literature.

The future of literature is in question. The novel is no longer, 11 for most people, the central means of expressing a culture. Poetry is read by only a few. Literary studies no longer stand at the centre of the university curriculum. Some of literature's tasks, such as social observation, are often accomplished better by movies and TV programs. Even in the bookstores, literature is often pushed aside by journalism, how-to manuals and cookbooks.

But literature remains the core of civilized life precisely 12 because it is the only reliable antidote to everything in our existence that diminishes us. Only the literary imagination can save us from the deadening influence of visual news and visual entertainment. When it works as it should, literature takes us beyond our parochialism into other minds and other cultures. It makes us know that even our enemies, even anonymous Argentinian sailors, are as humanly diverse as we are.

If we let it, literature can also save us from the narrowing 13 effect of politics. Politics teaches us to see the world in functional terms, defined by power blocs and national borders and pressure groups. Pretending to offer freedom, politics asks us to identify ourselves by ethnicity or gender or class or nationality. Literature, on the other hand, dares us to feel our way across all boundaries of thought and feeling.

One of the more beautiful stories I've read in recent years 14 was written by an Asian Trinidadian Canadian man, speaking in the voice of a Japanese woman: the writer, and his grateful readers, simply refused to be contained by the limits the world regards as normal. This is the immense power that literature puts in the hands of all of us.

In the same way, literature offers us the opportunity to escape 15 the two most pressing forms of bondage in our normal existence: time and ego. Emotionally and intellectually, literature dissolves the rules of time and beckons us toward Periclean Athens, Czarist Russia, Elizabethan England and a thousand other moments in the past. By lengthening our sense of time, it saves us from the maddening urgencies of the present. And when it succeeds on the highest level, it breaks the shell of our intense and tiresome self-consciousness. It forces itself inside the egotism fostered by the pressures of our lives and links us with human history and the vast ocean of humanity now on Earth. By taking us into other lives, it deepens our own.

Our clear task, if we hope to realize ourselves as a civilization, 16 is to cherish the writers who have done their work and nourish the writers who are still doing it. The literary imagination is not a grace of life or a diversion: it is the best way we have found of reaching for the meaning of existence.

Natalie Goldberg

■■■

The Rules of Writing Practice

For fifteen years now, at the beginning of every writing work- 1
shop, I have repeated the rules for writing practice. So, I will repeat them again here. And I want to say why I repeat them:
Because they are the bottom line, the beginning of all writing, the
foundation of learning to trust your own mind. Trusting your own
mind is essential for writing. Words come out of the mind.

And I believe in these rules. Perhaps I'm a little fanatical 2
about them.

A friend, teasing me, said, "You act as if they are the rules to 3
live by, as though they apply to everything."

I smiled. "Okay, let's try it. Do they apply to sex?" 4

I stuck up my thumb for rule number one. "Keep your hand 5
moving." I nodded yes.

Index finger, rule number two. "Be specific." I let out a yelp 6
of glee. It was working.

Finger number three. "Lose control." It was clear that sex 7
and writing were the same thing.

Then, number four. "Don't think," I said. Yes, for sex, too, I 8
nodded.

I proved my point. My friend and I laughed. 9

Go ahead, try these rules for tennis, hang gliding, driving a 10
car, making a grilled cheese sandwich, disciplining a dog or a
snake. Okay. They might not always work. They work for writing.
Try them.

1. *Keep your hand moving.* When you sit down to write, whether
    it's for ten minutes or an hour, once you begin, don't stop. If
    an atom bomb drops at your feet eight minutes after you
    have begun and you were going to write for ten minutes,
    don't budge. You'll go out writing.

What is the purpose of this? Most of the time when we write, 11 we mix up the editor and creator. Imagine your writing hand as the creator and the other hand as the editor. Now bring your two hands together and lock your fingers. This is what happens when we write. The writing hand wants to write about what she did Saturday night: "I drank whiskey straight all night and stared at a man's back across the bar. He was wearing a red T-shirt. I imagined him to have the face of Harry Belafonte. At three A.M., he finally turned my way and I spit into the ashtray when I saw him. He had the face of a wet mongrel who had lost his teeth." The writing hand is three words into writing this first sentence— "I drank whiskey ..."—when the other hand clenches her fingers tighter and the writing hand can't budge. The editor says to the creator, "Now, that's not nice, the whiskey and stuff. Don't let people know that. I have a better idea: 'Last night, I had a nice cup of warmed milk and then went to bed at nine o'clock.' Write that. Go ahead. I'll loosen my grip so you can."

If you keep your creator hand moving, the editor can't catch 12 up with it and lock it. It gets to write out what it wants. "Keep your hand moving" strengthens the creator and gives little space for the editor to jump in.

Keep your hand moving is the main structure for writing 13 practice.

2. *Lose control.* Say what you want to say. Don't worry if it's correct, polite, appropriate. Just let it rip. Allen Ginsberg was getting a master's degree from Columbia University. Back then, they were doing rhymed verse. He had a lot of practice in formal meter, and so forth. One night, he went home and said to himself that he was going to write whatever he wanted and forget about formalities. The result was "Howl." We shouldn't forget how much practice in writing he had prior to this, but it is remarkable how I can tell students, "Okay, say what you want, go for it," and their writing takes a substantial turn toward authenticity.

3. *Be specific.* Not car, but Cadillac. Not fruit, but apple. Not bird, but wren. Not a codependent, neurotic man, but Harry, who runs to open the refrigerator for his wife, thinking she wants an apple, when she is headed for the gas stove to light her cigarette. Be careful of those pop-psychology labels. Get below the label and be specific to the person.

But don't chastise yourself as you are writing, "I'm an idiot;   14
Natalie said to be specific and like a fool I wrote 'tree.'" Just
gently note that you wrote "tree," drop to a deeper level, and
next to "tree" write "sycamore." Be gentle with yourself. Don't
give room for the hard grip of the editor.

4. *Don't think.* We usually live in the realm of second or third
   thoughts, thoughts on thoughts, rather than in the realm of
   first thoughts, the real way we flash on something. Stay with
   the first flash. Writing practice will help you contact first
   thoughts. Just practice and forget everything else.

Now here are some rules that don't necessarily apply to sex,   15
though you can try to apply them to sex if you like.

5. *Don't worry about punctuation, spelling, grammar.*
6. *You are free to write the worst junk in America.* You can be more
   specific, if you like: the worst junk in Santa Fe; New York;
   Kalamazoo, Michigan; your city block; your pasture; your
   neighborhood restaurant; your family. Or you can get more
   cosmic: free to write the worst junk in the universe, galaxy,
   world, hemisphere, Sahara Desert.
7. *Go for the jugular.* If something scary comes up, go for it.
   That's where the energy is. Otherwise, you'll spend all your
   time writing around whatever makes you nervous. It will
   probably be abstract, bland writing because you're avoiding
   the truth. Hemingway said, "Write hard and clear about
   what hurts." Don't avoid it. It has all the energy. Don't
   worry, no one ever died of it. You might cry or laugh, but not
   die.

I am often asked, "Well, isn't there a time when we need to   16
stop our hand moving? You know, to figure out what we want
to say?"

It's better to figure out what you want to say in the actual act   17
of writing. For a long time, I was very strict with myself about
writing practice. I kept that hand moving no matter what. I wanted
to learn to cut through to first thoughts. Sure, you can stop for a
few moments, but it is a tricky business. It's good to stop if you
want, look up and get a better picture of what you're writing
about, but often I don't stay there. If I give myself a little gap, I'm
off for an hour daydreaming. You have to learn your own rhythm,
but make sure you do some focused, disciplined "keeping the
hand moving" to learn about cutting through resistance.

If you learn writing practice well, it is a good foundation for 18 all other writing.

When I was young, I played tennis. My arm wasn't very 19 strong, and I was impatient. I was so eager to play, I held the racquet up higher on the grip than I was supposed to in order to compensate. Unfortunately, I got used to using the racquet this way. I was a fine tennis player, but no matter how much I played, there was just so far I could improve, because I never mastered one of the important basics: the proper grip on the racquet.

I use this as an example for writing practice. Grow 20 comfortable with it in its basic form before you begin to veer off into your own manner and style. Trust it. It is as basic as drinking water.

Sometimes an interviewer asks me, "So writing practice is 21 old hat? Have you developed something new?"

And I say, "It would be like a Zen master teaching you 22 meditation one year and the next year saying, 'Forget compassion. Standing on our head is what's in.'"

The old essentials are still necessary. Stay with them under all 23 circumstances. It will make you stable—something unusual for a writer.

CREDITS

© 1992 "My Old Newcastle" by David Adams Richards. Reprinted with the permission of the author. • Sally Armstrong, "P4W," from *Homemakers*, September 1991, pp. 13–30. Reprinted by permission of the author. • Lesley Choyce, "Thin Edge of the Wedge," published in *Canadian Geographic* (March/April 1997). Reprinted with permission of the author. • Tomson Highway, "What a Certain Visionary Once Said." Copyright © 1992 by Tomson Highway. Reprinted by permission of the author and the Susan Schulman literary agency, 454 West 44th Street, New York, 10036. • "When Jannies Visited" by Ray Guy, from *Canadian Geographic* (Nov./Dec. 1993). • "A Home at the End of the Journey" by Allen Abel from *Maclean's* (Jan. 9, 1995). • "Elegy in Stone" by Steven Heighton from *Admen Move on Lhasa* by Steven Heighton. © Stoddart Publishing Co. Limited. Reprinted by permission. • "I Sing the Song of My Condo" by Evelyn Lau, from *The Globe and Mail* (June 17, 1994). © Evelyn Lau. • Brian Lewis, "Teeth." Originally published in *Up Here/Life in Canada's North*. Reprinted by permission of *Up Here/Life*. • "Touch the Dragon" by Karen Connelly. From *Touch the Dragon* by Karen Connelly, published by Turnstone Press, pp. 1–6. • "The Reel Thing" by Alfred LeBlanc, from *Equinox* (Sept./Oct. 1994). © Alfred LeBlanc. Reprinted by permission. • Cecil Foster, "Why Blacks Get Mad." Originally appeared in *Chatelaine Magazine*, November 1992. Reprinted by permission of the author. • Diane Francis, "Once a Kinder and Gentler Nation." Originally appeared in *Maclean's*, September 1990. Reprinted by permission of the author. • "Not Available in Stores" by Mark Kingwell, University of Toronto. Published in *Saturday Night*, (July/Aug. 1996). Reprinted by permission of the author. • Adrian Forsyth, "Little Plants of Horror", from *Equinox* (54), Nov./Dec. 1990. • Paul Quarrington, "Home Brew." Originally appeared in *Harrowsmith*, Vol. 17(1), (May/June 1992). Reprinted by permission of the author. • Jessica Mitford, "Behind the Formaldehyde Curtain," from *The American Way of Death*. Reprinted by permission of Jessica Mitford. All rights reserved. Copyright © 1963, 1978 by Jessica Mitford. • "You Are a Contract Painkiller" by Maureen Littlejohn, feature writer, editor, and journalist. Published in *Equinox* (April/May 1997). Reprinted with permission of the author. • "Breakfast in Bed" by Joe Fiorito, from *Comfort Me With Apples*, published by Nuage Editions. Reprinted by permission. • William Golding, "Thinking as a Hobby," from *The Borzoi College Reader*, eds. Charles Muscatine and Marlene Griffith, 1996. Originally published in *Holiday*, 1961. Copyright © 1961 by William Golding. Reprinted by permission of Alfred A. Knopf. • "Boomers Dance to a New Beat" by David Foot, Professor of Economics, University of Toronto, and co-author of *Boom, Bust & Echo 2000: Profiting from the Demographic Shift in the New Millennium*. Published in *The Globe and Mail*, Jan. 9, 1998. Reprinted by permission of the author. • Amy Willard Cross, "Life in the Stopwatch Lane," *The Globe and Mail*, July 5, 1990, p. A18. Reprinted by permission of the author. • Laura Millard, "Images of Canada: Canadian Bank Notes," first printed in *Border/Lines*, Issue 28, 1993 and is reprinted with the permission of the author. • Susan Swan, "Nine Ways of Looking at a Critic," © 1996 by Susan Swan. First published in *The Globe and Mail*, Nov. 30, 1996. • Charlotte Gray, "The Temple of Hygiene." Originally appeared in *Saturday Night Magazine*, September 1989. Reprinted by permission of the author. • "Save the Last Dance" by John Fraser. Originally appeared in *Saturday Night Magazine*, March 1993. Reprinted by permission of the author. • "The Sudbury Syndrome" from *Why I Hate Canadians* by Will Ferguson, © William Stener Ferguson 1997, published by Douglas & McIntyre. Reprinted by permission of the publisher. • Gloria Steinem, "The

Politics of Muscle" from *Moving Beyond Words*, by Gloria Steinem. Copyright ©
1994 by Gloria Steinem. Reprinted by permission of the author. • "The Babar
Factor" by Evan Solomon. © Evan Solomon. First published in *Shift* magazine,
Spring 1994. • Carol Krenz, "Food for Sloth." Originally appeared in *Montreal
Magazine* Jan./Feb. 1990. Reprinted by permission of the author. • Drew Hayden
Taylor, "Pretty Like a White Boy: The Adventures of a Blue Eyed Ojibway,"
from *An Anthology of Canadian Native Literature in English*, Oxford University
Press. First printed in *This Magazine*, August 1991. Copyright © by Drew Hayden
Taylor. • "I'm a Banana and Proud of It" by Wayson Choy, from *The Globe and
Mail* Facts and Arguments column. Reprinted by permission of the author. ©
Wayson Choy. All rights reserved by the author. • "Twice Struck" by Michael
Clugston, from *Equinox* (July/August 1991). © Michael Clugston. Reprinted by
permission. • "Pieces of Sky" by Neil Bissoondath from *If You Love This Country:
Fifteen Voices for a Unified Canada*. © Neil Bissoondath 1995. Reprinted with per-
mission of the author. • Stephen King, "Why We Crave Horror Movies," pub-
lished in *Playboy Magazine*, 1982. Reprinted with permission of the author's
agent, Arthur B. Greene, New York. • "Why We Crave Hot Stuff" by Trina
McQueen, President of Discovery Channel Canada. Published in *The Globe and
Mail* (Sept. 26, 1998). Reprinted by permission. • "Starving for the Gold" by
Laura Robinson, from *The Globe and Mail* (April 11, 1992). © Laura Robinson.
Reprinted by permission. • "You're Thinking of Getting a *What?*" from *I Love
Mom: An Irreverent History of the Tattoo* by John Gray. Reprinted by permission
of Key Porter Books Limited. • "The New Nature" by Tony Leighton, from
Equinox (December 1994). © Tony Leighton. Reprinted by permission. • "TV
Me Alone" by Jennifer Cowan, from *Shift* (July/August 1995). © Jennifer Cowan.
Reprinted by permission. • "Too Much Privacy Can Be Hazardous to the Person"
by Lawrence Solomon, editor of *The Next City*. Published in *The Next City*, sum-
mer 1998. Reprinted by permission. • "Kick 'Em Again" by Judy Rebick, from
Elm Street, September, 1998. Reprinted by permission. • "The Right Stuff" by
David Suzuki, from *Inventing the Future: Reflections on Science, Technology and
Nature*. Reprinted with the permission of Stoddart Publishing Co. Limited. •
"Stand Tall, and Pass The Ammunition" by Gerald W. Paul, published in
Canadian Funeral Director (February, 1985). • "Understanding Does Not Always
Lead to Tolerance" by Michele Lemon, from *The Globe and Mail* (Jan. 31, 1995).
• "My Body Is My Own Business" by Naheed Mustafa, from *The Globe and Mail*
(June 29, 1993). © Naheed Mustafa. Reprinted by permission. • Barbara
Ehrenreich, "The Ecstasy of War" from *Blood Rites: Origins and History of the
Passions of War* by Barbara Ehrenreich. Copyright © 1997 by Barbara Ehrenreich.
Reprinted by permission of Henry Holt and Company, Inc. •Jill Leslie
Rosenbaum and Meda Chesney-Lind, "Appearance and Delinquency: A
Research Note," from *Crime and Delinquency*. Copyright © 1994 by Rosenbaum
and Chesney-Lind. Reprinted with the permission of Sage Publications. •
Marilyn Dahl, "The Role of the Media in Promoting Images of Disability," from
the *Canadian Journal of Communication*. Reprinted by permission of the Canadian
Journal of Communication Inc. • Eudora Welty, "Listening." Reprinted by per-
mission of the publishers from *One Writer's Beginnings* by Eudora Welty,
Cambridge Mass.: Harvard University Press. Copyright © 1983, 1984 by Eudora
Welty. • David Smith, "Burying the Hatchet in Language" from *Peace Magazine*,
July/August 1997. Reprinted by permission. • "The Fading Power of the Written
Word" by Robert Fulford, from *The Globe and Mail* (Feb. 15, 1991). © Robert
Fulford. Reprinted by permission. • Natalie Goldberg, "The Rules of Writing
Practice" from *Wild Mind: Living the Writer's Life*. Copyright © 1977 by Natalie
Goldberg. Reprinted with the permission of Bantam Books.

INDEX OF AUTHORS AND TITLES